Neural Networks

in Finance

and Investing

Neural Networks

in Finance

and Investing

Using Artificial Intelligence to
Improve Real-World Performance

Revised Edition

Robert R. Trippi

Efraim Turban

EDITORS

IRWIN
Professional Publishing®
Chicago • London • Singapore

Times Mirror
Higher Education Group

Library of Congress Cataloging-in-Publication Data

Neural networks in finance and investing : using artificial
  intelligence to improve real-world performance / Robert R. Trippi
  and Efraim Turban, editors
      p.   cm.
  "a collection of survey and research articles"—pref.
  Includes index.
  ISBN 1-55738-919-5
      1. Finance—Decision making—Data processing.   2. Neural networks
          (Computer Science)   3. Artificial Intelligence.   I. Trippi, Robert
  R. II. Turban, Efraim.
  HG4012.5.N48   1996   96-3416
  332".0285"63—de20

Printed in the United States of America
1 2 3 4 5 4 6 7 8 9 0 BS 3 2 1 0 9 8 7 6

To my wife and best friend, Cecilia.

Robert R. Trippi

To my daughters, Daphne and Sharon.

Efraim Turban

CONTENTS

LIST OF FIGURES

LIST OF TABLES

Preface

Financial services firms are becoming more and more dependent on advanced computer technologies to establish and maintain competitiveness in a global economy. Neural networks represent an exciting new technology with a wide scope of potential financial applications, ranging from routine credit assessment operations to the driving of large scale portfolio management strategies. Many such applications have been reported to provide increases in profitability of 30 percent or more.

Neural Networks in Finance and Investing, revised edition,. is a thoroughly revised and expanded edition of the first book on the subject, published in 1992. It brings together from diverse sources a collection of survey and research articles that focus on the use of neural network technology to improve financial decision-making. This edition has been expanded by more than 50 percent over the first edition. It includes not only the latest thinking of recognized leaders in this field but also a number of earlier, widely cited papers that are now considered classics. Nearly all of the empirical papers in this volume have been subjected to peer review with respect to their technical correctness and methodological rigor.

Included with this edition is a complimentary special version of ThinksPro, a versatile full-featured neural network software package that can be used for many of the applications described in this book. Complete instructions for using the software can be found in its help file.

Initially, many of the first neural network researchers were inspired by the similarity between neural network architectures and learning paradigms and those of the brain. Neural networks were quickly recognized as useful for simulating intelligence in pattern recognition, association, and classification activities. These problems arise frequently in such areas as credit assessment, security investment, and financial forecasting. Unfortunately, most early attempts to apply neural networks to financial decision-making were naive, clumsy, and generally unsuccessful. However, recent innovations in the technology and improvements in our understanding of the strengths and weaknesses of neural networks vis-à-vis other forms of machine learning and human decision-making processes have resulted in many commercially successful systems. Although early neural network research was typically highly product-oriented, today most researchers and system implementors take a relatively hardware- and software-independent view of neural network-based decision support systems.

It is noteworthy that financial organizations are now second only to the Department of Defense in the sponsorship of research in neural network applications. Following a five-year research program that began in 1989, the D.O.D. is planning to spend an additional $15 million in neural network research over the period 1995–2000. In addition, the Japanese have embarked on a 10-year, $20 million program to further develop neural network technology, mainly in the commercial arena.

It is our hope that an updated collection of articles such as this, dealing exclusively with investment, risk assessment, forecasting, and other financial applications, will continue to be a useful addition to the libraries of financial analysts, information system professionals interested in or already working on such applications, and managers with financial decision-making responsibilities who wish to keep abreast of new developments in the field.

The editors wish to give thanks for their generous support in this endeavor to the Department of Economics and the Graduate School of International Relations and Pacific Studies at the University of California, San Diego, and to the College of Business Administration at California State University, Long Beach.

Robert R. Trippi
Efraim Turban

SOURCES AND ACKNOWLEDGMENTS

Chapter 1

"Neural Network Fundamentals for Financial Analysts," by Larry Medsker, Robert R. Trippi, and Efraim Turban. Printed by permission of the authors.

Chapter 2

"Artificial Neural Systems: A New Tool for Financial Decision-Making," by Delvin D. Hawley, John D. Johnson, and Dijjotam Raina. This article originally appeared in *Financial Analysts Journal*, November/December 1990, pp. 63–72. Reprinted with permission.

Chapter 3

"Applying Neural Networks," by Casimir C. "Casey" Klimasauskas. This article originally appeared in *PCAI*, January/February, 1991, pp. 30–33; March/April, 1991, pp. 27–34; and May/June, 1991, pp. 20–24. Reprinted with permission.

Chapter 4

"A Financial Neural Network Application," by Robert A. Marose. This article originally appeared in *AI Expert*, May 1990, pp. 50–53. Reprinted courtesy of Miller Freeman, Inc.

Chapter 5

"Analyzing Financial Health: Integrating Neural Networks with Expert Systems," by Don Barker. This article originally appeared in *PCAI*, May/June, 1990, pp. 24–27. Reprinted with permission.

Chapter 6

"Applying Neural Networks to the Extraction of Knowledge from Accounting Reports: A Classification Study," by R. H. Berry and Duarte Trigueiros. Printed with permission of the authors.

Chapter 7

"Artificial Neural Networks applied to Ratio Analysis in the Analytic Review Process," by Rames R. Coakley and Carol E. Brown. This article originally appeared in *Intelligent Systems in Accounting, Finance, and Management* 2 (1993), pp. 19–39. Reprinted with permission.

Chapter 8

"Recognizing Financial Distress Patterns Using a Neural Network tool," by Pamela K. Coats and L. Franklin Fant. This article originally appeared in *Financial Management*, Autumn 1993, pp. 142–155. Reprinted with permission.

Chapter 9

"Corporate Distress Diagnosis: comparisons Using Linear Discriminant Analysis and Neural Networks," by Edward I. Altman, G. Marco, and F. Varetto. This article originally appeared in *Journal of Banking and Finance* 18 (1994), pp. 505–529. Reprinted with permission.

Chapter 10

"A Neural Network Approach to Bankruptcy Prediction," by Wullianallur Raghupathi, Lawrence L. Schkade, and Bapi S. Raju. Reprinted with permission from *Proceedings of the IEEE 24th Annual Hawaii International Conference on Systems Sciences*, © 1991, IEEE.

Chapter 11

"Bankruptcy Prediction by Neural Network," by Eric Rahimian, Seema Singh, Thongchai Thammachote, and Rajiv Virmani. Printed with permission of the authors.

Chapter 12

"Neural Networks for Bankruptcy Prediction: The Power to Solve Financial Problems," by Kevin G. Coleman, Timothy J. Graettinger, and William F. Lawrence. This article originally appeared in *AI Review,* July/August, 1991, pp. 48–50. Reprinted courtesy of NeuralWare, Inc., Pittsburgh, PA.

Chapter 13

"Predicting Bank Failures: a Neural Network Approach," by Kar Yan Tam and Melody Y. Kiang. This article originally appeared in *Management Science* 38, no. 7 (July 1992), pp. 926–947, © 1992, The Institute of Management Sciences. Reprinted with permission.

Chapter 14

"Neural Networks: A New Tool for Predicting Thrift Failures," by Linda M. Salchenberger, E. Mine Cinar, and Nicholas A. Lash. This article originally appeared in *Decision Sciences* 23, No. 4, July/August, 1992, pp. 899–916. Reprinted with permission.

Chapter 15

"A Study of Using Artificial Neural Networks to Develop an Earnly Warning Warning Predictor for Credit Union Financial Distress with Comparison to the Probit Model," by Clarence N. W. Tan. Printed with permission of the author.

Chapter 16

"Bankruptcy Prediction Using Neural Networks," by Rick L. Wilson and Ramesh Sharda. This article originally appeared in *Decision Support Systems* 11 (1994), pp. 545–557. Reprinted with permission.

Chapter 17

"Bond Rating: A Nonconservative Application of Neural Networks," by Soumitra Dutta and Shashi Shekhar. Reprinted with permission from *Proceedings of the IEEE International Conference on Neural Networks*, pp. II443–II450, © July 1988, IEEE.

Chapter 18

"Neural Networks for Bond Rating Improved by Multiple Hidden Layers," by Alvin J. Surkan and J. Clay Singleton. Reprinted with permission from *Proceedings of the IEEE International Conference on Neural Networks*, pp. II163–II168, San Diego, CA, © 1990, IEEE.

Chapter 19

"Risk Assessment of Mortgage Applications with a Neural Network System: An Update as the Test Portfolio Ages," by Douglas L. Reilly, Edward Collins, Christopher Scofield, and Sushmito Ghosh. Reprinted with permission from *Proceedings of the IEEE International Conference on Neural Networks*, pp. II479–II482, © July 1991, IEEE.

Chapter 20

"Predicting Consumer Credit Performance: Can Neural Networks Outperform Traditional Statistical Methods?" by Leslie Richeson, Raymond A. Zimmerman, and Kevin G. Barnett. This article originally appeared in *International Journal of Applied Expert Systems* 2, no. 2 (1994), pp. 116–130. Reprinted with permission.

Chapter 21

"Using Neural Networks for Credit Scoring," by Herbert L. Jensen. This article originally appeared in *Managerial Finance* 18, no. 6 (1992), pp. 15–26. Reprinted with permission.

Chapter 22

"Economic Prediction Using Neural Networks: The Case of IBM Daily Stock Prices," by Halbert White. Reprinted with permission from *Pro-*

ceedings of the IEEE International Conference on Neural Networks, pp. II451–II458, © July 1988, IEEE.

Chapter 23

"Predicting Stock Price Performance: A Neural Network Approach," by Youngohc Yoon and George Swales. Reprinted with permission from *Proceedings of the IEEE 24th Annual Hawaii International Conference of Systems Sciences,* pp. 156–162, © January 1991, IEEE.

Chapter 24

"Stock Market Prediction System with Modular Neural Networks," by Takashi Kimoto, Kazuo Asakawa, Morio Yoda, and Masakazu Takeoka. Reprinted with permission from *Proceedings of the IEEE International Joint Conference on Neural Networks,* pp. I-1–I6, San Diego, CA, © 1990, IEEE.

Chapter 25

"Two Multilayer Perceptron Training Strategies for Low-Frequency S&P 500 Prediction," by Ypke Hiemstra and Christian Haefke. Printed with permission of the authors.

Chapter 26

"Using Artificial Neural Networks to Pick Stocks," by Lawrence Kryzanowski, Michael Galler, and David Wright. This article originally appeared in *Financial Analysts Journal,* July/August 1993, pp. 21–27. Reprinted with permission.

Chapter 27

"Testability of the Arbitrage Pricing Theory by Neural Network," by Hamid Ahmadi. Reprinted with permission from *Proceedings of the IEEE International Conference on Neural Networks,* pp. I385–I393, San Diego, CA, © 1990, IEEE.

Chapter 28

"Artificial Neural Network Models for Pricing Initial Public Offerings," by Bharat A. Jain and Barin N. Nag. This article originally appeared in

Decision Sciences 26, no. 3 (May/June 1995), pp. 283–299. Reprinted with permission. The *Deision Sciences* journal is published by the Decision Sciences Institute, located at Georgia State University.

Chapter 29

"A Commodity Trading Model Based on a Neural Network-Expert System Hybrid," by Karl Bergerson and Donald C. Wunsch, II. Reprinted with permission from *Proceedings of the IEEE International Conference on Neural Networks*, pp. I289–I293, Seattle, WA, © 1991, IEEE.

Chapter 30

"Commodity Trading with a Three Year Old," by J. E. Collard. Printed with permission of the author, acknowledging support from Gerber Inc., Schwieterman Inc., and Martingale Research Corp.

Chapter 31

"Trading Equity Index Futures with a Neural Network," by Robert R. Trippi and Duane DeSieno. This article originally appeared in the *Journal of Portfolio Management* 18, no. 5 (Fall 1992), pp. 27–33. Reprinted with permission.

Chapter 32

"Neural Networks for Predicting Options Volatility," by Mary Malliaris and Linda Salchenberger. Reprinted with permission from Proceedings of the 1994 World Congress on Neural Networks, San Diego, CA, June 5–9, 1994, pp. II-290–295.

Chapter 33

"A Nonparametric Approach to Pricing and Hedging Derivative Securities via Learning Networks," by James M. Hutchinson, Andrew W. Lo, and Tomaso Poggio. This article originally appeared in *The Journal of Finance* XLIX, no. 3 (July 1994), pp. 851–889. Reprinted with permission.

Chapter 34

"A Model-Selection Approach to Assessing the Information in the Term Structure Using Linear Models and Artificial Neural Networks," by Norman R. Swanson and Halbert White. This article orginally appeared in *Journal of Business and Economic Statistics* 13, no. 3 (July 1995), pp. 265–275. Reprinted with permission.

Chapter 35

"Performance of Neural Networks in Managerial Forecasting," by Won Chul Jhee and Jae Kyu Lee. This article originally appeared in *Intelligent Systems in Accounting, Finance, and Management* 2 (1993), pp. 55–71. Reprinted with permission.

Chapter 36

"Neural Network Models as an Alternative to Regression," by Leorey Marquez, Tim Hill, Reginald Worthley, and William Remus. A modified version of a paper from *Proceedings of the IEEE 24th Annual Hawaii International Conference on Systems Sciences,* vol. VI, pp. 129–135, © 1991, IEEE. Reprinted with permission.

Chapter 37

"A Connectionist Approach to Time Series Prediction—An Empirical Test," by Ramesh Sharda and Rajendra B. Patil. This article appeared in the *Journal of Intelligent Manufacturing,* published by Chapman and Hall, 1992. Reprinted with permission.

Chapter 38

"Time Series Prediction Using Minimally Structured Neural Networks: An Empirical Test," by Won Chul Jhee and Michael J. Shaw. Printed with permission of the authors.

Chapter 39

"Constructive Learning and Its Application to Currency Exchange Rate Forecasting," by A. N. Refenes. Printed with permission of the author.

CONTRIBUTORS

Hamid Ahmadi, California State University, Sacramento
Kazuo Asakawa, Fujitsu Laboratories Ltd.
E. I. Altman, New York University
Don Barker, Gonzaga University
Kevin G. Barnett, KPMG Peat Marwick
Karl Bergerson, Neural Trading Company
R. H. Berry, University of East Anglia
C. E. Brown, Oregon State University
E. Mine Cinar, Loyola University of Chicago
J. R. Coakley, Oregon State University
Pamela K. Coats, Florida State University
Kevin G. Coleman, Neuralware, Inc.
Edward Collins, Nestor, Inc.
Joseph Collard, GIST Technologies Corp.
Duane DeSieno, Logical Designs, Inc.
Soumitra Dutta, University of California, Berkeley
L. Franklin Fant, Florida State University
Michael Galler, McGill University
Sushmito Ghosh, Nestor, Inc.
Timothy J. Graettinger, Neuralware, Inc.
Christian Haefke, Institute for Advanced Studies, Vienna
Delvin D. Hawley, University of Mississippi
Ypke Hiemstra, Vrije Universiteit, Amsterdam
Tim Hill, University of Hawaii
James M. Hutchinson, PHZ Capital Partners
Herbert L. Jensen, California State University, Fullerton
Won Chul Jhee, Hong Ik University, South Korea
John D. Johnson, University of Mississippi, Oxford
Melody Y. Kiang, University of Texas at Austin
Takashi Kimoto, Fujitsu Laboratories Ltd.

Casimir C. Klimasauskas, Neuralware, Inc.
Lawrence Kryzanowski, Concordia University
Nicholas A. Lash, Loyola University of Chicago
William E. Lawrence, Neuralware, Inc.
Jae Kyu Lee, Korea Advanced Institute of Science and Technology
Andrew W. Lo, Massachusetts Institute of Technology
Mary Malliaris, Loyola University, Chicago
G. Marco, Centrale Dei Bilanci, Turin, Italy
Leorey Marquez, University of Hawaii
Larry Medsker, American University
Robert A. Morose, Hofstra University
Rajendra B. Patil, University of Oklahoma
Tomaso Poggio, Massachusetts Institute of Technology
Wullianallur Raghupathi, California State University, Chico
Eric Rahimian, Alabama A&M University
Dijjotam Raina, Mobile Telecommunications Technology, Inc.
Bapi S. Raju, University of Texas at Arlington
A. N. Refenes, University College London
Douglas L. Reilly, Nestor, Inc.
William Remus, University of Hawaii
Leslie Richeson, Trenton State College
Linda M. Salchenberger, Loyola University of Chicago
Lawrence L. Schkade, University of Texas at Arlington
Christopher Scofield, Nestor, Inc.
Ramesh Sharda, Oklahoma State University, Stillwater
Michael J. Shaw, University of Illinois at Urbana-Champaign
Shashi Shekhar, University of California, Berkeley
Seema Singh, University of Alabama at Huntsville
J. Clay Singleton, University of Nebraska
Alvin J. Surkan, University of Nebraska
George Swales, Southwest Missouri State University
Norman R. Swanson, University of California, San Diego
Masakazu Takeoka, The Nikko Securities Co., Ltd.
Kar Yan Tam, Hong Kong University of Science and Technology
Clarence N. W. Tan, Gold Coast University, Australia
Thongchai Thammachote, University of Alabama at Huntsville
Gonzago Trigueiros, University of East Anglia
Robert R. Trippi, University of California, San Diego

Efraim Turban, California State University, Long Beach
F. Varett., Centrale Dei Bilanci, Turin, Italy
Rajiv Virmani, University of Alabama at Huntsville
Rick L. Wilson, Oklahoma State University, Stillwater
Halbert White, University of California, San Diego
Reginald Worthley, University of Hawaii
David Wright, Marleau, Lemire Securities Co.
Donald C. Wunsch II, Neural Trading Company
Morio Yoda, The Nikko Securities Co., Ltd.
Youngohc Yoon, Southwest Missouri State University
Raymond A. Zimmerman, University of Texas at El Paso

PART I

NEURAL NETWORK OVERVIEW

NEURAL NETWORK FUNDAMENTALS FOR FINANCIAL ANALYSTS[1]

Larry Medsker, Efraim Turban, and Robert R. Trippi

INTRODUCTION

Over the past four decades, the field of artificial intelligence has made great progress toward computerizing human reasoning. Nevertheless, the tools of AI have been mostly restricted to sequential processing and only certain representations of knowledge and logic. A different approach to intelligent systems involves constructing computers with architectures and processing capabilities that mimic the processing characteristics of the brain. The results may be knowledge representations based on massive parallel processing, fast retrieval of large amounts of information, and the ability to recognize patterns based on experience. The technology that attempts to achieve these results is called *neural computing* or *artificial neural networks* (ANN).

Artificial neural networks are an information processing technology inspired by studies of the brain and nervous system. After falling into disfavor in the 1970s, the field of neural networks experienced a dramatic resurgence in the late 1980s. The renewed interest developed because of the need for brainlike information processing, advances in computer technology, and progress in neuroscience toward better understanding of the mechanisms of the brain. Declared the Decade of the Brain by the U.S. government, the 1990s look extremely promising for understanding the brain and the mind. Neural computing should have an important role in this research area, which initially was oriented toward medical research. In many financial decision-making as well as other application areas, ANN are supplementing or taking the place of statistical and conventional expert systems (ES) approaches, as the ANN approach provides features and performance advantages not available in the other types of systems.

THE BIOLOGICAL ANALOGY

Biological Neural Networks

The human (and animal) brain is composed of cells called *neurons*, which are unique in that they do not die—all other cells reproduce to replace themselves, then die. This phenomenon may explain why we retain information. Estimates of the number of neurons in a human brain range up to 100 billion, and more than a hundred different kinds of neurons are known. Neurons function in groups called networks. Each group contains several thousand highly interconnected neurons. Thus, the brain can be viewed as a collection of neural networks.

Thinking and intelligent behavior are controlled by the brain and the central nervous system. The ability to learn and react to changes in our environment requires intelligence. Those who suffer brain damage, for example, have difficulty learning and reacting to changing environments.

A portion of a network composed of two cells is shown in Figure 1.1. The cell itself includes a *nucleus* (at the center). On the left of Neuron 1, note the *dendrites,* which provide inputs to the cell. On the right is the *axon*, which sends signals (outputs) via the axon terminals to Neuron 2. These axon terminals are shown merging with the dendrites of Neuron 2. Signals can be transmitted unchanged, or they can be transmitted over synapses. A *synapse* is able to increase or decrease its strength of connection and causes excitation or inhibition of a subsequent neuron.

Figure 1.1

Two Interconnected Biological Cells

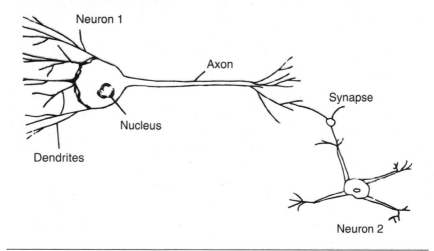

Artificial Neural Networks

An *artificial* neural network is a *model* that emulates a biological neural network. Today's neural computing uses a very limited set of concepts based on our knowledge of biological neural systems. The concepts are used to implement software simulations of massively parallel processes involving processing elements (also called artificial neurons or neurodes) interconnected in a network architecture. The artificial neuron is analogous to the biological neuron. It receives inputs analogous to the electrochemical impulses that the dendrites of biological neurons receive from other neurons. The output of the artificial neuron corresponds to signals sent out from a biological neuron over its axon. These artificial signals can be changed similarly to the change occurring at the synapses.

The state of the art in neural computing is not necessarily limited by our understanding of biological neural networks. Despite extensive research in neurobiology and psychology, important questions remain about how the brain and the mind work. This is just one reason why neural computing models are not very close to actual biological systems. Nevertheless, research and development in the area of ANN are producing interesting and useful systems that borrow some features from the biological systems, even though we are far from having an artificial brainlike machine.

NEURAL NETWORK COMPONENTS AND STRUCTURES

A network is composed of processing elements that can be organized in different ways or architectures.

Processing Elements

An ANN is composed of artificial neurons (to be referred to as neurons); these are the *processing elements* (PEs). Each of the neurons receives input(s), processes the input(s), and delivers a single output. This process is shown in Figure 1.2. The input can be raw data or output of other processing elements. The output can be the final product, or it can be an input to another neuron.

A Network

Each ANN is composed of a collection of neurons grouped in layers. A basic structure is shown in Figure 1.3. Note the three layers in this example: input, intermediate (called the hidden layer), and output.

Network Structure

Similar to biological networks, an ANN can be organized in several different ways (topologies); that is, the neurons can be interconnected in different ways. Therefore, ANN appear in many shapes. In processing information, many of the processing elements perform their computations simultaneously. This *parallel processing* resembles the way the brain works and contrasts with the serial processing of conventional computing.

Processing Information in the Network

Once the structure of a network is established, the relevant information can be processed. The major elements participating in the processing are inputs, outputs, and weights.

Inputs. Each input corresponds to a single attribute. For example, if the problem is to decide on the approval or disapproval of a loan, an attribute can be an income level, age, or ownership of a house. The *value* of an

Figure 1.2

A Neural Processing Element

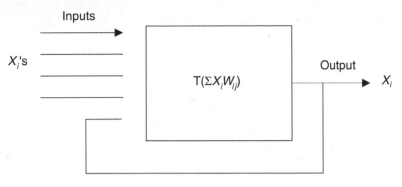

Figure 1.3

Three-Layer Network

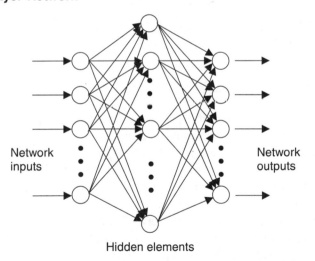

attribute is the input to the network. Although input data are numerically valued, in some applications numbers may actually represent qualitative data such as "yes," "no"; "up," "down"; or "pass," "fail."

Outputs. The output of the network is the solution to a problem. For example, in the case of a loan application it may be "yes" or "no." The ANN assigns numeric values, for example, +1 for yes and 0 for no. The purpose of the network is to compute the value of the output.

Weights. Key elements in an ANN, *weights* express the *relative strength* (or mathematical value) of the initial entering data or the various connections that transfer data from layer to layer. In other words, weights express the *relative importance* of each input to a processing element. Weights are crucial; it is through repeated adjustments of weights that the network "learns."

Summation Function

The *summation function* finds the weighted average of all the input elements to each processing element. A summation function multiplies the input values (Xs) by the weights (Ws) and totals them together for a weighted sum, Y. For N inputs i into one processing element j, we have:

$$Y_j = \sum_{j}^{n} X_i W_{ij}$$

Transformation (Transfer) Function

The summation function computes the internal stimulation, or activation level, of the neuron. (Sometimes it is referred to as the activation function.) Based on this level, the neuron may or may not produce an output. The relationship between the internal activation level and the output may be linear or nonlinear. Such relationships are expressed by a *transformation (transfer) function*, and there are several different types. The selection of the specific function determines the network's operation. One very popular nonlinear transfer function is called a *sigmoid function*:

$$Y_T = \frac{1}{1 + e^{-y}}$$

where Y_T is the transformed (or normalized) value of Y.

The purpose of this transformation is to modify the output levels to a reasonable value (e.g., between 0 and 1). This transformation is done *before* the output reaches the next level. Without such transformation, the value of the output may be very large, especially when several layers are involved. Sometimes instead of a continuous transformation function, a *threshold detector* is used. For example, any value of 0.5 (or other fixed number) or less is changed to zero; any value above 0.5 is changed to one. A transformation can occur at the output of each processing element, or it can be performed at the final output of the network. An example of a PE using a sigmoid transfer function is the following:

$x_1 = 3$ $w_1 = .2$

$x_2 = 1$ $w_2 = .4$ PE $y = .77$

$x_3 = 2$ $w_3 = .1$

Note that the summation function results in:

$$y = 3(.2) + 1(.4) + 2(.1) = 1.2$$

and the sigmoid transformation results in:

$$Y_T = \frac{1}{1 + e^{-1.2}} = .77$$

Learning

An ANN learns from its mistakes. The usual process of learning (or training) involves three tasks:

1. Compute outputs.

2. Compare outputs with desired answers.

3. Adjust the weights and repeat the process.

The learning process usually starts by setting the weights randomly. The difference between the actual output (Y or Y_T) and the desired output (Z) is called Δ. The objective is to minimize Δ (or better, to reduce it to zero). The reduction of Δ is done by incrementally changing the weights.

Information processing with ANN consists of analyzing patterns of activities (*pattern recognition*) with learned information stored as the neuron's connection weights. A common characteristic of systems is the ability to classify streams of input data without the explicit knowledge of rules and to use arbitrary patterns of weights to represent the memory of categories. During the learning stages, the interconnection weights change in response to training data presented to the system. Different ANN compute the error in different ways, depending on the learning algorithm that is being used. More than a hundred learning algorithms are available for various situations and configurations. In training a network, the training data set is divided into two categories: test cases and training cases.

ANN STRENGTHS AND WEAKNESSES

Neural network technology has significant advantages over conventional rule—or frame-based ES approaches—in some applications. For one, since neural networks do not require knowledge to be formalized, they are appropriate to domains in which knowledge is scanty. Conventional expert systems map input responses into progressively refined but linearly separable spaces. Neural networks, on the other hand, can develop input/output map boundaries that are highly nonlinear (Figure 1.4). Some types of problems benefit from this capability. Also, although most conventional ES software permits classification probabilities to be incorporated into rules, ordinarily they must be explicitly entered. Some types of neural networks are able to deduce these probabilities through training. It is difficult for rule-based ESs to develop rules from historical data when the inputs are highly correlated. Neural network learning paradigms do not suffer from this problem. Finally, the per-case processing time of neural networks can be faster than that of conventional systems, since the network examines all of the information available about a problem at once. This facilitates a more highly automated input interface.

Neural networks have several other benefits:

❖ *Fault tolerance.* Since there are many processing nodes, each with primarily local connections, damage to a few nodes or links does not bring the system to a halt.

❖ *Generalization.* When a neural network is presented with noisy, incomplete, or previously unseen input, it generates a reasonable response.

❖ *Adaptability.* Since the network learns in new environments, training can occur continuously over its useful life and occur concurrently with the deployment of the network.

Figure 1.4

Input–Output Maps (with outputs A, B, C, D)

a.

Orthogonal

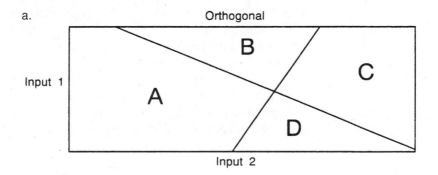

b.

Linearly Separable

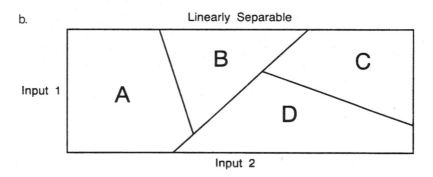

c.

Nonlinearly Separable

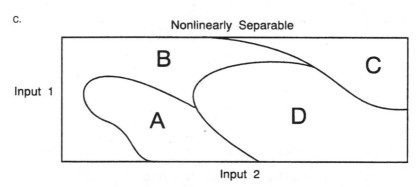

Source: R. R. Trippi and E. Turban, "Auto-Learning Approaches for Building Expert Systems," *Computers and Operations Research* 17, no. 6 (June 1990), pp. 553–60.

Neural networks have their weaknesses. Not every potential ES application will benefit from the advantages of neural networks or be worth the additional cost and complexity. A vexing and sometimes unacceptable characteristic of neural network ESs is that they can identify as important for decision-making factors that appear to be irrelevant or even factors that conflict with traditional theories in the knowledge domain. Since the scope of training is always to some extent limited by economics and time, networks that contradict accepted theory run the risk of lacking generality, functioning well only on data with a structure similar to that of the training set.

Most neural network systems lack explanation facilities. Justifications for results are difficult to obtain because the connection weights do not usually have obvious interpretations. This is particularly true in pattern recognition where it is very difficult or even impossible to explain the logic behind specific decisions. With current technologies, training times can be excessive and tedious; thus, the need for frequent retraining may make a particular application impractical. The best way to represent input data and the choice of architecture is still mostly subject to trial and error. Neural computing usually requires large amounts of data and lengthy training times.

Also, most neural networks cannot guarantee an optimal solution to a problem, a completely certain solution, or sometimes even repeatability with the same input data. However, properly configured and trained neural networks can often make consistently good classifications, generalizations, or decisions, in a statistical sense.

Neural networks can be used effectively to automate both routine and ad hoc financial analysis tasks. Prototype neural network-based decision aids have been built for the following applications:

- ❖ Credit authorization screening.

- ❖ Mortgage risk assessment.

- ❖ Project management and bidding strategy.

- ❖ Financial and economic forecasting.

- ❖ Risk rating of exchange-traded, fixed-income investments.

- ❖ Detection of regularities in security price movements.

- ❖ Prediction of default and bankruptcy.

Other potential applications meriting further research, development, and evaluation are the following:

❖   Portfolio selection and diversification.

❖   Simulation of market behavior.

❖   Index construction.

❖   Identification of explanatory economic factors.

❖   "Mining" of financial and economic databases.

DEVELOPING NEURAL NETWORK APPLICATIONS

Neural network applications are in use enough to allow identification of practical guidelines for their development. The first two steps in the ANN development process involve collecting data and separating it into a training set and a test set. These tasks must be based on a thorough analysis of the application so that the problem is well bounded and the functionality of the system and the context of the neural networks are well understood.

In conjunction with a domain expert, the developer must identify and clarify data relevant to the problem. This means formulating and conceptualizing the task in a data-oriented way that will be amenable to a neural network solution. For example, textual descriptions need to be reformulated to allow the knowledge to be described numerically. The developer needs to avoid biases due to the particular way the data are represented. Other considerations are the stability of the input and the extent to which environmental conditions might require changes in the number of input nodes to the neural network. At this point, a difficulty in expressing data in the form needed for a neural network might lead to cancellation of the project.

The anticipated structure of the neural network and the learning algorithm determine the data type, such as binary or continuous. High-quality data collection requires care to minimize ambiguity, errors, and randomness in data. The data should be collected to cover the widest range of the problem domain; it should cover not only routine operations, but also exceptions and conditions at the boundaries of the problem domain. Another task is to confirm reliability by using multiple sources of data; even so, ambiguities will have to be resolved. In general, the more data used, the better—as long as quality is not sacrificed. Larger data sets increase processing times during training, but better data improve the accuracy of the training and could lead to faster convergence to a good set of weights.

Normally, training a neural network begins with *data separation*. The data sets are randomly separated into two categories: training cases and testing cases. The training cases are used to adjust the weights. The test cases are used for validation of the network. The number of cases needed for each category can be computed by considering several factors.[2-4]

NETWORK STRUCTURES

Many different neural network models and implementations are being developed and studied today.[3, 5] Three representative architectures are shown in Figure 1.5 and are discussed below.

Associative Memory Systems

Associative memory is the ability to recall complete situations from partial information. These systems correlate input data with information stored in memory. Information can be recalled from incomplete or "noisy" input, and performance degrades only slowly as neurons fail. Associative memory systems can detect similarities between new input and stored patterns. Most neural network architectures can be used as associative memories, and a prime example of a single-layer system is the Hopfield network,[6] which uses the collective properties of the network and minimization of an energy function to classify input patterns.

Hidden Layer

Associative memory systems can have one or more intermediate (hidden) layers. An example of a simple network was shown in Figure 1.3. Many of today's multilayer networks use the back-propagation learning algorithm. Another type of unsupervised learning, competitive filter associative memory, is capable of learning by changing its weights in recognition of categories of input data without being provided examples by an external trainer. A leading example of such a single-layer, self-organizing system for a fixed number of classes in the inputs is the Kohonen network.[7]

Double-Layer Structure

A double-layer structure, exemplified by the adaptive resonance theory (ART) approach, does not require the knowledge of a precise number of

Figure 1.5

Neural Network Structures

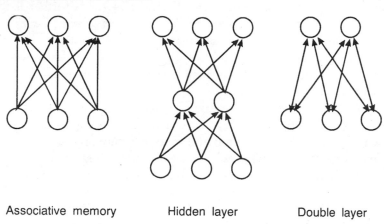

Associative memory   Hidden layer   Double layer

classes in the training data.[8] Instead, it uses feed-forward and feed-backward to adjust parameters as data are analyzed to establish arbitrary numbers of categories that represent the data presented to the system. Parameters can be adjusted to tune the sensitivity of the system and produce meaningful categories.

For more complex neural computing applications, neurons are combined in various architectures useful for information processing. Practical applications require one or more (hidden) layers between the input and output neurons and a correspondingly large number of weights. Most commercial ANN include three, or rarely four or five, layers, each containing from 10 to a thousand processing elements. Some experimental ANN include millions of processing elements. The use of more than three layers is not necessary in most commercial systems. The amount of computation added with each layer increases very rapidly.

LEARNING ALGORITHMS

An important consideration in ANN is the appropriate use of algorithms for learning (or training). Such algorithms are called learning algorithms (or paradigms), and more than a hundred of them are known. A taxonomy of these algorithms has been proposed by Lippman,[9] who distinguishes between two major categories based on the input format: binary-valued input (0's and 1's) or continuous-valued input. Each of these can be further divided into two basic categories: *supervised learning* and *unsupervised learning*.

Supervised learning uses a set of inputs for which the appropriate (desired) outputs are known. In one type, the difference between the desired and actual output is used to calculate corrections to the weights of the neural network. A variation of that approach simply acknowledges for each input trial whether or not the output is correct as the network adjusts weights in an attempt to achieve correct results. Examples of this type of learning are back-propagation and Hopfield network.

In unsupervised learning, only input stimuli are shown to the network. The network is self-organizing; that is, it organizes itself internally so that each hidden processing element responds strategically to a different set of input stimuli (or groups of stimuli). No knowledge is supplied about what classifications (outputs) are correct, and those that the network derives may or may not be meaningful to the person training the network. However, the number of categories into which the network classifies the inputs can be controlled by varying certain parameters in the model. In any case, a human must examine the final categories to assign meaning and to determine the usefulness of the results. Examples of this type of learning are the adaptive resonance theory and Kohonen self-organizing feature maps.

HOW A NETWORK LEARNS

Consider a single neuron that learns the inclusive OR operation—a classic problem in symbolic logic. Consider two input elements, X_1 and X_2. If either of them or both have a positive value (or a certain value), then the result is also positive. This can be shown as follows.

Case	Inputs		Desired Results	
	X_1	X_2		
1	0	0	0	
2	0	1	1	(positive)
3	1	0	1	(positive)
4	1	1	1	(positive)

The neuron must be trained to recognize the input patterns and classify them to give the corresponding outputs. The procedure is to present to the neuron the sequence of the four input patterns so that the weights are adjusted by the computer after each iteration. This operation is repeated until the weights converge to one set of values that allows the neuron to correctly classify each of the four inputs. The results shown in Table 1.1 were produced by using a spreadsheet to execute the calculations.

In this simple example, a step function is used to evaluate the summation of input values. After calculating outputs, a measure of the error Δ between the output and the desired values is used to update the weights,

Table 1.1
Example of Supervised Learning

Parameters: $\alpha = 0.2$; Threshold = 0.5

Iteration	X_1	X_2	Z	Initial W_1	W_2	Y	Δ	Final W_1	W_2
1	0	0	0	0.1	0.3	0	0.0	0.1	0.3
	0	1	1	0.1	0.3	0	1.0	0.1	0.5
	1	0	1	0.1	0.5	0	1.0	0.3	0.5
	1	1	1	0.3	0.5	1	0.0	0.3	0.5
2	0	0	0	0.3	0.5	0	0.0	0.3	0.5
	0	1	1	0.3	0.5	0	1.0	0.3	0.7
	1	0	1	0.3	0.7	0	1.0	0.5	0.7
	1	1	1	0.5	0.7	1	0.0	0.5	0.7
3	0	0	0	0.5	0.7	0	0.0	0.5	0.7
	0	1	1	0.5	0.7	1	0.0	0.5	0.7
	1	0	1	0.5	0.7	0	1.0	0.7	0.7
	1	1	1	0.7	0.7	1	0.0	0.7	0.7
4	0	0	0	0.7	0.7	0	0.0	0.7	0.7
	0	1	1	0.7	0.7	1	0.0	0.7	0.7
	1	0	1	0.7	0.7	1	0.0	0.7	0.7
	1	1	1	0.7	0.7	1	0.0	0.7	0.7

subsequently reinforcing correct results. At any iteration in the process for a neuron, j, we get

$$\Delta = Z_j - Y_j$$

where Z and Y are the desired and actual outputs, respectively. Then, the updated weights are:

$$W_i \text{ (Final)} = W_i \text{ (Initial)} + \alpha \Delta X_i$$

where α is a parameter that controls how fast the learning takes place.

As shown in Table 1.1, each calculation uses one of the X_1 and X_2 pairs and the corresponding value for the OR operation along with initial values, W_1 and W_2, of the neuron's weights. In this example, the weights are assigned random values at the beginning and a *learning rate* (a parameter), α, is set to be relatively low. Δ is used to derive the final weights, which then become the initial weights in the next row.

The initial values of weights for each input are transformed using the equation above to values that are used with the next input (row). The threshold value (another parameter) causes the Y value to be 1 in the next row if the weighted sum of inputs is greater than 0.5; otherwise, the output is set to 0. In this example, in the first iteration two of the four outputs are incorrect ($\Delta = 1$), and no consistent set of weights has been found. In the subsequent iterations, the learning algorithm improves the results until it finally produces a set of weights that give the correct results. Once determined, a neuron with those weight values can quickly perform the OR operation.

In developing ANN, an attempt is made to fit the problem characteristic to one of the known learning algorithms. Software exists for all the most common algorithms, but it is best to use a well-known and well-characterized one, such as back-propagation.

TRAINING THE NETWORK

This phase consists of presenting the training data set to the network so that the weights can be adjusted to produce the desired output for each of the inputs. Weights are adjusted after each input vector is presented, so several iterations of the complete training set will be required until a consistent set of weights that works for *all* the training data is derived.

The choice of the network's structure (e.g., the number of nodes and layers), as well as the selection of the initial conditions of the network, determines the time needed for training. Therefore, these choices are important and require careful consideration at the outset of the process.

In the ideal case, the network can learn the features of the input data without learning irrelevant details. Thus, with the presentation of novel inputs that are not identical to those in the training set, the network would be able to make correct classifications.

In the first step of the development process, the available data are divided into training and testing data. After the training has been performed, it is necessary to test the network. The testing phase examines the performance of the network using the derived weights by measuring the ability of the network to classify the test data correctly. Black-box testing (comparing test results to actual historical results) is the primary approach to verify that inputs produce appropriate outputs.

In many cases, the network is not expected to perform perfectly, and only a certain level of quality is required. Usually, the neural network application is an alternative to another method that can be used as a standard. For example, a statistical technique or other quantitative methods may be known to classify inputs correctly 70 percent of the time. The neural network implementation often improves on that percentage. If the neural network is replacing manual operations, performance levels of human processing may be the standard for deciding if the testing phase is successful.

The test plan should include routine cases as well as potentially problematic situations, for example, at the boundaries of the problem domain. If the testing reveals large deviations, the training set needs to be reexamined, and the training process may have to be reactivated.

In some cases, other methods can supplement straightforward blackbox testing. For example, the weights can be analyzed statistically to look for unusually large values that indicate overtraining or unusually small weights that indicate unnecessary nodes, which can be eliminated. Also, certain weights that represent major factors in the input vector can be selectively activated to make sure that corresponding outputs respond properly.

Even at a performance level equal to that of a traditional method, the ANN may have other advantages. For example, the network is easily modified by retraining with new data. Other computerized techniques may require extensive reprogramming when changes are needed.

IMPLEMENTATION

The implementation of an ANN frequently requires proper interfaces to other computer-based information systems and training of the users. Ongoing monitoring and feedback to the developers are recommended for system improvements and long-term success. An important consideration is to gain confidence of the users and management early in the deployment to ensure that the system is accepted and used properly.

If it is a part of a larger system, the ANN will need convenient interfaces to other information systems, input/output (I/O) devices, and manual operations of the users. The system may need I/O manipulation subsystems such as signal digitizers and file conversion modules. Good documentation and user training are necessary to ensure successful integration into the mainstream operations. A convenient procedure must be planned for updating the training sets and initiating periodic retraining of the network. This includes the ability to recognize and include new cases that are discovered when the system is used routinely.

Ongoing monitoring and feedback to the developers is necessary for maintaining the neural network system. Periodic evaluation of system performance may reveal environmental changes or previously missed bugs that require changes in the network. Enhancements may be suggested as users become more familiar with the system, and feedback may be useful in the design of future versions or in new products.

NEURAL COMPUTING PARADIGMS

In building an artificial neural network, the builder must make many decisions. The most important decisions concern the following issues:

❖ Size of training and test data.

❖ Learning algorithms.

❖ Topology—Number of processing elements and their configurations (inputs, layers, outputs).

❖ Transformation (transfer) function to be used.

❖ Learning rate for each layer.

❖ Selecting diagnostic and validation tools.

A specific collection of configurations determined by these decisions is referred to as the network's paradigm.

PROGRAMMING NEURAL NETWORKS

Artificial neural networks are basically software applications that need to be programmed. Like any other application, ANN can be programmed with a programming language, a tool, or both.

A major portion of the programming deals with the training algorithms and the transfer and summation functions. It makes sense, therefore, to use development tools in which these standard computations are pre-programmed. Indeed, several dozen development tools are on the market. Some of these tools are similar to expert system shells. Even with the help of ANN tools, however, the job of developing a neural network may not be so simple. Specifically, it may be necessary to program the layout of the database, to partition the data (test data, training data), and to transfer the data to files suitable for input to an ANN tool.

Most development tools can support several network paradigms (up to several dozen). In addition to the standard products, many specialized products are available. For example, several products are based on spread-sheets (e.g., NNetSheet). Other products are designed to work with expert systems as hybrid development products.

The user of these tools is constrained by the configuration of the tool. Therefore, builders may prefer to use programming languages such as C, or to use spreadsheets to program the model and execute the calculations.

NEURAL NETWORK HARDWARE

Most current neural network applications involve software simulations that run on conventional sequential processors. Simulating a neural network means mathematically defining the nodes and weights assigned to it. So instead of using one CPU for each neuron, one CPU is used for all of the neurons. This simulation may require long processing times. Advances in hardware technology will greatly enhance the performance of future neural network systems by exploiting the inherent advantage of *massively parallel processing*. Hardware improvements will meet the higher require-ments for memory and processing speed and thus allow shorter training times of larger networks.

Each processing element computes node outputs from the weights and input signals from other processors. Together, the network of neurons can store information that may be recalled to interpret and classify future inputs to the network.

To reduce the computational work of ANN, which can consist of hundreds of thousands of manipulations when the work is done on regular computers, one of three approaches is applicable:

1. *Faster machines.* For example, a machine supplemented by a faster math coprocessor can expedite work, but not too much (e.g., 2 to 10 times faster).

2. *Neural chips.* Most of today's special semiconductor chips can execute computations very fast, but they cannot be used to train the network. So it is necessary to train "off the chip." This problem is expected to be overcome soon; in the interim, acceleration boards are useful. The idea is to provide implementation of neural network data structures through hardware rather than software, using an analog device (e.g., Intel 80170 Electronically Trainable ANN) or a digital device, or even an optical one.[10] (See Caudill [1991] for details.) Most hardware-implemented neural networks are still in the developmental stage.

3. *Accelerator boards.* These are dedicated multichip processors that can be added to regular computers; they function similarly to a math coprocessor. Because they are especially designed for ANN, they are very fast in this application. (For example, such a processor can be 10 to 100 times faster than the 80486 processor.) Acceleration boards are currently the good approach to speeding up computations. Some examples are the BrainMaker Accelerator Board, Balboa/860 boards, and NeuroBoard, which is at least 100 times faster than the 80486 processor. Accelerator boards are extremely useful because they reduce training time, which usually is long. For example, independent testing with the NeuroBoard accelerator showed a reduced training time from seven minutes to one second.

CONCLUSION

Artificial neural networks represent a radically different form of computation from the more common algorithmic model. Neural computation is massively parallel, typically employing from several thousand to many millions of individual simple processors, arranged in a communicative network. ANN technology can deliver performance demonstrably superior to conventional problem-solving approaches in a wide variety of areas. Although numerous neural network models and products supporting those models are currently available, the deployment of neural network-based systems to aid in making business decisions is at a relatively early stage of development, with much of the current activity still taking place at the research level.

The unique learning capabilities of ANN promise benefits in many aspects of investment and financial decision-making, which involve the recognition of patterns and in which adequate representation of knowledge is difficult or impossible. Commercial applications likely to be most successful are those that directly assist finance professionals in one or more specific aspects of their work, such as implementation of a particular strategy, or that provide improved results relative to statistical and other conventional forms of analysis when used for more routine operations such as credit, risk, and exception assessment.

ENDNOTES

1. The material in this chapter is based largely on the work of L. Medsker as it appears in E. Turban, *Expert Systems and Applied Artificial Intelligence* (New York: Macmillan Publishing Co., 1992) Chapter 18; and in part on the work of R. R. Trippi, "Intelligent Systems for Investment Decision Making," in *Managing Institutional Assets*, ed. F. Fabozzi (Harper and Row, 1990).

2. M. Caudill and C. Butler, *Naturally Intelligent Systems* (Cambridge, MA: MIT Press, 1990).

3. R. Hecht-Nielson, *Neurocomputing* (Reading, MA: Addison Wesley, 1990).

4. T. Khanna, *Foundations of Neural Networks* (Reading, MA: Addison Wesley, 1990).

5. R. Beale and T. Jackson, *Neural Computing* (Bristol, England: Adam Hilger, 1990).

6. J. Hopfield, "Neural Networks and Physical Systems with Emergent Collective Computational Abilities," *Proceedings of the National Academy of Science USA* 79 (1985), pp. 141–52.

7. T. Kohonen, *Self-Organization and Associative Memory* (Berlin: Springer-Verlag, 1984).

8. G. Carpenter and S. Grossberg, "A Massively Parallel Architecture for a Self-Organizing Neural Pattern Recognition Machine," *Computer Vision, Graphics and Image Processing* 37 (1987), pp. 54–115.

9. R. P. Lippman, "Review of Neural Networks for Speech Recognition," *Neural Computation* 1, no. 1 (1989), pp. 1–38.

10. M. Caudill, "Embedded Neural Networks," *AI Expert*, December 1989, April 1990, June 1990, July 1990, September 1990, December 1990, April 1991.

2

ARTIFICIAL NEURAL SYSTEMS: A NEW TOOL FOR FINANCIAL DECISION-MAKING

Delvin D. Hawley, John D. Johnson, Dijjotam Raina

INTRODUCTION

The financial press has largely confined its coverage of artificial intelligence applications to so-called "expert systems." While expert systems have been successfully applied to some financial decision tasks, many others are beyond the scope of expert systems technology. The disadvantages of expert systems include the difficulty of programming and maintaining the system, the enormous time and effort required to extract the knowledge base from human experts and translate it into the if-then rules upon which the system is based, and the inability of an expert system to use inductive

This article originally appeared in *Financial Analysts Journal*, November/December 1990, pp. 63–72. Reprinted with permission.

learning and inference to adapt the rule base to changing situations. These problems may be particularly troublesome in financial analysis and management environments.

Many of these problems could be overcome with another product of artificial intelligence research: the artificial neural system, also known as an artificial neural network, electronic neural network, or simply neural net. Neural networks attempt to model human intuition by simulating the physical process upon which intuition is based; that is, by simulating the process of adaptive biological learning (although on a much less complex scale). A neural network is theoretically capable of producing a proper response to a given problem (or the best possible response when more than one response is applicable) even when the information is noisy or incomplete or when no set procedure exists for solving the problem.

THE DECISION ENVIRONMENT

Simon has classified managerial decisions along a continuum from highly structured to highly unstructured.[1] In structured decisions, the procedures for obtaining the best (or at least a good enough) solution are best known in advance, and the objectives are clearly specified. Managers can call on predefined models, whether conceptual or computer-based, to assist in the decision process. In unstructured problems, however, intuition plays a larger role in decision-making. The manager may seek help from experts, but the final decision generally involves ad hoc analysis and a substantial subjective element.

Many highly structured, routine tasks can be handled effectively by basic computer systems, readily available commercial software, and lower-level management or even clerical personnel. Most decisions faced by top-level financial managers, however, are highly unstructured in nature and not easily adapted to conventional methods of computer-aided analysis and decision support. In addition, many of these decisions are largely unique in character.

In such cases, the manager may have to draw upon incomplete, ambiguous, partially incorrect, or irrelevant information and analyze it in a highly subjective and ad hoc manner. The manager may not be able to objectify his decision process or to break it down in a step-by-step manner.

Computer technology, at its current state of development, has little to offer decision-makers faced with unstructured problems. CFOs, for example, may call on corporate computer information systems or external on-line data sources such as Dow-Jones News Retrieval to acquire information and spreadsheet programs or other software to analyze the information. If more formal or complicated software is required, however, it must be created from scratch by internal or external programmers. This can take many weeks or months and usually involves great expense. In addition, the resulting program may have to be reworked each time it is applied to a new problem. Because most financial decisions must be made very quickly, this is simply not a viable alternative for decision-makers in many cases.

As a consequence, top-level financial decision-makers have obtained very little direct benefit from the tremendous advances in computer technology over the past decade, despite the arrival of decision support systems and expert systems. Decision support systems aim to assist the decision-maker without constraining the decision process. Expert systems attempt to model the decision-making ability of human experts. The intuition or knowledge base of the experts must be programmed into an expert system, however, and the creation of the knowledge base is a long and expensive process. Expert systems thus simply are not economical for one-time decision problems. Furthermore, it is rarely clear what an expert's knowledge base includes and what heuristics must be used to model it.

In unstructured decision environments, artificial neural systems offer distinct advantages over decision support and expert systems. Neural nets can be defined as "highly simplified models of the human nervous system, exhibiting abilities such as learning, generalization, and abstraction."[2] While the concept of such systems is not new, only recently have technological advances made artificial neural systems a viable alternative for many financial problems.

NEURAL NETWORKS

An artificial neural system (ANS) models (or reproduces), in a very simplified way, the biological systems of the human brain. It does so by mimicking the basic functions of the major component of the human brain: the neuron. Simulated neurons serve as the basic functional unit of the ANS, in much the same way that binary electronic switches serve as the basic units in digital computers.

A neuron, illustrated in Figure 2.1, is a simple structure that performs three basic functions: the input, processing, and output of signals. The input components (called dendrites) receive electrochemical impulses

Figure 2.1

A Single Neuron

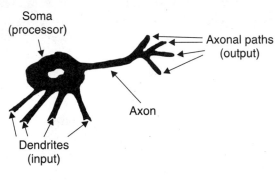

(through synaptic links) from the output components (called axons) of other neurons. Each neuron may be connected to 1,000 or more neighbors via a network of dendrites and axons.

The processor component of the neuron (called the nucleus or soma) works very simply. The neuron's many dendrites receive impulses from other neurons and transfer these impulses to the soma. (All dendrites do not receive impulses simultaneously; each dendrite can receive an impulse at any point in time from any of the axons to which it is connected.) The soma collects these impulses, sums them, and compares the sum to an output threshold or "action potential." This action potential is the level of stimulation (called the "activation level") necessary for the neuron to "fire" or send an impulse through its axon to other connected neurons.

A neuron is a much slower mechanism (possibly a thousand times slower) than the digital switches in conventional computers. Even so, the brain is capable of solving difficult pattern-recognition problems (vision and language, for example) in about one-half second, while even simple pattern-recognition tasks are beyond the capabilities of conventional digital computers. The brain achieves its processing speed and power by linking tremendous numbers of inherently slow neurons into an immensely complex network that allows many individual neurons to function simultaneously. (This process of subdividing tasks for simultaneous completion is referred to as parallel distributed processing.)

Artificial Neurons

Like the brain itself, an ANS depends for power and speed on the simultaneous functioning of its individual neural units. In most cases, the ANS requires computer hardware with parallel processing (as opposed to the standard serial) capabilities. Because the outputs of an ANS are parallel (involving simultaneous transmission of data vectors), ANS implementations usually require specialized hardware, sometimes referred to as neurocomputers, designed to facilitate parallel processing. The parallel inputs required by neural networks may also require the installation of special-purpose preprocessors, or "front-ends."[3]

Neural net systems differ from traditional computer applications, including most expert systems, in many other ways. Neural nets are not "programmed" in the traditional sense. An ANS is not provided with quantitative descriptions of objects or patterns to be recognized or with logical criteria for distinguishing such objects from similar objects. Instead, it is presented with repetitive examples that display variety: Cars come in all shapes and sizes, mammals include cows and mice but not alligators, and so on. The ANS "discovers" the relationships between inputs by observing the examples and progressively refining an internal matrix of weights governing the relationships between its simulated neurons. The ANS thus learns through adaptation—the major difference between ANS and expert system applications. Expert systems are based on inference from accurate representation of the problem environment; they generally have little or no learning capability.

An ANS has three major components: a network topology, a spreading activation method, and a training mechanism. The network topology consists of a set of nodes connected via links. Nodes directly linked to one another are said to be neighbors. Nodes are connected in parallel; that is, each node is connected to many others. Furthermore, the flow of information through the system need not be unidirectional; information can flow in either direction along any link.

Figure 2.2 shows a simple artificial neuron consisting of a node (Y) and its associated links. Input signals—the ys in Figure 2.2—are received from the node's links, assigned weights (the ws), and added. The value of the node, Y, is the sum of all the weighted input signals. This value is compared with the node's threshold activation level. When the value meets the threshold level, the node transmits a signal to its neighbors.

Figure 2.2

A Single Artificial Neuron

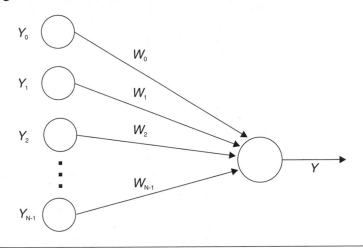

The activation level of any node depends on the node's previous activation level and on the activation levels of its neighbors. A node's activation level is communicated to its neighbors at each point in time via the system's spreading activation method. The neighbors use the activation level to update their own levels of activation. Weights, which are numeric estimates of connection strengths, are assigned to the links between nodes.

If the activation level of one node tends to increase (decrease) the activation level of a neighboring node, then the connection is designated as an excitatory (inhibitory) link and is assigned a positive (negative) weight. These weights—numeric estimates of the direction and strength of connections between nodes—are the instrumental elements of the ANS "learning" process.[4]

The learning process of an ANS is actually a training process. An animal can be trained by rewarding desired responses and punishing undesired responses. The ANS training process can also be thought of as involving rewards and punishments. When the system responds correctly to an input, the "reward" consists of a strengthening of the current matrix of nodal weights. This makes it more likely that a similar response will be produced by similar inputs in the future. When the system responds incorrectly, the "punishment" calls for the adjustment of the nodal weights based on the particular learning algorithm employed so that the system will respond differently when it encounters similar inputs again. Desirable actions are thus progressively reinforced, while undesirable actions are progressively inhibited.

An ANS can be trained using either a supervised or an unsupervised methodology. In supervised training, an input information vector is paired with a desired output or target vector.[5] For example, the input vector might contain a series of numbers, while the output vector contains the product of the numbers. The objective of the training process in this case would be for the ANS to discover the pattern underlying the relationship between the input and the target output.

Prior to training, the system may have no knowledge of numbers, their relative magnitudes, or mathematical operations; in the terminology of psychology, it is a *tabula rasa* or "blank slate," consisting only of a matrix of arbitrarily assigned nodal weights. The system would need to discover that the symbol 6 implies something different from the symbol 2, and that the symbol 12 is related to them in some consistent manner. It would also need to discover that the symbol 12 can be related to 3 and 4 in a similar and consistent manner.

In unsupervised training, the system is presented with only the input vector; no target vector exists. The ANS objective is to detect and identify patterns in the input. The system self-organizes until a consistent output is produced whenever the input vector is applied. The characteristics of the output may be quite unpredictable prior to training.[6] As with supervised learning, the system in unsupervised training discovers recurring patterns in the input information, but it must do so without any information about the desirable or correct output. Such a system could be trained, for example, to recognize and identify specific musicians in recordings of symphonic music.

ANS VERSUS ES

An expert system (ES) depends on the representation of the expert's knowledge as a series of if-then conditions or rules, known as the knowledge base. These rules must first be determined by observing human experts, then programmed into the ES using special languages such as PROLOG, or shells such as Knowledge Craft, ART, or KEE. This process can be time-consuming and expensive. Coats points out that ES programmers, or knowledge engineers, "spend weeks, months, sometimes years with experts, coaxing them to articulate the objective and subjective factors, rules, and thought processes used in problem solving . . . The fact is that extracting knowledge from the experts presents a very serious bottleneck."[7] Furthermore, once the system is functional, making even minor changes to the knowledge base can be a complex and expensive process because of the intricate relations between the rules forming the knowledge base.[8] Thus, expert systems are generally cost-effective only for frequently recurring problems of a very narrow scope that can be solved by a knowledge base that is essentially static.

Neural net systems do not exhibit these same shortcomings, primarily because they do not require a predefined knowledge base. Changes in the problem do not require reprogramming the ANS; the system simply retrains itself based on the new information. The ANS creates its own knowledge system based on the inputs (and possibly outputs) to which it is exposed. It is also self-maintaining, responding automatically to changes in the problem environment by adjusting nodal weights. Best of all, it is fundamentally a dynamic, rather than a static, system. It continues to adapt and improve as it is exposed to new information.

Neural nets will certainly not replace programmers in the foreseeable future, but they do offer a much more powerful and expedient alternative in some applications, particularly those involving pattern recognition.[9] The abilities of an ANS to self-organize and to function without a preprogrammed knowledge base give it an important additional advantage in business applications: protection of sensitive information.

Another problem with expert systems, as pointed out by Coats, is that "ES cannot really deal with erroneous, inconsistent, or incomplete knowledge because most ES rely on rules that represent abstracted knowledge of the domain [i.e., the problem space] and thus the ES are not able to reason from basic principles."[10] In other words, a fairly complete understanding of the human expert's knowledge is a prerequisite to creating the knowledge base for the ES. The system is not able to make educated guesses or employ common sense as a human expert would when presented with a problem that did not have a clear solution path. It is also unable to perform effectively when the input information is incomplete, ambiguous (noisy), or partially erroneous.

It is in this area that neural net systems may offer the clearest advantage over expert systems. The ANS can accommodate variations in inputs.

That is to say, the ANS is very good at filtering out noise and isolating useful input information. People are very good at this, too. A human reader, for example, can often make sense of a text that is largely illegible or incorrect.

The real world rarely obliges financial decision-makers by presenting them with clearly defined and precise information. Much of the information they receive is noisy, incomplete, and full of error. Conventional computers and expert systems can be programmed to tolerate noisy inputs, but the necessary algorithms involve such an enormous computational load that their use is often impractical. Neural networks, however, can work with noisy and incomplete inputs and produce the correct output by making use of context and generalizing or "filling in the gaps" in incomplete information. This ability to generalize is based on the adaptive structure of the neural net system, rather than on complex programming.

Neural nets are also capable of abstraction—inferring the "ideal set" from a nonideal training set. This process involves determining the most prominent characteristics of the training set, then using those characteristics to construct an internal representation of the ideal or archetypical pattern.[11]

It is the nature of an ANS to make educated guesses, inferring as much as possible from previous inputs and experience. In the early training stages of an ANS, the educated guesses will undoubtedly range very wide of the mark because the system has had very little education. As the training process progresses, however, the experiential basis for the educated guesses will become more refined, and the quality of the guesses will, on average, improve. In fact, an ANS, unlike an ES, can potentially exceed the ability of human experts. A well-trained ANS, for example, may be able to discern patterns that human experts would miss and to recognize patterns with a higher degree of consistency.

ANS Disadvantages

A major and inherent problem of artificial neural systems is that the internal structure of the neural network makes it difficult to trace the steps by which the output is reached. In other words, an ANS cannot tell the user how it processed the input information or reached a conclusion. That process is represented only in the matrix of connected weights, which, at least at present, cannot be translated into an algorithm that would be intelligible or useful outside the ANS.[12] The output cannot be decomposed into discrete steps or series of operations, as would be possible with an

ES rule base or any conventional computer program.[13] It is thus not possible to check intermediate computations or to debug an ANS in the traditional sense. The only way to test the system for consistency and reliability is to monitor the output.

The absence of a clearly identifiable internal logic could be a severe stumbling block in the acceptance of neural networks, at least for some applications. Where is the accountability? How does the user know if the system malfunctions? It would be ill-advised, given the current state of technology, to use an ANS to control nuclear weapons on a warship.

Many important business decisions made by humans suffer from the same shortcoming. An executive can rarely recognize and understand *all* the steps that went into a given decision, let alone be able to explain the process to another person. It is the average effectiveness of the executive's decisions—the dependability of the output—that counts, not the intricacies of the intermediate processes. Although this standard may apply to human decision-makers, many people are going to be uncomfortable applying it to computer-based systems.

Finally, the ANS learning process requires a large number of training examples and hence can involve substantial time and effort. For most conceivable financial applications, however, ample training examples would be readily available, so relatively little time or effort would be involved in data collection. Furthermore, the time and effort required to train an ANS would be much less than that required to extract and translate an expert's knowledge base for an ES.

ANS APPLICATIONS

Neural net systems are most effectively applied to three tasks (all based primarily on pattern recognition): classification, associative memory, and clustering.[14] Classification involves the assignment of input vectors to *pre-defined* groups or classes based on patterns that exist in the input information. An ANS should be successful in this task even if the inputs are incomplete or have been corrupted. If the input vector consists of sounds of a musician playing an instrument in a busy subway station, for example, an ANS should be able to pick out the sounds of the instrument and classify it as a saxophone, a piano, or a bagpipe.

The recognition of handwritten characters is another example of a classification task. The recognition and identification of underwater targets by sonar would be a very appropriate ANS application.[15] In finance, an example of classification would be the grouping of bonds, based on patterns in the issuers' financial data, into categories that match the agency ratings assigned to those bonds.

An ANS can also function as associative memory (also referred to as content-addressable memory). In this task, the class exemplar is desired, and the input pattern is used to determine which exemplar to produce. Content-addressable memory is useful when only part of a pattern is available and the complete pattern is required. As an example, the input vector may consist of a digitized picture of a smudged fingerprint, and the desired output would be a reconstruction of the complete fingerprint.

In clustering, the ANS is used to group or "vector-quantitize" a large number of diverse inputs, each of which has elements of similarity with other inputs. This function is useful in compressing or filtering input data without losing important information. An example would be clustering corporate bonds into homogeneous risk classes based on financial statement data. In this case, the number and composition of the risk classes would be determined by the ANS, not by the user. This differs from classification, discussed above, in that the categories are not predefined.

ANS in Use

Researchers are currently working on many projects using ANS technology. Sejnowski and Rosenberg have created a neural network, NETtalk, that learned the correct pronunciation of words from written text (ASCII characters) even though it began with no linguistic rules.[16] The ANS taught itself pronunciation skills (approximately equivalent to those of a six-year-old child) *overnight*, simply by listening to the correct pronunciation of speech from text. In contrast, Digital Equipment Corporation designed an expert system called DECtalk that serves the same function but required 20 *years* of linguistic research to devise the necessary knowledge base.[17] Current ANS research is directed toward the recognition of radar and sonar targets and the detection of plastic explosives in airline baggage.[18] In the business and finance areas, researchers are working on the development of neural networks that can assess the risk of mortgage loans and rate the quality of corporate bonds.[19]

While a good deal of ANS research has focused on the behavior of stock prices, it has had only moderate success to date. Halbert White of the University of California at San Diego, for example, provided an ANS with daily returns for IBM common stock over 500 days in the mid-1970s, the objective being to extract predictable fluctuations in the stock price.[20] However, only random movements were evident. White points out that "it won't be easy to uncover predictable stock market fluctuations with neural nets, and if you succeed, you'll want to keep it secret." Of course, this application presupposes that predictable patterns in stock prices exist, contrary to a preponderance of empirical evidence supporting weak-form market efficiency.

The inability of an ANS to discover stock price patterns does not necessarily imply a failure of the system; it could be construed simply as additional evidence supporting market efficiency. Unfortunately, there is no way to know which conclusion is correct. The situation is similar to that of scientists monitoring radio signals in space. The absence of nonrandom signals does not necessarily imply that intelligent extraterrestrial life does not exist; the search may simply not be focused in the proper place, or the technology may be incorrectly applied.

APPLICATIONS IN FINANCE

Tasks requiring accuracy of computational results or intensive calculations are best left to conventional computer applications. As we have noted, artificial neural networks are best applied to problem environments that are highly unstructured, require some form of pattern recognition, and may involve incomplete or corrupted data. Below, we outline some potential applications of ANS to problems faced by corporate financial managers, financial institutions, and professional investors.

Corporate Finance

Financial Simulation. The financial structure of any business operation constitutes an immensely complex and dynamic environment. While financial management tasks can be broken down conceptually and functionally into a number of subtasks, the interrelations between these subtasks are still enormously complex. Artificial neural systems can be used to create models of segments of the corporate financial environment. Such models can be (1) specific to a particular company, (2) dynamic with respect to changes in the financial structure of the company over time, and (3) reflective of the relations between the segment modeled, other financial and nonfinancial segments of the company, and the external environment.

An ANS might, for example, be created to simulate the behavior of a firm's credit customers as economic conditions change. The input vectors could consist of economic data and customer-specific data, and the output could be the expected purchase/payment behavior of the customer given the input conditions. Training data would be based on actual behavior of customers in the past. Such a system would be useful for planning for bad-debt expenses and the cyclical expansion and contraction of accounts receivable and for evaluating the credit terms and limits assigned to individual customers.

Neural net simulations might also be designed for many other segments of the firm's financial environment, such as cash management, evaluation of capital investments, asset and personnel risk management (insurance), exchange rate risk management, and prediction of credit costs and availability based on the firm's financial data. The richest potential for ANS applications in corporate financial management may well lie in simulations of this sort.

Prediction. Some tasks involving financial forecasting can be performed more efficiently using conventional computers and software rather than neural networks. This is particularly true of those tasks involving complex numerical calculations in well-identified models. However, the financial analyst is always concerned with the effects of certain actions on the behavior of investors.

Investors do not react to isolated bits of information about a company; they are, rather, influenced by the comprehensive body of information concerning all aspects of the company. It may be possible to train an ANS to mimic the behavior of investors in response to changes in the collective financial condition or policies of the company. Using actual investors as training models, one might create an ANS that could simulate investors' reactions to, say, changes in dividend policy, accounting methods, reported earnings, capital structure, or any other items of interest. Past studies of this sort have relied primarily on changes in stock price to gauge investor reaction, but investors may react in many ways other than buying or selling stock. An ANS could improve the financial analyst's ability to predict investor reactions to changes in corporate financial policy.

Evaluation. It should be possible to train an ANS to estimate a value for acquisition targets based on the target's financial information. The training procedure would involve both an input vector consisting of financial information concerning the target company and a target output consisting of the acquisition value estimate of a human expert. The objective of the ANS would be to simulate the valuation processes used by the human expert in order to derive for any target a value estimate that would be comparable to the estimates of a human expert.

The system could also be trained to select desirable acquisition targets on the basis of criteria other than simple valuation; criteria, for example, known only to the human expert and involving perhaps "hunches" or personal preferences. That is, the system would learn to mimic the idiosyncracies and intuition of the human expert without depending on definable rules or programmable logic in the process. The numerous benefits of such a system would include the following:

1. The system could be used to screen a very large number of companies for undervaluation or desirability for acquisition. The decision-maker would save much time by looking only at companies that were closest to the "ideal" acquisition target.

2. Because the system would not depend on preprogrammed rules or a set knowledge base, it could easily adapt to mimic the evaluation techniques of any decision-maker.

3. The system would automatically adapt to changes in a decision-maker's analytical procedures and selection criteria over time.

An expert system could conceivably perform a similar task, but it would be severely limited in comparison with an ANS. The ES would require a knowledge base extracted from the human expert, and it is unlikely that such a knowledge base would incorporate all of the subjective elements and idiosyncracies of the expert's decision process. Even if it did, the resulting ES could not adapt to changes in personal preferences or selection criteria (or could not be adapted without substantial reprogramming costs and delays).

Credit Approval. While the task of approving customers for credit and assigning credit limits is generally delegated to lower-level financial staff, it is still a labor-intensive and time-consuming process that has a significant impact on the profitability of most companies. Approval procedures based on credit scoring can be successfully implemented with conventional computer equipment and software, but such systems cannot incorporate the subjective and otherwise nonquantifiable elements of a human's decision process. In addition, much of the information concerning customers does not come to the decision-maker in a standard format (e.g., Dun & Bradstreet credit reports have a standardized form, but financial statements display a remarkable diversity).

An ANS could be trained using customer data as the input vector and the actual decisions of the credit analyst as the desired output vector. The objective of the system would be to mimic the human decision-maker in granting or revoking credit and setting credit limits. In addition, the system would be able to deal with the diversity of input information without requiring that the information be restated in a standard form.

Financial Institutions

Assessing Lending/Bankruptcy Risk.   The credit-approval system described above would be applicable in commercial and consumer lending as well. The diversity of loan applicants and lending arrangements encountered by most lending institutions could be handled quite efficiently in an ANS environment. While the ANS may not be used to make the final decision on loans of major importance to the institution, its output could be viewed as one more expert opinion included in the decision process.

Security/Asset Portfolio Management.   Financial institutions must manage a wide variety of investment portfolios involving many types of assets: stocks, bonds, mortgages, real estate, and so on. Decisions concerning risk adjustments, market timing, tax effects, maturity structure, and many other variables must be made almost continuously. For trust departments in large banks, this can be an enormously complex task involving many people. The task is complicated even more by the constant fluctuation of the financial and economic environment. Given the unstructured nature of the portfolio manager's decision processes, the uncertainty of the economic environment, and the diversity of information involved, this would be an appropriate arena for a neural network implementation.

Pricing IPOs. The pricing of new securities by investment bankers is always a difficult and complicated process that has a direct impact on the profitability of the firm. For initial public offerings of common stock, however, the pricing process is most difficult. Information concerning the issuer may be incomplete, in a nonstandard format, and cover only a short time period. Information about similar companies and the industry will need to be considered, as well as information about current and future economic conditions. In addition, there are many subjective elements involved in gauging investors' level of receptiveness and in determining the most opportune time to release the issue.

Here again, an ANS could be trained to mimic the decisions of the expert(s) by observing the inputs and outputs of actual decisions made in the past. In addition, in this environment, the system has the potential to improve on the expert's performance because the input data can include actual price performance and selling activity subsequent to a security's issuance. The system thus has the potential for learning directly from the decision-maker and also from the actual results in the decision. The ANS might thus discover relationships that were overlooked or misinterpreted by the expert. In addition, such a system will continue to serve the firm even if the human expert leaves, thus perpetuating the expert's knowledge and valuable experience.

Professional Investors

Identification of Arbitrage Opportunities. Consider an analyst who specializes in the identification of hostile takeover targets in advance of tender offer announcements. This analyst's selection of likely targets, and therefore desirable investments, depends on many bits of information and a good amount of personal experience and judgment. An ANS could be trained to assist the analyst in the identification task by observing the actual decisions he or she makes and the errors that those decisions have produced. After training, the ANS could improve upon the efficiency of the analyst by increasing the number of companies that can be examined in a given time span, thus allowing more thorough screening and more frequent updating of each company's evaluation. Even a small improvement in the performance of the decision-maker could result in a substantial improvement in profitability.

Technical Analysis. Technical analysis, with the objective of predicting future short-term movements in stock prices based on patterns in *ex post* price and volume data, has been the subject of much research but has achieved almost no empirical support. Even so, many professional and private investors use technical analysis as a primary investment-selection tool. This group has long voiced the opinion that empirical studies of technical analysis have failed to corroborate its usefulness because they applied it in an isolated, incomplete, or erroneous manner and because the researchers lack the necessary level of experience, and the intuition it brings, to use technical analysis effectively. These investors believe that the intuition of the experienced analyst, not the blind application of a selection procedure or formula, is the key to success; someone has to interpret the data, recognize the important patterns, and make the predictions. Market technicians may also argue that a successful technical analyst is unlikely to divulge the nature of his or her techniques to researchers because any "edge" the techniques afford the analyst may be destroyed if other investors begin to use them. Consequently, researchers may have been studying a set of analysis tools that is missing the most important parts.

While the pattern-recognition capabilities of neural nets suggest possibilities for the application of ANS technology to research studies concerning technical analysis, it is likely that the most beneficial applications would be designed by and for the technicians themselves. If an ANS could be trained to simulate the experience-based intuition of a successful technician, it could result in a substantial increase in the number of stocks that could be analyzed in real time. While a similar result could probably be achieved with an expert system, the technician would have to divulge valuable information to a knowledge engineer, and the resulting system could not be easily adapted to changes in the market environment or the prerogatives of the analyst. The special abilities of neural nets would be very well adapted to this particular application.

Fundamental Analysis. Insofar as fundamental analysis also requires judgment and intuition based on experience (although possibly to a lesser extent than technical analysis), this area also offers great promise for successful ANS applications. Given the vast amount of information that can be involved for each company at each time point, the parallel processing capability of artificial neural systems offer a very important potential advantage in this area. Much more so than for technical analysis, the inputs for fundamental analysis are parallel in nature. An input data vector for one company could include all the raw data from many years of financial statements, current and historical market and economic data, industry averages, and more. The ANS could be trained to evaluate stocks using these inputs and the analyst's own evaluations as the target output vector. As with technical analysis, the goal of the system would be to improve upon the efficiency of the analyst by allowing analysis of a greater number of stocks and more frequent updates.

CONCLUSION

We hope that the preceding discussion will stimulate financial managers and researchers to recognize that artificial neural nets offer great potential for improvements in productivity and efficiency. The necessary technology exists, and significant improvements will certainly continue in the years ahead. It is quite possible that the development of artificial neural networks will prove to be one of the most important, practical, and fruitful endeavors in finance in the next decade. There would seem to be no area of business management that is better suited for successful ANS applications nor any that is so likely to benefit from them.[21]

ENDNOTES

1. H. Simon, *The New Science of Management Decision* (New York: Harper and Row, 1960).

2. P. D. Wasserman and T. Schwartz, "Neural Network, Part 1," *IEEE Expert*, Winter 1987, p. 10.

3. It should be noted that neural network topologies can be simulated with software in order to build working prototypes. For a list of available software and hardware products, see the August 1989 issue of *Byte*.

4. A technical discussion of the ANS training process is available from the authors on request.

5. P. D. Wasserman and T. Schwartz, "Neural Network, Part 2," *IEEE Expert*, Spring 1988, p. 12.

6. *Ibid.*

7. P. K. Coats, "Why Expert Systems Fail," *Financial Management*, August 1988, p. 81.

8. *Ibid.*, p. 80.

9. Wasserman and Schwartz, "Neural Network, Part 2," *op. cit.*, p. 11.

10. Coats, "Why Expert Systems Fail," *op. cit.*, p. 80.

11. Wasserman and Schwartz, "Neural Network, Part 2," *op. cit.*, p. 11.

12. It should be noted that a number of researchers are currently addressing this problem.

13. See Y. S. Abu-Mostafa and D. Pslatis, "Optical Neural Computers," *Scientific American*, March 1989; and J. A. Anderson, E. J. Wisniewski, and S. R. Viscuso, "Software for Neural Networks," *ACM Computer Architecture Transactions*, forthcoming.

14. Simon, *The New Science of Management Decision, op. cit.*

15. K. K. Obermeier and J. J. Barron, "Time to Get Fired Up," *Byte*, August 1989.

16. T. Sejnowski and C. R. Rosenberg, "NETtalk: A Parallel Network that Learns to Read Aloud" (John Hopkins University Technical Report 1, 1986).

17. J. Giarratano and G. Riley, *Expert Systems* (Boston: PWS-KENT Publishing, 1989).

18. *Ibid.*, and Obermeier and Barron, "Time to Get Fired Up," *op. cit.*, p. 220.

19. B. Bower, "Neural Networks: The Buck Stops Here," *Science*, August 6, 1988.

20. H. White, "Neural Network Learning and Statistics," *AI Expert*, December 1989.

21. The authors of this chapter thank Pamela Coats, Van Harlow, and colleagues at the University of Mississippi for their helpful comments.

3

APPLYING NEURAL NETWORKS

Casimir C. "Casey" Klimasauskas

Section I: An Overview

BASIC CONCEPTS IN NEURAL NETWORKS

Before looking at the application process, let us establish some basic concepts. First, a definition. *Neural networks* (artificial neural systems) are an information processing technology inspired by studies of the brain and nervous system.

As an information processing technology, a neural network accepts several inputs, performs a series of operations on them, and produces one or more outputs. In this sense, they are just like a subroutine.

Where does the term *neural network* come from? In personal computers, a local area network connects several computers into an inter-

This article originally appeared in *PCAI*, January/February, 1991, pp. 30–33, March/April, 1991, pp. 27–34, and May/June, 1991, pp. 20–24. Reprinted with permission.

related, functioning whole. Within the brain, the elemental computing units called neurons are connected together into a functioning whole as well. Technologies inspired by studies of the brain use the basic concept of neurons connected together into a functioning whole. Hence the term *neural networks*.

One key difference between neural networks and other technologies (database, expert systems, programming languages) is that the method for how the inputs are processed is developed by showing the network examples of inputs and what the outputs should be. You might think of an untrained neural network as a lump of clay on the potter's wheel. As the network is shown examples of how it should respond to various inputs, the clay is shaped until it reflects the subtle relationships between the inputs and the outputs. The actual process that occurs is that the neural network designer selects a basic architecture in which the problem is to be solved. This basic architecture is shown an example set of inputs. It uses these inputs to devise an output (actual output). The network output (actual output) is compared to what the answer should have been (desired output). The difference between these is the error. The error is used to adjust various parameters in the basic architecture so that the next time the neural network is shown this example, it will produce more nearly the correct answer. This process is repeated several times for each example in the training set.

WHAT PROBLEMS SHOULD NEURAL NETWORKS BE CONSIDERED FOR?

It is important to recognize that neural networks are an evolutionary technology. They are able to improve the performance of several existing technologies. When used in conjunction with or as a replacement of these technologies in high-value or high-volume applications, the financial impact can be tremendous. Examples of the areas where neural networks work best include classifying data, modeling and forecasting, and signal processing.

Classifying data is currently one of the most widely used capabilities of neural networks. Examples include targeted marketing (deciding who to send mail-order catalogs), credit approval (deciding who gets credit or how much credit should be granted to an individual), stock picking (ranking by predicted performance), automated trading, picking winning football teams, predicting future job performance based on aptitude tests, classifying sonar signals (deciding if the sonar return signal is from an underwater mine or a rock), predicting solar flares (very important to the power industry), sorting syringes (needles) into good or bad, testing electric motors for proper operation, diagnosing problems with automobile engines, and so forth. Neural networks used in these applications typically replace statistically based systems or a variety of other pattern classification systems. Performance improvements range from 5 percent to 50 percent reduction in error. In some instances where the problem is well understood, although neural networks will match or approximate the performance of statistical or pattern classification systems, they may not do any better.

Modeling and forecasting are concerned with developing mathematical relationships between several continuous input variables and typically one, though possibly more, output variables. In forecasting, the input variables consist of samples of the data to predict at several points back in time. Examples of modeling include developing models of chemical processes for optimizing performance, building models of very complex programs for designing electric generators, or predicting interest rates or inventory levels. The technologies currently used in these applications include linear and polynomial regression techniques, auto-regressive (integrated) moving average (ARMA & ARIMA), and Box-Jenkins. Where these techniques are being used or considered, neural networks should also be considered. As an example of how well these techniques do, Lapedes & Farber at Los Alamos National Laboratories found that neural network approaches substantially outperformed all existing techniques for forecasting chaotic time series. In another instance, a neural network was trained to predict the direction of a fractal dimension 13 time series (stock price) two steps in advance. It was successful in doing this 87 percent of the time. This is quite a feat!

In the area of signal processing, neural networks, in particular back-propagation and related networks, may be thought of as techniques for developing a multilevel convolver. This results in the ability to create better signal discriminant systems, which can be used in classifying sounds, for speech recognition, and as a replacement for various single-level convolutional filters.

In summary, the most exciting aspect of neural network technology is that it represents a fundamental breakthrough in the ability to approximate complex mathematical mappings. The practical side of this is the wide range of applications that incrementally benefit from this breakthrough.

AN OVERVIEW OF THE APPLICATION PROCESS

In this chapter, we will focus on a pattern classification application: solving the credit-approval problem. This particular problem was chosen for the richness of the concepts that it can be used to illustrate.

The basic application process consists of the following steps:

1. Collect all the data in one place.

2. Separate the data into training and test sets.

3. Transform the data into network-appropriate inputs.

4. Select, train, and test the network.

5. Repeat steps 1, 2, 3, and 4 as required.

6. Deploy the developed network in your application.

To begin the process, examine the credit-approval problem and see briefly how each of these steps applies.

THE CREDIT-APPROVAL PROBLEM

Figure 3.1 shows a basic credit card application. Data are abstracted from this application and entered into a database. The database definition for a basic credit card application is shown in Figure 3.2. For purposes of this example, these are assumed to be fixed-length records. If data are not available, the field will be blank (if character type) or zero (if numeric type). All data are stored in ASCII. Note, however, that this example makes quite a number of simplifying assumptions about the credit approval problem for purposes of illustrating the neural network application process.

Comparing the fields in the database, notice that they do not correspond exactly to what is on the credit card application. The credit cards have been counted by type and entered into the database. The total monthly expenses have been computed by adding up the monthly credit card payments plus the mortgage payment. The occupation is entered into the database along with a "standard occupation code" derived from a standard job description catalog. All of this "preprocessing" of the application has been done manually prior to data entry.

The field "late payments" indicates the number of weeks late a particular payment was. Each field corresponds to one of the past 12 months.

Figure 3.1

A Simplified Application Designed for Illustrating How Neural Networks Are Applied

Name:_____ Home Phone:_____Work Phone:_____
Address:_____
      City:_____ State:_____ Zip:_____
      Social Security Number:_____ Sex: __M __F
      Marital Status:__Single __Married __Widowed __Divorced
      Number of Children:____
Job Information:
      Employer:_____ Years:____
      Occupation:_____
Financial Information:
      Home: __Own __Rent   Purchase Price:_____ Date:____
      Monthly Income:_____
      Checking Account: Number:_____ Bank:_____
                Balance:_____
      Savings Account: Number:_____ Bank:_____
                Balance:_____

	Total Amount	Monthly Payment
Mortgage Expense:	_____	_____
Car Loans:		
_____	_____	_____
_____	_____	_____
Credit Cards:		
_____	_____	_____
_____	_____	_____
_____	_____	_____
_____	_____	_____

Each month, the field is shifted over one digit and the current month's status appended. This field will be used to determine whether this person is a good risk. The neural network will be trained so that when it sees

Figure 3.2

Database Description for Credit Card Application

The data in this record are collected directly from the credit card application itself.

Field Name	Len	Type	Description
Name:	24	char	Last, first
Address:	32	char	
Zip code:	5	digits	
Home tel:	10	char	
Work tel:	10	char	
SS#:	11	char	Social Security number
Sex:	1	char	M/F
Marital status:	1	char	Single, married, widowed, divorced
Children:	1	digit	Number of children under 18 at home
Occupation:	12	char	Description of occupation
Occ code:	4	digits	Standard occupation code
Home:	1	letter	Own/rent
Monthly income:	6	digits	
Monthly expenses:	6	digits	
Checking account:	1	char	Y/N
Savings account:	1	char	Y/N
Master Card:	1	digit	Number of MCs
Visa:	1	digit	Number of Visas
American Express:	1	digit	Number of AMEX (Amex, Optima, etc.)
Merchant cards:	1	digit	Number of merchant cards
Late payments:	12	digit	1 digit for each of past 12 months

a particular set of input data, it will learn how to predict whether this individual will be a good-paying or poor-paying (good-risk or poor-risk) customer.

The process used to build the neural network credit authorizer is as follows:

1. *Collect the data.* The first step is to gather all of the pertinent data in one place. In this example, all of the data already are in a single database. However, since redlining (denying credit based on geographic location) is illegal, it might be helpful to learn more about the individual by using a "zip code overlay" of census data. If a zip code overlay of census data were used, it would be necessary to append the applicable census data fields to the credit data record (or at least make them readily accessible on the same machine).

2. *Separate the data into training and test sets.* Since neural networks learn from experience, it is important to provide them both with experience and a way to see if they have "learned" ("generalize well") or "memorized" ("generalize poorly") what they have been shown. The only way to do this is to divide the available data into two (or more) sets. This procedure will be described further in Section III.

3. *Transform the data into network-appropriate inputs.* Neural networks *only* accept numeric inputs. How do you convert "occupation" into a number? The process of transforming numeric and symbolic inputs into purely numeric inputs is called preprocessing. For me, this was the one area that seemed like magic. In Section II, the magic will be dispelled.

4. *Select, train, and test a network.* Picking the right network configuration can have a substantial impact on the performance of the resulting system. The process of debugging a neural network is still an art, but much easier with the powerful tools that are becoming commercially available. Section III describes this process and provides a number of helpful hints to get the most out of your neural network.

5. *Deploy the developed network in your application.* Once the development is done, how do you make a neural network part of an application?

Section II: A Walk through the Application Process

REVIEW

The basic process of developing a neural network consists of the following steps:

1. Collect all the data in one place.

2. Separate the data into training and testing sets.

3. Transform the data into network-appropriate inputs.

4. Select, train, and test the network.

5. Repeat steps 1, 2, 3, 4 as required.

6. Deploy the developed network in your application.

Actually, before taking any of these steps, we need to know what our objective is. The problem selected to illustrate these steps is the credit-approval problem: Who should we give credit to? In an ideal world, the resulting neural network should give us a simple approve-disapprove signal.

COLLECT ALL THE DATA IN ONE PLACE

The process of training a neural network entails looking at all of the possible or potentially useful information about the problem and using that to predict a certain behavior or other characteristic. For purposes of generating training and test sets, all of this information must be brought together. This process is similar to what is required to develop statistically based or behavioral scoring models.

In many applications where the objective is to predict the behavior of a specific individual, zip-code or block-code overlays are used to provide additional information about the individual. Block-code overlays typically start with the U.S. Census Bureau data. The Census Bureau has divided the entire United States into "blocks." Each block consists of approximately 30 families. When census data is collected every 10 years, it is summarized by block. This data is available directly from the Census Bureau as well as various third-party companies who merge other information into it. The census data includes estimates of income, number of children, type of employment, and so on—everything that is asked on the census report. However, in accord with privacy laws, the data provided by the Census Bureau does not reference individuals. The third-party companies start with the census data and will rent mailing lists from various magazines, clubs, and other organizations and match them against the "block groups" to enhance the amount of information known about a block group.

Credit bureaus often match customers in their database to block groups and incorporate specific fields from the census data into the customer record for purposes of developing creditworthiness or bankruptcy-likely scores. In a large company, various components of the customer database may be managed by different groups within the company. For purposes of developing a neural network model, selected fields from the various databases may need to be merged.

Sometimes, information might be captured at one point, then stripped from the master record and archived. If you think this information is pertinent, it should be remerged into the master records.

SEPARATE THE DATABASE INTO TRAINING AND TEST SETS

Why not use all of the data available to train and test a neural network? First, doing so prevents determining whether the neural network has memorized the data or learned something about the relationships between the inputs and the predicted output. Memorizing the relationship between the inputs and outputs may result in poor or erratic response to new or novel situations. Setting aside a certain number of examples increases our confidence in the performance of the trained neural network. Second, depending on the particular problem, certain neural networks may not learn well if the data is not properly distributed between possible outcomes. As such, it becomes important to carefully select the cases to be used for training. For testing purposes, an "Nth" item subset provides the best picture of how the network will perform overall.

Why is it so important to have about the same number of training items in each output category? Part of the answer is that many neural networks are basically lazy. They will attempt to find the easiest way to solve a particular problem. If 95 percent of the examples are "good" and 5 percent "bad," the network may discover that it is right most of the time by classifying everything as good. This kind of swamping effect is even more pronounced when the boundaries between good and bad are fuzzy.

What is the ideal training set? For the most popular class of neural networks, back-propagation, the ideal training set is equally distributed among each of the possible outcomes. The ideal test set is one that is representative of the data as a whole. In practical terms, it is often easier to extract a test set first, then select a training set from the remaining examples.

For example, suppose that the database has about 31,000 examples in it. Each of the examples has been categorized into one of three possible outcomes: good risk, poor risk, and indeterminate risk. An analysis of the frequency of each of these is shown in column 2 of Figure 3.3.

The first step is to extract a test set. For our purposes, 10 percent will be sufficient. The test set will be extracted by sequentially going through the data and picking out every tenth example. The results are shown in column 3 of Figure 3.3.

The second step is to select the training set. The smallest single outcome is "poor risk." After selecting the test set, there are 6,179 (6,851–672) poor-risk examples left. Of the remaining elements, randomly pick examples until 6,179 of each category are selected. When a particular category is full, reject any new examples picked for it. Include all of the examples for the poor-risk category. The results are shown in column 4 of Figure 3.3.

Figure 3.3

Frequency of Occurrence of Each of the Three Possible Outcomes in the Database Distributed among the Test and Training Sets

Category	Initial Data	Test Dataset	Training Dataset	Unused Examples
Good risk	17,284	1,739	6,179	9,366
Indeterminate risk	7,523	755	6,179	589
Poor risk	6,851	672	6,179	0
Total:	31,658	3,166	18,537	9,955

Training examples are picked randomly to remove any bias that might exist in the natural ordering of the master database.

As a general rule, the more training examples available, the better the network will ultimately perform. For a variety of problems that we have solved using neural networks, 30,000 to 40,000 training examples have been adequate. Little additional improvement has been seen with more examples. For simple problems with few inputs and well-defined boundaries, as few as 50 or 100 examples may be adequate.

TRANSFORM THE DATA INTO NETWORK-APPROPRIATE INPUTS

When I began to learn about neural networks, this was perhaps the most bewildering element of the application process. It seemed like magic that symbolic and numeric data could be mapped into a vector of numbers. As with most "magic," when understood, the process is straightforward.

As described elsewhere, neural networks typically work with inputs in the range 0 to 1 or −1 to +1. Each of the fields in our database must be mapped into one or more network inputs, each in the appropriate range. This section covers basic concepts in mapping data into a neural network.

A description of the database is provided in Listing 1 in the Appendix to this part. Our mission is to find a way to map that database into a form suitable for input to a neural network. Notice that the database consists primarily of three types of data: numeric (income, expense, number of MCs, etc.), category (sex, rent/own, checking account, etc.), and free-form text (occupation, name, address, etc.). Let us go through each of the database fields individually and see how we can use them.

"NameCA" identifies the individual and probably does not have a significant bearing on the creditworthiness of the person. Address ("AddrCA") and zip code ("ZipCA") could be useful for integrating geographic block-code overlay data. However, it is illegal to use zip code as an input by itself. (This is known as redlining.) Social Security number ("SSNCA") could be useful as a key into other databases but is not directly useful. Sex ("SexC") is another field that cannot be used as network input because it is illegal to discriminate against an individual based on sex when issuing credit.

Marital status ("MStatusC") can take on one of four values (M=married, S=single, W=widowed, D=divorced). This type of "category" record is typically encoded using a "one of N" coding. In a "one of N" coding, each category will be assigned to a separate neural network input. Since there are four categories, this database element would map to four inputs. For these four inputs, only one of them would be "on" (its value set to 1) at a time. All of the others would be off (value set to 0).

Number of children ("NChildrenC") will range from 0 to 9. Since this is a number, it can be rescaled into the range 0 to 1 and input directly to the network.

Occupation creates some problems. In this database, there are several occupations. A listing of them is shown in Figure 3.4. One way of approaching the encoding of occupation is to use the "one of N" encoding used for marital status. The difficulty with that approach is that there are over 3,000 standard occupations and likely very few examples of most in the database. Another solution is to group them into some larger set of categories such as principal, management, professional, skilled labor, unskilled labor. These categories were chosen because they seem as though they might be significant in determining creditworthiness. Since they were chosen somewhat intuitively, and the grouping of titles under each category is somewhat arbitrary, other categories and groupings may work better. However, this is a start.

Home ownership takes on one of two categories: rent or own. This encodes nicely into a "one of N" encoding.

Monthly income and expenses are both numbers and could be rescaled and passed directly to the network as inputs.

Checking account and savings account contain either a Y=yes or N=no flag. In the mapping program, Y=yes is translated to a 1, and N=no to a 0. Another way these fields could be treated is to consider them as each containing two categories and encode them each into two inputs. This has advantages in some instances.

The number of credit cards of each category has been directly passed through to the training file, with the expectation that they will be appropriately scaled by the neural network development tool.

Payment history has already been preprocessed into a rating. If more than 9 out of 12 payments were made on time, the rating is G=good. If fewer than 6, the rating is poor. Otherwise, it is indeterminate. The "RatingC" field is mapped to three outputs, one for each of the possible categories of good, poor, or indeterminate.

To review the process of mapping database inputs to neural network inputs:

Figure 3.4

A Listing of the Kinds of Occupations that Occur in the Credit Database and One Possible Way of Grouping Them Together

Principal:	President
	Store owner
	Contractor
Management:	Vice president
	Senior manager
	Manager
	Plant manager
	Office manager
	EDP manager
Professional:	Software engineer
	Accountant
	Doctor
	Professor
Skilled labor:	Draftsman
	Mechanic
	Electrician
	Plumber
Unskilled labor:	Laborer
	Farmhand
	Trucker
	Cabbie

1. Do not attempt to map information that does not seem likely to apply or that may otherwise be illegal to use in making a decision.

2. Numeric inputs can be used directly as is.

3. Symbolic fields may be mapped directly with a "1 of N" code or indirectly by regrouping them into larger conceptual groups first.

4. Network "desired outputs" are mapped in much the same way as network inputs.

SELECT A NETWORK ARCHITECTURE

Back-propagation has almost universally become the standard network paradigm for modeling, forecasting, and classification. Selecting an optimal back-propagation architecture is one of the areas that is receiving substantial research. Some of the key questions are How many hidden units? Which transfer function? Which learning rule? What should the learning rates be?

TRAIN AND TEST THE NETWORK

Depending on the dataset, the training process may be very slow. The basic training process consists of showing the network a set of inputs and what the output should be. The network uses the current inputs to produce an output. This is compared to what the network should have produced. The error is used to modify the weights so that the network gives a more nearly correct answer the next time. During training, several diagnostic tools are helpful in particular: (1) measuring the mean square error of the entire output layer, (2) a histogram of all of the weights in the network, and (3) Pearson's R coefficient for each of the outputs. These diagnostic tools facilitate understanding how the network is training.

During the testing process, the test database is used to determine how well the network performs on data it has not previously seen during training. A properly architected and trained network will exhibit similar levels of performance on *both* the training and testing sets. If performance differs widely, appropriate corrective action should be taken to the architecture, composition, or size of the training and testing sets.

DEPLOY THE NETWORK

Once trained to your satisfaction, the final step is to convert the network into a form that can be deployed with your application.

SUMMARY

Selecting appropriate test and training sets is an essential step in developing a neural network application. Once selected, developing a mapping from the symbolic and numeric fields in the database is relatively straightforward.

APPENDIX TO SECTION II

Listing 1 - "network.h" describes the layout of the database

```
/* 12:00 14-Jan-91 (Network.H) "credit card" database definition */
/*****************************************************************************
**
*Database Record Description*
**
*****************************************************************************
*/
typedef struct_cdb {/* credit card database record */
char NameCA[24];/* name */
char AddrCA[32];/* address */
char ZipCA[5];/* zip code */
char SSNCA[11];/* social security code number */
char SexC;/* sex (M/F) */
char MStatusC;/* marital status */
char NChildrenC;/* # of children */
char OccupationCA[12];/* occupation */
char HomeOwnC;/* rent/own */
char IncomeCA[6];/* monthly income */
char ExpenseCA[6];/* monthly expenses */
char CheckingActC;/* checking account Y/N */
char SavingsActC;/* savings account Y/N */
char NMCsC;/* # of Master cards */
char NVISAsC;/* # of Visa cards */
char NAmexC;/* # of American Express cards */
char NMerchC;/* # of merchant cards */
char PmtHisCA[12];/* payment regularity for past 12 mos */
char RatingC;/* G=good risk, P=poor risk, I=indeterminate */
char LFCharC;/* line-feed at end of record */
}CDB;
```

Compiling and Running Programs for Generating Test and Training Sets

1. *Compile the program.* The author used Zortech "C" version 2.00.

    ```
    C>ztc select.c
    ```

2. *Execute the select program to create the test and training databases.* The main database is "db."

    ```
    C>select db test.db train.db
    ```

3. *Compile the conversion program to map the test and training databases into network input files.*

    ```
    C>ztc xformc.c
    ```

4. *Transform the test database into network inputs.* The resulting ".nna" file is suitable for input to NeuralWare's NeuralWorks Explorer or NeuralWorks Professional II; Ward System's NeuroShell; or California Scientific's BrainMaker.

    ```
    C>xformc test.db test.nna
    ```

5. *Transform the training database into network inputs.*

    ```
    C>xformc train.db train.nna
    ```

6. *You are now ready to train the network of your choice.* This will be described in more detail in Section III of this chapter.

Section III: Training a Neural Network

THE TRAINING PROCESS

In Section I, a database for credit application evaluation was described. In Section II, various techniques were described and applied to convert the various symbolic and numeric fields into values appropriate for neural network input. In particular, each of the fields in the database was converted to a numeric value. Prior to conversion, the database was divided into two parts: a *training* and a *testing* set. The training set was chosen so that it represented equally the likelihood of each outcome. The test set was chosen to represent the entire population.

After transforming the database, there were 20 numeric inputs and three numeric outputs. Any network built to learn the relationship between the inputs and the outputs will have 20 inputs and three outputs. The outputs represented a poor, good, or indeterminate risk. This was based on a very primitive analysis of payment history. The training data was written to an ASCII file (using xformc.exe) in a format suitable for input to a variety of neural network tools readily available.

Architecting the Network

When building a back-propagation network, a series of decisions must be made. These are listed in Table 3.1. The problem-specific parameters are defined by the problem. In particular, the number of inputs is 20, the number of outputs is 3, and a min–max table is required to automatically scale all of the data into the appropriate range for input to the network (Table 3.2).

The network decisions are determined by a combination of analysis of the data and trial and error.

Transfer Function

Selecting a transfer function is determined by the nature of the data and what the network is trying to learn. The key observation that leads to the selection of a transfer function is to observe that when the input to a processing element is 0, no learning occurs on that particular connection. In a typical application, several of the inputs will be coded as either 0 or 1. With sigmoidal transfer functions, the limits of the output of the processing element are 0 and 1. With a hyperbolic tangent transfer function, the limits are –1 and 1. As a result, if the problem involves learning about "average" behavior, sigmoid transfer functions work best. However, if the problem involves learning about "deviations" from the average, hyperbolic tangent works best. For example, bankruptcy prediction and stock picking are examples of problems where the objective is to learn to pick out "exceptional" situations, and hyperbolic tangent works best. In the case of learning to classify respondents from nonrespondents for a direct-mail application, the sigmoid works well. In this case, the sigmoid transfer function is a good starting point.

Table 3.1

Parameters for Back-Propagation Networks

Network Decisions:

Transfer functions:	Sigmoid
	Hyperbolic tangent
	Sine
Learning rules:	Delta rule
	Cumulative delta rule
	Normalized cumulative delta rule
Topology:	Number of hidden layers
	Number of PEs per layer
	Functional link layer (if any)
	Connection to prior layers
Learning rates:	Learning rates for each layer

Problem Specific Parameters:

Number of input PEs:	Number of inputs to network
Number of output PEs:	Number of outputs from the
	network
Min–max table:	Required to normalize data
Instruments:	RMS error, confusion matrix

Learning Rule

The original learning rule developed by Rummelhart and described in Chapter 8 of *Parallel Distributed Processing: Explorations in the Microstructure of Cognition,* Volume I (MIT Press, 1986) is the delta rule. Two very popular extensions of this are the cumulative delta rule (which accumulates weight changes over several examples) and the normalized cumulative delta rule. In general, the normalized cumulative delta rule works very well. Typically, the epoch (the number of presentations over which weight changes are accumulated) is set to 16. In circumstances where the data are very noisy, this may need to be adjusted.

Table 3.2

Initial Network Decisions

This table shows the experience of the author in developing an initial design for a back-propagation neural network.

1. Create the training and test sets.

2. Transform the training and test sets to numeric values suitable for network inputs.

3. Select a transfer function:
   Exceptions are more important than average.
   Hyperbolic tangent average is more important than exceptions.
   Sigmoid.

4. Select a learning rule:
   Normalized cumulative delta rule.
   Default learning parameters. (Optimize later)
   Epoch = 16 (Optimize later)

5. Topology:
   One hidden layer.
   Number of hidden units selected so total weights are much less than the number of training examples.

6. Diagnostic tools:
   RMS error for output layer.
   Confusion matrix for each output.
   Histogram of weights for each layer.

Epoch Size

The procedure for adjusting the epoch size is as follows: (1) Pick an initial value; (2) train the network for 10,000 (or some preestablished number) interactions; (3) test the network and record the accuracy (or Pearson's R-Coefficient). Repeat this process three or four times for each of several epoch sizes. If you plot out the results, you will discover that the network performance peaks for a certain epoch size. This represents the fundamental "frequency" of certain dominant components of the underlying noise. Use this new epoch size for all further training.

Topology Issues

Three basic questions arise under topology issues. The first is, "How many hidden layers?" Closely associated with this is, "How many PEs in each hidden layer?" Typically, start with a single hidden layer. Most problems can be solved with a single hidden layer. If you do use more than one hidden layer, make sure to connect each layer to all prior layers. This promotes learning and increases the complexity of patterns that can be learned without adding additional processing elements. When starting out on solving a problem, it is usually helpful to try connecting the output layer directly to the input layer (connect prior layers). If the problem was reasonably solved using conventional statistical methods, this is often very effective.

How many hidden units? In general, the fewer the number of processing elements in the hidden layers, the better the network will "generalize." Generalization is the ability to interpolate between previously seen examples. Procedures have been developed to "prune" out superfluous hidden units as well as methods for adding additional hidden units to improve performance. From an information perspective, a theoretical upper bound for the number of hidden units can be determined by the number of training examples. The rule is that there should be at least five examples for each weight. In a network with 20 inputs, five hidden units, and three outputs, there are $(20+1)*5 + (5+1)*3 = 123$ weights. There are 264 examples in the training set, so five hidden units may be a bit many. Even so, for this example we will use one hidden layer with five hidden units.

Functional Link Layer

Pao made the observation that the hidden layer in a back-propagation network "transforms" the input space into a new space in which the classes are more nearly linearly separable. Based on this, he suggested that this could be done artificially by computing the pairwise product of each of the inputs. Sometimes this works very well. When using functional links, the first step is to use no hidden layer and to connect all processing elements to both the input as well as the functional link layer (connect prior). This in essence augments the input layer with $N*(N-1)$ additional parameters representing the pairwise product of the inputs. If this does not work well, it is usually better to not use a functional link layer at all.

Learning rates are the final key decision that must be made. Most vendors provide a set of "ready-made" learning rates. These typically work. As a rule of thumb, the learning rate for the last hidden layer should be twice that of the output layer. If there are no connections that jump layers, the learning rates for each prior hidden layer should be twice that of the prior hidden layer. If connections do jump layers (prior layer connections), learning rates should be 20 percent to 30 percent less than the hidden layer above. Optimal learning rates (those that result in networks with maximum performance) result in smooth RMS error graphs and weight histograms for each layer, which spread at about the same rate. If the weights for one layer grow larger faster than another layer, the network may get caught in a very long, shallow trough. The learning rates for the layer that is growing faster can be reduced to balance out the evolution of the network. If the RMS error graph jumps around a lot, reduce the learning rates for all layers proportionately. This, in a nutshell, is the condensed wisdom of several thousand tests.

Figure 3.5 shows how NeuralWorks Professional II/PLUS can be used to build a network for solving the credit approval problem. The learning coefficients and momentum parameters are the manufacturer's default values. The training and testing files have been selected along with other options.

GAME PLAN FOR NETWORK OPTIMIZATION

Once the network is built, there are three key areas that need to be optimized: learning rates, epoch size, and hidden layer size (Table 3.3). There are a series of heuristics for optimizing each of these parameters for a particular problem. The basic principles for optimizing learning rates and epoch size have already been discussed above. There are two basic approaches to optimizing hidden layer size: constructive and destructive.

The constructive approach to hidden layer size is to start with a network with no hidden units. The inputs are connected directly to the outputs. Train the weights until the error "stabilizes." Fix these weights and add a hidden unit connected to the input and all prior hidden layers. The output of this new unit is connected to the output. Continue training. Eventually, the network will make no mistakes on the training data. One of the keys to the constructive approach is to decide when to stop adding hidden units. The answer is that at each decision point, the network is

Figure 3.5

Setting Up a Back-Propagation Network to Solve the Credit Rating Problem Using NeuralWorks Professional II PLUS "Back-Prop Builder"

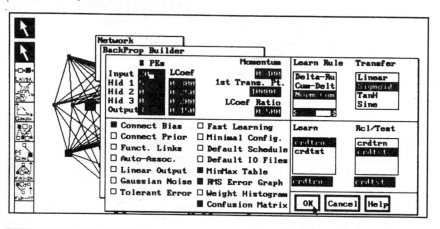

tested on both the training and test sets. Performance on both is plotted. If the performance on both does not improve, remove the last hidden unit added and stop. Why? The network is starting to "memorize" the training set to the detriment of the test set.

The destructive approach to hidden layer size is to start with a network with a large population of hidden units. Train the network for a while and then test it on both the training and test sets. For each unit in the hidden layer, (1) disable the unit, setting its output to zero; (2) retest the network on both the training and test sets; and (3) record the results. If disabling the unit improved *both* the performance on both the training and test sets, leave it disabled. Use the new results for the standard to measure the effect of each succeeding unit. Then, continue the training process.

During training, a few common problems often occur. The first is that the weights in the network grow large very rapidly. This shows up very graphically on the weight histogram and is usually easily detected in the RMS error plot as well. The underlying cause of this problem is that the learning rates are set too high, the training set is not adequately randomized, or the inputs are not properly scaled. First, make sure that the training presentations are randomized. If they are not, the network may very quickly learn about how to classify data in one particular mode

---
Table 3.3

Optimizing the Network Parameters

1. **Optimize learning rates.**
   Initialize the network and train it for 10,000 iterations.
   Simultaneously:
   Lower all of the learning rates so that the RMS error plot is smooth.
   Change the relative magnitude of the learning rates so that the weight histograms for each layer spread at the same rates.

2. **Optimize the epoch size.**
   Start with an initial epoch.
   Train the network for 10,000 iterations.
   Test the network and record the R-Coefficient for each output.
   Repeat the above process for a variety of epoch sizes.
   Plot out the R-Coefficients and pick the epoch that produces the highest value.

3. **Optimize the hidden layer size.**
   Use one of the following procedures:
   Start with a "minimum" number of hidden units and add more as the training process proceeds.
   Start with the "maximum" number of hidden units and prune out marginal ones.

(all good) and, due to the effects of momentum, move quickly in that direction. When data of another class eventually appear, the network has become "locked" up and does not effectively learn the new data. The second check is to see that the inputs have all been scaled into a range appropriate for the type of network (0 to 1 for sigmoid or –1 to 1 for hyperbolic tangent). An easy way to do this is to use a min-max table that will compute the minimum and maximum of each training example. These values are used to scale the inputs into the appropriate range automatically. Finally, try reducing the learning rates.

Another problem that sometimes occurs is that the RMS error does not seem to decrease. Sometimes this is a problem and sometimes it is not. If the training data are particularly noisy, the RMS error may not decrease much over the training process. In this case, the confusion matrix can be used to determine where the problem is. In some cases, the error may be caused by one particular output that is of little concern.

Figure 3.6 shows a network that has been trained for 16,000 iterations. (This problem actually requires about 50,000 iterations for best performance.) This took about 10 minutes on a Toshiba 5200. Notice that the RMS error has not dropped very much and that it is quite "jagged." From prior discussions, the learning rates should be reduced. Though it would be helpful, weight histograms for each of the layers are not being used. For each output, there is a confusion matrix. The confusion matrix is a graphical way of understanding how the network is performing. Along the x-axis is the "desired output": what the network should be producing. Along the y-axis is the actual output of the network. Both the desired output and the actual outputs have been discretized into bins. The bars in one column of the interior of the confusion matrix show the distribution of actual network outputs for a particular desired output. If the network

Figure 3.6
Trained Network

This network has run through 50,000 training iterations. The RMS error graph shows how well the network is performing.

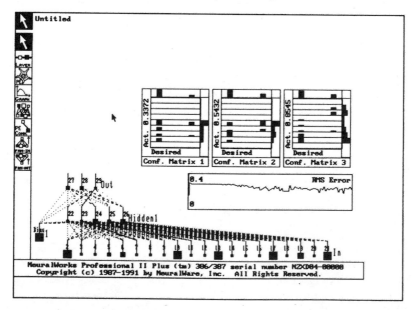

were performing perfectly, the only interior quadrants would be the lower left and upper right of the interior area. From this, the network is starting to learn to distinguish good from nongood (Conf. Matrix 3). However, it is quite confused in both of the other categories.

The number along the y-axis is Pearson's R-coefficient. This is a correlation coefficient that measures how well the desired output and actual outputs are correlated. A perfect correlation results in a score of 1.0. The scores shown are poor = 0.3372, indeterminate = 0.5432, good = 0.8545. This is a numerical method to represent what is happening graphically.

SUMMARY

In Part III, the basic process of architecting and training a network has been discussed. The procedures used are those that have been developed by the author through trial and error. Following the steps outlined usually results in success.

Sources, sample data, and copies of the network shown are available from the author.

PART II

ANALYSIS OF FINANCIAL CONDITION

4

A FINANCIAL NEURAL NETWORK APPLICATION

Robert A. Marose

INTRODUCTION

A statistical-based hybrid neural network at Chase Manhattan Bank is one of the largest and most successful AI applications in the United States. It addresses a critical success factor in the bank's strategic plan: reducing losses on loans made to public and private corporations.

Most of Chase's business for corporations involves assessing their creditworthiness. Chase loans $300 million annually and has long searched for tools to improve loan assessment. This assessment allows Chase to mitigate risk and seek out new business opportunities. Financial-restructuring deals are promising business opportunities for the bank.

In 1985, Chase began a search for new quantitative techniques to assist senior loan officers in forecasting the creditworthiness of corporate

Reprinted with permission from *AI Expert*, May 1990, pp. 50–53.

73

loan candidates. Chase located Inductive Inference Inc. (headed by Dr. David Rothenberg), a New York City company with a history of successfully applying neural-network technology to statistical pattern analysis. A test model was built, evaluated, and independently audited. The results were reviewed by the Chase CEO committee in 1987, and Inductive Inference was granted a multimillion dollar contract. Consequently, Chase established a 36-member internal consulting organization called Chase Financial Technologies to oversee the development of pattern-analysis network models for evaluating corporate loan risk.

The resulting models, called the Creditview system, perform three-year forecasts that indicate the likelihood of a company being assigned a Chase risk classification of *good, criticized,* or *charged-off.* In addition to the overall forecast, Creditview provides a detailed listing of the items that significantly contributed to the forecast, an expert-system-generated interpretation of those items, and several comparison reports. This article focuses on the public company loan model (PCLM).

Creditview models run on a Chase Financial Technologies host computer. A user system resides at each user's PC and communicates with the host through telephone lines. In addition, conventional financial statement analysis may be performed using Chase's Financial Reporting System, an independent financial spreading and analysis package designed for conventional financial statement analysis. The Financial Reporting System also resides on the user's PC and permits a company's standard financial statements to be accessed and displayed. System data is obtained from COMPUSTAT.

It took 15 years for Inductive Inference to develop ADAM, a tool that generates the models such as those used in Creditview. ADAM is a statistically based technique that extracts a collection of Boolean formulae from historical data and captures rules most significant in determining the obligor's creditworthiness. ADAM identifies rules and their combinations that, based on historical data, may be expected to do three-year forecasts reliably. The historical data are also used to embed the Boolean formula in a network that evaluates the significance of each possible formula combination that may be satisfied by a particular company.

ADAM's pattern-analysis technology provides the ability to construct a hybrid neural network (the Forecaster) if enough high-quality historical data are available. Each forecaster represents a separate "model" produced by ADAM (Figure 4.1). PCLM, the first model implemented at Chase,

Figure 4.1

ADAM and PCLM

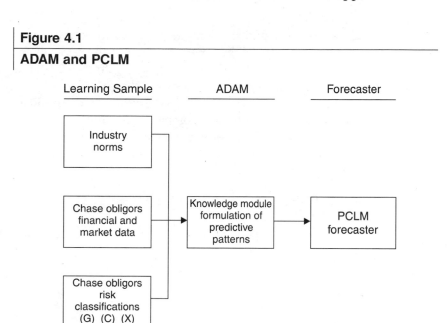

derives from Chase's extensive loan history of large, publicly traded companies and their past financial data. (Chase has both publicly and privately owned corporations in its base of clients and prospects. Separate credit-risk forecasting models will be developed for public and private companies because their particular characteristics will probably mandate separate assessments and analysis by the bank.)

The input to ADAM includes the following:

❖ Historical financial-statement data on *good* and *bad* obligors (the learning sample).

❖ Industry norms calculated using financial-statement data from companies in specific industries (obtained from COMPUSTAT). These norms reflect industry characteristics.

The historical data analyzed by ADAM to produce forecasting models consist of a large collection of data units. Each data unit contains as much as six years of consecutive financial data for a particular company, corresponding industry norms, and the company's status three years after the last year of data. (The last of the six years is called the "year of the data unit.") The data unit's status is the company's rating — G stands for *good*, C stands for *criticized*, and X stands for *charged-off*.

ADAM uses this data to construct a large set (say, 1,000) of candidate variables that may or may not indicate a company's future financial condition. These variables are used to form patterns.

DEFINITION OF PATTERNS

A pattern is fundamentally a statement about the value of a particular financial variable or set of variables. A very simple pattern may have the form:

$$C1 < V1 < C2$$

or

$$V1 < C1$$

where V1 is a financial variable and C1 and C2 are constants. For example:

$$1.75 < \text{QuickRatio} < 2.00$$

could be a simple pattern. Typically, patterns are more complex; they have several elements of this kind and are combined by using AND, OR, and NOT. This example could be one of a small complex pattern:

$$C1 < V1 < C2$$
$$V2 < C3$$
$$C4 < V3 < C5 \text{ .AND. } C6 < V4 < C7$$
$$C8 \leq V5 \leq C9$$

where all the Cs are constants and the Vs are financial variables.

Candidate variables are arranged into thousands of complex patterns and analyzed by ADAM to produce an optimal set of variables and patterns that form a pattern network called the Forecaster. The criteria for selection of patterns include score, complexity, and spuriousness.

Score

The score (as observed in the historical data) measures the ability of the pattern to differentiate between the categories *good, criticized,* and *charged-off*—in other words, the ability of the pattern to classify correctly.

Complexity

Complexity is a measure of how complicated the pattern is (in terms of number of variables), simple patterns within it, and the amount of historical data it satisfies.

Spuriousness

A measure of the likelihood that the pattern's score (how well it predicts) is due solely to chance.

These statistics are used to evaluate the predictive power of the patterns and ensure that whatever predictive power is uncovered is not by chance. To each pattern and status a probability (called the "precision") exists that a data unit corresponding to the pattern will have that status. ADAM uses a proprietary network-balancing technique that selects the patterns for the network to maximize precision and minimize bias.

ADAM was used to develop the PCLM, an expert system based on historical data that can predict the likelihood of a public firm being rated *good, criticized,* or *charged-off* three years in advance. Among other features, PCLM does the following:

❖ Accepts six years of past financial data for the firm under consideration.

❖ Uses the lattice (network) of Boolean expressions developed by ADAM to determine nodes that best match the firm under analysis.

❖ Calculates the probability for each rating based on the expressions matched and the characteristics of these patterns.

❖ Produces extensive reports, including a text explanation of the analysis, based on the characteristics of the matched pattern and other companies that have matched these expressions.

The PCLM comprises two parts: the Forecaster, built by the ADAM technology from large publicly traded companies (residing on a Chase host computer), and a PC-based user system that allows access to the model on the host computer to generate forecasts for particular companies, perform various analyses, and print reports (Figure 4.2). Note that information about an obligor's specific credit facility (whether the facility is secured, covenants, and so on) is not considered by the PCLM. The system evaluates the company itself rather than the risk of its defaulting on specific credit payments.

PCLM MODEL OUTPUT

The PCLM produces these reports: Contributing Variables, Expert-System Interpretation, Two-Year Comparison: Items of Increased Significance, Two-Year Comparison: Items of Decreased Significance, and Two-Year Comparison: Items That Changed Risk Category. Of these reports, Contributing Variables contains PCLM's primary output; the others derive from the data contained in it. Contributing Variables comprises an overall forecast

Figure 4.2

PCLM Model Process

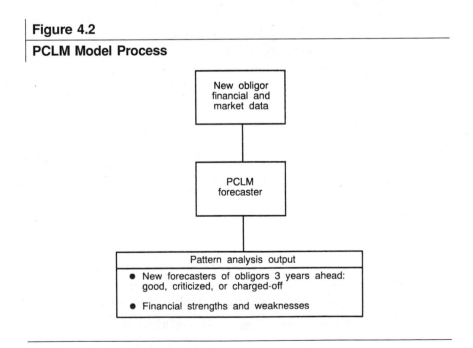

for the company in question along with a list of the variables that most strongly contributed to the forecast. The basic report consists of five sections.

Section 1

General information. Contains the company name, forecast year, standard industrial classification (SIC), data source, date, and years of data that were used in generating the forecast.

Section 2

Industry peer group. Defines the industry peer group as determined by the model for the company. The company's asset size and geographic location are shown in this section. Information on the industry peer group consists of its SIC, the latest year for which industry norms were calculated, the number of firms in the peer group, and the peer-group reference number (useful in determining the peer group's members).

Section 3

Overall forecast. Shows the forecast rating for the company (*G, C,* or *X*). These ratings are mathematically combined into a single "vulnerability index" that helps compare the relative risk among different forecasts (different companies or years for the same company). In addition, to assist the analyst in evaluating the forecast's significance, the company's forecast compared to others in Chase's experience is shown in several ways. Chase rank shows the relative percentile of this company's *good* rating compared to all Chase obligors in the years 1986 through 1988. For example, if the company's Chase rank was 25 percent for all Chase obligors from 1986 through 1988, 75 percent have a higher and 25 percent have a lower rating than *good*. The percentage going to *criticized* and *charged-off* shows the historical outcome of similarly ranked companies.

Section 4

A list of contributing variables most strongly influencing the forecast. These variables are organized into categories and by contributions to strength and weakness within each category: *profitability, asset efficiency, cash flow, capital structure and liquidity,* and *market.*

Section 5

A list of contributing variables compared to the best or worst quartile of companies in the industry (defined as its peer group) that most strongly influence the forecast.

Other reports can also be generated by the user system:

❖ *Expert system interpretation.* The PCLM can use its network to output the various factors accounting for its conclusions. This output permits the model to explain its decision in an under-standable, text-generated manner.

❖ *Two-year comparison reports.* These reports automatically com-pare the forecasts for two (not necessarily consecutive) years and show items that appear in the second but not the first year (Items of Increased Significance Report), items that appear in the first but not the second year (Items of Decreased Significance Report), and items that appear in both years but have changed their risk cate-gory (Items That Changed Risk Category Report).

SYSTEM SUCCESS

PCLM benefits the user because it identifies the strengths and vulnerabilities in the financial structure of the obligor and forecasts the impact of these factors on the firm's financial health three years into the future. Chase tested the system extensively and, having identified many potentially trou-blesome loans, the bank is now implementing it.

From a statistician's viewpoint, a major distinction between ADAM and classical neural networks, as shown in Table 4.1, is that neural networks weigh values that maximize the accuracy in the classification of the historical data. ADAM, however, maximizes the accuracy of the classification after discounting bias.

A new, more robust PCLM is being developed as a sister model for private companies, and a user-friendly shell has been created to facilitate the use of both models by bank officers from their PCs. Feasibility studies have concluded that the ADAM technology can be applied successfully to corporate planning, investment portfolio analysis, and oil-exploration models.

Table 4.1

Expert Systems, Neural Networks, and ADAM

Feature	Expert System	Neural Network	ADAM Model
Model financial data and use the results to evaluate new information	No	Yes	Yes
Automatically model and use the unconscious knowledge and experience of experts	No	Yes	Yes
Automatically adapt to changing economic and market conditions	No	Yes	Yes
Explain, in English, the reason for their evaluations	Yes	No	Yes
Accommodate missing information	Yes	Yes	Yes
Discover unknown significant rare events	No	Yes	Yes
Resistant to data errors	Sometimes	Sometimes	Yes

5

ANALYZING FINANCIAL HEALTH: INTEGRATING NEURAL NETWORKS AND EXPERT SYSTEMS

Don Barker

INTRODUCTION

The application presented here was developed using KnowledgePro, NeuroShell, and dBase III Plus. These software environments require little programming experience and provide for quick and simple data exchanges. As a result, practically anyone wishing to employ the flexibility and power of integrated knowledge processing would be able to exploit the concepts detailed below.

As we begin the last decade of this millennium, true machine intelligence still eludes us and remains confined to the imaginations of science fiction writers. Unquestionably, significant strides have been made in developing systems for solving problems that previously required human reasoning. Feigenbaum, McCorduck, and Nil document hundreds of such programs in their book *The Rise of the Expert Company*.[1] The expert systems

This article originally appeared in *PCAI*, May/June, 1990, pp. 24–27. Reprinted with permission.

83

they describe work by storing the knowledge of human specialists in the form of rules and applying the tenets of logic to produce answers to a myriad of business concerns.

Although expert systems function well within their limited areas of competency, they perform quite poorly outside these boundaries. When confronted with circumstances where heuristics are either unclear or questionable, expert systems, because of their deterministic nature, are simply impractical solutions for automating the reasoning process. Since many "real-world" problems lack a distinct set of decision rules, it is little wonder that AI has progressed slowly.

Fortunately, a new genre of AI software, neural networks, is now making itself felt in the marketplace. These programs rely on classification and association to reach likely solutions. They are able to "learn" from a set of sample decisions and classify new cases according to the similarities associated with the "memorized" patterns. The method by which these patterns are stored and identified is called parallel distributed processing (PDP). It is termed "parallel" because multiple aspects of a pattern are considered simultaneously, and "distributed" because the results are stored throughout the network.

However, neural networks suffer from several limitations of their own. They lack the capacity to explain their conclusions and, perhaps more important, they are unable to reason in a sequential or stepwise manner that results in precise conclusions. These restrictions can be critical when dealing with situations that demand exact answers and lucid justifications. Because expert systems use symbolic processing to logically derive a conclusion, they excel at explaining their line of reasoning and producing precise recommendations.

From the previous discussion, it should now be apparent that symbolic and parallel distributed processing are not competing AI strategies but complimentary. By uniting them, we can avoid many of the weaknesses inherent in each method while capitalizing on their unique strengths. The program described below provides an example of effectively combining these two dissimilar knowledge-processing strategies.

RATIO ANALYSIS OF SMALL BUSINESS

Like large corporations, every small business must produce financial statements, if for no other reason than tax purposes. However, these statements can provide useful information about the financial health of the company.

One common way of analyzing the data in financial statements is to convert them into ratios. A ratio is simply a means of transforming two numbers into one. Interpretation of the new number depends upon comparisons. Comparing a firm's ratios to industrywide average ratios can reveal the relative financial condition of the company.

We are going to examine a system that analyzes the ratios of small firms. It performs two main tasks: (1) interpreting the ratios of a company and (2) estimating the likelihood that a firm will be able to acquire additional capital through borrowing. Both the heuristics and the facts necessary for performing the first task are unambiguous and reliable, making it an ideal choice for an expert system solution.

However, estimating a company's borrowing ability is a bit more tricky. Rules for making a loan decision are obscure and, although sample cases do exist, they have inconsistencies. (These inconsistencies result from the various lending institutions applying different criteria in making loan decisions.) In the absence of clear rules or precise data, a neural network approach has the best chance of producing plausible results.

Figure 5.1 shows the design for a hybrid expert system that addresses all the facets of our problem. It contains elements for communicating with the user and for processing knowledge in both a symbolic and parallel distributed fashion, and a database to store relevant facts. Notice that the symbolic processing component has access to both its rule base and a shared database. Access to the database is necessary because the industry average ratios required for analysis are stored there. The rule base contains the expertise necessary to interpret a company's ratios by comparing them with the average ratios obtained from the database.

The parallel distributed processing segment also shares a connection with the database. This allows the neural network to train on sample loan decisions stored in the database. The PDP element uses the trained neural network to classify new cases in order to make predictions about loan possibilities.

PUTTING THE SYSTEM ON THE COMPUTER

Since there is presently no software package that incorporates symbolic processing, PDP, and a database, three separate development tools are necessary for putting our hybrid expert system on the computer. These programs must communicate with each other and transfer relevant data. They should also allow for the creation of a "seamless" interface to minimize

Figure 5.1

Diagram of a Hybrid Expert System for Evaluating Business Ratios

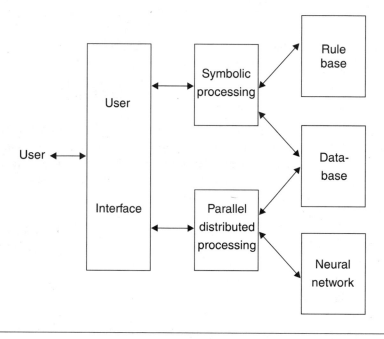

user confusion. Finally, to reduce development time and make this technology more widely available, it is desirable that the programs provide most of the procedural code necessary to implement the system.

NeuroShell, by Ward Systems, Inc., is used to construct the neural network portion of the program. It employs one of the most powerful algorithms for performing parallel distributed processing (backward error propagation). NeuroShell stores data in standard ASCII files, making data transfer a simple operation. Another important feature is a run-time version that can be evoked from inside another program and run in the background. This contributes greatly to the goal of a seamless user interface. NeuroShell is constructed around the same idea that has made expert system shells so popular. By including all the fundamental components necessary for building a neural network and offering menu-driven controls, it releases the developer to concentrate on the critical job of crafting a quality neural network.

KnowledgePro, a product of Knowledge Garden, Inc., is an expert system shell with an extensive command language for manipulating symbols. These commands enable data from imported files to be parsed and organized for symbolic processing. They also make it possible to format data for export to other programs with different file structures. In addition, facilities exist for executing external programs from within a KnowledgePro application. Like other expert system shells, KnowledgePro comes with an inference mechanism for directing reasoning efforts and a user interface for communicating with the outside world. This allows the developer to ignore the procedural aspects of building an expert system and to focus on gathering the expertise necessary to create a rule base for solving a particular problem.

KnowledgePro uses the concept of "topics" for organizing and processing related "chunks" of knowledge. Topics are similar to procedures in traditional programming languages in that they act to separate tasks or functions within a program. For instance, Figure 5.2 displays the topic named "main." Its purpose is to control the execution of all the other topics that comprise our hybrid expert system. When KnowledgePro encounters the command "do (main)," it begins execution of the topic. This, in turn, causes the sequential activation of the eight topics contained in "main." As each topic terminates, control is returned to "main" so that the next topic can be run.

The first topic to be executed is "instructions." This topic presents the user with an explanation of how the system operates. When the user finishes reading these instructions, the topic "identify business type" is activated. Here the user is asked to select the industry category that most closely matches the business being evaluated. (This information is used later to search the database for the industry average ratios that correspond to the business.) The third topic, "gather financial facts," queries the user for a series of numbers drawn from the financial statements of the company under examination. These numbers are converted into ratios in the topic "compute ratios for firm" (see the Appendix—Business Ratios). The next three topics in "main" are the heart of the system. We will investigate them in more detail.

Figure 5.2

The "Main" Topic (routine) for the Hybrid Expert System Dubbed the "Ratio Evaluator"

```
(* Ratio evaluator *)

do (main).

topic main. (* driver routine for system *)

   window ('Ratio Evaluator', white, blue, yellow, 2,2,78,19).

   do (instructions).
   do ('identify business type').
   do ('gather financial facts').
   do ('compute ratios for firm').
   do ('get industry ratios').
   do ('estimate borrowing probability').
   do ('interpret ratios').
   do (continue).

end. (* main *)
```

SEARCHING THE DATABASE

Figure 5.3 is a listing of the topic "get industry ratios." Its function, as the name implies, is to retrieve industry average ratios from a database. dBase III Plus was chosen to create the data files for this program because both KnowledgePro and NeuroShell are able (through additional utilities) to read these files. Table 5.1 shows the structure and some sample records from the database "RATIOS.DBF." The "TYPE" field holds the name of each industry category, while the other four fields contain the associated ratios.

The first instruction in Figure 5.3 tells KnowledgePro to open the file "c:\garden\ratios" and read its structure. The subsequent line stores the field names from the database in the variable "field_list." These field names are used in the subtopic "locate," which is activated by the command

Figure 5.3

A Procedure for Extracting Database Records

Topic 'get industry ratios'. (* data base access *)

```
db_desc = open_dbf('c:\garden\ratios').
field_list = element(?db_desc,5).
locate( ).
close_dbf(?db_desc).

topic locate ( ).

    eof = number_to_char(26).
    data_list = #s.
    data = read_dbf(?db_desc).
    While ?data<>?eof
        then ?field_list is _c ?data and
        (If ?TYPE = ?business_type
        then data_string gets
        [?QUICK,?DEBT_WORTH,?SALES_REC,?PROFIT_WTH]
        and data = number_to_char(26)
        else data = read_dbf(?db_desc)).

end. (* locate *)

record_list = string_to_list (?data_string).

average_quick_ratio is element (?record_list,1).
average_debt_to_worth is element (?record_list,2).
average_sales_to_receivables is element (?record_list,3).
average_profit_to_worth is element (?record_list,4).

end. (* get industry ratios *)
```

"locate( )." (A question mark appearing in front of a word or phrase signifies that it is a variable name and causes the program to examine the value assigned to it and not the variable name itself.)

Topic "locate" performs a sequential search of the database to find the record that matches the industry type identified earlier. Once the record is found, its contents are stored in the variable "data_string," and the subtopic terminates. The database is then closed, and the data string is converted into a list. This is done so that each ratio can be extracted from the list and assigned to a variable (see the lower portion of Table 5.1). The procedure for accessing the database then concludes, and control is returned to the topic "main."

Table 5.1

The File Structure and Sample Listing of the Database Containing the Industry Financial Ratios

Structure for database: C: ratios, dbf
Number of data record: 7
Date of last update: 12/15/89

Field	Field Name	Type	Width	Dec
1	TYPE	Character	20	
2	QUICK	Numeric	5	1
3	DEBT_WORTH	Numeric	5	1
4	SALES_REC	Numeric	5	1
5	PROFIT_WTH	Numeric	5	1
Total			41	

Record #	TYPE	QUICK	DEBT_ WORTH	SALES_ REC	PROFIT_ WTH
1	Apparel	0.8	66.1	16.0	20.6
2	Computer stores	0.8	97.6	11.5	38.2
3	Farm equipment	0.6	123.4	24.8	16.1
4	Fuel oil	1.6	60.8	19.6	14.1
5	Gift shops	0.9	63.9	11.2	36.3
6	Hardware	0.9	76.0	13.6	13.6
7	Office supplies	1.2	90.1	10.6	16.1

PARALLEL DISTRIBUTED PROCESSING

The next step in our analysis is to estimate the probability of the firm obtaining capital through additional debt. A neural network is used to process the firm's ratios and produce a plausible guess concerning the likelihood of a loan. The training set for this network is shown in Table 5.2. (These sample cases are only for demonstration purposes. A much larger set of actual cases would be needed to accurately train a network.) As you look at Table 5.2, notice that when the debt-to-worth ratio is high, the loan is denied. This is because an elevated debt-to-worth means that creditors are sharing a greater degree of risk than the owners. Future creditors are quite reluctant to extend more financing in this situation. Thus, we can safely expect the neural network to assign a low borrowing probability to companies with an elevated debt-to-worth ratio.

Figure 5.4 lists the topic "estimate borrowing probability." The first four lines of code instruct the program to create a file and place the ratios for the firm in it. The commands "#s" and "#x" are used to format the values in the file so that NeuroShell will be able to read it. The purpose of the next group of instructions is to invoke the batch version of NeuroShell, telling it to process the file "ratios.in" and then call a subtopic to read the results. In this

---

Table 5.2

Training Cases for the Neural Network

Quick Ratio	Debt-to-Worth	Sales-to-Receivables	Profit-to-Worth	Loan Probability
0.5	220.0	25.0	140.0	0.0
0.6	41.2	22.7	61.4	100.0
0.5	261.4	27.8	159.1	0.0
0.8	35.0	20.8	58.3	100.0
0.5	243.5	31.3	152.2	0.0
1.0	34.1	16.7	56.9	100.0

0.0 = Loan denied
100.0 = Loan approved

Figure 5.4

The Procedure for Accessing the Neural Network from within KnowledgePro

---

```
topic 'estimate borrowing probability'. (* parallel distributed
  processing *)

  new_file ('ratios.in').
  write(['ratios.in'],#x1,?quick_ratio,#s#x10,?debt_to_worth,#s#x20,
  ?sales_to_receivables,#s#x30,?profit_to_worth,#s#x40).
  close_all().

  NeuroShell = ('c:\garden\banalog.exe ratios').
  if run (?NeuroShell)<0
  then say ('Sorry, it was impossible to load NeuroShell')
  else do ('get output patterns from ratios').

  topic 'get output patterns from ratios'.
    output is read_line ('ratios.prn').
    close_all().

    number = string_to_list (?output).
    estimation = ((?number + 0.5) div 1).
  end. (* topic get output patterns from ratios *)

end. (* estimate borrowing probability *)
```

---

subtopic, the rounded output from the neural network is assigned to the variable "estimation." This ends the parallel distributed processing portion of the program and reinstates control to the "main" topic.

SYMBOLIC PROCESSING

With all the necessary data gathered, it is now possible to complete the ratio evaluation. Table 5.3 provides a complete picture of the rules for interpreting a firm's ratios in comparison with industry averages. The rules are displayed in the form of a decision table. Decision tables are

Table 5.3

Decision Table for Ratio Analysis

	1	2	3	4	5	6	7	8	9	10	11	12	13	14	15	16
Quick ratio	F	U	U	U	U	F	F	F	F	U	F	F	F	U	U	U
Debt-to-worth	F	F	U	U	U	F	F	U	U	F	F	U	U	F	F	U
Sales-to-receivables	F	F	F	U	U	F	U	U	U	F	U	F	F	U	U	F
Profit-to-worth	F	F	F	F	U	U	U	U	F	U	F	F	U	F	U	U
Liquidity	F	U	U	U	U	F	F	F	F	U	F	F	F	U	U	U
Leverage	F	F	U	U	U	F	F	U	U	F	F	U	U	F	F	U
Activity	F	F	F	U	U	F	U	U	U	F	U	F	F	U	U	F
Profitability	F	F	F	F	U	U	U	U	F	U	F	F	U	F	U	U

F = Favorable
U = Unfavorable

---

extremely useful devices for viewing judgments in a very compact form. Each column in Table 5.3 represents a complete and sometimes complex rule. For example, column 1 of the decision table is read as follows:

> If the quick ratio is favorable
>   and debt-to-worth is favorable
>   and sales-to-receivables is favorable
>   and profit-to-worth is favorable,
> then liquidity is favorable
>   and leverage is favorable
>   and activity is favorable
>   and profitability is favorable.

Since there are four conditions in the *if* part or antecedent of each conditional, our decision table needs to cover 16 possible combinations or rules (4^2). Columns 2 through 16 cover the remaining possibilities. KnowledgePro processes rules derived from the decision table. For example, one rule checks to see if the company's ratios are favorable in comparison to the industry ratios. When all four ratios are favorable, the rule fires, and the procedure displays the results of the analysis to the user along with an estimation of the company's chances of acquiring a loan.

At this point, the last theme in the topic "main" is executed. This final topic prompts the user to either end the session or continue by submitting another case.

CONSULTING THE SYSTEM

Let us now step through a consultation with the system to see how it appears from the outside. We'll use the imaginary company "Computers R US" to test the program. The relevant financial data for the business are exhibited in Table 5.4. The first display to appear contains information about the system (Figure 5.5). Once familiar with this overview, the <Enter> key is pressed to begin the session. We are then asked to select the business sector that most closely matches the firm under study (Figure 5.6). Because Computers R US is a small storefront operation selling directly to the public, the "retailers" option is chosen. We are then presented with another list containing a further breakdown of the selected business sector. Picking "computer stores" starts a series of window prompts that collect all the necessary numbers for completing the ratio evaluation (see Figure 5.7 as an example of these query windows).

After all the entries have been made, the program analyzes the inputs by executing its parallel distributed and symbolic processing components. Figure 5.8 displays the system's final conclusion. Observe that in every case, with the exception of the debt-to-worth ratio (137.2 percent), our computer company has favorable ratios in comparison with the industry averages. But because the debt-to-worth rating carries a great deal of weight with creditors, the firm's other positive ratios have only managed to garner it a 52 percent chance of acquiring capital through new loans. This concludes the consultation. One last screen appears, giving us the opportunity to either evaluate another company or exit the program.

Table 5.4

Financial Data for the Imaginary Company "Computers R US"

COMPUTERS R US INCOME DATA

Sales	$250,000
Cost of Goods Sold	120,000
Gross Margin	$130,000
Expenses	60,000
Profit (pretax)	$ 70,000
Income Tax	28,000
Profit (after tax)	$ 42,000

ASSETS

Inventory	$ 90,000
Accounts Receivable	15,000
Current Assets	$105,000
Leasehold Improvements	$ 50,000
Equipment	30,000
Fixed Assets	$ 80,000
Total Assets	$185,000

LIABILITIES AND CAPITAL

Accounts Payable	$ 7,000
Short-Term Bank Loans	10,000
Current Debt	$ 17,000
Notes Payable	$ 20,000
Long-Term Bank Loans	70,000
Long-Term Debt	$ 90,000
Total Debt	$107,000
Common Stock	$ 36,000
Retained Earnings	42,000
Net Worth	$ 78,000

Figure 5.5

Information about the System

Ratio Evaluator

Welcome to the Ratio Evaluator. This system is only for the purposes of demonstration, and its recommendations should not be taken seriously. It is designed to show how neural technology can be used in concert with a rule-based expert system and a database to provide a more complete decision support system.

A consultant with the Ratio Evaluator begins with the system asking you for financial numbers from the firm under study. This information is used to compute a set of ratios designed to reveal the financial health of the firm. These ratios are evaluated in comparison to numbers drawn from a database of industry average ratios. Some of these figures are also used to produce an estimate of how likely it is that the company will be able to acquire additional debt in the near future. Important variances are noted, and a final report is issued containing the results of the analysis.

Press the Enter key to begin the consultation.

F1 Help	F5 Evaluate	F7 Edit	Pg 1 of 1
Space Cont.	F6 Display KB	F8 DOS	F10 Quit

CONCLUSION

Our example application has shown that instead of being mutually exclusive, expert systems and neural networks are actually complimentary reasoning mechanisms that can be joined to form a versatile tool for tackling especially perplexing problems that, because of their diverse nature, have resisted solution by any single AI technology.

This chapter only touches on one possible application of integrating these two approaches to problem solving. Perhaps the ideas presented here will encourage further investigation of other interesting combinations for automating the reasoning process.

Figure 5.6

List of the Possible Business Sectors in Which a Firm Might "Fit"

Ratio Evaluator

Please choose a general business sector:

```
Retailers
Wholesalers
Services
Contractors
Professional services
Manufacturers
```

F1 Help	F5 Evaluate	F7 Edit	
	F6 Display KB	F8 DOS	F10 Quit

Figure 5.7

The Numbers Required to Compute the Firm's Ratios

Ratio Evaluator

```
Query
Enter current assets:
=> 105000
```

F1 Help	F5 Evaluate	F7 Edit	
Enter Accept	F6 Display KB	F8 DOS	F10 Quit

Figure 5.8

Results of the Analysis

Ratio Evaluator

ASSESSMENT

	Quick Ratio	Debt/ Worth	Sales/ Receivables	Profit/ Worth
Firm:	0.9	137.2	16.7	89.7
Std:	0.8	97.6	11.5	38.2

The quick ratio is greater than or equal to the industry average, signaling that the firm should have the liquidity to meet its short-term obligations.

The debt-to-worth ratio is greater than the industry average, indicating that the firm is heavily leveraged, which increases the risk to the creditors.

The sales-to-receivables ratio is greater than or equal to the industry average, which implies a sound receivables management policy.

The profit-to-worth ratio is greater than or equal to the industry average, signaling that the owners are getting a solid return on their investments.

The likelihood of raising capital by borrowing is 52 percent.

| F1 Help | F5 Evaluate | F7 Edit | Pg 1 of 1 |
| Space Cont. | F6 Display KB | F8 DOS | F10 Quit |

NOTE

1. Edward A. Feigenbaum et al., *The Rise of the Expert Company: How Visionary Companies Are Using Artificial Intelligence to Achieve Higher Productivity and Profits* (New York: Random House, 1988).

APPENDIX

Business Ratios

Although there are many types of ratios, they can generally be placed into one of four categories, depending on what they are trying to measure: liquidity, leveraging, activity, and profitability. Liquidity ratios test a firm's ability to meet its short-term or current financial obligations; leverage ratios indicate the proportion of funds provided by owners and creditors; activity ratios reveal how effectively a firm utilizes the resources at its disposal; and profitability ratios measure the overall net effect of the managerial efficiency of a firm. For our purposes here, we will use only a single ratio from each of the four categories. They are listed below with a brief description of each.

$$\text{Quick ratio} = \frac{\text{Current assets} - \text{Inventory}}{\text{Current debt}}$$

The quick ratio indicates the amount of liquid assets available to meet a firm's current obligations. Assuming current assets can be liquidated at or near book value, the higher the ratio, the greater the firm's liquidity.

$$\text{Debt-to-worth} = \frac{\text{Total debt}}{\text{Net worth}} \times 100\%$$

The debt-to-worth ratio shows the proportion of capital contributed by creditors as compared to the funds contributed by the owners. A high value indicates that the firm is strongly leveraged, indicating a greater risk for the creditors. Servicing an inordinate amount of debt can strain the resources of any organization.

$$\text{Sales-to-receivables} = \frac{\text{Sales}}{\text{Receivables}}$$

The sales-to-receivables ratio measures an important business activity. It relates the revenues generated to the level of outstanding receivables carried. A high number implies a sound receivables management policy. By turning over receivables quickly and keeping noncash sales to a minimum, a company benefits in terms of an improved cash flow and fewer collection problems.

$$\text{Profit-to-worth} = \frac{\text{Profit (pretax)}}{\text{Net worth}} \times 100\%$$

The profit-to-worth ratio shows the return the owners are receiving on their investment. The higher the ratio, the more profitable their investment.

6

APPLYING NEURAL NETWORKS TO THE EXTRACTION OF KNOWLEDGE FROM ACCOUNTING REPORTS: A CLASSIFICATION STUDY

R. H. Berry and Duarte Trigueiros

INTRODUCTION

This study develops a new approach to the problem of extracting meaningful information from samples of accounting reports. Neural networks are shown to be capable of building structures similar to financial ratios, which are optimal in the context of the particular problem being dealt with. This approach removes the need for an analyst to search for appropriate ratios before model building can begin.

The internal organization of a neural network model helps identify key features of accounting data and provides new insights into the relative importance of variables for particular modeling tasks. The lack of inter-

Printed with permission of the authors.

pretability of neural network parameters so often reported in other applications of the approach is removed in the accounting context. Much of the internal operation of the networks involves the construction of generalizations of the ratio concepts with which accountants are familiar. Thus, traditional modes of understanding can be brought to bear.

ACCOUNTING DECISION MODELS

Accounting reports are an important source of information for managers, investors, and financial analysts. Statistical techniques have often been used to extract information from them. The aim of such exercises is to construct models suitable for predictive or classification purposes or for isolating key features of the data. Well-known examples include, in the U.S. context, Altman et al.[1] and, in the U.K. context, Taffler.[2]

The procedures used in this vast body of literature are generally similar. The first stage consists of forming a set of ratios from selected items in a set of accounting reports. This selection typically is made in accordance with the prior beliefs of researchers. Next, the normality of these ratio variables is examined and transformations applied, where necessary, to bring it about. Finally, some linear modeling technique is used to find optimal parameters in the least-square sense. Linear regression and Fisher's multiple discriminant analysis are the most popular algorithms. However, logistic regression can also be found in some studies. Foster[3] provides a review of the general area of statistical modeling applied to accounting variables.

The widespread use of ratios as input variables is particularly significant in the present context. This seems to be an extension of their normal use in financial statement analysis. However, there is a problem. There are many possible ratios. Consequently, some researchers utilize a large number of ratios as explanatory variables, others use representative ratios, and still others use factor analysis to cope with the mass of ratio variables and their linear dependence.

THE STATISTICAL CHARACTERIZATION
OF ACCOUNTING VARIABLES

The statistical distribution of accounting ratios has been the object of considerable study. The common finding is that ratio distributions are skewed. Horrigan,[4] in an early work on this subject, reports positive skewness of ratios and explains it as the result of effective lower limits of zero on many ratios. Barnes,[5] in a discussion of the link between firm size and ratio values, suggests that skewness of ratios could be the result of deviations from strict proportionality between the numerator and the denominator variables in the ratio. The underlying idea here, that interest should center on the behavior of the component accounting variables and not on the ratios that they have traditionally been used to form, is basic to the present research.

Mcleay,[6] in one of the few studies of distributions of accounting variables as opposed to ratios of such variables, reports that accounting variables that are sums of similar transactions with the same sign, such as sales, stocks, creditors, or current assets, exhibit cross-section lognormality. Empirical work carried out during the current research project confirms this finding and suggests that the phenomenon of lognormality is much more widespread. Many other positive-valued accounting variables have cross-section distributions that are approximately log normal. Furthermore, where variables can take on positive and negative values, then lognormality can be observed in the subset of positive values and also in the absolute values of the negative subset. Size-related nonfinancial variables such as number of employees also seem to exhibit lognormality. Distributional evidence for 18 accounting and other items for 14 industry groups over a five-year period can be found in Trigueiros.[7] In this chapter, lognormality is viewed as a universal distributional form for the cross-section behavior of those variables used as inputs to the neural networks that have been built.

The lognormal distribution is characterized by a lower bound of zero and a tail consisting of a few relatively large values. In any statistical analysis of such variables, based on the least-squares criterion, these few large values will dominate coefficient estimates. Consequently, an analyst is well advised to apply the logarithmic transformation to accounting variables that are to be inputs to least-squares-based techniques to counteract this effect. In what follows, logs of accounting variables will appear in various linear combinations, having the general form:

$$z = a_1\log(x_1) + a_2\log(x_2) - b_1\log(y_1) - b_2\log(y_2) \qquad (1)$$

If the logarithmic transformation is reversed, this linear combination is seen to be equivalent to:

$$k = \frac{x_1^{a_1} \quad x_2^{a_2}}{y_1^{b_1} \quad y_2^{b_2}} \qquad (2)$$

This is a complex ratio form. Had the linear combination been restricted to the difference between two variables, and the coefficients to the value one, then a simple ratio of two variables would have been produced by reversing the logarithmic transformation. The observation that a linear combination, including both positive and negative coefficients, in log space is equivalent to a ratio form in ordinary space is fundamental to the interpretation of the neural network coefficients presented in this chapter.

NEURAL NETWORKS

A neural network is a collection of simple computational elements—neurons—that are interconnected. The connections between neurons have weights attached to them. A neuron can receive inputs from other neurons or from sources outside the network; form a weighted combination of these inputs (often called NET), the weights being those assigned to the connections along with the inputs travel; and produce an output (often called OUT) that is sent to other neurons. The output may be simply the weighted combination of inputs, NET, or a nonlinear transformation of NET. This nonlinear transformation is known as a transfer, or squashing, function. The number and pattern of interconnection of the neurons in a network determine the task a network is capable of performing.

The particular network form used in this chapter is known as a multilayer perceptron (MLP). A simple example is shown in Figure 6.1. There are three layers of neurons (each neuron being represented by a rectangle): an input layer, a hidden layer, and an output layer. The neurons in the input layer do not perform weighting or nonlinear transformation. They simply send inputs from the world outside the network to the hidden-layer neurons. In Figure 6.1, each input neuron sends its signal to each of the neurons in the hidden layer. Each of these hidden-layer neurons forms a weighted linear combination of the input values and then applies a nonlinear transformation to generate its own output. A common transfer function is the sigmoid, which generates a signal $0 \leq OUT \leq 1$:

$$OUT = \frac{1}{1 + e^{-NET}} \tag{3}$$

The signals from the hidden-layer neurons are sent to the output-layer neurons. In Figure 6.1, each output-layer neuron receives input from each hidden-layer neuron. The neurons in the output layer each form linear

Figure 6.1

A Multilayer Perceptron

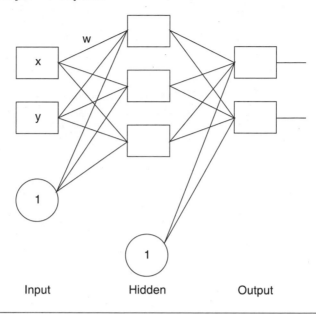

| Input | Hidden | Output |

combinations of their inputs and apply a nonlinear transformation before sending their own signals onward, in their case to the outside world. The sigmoid function again serves as the nonlinear transformation. The circles in Figure 6.1 do not represent neurons. They each send a signal that has a constant value of 1 along weighted connections. This weighted signal becomes part of NET for each receiving neuron. This has the effect of generating a threshold value of NET in each neuron's OUT calculation, above which OUT rises rapidly.

The particular MLP shown in Figure 6.1 is capable of performing a relatively complex classification task, given that appropriate weights have been attached to the interconnections between neurons. Figure 6.2 shows a convex set of (x,y) values. The convex region is formed by the intersection of three half-spaces, each defined by a linear inequality. Each of the three linear relations that define the convex set can be represented by a linear combination of (x,y) values. Thus, each can be represented by one of the three neurons in the hidden layer of the MLP shown in Figure 6.1. Each

Figure 6.2
Classification Problem

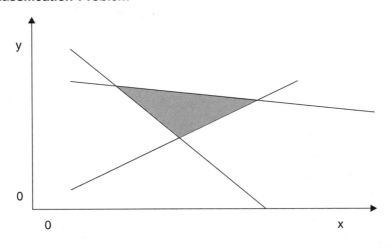

output-layer neuron then receives over/under signals from the hidden-layer neurons and, again by weighting and transforming the signals, carries out AND/OR operations to produce an output.

In the network shown in Figure 6.1, one output neuron will produce a value close to 1 if the (x,y) pair being input lies within the convex region. The other will produce a value close to 0 in these circumstances. The input of an (x,y) pair outside the convex region will cause a reversal of this output pattern. (Given the binary nature of the output signal required, one output neuron could theoretically do the job. However, computational experience shows that economizing on output neurons is a mistake.) In order to model more difficult nonlinear boundaries, additional hidden layers of neurons might have to be added to the network.

The problem left unresolved in the preceding description of the operation of the MLP is where do the values of the interconnection weights come from? To carry out the classification task appropriately, each interconnection must have an appropriate weight.

The network learns these weights during a training process. To build a network capable of performing a particular classification task, the following actions must be undertaken:

1. The network topology (number of layers and number of neurons in each layer) must be specified.

2. A data set must be collected to allow network training. In the example under discussion, this training set would consist of (x,y) pairs and for each pair a target value vector $(1,0)$ if the pair lies in the convex region of interest, $(0,1)$ if it does not.

3. Random, small weights are assigned to each interconnection.

4. An (x,y) pair is input to the network.

5. The vector of OUT values from the output neurons is compared with the appropriate target value vector.

6. Any errors are used to revise the interconnection weights.

The training set is processed repeatedly until a measure of network performance based on prediction errors for the whole training set reaches an acceptably low level. Once training has been completed, the network can be used for predictive purposes. There are two styles of training. In the first, weight updating occurs after each individual element of the training set is processed through the MLP. In the second, the entire training set is processed before updating occurs.

The algorithm used to adjust interconnection weights, known as the generalized delta rule or as the back-propagation method, is usually associated with Rumelhart et al.[8] This algorithm is an enhanced version of the stochastic gradient-descent optimization procedure. Its virtue is that it is able to propagate deviations backwards through more than one layer of nodes. Thus, it can train networks with one or more hidden layers. For the algorithm to work, the transfer function used in the MLP must be differentiable. Good descriptions of the algorithm exist in several sources, including Pao[9] and Wasserman.[10] Wasserman's approach plays down the mathematics and emphasizes the computational steps.

Minimum least-squares deviation is one possible success criterion that could be used to decide when to curtail the training process. However, there are others, such as likelihood maximization. In this case, the weights are adjusted to maximize the probability of obtaining the input/output data that constitute the training set.

In general, if the number of nodes in hidden layers is large compared with the number of important features in the data, the MLP behaves just like a storage device. It learns the noise present in the training set, as well as the key structures. No generalization ability can be expected in these circumstances. Restricting the number of hidden-layer neurons, however, makes the MLP extract only the main features of the training set. Thus, a generalization ability appears.

It is its hidden layers of neurons that make the multilayer perceptron attractive as a statistical modeling tool. The outputs of hidden neurons can be considered as new variables, which can contain interesting information about the relationship being modeled. Such new variables, known as internal representations, along with the net topology, can make the modeling process self-explanatory, and so the neural network approach becomes attractive as a form of machine learning.

As stated earlier, if variables are subjected to a logarithmic transformation, then a linear combination of such variables is equivalent to a complex ratio form. If the values input to an MLP are the logs of variable values, then the neurons in the (first, if there are more than one) hidden layer produce NETs that represent complex ratios. The nonlinear transformation effectively reverses the logarithmic transformation, so these complex ratios are inputs to the next layer of neurons where they are linearly combined to model the relation being investigated.

The hidden layer of neurons in the MLP discussed in this chapter is, then, dedicated to building appropriate ratios. The problem of choosing the best ratios for a particular task, which has taxed so many researchers, is thus avoided. The best ratios are discovered by the modeling algorithm, not imposed by the analyst. It will be shown later that by using an appropriate training scheme these extended ratios can be encouraged to assume a simple and therefore potentially more interpretable form.

AN APPLICATION: MODELING INDUSTRY HOMOGENEITY

The approach described above is now applied to the problem of classifying firms to industries on the basis of financial statement data. The neural network's performance is compared to that of a more traditional discriminant analysis-based approach. To ensure that the discriminant analysis exercise is more than a "straw man," an existing, reputable study based on discriminant analysis is replicated. The neural network approach is then applied using the same raw data.

All companies quoted on the London Stock Exchange are classified into different industry groups according to the Stock Exchange Industrial

Classification (SEIC), which groups together companies whose results are likely to be affected by the same economic, political, and trade influences.[11] Although the declared criteria are ambitious, the practice seems to be more trivial, consisting of classifying firms mainly on an end-product basis. The aim here is to attempt to mimic the classification process using accounting variables.

The data for exercises were drawn from the Micro-EXSTAT database of company financial information provided by EXTEL Statistical Services Ltd. This covers the top 70 percent of U.K. industrial companies. Fourteen manufacturing groups were selected according to the SEIC criteria. The list of member firms was then pruned to exclude firms known to be distressed, and nonmanufacturing representatives of foreign companies that had recently merged, or were highly diversified. After pruning, data on 297 firms remained for a six-year period (1982–1987) and a bigger sample (502 cases) for the year 1984. The distribution of firms by industry in this sample is shown in Table 6.1.

The initial analysis of this data followed the traditional statistical modeling approach. This consisted of, first, "forming 18 financial ratios chosen as to reflect a broad range of important characteristics relating to the economic, financial and trade structure of industries."[12] Eight principal components were then extracted to form new variables. Next, these new variables were used as inputs to a multiple discriminant analysis. Only a randomly selected half of the data set was used during this estimation phase of the discriminant analysis.

The other half was used as a holdout sample to measure the classification accuracy of the resulting model. The exercise was repeated reversing the role of the two half-data sets. Lack of consistency of results here would have raised doubts about the appropriateness of the sampling activity undertaken. A detailed description of the ratios used and the modeling procedure adopted can be found in Sundarsanam and Taffler.[13] The results of this exercise were found to be similar to those achieved by Sundarsanam and Taffler.[14] Thus, it was decided that they were an acceptable base case against which to compare the results achieved by an MLP constructed with the same data.

The input data for the neural network approach consisted of eight of the accounting variables that had been building blocks for the 18 ratios previously calculated. The number eight was selected simply to mimic the number of explanatory variables in the discriminant analysis. It must be emphasized that basic accounting variables, not ratios, were used. The

Table 6.1

Industry Groups and Number of Cases in the One-Year (1984) Data Set

Group	Name	Cases	Percent
1	Building materials	31	6.2
2	Metallurgy	19	3.8
3	Paper, packaging	46	9.2
4	Chemicals	45	9.0
5	Electrical	34	6.8
6	Industrial plants	17	3.4
7	Machine tools	21	4.2
8	Electronics	79	15.7
9	Motor components	23	4.6
10	Clothing	42	8.4
11	Wool	19	3.8
12	Misc. textiles	30	6.0
13	Leather	16	3.2
14	Food	80	15.9

selected items were fixed assets (FA), inventory (I), debtors (D), creditors (C), long-term debt (DB), net worth (NW), wages (W), and operating expenses less wages (EX). The variables were chosen to represent the key balance sheet elements and a rudimentary picture of cost structure.

A logarithmic transformation was applied to these variables. Many of these accounting variables were well suited for a logarithmic transformation. However, some caused problems because of the presence of zero or negative values. In order to transform the negative values of such variables, the following rule was applied:

$$x \to \log(x), \quad \text{for } x > 0$$
$$x \to -\log(|x|), \quad \text{for } x < 0$$

This corresponds to the assumption that negative cases are lognormally distributed in a negative direction.

To avoid the problem of zero values, instead of log 0, a very small number, log 1 = 0, was used. Such an approach is acceptable if the unit of measurement is not far away from the typical value in the data set. An alternative approach to (some) such problem variables would be to ensure that their pattern of variation is reflected in the model by using as input variables some that in combination define the problem variable but which are themselves amenable to the logarithmic transformation. The variability of profit, say, could be brought to the model by the introduction of both sales and expenses.

The base of logarithms to be used can be selected in a way that avoids the need for further scaling. The aim of the transformation is to avoid extreme values. With natural logs, the transformed values of the variables being examined ranged from 2 to 18, approximately. Base 10 logs generated a range between 3 and 7. Given the transfer function in use, 2 to 18 is too great a range. The training process would break down. Thus, base 10 logs were used, and the resulting variable values centered on zero for submission to the network.

The eight variables were then input to a succession of differently structured MLPs. The basic format consisted of an input layer of eight neurons, one or two hidden layers with relatively few neurons in each, and an output layer with 14 neurons. Once again the networks were trained using only half the data set, the other half being used to test classification performance. As with the discriminant analysis, the roles of training and testing set were reversed and the consistency of the resulting models examined. The most successful network topology involved one hidden layer with six nodes. The method of determining this optimal topology, its performance, and the interpretation of its weights is discussed below.

INTERPRETING AND POSTPROCESSING THE OUTPUTS OF AN MLP

There is a problem when using an MLP with multiple output neurons. The implied industry classification, given a set of inputs, may not be easy to identify. This has implications for both network training and use. Each output neuron produces an output value between 0 and 1. It would be most unusual to find 13 zeros and a single 1 (one) in the vector of outputs. Therefore, identifying the predicted classification when overlapping distributions are present requires a probabilistic interpretation of outputs. In accounting applications, population proportions generally bear no relation to the proportions observed in the sample. Therefore, the approaches adopted by other neural network researchers in other application areas, where population and sample probabilities coincide, may not be appropriate. In particular, it is most unlikely that sample proportions can be viewed as good estimates of prior probabilities.

Following Baum and Wilczek,[15] several authors advocate a direct interpretation of outputs as probabilities and show how the usual squared-error criterion can be corrected to achieve likelihood maximization.[16,17] In such cases, the connection weights in the network are adjusted in the gradient direction of the log likelihood rather than the squared error.

An alternative approach is to interpret the outputs of the MLP as a multidimensional measure of distance to targets. If departures from normality are not severe, this interpretation can be carried out using conventional statistics such as chi-square, Penrose, or Mahalanobis distances. Such measures can be regarded as scores, and conditional probabilities can be deduced from them, allowing further Bayesian corrections if required, independent of the proportions observed in the sample. A Bayesian correction independent of the sample proportions could of course also be applied directly to the MLP's outputs if they were interpreted as probabilities.

In this application, it was found that interpreting neuron outputs directly as probabilities produced a clear reduction in classification accuracy. There was a severe loss of ability to identify firms belonging to the smaller industry groups. A Bayesian correction independent of sample proportions was not pursued.

Results are reported in Figure 6.3. Direct interpretation, shown in Figure 6.3a, ignores nine of the 14 industry groups but finally achieves a good global performance by classifying the remaining five groups, which are the bigger ones, very well. Figure 6.3b shows classification performance when neuron outputs are postprocessed to produce a multidimensional distance measure. As can be seen, this allows the smaller industry groupings to appear. Therefore, although for the sake of efficiency of convergence the likelihood cost function was adopted during training, node outputs were postprocessed as distances.

A relatively simple approach was taken to the definition of a multidimensional distance. For a training set with N cases, consider o_{im}, the output signal produced in output layer neuron m, $1 \leq m \leq M$ by case i, $1 \leq i \leq N$. Compute K square deviations, d_{kim}, between neuron m's output for that input vector and each possible target value, t_{km} for that neuron: $d_{kim} = (t_{km} - o_{im})^2$, with k, $1 \leq k \leq K$. The mean sum of squared deviations from the kth target at neuron m over the whole training set will be:

Figure 6.3
The Impact of Postprocessing Outputs on Classifications

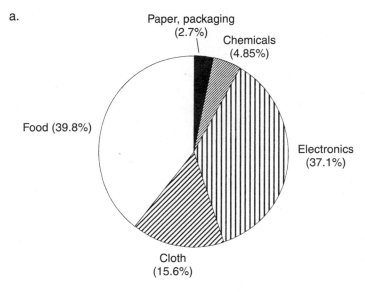

a.

Paper, packaging
(2.7%)

Chemicals
(4.85%)

Food (39.8%)

Electronics
(37.1%)

Cloth
(15.6%)

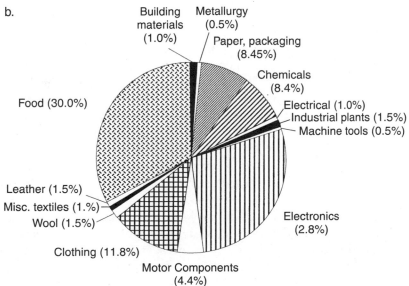

b.

Building
materials
(1.0%)

Metallurgy
(0.5%)

Paper, packaging
(8.45%)

Chemicals
(8.4%)

Food (30.0%)

Electrical (1.0%)
Industrial plants (1.5%)
Machine tools (0.5%)

Leather (1.5%)
Misc. textiles (1.%)
Wool (1.5%)

Electronics
(2.8%)

Clothing (11.8%)

Motor Components
(4.4%)

$$\sigma_{km}^2 = \sum_{i=1}^{N} \frac{d_{kim}}{(N-1)} \tag{4}$$

The standardized distances between a neuron's output and the kth target can be added over all nodes to give:

$$D_{ki} = \sum_{m=1}^{M} \frac{d_{kim}}{\sigma_{km}^2} \tag{5}$$

D_{ki} is then the distance between the output vector generated by the ith case in the training set and the kth target. The minimum of these distances identifies the appropriate classification if no Bayesian corrections are needed, that is, if the assumption of equal prior probabilities is acceptable. As part of this research effort, this distance measure's performance has been compared with that of a more elaborate measure, the Mahalanobis distance. The use of the Mahalanobis distance did not produce improved performance.

DETERMINING NETWORK TOPOLOGY

The literature gives little guidance on selecting the number of hidden layers or the number of nodes per hidden layer. Nor is there much advice on the number of times the training set should pass through the network before training is complete. The most common approach to the latter problem is to choose a target value for the training set error and repeat submission of the training set until this target value is achieved.

For the former problem, a reasonable approach would seem to be to subdivide the training set into two parts, A and B. Training set A is used in the connection weight updating procedure as usual. Different topologies can be trained using this training set. The classification performance of each of these topologies on training set B can then be examined. The topology that gives the best performance is then selected for further work. It is this topology that can then be retrained to generate a simplified structure as described in the next section. The true generalization ability of the network topology can then be checked on the as yet unused testing set.

THE PROCESS OF NETWORK TRAINING

One of the major goals of this research was the evaluation and improvement of the interpretability of multilayer perceptron models. MLPs are often considered unsuitable in applications where self-explanatory power is required. However, in the case of accounting variables, it seems possible to interpret the way the relation has been modeled by looking at the weights connecting input variables with the hidden layer's neurons. These weights are the exponents of the extended ratios involved in the optimal solution.

In order to enhance interpretability, the normal process of training interconnection weights was amended in two ways. First, it was decided to assign to one hidden-layer neuron the task of dealing with the scale effect in financial variables. The failure of ratios to cope with scale effects has been widely discussed in the literature. The weights on connections from input neurons to this hidden-layer neuron were fixed at either 0 or 1 from the outset. Connections with unit weights linked the hidden-layer neuron to only those inputs that were seen as size related. Dedicating one neuron of the hidden layer to representing this scale effect generated as a bonus an improvement in speed of convergence of the training process.

The weight generation process was also amended in a second way. During training, whenever a new presentation of the entire training set was to begin, one of the neurons of the hidden layer was randomly selected, and the connection weights linking it to the input neurons were examined. Any inhibitory weights (close to 0) were penalized by a small factor, typically 0.98. As has been said, the aim was to reduce the number of variables featuring in each of the complex ratios being formed. In a neural network, each neuron acts as a modeling unit with a certain number of free parameters. The same output can be obtained with very different combinations of these parameters. Inhibitory weights connecting inputs with the hidden layer appear when the network tries to weaken the contribution of a variable. Therefore, by randomly introducing small penalizations of inhibitory weights during the training, the inhibitory weights were encouraged to remain inhibitory. As a byproduct, the noninhibitory weights were encouraged to become even less inhibitory. Before the end of training, all the weights connecting inputs to the hidden layer and exhibiting strong inhibitory values were set to 0 and fixed. While this procedure served its purpose, it should only be applied when the basic network topology is known with some confidence.

The results produced in the neural network can be seen in Table 6.2. This shows the extended ratios formed in an MLP with eight inputs, six nodes in one hidden layer, and 14 output nodes, trained with 1984 data. Only two hidden-layer neurons produce ratio forms of substantial complexity. The relative simplicity of the ratio structures achieved bodes well for other applications in the accounting and finance area.

Interpretation of the resulting ratios unfortunately is unclear. One possible explanation for this is that the data set being used does not include an economic basis for the classification decision. Financial statement data is hardly an ideal data set for the application in question; variables such as product type are obviously more relevant. However, the fact that traditional ratios have not been formed does not indicate a failure of the approach. It indicates the unsuitability of these traditional ratio constructs and the need for alternatives.

Apart from these nonstandard training features that stem from the particular application area, two further enhancements to the training process described in the literature were also applied. The first was the utilization of a learning rate particular to each weight.[18,19] The second was, as has already been mentioned, likelihood maximization instead of squared-deviations minimization.

Table 6.2

Values of Weights Connecting Input Variables Hidden Nodes after Training with Penalties

	Node Number				
Variable	2	3	4	5	6
DB			− 6		
NW	8				
W	1			− 6	
I	8				
D	2				− 2
C				3	
FA	− 9	− 4		6	− 4
EX	−10	4	8	− 2	3

MLP CLASSIFICATION PERFORMANCE

In order to obtain an estimate of the generalization capacity associated with the MLPs examined here, the original samples were divided randomly into two subsamples of approximately equal size. All models were constructed twice, first with one-half of the sample and a check carried out with the other half, and then by reversing the roles of the two half-data sets. Results were considered acceptable if both models, when validated with the half sample not used to build them, produced consistent results.

All classification results reported here concern the test set, not the training set. That is, they were obtained by measuring the rate of correct classification the model produced when evaluated by the half set not used to train it. The classification performance on the set used for training depends solely on the number of free parameters and can be increased simply by introducing more neurons into the hidden layers. Such results are therefore uninteresting and are not presented here.

The normal approach to testing a model, by deleting a single observation and predicting its value with the model estimated on the rest of the data set and then repeating this procedure, is infeasible here. This is because the training of a neural network is time-consuming. However, the procedure adopted here will work acceptably with a large enough data set.

It was found that the generalization capacity of the neural MLP was very much dependent on the topology of the net. The number of nodes in the hidden layer seemed to determine the ability of the net to properly generalize. Persistently, good generalizations were obtained whenever the hidden layer had six nodes. Both the 1984 and the six-year data sets exhibited such a feature. Figure 6.4 shows some classification results for different numbers of nodes in the hidden layer when using the six-year data set. Similar patterns, though not showing so great a contrast, were observed when using the 1984 set.

Table 6.3 shows the best generalization results achieved with the traditional methodology (discriminant analysis and ratios) and also with the neural network. As can be seen, the neural network achieved a better performance, with half the number of input variables and within a much simpler framework.

The need for forming appropriate ratios was avoided as well as the blind pruning of outliers and the extraction of an arbitrary number of factors.

Figure 6.4

Proportion of Correct Classifications versus Hidden-Layer Structure: 6-Year Data Set

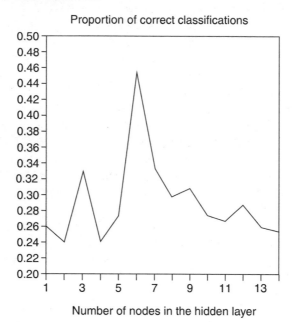

Proportion of correct classifications

Number of nodes in the hidden layer

Table 6.3

Classification Results of MLP (Multilayer Perceptron) Compared with MDA (Multiple Discriminant Analysis)

Input	1984 Data (%)		Six-Year Data (%)	
	MDA	MLP	MDA	MLP
18 ratios	29		30	
8 variables		38		45

CONCLUSION

So far, most applications of neural networks have related to the modeling of difficult relations (pattern recognition) or the mimicking of brain functions. There has been little emphasis on their potential explanatory power. Here, however, it has been argued that, in accounting-based applications, networks could generate meaningful internal representations. Numerical, continuous-valued observations such as those found in stock returns or data organized in accounting reports cannot be efficiently used by traditional expert systems knowledge-acquisition tools. Neural networks can now be seen as an alternative self-explanatory tool. In this application, hidden units formed ratios very different to those commonly used. If repeated in other application areas, this could shed light on many important issues.

The emphasis on interpretation should not obscure the other finding of the study. The MLP proved able to outperform the classification performance of a traditional discriminant analysis approach. Neither method came close to adequately classifying the testing sets, but there was a substantial improvement when the MLP was used. The fact that there was a potential for improvement was a key fact in determining the particular application area to be studied. It is perhaps worth pointing out that redoing the discriminant analysis, using representations of the ratios produced by the MLP, captured some but not all of the MLP-based improvement. The remainder may well have related to the ability of the MLP to cope with nonlinear boundaries.

The importance of the MLP's topology cannot be overemphasized. The number of hidden layers, and hidden-layer neurons, can be selected by splitting the training set and adopting a two-phase training process. However, the principle of parsimony should always be borne in mind. If there are too many hidden neurons, the MLP will fail to identify key features and will model the noise in the data set as well. Generalization ability will then be lost.

ENDNOTES

1. A. Altman, R. Haldeman, and P. Narayanan, "Zeta Analysis: A New Model for Bankruptcy Risk of Corporations," *Journal of Banking and Finance*, 1977.

2. R. Taffler, "Forecasting Company Failure in the U.K. Using Discriminant Analysis and Financial Ratios Data," *Journal of the Royal Statistical Society*, 1982.

3. G. Foster, *Financial Statement Analysis* (Englewood Cliffs, NJ: Prentice Hall, 1986).

4. J. Horrigan, "The Determination of Long-Term Credit Standing with Financial Ratios," *Journal of Accounting Research, Supplement. Empirical Research in Accounting: Selected Studies*, 1966.

5. P. Barnes, "Methodological Implications of Non-Normally Distributed Financial Ratios," *Journal of Business, Finance and Accounting* 6, 1982.

6. S. Mcleary, "The Ratio of Means, the Means of Ratios, and Other Benchmarks," *Finance, Journal of the French Finance Society*, 1986.

7. D. Trigueiros, "The Cross-Section Distribution of Accounting Variables" (University of East Anglia: unpublished working paper, 1991).

8. D. Rumelhart, G. Hinton, and R. Williams, "Learning Internal Representations by Error Propagation," in *Parallel Distributed Processing* (MIT Press, 1986).

9. Y. H. Pao, *Adaptive Pattern Recognition and Neural Networks* (Reading, MA: Addison-Wesley, 1989).

10. P. D. Wasserman, *Neural Computing: Theory and Practice* (New York: Van Nostrand Reinhold, 1989).

11. J. Plymen, "Classification of Stock Exchange Securities by Industry," *Journal of the Institute of Actuaries*, 1971.

12. P. Sudarsanam and R. Taffler, "Industrial Classification in U.K. Capital Markets: A Test of Economic Homogeneity," *Applied Economics*, 1985.

13. *Ibid.*

14. *Ibid.*

15. E. Baum and F. Wilkzek, "Supervised Learning of Probability Distributions by Neural Networks," *IEEE Conference on Neural Information Processing Systems—Natural and Synthetic*, Denver, 1987.

16. J. Hopfield, "Learning Algorithms and Probability Distributions in Feedforward and Feed-back Networks," *Proceedings of the National Academy of Science USA*, 1987.

17. S. Solla, E. Levin, and M. Fleisher, "Accelerated Learning in Layered Neural Networks," *Complex Systems*, 1988.

18. R. Jacobs, "Increased Rates of Convergence Through Learning Rate Adaptation," *Neural Networks*, 1988.

19. F. Silva and L. Almeida, "Speeding Up Backpropagation," INESC (Lisbon: R. Alves Redol, 1990).

7

ARTIFICIAL NEURAL NETWORKS APPLIED TO RATIO ANALYSIS IN THE ANALYTICAL REVIEW PROCESS

James R. Coakley and Carol E. Brown

INTRODUCTION

Auditors commonly use statistical procedures to analyze and evaluate financial information by examining relationships among financial and non-financial data for plausibility. These analytical procedures play an important role in the preliminary audit process (Cushing and Loebbecke 1986; Tabor and Willis 1985). In addition, *Statement on Auditing Standards No. 56* requires that auditors use analytical procedures to help in planning "the nature, timing and extent of other auditing procedures" (American Institute of Certified Public Accountants 1988, SAS 56, AU 329.04).

Much audit research evaluates the effectiveness of alternative analytical review procedures in terms of their ability to direct attention toward financial account balances containing material errors. Analytical review procedures are essentially tests of reasonableness that involve a comparison of the client's unaudited book values to the auditor's expectations about what those values should be, giving consideration to known circumstances that affect the financial status of the firm.

Analytical review activities generally are governed by pattern-recognition tasks: Various fluctuations in account balances are interpreted as being unusual, thereby signaling the need for additional investigation. Financial accounts usually exhibit fluctuations in balances from month to month, making it likely that pattern-recognition procedures will produce ambiguous interpretations. These ambiguous interpretations also require additional investigation, but they may not be distinguished from valid interpretations resulting from unusual fluctuations. Unnecessary investigations add to the overall cost of the audit without providing additional substantial evidence about the reasonableness of financial accounts.

In practice, auditors usually employ prediction models for analytical procedures (Coakley 1982; Daroca and Holder 1985; Harper et al. 1990; Holder 1983; Spires and Yardley 1989; Wright and Ashton 1989). Published research evaluates numerous alternative methodologies for conducting analytical review, including trend analysis, ratio analysis, regression analysis, and univariate and bivariate Box–Jenkins time series analysis (Albrecht and McKeown 1978; Coakley 1982; Daroca and Holder 1985; Holder 1983; Kinney 1978, 1979, 1987; Kinney and Salamon 1978, 1982; Knechel 1986, 1988a, b; Loebbecke and Steinbart 1987; Neter 1979; Stringer 1975; Wright and Ashton 1989). Of the evaluated methodologies, regression analysis and bivariate Box–Jenkins time-series analysis appear to perform well in identifying unusual fluctuations in the financial statements that need detailed investigation. However, Loebbecke and Steinbart (1987) conclude that while these methodologies may be good at spotting fluctuations resulting from the presence of material monetary errors in the account balances, they do not reliably indicate the absence of material monetary errors.

Research on the judgmental process used by auditors suggests that recognition of patterns in financial ratios is an important part of the analytical review process. Libby (1985) argues that the detection of audit errors is a diagnostic problem. Using protocol analysis of four auditors from two firms, Biggs et al. (1988) find that auditors use financial ratios to investigate audit problems and opportunities in a complex, realistic task setting. Biggs and Wild (1985) note that auditors could identify patterns in financial data; they concluded, "this evidence suggests that pattern recognition is an important part of the auditor's analytical review" (p. 631). Bedard and Biggs (1991) found that auditors sometimes fail to include the combination of all crucial cues during pattern-recognition tasks. They suggest that the subject's lack of pattern recognition seems plausible given Kinney's (1987) conclusion that analytical procedures as performed in practice do not stress the use of data in combination.

The use of pattern recognition by auditors in the analytical review process suggests that artificial neural networks (ANNs) might prove useful for those same tasks. ANNs, a type of artificial intelligence technology, have been used to analyze bankruptcy prediction (Odom and Sharda 1990), bond rating (Surkan and Singleton 1990), and the going-concern problem (Hansen and Messier 1991). Several firms are exploring the commercial use of neural networks for predicting commercial bank failure (Bell et al. 1989), detecting credit card fraud (Rochester 1990), and verifying signatures (Francett 1989). For accounting and auditing problems, however, application of ANN technology has been limited.

Many reasons explain why an ANN approach may produce results superior to regression-based approaches for analysis of financial data. For example, ANNs are able to recognize patterns in accounts even when the data are noisy, ambiguous, distorted, or variable. ANNs continue to perform well even with missing or incomplete data—a task most difficult for regression. Also, an ANN is capable of discovering data relationships, whereas regression model-building presumes knowledge of the underlying relationships. Since the ANN incorporates these relationships, the generated outputs are not sensitive to minor variations in the input patterns (Hecht-Nielsen 1989). This robustness is a very important feature when performing analysis of financial statements since monthly variations in the account balances almost always occur.

According to Hecht-Nielsen (1989), the primary advantage of ANNs over classical statistical regression analysis is that ANNs have more general functional forms than do other well-developed statistical methods. ANNs do not depend on linear superposition and orthogonal functions, which linear statistical regression approaches must use. As a result, the function approximations that arise from properly applied ANNs are usually better than those provided by regression techniques. This difference is particularly important in high-dimensional spaces where many of the more "automated" regression techniques often fail to produce an appropriate approximation. Providing a large number of input parameters to an ANN does not pose a model structure problem as in regression—If the data turns out to be unimportant in solving the problem, the ANN will learn to ignore it by assigning near-zero values to weight the data (Hecht-Nielsen 1989). Thus, ANNs may provide an enhanced capability to analyze financial statements composed of numerous, linearly dependent accounts and aggregates.

The objective of this research was to identify new approaches to analytical review that provide robust attention-directing procedures that can be applied to a variety of organizations and industries. Extending prior studies that assess the effectiveness of the analytical review procedures, the current research varied many factors, including the size of monetary errors, statistical levels of confidence placed on analytical review, and sources of material errors. This study differs from prior research because it includes an ANN to perform the statistical analytical review procedure.

The research question for this study was whether an ANN would produce more appropriate investigation signals for the fluctuating data typically contained in financial statements.

METHODOLOGY

The methodology for the study involved two processes: first, developing a realistic model with financial data and, second, defining alternative statistical, analytical review techniques. Model development encompassed four areas:

❖   Specification of a financial model of the firm.

❖   Definition of sources of error.

❖   Description of the firm in the case study.

❖   Selection of decision rules.

Evaluation of ANN performance required comparison with alternative statistical analytical review techniques. Thus, three procedures were specified:

❖   Financial ratio procedures.

❖   Regression procedures.

❖   Artificial neural network procedures.

Financial Model of the Firm

Financial statements of any firm contain numerous accounts. For each account, many individual transactions constitute the book or reported balance for each annual reporting period. This reported balance can be partitioned into 12 monthly balances.

An auditor needs to determine if an account balance is free of material errors that require an adjustment to the financial statements. If x_{at} reflects the recorded balance (also referred to as the book value) in account a for month t, and y_{at} reflects the correct but unknown balance of account a for month t, then the error in the account prior to the audit is represented by e_{at}:

$$(e_{at} = x_{at} - y_{at}) \tag{1}$$

Alternative analytical review techniques are applied to estimate the expected balance in the account, $\hat{y}_{at}$. This expected balance is compared with the actual book value (x_{at}) to determine if a discrepancy exists. Four decisions could result from this analysis (Table 7.1).

A Type I error is an incorrect decision to investigate, which occurs if the analytical review procedure signals the existence of an error when no material error is present in the account. The Type I error rate provides a measure of efficiency. A large number of Type I errors may reduce

Table 7.1

Types of Attention-Directing Decisions

Size of Error in Account Balance	Results of Analytical Review Procedure	
	Investigation Not Signaled	Investigation Signaled
Less than materiality threshold	Correct decision	Type I error
Greater than materiality threshold	Type II error	Correct decision

the efficiency of the audit since additional accounts may be needlessly investigated. A Type II error is an incorrect decision not to investigate, which occurs when the analytical review procedure fails to signal the existence of a material error when one actually exists. The Type II error rate provides a measure of the reliability of the analytical review procedure and is consistent with the audit risk model in SAS 47 (AICPA 1983) that attempts to control the risk of concluding that an account balance is correct when it actually contains a material error.

Using a method discussed by Loebbecke and Steinbart (1987), researchers can assess the effectiveness of the analytical review procedure by comparing the sum of the Type I and Type II error rates to a benchmark value of 1.0. If a purely random process were used to signal investigations, the expected value of the sum of the error rates would equal 1.0. An effective analytical review procedure would improve on a purely random process by providing Type I and Type II error rates that sum to less than 1.0.

To summarize, a lower Type I error rate would indicate that a procedure is more efficient, a lower Type II error rate would indicate that a procedure is more reliable, and a lower combination of Type I and Type II error rates would indicate that a procedure is more effective. The baseline for comparing the effectiveness of a procedure is 1.0, since that is the expected value of the Type I and Type II error rates from a procedure based on a purely random process.

Definition of Sources of Error

Two sources of errors were used to affect analyses of the financial accounts: (1) unrecorded purchase of merchandise on account and (2) recorded fictitious sales on account. Coakley and Loebbecke (1985) report that these sources of error are among the most frequently encountered in practice. Also, affected accounts typically require adjustments (Hylas and Ashton 1982; Kinney 1987).

Unrecorded purchase of merchandise on account and recorded fictitious sales on account usually occur due to an error in the time at which a legitimate transaction is recorded. Financial reporting requires that a continuous process be artificially divided into segments—months or years. Transactions occur either before the end of a period or after the end of the period. Merchandise purchased and delivered shortly before the end of accounting period one may not be recorded until accounting period two. Sales occurring at the beginning of accounting period two may be inadvertently recorded as occurring during accounting period one, thus creating "fictitious" sales in accounting period one. Errors such as these, that occur because transactions are recorded in the wrong accounting period, are termed "cutoff" errors. Cutoff errors are self-correcting. If a purchase is not recorded in accounting period one and instead recorded in accounting period two, the purchases for accounting period one will be understated, and the purchases for accounting period two will be overstated. When the two accounting periods are combined, the errors offset each other, leaving the totals correct.

Normally, at the end of a fiscal year the inventory is physically counted, and the accounting records are adjusted to match what is actually on hand. Because counting the inventory is so much work, it is usually only done once a year rather than every month. For periods that are not the end of a fiscal year, the ending inventory is estimated based on the accounting records. The effect of cutoff errors is different when the inventory is adjusted to match a physical count and when no adjustment is made. If the merchandise is physically present at year-end, it will be included along with the rest of the inventory when a physical count of inventory is taken and thus will be included in the adjusted inventory amount. If no physical inventory is taken, the inventory amount will not be adjusted.

The impact of cutoff errors on the financial accounts depends on whether a physical count of inventory was taken. If it was, the inventory account is adjusted to match the physical count. (This assumption was used by Kinney (1987).) If a physical count of inventory was not taken, the inventory account is not adjusted. (This assumption matches the process used by the firm for interim statements.) An analysis of the two sources of error was provided for each of the two inventory conditions (Table 7.2).

In a perpetual inventory system, when purchases on an account are not recorded, both inventory and payables are understated by the amount of unrecorded purchases. As a result of aggregation, current assets and current liabilities are understated. If a physical inventory is taken and the inventory is adjusted to match the actual count, the error is forced into cost of sales as an understatement. As a result of aggregation, current liabilities are understated.

When fictitious sales on an account are recorded, both sales and receivables are overstated by the amount of fictitious sales recorded. If a perpetual inventory system is used, the actual cost of the items sold would

Table 7.2

Sources of Error

	Source of Error			
	Purchase on Account not Recorded		Fictitious Sales on Account Recorded	
Financial Accounts	**Inventory Adjusted to Physical Count**	**No Physical Count of Inventory**	**Inventory Adjusted to Physical Count**	**No Physical Count of Inventory**
Receivables			Overstate by S	Overstate by S
Inventory		Understate		Understate by C
Payables	Understate	Understate		
Sales			Overstate by S	Overstate by S
Cost of sales	Understate			Overstate by C
Current assets		Understate	Overstate by S	Overstate by S
Current liabilities	Understate	Understate		Overstate by S-C

Note: The firm uses a perpetual inventory system.
S: Sales revenue for items sold.
C: Cost associated with items sold.

be recorded to the inventory and cost of sales accounts. The error in these accounts, on average, will equal the gross margin times the actual error. As a result of aggregation, current assets are also affected by an amount equal to the difference between the sales revenue and the cost. If a physical count of inventory is taken and the inventory account is adjusted to match the physical count, the errors to the inventory and cost of sales accounts are corrected, leaving only the error to receivables and sales.

Description of the Firm in the Case Study

Actual month-end balances were obtained for a wholesale distributor for four calendar years. The firm under study has a single, disaggregated operation that produces revenues of approximately $25 million per year. No changes of accounting methods or other unusual circumstances occurred in the four-year period. For the purposes of this exploratory study, only internal financial data were examined; no external industry, economic indicators, or operating data were included.

Although each of the four years was audited, the monthly balances were not audited individually. During the audit, an error in a monthly account balance that was material to the annual balance would most likely be corrected. However, certain types of errors may be material to the month but not material to the annual balance. Such errors are probably not ordinarily corrected (Kinney 1978). The firm uses good internal accounting controls and there were no audit adjustments to the financial statements. Thus, it was reasonable to assume that the monthly balances were free of material error.

To simulate unaudited values to which the auditor would apply analytical review procedures, the balances for each month were seeded with a "material" accounting error. The procedures for seeding errors were consistent with previous studies (Coakley 1982; Kinney 1987; Knechel 1986, 1988; Loebbecke and Steinbart 1987).

Since this was an exploratory study, only the pertinent income statement and balance sheet accounts or aggregates related to the sources of errors were included. Additional accounts that were identified as predictor variables during the regression model specification (discussed below) were also included. This resulted in 15 income statement and balance sheet accounts or aggregates selected for the study. The average balance and coefficient of variation were calculated over the three-year base period for the 15 accounts or aggregates (Table 7.3).

Table 7.3

Financial Accounts Included in the Study

Financial Account	Average Account Balance over Three-Year Base Period	Coefficient of Variation
Cash	50,053	0.648
Receivables (trade accounts receivable)	4,727,090	0.213
Other accounts receivable	−118,285	1.537
Total receivables*	4,496,426	0.181
Inventory	1,515,267	0.343
Allowance for inventory obsolescence	1,668	0.239
Current assets*	6,213,770	0.209
Property, plant & equipment (PP&E)	285,169	0.135
Accumulated depreciation	145,325	0.306
Deferred charges & intangibles	466,245	0.283
Payables	3,065,869	0.224
Accrued salaries & wages	70,599	0.213
Current liabilities*	6,363,187	0.168
Sales	1,595,985	0.205
Cost of sales	1,157,543	0.227

*Aggregates.

Five accounts were directly impacted by the sources of error applied in this study. Figure 7.1 depicts the audited book value balances for these five accounts over the 36-month base period and the 12-month prediction

Figure 8.1

Simple Six-Node Cascade-Correlation Neural Network

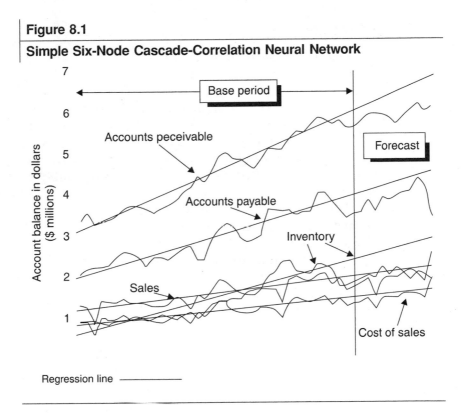

Regression line ⎯⎯⎯⎯⎯

period. As Figure 7.1 depicts, the inventory account has the greatest degree of variability. All accounts indicated an upward growth trend, depicted in Figure 7.1 with the fitted regression lines. Note, however, that the growth rate declined in the prediction period. This is most evident in the receivables and payables accounts.

Three unusual fluctuations appear during the prediction period in the sales and cost of sales accounts: a downward fluctuation in the fourth and eleventh months and an upward fluctuation in the last month. The researchers anticipated that the analytical review procedures would detect these fluctuations and signal these months for additional investigation. Since these balances are the audited book values, these signals to investigate would be erroneous, resulting in a Type I error.

Selection of Decision Rules

An auditor's actions following application of an analytical review procedure depend on the decision rule used with the procedure. Many alternative decision rules are investigated in the literature (Albrecht and McKeown 1978; Coakley 1982; Kinney 1978, 1979, 1987; Kinney and Salamon 1978, 1982; Knechel 1986, 1988a, b; Loebbecke and Steinbart 1987; Neter 1979). For the purpose of this study, a single decision rule was selected for each type of analytical review procedure based on the overall performance in past studies and the applicability to the data analyzed.

Each of the alternative decision rules, in turn, depended on the desired level of overall materiality (M) and the α level for the confidence interval of the error. The amount defined as "material" is based on the functional relationship developed by Warren and Elliot (1986):

$$\text{Materiality } (M) = 0.038657 * (\text{Revenues})^{2/3} \qquad (2)$$

Icerman and Hillison (1991) compare material amounts derived from the formula in equation (2) with empirical data collected from 49 manufacturing firms. Their analysis reports that the formula produced values consistent with the size of individual errors that resulted in adjustments to the financial statements. Relying on their study, the formula in equation (2) is used to provide a reasonable approximation for materiality.

According to Icerman and Hillison (1991), adjustments to financial accounts result from both overstatement and understatement errors. Many of the previous studies (Kinney 1987; Kinney and Salamon 1978; Knechel 1986) limited the analysis to overstatement errors, which may not provide an adequate evaluation of the analytical review technique. In this study, both overstatement and understatement errors are considered.

In addition, the α level represents the allowable probability that an incorrect account is being accepted as correct. The α level is used to calculate the upper and lower precision limits (UPL and LPL) of an $1-\alpha$ confidence interval for the errors. When overstatement errors are anticipated, further investigation is warranted when the $UPL_{1-\alpha/2}$ exceeds M. When understatement errors are anticipated, further investigation is warranted when the $LPL_{1-\alpha/2}$ is less than $-M$.

Financial Ratio Procedure

Financial ratios were used in this study to provide a benchmark for comparing the regression and ANN techniques. Five ratios were selected based on the ability of the ratio to reflect changes in the account balances due to the sources of error (Table 7.4).

Table 7.4

Impact of Source of Error on Evaluated Financial Ratios

| | Source of Error | | | |
| | Purchase on Account Not Recorded | | Fictitious Sales on Account Recorded | |
Financial ratios	Inventory Adjusted to Physical Count	No Physical Count of Inventory	Inventory Adjusted to Physical Count	No Physical Count of Inventory
Receivables turnover			Up[*]	Up[*]
Sales/Receivables				
Inventory turnover	Down	Up		Down
Cost of sales/ Inventory				
Cost of sales ratio	Down		Down	Up[*]
Cost of sales/Sales				
Accruals ratio	Up	Up	Up	Up
Receivables/ Payables				
Quick ratio	Up	Up	Up	Up
(Cash + Receivables)/Current liabilities				

[*]Ratio value is less than 1 for all data in this study.

These ratios (or variants) have previously been evaluated to determine their effectiveness as analytical review procedures (Coakley 1982; Kinney 1987). Generally, prior research finds that financial ratios do not reliably indicate the presence of "just material" errors but may be useful in signaling the presence of larger errors. Thus, the usefulness of financial ratios as an analytical technique has been limited to directing attention to large material errors.

Ending balances were used in computing all ratios. Ending balances are preferred in auditing over the traditional financial method of using average balances. If a material error is present in the ending balance of an account, averaging the ending balance with the beginning balance will dilute the effect of the error, making it more difficult to detect.

The model for evaluating the effect of errors on financial ratios is based on a statistical rule proposed by Kinney (1987). This rule triggers an investigation when the difference between book values for the test month and the expected audited value is so large in relation to past differences that it is unlikely that the difference can be attributed to chance. Let r_t represent the book value of a ratio in month t. The expected audit value of the ratio for month t (denoted $\hat{r}_t$) is assumed to be the average audited value of the same ratio for the previous audit year, adjusted for changes in the industry. Finally, let s_r represent the standard deviation of the audited monthly values of ratio r for the previous audit period. Then:

$$Test\ statistic = (r_t - \hat{r}_t)/s_r \tag{3}$$

The decision rule is to investigate the accounts comprising the ratio if the calculated test statistic exceeds a preset critical value for the deviation. If the distribution of standardized changes is normal (which is assumed), a Z-value based on a risk level specified by the auditor may be used as the critical value. Thus, the auditor investigates the accounts if the test statistic in equation (2) is greater than $Z_{1-\alpha/2}$ or is less than $-Z_{1-\alpha/2}$, where α is the probability of a Type I error.

Regression Procedure

The ordinary least-squares regression model in equation (4) has been evaluated as an analytical review procedure in numerous previous studies (Albrecht and McKeown 1978; Coakley 1982; Kinney 1978, 1979, 1987; Kinney and Salamon 1978, 1982; Knechel 1986, 1988a, b; Loebbecke and Steinbart 1987; Neter 1979; Stringer 1975):

$$Y = X\beta + \varepsilon \qquad (4)$$

The parameters for the model are generated over a base period (usually 36 or 48 months) and then applied to predict values in the current audit period (equation (5)). The process is valid assuming that there were no changes in the economic generating process from the base period to the audit period:

$$\hat{Y} = X\beta \qquad (5)$$

The actual observed value of Y varies about the true mean value with variance σ^2. A predicted value of an individual observation will still be given by $\hat{Y}$ in equation (5), but the variance will be larger since there is more uncertainty in prediction than in estimation (Devore 1982; Draper and Smith 1982). The variance of the error between the observed value and the predicted value (equation (6)) can be used to establish a prediction interval:

$$\text{Var}(Y - \hat{Y}) = (1 + X_0'(X'X)^{-1}X_0)\sigma^2 \qquad (6)$$

If the upper precision limit of the prediction interval is less than M (a material amount), the auditor can be at least $1-\alpha/2$ confident that the total overstatement error is less than a material amount. Likewise, if the lower precision limit of the prediction interval is greater than $-M$, the auditor can be at least $1-\alpha/2$ confident that the total understatement error is less than a material amount.

Regression models were developed for five accounts and two aggregates: receivables, inventory, payables, sales, cost of sales, current assets and current liabilities. Each account or aggregate was affected by the sources of errors used in the study (see Table 7.2). Stepwise regression techniques were applied using lagged data of one and two months of the internal financial data and a period indicator as the independent variables. The resulting models and associated multiple coefficient of determination (adjusted R^2) values are depicted in Table 7.5. The regression model provides a reasonable explanation of the variation for the receivables, inventory and payables accounts and for the current assets and

Table 7.5

Parameters and Coefficient of Multiple Determination for Regression Models.

Financial Account	Model	Adjusted R^2
Receivables$_t$	$= 1461074$ $+ 0.76$ receivables$_{t-1}$ $- 0.61$ other receivables$_{t-2}$ $- 0.38$ payables$_{t-2}$ $+ 33402{*}t$ (period adjustment)	0.974
Inventory$_t$	$= -87166$ $+ 1.10$ Inventory$_{t-1}$ $+ 0.87$ Receivables$_{t-2}$	0.943
Payables$_t$	$= 1512282$ $+ 0.61$ current assets$_{t-1}$ $= 1.02$ deferred charges & intangibles$_{t-1}$ $- 0.55$ total receivables$_{t-2}$ $+ 0.42$ sales$_{t-2}$	0.925
Sales$_t$	$= 410123$ $+ 0.22$ current liabilities$_{t-1}$ $+ 1.08$ other receivables$_{t-1}$ $- 1.58$ other receivables$_{t-2}$ $- 3.61$ accrued salaries & wages$_{t-2}$	0.783
Cost of sales$_t$	$= 220502$ $+ 0.17$ current liabilities$_{t-1}$ $+ 0.79$ other receivables$_{t-1}$ $- 1.16$ other receivables$_{t-2}$ $- 2.46$ accrued salaries & wages$_{t-2}$	0.761
Current assets$_t$	$= 1033563$ $+ 0.84$ current assets$_{t-1}$ $- 1.61$ cash$_{t-1}$ $+ 11.07$ accumulated depreciation$_{t-2}$ $- 0.47$ payables$_{t-2}$	0.976

Figure 7.1		
(concluded)		

Financial Account	Model	Adjusted R^2
Current liabilities$_t$	$= 2537316$ $+ 0.83$ current liabilities$_{t-1}$ $- 0.74$ other receivables$_{t-1}$ $- 0.90$ payables$_{t-2}$ $+ 50285^*t$ (period adjustment)	0.963

current liabilities aggregates. The lack of external economic indicators may account for the lower explanatory ability of the regression method for the sales and cost of sales accounts.

Artificial Neural Network Procedure

Developing an analytical review procedure using an ANN model involved selecting the appropriate ANN model, preparing the input data, training the model, and developing the statistical decision rules.

Selection of the ANN Model

Numerous published descriptions provide insights into various ANN models (Anderson and Rosenfeld 1988; Hecht-Nielsen 1989; Hoptroff et al. 1991; Lawrence 1991; Rumelhart and McClelland 1986; Waite and Hardenbergh 1989; Wasserman 1989). Definition of an ANN model requires specification of a training algorithm, an architecture, and an activation rule.

Training algorithm. The current study used a back-propagation model. Back-propagation is the predominant training algorithm referenced in the literature (Anderson and Rosenfeld 1988; Hecht-Nielsen 1989; Hoptroff et al. 1991; Lawrence 1991; Rumelhart and McClelland 1986; Waite and Hardenbergh 1989; Wasserman 1989). The model was derived from a discussion of the mathematics in a back-propagation training algorithm

(Lawrence 1991), and developed using Turbo Pascal on an Intel 386-based microcomputer. The program was thoroughly tested using examples from the literature.

ANN model architecture. A feedforward, multilayer architecture was selected for this exploratory study. Numerous experiments were conducted to find the network architecture that minimized the total mean square error between the input account balances and the predicted output balances for the 12-month prediction set (Hecht-Nielsen 1989). These experiments encompassed altering the method for designating the period (12 neurons, a single neuron, or no period indicator), the number of hidden layers (one versus two) and the number of nodes per hidden layer (7 versus 15 versus 31).

The autoassociative architectures (similar to statistical prediction models based on autoregression) were considered but not used. The financial ratio and regression procedures included in this study did not use autoregressive methods. Hence, using autoregressive methods in the ANN model might have biased the comparisons.

The ANN model was used to make a single period prediction based on trends. To train the model, the ANN has to simultaneously see the current target value and the past input data within each training set. This required 30 input data streams to represent the data from the previous two months for each of the 15 financial accounts or aggregates (this corresponded to the two months of lagged data used for the regression models). Fifteen nodes were used to represent the output layer, one for each financial account or aggregate.

An additional 12 input neurons were added to designate the month for the financial data. The input value of a neuron was set to one if the neuron corresponded to the month of the data, and zero otherwise. Another alternative investigated was using one neuron to designate the month with the possible input values of 1 to 12. In this situation, the network would interpret July (7) as being larger than January (1). Using a single neuron to designate the month does incorporate a linear trend into the model. However, for this set of financial data, the architecture using 12 neurons to represent the month outperformed the architecture using a single neuron to represent the month.

There are no general rules in the literature that define the number of hidden layers or the number of neurons per hidden layer. Most studies of the back-propagation training algorithm have found that no more than two hidden layers are required (Hecht-Nielsen 1989; Lawrence, 1991; Ru-melhart and McClelland 1986; Wasserman 1989). The number of neurons per hidden layer has also varied greatly in the experiments reported in the literature. This study evaluated 7, 15, and 31 neurons in each of the hidden layers. (This corresponds to $n/2$, n, and $2n + 1$, where n is the number of neurons in the output layer.) The final configuration selected had one hidden layer with 15 neurons.

ANN model activation rule. The preliminary experiments also evaluated three alternative activation rules (sigmoid, modified sigmoid, or hyperbolic tangent). The modified sigmoid activation rule provided the lowest mean square for error (MSE) for these data. (The MSE was derived from the squared difference between the predicted output value and the target value.) As Stornetta and Huberman (1987) point out, the conventional sigmoid function may not be optimal for all sets of data. The magnitude of a weight adjustment is proportional to the output level of the neuron from which it originates. With the conventional (0-1) range on the input data and hidden neuron node output values, a level of 0 results in no weight modification. Hence, the standard sigmoid function appears to be inappropriate for financial accounts where both overstatement and un-derstatement errors are possible. The alternative approach is to change the input range to $\pm\frac{1}{2}$ and add a bias to the activation rule to modify the neuron output range to $+\frac{1}{2}$:

$$OUT = -\frac{1}{2} + 1/(e^{-NET} + 1) \tag{7}$$

This modified sigmoid function will place less weight on those account balances close to the mean yet should provide an improved capability for explaining under- and overstated account balances.

Input Data Preparation

Monthly account balances were first scaled to a $\pm\frac{1}{2}$ range and then nor-malized to produce the input patterns and desired output patterns. De-veloping a statistical decision rule for the ANN (discussed in the next section) required a near-linear relationship between the layers. To achieve a near-linear relationship, it was necessary to normalize all input vectors before applying them to the network. Each component of an input vector was divided by that vector's length, an operation that converted an input vector into a unit vector pointed in the same direction. This constrained the ANN to the near-linear portions of the sigmoid function.

ANN Model Training Procedures

ANNs effectively filter input to produce output. More specifically, an ANN looks for patterns in a set of examples and learns from those examples to produce new patterns, the output. The ANN then compares target values to output patterns to classify a new set of examples. This "training" process repeats until the difference between the target values and output patterns across an entire set of examples converges at a minimal value. The model was trained using the 36 months of financial data in the base period and evaluated using the 12 months of financial data in the prediction period. The training was stopped when the selected set of model parameters minimized the mean squared error between the target values and output patterns in the prediction period (the prediction period corresponds to a **training test set** as described by Hecht-Nielsen 1989).

Training sets are usually presented to the network in a random order. When data are presented in a chronological order, the network will attempt to incorporate the directional trends in financial data into the solution. If the financial trends for the data contain numerous changes in directional trend, a random order would be more appropriate since it would force the network to generalize over the entire training set. Since a general upward trend was present across four years of financial data for this firm, the chronological ordering method was used.

To provide a basis comparison with the regression model, the coefficient of multiple determination (adjusted R^2) was calculated for each output node (financial account) in the network and listed in Table 7.6. A comparison with the adjusted R^2 values for the regression (Table 7.5) clearly shows that the ANN model explains a larger portion of the variation in the financial account balances.

There is a danger in relying on R^2 as a performance measure when using ANNs. With any model, R^2 can be made unity simply by employing n properly selected coefficients in the model. For example, a cubic polynomial applied to model four observations would produce a solution that would exactly pass through each point. In this study, a relatively small pattern set (36 patterns) was used with 15 variables. High R^2 values may result because the number of parameters is approaching the saturation

Table 7.6

Adjusted R^2 Values of Financial Accounts from Neural Network Analysis

Financial Account	Adjusted R^2
Cash	0.9920
Receivables	0.9984
Other accounts receivable	0.9910
Total receivables*	0.9979
Inventory	0.9988
Allowance for inventory obsolescence	0.3396
Current assets*	0.9982
Property, plant & equipment	0.9981
Accumulated depreciation	0.9989
Deferred charges & intangible	0.9990
Payables	0.9993
Accrued salaries & wages	0.9993
Current liabilities*	0.9922
Sales	0.9959
Cost of sales	0.9969

*Aggregates.

point. The adjusted R^2 attempts to compensate for this phenomenon by reducing the degrees of freedom (Draper and Smith 1982).

Developing the Statistical Decision Rule

A statistical decision rule was needed to apply the ANN method as an analytical review procedure. The decision rule develops a prediction interval for each output node. Since the output value derived for a single output node of the network is, in essence, a linear combination of the outputs from the last hidden layer, the ANN was considered a variant of the general linear model. With this interpretation, the other hidden layers were considered a transformation process applied to the input vector.

To develop a prediction interval, an estimate of the variance of the predicted values had to be derived. As with the general linear model, the ANN model attempts to minimize the squared error, that is, the deviations between the actual value and the predicted value. An estimate of variance in the error associated with each output node can be obtained by dividing the sum of the squared deviations by the degrees of freedom. For the ANN, the degrees of freedom were equal to the number of active nodes in the final hidden layer of the model with nonzero weights. If a node has a near zero weight, it is not making a contribution to the solution. Since this node may contribute to the solution for another output node, it cannot be "trimmed" from the network. One could assume that all nodes in the final hidden layer contribute to the solution. This would be a conservative approach that would result in a lower value for the degrees of freedom and a higher value for the estimated variance.

Once an estimate of the variance was derived, equation (6) could be applied to estimate the variance for a predicted output value given an input vector. Using this estimated variance, a prediction interval could be constructed. (According to Draper and Smith 1982, equations (5) and (6) are robust and can be used to estimate the predicted value and its associated variance even if the error terms are not normally distributed.) Using this prediction interval, the ANN model can be evaluated as an analytical review procedure using the same decision rules that were applied to evaluate the regression model.

EXPERIMENTAL PROCEDURES

A simulation was performed to evaluate the effectiveness of alternative models in signaling the presence of material errors. The simulation process seeded audited account balances with a monthly cutoff error. This error then propagated through the various accounts due to the aggregation process of generating monthly financial reports. Since cutoff errors are self-correcting, the errors were only reflected in the seeded months. If the analytical review technique was reliable, it should have signaled the need for further investigation whenever material errors were seeded. If no material errors were seeded, an efficient analytical review procedure would not signal further investigation.

Three factors were varied during the simulation: the size of the monetary error, the statistical level of confidence placed on analytical review, and the sources of material errors. The distribution of the material error across monthly balances was not varied since only two types of cutoff errors were evaluated.

The size of the monetary error was varied from 0, 0.5, 1.0, 1.5, and 2.0 times the material amount. As the size of the error was raised from 0 to 0.5 times materiality, researchers expected the number of Type I errors to increase. The procedures were more efficient at detecting the error, but since the error was less than a material amount, an investigation should not have been signaled. As the size of the error was raised from 1.0 to 2.0 times materiality, the number of Type II errors should have decreased. The larger errors should have been easier to detect.

The statistical level of confidence affects the width of the prediction interval. Lower values of α yield wider prediction intervals, which should result in fewer signals to investigate. Thus, increasing α should result in more Type I but fewer Type II errors. Based on the results of previous research (Coakley 1982; Kinney 1978, 1979, 1987; Kinney and Salamon 1978, 1982; Loebbecke and Steinbart 1987), α levels of 0.10 and 0.33 were applied in this study.

Two types of error were introduced: (1) unrecorded purchase on account and (2) recorded fictitious sales on account. To provide a valid comparison of the financial ratios with the results of the Kinney (1987) study, it was assumed that a physical count of inventory was taken and that the inventory account was adjusted to match the physical count. For the remainder of the analysis, the assumption that the inventory accounts were not corrected to a physical count was used since it was consistent with the actual procedures used in the firm.

RESULTS

Results in this study have been divided into findings based on the following:

❖ Financial ratios.

❖ Comparison of methods.

❖ Effect of error size.

❖ Effect of statistical level of confidence.

❖ Effect of sources of material error.

❖   Applying methods to base period.

Financial Ratios

Results from applying financial ratios to the 48 months of data in the current study were compared to the results from Kinney's research (1987) and listed in Tables 7.7 and 7.8. Table 7.7 indicates that the means and standard deviations of monthly ratios are similar for both firms. Table 7.8 illustrates comparisons between Type I error rates when no error was seeded into the accounts and Type II error rates when an error twice materiality was seeded into accounts.

The first two turnover ratios relate an income statement account to a balance sheet account. Applying those financial ratios to the data within this study resulted in higher Type II error rates compared with Kinney's results. For the cost of sales and accruals ratios, the data within this study produced higher Type I error rates yet similar Type II error rates. The quick ratio was not investigated in the Kinney study and is presented only for comparison purposes with the other ratios (Kinney 1987).

Even though the financial ratios had similar variation across the two studies, it was much more difficult to distinguish the fluctuations caused by seeded errors from those that normally occurred in the financial data of the firm used in this study. One possible explanation is that a different formula was used to derive a material amount. Kinney (1987) used one-half

Table 7.7

Comparison of Means and Standard Deviations of the Monthly Ratios

Financial Ratios	Kinney (1987)		Case Study	
	Mean	Std. Dev.	Mean	Std. Dev.
Receivables turnover	0.35	0.03	0.35	0.03
Inventory turnover	0.86	0.17	0.84	0.20
Cost of sales ratio	0.72	0.02	0.71	0.02
Accruals ratio	1.62	0.12	1.55	0.10
Quick ratio	n/a	n/a	0.72	0.04

Table 7.8

Comparison of Financial Ratio Analysis

Financial Ratios	Kinney (1987)		Case study	
	Type I	Type II	Type I	Type II
Receivables turnover	0.38	0.21	0.26	0.72
Inventory turnover	0.35	0.19	0.59	0.40
Cost of sales ratio	0.29	0.00	0.56	0.00
Accruals ratio	0.33	0.40	0.44	0.42
Quick ratio	n/a	n/a	0.72	0.26

of 1 percent of last year's audited sales, adjusted for the sales growth rate for the industry. The resulting value for a material error was approximately twice as large as the value derived from materiality formula (equation (2)) used in this study. The lower materiality threshold used would explain the higher Type II error rates since larger errors should be easier to detect. However, changes in the materiality threshold would not explain the differences in the Type I error rates since materiality does not affect the decision rule for the financial ratios.

The differences in the Type I error rates are most likely due to the variability in the monthly account balances. Figure 7.2 depicts the calculated ratios for the four audit periods. Recall that the decision rule compares the value of the financial ratio in the current month with the average of the financial ratio values from the previous audit period, adjusting for the variation in the previous audit period. High variability in the calculated inventory turnover ratio values results in numerous false signals to investigate. Although the values for the cost of sales ratio appear consistent across the audit periods, the very low variance causes small fluctuations to be interpreted as signals to investigate even though material errors are not present. The consistency and low variation of the cost of sales ratio also enables a high detection capability for seeded errors resulting in very low Type II error rates. The averaged values for the accruals ratio also appear consistent across the audit periods, but the wide variation across the individual monthly values produces many erroneous signals to investigate.

Figure 7.2

Financial Ratios Calculated from Audited Balances

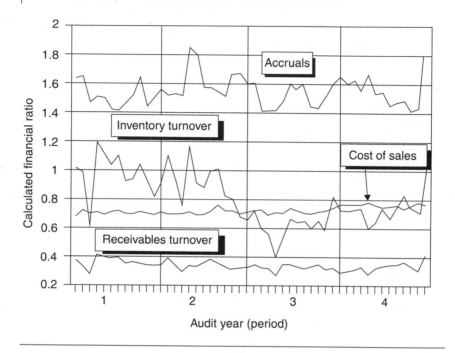

The Kinney (1987) study found the four financial ratios to be much more effective analytical review procedures. The results from this study are more consistent with the conclusions of Loebbecke and Steinbart (1987), which found that financial ratios do not reliably indicate the absence of errors. The implication is that financial rates applied as analytical review procedures may produce inconsistent results even when applied across similar firms.

Comparison of Methods within this Study

A comparison of the average results across the three factors are presented in Figure 7.3 for the financial ratio, regression, and ANN methods.

Results are presented for both inventory assumptions, annotated on the graph as *NC* for the assumption that no physical count was taken

Figure 7.3

Comparison of Analytical Review Methods

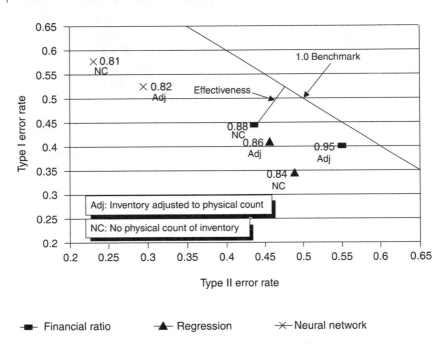

and as *Adj* for the assumption that inventory values were adjusted to the physical count. The solid line in the upper right-hand corner of the graph represents the 1.0 benchmark (Loebbecke and Steinbart 1987). An effective analytical review procedure will have Type I and Type II error rates that sum to less than 1.0. The actual sum of the error rates is annotated on the graph below each point.

For the regression and ANN methods, there was a slight, but insignificant, increase in the overall effectiveness when it was assumed that inventory values were adjusted for physical counts. A more noticeable difference occurred in the effectiveness of the financial ratios due to the sensitivity of the inventory turnover and cost of sales ratios to the two assumptions (Table 7.4). The assumption of adjusting the inventory to the physical count lowers the inventory turnover ratio. Seeding this error into audit period 4 will further reduce the monthly ratio values, making them more consistent with the average value from period 3. Thus the Type I error rate should be reduced. When it is assumed that the inventory accounts are not adjusted to a physical count, the inventory turnover ratio is increased. This increases the likelihood that the monthly ratio values in audit period 4 are higher than the averaged values of the third audit period, thus increasing the Type I error rate. The assumption of not adjusting inventory to the physical count also removes the effect on the cost of sales ratio, which eliminates the error rates of this ratio from the average. This would raise the average Type II error rate since the cost of sales ratio is very reliable.

The ANN approach provided enhanced reliability (lower Type II error rates) yet lower efficiency (higher Type I error rates) compared to the other approaches. Based on the averaged error rates, the ANN approach is slightly more effective (Figure 7.3). That is, the composite Type I and Type II error rates are lower. However, none of the three approaches provides a significant improvement in effectiveness over a purely random process.

Effect of Error Size

The effect of the size of the error seeded into the financial accounts on the Type I and Type II error rates is shown in Figure 7.4. The values depicted are averaged over the two sources of error and two statistical levels of confidence. The regression and ANN procedures result in higher Type I error rates when errors of less than a material amount are seeded. However, the financial ratio approach did not perform as expected and resulted in a lower Type I error rate. This anomaly is most likely due to the fluctuating nature of the data over the test period (last two years). As expected, all procedures became more reliable when larger errors were seeded. There appears to be very little difference in the improvements across the three methods.

Effect of Statistical Level of Confidence

The effect of varying the statistical level of confidence (alpha risk level) is presented in Figure 7.5. The depicted values were averaged over the seeded error size and the source of error. The ANN approach is less sen-

Figure 7.4

Effect of Error Size on Type I and Type II Error Rates

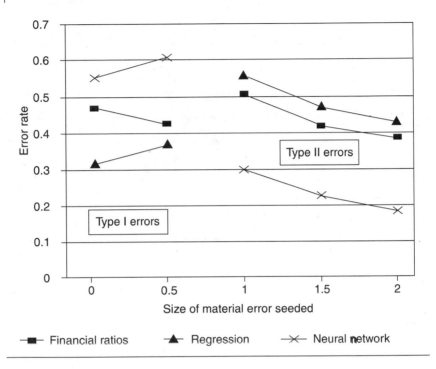

sitive to varying the alpha risk. This reduced sensitivity was anticipated since the ANN produced higher R^2 values with lower variation in the predicted values. Since the prediction interval is a function of the alpha risk and the variation, the smaller variations would produce tighter prediction intervals.

The results suggest that all approaches have similar overall effectiveness when the alpha risk is increased. The slope of all the lines is nearly parallel to the 1.0 benchmark line. Thus, as the alpha risk is raised from 0.10 to 0.33, the various procedures trade off Type I and Type II errors. Since the ANN approach has less variation in the predicted values, there is less trade-off available.

Figure 7.5

Effect of Alpha Risk Level on Type I and Type II Error Rates

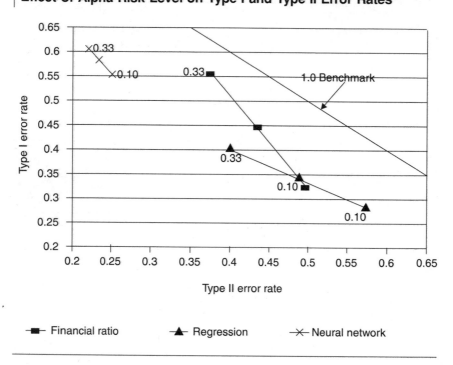

Effect of Sources of Material Error

The effect of the source of material error on the Type I and Type II error rates is displayed in Figure 7.6. The values depicted were averaged across the size of error seeded and the alpha risk levels. In Figure 7.6, the lines depicting the range of error rates for each method are approximately parallel to the 1.0 benchmark. This implies that the methods had similar effectiveness across both error types, with the difference being a trade-off between the Type I and Type II error rates.

The regression and ANN approaches appear to have similar effectiveness with the purchases not recorded (PNR) error but an almost opposite effect with the fictitious sales (FS) error. With reference to Figures 7.7 and 7.8, it can be seen that the ANN approach produces more effective signaling for the receivables (AR), inventory (Inv), and

Figure 7.6

Effect of Source of Error on Type I and Type II Error Rates

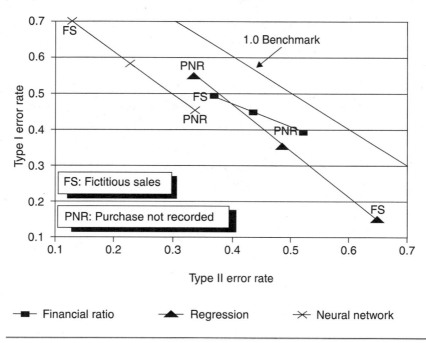

payables (AP) accounts, while being slightly less effective for the current assets (CA) and current liabilities (CL) aggregates. The regression method is more effective in signaling investigations in the sales and cost of sales (COS) accounts.

The fictitious sales error directly affects the receivables, inventory, sales and cost of sales accounts. The difference in performance between the two methods for this error source is driven by the difference in their ability to signal errors in these four accounts: the high Type II error rates in the receivables and inventory accounts biased the average Type II error rate for the regression method, and the high Type I error rates in the sales and cost of sales accounts biased the average Type I error rate for the ANN method.

For the "purchases not recorded" error, the major accounts affected are payables, inventory, and cost of sales. The regression method has high Type

Figure 7.7

Regression Method Error Rates by Individual Financial Account

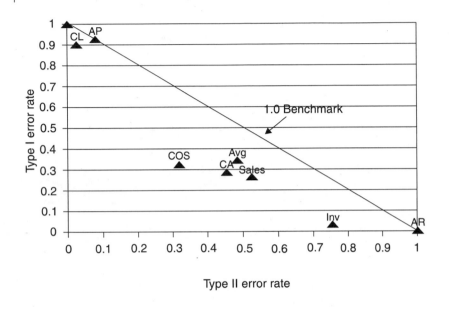

—▲— Regression

I error rates for the payables accounts, which is offset by averaging with the low Type I error rates for the inventory account. The average for the ANN is driven by the more effective inventory and payables accounts.

Applying Methods to Base Period

It was anticipated that the greater predictive ability of the ANN method would significantly increase the effectiveness when applied as an analytical review procedure. After reviewing the results of the previous experiment, the regression and ANN approaches were applied to the last year of the base period to determine whether the reduced effectiveness was a model problem or a data problem. Since the financial data within the last year of the base period are within the range where the model parameters were estimated, the overall performance should improve.

Figure 7.8

Artificial Neural Network Method Error Rates by Individual Financial Account

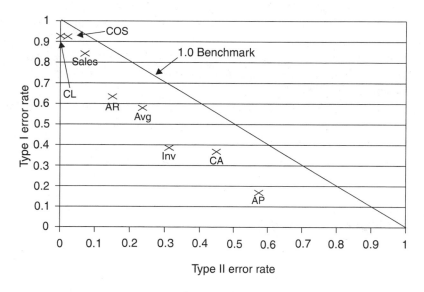

✕ Neural network

The overall effectiveness of the regression model did improve. However, the regression method still produced high average error rates: 0.32 for Type I errors and 0.46 for Type II errors. The ANN model proved extremely effective with no Type I or Type II errors discovered.

CONCLUSIONS

The ANN approach applied to extrapolate financial trends provided enhanced reliability (lower Type II error rates) yet lower efficiency (higher Type I error rates) compared to the regression and financial ratio approaches. Based on the averaged error rates, the ANN approach is slightly more effective. That is, the composite Type I and Type II error rates are lower. However, none of the three approaches provide a significant improvement in effectiveness over a purely random process. These results are consistent with those found by Loebbecke and Steinbart (1987).

The ANN approach was less sensitive to changes in the statistical level of confidence (variations of the alpha risk). This reduced sensitivity was anticipated since the ANN produced lower variation in the predicted values. Since the prediction interval is a function of the alpha risk and the variation, the smaller variations would produce tighter prediction intervals. The alternative methods had similar effectiveness across both of the error sources investigated. Differences were due to trade-offs between the Type I and Type II error rates.

These results tentatively suggest that the ANN was able to extrapolate financial trends more effectively than the other statistical procedures due to its ability to recognize patterns within the financial accounts. Compared to financial ratio and regression methods, the ANN demonstrated superior predictive ability with less overall variation in the predicted values.

EXTENDING THE RESEARCH

This study examined how an ANN process performed within the framework of a single case study, consisting of data for a single firm over a 48-month period. Many variations on this research need to be investigated before any general conclusions can be drawn concerning the overall effectiveness of ANNs as an analytical review procedure.

Additional research is needed in these areas. First, the preliminary experiments should be extended to do the following:

❖   Expand the data set used for testing to include multiple firms and multiple four-year periods for each firm.

❖   Expand the data set used for testing to include all the detail in a complete income statement and balance sheet.

❖   Examine the performance of the ANN method in identifying material errors resulting from additional sources of errors seeded into the data streams, varying the size of the error, the statistical level of confidence placed in the test, and the distribution of the error across the financial accounts.

❖   Develop appropriate procedures for building ANN configurations used to study financial data.

❖   Investigate alternate ANN models to determine their relative robustness for deriving pattern associations in financial data.

ANNs seem useful for analyzing patterns that can indicate the need for investigations of a firm's unaudited financial data. However, the normal fluctuations present in some sets of financial data cannot be effectively analyzed by any known forecasting method. This leads to the second area of additional research:

❖   Investigate whether the ANN approach can be used to analyze the complex patterns (or cues) in the financial accounts to identify the source of material error.

This concept was briefly investigated by Kinney (1987), who found that patterns of deviations from expectation over several related financial ratios were useful in identifying the cause of an error. Thus, the patterns of related fluctuations across numerous financial accounts may provide a more reliable indication of the presence of material errors as well as providing insight into the plausible causes of the error.

Additional research is also needed to contrast ANN methods with other traditional methods of performing analytical review. This study focused on predicting the monthly balances in individual accounts. ANNs could be used to forecast the values of the financial ratio, versus the values of the accounts that comprise the financial ratio. ANNs may be more robust compared to other techniques when the input data are derived from audited quarterly financial statements versus unaudited monthly account balances.

CONCLUDING COMMENT

Even if the ANN approach does provide superior capability to correctly signal financial accounts for investigation, the cost of performing these procedures must be weighed against the benefit from applying them during preliminary analytical review. Statistically significant improvements in effectiveness may not justify the added costs of performing these procedures. The results of these preliminary experiments indicate that it is worth pursuing the question of whether ANNs are useful as an analytical procedure in auditing.

Acknowledgments

The authors wish to thank James K. Loebbecke, James V. Hansen, and three anonymous reviewers for their insightful comments and suggestions.

REFERENCES

Albrecht, W.S. and J.C. and McKeown. 1978. *Toward an Extended Use of Statistical Analytical Reviews in the Audit,* Symposium on Auditing Research II. Urbana: University of Illinois Trustees, pp. 53–69.

American Institute of Certified Public Accountants. 1983. *Statement on Auditing Standards No. 47: Audit Risk and Materiality in Conducting an Audit.* New York: American Institute of Certified Public Accountants.

American Institute of Certified Public Accountants. 1988. *Statement on Auditing Standards No. 56: Analytical Procedures.* New York: American Institute of Certified Public Accountants.

Anderson, J.A. and E. Rosenfeld. 1988. *Neurocomputing: Foundations of Research.* Cambridge, MA: MIT Press.

Bedard, J.C. and S.F. Biggs. 1991. "Pattern Recognition, Hypothesis Generation, and Auditor Performance in an Analytical Task," *The Accounting Review* LXVI, no. 3, pp. 622-42.

Bell, T.B., G.S. Ribar, and J. Verchio. 1990. "Neural Nets versus Logistic Regression: A Comparison of Each Model's Ability to Predict Commercial Bank Failures," in *Auditing Symposium X—Deloitte & Touche/University of Kansas Symposium on Auditing Problems,* ed. R. P. Srivastava. Lawrence, KS: University of Kansas, pp. 29–53.

Biggs, S.F., T. Mock, and P. Watkins. 1988. "Auditor's Use of Analytical Review in Audit Program Design," *The Accounting Review* LXIII, no. 1, pp. 148–61.

Biggs, S. and J. Wild. 1985. "An Investigation of Auditor Judgment in Analytical Review," *The Accounting Review* LX, no. 4, pp. 607–33.

Coakley, J.R. 1982. *Analytical review: A Comparison of Procedures and Techniques Used in Auditing.* Unpublished dissertation. University of Utah.

Coakley, J.R. and J.E. Loebbecke. 1985. "The Expectation of Accounting Errors in Medium-Sized Manufacturing Firms," *Advances in Accounting* 2, pp. 199–246.

Cushing, B.E. and J.K. Loebbecke. 1986. *Studies in Accounting Research no. 26, Comparison of Audit Methodologies of Large Accounting Firms.* Sarasota, FL: American Accounting Association.

Daroca, F. and W.W. Holder. 1985. "Analytical Review Procedures in Planning the Audit: An Application Study," *Auditing: A Journal of Practice and Theory* 4, no. 2, pp. 100–107.

Devore, J.L. 1982. *Probability and Statistics for Engineering and the Sciences.* Monterey, CA: Brooks/Cole Publishing.

Draper, N.R. and H. Smith. 1982. *Applied Regression Analysis,* 2nd ed. New York: John Wiley.

Francett, B. 1989. "Neural Nets Arrive," *Computer Decisions* 21, no. 1, pp. 58–62.

Hansen, J.V. and W.F. Messier. 1991. "Artificial Neural Networks: Foundations and Applications to a Decision Problem," *Expert Systems with Applications: An International Journal* 3, no. 1, pp. 135–41.

Harper, R.M., J.R. Strawser, and K. Tang. 1990. "Establishing Investigation Thresholds for Preliminary Analytical Procedures," *Auditing: A Journal of Practice and Theory* 9, no. 3, pp. 115–33.

Hecht-Nielsen, R. 1989. *Neurocomputing,* Reading, MA: Addison-Wesley.

Holder, W.W. (1983) "Analytical Review Procedures in Planning the Audit: An Application Study," *Auditing: A Journal of Practice & Theory* 2, no. 2, pp. 100–107.

Hoptroff, R., T. Hall, and M.J. Bramson, (1991) "Forecasting Economic Turning Points with Neural Nets," *Proceedings of the International Joint Conference on Neural Networks.* Piscataway, NJ: IEEE Service Center, pp. II.347–II.352.

Hylas, R.E. and R.H. Ashton. 1982. "Audit Detection of Financial Statement Errors," *The Accounting Review* 57, pp. 751–65.

Icerman, R.C. and W.A. Hillison. 1991. "Disposition of Audit-detected Errors: Some Evidence on Evaluative Materiality," *Auditing: A Journal of Practice and Theory* 10, pp. 22–34.

Kinney, W.R., Jr. 1978. "ARIMA and Regression in Analytical Review: An Empirical Test," *The Accounting Review* 58, pp. 48–60.

Kinney, W.R., Jr. 1979. "Integrated Audit Tests: Regression Analysis and Partitioned DUR," *Journal of Accounting Research* 17, pp. 456–75.

Kinney, W.R., Jr. 1987. "Attention-Directing Analytical Review Using Accounting Ratios: A Case Study," *Auditing: A Journal of Practice and Theory* 6, no. 2, pp. 59–73.

Kinney, W.R., Jr. and G.L. Salamon. 1978. "The Effect of Measurement Error on Regression Results in Analytical Review," *Symposium on Auditing Research III.* Urbana: University of Illinois Trustees, pp. 49-64.

Kinney, W.R. Jr. and G.L. Salamon. 1982. "Regression Analysis in Auditing: A Comparison of Alternative Investigation Rules," *Journal of Accounting Research* 20 (Part 1), pp. 350–66.

Knechel, W.R. 1986. "A Simulation Study of the Relative Effectiveness of Alternative Analytical Review Procedures," *Decision Sciences* 17, pp. 376–94.

Knechel, W.R. 1988a. "The Effectiveness of Statistical Analytical Review as a Substantive Auditing Procedure: A Simulation Analysis." *The Accounting Review* LXIII, pp. 74–95.

Knechel, W.R. 1988b. "The Effectiveness of Nonstatistical Analytical Review Procedures Used as Substantive Audit Tests," *Auditing: A Journal of Practice and Theory* 8, pp. 59–73.

Lawrence, J. 1991. *Introduction to Neural Networks.* Grass Valley, CA: California Scientific Software.

Libby, R. 1985. "Availability and the Generation of Hypotheses in Analytical Review," *Journal of Accounting Research* 23, no. 2, pp. 648–67.

Loebbecke, J.K. and P.J. Steinbart. 1987. "An Investigation of the Use of Preliminary Analytical Review to Provide Substantive Audit Evidence," *Auditing: A Journal of Practice and Theory* 6, pp. 74–89.

Neter, J. 1979. "Two Case Studies on Use of Regression for Analytic Review," *Symposium on Auditing Research IV.* Urbana: University of Illinois Trustees, pp. 291–337.

Odom, M. and R. Sharda. 1990. "Neural Network Model for Bankruptcy Prediction," *Proceedings of the International Joint Conference on Neural Networks* 2, pp. 163–68.

Rochester, J.B. 1990. "New Businesses for Neurocomputing," *I/S Analyzer* 28, no. 1, pp. 1–12.

Rumelhart, D.E. and J.L. McClelland. 1986. *Parallel Distributed Proceeding, Explorations in the Microstructure of Cognition,* Volume 1: *Foundations.* Cambridge, MA: MIT Press.

Spires, E. and J. Yardley. 1989. "Empirical Evidence on the Reliability of Auditing Procedures," *Journal of Accounting Literature* 8, pp. 49–75.

Stornetta, W.S. and B.A. Huberman. 1987. "An Improved Three-layer Backpropagation Algorithm," *Proceedings of the IEEE First International Conference on Neural Networks.* San Diego, CA: SOS Printing.

Stringer, K.W. 1975. "A Statistical Technique for Analytical Review," *Journal of Accounting Research* 13(Sup), pp. 1–9.

Surkan, A.J. and J.C. Singleton. 1990. "Neural Networks for Bond Rating Improved by Multiple Hidden Layers," *Proceedings of the International Joint Conference on Neural Networks* 2, pp. 157–62.

Tabor, R.H. and J.T. Willis. 1985. "Empirical Evidence in the Changing Role of Analytical Review Procedures," *Auditing: A Journal of Practice and Theory* 4, no. 2, pp. 93–108.

Waite, T. and H. Hardenbergh. 1989. "Neural Nets," *Programmer's Journal* 7, no. 3, pp. 10–22.

Warren, C.S. and R.K. Elliot. 1986. "Materiality and Audit Risk—A Descriptive Study." Working paper, 23 August.

Wasserman, P.D. 1989. *Neural Computing: Theory and Practice.* New York: Van Nostrand Reinhold.

Wright, A. and W.H. Ashton. 1989. "Identifying Audit Adjustments with Attention-Directing Procedures," *The Accounting Review* LXIV, no. 4, pp. 710–28.

8

RECOGNIZING FINANCIAL DISTRESS PATTERNS USING A NEURAL NETWORK TOOL

Pamela K. Coats and L. Franklin Fant

The traditional approach and present standard for predicting financial distress uses multiple discriminant analysis (MDA) to weight the relative value of information provided by a combination of financial ratios.[1] But MDA has been sharply criticized because the validity of its results hinges on restrictive assumptions (Werbos [37], Eisenbeis [11], Altman and Eisenbeis [3], Scott [29], Tollefson and Joy [32], Sheth [31], Ohlson [26], Pinches [27], Zmijewski [41], Zavgren [39], Karels and Prakash [17], and Odom and Sharda [25]). Two assumptions are particularly problematic for ratio analysis. First, MDA requires that the decision set used to distinguish between distressed and viable firms must be linearly separable. For a single ratio, this means that a value above or below a given threshold point must always signal either distress or good health. In the instance

The authors recognize and thank R. C. Lacher and S. C. Sharma for their contributions, and I. Locke, D. Pagach, and three anonymous *Financial Management* reviewers for their insightful comments.

where two ratios are considered together, the threshold separating the classification regions is a line; where more than two ratios, a plane. Second, MDA does not allow for a ratio's signal to vacillate depending on its relationship to another ratio or set of ratios. In other words, ratios are treated as completely independent.

Unfortunately, these restrictions violate common sense. In practice, a ratio may signal distress both when it is higher than normal and when it is lower than normal, or a ratio's value may be considered acceptable under some conditions yet risky under others. These problems and others (e.g., bias of extreme data points, multivariate normality assumption, and equal group covariances assumption) make MDA incompatible with the complex nature, boundaries, and interrelationships of financial ratios. The power of MDA for financial ratio analysis is compromised, and the results may be erroneous (Karels and Prakash [17]).

Our research is motivated by the fact that a "neural network" (NN) analysis of the same ratios used by MDA, for the same objective, is possible without any of the circumscription that binds MDA.[2] Moreover, studies indicate that neural network models are at least as successful as MDA in terms of overall accuracy (Williams [38]; Cottrel, Munro, and Zipser [9]; Odom and Sharda [25]; Webb and Lowe [36]; and Utans and Moody [57]).

The question asked by our study is, How successfully can neural networks discern patterns or trends in financial data and use them as early warning signals of distressful conditions in currently viable firms? Being able to form highly reliable early forecasts of the future health of firms is, of course, critically important to bank lending officers, investors, market analysts, portfolio managers, auditors, insurers, and many others in the field of finance.

Our approach creates NN models that glean and learn relationships in raw data from processing examples of conclusions reached by experts (auditors) who have analyzed the same data. The experts, in making their assessments, have implicitly imposed their insights and intuition cultivated over years of on-the-job experience. Our research objective is to *formalize* this ingrained, unarticulated knowledge of the experts by uncovering consistencies between the experts' conclusions and the recurring patterns in the financial data. To evaluate our results, we measure our neural networks' success in using a limited number of financial ratios to duplicate the going-concern determinations rendered by auditors.[3,4]

The test results in this study suggest that the NN approach is more effective than MDA for the early detection of financial distress developing in firms. The NN models consistently correctly predict auditors' findings of distress at least 80 percent of the time over an effective lead time of up to four years. A statistical comparison of results shows that the neural networks are always better than the MDA models for identifying firms that eventually receive going-concern opinions.

The neural network we use is a mathematical algorithm for creating a perfect mapping between the input and output values for a set of training data. The NN training process incrementally captures knowledge about the relationship between the output and the patterns in the input in order to correctly categorize the training situations. Once training is complete, the patterns found by the NN can be used to forecast situations where the outcome is unknown.

MDA can be considered equivalent to a special use of NN, and the two approaches give identical results when the input variables are linearly separable. However, the NN model is not subject to MDA's constraining assumptions, such as linear separability and independence of the predictive variables. This allows a neural network to achieve better results than MDA when patterns are complex.

The remainder of this chapter is organized as follows. Section I provides an overview of the particular type of neural network used for our research, namely Cascade-Correlation, and details its method of training. Section II presents the research design that focuses on neural networks and MDA comparison models and describes the collection of the data and the selection of the samples used by the neural networks and MDA models for training and testing. Section III presents the neural network results, makes comparisons with the test results for MDA models, and offers interpretations. Section IV summarizes our findings and the direction of further research.

SECTION I. OVERVIEW OF NEURAL NETWORK METHODOLOGY

Artificial neural networks are inspired by neurobiological systems. Robert Hecht-Nielsen, inventor of one of the earliest neurocomputers, defines a neural network as a computing system made up of a number of simple, highly interconnected processing elements that process information by their dynamic state responses to external inputs (Caudill [8]). This definition brings out the two key elements in a neural network: *processing elements* and *interconnections.*

Each processing element receives and combines input signals and transforms them into a single output signal. Each output signal, in turn, is sent (from its processing element) as an input signal to many other processing elements (and possibly back to itself). Signals are passed around the network via weighted interconnections (links) between processing elements. Network knowledge is stored both in the way the processing elements connect in order to transfer signals and in the nature and strength of the interconnections.

Many types of neural networks exist, with certain types more suited to particular problems than others. We use a learning paradigm called Cascade-Correlation (or Cascor) (Fahlman and Lebiere [13]). It is a mathematical algorithm for training a network to detect relationships between data and output values in order to correctly categorize situations. Cascor overcomes several limitations of the more common back-propagation approach.[5]

A. Structure

Figure 8.1 shows a diagram of a simple Cascade-Correlation neural network consisting of six processing elements, called nodes, and their weighted interconnections. This elementary network connects an input layer of three nodes, an output layer of one node, and two hidden (or internal) nodes.

The input layer is composed of pieces of input data that describe the situation being studied. For example, each input node may refer to a particular financial ratio. Taken together, the values for these three input nodes represent one pattern to be studied by the network. These node values provide the initial signals to the NN. Since neural networks do not impose a linearity constraint, qualitative data (denoting, for example, a firm's nationality, region of operation, market segments, employee satisfaction, severity of strikes, or spurious market behaviors) can be dealt with in the same fashion as numeric input.

The output layer is composed of a single response or condition node, which reflects the situation's known outcome. As an example, the output node may be used to denote a firm as being either healthy or distressed. Neural systems generate either categorical (e.g., groups A, B, C, or D; small, medium, or large) or relational (e.g., better than/worse than; greater than/less than) output.

Figure 8.1

Simple Six-Node Cascade-Correlation Neural Network

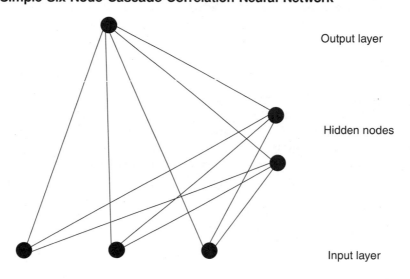

Output layer

Hidden nodes

Input layer

Notes:
Lines denote numeric connection weights between nodes.
● denotes a node.
Processing is directional from bottom to top.

There can be any number of hidden nodes, depending on (and increasing with) the complexity of the pattern in the input data. Each hidden node is fully connected *from* all input nodes and previously installed hidden nodes and *to* all output nodes. Cascor begins with no hidden nodes, and then incrementally creates and installs hidden nodes (one at a time) to improve the network's ability to categorize. It is the hidden nodes, and their manner of connection with every input and output node and to each other, that make a Cascor NN capable of elaborating on hidden structures in the data. One of the advantages of Cascade-Correlation over previous neural network designs is that Cascor automatically self-determines the number of hidden nodes necessary to detect all of the features of the pattern (see Section I.C., Training). With other NN methods, extensive human trial and error is usually needed to discover the number of hidden nodes that best enables good predictions.[6]

The numeric weight assigned to the connection of any two nodes reflects the direction (positive or negative) and relative strength of the relationship between the nodes. Determining these weights is the focus of the neural network's computational process. In essence, the network's knowledge about one node's influence on another is encoded in the connection weights.

B. Classification

What type of patterns can Cascor neural nets represent? This is equivalent to asking, How many distinct regions can be formed within a decision space and how are they separated? To help the reader visualize the classification abilities of Cascor neural nets, several nets are portrayed graphically in Figure 8.2 for the two-dimensional (i.e., two-input) case.

A neural net with no hidden nodes is equivalent to a multiple discriminant analysis. As with MDA, the decision (or categorization)

Figure 8.2

Cascor Decision Regions

a. Cascor Decision Regions with No Hidden Nodes

Ratio 1

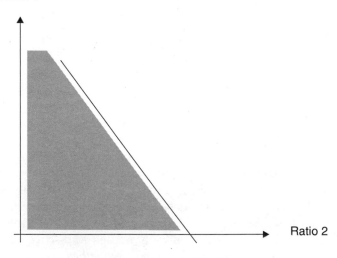

Ratio 2

Figure 8.2

(concluded)

b. Cascor Decision Regions with One or More Hidden Nodes

Ratio 1

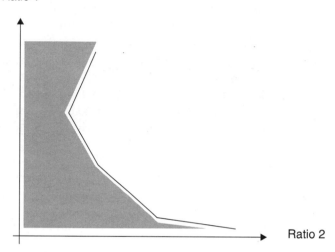

Ratio 2

c. Cascor Decision Regions with Many Hidden Nodes

Ratio 1

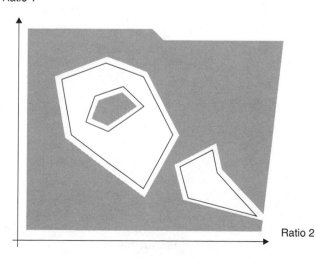

Ratio 2

regions can only be separated by a single straight line, as shown in Figure 8.2a. As noted earlier, when discriminating variables are *not* linearly separable, MDA (as well as a neural net with no hidden nodes) may not be appropriate.

A Cascor net with one hidden node has the ability to separate the decision (or categorization) space into regions by an angular surface (either open or closed), rather than a straight line (see Figure 8.2b). Because of the hidden node, individual input nodes can interact (pass information and influence each other's output signals). This facilitates a flexible mapping.

As more hidden nodes are added, the net becomes completely general and can separate the decision space into an arbitrary number of regions defined by complex boundaries, as the examples in Figure 8.2c indicate (Lacher [19]).

C. Training

The objective of the training process is to autonomously *learn*[7] the relationship between the output and patterns in the input and to incrementally capture that knowledge in a unique structure of hidden nodes and connection weights that produce correct categorizations. This process of working toward accurate mappings is called "convergence." According to a mathematical theorem proved by Kolmogorov in the 1950s (Lorentz [21]) (and restated for back-propagation neural networks by Hecht-Nielsen in the late 1980s (Caudill [7]) and for Cascor neural networks by Lacher in the early 1990s (Lacher [19])), the network will always eventually figure out how to make perfect mappings of the data on which the NN is being trained.[8]

Initially, the network is organized into two layers of nodes. The input layer presents the variety of patterns. In our research experiments, for example, each pattern represents a different firm's set of five financial ratios for a given year of operation, in other words, five input nodes. The output layer is a one-node response (either -1 for distressed or +1 for healthy) associated with a given input pattern. It is the association of pattern and response that the network attempts to learn through its internal nodes. The actual number of hidden nodes and the connection weights are determined by the neural net.

As the training process begins, the network is furnished with the entire set of training patterns. At this point, the NN has no hidden nodes and seeks to determine a set of connection weights that, when combined with the values of their respective input nodes,[9] provide a linear mapping to the associated output node. The NN works by minimizing the average residual forecast error for the training set. In the initial network, with no hidden nodes, the system of input nodes, output nodes, and connection weights is precisely equivalent to the system of coefficients and independent variables in a discriminant analysis (Webb and Lowe [36]); in other words, the solution forms a linear frontier, as in Figure 8.2a, and the classification accuracy of the NN and the MDA are identical.

Once the network has looked at all of the patterns in the training sample (one pass through the entire set of training examples is called an "epoch"), the network starts over again and cycles through the set. When further adjustment of the weights produces no significant error reduction after a certain number of training cycles (set by the user[10]), training of the connection weights stops. The network runs one more time over the training set to measure the error. If the user is satisfied with the network's performance,[11] processing stops. If the residual forecast error is unacceptable, Cascor starts creating hidden nodes one at a time.

To create a new hidden node, Cascor starts with a "candidate node" not yet permanently connected to the network. The candidate node receives trainable input connections from all of the nodes in the network's input layer and from all preexisting hidden nodes. Cascor runs several passes over the training patterns, adjusting the candidate node's input weights, or connections, after each pass. The goal of the adjustment is to maximize the magnitude of the correlation between the candidate node's output and the residual forecast error that the network is trying to eliminate. Thus, the new hidden node is intended to cancel a portion of the forecast error when the node is installed permanently into the network. The new node's input weights are frozen, and all of the output weights are once again trained to the error remaining at the output layer, using a predetermined training, or learning, algorithm for adjusting weights.

This cycle of adding hidden nodes one by one repeats until a steady state is reached; that is, the process continues either until the model can fit all of the sample patterns, until further addition of hidden nodes no longer reduces forecast error, or until the forecast error is within a tolerable range determined by the user. Thus, "training" is the process of creating and installing new hidden nodes until the residual forecast error is eliminated or tolerable. To implement the Cascor neural network, the software NeuralWorks Professional[TM] II/PLUS (*Neural Computing* [24]) was used. For a listing of the specific C computer code, see Crowder [10].

Although a detailed explanation of the mathematics of Cascor's learning process is beyond the scope of this paper, a general, somewhat intuitive explanation is certainly desirable. When training, the network is presented with one observation from the data at a time. The network generates an output value based on that data (in our case, makes a classification decision) and compares this output to the true, correct output value. The difference between the output of the network and the correct output is the error. In essence, the training set presents a hyperdimensional surface to the network, which is the prediction error. The neural network's task in training is to seek out the global minimum of this error function. By using the input data to calculate an output value, and comparing this to the true value, the network generates a point on the surface of the error function. The algorithm adjusts itself by moving in the direction of steepest descent, which is the negative of the gradient at that point. This adjustment is accomplished by updating the coefficients in the function generating the output (which involves gradient ascent and the chain rule in calculus). Those familiar with estimation of nonlinear econometric models will see that their optimization is similar to the optimization described here.[12]

SECTION II. RESEARCH DESIGN

A. Models

Our research builds and test four Cascor models for predicting financial distress. The models are trained on historic financial data for many firms, some of which were cited by their auditors as being likely candidates for financial distress and the remainder being free from such designation. The four models represent four different lead times: the year for which distressful conditions in a firm are reported by auditors, and the one, two, and three years prior.

The financial information we chose to describe each firm is the set of five ratios from Altman's Z score model (Altman [1], [2]). We also built four MDA models, again based on Altman's Z score ratios and using the same data as the Cascor models, to serve as benchmarks to compare with our neural network approach to the pattern-classification of healthy and distressed firms. We use Altman's ratios throughout because Altman's findings have been the most widely and consistently referenced and used to date by both researchers and practitioners.

The five ratios chosen by Altman to explain business viability are:

$$Z = f(x_1, x_2, x_3, x_4, x_5) \tag{1}$$

where

x_1 = Working capital/total assets.
x_2 = Retained earnings/total assets.
x_3 = Earnings before interest and taxes/total assets.
x_4 = Market value of equity/book value of total debt.
x_5 = Sales/total assets.
Z = Overall index (known as Altman's Z score).

B. Criterion for Distress

To identify financially troubled firms, we used auditors' reports rather than the traditional bankruptcy filings because auditors' reports offer an earlier warning of "developing" distressful conditions (Altman and McGough [4]). An underlying assumption of financial statements examined by auditors is that the firm has the ability and intent to continue as a viable operating entity, in other words, as a going-concern, for the indefinite future. If facts uncovered during an audit cast substantial doubt on the firm's ability to continue as a going concern (for one year following the date of the financial statements), the firm's independent public accountants must consider modifying their report that accompanies the financial statements. During the period our study covers, this modification generally took the form of a disclaimer report, informally referred to as a "going-concern opinion."[13]

Our decision to use the auditors' report rather than a bankruptcy filing as our indicator of financial distress was based on a desire to capture the "practical" relevance of the predicted event. Bankruptcy of a firm may also occur after a prolonged period of financial distress. At this point, there is little practical use for a predictive algorithm since the distressed nature of the firm is obvious to virtually all of the firm's stakeholders—shareholders, employees, vendors, and so on. On the other hand, the issuance of a going-concern opinion is expected to precede bankruptcy, perhaps quite substantially, considering the sequences of events that may lead a firm from financial viability into bankruptcy. Another reason that issuance of a going-concern opinion is preferable to a bankruptcy filing as the predicted event is that bankruptcy is only one outcome of financial distress. Others include reorganization, liquidation, and acquisition by a viable firm. Regardless of the eventual outcome, losses and downside risks preceding the final resolution are likely to be incurred by stake-holders, considering predistress asset values and risk. Bad audit reports can cause bond ratings to be lowered, lines of credit to dry up, and other business relationships to be disrupted. Thus, use of the disclaimer report as a prediction criterion covers a broader range of events than does a bankruptcy filing and should have more relevance to decision-makers.

C. Data

The data were collected from the Standard & Poor's COMPUSTAT fi-nancial database covering the period 1970–1989. Two groups of firms were drawn: a group identified as financially distressed companies and a group identified as financially viable companies, named the "distressed group" and the "viable group," respectively. The distressed group was culled from the Industrial Research File, which only lists firms that have ceased operations. To be in the distressed group, a firm must have received a going-concern opinion and passed a screening process that posed certain "sanity checks" designed to weed out erroneous data and make sure that all of the information necessary to calculate the five ratios for Altman's model for the year of the going-concern opinion and the three years prior thereto was available.[14] There were 94 suitable distressed firms after the screening process.[15]

To serve as counterexamples to the distressed firms, a group of 188 viable firms (two viable firms for every distressed firm) was chosen ran-domly at large from the full-coverage file. These firms were matched 2-to-1 to the distressed group only with regard to each distressed firm's year of going-concern opinion. To be considered viable, a firm must not have received a going-concern opinion for the year of match or for any of the previous three years. And to ensure that firms on the brink of distress were not selected as viable, any firm that received a going-concern opinion within two years after the going-concern opinion for its match in the distressed group was rejected from consideration.[16] The viable group also had to pass the same screening process as the distressed group. The viable firms were drawn entirely from the manufacturing sector, but data relating to distressed firms in our database run the gamut of industries and services. We felt that the number of distressed firms (51) available from COMPUSTAT's manufacturing sector alone was insufficient to adequately train *and* test the neural network,[17] so 46 percent of the distressed group comes from outside the manufacturing sector. This does not bias the comparison of NN versus MDA since the methods use identical data.

After the sample of firms were selected, data from the two sample groups were randomized and recombined to form eight nonoverlapping sets. There were two sets for each of four years. Each set contained one year of data for 47 distressed forms and 94 viable firms. The data represent the year of the going-concern opinion (y_0), the year before the going-concern opinion (y_{-1}), two years before the going-concern opinion (y_{-2}), and three years before the going-concern opinion (y_{-3}). Half of the randomly selected sets were used to train the NN to recognize patterns that explained auditors' going-concern opinions. The remaining sets were treated as holdout samples for testing the network's predictive ability. MDA models for each of the four years were built using the same data on which the NN trained and were tested on the identical holdout samples used by the NN.

Table 8.1 gives a summary of univariate statistics describing the data. There are distinct differences between the distribution of the ratios for the distressed and viable firms. With respect to the distressed firms, there is a marked deterioration in the means and medians for ratios x_1, x_2, and x_3 as the year of the going-concern opinion (y_0) approaches. The standard deviations of ratios x_1, x_2, and x_3 consistently increase over time, and there is also a clear tendency for these ratios to become increasingly negatively skewed with time. Changes in the ratios x_4 and x_5 over time are not as consistent or striking. Comparing distressed firms in the training sample to those in the testing sample reveals that there are some differences in the two sets of statistics, but these are simply due to the random assignment of the distressed firms to the two samples. In contrast, statistics for the viable firms do not exhibit any significant changes across time. The ratio x_4 is heavily skewed to the right, much more so than it is for the distressed firms. For the viable firms, this is the only ratio that displays

Table 8.1

Univariate Statistics for Ratios Used to Distinguish Distressed and Viable Firms

a. Distressed Firms

Year	Training Set Ratios					Test Set Ratios				
	x_1	x_2	x_3	x_4	x_5	x_1	x_2	x_3	x_4	x_5
y_0										
Mean	-0.72	-2.30	-0.56	1.97	2.09	-0.39	-1.99	-0.30	1.60	1.62
Standard deviation	1.48	4.39	0.84	4.47	1.88	0.73	3.93	0.61	2.29	1.34
Maximum	0.58	0.38	0.36	28.53	9.10	0.64	0.44	0.51	12.22	5.55
Median	-0.45	-0.66	-0.25	0.46	1.67	-0.19	-0.57	-0.15	0.80	1.30
Minimum	-9.47	-22.64	-4.55	0.01	0.02	-3.16	-22.42	-2.64	0.03	0.07
y_{-1}										
Mean	-0.04	-0.98	-0.26	1.74	1.46	-0.04	-1.27	-0.17	1.92	1.58
Standard deviation	0.50	2.84	0.96	3.95	0.90	0.50	3.16	0.44	4.74	1.13
Maximum	0.63	0.40	0.17	25.70	4.45	0.63	0.50	0.37	32.39	5.30
Median	0.06	-0.17	-0.02	0.42	1.40	0.05	-0.27	-0.02	0.64	1.54
Minimum	-2.00	-18.44	-6.21	0.01	0.14	-2.30	-19.46	-1.89	0.01	0.05
y_{-2}										
Mean	0.11	-0.40	-0.03	1.51	1.36	0.15	-0.64	-0.12	1.62	1.58
Standard deviation	0.31	0.93	0.28	3.33	-0.72	0.28	1.59	0.40	2.50	1.23
Maximum	0.81	0.55	0.74	21.52	3.59	0.77	0.49	0.15	15.26	5.77
Median	0.15	-0.03	0.01	0.38	1.32	0.14	-0.20	0.00	0.88	1.38
Minimum	-0.64	-4.55	-0.95	0.01	0.24	-1.14	-9.50	-1.88	0.04	0.03
y_{-3}										
Mean	0.16	-0.27	0.00	1.36	1.34	0.22	-0.38	-0.05	1.87	1.57
Standard deviation	0.30	0.68	0.24	3.07	0.63	0.26	0.89	0.28	3.96	1.20
Maximum	0.85	0.54	0.48	18.47	2.55	0.68	0.51	0.79	26.19	5.78
Median	0.17	0.03	0.05	0.43	1.26	0.22	-0.08	0.01	0.61	1.42
Minimum	-0.73	-2.01	-0.71	0.01	0.16	-0.65	-3.80	-0.93	0.03	0.07

Table 8.1

(concluded)

b. Viable Firms

Year	Training Set Ratios					Test Set Ratios				
	x_1	x_2	x_3	x_4	x_5	x_1	x_2	x_3	x_4	x_5
y_0										
Mean	0.34	0.43	0.16	15.83	1.48	0.35	0.39	0.17	9.91	1.42
Standard deviation	0.16	0.17	0.08	34.75	0.48	0.17	0.19	0.08	13.46	0.42
Maximum	0.73	0.81	0.45	290.75	3.94	0.69	0.85	0.63	61.13	2.76
Median	0.36	0.43	0.15	4.97	1.44	0.36	0.38	0.17	4.18	1.38
Minimum	0.02	-0.02	0.00	0.15	0.45	0.01	-0.37	0.00	0.02	0.57
y_{-1}										
Mean	0.35	0.43	0.19	13.12	1.50	0.35	0.38	0.17	9.68	1.44
Standard deviation	0.16	0.16	0.14	20.62	0.46	0.17	0.18	0.07	13.09	0.44
Maximum	0.74	0.83	1.30	111.54	3.88	0.70	0.85	0.34	58.97	2.74
Median	0.37	0.42	0.17	4.63	1.48	0.37	0.36	0.16	4.08	1.40
Minimum	-0.02	0.02	0.03	0.21	0.53	0.00	-0.22	0.01	0.01	0.58
y_{-2}										
Mean	0.36	0.43	0.17	12.32	1.52	0.35	0.37	0.17	8.76	1.41
Standard deviation	0.16	0.16	0.08	20.03	0.44	0.16	0.19	0.08	13.08	0.42
Maximum	0.75	0.81	0.46	133.44	3.25	0.70	0.84	0.47	62.40	2.48
Median	0.37	0.41	0.17	3.90	1.51	0.37	0.36	0.16	3.37	1.39
Minimum	0.01	-0.15	0.00	0.19	0.53	0.01	-0.28	0.02	0.01	0.34
y_{-3}										
Mean	0.36	0.41	0.17	11.04	1.53	0.35	0.34	0.17	9.06	1.45
Standard deviation	0.16	0.16	0.08	18.02	0.43	0.15	0.26	0.09	15.33	0.42
Maximum	0.71	0.78	0.48	96.09	2.98	0.71	0.81	0.61	70.24	2.70
Median	0.37	0.40	0.17	3.80	1.55	0.37	0.36	0.16	2.96	1.36
Minimum	-0.07	-0.07	0.01	0.11	0.51	0.04	-1.28	0.05	0.02	0.42

177

much asymmetry. Comparing the statistics for the distressed firms to those for viable firms, it can be seen that the mean and median of x_1 through x_4 are consistently larger for the distressed firms than for the viable firms. In addition, the standard deviations for all ratios except x_4 are consistently larger for the distressed firms than for the viable firms.

SECTION III. PREDICTION RESULTS

A. Training Results

Using the training sets, the Cascor software determined a unique NN for each year. Each NN was trained until it delivered 100 percent classification accuracy for its year. In other words, each trained network eventually correctly identified all 47 of the distressed firms as being distressed and all 94 of the healthy firms as being healthy. Some networks required up to 1,400 training cycles and installed as many as eight hidden nodes.

Statistics for the MDA models for each of the four years appear in Table 8.2. The table shows, by year, the coefficients for each ratio and the midpoint score used for predicting viability or distress. We used the software Mathcad (Version 3.0) to implement Fisher's linear discriminant.

Table 8.2
Coefficients for MDA Models

Year	x_1	x_2	x_3	x_4	x_5	$\hat{m}^*$
y_0	−0.733	−0.198	−2.259	−0.018	−0.154	0.35
y_{-1}	−5.168	−0.849	2.594	−0.057	−0.409	−1.71
y_{-2}	−5.752	−1.958	−3.396	−0.061	−0.540	−2.84
y_{-3}	−4.056	−2.884	−2.768	−0.058	−0.292	−2.26

*This statistic represents the estimated midpoint between the two populations (distressed and viable). The discriminant function is $y = X\delta$, where X is a 1-by-5 vector of the ratios x_1, through x_5, and δ is the 5-by-1 vector of estimated coefficients. The allocation rule was to classify firm i as failed if $y_i \geq \hat{m}$.

B. Test Results and Implications

Holdout samples were used to test the robustness for the neural networks for prediction. We collected statistics on the percentages of accurate forecasts made by the trained networks. The MDA models were also tested on the holdout samples, and the results were used as benchmarks to assess the performance of the neural networks.

Parts a and b of Table 8.3 compare the classification test results of Cascor and MDA. A "Type I hit" is one in which a distressed firm is correctly classified, and a "Type II hit" is the correct classification of a viable firm. Conversely, a "Type I error" is one in which a distressed firm is misclassified by the predictor as viable, and a "Type II error" is the misclassification of a viable firm as distressed. An "overall hit" refers to the total correct classifications for the set, regardless of type. Rate, in each case, is the ratio of the number of hits for a given classification over the total number of actual patterns in that classification.

We note that MDA has good success with Type II hits, although not with Type I hits. Type II hit rates for MDA were all above 90 percent over the four-year test horizon; Type I hit rates for MDA range between 63.8 percent and 70.2 percent. On the other hand, Cascor achieved quite high scores for Type II hits while, in addition, showing consistently high Type I hit rates, consistently high overall hit rates, and robustness in terms of a longer effective lead time for all predictions.

Test were performed to determine if the two population proportions were equal. Specifically, the null hypothesis was that the proportion of hits, in other words, accuracy for the MDA model of a given year is greater than or equal to the proportion of hits for the neural network model of the same year:

$$H_0: p_{MDA} \geq p_{NN} \tag{2}$$

where p is the percentage of hits for either MDA or the Cascor neural network (NN). The following test statistic (which is normally distributed) is appropriate:

$$z = \frac{(\hat{p}_{NN} - \hat{p}_{MDA}) - 0}{\left(\dfrac{\hat{p}_{NN}\,\hat{q}_{NN} + \hat{p}_{MDA}\,\hat{q}_{MDA}}{n}\right)^{\frac{1}{2}}} \tag{3}$$

Table 8.3

Classification Hit Rates and Error Rates for Cascor vs. MDA Test Results

a. Classification Hit Rates for Cascor vs. MDA Test Results

Year	Cascor			MDA		
	Type I	Type II	Overall	Type I	Type II	Overall
y0	89.4	97.9	95.0	63.8	100.0	87.9
y-1	83.0	97.9	92.9	68.1	90.4	83.0
y-2	89.4	83.0	86.2	70.2	90.4	83.7
y-3	80.9	83.0	81.9	66.0	92.6	83.7

b. Classification Error Rates for Cascor vs. MDA Test Results

Year	Cascor			MDA		
	Type I	Type II	Overall	Type I	Type II	Overall
y0	10.6	2.1	5.0	36.2	0.0	12.1
y-1	17.0	2.1	7.1	31.9	9.6	17.0
y-2	10.6	17.0	13.8	29.8	9.6	16.3
y-3	19.1	17.0	18.1	34.0	7.4	16.3

Note: Numbers are expressed as percentages.

Table 8.4

Test for Differences Between Proportions

$$H_0: p_{MDA} \geq p_{NN} \text{ versus } H_a: p_{MDA} < p_{NN}$$

a. Percentage of Hits for Distressed Firms

n	Neural Network (Cascor)	MDA	z	p-Value
47	89.4	63.8	3.08*	0.001
47	83.0	68.1	1.71*	0.044
47	89.4	70.2	2.39*	0.008
47	80.9	66.0	1.66*	0.049

b. Percentage of Hits for Viable Firms

n	Neural Network (Cascor)	MDA	z	p-Value
94	97.9	100.0	-1.42	0.922
94	97.9	90.4	2.22*	0.013
94	83.0	90.4	-1.50	0.934
94	83.0	92.6	-2.03	0.979

Notes:

p is the percentage of hits for either multiple discriminant analysis (MDA) or the Cascor neural network (NN).

* Denotes significance at the 5 percent level.

where $\hat{p}$ refers to the sample percentage of hits, $\hat{q}$ refers to the sample percentage of misses (thus $\hat{p} + \hat{q} = 1$), and n is the number of firms. The results appear in Table 8.4. From the p-values of this one-tailed test, it can be seen that the null hypothesis is rejected (at the 5 percent level of significance) for all four tests concerning the group of distressed firms. That is, the neural network outpredicts MDA when the firm in question has or will receive a going-concern opinion. As regards classification of financially healthy firms, the null hypothesis is rejected only once out of four tests. Therefore, we do not claim any better prediction ability for neural networks over MDA for the group of viable firms alone.

What do these results imply about the relative contribution of neural networks versus MDA? If the user is simply concerned with making a correct classification, either tool suffices. But, since being wrong is not a problem when the cost is small, decision-makers must also consider the magnitude of costs and benefits of their decisions. Once the relative costs of misclassification for each group are considered, the results of our analysis indicate that Cascor makes a notable contribution over MDA as a practitioner's decision-making tool. We expect that the costs of misclassifying a viable firm as distressed (Type II error) are typically small. Consider a financial analyst comparing potential investments or a bank loan officer reviewing loan applications. In an environment where there is a reasonably large number of viable firms from which to choose, there is little cost to misclassifying a viable firm. There are many other firms with which to transact. On the other hand, the cost of misclassifying a distressed firm (Type I error) can be substantial. To be more specific, the decision-making framework we envision as most appropriate for Cascor is a form of Bayesian hypothesis testing,[18] where costs of errors and probabilities of population membership both explicitly enter into the final classification decision.

SECTION IV. CONCLUDING COMMENTS

The spirit of this research is discovery. We compared the results of the established MDA approach, which makes a priori assumptions about the discriminating variables against a new, more robust neural network approach. Our objective was to showcase the advantages of the NN for recognizing complex patters in data.

Test results suggest that the NN approach is more effective than MDA for pattern classification. The MDA model produces excellent results for the year of the going-concern opinion. However, Cascor does better by comparison in the earlier years' classification, sustaining reliability even as we move away form y_0. Although the MDA method produces high Type II hit rates through y_{-3}, the Type I hit rates are notably less reliable. We believe that Cascor's robust prediction of distress, in the shape of

Type I hit rates consistently above 80 percent over a four-year effective lead time, is worth pursuing.

Our plans for further studies in this area include using quarterly data in place of annual data and using several time periods in conjunction to look for time series patterns in the magnitude of changes (or combinations of changes) in ratios. Also, the ratios we used in our current tests were based on Altman's 1968 bankruptcy study, and different ratios may perform better today or may be more appropriate for going-concern opinions. Finally, we believe that Cascor's already high hit rates may be improved by further experimentation with the parameters, such as the number of input and output nodes, the training algorithm, and the activation function.[19] The choice of activation function is of particular interest because it appears to be the key to enabling Cascor networks to generate precise analog forecasts rather than only binary classifications (Fahlman and Lebiere [13]). This capability is experimental at present, but has the potential for providing a forecast of gradations (or degrees or categories) of financial health, rather than just the bipolar choices of viable or distressed.

REFERENCES

1. E.I. Altman. "Financial Ratios Discriminant Analysis, and the Prediction of Corporate Bankruptcy." *Journal of Finance,* September 1968, pp. 589–609.

2. E.I. Altman. *Corporate Distress: A Complete Guide to Predicting, Avoiding, and Dealing with Bankruptcy.* New York: John Wiley & Sons, 1983.

3. E.I. Altman and R.A. Eisenbeis. "Financial Discriminant Analysis: A Clarification." *Journal of Financial and Quantitative Analysis,* March 1978, pp. 185–195.

4. E.I. Altman and T.P. McGough. "Evaluation of a Company as a Going Concern." *Journal of Accounting,* December 1974, pp. 50–57.

5. R. Barniv and A. Raveh. "Identifying Financial Distress: A New Nonparametric Approach." *Journal of Business Finance and Accounting,* Summer 1989, pp. 361–83.

6. L. Breiman, J.H. Friedman, R.A. Olshen, and C.J. Stone. *Classification and Regression Trees.* Belmont, CA: Wadsworth, 1984.

7. M. Caudill. "Neural Networks Primer, Part III." *AI Expert,* June 1988, pp. 53–59.

8. M. Caudill. "Neural Networks Primer." *The Magazine of Artificial Intelligence in Practice.* San Francisco: Miller Freeman Publications, 1989.

9. G.W. Cottrel, A. Munro, and D. Zipser. "Learning Internal Representations from Gray-Scale Images: An Example of Extensional Programming." *Proceedings of the 9th Annual Conference of the Cognitive Science Society,* 1987, pp. 461–73.

10. R.S. Crowder. "Software Implementing the Cascade-Correlation Learning Algorithm in C." Pittsburgh: Carnegie Mellon University, June 1990.

11. R.A. Eisenbeis. "Pitfalls in the Application of Discriminant Analysis in Business Finance and Analysis." *Journal of Finance,* June 1977, pp. 875–900.

12. P.J. Elmer and D.M. Borowski. "An Expert System Approach to Financial Analysis: The Case of S&L Bankruptcy." *Financial Management,* Autumn 1988, pp. 66–76.

13. S.E. Fahlman and C. Lebiere. *The Cascade-Correlation Learning Architecture.* Technical Report: CMU-CS-90-100. Pittsburgh: Carnegie Mellon University, February 1990.

14. H. Frydman, E.I. Altman, and D. Kao. "Introducing Recursive Partitioning for Financial Classification: The Case of Financial Distress." *Journal of Finance,* March 1985, pp. 269–91.

15. E. Goss, A. Whitten, and V. Sundaraiyer. "Forecasting with Lotus-based Logit Regression Models." *Journal of Business Forecasting,* Spring 1991, pp. 19–22.

16. D.D. Hawley, J.D. Johnson and D. Raina. "Artificial Neural Systems: A New Tool for Financial Decision-Making." *Financial Analysts Journal,* November/December 1990, pp. 63–72.

17. G.V. Karels and A. Prakash. "Multivariate Normality and Forecasting of Business Bankruptcy." *Journal of Business Finance and Accounting,* Winter 1987, pp. 573–93.

18. K. Knight. "Connectionist Ideas and Algorithms." *Communications of the ACM,* November 1990, pp. 59–74.

19. R.C. Lacher. "Artificial Neural Networks: An Introduction to the Theory and Practice." Monograph in progress. Tallahassee: Department of Computer Science, Florida State University, 1992.

20. R.C. Lippmann. "An Introduction to Computing with Neural Nets." *IEEE ASSP Magazine,* April 1987, pp. 4–22.

21. G.G. Lorentz. "The 13th Problem of Hilbert." in *Mathematical Developments Arising from Hilbert Problems.* ed. F.E. Browder. Providence, RI: American Mathematical Society, 1976.

22. D. McFadden. "A Comment on Discriminant Analysis versus Logit Analysis." *Annals of Economic and Social Measurement,* 1976, pp. 511–23.

23. M. Minsky and S. Papert. *Perceptions.* Cambridge: MIT Press, 1969.

24. *Neural Computing.* Users Manual to Accompany NeuralWorks Professional^{TM} II/PLUS Neural Network Software. Pittsburgh: NeuralWare, Inc., 1990.

25. M.D. Odom and R. Sharda. "A Neural Network Model for Bankruptcy Prediction." In *Proceedings of the International Joint Conference on Neural Networks,* 1990.

26. J.A. Ohlson. "Financial Ratios and the Probabilistic Prediction of Bankruptcy." *Journal of Accounting Research,* Spring 1980, pp. 109–31.

27. G.E. Pinches. "Factors Influencing Classification Results from Multiple Discriminant Analysis." *Journal of Business Research,* December 1980, pp. 429–56.

28. D.E. Rumelhart and J.L. McClelland. *Parallel Distributed Processing: Explorations in the Microstructure of Cognition.* Cambridge, MA, and London: MIT Press, 1986.

29. E. Scott. "On the Financial Application of Discriminant Analysis: Comment." *Journal of Financial and Quantitative Analysis,* March 1978, pp. 201–205.

30. M. Selfridge and F. Biggs. "The Architecture of Expertise: The Auditor's Going-Concern Judgment." *Expert Systems Review* 2, no. 3 (1990), pp. 3–18.

31. J.N. Sheth. "How to Get the Most Out of Multivariate Methods." In *Multivariate Data Analysis.* eds. Hair, Anderson, Tatham, and Grablowsky. Tulsa, OK: Petroleum Publishing Company, 1979, ch. 1.

32. J.O. Tollefson and O.M. Joy. "Some Clarifying Comments on Discriminant Analysis." *Journal of Financial and Quantitative Analysis,* March 1978, pp. 197–200.

33. J. Utans and J. Moody. "Selecting Neural Network Architectures via the Prediction Risk: Application to Corporate Bond Rating Prediction." *IEEE,* June 1991, pp. 35–41.

34. P.D. Wasserman and T. Schwartz. "Neural Networks, Part 1." *IEEE Expert,* Winter 1987, pp. 10–12.

35. P.D. Wasserman and T. Schwartz. "Neural Networks, Part 2." *IEEE Expert,* Spring 1988, pp. 10–15.

36. A.R. Webb and D. Lowe. "The Optimized Internal Representation of Multilayer Classifier Networks Performs Nonlinear Discriminant Analysis." *Neural Networks* 3 (1990), pp. 367–75.

37. P.J. Werbos. "Beyond Regression: New Tools for Prediction and Analysis in the Behavioral Sciences." Ph.D. Dissertation. Harvard University, 1974.

38. R.J. Williams. *Learning Internal Representations by Error Propagation.* Institute for Cognitive Science Report 8506. San Diego: University of California, 1985.

39. C.V. Zavgren. "The Prediction of Corporate Failure: The State of the Art." *Journal of Accounting Literature,* Spring 1983, pp. 1–38.

40. A. Zellner. *An Introduction to Bayesian Inference in Econometrics.* New York: John Wiley & Sons, 1971.

41. M.E. Zmiljewski. "Methodological Issues Related to the Estimation of Financial Distress Prediction Models." *Journal of Accounting Research* (Supplement 1984), pp. 59–82.

APPENDIX: EXAMPLE OF CASCOR PREDICTION COMPUTATIONS

Each hidden node is an information processor having n inputs, n input connection weights, and a single output. Each node forms a weighted sum of its n inputs, and each weighted sum is transformed by a nonlinear activation function to compute the output. In other words, the output is a nonlinear function of a scalar product of the input values. This transformation may be as simple as providing and "ON" indication if the sum exceeds a certain threshold or may be more complicated, such as a sigmoidal, Gaussian, or exponential function. Just as the activation function is not limited to a simple on/off, inputs may be analog, Boolean, or discrete.

Table 8A.1 is an abbreviated example of corporate financial input data in the format used in our Cascor trials. Each row of the table is one pattern that represents financial data relating to one firm, namely:

❖ One set of five ratios for the Altman Z score model.

❖ An actual output of –1 for a financially distressed firm and +1 for a viable firm, as determined by the auditors' going-concern opinion.

Figure 8A.1 displays the nodal architecture for predicting the output for Pattern 1 in the example data file. The five ratios and the bias[20] node are nodes No. 1 to No. 6. When the hidden node is added, it becomes node No. 7. The output is represented by node No. 8. The computations of the value of the hidden node and the value of the output node are shown in Table 8A.2. We used the symmetric sigmoidal activation function for computing the value of the hidden node and the value of the output node. The equation is:

$$Activation\ value of node = \frac{1}{\left(1 + e^{-(SUM)}\right)}$$

where SUM is the weighted sum of the inputs to the node. Cascor's prediction of an output of +1 for Pattern 1 is correct according to the actual output for this viable firm.

188   Chapter 8

Table 8A.1

Example Data File

Patterns	Financial Ratios					Actual Outcomes
	x_1	x_2	x_3	x_4	x_5	
1	0.56	0.40	0.09	1.48	1.77	+1
2	0.26	0.40	0.11	24.76	1.20	+1
3	−0.52	−0.44	−0.25	0.38	1.35	−1

Notes: +1: viable; −1: distressed

Figure 8A.1

Cascor Architecture for Pattern 1 of Example Data File

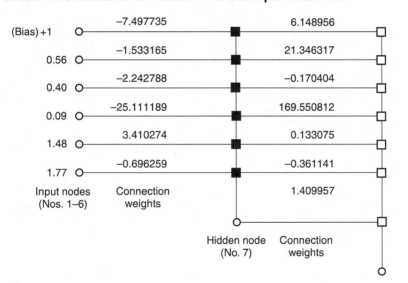

O represents a node.
■ represents a frozen connection weight.
☐ represents a connection weight that is trained repeatedly.
Vertical lines sum all incoming activation.

Figure 8A.2

Cascor Execution Worksheet for Pattern 1 of Example Data File

a. Computed Activation Value of Hidden Node (No. 7)

Input Nodes		Connection Weights		
+1	*	−7.4977350	=	−7.497735
0.56	*	−1.5331650	=	−0.858572
0.40	*	−2.2427880	=	−0.897115
0.09	*	−25.1111890	=	−2.260007
1.48	*	3.41022740	=	5.047206
1.77	*	−0.6962590	=	−1.232378
		SUM	=	−7.698601

$$\text{Hidden node's activation value} = \frac{1}{\left(1 + e^{-(-7.69801)}\right)} - 0.5 = -0.5.$$

b. Computed Activation Value of Output Node (No. 8)

Input Nodes		Connection Weights		
+1	*	6.148956	=	6.148956
0.56	*	21.346317	=	11.953937
0.40	*	−0.170404	=	−0.068161
0.09	*	169.550812	=	15.259572
1.48	*	0.133075	=	0.196951
1.77	*	−0.361141	=	−0.639220
−0.50	*	1.409957	=	−0.704339
		SUM		15

$$\text{Output node's activation value} = 2\left[\frac{1}{\left(1 + e^{-(15)}\right)} - 0.5\right] = +1.$$

Note: Just as the output node has a user-determined range of −1 to +1, there is a user-determined range of −0.5 to +0.5 for the hidden node(s). In the example above, 0.5 is subtracted from the hidden node's activation value and the output node's activation value, and the output node's activation value is multiplied by 2. These are simply scale adjustments to keep the values within their prescribed boundaries.

ENDNOTES

1. While other studies have suggested alternatives to MDA, including logit (McFadden [22]; Goss et al. [15]); probit (McFadden [22]); recursive partitioning (Breiman et al. [6]; Frydman, Altman, and Kao [14]); expert systems (Elmer and Borowski [12]); and nonparametric models (Barniv and Raveh [5]), none of these approaches has replaced MDA as the standard for comparison.

2. Since neural networks do not impose a linearity constraint, nonnumeric data that denote, for example, a firm's nationality, region of operation, market segments, employee satisfaction, severity of strikes, or spurious market behaviors can be dealt with in the same fashion as numeric input.

3. Part of the independent auditors' responsibility in a corporate audit is to assess the capability of the firm to continue in existence, i.e., as a going concern, through the following fiscal year-end. If the auditors have sufficient doubt as to this capability, they will issue a disclaimer report to that effect. This report is frequently referred to as a "going-concern opinion."

4. No published research to date has sought to fit a model to emulate the past performance of auditors in assessing financial distress. Selfridge and Biggs [30] have, however, examined the nature of auditors' knowledge and have proposed a cognitive model that identifies the types and relationships of the knowledge involved.

5. Cascor has been shown to have several advantages over back-propagation and other existing neutral network algorithms: The Cascor network learns very quickly, it determines its own size and design, it retains the structure it has built even if the training set changes, and it requires no back-propagation of error signals through the connections of the network (Fahlman and Lebiere [13]).

6. This task of reducing the weights to avoid "overfitting" is described by Utans and Moody [33]. (See also note 17.)

7. "The learning process is actually a training process. An animal can be trained by rewarding desired responses and punishing undesired responses. The (neural network) training process can also be thought of as involving rewards and punishments. When the system responds correctly to an input, the 'reward' consists of a strengthening of the current. . . model weights. This makes it more likely that a similar response will be produced by similar inputs in the future. When the system responds incorrectly, the 'punishment' calls for the adjustment of the model weights based on the particular learning algorithm employed so that the system will respond differently when it encounters similar inputs again. Desirable actions are

thus progressively reinforced, while undesirable actions are progressively inhibited" (Hawley, Johnson, and Raina [16]).

8. A network exists that can produce a mapping between inputs and outputs consistent with any underlying functional relationship. In addition, the inputs need not be real values (Lorentz [21]).

9. See the Appendix for a numerical example of how the connection weights and input values are combined to form a forecast of the output.

10. The user sets parameters for the error reduction threshold and the number of training cycles.

11. Performance satisfaction is a judgment by the user.

12. This is an intuitive representation of the Cascor training process, adapted from Fahlman and Lebiere [13]. For a mathematical presentation of the process, see Fahlman and Lebiere [13] and Lacher [19]. For further details on neural networks in general, see Minsky and Papert [23]; Rumelhart and McClelland [28]; Lippman [20]; Wasserman and Schwartz [34], [35]; Knight [18]; and Lacher [19].

13. Issuance of a going-concern opinion does not mean that the auditors *predict* failure within the coming year. Nor does the issuance of an unqualified opinion (sometimes referred to as a "clean" opinion) represent any guarantee that the firm will not fail during the coming year. A clean opinion simply means that nothing came to the auditors' attention during the course of their work that brought the going-concern assumption into question, whereas a going-concern opinion indicates the finding of facts that conflict with that assumption.

14. Screening involved checking for blank or zero fields and testing for ratio values that were unreasonably large or small as to suggest an error in the COMPUSTAT database. Also, pre-1980 data were adjusted to capitalize financial leases (Frydman et al. [14, p. 279]).

15. These 94 distressed firms were reported as ceasing operations for the following reasons: acquisition or merger (15), bankruptcy (13), liquidation (7), reverse acquisition (1), privatization (6), and other (52).

16. The practice of removing unusual and potentially misleading observations from the training data many seem improper to readers accustomed to performing statistical analysis and hypotheses testing. Readers must keep in mind, however, that the Cascor algorithm is not a statistical tool. One does not make statements of probability based on the output of the network. It may help to think of the Cascor approach (and indeed most other neural network architecture) as being more related to polynomial interpolation than to a statistical model such as linear regression. In fact, one

of the uses of neural networks is as a sophisticated approach to fitting a function to a set of ill-behaved, multidimensional data. The fitted function can then be analyzed for its properties.

17. A small number of training observations leads to overfitting. In this situation, the NN learns to recognize individual cases rather than generalizing. The experiences of previous NN categorization studies indicate that the training sample size of any given category should not be less than 30. For examples, see Odom and Sharda [25] and Utans and Moody [33].

18. See Zellner [40, ch. 10] for a review of this procedure.

19. See the Appendix concerning the role of the activation function.

20. For Cascor networks, one of the n inputs must always be a constant term (known as the "bias") permanently set to +1 (Fahlman and Lebiere [13]).

CORPORATE DISTRESS DIAGNOSIS: COMPARISONS USING LINEAR DISCRIMINANT ANALYSIS AND NEURAL NETWORKS[*]

Edward I. Altman, Giancarlo Marco, and Franco Varetto

INTRODUCTION

The Centrale dei Bilanci (CB) is an organization established in 1983 by the Banca d'Italia, the Associazione Bancaria Italiana, and over 40 leading banks and special credit institutions in Italy. In 1993, the "Sistema In-

[*] Reprinted with permission of the authors from the *Journal of Banking and Finance* 18 (1994), pp. 505–29, North Holland. We would like to thank Professor P. Coats of Florida State University for the documents she kindly supplied us, and Professor L. Saitta of the University of Turin for the numerous and profitable discussions about neural networks and the applications of artificial intelligence. We have profited by the comments of Professor Piero Terna and Professor Francesco Borazzo of the University of Turin. An earlier version of the paper was presented at the International Seminar on European Financial Statement Data Bases: Methods and Perspectives, Bressanone, Italy, September 16-17, 1993.

formativo Economico e Finanziario" (the Economic and Financial Information System of the CB, which monitors Italian businesses) included approximately 70 members.[1]

One of the "products" of the CB is a system designed to provide banks with a tool to quickly identify companies that are in financial trouble. The development of this system commenced in 1988 with the creation of an initial version based on a pair of linear discriminant functions, working parallel to one another and adapted to the industrial sector. The functions were estimated from a sample of 213 unsound (distressed) companies compared to a sample group of the same number of healthy companies; the estimation was made on the second year prior to the time that the state of distress was recognized.[2] This system correctly classified, in the year immediately prior to distress, 87.6 percent cases of healthy companies and 92.6 percent cases of unsound companies. For a description of the features of this initial system, see Varetto (1990). In 1989, the system was distributed to half of the banks belonging to CB for actual application in credit analysis at their head offices. The result of the experiment confirmed the system's soundness. In practical terms, automatic diagnosis systems can be used to preselect businesses to examine more thoroughly, quickly, and inexpensively, thereby managing the financial analyst's time efficiently. These systems can also be used to check and monitor the uniformity of the judgments made about businesses by the various branches of the bank, without replacing credit analyst personnel.

On the basis of the experiments performed and making use of an extended database, the CB created a second version of the diagnostic system that was completed and distributed to the banks belonging to Centrale's information system during 1991. In the same year, initial tests were conducted into the use of neural networks for the identification of businesses showing economic and financial distress.

The aim of this chapter is to illustrate the results achieved with neural networks, comparing them with discriminant analysis results and its applications. The next section gives a brief description of the existing version of the diagnostic system obtained, using what is now recognized as traditional statistical discriminant analysis methodology. The third section examines the essential aspects of the neural network approach. The main conclusions that can be drawn from the experiments in the use of the neural networks (NN) may be summed up as follows:

❖ Neural networks are able to approximate the *numeric* values of the scores generated by the discriminant functions even with a different set of business indicators from the set used by the discriminant functions.

❖ Neural networks are able to accurately classify groups of businesses as to their financial and operating health, with results that are very close to or, in some cases, even better than those of the discriminant analysis.

❖ The use of integrated families of simple networks and networks with a "memory" has shown considerable power and flexibility. Their performance has almost always been superior to the performance of single networks with complex architecture.

❖ The long processing time for completing the NN training phase, the need to carry out a large number of tests to identify the NN structure, and the trap of "overfitting" can considerably limit the use of NNs. The resulting weights inherent in the system are not transparent and are sensitive to structural changes.

❖ The possibility of deriving an illogical network behavior in response to different variations of the input values constitutes an important problem from a financial analysis point of view.

❖ In the comparison with neural networks, discriminant analysis proves to be a very effective tool that has the significant advantage for the financial analyst of making the underlying economic and financial model transparent and easy to interpret.

❖ We recommend that the two systems be used in tandem.

Perhaps the main conclusion of this study is that neural networks are *not* a clearly dominant mathematical technique compared to traditional statistical techniques such as discriminant analysis. The tendency for recently published articles on the use of NN approaches in financial distress classification (a number of references to these studies follows shortly) is that this "new" technique is clearly superior. We find that a more balanced conclusion is appropriate, indicating advantages and disadvantages of the "black-box" NN technique.

In addition, our study is being applied and tested within an operation that has the potential for being implemented in an actual business and financial context by concerned practitioners. Finally, our sample, consisting of over 1,000 Italian firms, is by far the largest of any distressed prediction study to date—including those using discriminant analysis or NN approaches.

CENTRALE DEL BILANCI'S SYSTEM OF DIAGNOSTIC RISK OF DISTRESS

Distressed firm risk analysis is one of the CB's permanent projects aimed at developing analytical methodologies concerning business credit. This project allows for the periodic updating of the discriminant functions to maintain or enhance their diagnostic capabilities. The integral parts of the project are the construction and maintenance of a specific database of unsound companies and the development of research on the companies' dynamics of economic decline leading to distress and bankruptcy.

The system is based on the application of the traditional linear discriminant analysis methodology on the basis of two samples of businesses representative of healthy and unsound companies.[3] A numerical score is obtained from the discriminant function that expresses the "risk profile" of the business.

Unlike the first version of the system, the new release includes special models for trading and construction companies as well as the industrial model developed earlier.[4] Work discussed in this study only refers to the existing model for industrial companies. The essential points are discussed below.

1. The diagnostic system has been designed and set up to be applied to the medium and small businesses in Italy. For this reason, companies with sales of more than 100 billion lira (i.e., 60 million U.S. dollars) have been excluded from the sample. Our tests involve data covering the period 1985–1992.

2. We have utilized a balanced sample of healthy and unsound companies rather than considering all the collected companies in the files of the CB (around 37,000 companies a year) since our sample is quite large in and of itself. This methodological line is common to other models of discriminant analysis.

3. The discriminant models had only modest ex post accuracies when using large samples of "healthy" (nonbankrupt) businesses because these companies are broken down into at least three large subsets: outstanding, normal, and vulnerable companies. And the breadth of

these categories, just as their features, varies over time. The discriminant analysis model seems limited in its ability to differentiate between unsound companies and companies that are "live" but belong to the vulnerable subset. Certainly, it is far more difficult to discriminate between two "sick" firm samples (unsound and vulnerable) than between the clearly healthy versus unsound firms. Consequently, with the increase in the size and industrial scope of the sample, rates of recognition decrease because of the increase in the variability of possible situations. The accuracy does not improve even if use is made of more sophisticated Bayesian-type statistical methodologies.

4. To tackle this problem, it was decided to take another path in the revised version of the system. The diagnostic system was broken down into two submodels working in sequence. The first model (F1) was estimated on samples of 404 unsound companies and 404 healthy companies: The former were identified from the entire population of companies collected in the files of Centrale dei Bilanci that (a) underwent some form of bankruptcy proceeding, (b) were wound up in temporary receivership, or (c) had stated they were in dire straits with regard to their payments to the banks. The sound-firm sample was obtained from the "live" company file, excluding "vulnerable" businesses identified through the use of tests on a restricted number of business ratios over the span of a few years. These ratios are not part of those included in the discriminant functions. The sample of businesses "running normally" was obtained by matching with similar distressed companies by size (in terms of net assets), industry, and location. The first model consisted of a nine-ratio linear function (F1) that distinguished between healthy businesses and unsound or vulnerable businesses (Figure 9.1).

5. The second phase of the model (F2) comes into play after F1 has diagnosed the business to be unsound. The second discriminant function was estimated from two balanced samples, again each of 404 businesses, of unsound (the same ones used for the F1 estimation) and vulnerable companies. The latter were extracted from among the live sample but found to be diagnostically unsound by F1. Both functions have been estimated based on ratio values from the annual report of the third year prior to the distress date.

6. All variables of the F1 and F2 models that contained coefficients with counterintuitive signs were eliminated (even if they were statistically

---

Figure 9.1

Diagnostic System Flow

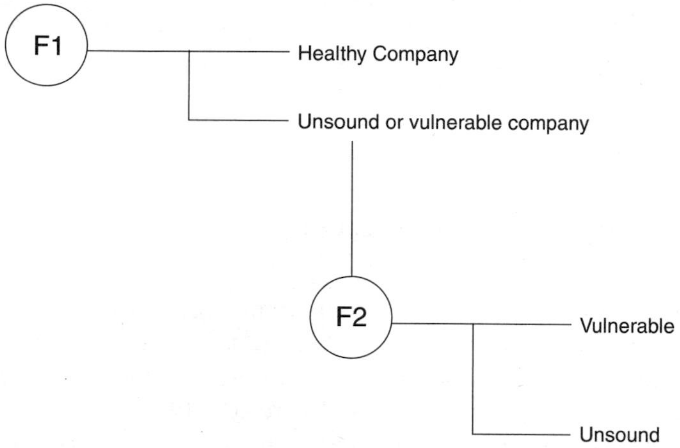

Note: This chart indicates the basic progression of discriminant analysis models performed within the corporate monitoring system at the Centrale dei Bilanci, Torino, Italy.

---

significant). Variables with unstable behavior were eliminated and only those that increased the capacity to classify the unsound companies as the time prior to distress approached and also maintained (or increased) the capacity to classify healthy businesses were retained.

7. Estimations were made using logit as well as discriminant analysis but no significant progress was made on ex post classification. Therefore, we retained the discriminant functions.

8. The discriminatory capacity of the principal function (F1), on which most of the experiments with neural networks are compared, is shown in Table 9.1.

The percentage of correct ex post classification improves as distress approaches; for the unsound companies it goes from 86.4 percent in T-3 (estimation period) to 96.5 percent in period T-1. The accuracy of the classification was checked with a holdout sample of 150 unsound businesses and 150 healthy ones, obtaining results that were similar to the estimation sample (90 percent in T-3 and 95 percent in period T-1).

Table 9.1

Rate of Successful Recognition (F1 Discriminant Function)

Estimation Sample (404 Companies in Each Group)		Healthy Firms	Unsound Firms
Estimation period	T-3	90.3%	86.4%
Control period	T-1	92.8	96.5
Holdout sample (150 companies in each group)	T-1	90.3	95.1

Table 9.2

Rate of Successful Recognition (F2 Discriminant Function)

Estimation Sample (404 Companies)		Vulnerable Firms	Unsound Firms
Estimation period	T-3	99.0%	60.1%
Control period	T-1	97.8	82.7
Holdout sample (150 companies)	T-1	96.8	81.0

The second function, as expected, has a lower discriminant capacity, especially for the unsound firms. Table 9.2 lists the F2 function results showing 82.7 percent correct classification of the unsound firms in the control period (T-1) and 81.0 percent in the holdout sample for that group (versus about 95 percent in the F1 function).

To make it easier to interpret the results, the scores of the functions are represented on graphs where the business under examination is positioned on the two different reference systems: Figure 9.2a is an example of an unsound business monitored over the last five years of its life (1985-1989). From F1, the firm is identified as a distressed company in the fifth year prior to failure. At this stage, the system does not yet distinguish if the unsound business is simply vulnerable (with greater or lesser degree of vulnerability) or if it belongs to the set of unsound companies. Figure 9.2b shows the diagnosis of the same firm made by F2 and places the business in the uncertain area between vulnerability and risk of bankruptcy in the first two years of the series and then signals a rapid decline into

Figure 9.2

Examples of an Unsound Company

a. Function 1

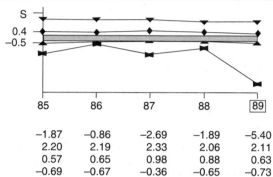

SOLIDITA' ECONOMICO-FINANZIARIA A BREVE TERMINE

	85	86	87	88	89
⋈ Company	−1.87	−0.86	−2.69	−1.89	−5.40
▼ Third	2.20	2.19	2.33	2.06	2.11
◆ Median	0.57	0.65	0.98	0.88	0.63
▲ First Quartile	−0.69	−0.67	−0.36	−0.65	−0.73

b. Function 2

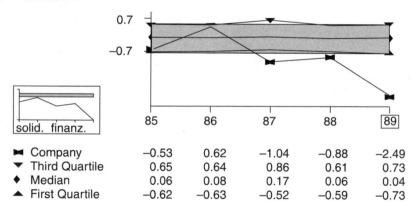

	85	86	87	88	89
⋈ Company	−0.53	0.62	−1.04	−0.88	−2.49
▼ Third Quartile	0.65	0.64	0.86	0.61	0.73
◆ Median	0.06	0.08	0.17	0.06	0.04
▲ First Quartile	−0.62	−0.63	−0.52	−0.59	−0.73

the higher-risk bankruptcy zone. As can be seen, the diagnosis of the company is carried out on the basis of a joint analysis of the two functions, with additional reference points supplied by quartile comparisons with the entire CB database of comparable companies.

The classificatory space described by F1 has been divided into five zones on the basis of the distribution of healthy, vulnerable, and unsound companies. These include (a1) high security, (b1) security, (c1) uncertainty between security and vulnerability, (d1) vulnerability, and (e1) intense vulnerability. Function F2 is calculated as soon as F1's score falls into one of the zones (c1), (d1) or (e1): F2 has been split into zones of (a2) high vulnerability; (b2) vulnerability; (c2) uncertainty between vulnerability and risk; (d2) risk; and (e2) high risk of bankruptcy.

Score values separating the different zones constitute the ordinates of the fixed classification system shown on the graphs.[5]

NEURAL NETWORKS

For many years, neural network models have been analyzed both by academics and practitioners, including those efforts outside the circle of artificial intelligence experts.[6] It is too early to say whether the use of experimental NN is simply a fad or if it will result in something more permanent. Some aspects of the neural networks, however, do seem promising in the area of business and finance applications.[7]

The application of the NN approach to company distress prediction, although relatively new, has seen a number of researchers attempt to improve upon the traditional discriminant analysis technique. An interesting procedure by Coats and Fant (1993) used a limited number of financial ratios to duplicate the going-concern determination by accounting auditors. They utilize the cascade-correlation NN approach (Fahlman and Lebiere 1992) to duplicate the auditor-expert conclusion on a sample of 94 manufacturing and nonmanufacturing failed firms and conclude that it clearly dominates the LDA method in this application.[8] In addition, studies by Karels and Prakash (1987), Odom and Sharda (1990), Ragupathi et al. (1991), and Rahimian et al. (1992) have all assessed NN for bankruptcy prediction. Interestingly, at least three of the above studies utilized the same five financial variables found in Altman's (1968) study.

This paper will explore the basic theory of neural networks, but we do not plan to discuss in detail the reasons that inspired the connectionist approach. Connectionist processing models (neural networks) consist of a potentially large number of elementary processing units; every unit is interconnected with other units and each is able to perform relatively simple calculations. The network's processing result derives from their collective behavior rather than from the specific behavior of a single unit. The links are not rigid but can be modified through learning processes

Figure 9.3

General Scheme of Neural Unit

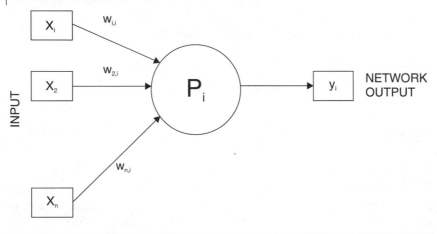

generated by the network's interaction with the outside world or with a set of symbolic signals.

The individual units and the connections linking them can be shown as in Figure 9.3: Each unit (i) receives an input (X_i) from the outside, or from other neurons with which it is linked, with an intensity (weight) equal to W_{ji}. The overall input that the ith neuron receives equals an assumed potential (P_i) equal to:

$$P_i = \sum_j nW_{ji} * X_i - S_i$$

where S_i represents an excitation threshold value that limits the neuron's degree of response to the stimuli received; for example, the neurons give a response signal in the "jump-type" response function only if the total input arriving from outside and/or other neurons is greater than S_i. It is possible to eliminate the S_i threshold and replace it with a dummy input (k) of a value equal to 1 ($X_k = 1$) and by setting $W_{ki} = -S_i$, obtaining the general expression:

$$P_i = \sum_j W_{ji}X_j, \text{ where } k \text{ is included in } X_j$$

The neuron's response (Y_i) depends on the transfer of potential (P_i) to the output function. One of the most widely used functions in the literature and in our tests is the logistic function, according to which

$$Y_i = \frac{1}{1 + e^{-P_i}}$$

Generally, the response function determines values between a minimum and a maximum; in our case Y_i is included between 0 and 1. Output (Y_i) of the neuron can be either a total response value of the network (if it is the final output value) or an input for further neuron units. The network, made up of many elementary units of the ith type, can have different degrees of complexity. The simpler networks consist of a single neuron layer (in extreme cases by a single neuron), each of which is in direct contact with the outside stimuli i and generates output from the network directly. A slightly more complicated network has two layers: an intermediate, hidden layer that receives stimuli from outside the network, and an output layer that generates the network's responses. Networks can be constructed with circuits for feedback between neurons from one layer to those of previous levels, just like self-connecting links.

Considerable limitations of a single-layer network have been shown. Networks with one layer, in addition to the input layer, can only perform linear separations of the input space. Two layer networks can generate convex geometrical shapes, while networks with at least three layers enable the input space to be separated into shapes of any configuration. (The complexity of the regions is determined by the number of neurons.) There are no general rules to establish the optimal degree of network complexity.

The crucial aspect of neural networks lies in the fact that the weightings of the connections are not fixed but can be modified on the basis of a learning procedure derived from the comparison of the network responses with those required by actual results. The network, in other words, behaves as an adaptive dynamic system that reacts to response differences.

The network is given a set of inputs generating a response that is compared with the response required; the weightings are not changed if the response obtained corresponds with the response required. If the difference exceeds a certain tolerance level, revisions are introduced into the weightings, and learning starts again; then a new case is input. The analysis of all the cases supplied constitutes the maximum extension learning cycle. After the interaction of a large number of cycles, the error is reduced to acceptable levels and, once the holdout set accuracy has been exceeded, the learning ends and the weightings are locked. The network has achieved a stable equilibrium configuration that represents "its capacity to solve a problem."

However, the learning mechanism involves a number of problems:

❖ The learning stage can be very long (slow learning).

❖ The system might not achieve a stable absolute minimum configuration (optimal error reduction) but might lock on local minimums without being able to move to the optimum.

❖ The system might give rise to oscillating behavior in the learning phase—when the minimum point is reached and then exceeded. Hence, it then returns to the previous point.

❖ When the actual situation is significantly different, or changes, compared to the situation implicit in the training examples, it is then necessary to repeat the learning phase. The same applies when the set of examples is not representative of the reality of the problem or concept to be learned.

❖ The analysis of the weightings is complex and difficult to interpret. There is, in other words, little network transparency as far as the examination of the system's logic is concerned. This makes it difficult to identify the causes of the errors or defective responses.

The algorithm determining the network's learning is of fundamental importance for the final performance of the network itself.[9]

Neural networks do not require the prespecification of a functional form nor the adoption of restrictive assumptions about the characteristics of statistical distributions of the variables and errors of the model. Moreover, by their nature, NN make it possible to work with imprecise variables and with changes of the models over time, and are thus able to adapt gradually to the appearance of new cases representing changes in the situation. As noted earlier, the price to be paid for using networks of neurons is their lack of transparency in the use of the variables within the network connections. While one is able to identify the explanatory importance of each variable with the usual estimation techniques, signs of influence on the endogenous variables and the degree of their mutual correlation with each neuron remains unclear.

We know many things about how companies can fall into economic distress, about crisis processes, and company decline, but we do not have a complete theory. One of the ways of tackling this problem in operative terms is to use company classification techniques that use the tools that statistical methodology supplies. Multiple discriminant analysis is one of the tools most often used and was described earlier in our F1 and F2 functions.

Results obtained appear very promising. Linear discriminant analysis can be considered equivalent to a network made up of a single neuron that receives signals from the set of indicators and generates an output with a linear transfer function without transformation, $Y_i = P_i$. To exploit the advantages offered by the network of neurons, we have used a three-layer network based on a combination of simple (two-layer) elementary networks in a "cascade" fashion. Figure 9.4 illustrates the differences between discriminant analysis and a multilayer neural network system.

The experimental program is subdivided into four parts:

Part 1: Check the capacity of a neural network to reproduce the numeric values of the scores obtained using linear discriminant analysis, receiving, as input, the signals of ratios *different* from those employed in discriminant analysis. Note that in this first experiment, the multilayer network has been forced to behave linearly, not exploiting its wealth of descriptive potential. Nonetheless, within this constraint, we can verify the network's capacity to approximate the discriminant analysis' linear functions using a different set of ratios.

Part 2: Check the capacity of the neural network to separate the samples between bankrupt and healthy companies. The network's output unit is not the value of a score as in the previous section but simply the binary values 0 (=healthy) and 1 (=unsound). The network's training stage was carried out in period T-3, while the test of its correct recognition was done in either period T-1 of the training sample or on an independent sample.

Part 3: This section considers the change in company performance over time. One of the problems involved in identifying distressed companies is making the classificatory functions sensitive to the passing of time and the changes of the companies' business patterns. See the work of Theodossiou (1993) for an analysis of the time series properties of distressed prediction. An attempt was made to capture these aspects by constructing complex networks divided into three segments.

Figure 9.4

Discriminant Analysis and Multilayer Neural Network (NN)

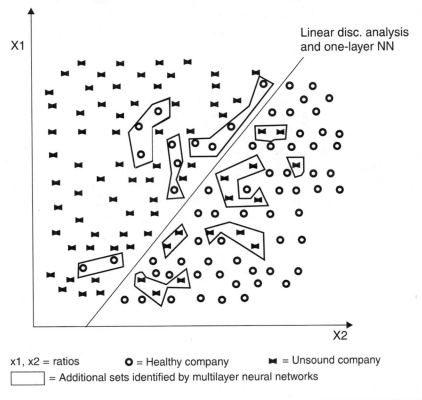

x1, x2 = ratios   O = Healthy company   ◄ = Unsound company
☐ = Additional sets identified by multilayer neural networks

The output of the first subnetwork summarizes the conclusions about the economic and financial profile observed in period T-3; these are linked to the conclusions relating to period T-2. If, during this period, the profile follows a trend that is consistent (inconsistent) with the trend in the prior period, the conclusions come out reinforced (weakened). The same applies to the pattern of period T-1. An alternative way of tackling the problem of time pattern analysis lies in using networks with "memories"; the simplest network of this type includes among the input data the change in value of the variables. Figure 9.5 illustrates an example of such a network "with memory."

Figure 9.5

Networks with Memory of Input

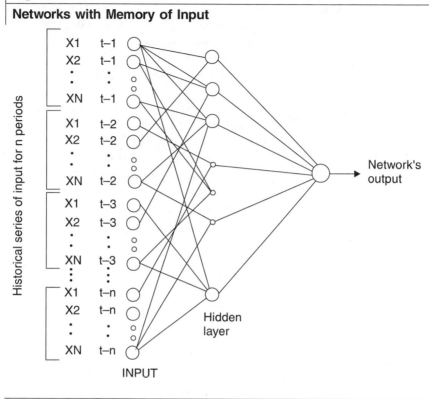

From an economic-logic point of view, it is as if there has been an attempt to reproduce the reasoning of the financial analyst when he or she examines a historical series of business data. The analyst forms an opinion on the state of business by observing how it has evolved over the entire time span available.

Part 4: The aim of this section is to check the capacity of networks to separate the three categories of companies: healthy, vulnerable, and unsound. The networks used for this section have an output level comprising two output neurons: The first distinguishes the healthy businesses from the unsound ones, while the second separates the unsound businesses from the vulnerable and unsound businesses. The two neurons have the same role as the two functions F1 and F2.

Two types of experiment were carried out for this purpose: In the first case, network training was carried out over period T-3, while the check of the capacity for generalization was conducted on period T-1 and on an independent sample. In the second case, networks with memories were used over the whole three-year monitoring period, while the control sample was limited to healthy and vulnerable companies extracted from the continuing company database.

All the experiments were carried out on the same samples used to fine-tune the discriminant functions. An initial sample involved 1,212 businesses: 404 each of healthy, unsound, and vulnerable firms. A second independent sample of 453 companies was used, 151 of each type, with data limited to the last year prior to bankruptcy. A final sample, independent of the other two, was analyzed comprising 900 healthy and 900 vulnerable companies for three years of historical series. These were taken from the files of live companies.

RESULTS

Healthy versus Unsound Firms

The first tests were conducted to estimate the accuracy of the numeric values of the linear discriminant function. We limited the analysis to approximating the function that separates the healthy from unsound companies (F1) for period T-3. If these approximations can be obtained with a smaller set of indicators (input signals) than what was used for the estimation of the discriminant function, it will be a direct check of the neural network's capacity for adaptation and simplification. The experiments were conducted using networks of varying complexity in terms of the number of input indicators, the number of layers, and the number of connections.

The best results were obtained with a three-layer network: one initial hidden layer of 10 neurons, a second hidden layer with 4 neurons, and an output layer consisting of a single neuron. The input comprised 10 financial ratios: 4 relative to the firms' financial structure and indebtedness, 2 to liquidity, and 4 representative of company profitability and internal financing.

The network neurons are totally interconnected. This means that each neuron on a layer is connected to all the others on the next level, including the input signals, which are connected to all of the neurons on the first layer. Training was interrupted after 1,000 learning cycles, each of which examined 808 companies, adjusting the weighting after each cycle. The resulting profile was extremely close to the desired level.

Another measure of the network results is summarized in Table 9.3. This shows the distribution of the categorization of company creditworthiness by score intervals. The classification differences based on the scores and the actual categories seem small and concentrated mainly toward positive values near one (best credits).

Results obtained after 1,000 learning cycles are quite encouraging and lead one to believe that if the learning phase lasted longer the error could be reduced still further. It should be noted that the network built to replicate the discriminant function is comprised of completely different indicators from those included in the functions. The latter's selection required a significant number of worker-hours. In the case of the neural network, machine-hours were used more, while the selection of indicators, albeit careful and well thought out, required a tiny fraction of the total time. This is a clear indication of the network's capacity for adaptation.

Multilayer Networks

Networks with varying degrees of complexity were trained using ratios from period T-3 followed by testing in period T-1 from the same sample and also an independent sample. The most satisfactory results were ob-

Table 9.3

Distribution of Companies by Score Intervals

	Score Required	Score Calculated
High security	15.2	10.2
Security	34.5	37.2
Uncertainty	11.3	12.0
Vulnerability	23.8	25.4
High level of vulnerability	15.2	15.2
Total	100.0%	100.0%

tained with a three-layer network, comprising 15 neurons in the first hidden layer, 6 neurons in the second hidden layer, and 1 neuron in the output layer. The full interconnected network is fed with the numeric values of 15 business ratios; these are a broader set than the one in the 10-ratio network described in the previous section. Not having observed substantial benefits with using a random selection of cases, we used a sequential ordering of the observations.

Although the network training used slightly greater than 2,000 cycles, the analysis of the error sequence indicated a typical oscillating phenomenon.[10] At the end of the training period, the network was able to recognize correctly 97.7 percent of healthy and 97.0 percent of unsound companies. All the other networks that used a lower degree of complexity, even if trained with a higher number of cycles, did not achieve the same recognition capability as obtained using the 15, 4, 1 network.[11] This compares favorably with the recognition rates obtained by the linear discriminant function F1 in period T-3: 90.3 percent of healthy companies and 86.4 percent of unsound ones.

The network's identification capability is clearly greater than the discriminant function's although it is obtained with a higher number of indicators: 15 as opposed to 9. This aspect is important since the network is more complicated and uses a large number of learning cycles. The results of the learning, however, behave erratically. There are great and rapid improvements in the capacity to identify the two groups with the first cycles; nevertheless, as the cycle procedure continues, the convergence becomes slower, with frequent oscillations and jumps backward and with deterioration in the recognition rates that are sometimes significant. As can be seen, the network had already achieved recognition levels that were not far off the final results, especially in the healthy group, in the earlier cycles. The unsound firm errors were reduced considerably as the number of cycles increased until the last 560 cycles, when the classification accuracy became erratic.

This network, trained in period T-3, showed a lower recognition capacity than the one in the training period using period T-1; period T-1's identification error was 10.6 percent for healthy businesses and 5.2 percent for unsound firms. Compare these rates of error with those obtained with the discriminant functions: 7.2 percent for healthy and 3.5 percent for unsound companies (Table 9.1).

This neural network shows a *lower* capacity for generalization than the traditional discriminant function's. This conclusion is reinforced by the results obtained on the independent samples of 302 companies for period T-1: rates of error are 15.9 percent for the healthy and 9.5 percent for the unsound companies as opposed to the 9.7 percent and 4.9 percent, respectively, obtained with the discriminant functions.[12]

The simpler network's results are more modest than the ones obtained from traditional discriminant analysis but show a greater capacity for generalization than the more complex networks. This confirms what others have shown: The network judged to be most effective at the end of the learning cycle might not be as suitable with other sets of independent cases. The network is the victim of a phenomenon know as "overfitting." We encountered a similar phenomenon when we observed the holdout sample accuracy of quadratic discriminant functions versus the less complex linear function (see Altman et al. 1977).

Multilayer Networks with Discriminant Function Ratios

The results obtained in the previous section use networks fed with ratios different from the ones used in discriminant functions. The reason for this choice is the need to estimate the classification capacity of the networks using a standard information base (ratios) such as are normally available in financial analysis reports published by the CB. In a related test, 9 of the 11 F1 discriminant function's indicators are utilized with networks of differing complexity. The intention was to check the network's capacity to reproduce the knowledge built into the discriminant functions and convert it into knowledge distributed over the neural connections.

The best result was obtained with a 9, 5, 1 network after 4,030 learning cycles with a 0.75 learning rate and 0.30 momentum.[13] Table 9.4 shows

Table 9.4

Comparison of Recognition Rates: NN vs. LDA

Sample size = 404 in each group		Neural Network		Linear Discriminant Function (F1)	
		Healthy	Unsound	Healthy	Unsound
Estimation period	T-3	89.4%	86.2%	90.3%	86.4%
Control period	T-1	91.8	95.3	92.8	96.5

the rates of recognition of businesses in the T-3 period (network estimation) and period T-1 (control period). The results are not dissimilar, although slightly lower, from those obtained using the discriminant function. It is not, however, certain that the formalization of the knowledge built into the network is totally equivalent to the knowledge of the linear function since companies that the network recognized incorrectly were, in part, different from those incorrectly recognized by the discriminant function. Moreover, while the discriminant function always behaves in the same way when the values of the exogenous variables vary, with the use of the network we have seen behavior that is not always consistent when the input changes. We will postpone this discussion until the next section, where it can be treated more thoroughly.

Simple Network Connections

Neural networks can have difficulty when tackling particularly complex problems. In our case, the complexity derives from the nature of the problem and from the wide range of observations. While the wealth of data makes it possible to construct a model that is general and robust, it also tends to make the training of the network more difficult. Complex networks with numerous inputs and neurons are perhaps better able to classify a more heterogeneous sample of firms but have the disadvantage of sometimes making the time (and expense) required for training prohibitive. Moreover, these networks tend to adopt oscillating or nonconvergent behavior as well as often being victims of the overfitting trap.

One methodology for tackling these problems might be breaking down the total network into simpler networks connected to each other. We carried out experiments along these lines, starting with the generation of elementary networks, which were then connected to each other in a second-level network. Every elementary network (e.g., leverage) is fed with a number of ratios that are representative of that characteristic.

The second-level network coordinates the results of the eight elementary networks in order to generate the system's final response. That is, it is trained to combine the conclusions reached by the elementary networks. This is equivalent to a multivariate discriminant or logit analysis with the same potential benefits over a univariate structure.

The results obtained are shown in Table 9.5. As expected, the classification accuracy of the elementary networks differs greatly from network to network and generally is not very high. Furthermore, it does not always increase when passing from the estimation period (T-3) to the control period (T-1). The second-level network, however, which generates the system's overall responses, performs very well, with correct classification of healthy companies of 98.3 percent and unsound companies of 92.5 percent in the estimation period (T-3). This result is considerably better than that achieved through discriminant analysis (Table 9.1). In addition, the system of networks applied to the control period (T-1) gives outstanding results in this case, too, with 92.8 percent of healthy companies and 94.5 percent of unsound companies classified correctly.

On the whole, the test of the simple network system's capacity for generalization on the independent sample of 302 companies in period T-1 is also good. In the face of significant reduction in first-level elementary rates of identification, second-level networks generate correct classification rates of 93.6 percent for the healthy companies and 89.1 percent for unsound companies. Compared with results obtained with discriminant functions, there is a significant drop in the number of unsound companies identified correctly (– 6 percent) but not enough to cancel out the effectiveness of the system.

These results are encouraging for the use of neural networks. Note that the system's classification was obtained with a small effort on the part of the analyst and by using annual report ratios that are not particularly complex.

Analysis of Simple Network Systems—Some Concerns

As mentioned earlier, a problem that arises in the use of neural networks concerns the low level of intelligibility of the knowledge base spread over the network and built into the weighting of the connections. We carried out an analysis of elementary and second-level networks to try to better understand how they work. Distributed knowledge mapping (see Hinton et al. 1986) implicit in the weighting values of the network can be studied from various points of view, including the identification of the significance assumed by the various neurons and the analysis of the network's behavior when input conditions change.

The significance of the neurons can be identified either by examining the weightings matrix, in the simplest cases, or by studying the role that individual neurons play in determining the output.[14] By modifying the

Table 9.5

Connection of Simple Neural Networks with One Output

	Number of Learning Cycles	Correct Classification (%)					
		Sample of 808 Companies				Holdout Sample of 302 Companies, Period T-1	
		Period T-3 Estimated		Period T-1 (Control)			
Variable Types Analyzed		Healthy	Unsound	Healthy	Unsound	Healthy	Unsound
Specialized elementary NN							
1) Leverage; assets/liabilities	4,640	76.98%	82.21%	73.76%	91.04%	76.80%	90.48%
2) Ability to bear debt	3,800	74.50	79.20	69.06	92.04	35.20	97.28
3) Liquidity	4,950	69.31	84.96	71.29	90.80	36.00	97.96
4) Profitability, internal finance	4,770	87.87	85.71	84.90	92.29	56.80	96.60
5) Profit accumulation	4,050	81.44	75.94	88.61	71.14	59.20	85.03
6) Ability to bear cost of debt	5,000	75.25	87.97	76.73	95.77	67.20	99.32
7) General efficiency	1,260	62.38	60.40	65.10	69.65	63.20	57.82
8) Trade indebtedness	900	59.90	69.92	60.15	79.60	73.60	66.67
Second-Level NN	2,850	98.27	92.48	92.82	94.53	93.60	89.12

NN trained at T-3 with learning rate = 0.75 and momentum = 0.25. The revision of the weight is done for each company; in each cycle there are 808 revisions.

initial weightings and repeating the learning process, the weightings matrix is modified, which might also change the role of the various neurons.

Generally speaking, the behavior of a network can be studied on the basis of the derivatives (or elasticities) of the output compared with the individual inputs. Where more than one input is changed at the same time, it is possible to refer to the total differential of the output compared with the inputs.

From a mathematical point of view, the neural network is a nonlinear system. Its input/output derivatives depend on the input value configuration vector. Therefore, the network's capacity to react to input changes is not always the same but strictly depends on the starting position. This factor makes the identification of the individual contributions of the inputs to the formation of the output complex and uncertain.

Even in its simplicity, the second-level network shows peculiar behavior patterns. We examined the values of the partial derivatives between the output and the individual inputs in the case of different starting configurations. The calculation of the partial derivatives showed significant dependence on the base conditions, with sudden changes of sign. This feature of the networks is particularly awkward for the financial analyst because the behavior of the network may be unpredictable and contrary to business logic. For example, for a business to be considered unsound by the network, it only needs to have a very modest general efficiency, a relatively high leverage, and an uncertain ability to bear financial indebtedness while having outstanding ratings in the other inputs. If the level of liquidity is worsened under this profile, the network shows an improvement in the output and, under some conditions, the company goes from being unsound to healthy, thus altering the initial conclusions! Such behavior does not occur if the profitability is worsened, but it reappears in the case of increased commercial indebtedness.

Interconnection of Simple Networks with Memories

The next experiment made use of the logic of networks with memories on the inputs (see Figure 9.5 for a general description of such a structure). The inputs of this type of network include the entire three-year historical series of the indicators used. The network is trained to consider all the data available about the company at the same time. This is like a financial analyst examining the historical time series of financial statements.

The correct recognition rates of healthy and unsound companies is high, even in several elementary networks, rising to over 99 percent in the second-level network. The overall accuracy of the interconnected system of elementary networks with memories commits errors of four healthy companies (out of 404) and one unsound company (out of 404).[15]

We did analyze the overall functioning of the system on simple, interconnected networks with memories. We found, in the second-level network, the same nonacceptable behavioral problems already identified above, with a frequent inversion of the output value when the inputs are uniformly modified either individually or in limited subsets.

Multigroup Analysis

The last set of experiments is aimed at the generation of a two-output network for the simultaneous, not sequential, separation of healthy, vulnerable, and unsound companies. This test was very severe because of the difficulty in identifying in a single solution the characteristics separating the three groups of businesses. The best results were achieved with a network using families of simple NNs with memory consisting of three layers: one hidden layer with 15 neurons, a second hidden layer with 12 neurons, and 1 output layer with 2 neurons. This is somewhat analogous to the three-group simultaneous distress S&L analysis of Altman (1977). Since these results are still experimental and not germane to our overall conclusions, we refer the reader to a lengthier working paper, Varetto and Marco (1993).

CONCLUSION

In light of the experiments carried out, neural networks are a very interesting tool and have great potential capacities that undoubtedly make them attractive for application to the field of business classification. The networks assessed on our samples have shown significant capacities for recognizing the health of companies, with results that are, in many cases, near or superior to the results obtained through discriminant analysis. The results of the two-output networks trained to simultaneously recognize the three types of company performance—healthy, vulnerable, and unsound—also proved very interesting. Nonetheless, taking into account the results obtained in the control periods and in the holdout samples, discriminant analysis was deemed better, on the whole, than the networks trained in our experiments.

The greatest problem concerns the existence of nonacceptable types of behavior in the network. These are intrinsic to the nonlinear nature of the mathematical model underlying the network, combining a large number of variables several times over in a complex fashion. These behavior patterns are characteristic of networks of any complexity that have at least two inputs.

The extent and frequency of illogical types of behavior (in the judgment of the financial analyst) grow with the increase in the complexity of the network architecture. Only extremely simple networks limit the probability of meeting these unacceptable results. The construction of ultrasimplified networks cannot be a solution, however, because the problem is only delayed. It does in fact crop up again as a result of the need to coordinate simple networks with others of higher level.

The problem of understanding these types of behavior and how to remedy them is not easy to solve. As well as using real examples, it would be possible, for example, to train the network with artificial cases constructed to represent other possible combinations. Given the high number of artificial cases required, the network's capacity for analyzing real cases could be totally distorted if errors are committed at this stage.

On the whole, linear discriminant analysis compares rather well with neural networks. The fine-tuning of the discriminant function does take longer, but the greater estimation speed makes it possible to carry out careful tuning at relatively low cost. Furthermore, the linear form, albeit with the limitations of its ability to perform well, ensures consistent behavior for any type of variable. This makes it possible to interpret the model's operating logic on the basis of the coefficients.

In the neural network, it is not possible to ascertain whether a particular variable comes into the interpretative model with the wrong sign and whether or not to eliminate or replace it, as can be accomplished with traditional econometric and statistical tools. With discriminant analysis, it is possible to learn what the most important variables are for explaining the differences between the companies in the sample. In the network fine-tuning process, the length of the training process, the rate of mean-error decline, and the results on the recognition rates are the keys for estimating the soundness of the variables, ex post.

Our conclusions on the use of neural networks are not straightforward, and they recognize the undoubted advantages such networks have. A path we intend to adopt in the future is to integrate networks and discriminant functions, applying the former to less clear and more complex problems of classification in which the flexibility of networks and their capacity for structuring into simple, integrated families could prove very useful. The key determinant as to whether neural networks, in conjunction or not with traditional classification procedures, will be integrated into practitioner decisions is the accuracy, logic, and understandability of the process and its components. It must be emphasized again, however, that we have found illogical behavior patterns in all of the many NN systems tried in our research. These results have not been emphasized enough in previous applications of NN systems to business-related problems.

Neural networks have shown enough promising features to provide an incentive for more thorough and creative testing. Analysts' fascination with artificial intelligence models will, no doubt, motivate continued firm-related investigations.

REFERENCES

Altman, E. 1968. "Financial Ratios, Discriminant Analysis and the Prediction of Corporate Bankruptcy." *Journal of Finance* (Sept.), pp. 589–609.

Altman, E. 1993. *Corporate Financial Distress and Bankruptcy,* 2nd ed. New York: John Wiley and Sons.

Altman, E. and T. McGough. 1974. "Evaluation of a Company as a Going Concern." *Journal of Accountancy* (Dec.), pp. 50–57.

Altman, E., R. Haldeman, and P. Narayanan. 1977. "ZETA Analysis, a New Model to Identify Bankruptcy Risk of Corporations." *Journal of Banking and Finance* 1, pp. 29–54.

Altman, E. 1977. "Predicting Performance in the S&L Industry." *Journal of Monetary Economics* (Oct.).

Bell, T., G. Ribar, and J. Verchio. 1990. "Neural Networks versus Logistic Regression in Predicting Bank Failures." in: P. Srivastava, ed., Auditing Symposium X. University of Kansas.

Cadden, D. 1991. "Neural Networks and the Mathematics of Chaos - an Investigation of the Methodologies as Accurate Predictors of Corporate Bankruptcy." *IEEE.*

Cammarata, S. 1990. "Reti Neuronali" *Etas Kompass.*

Chung, H. and K.Y. Tam. 1993. "A Comparative Analysis of Inductive Learning Algorithms. *Intelligence Systems in Accounting, Finance and Management.*

Coakley, J. and C. Brown. 1993. "Artificial Neural Networks Applied to Ratio Analysis in the Analytical Review Process." *Intelligent System in Accounts, Finance and Management* (Jan.).

Coats, P. and L. Fant. 1993. "Recognizing Financial Distress Patterns Using a Neural Network Tool." *Financial Management* (Nov.), pp. 142–55.

Coleman, G., T. Graettinger, and W. Lawrence. 1992. "Neural Networks for Bankruptcy Prediction: The Power to Solve Financial Problems." *AI Review.* July/August 1991, pp. 48–50. (See Chapter 12 of this book.)

Dutta, S., and S. Shekhar. 1992. "Generalization with Neural Networks: An Application to the Financial Domain." Working Paper 92/30. INSEAD, Fontainebleau, France.

Fahlman, S. and C. Lebiere. 1992. "The Cascade-Correlation Learning Architecture Technical Report: CMU-90-100." Carnegie Mellon University. (Feb.).

Freeman, J. and D. Skapura. 1991. *Neural networks.* Reading, MA: Addison Wesley.

Hertz, J., A. Krogh, and R. Palmer. 1991. *Introduction to the Theory of Neural Computing.* Reading, MA: Addison Wesley.

Hinton, G., J. McClelland, and D. Rumelhart. 1986. "Distributed Representations." in D. Rumelhart and J. McClelland, *Parallel Distributed Processing: Exploration in Cognition.* Cambridge, MA: MIT Press.

Karels, G.V. and A. Prakash. 1987. "Multivariate Normality and Forecasting of Business Bankruptcy." *Journal of Business, Finance and Accounting* (Winter), pp. 573–93.

Kryzanowski, L., M. Galler, and D. Wright. 1989. "Using Artificial Neural Networks to Pick Stocks." *Financial Analysts Journal* (July/Aug.), pp. 21–27.

Kryzanowski, L. and M. Galler. 1994. "Analysis of Small Business Financial Statements Using Neural Nets." *Journal of Accounting, Auditing and Finance.* Forthcoming.

Liang, T., J. Chandler, I. Han, and J. Roan. 1992. "An Empirical Investigation of Some Data Effects on the Classification Accuracy of Probit, ID3 and Neural Networks." in *Cont. Acc. Res.,* Fall.

Odom, M. and R. Sharda. 1990. "A Neural Network Model for Bankruptcy Prediction." Proceedings of the IEEE International Conference on Neural Networks. San Diego, CA. pp. 163–68.

Pau, L. and C. Gianotti. 1990. *Economic and Financial Knowledge-Based Processing.* Berlin: Springer.

Raghupathi, W., L. Schleade, and B. Raju. 1991. "A Neural Network Approach to Bankruptcy Prediction." Proceedings of the IEEE 24th International Conference on System Sciences. Hawaii. (See Chapter 10 of this book.)

Rahimian, E., S. Singh, T. Thammachofe, and R. Virmani. 1992. "Bankruptcy Prediction by Neural Network." (See Chapter 11 of this book.)

Rumelhart, D. and J. McClelland. 1986. *Parallel Distributed Processing: Exploration in the Cognition.* Cambridge, MA: MIT Press.

Rumelhart, D., G. Hinton, and R. Williams. 1986. "Learning Internal Representations by Error Propagation, in Parallel Distributed Processing." Cambridge, MA: MIT Press, pp. 318–62.

Swales, G. and Y. Yoon. 1992. "Applying Artificial Networks to Investment Analysis." *Financial Analysts Journal* (Sept./Oct.).

Theodossiou, P. 1993. "Predicting Shifts in the Mean of a Multivariate Time Series Process: An Application in Predicting Business Failures." *Journal of the American Statistical Association* 88, no. 422, pp. 441–49.

Trippi, R. and D. de Sieno. 1992. "Trading Equity Index Futures with a Neural Network." *Journal of Portfolio Management* (Fall).

Varetto, F. and G. Marco. 1993. "Diagnosi delle Insolvenze e Reti Neurali: esperimenti e Confronti con l'Analisi Discriminante Lineare." *W.P. Centrale dei Bilanci,* Sept. 1993, and forthcoming *Economia Aziendale.*

Varetto, F. 1990. Il Sistema di Diagnosi dei Rischi di Insolvenza della Centrale dei Bilanci, Bancaria ed. Rome.

Wong, F., P. Wang, T. Goh, and B. Quek. 1992. *Fuzzy Neural Systems for Stock Selection." Financial Analysts Journal* (Jan./Feb.).

ENDNOTES

1. In addition to the management of databases with information on the financial statements of over 37,000 companies collected every year, the Centrale dei Bilanci is actively engaged in several lines of operation: the development of financial analysis methodology, production of user software, management education, and industrial economic research.

2. At the time that the distressed state is recognized, there is a break in the historical series of the annual reports in the data base. For companies subject to the law governing bankruptcy and failure, a period of time passes between the suspension of the availability of balance sheets and the moment of the final declaration of bankruptcy or composition.

3. For a description of the methodological aspects of discriminant analysis and the main models available in different countries, see Altman (1993).

4. The trading and building sector models are still being tested and will be reported on in a subsequent publication.

5. The coefficients of all the functions are protected by secrecy for the purpose of safeguarding the investments of the *CB's* owners made in research, testing, and database creation. This latest version of the two-function system has been inserted in a procedure on the PC and distributed to around 30 of the member banks. Actual application in the field is underway and has already given significant, favorable signs.

6. For an introduction to the theory of neural networks and the operating mechanisms, see Rumelhart and McClelland (1989); Cammarata (1990); Khana (1991); Freeman and Skapura (1991); and Hertz et al. (1991).

7. In the area of finance, there have been a number of recent attempts to apply NN. Cadden (1991) has applied neural networks to insolvency analysis by adopting a Boolean transformation of the financial ratios di-

vided into quartiles; Chung and Tam (1993) have compared the performance of the neural networks with that of other inductive learning algorithms for bankruptcy forecasting in the banking industry; Bell et al. (1990) have compared neural networks with logistic regression for the prediction of bank failures. The networks have also been assigned to the rating of bonds (Dutta nd Shelber 1992), to the prediction of the progress of historical series of company data, to the selection of investments, and to operations on the financial market (Swales and Yoon 1992; Wong et al 1993; and Trippi and de Sieno 1992); and the recognition of accounting data patterns (Liang et al. 1993). Kryzanowski, Galler, and Wright (1993) applied NN for positive versus negative common stock return predictions and Kryzanowski and Galler (1994) have analyzed the financial statements of small businesses using neural nets. For a partial list of applications in the financial field, see Pau and Gianotti (1990) and Trippi and Turban (1993).

8.   While the Coats and Fant (1993) analysis is relevant, we must point out that the auditors' qualification is itself an inexact and subjective process and, as we have shown in an earlier study (Altman and McGough 1974), the discriminant analysis Z-score approach was far more accurate in predicting the actual bankruptcy of a sample of failed firms than was the so-called accountant-expert. Still, the auditing disclaimer report is an unambiguous, although possibly incorrect, indicator of distress. And the distressed firms in the Coats and Fant sample were those that discontinued operations after receiving a going-concern qualification.

9.   The method considered here is the well-known error -back- propagation algorithm by Rumelhart et al. (1986).

10. Training was conducted with a 0.75 learning rate and null momentum. These values were obtained on the basis of the results of experiments with alternative learning and momentum rates.

11. Experiments were also conducted, among others, using Cascade-Correlation, but we did not obtain superior results; for the methodological aspects relating to Cascade-Correlation, see Fahlman and Lebiere (1992).

12. Increased generalization was achieved with the simpler, 10, 4, 1 type networks, fed with the ten ratios used in the first section of experiments. After 2,000 learning cycles, this network showed a recognition capacity of 93.3 percent for healthy companies and 84.7 percent for unsound companies in period T-3, far lower than results obtained with the more complex 15, 6, 1 network. Nonetheless, the simpler network was able to limit the errors on the T-1 sample to 8.2 percent and 3.7 percent, respectively and, on the independent sample, to 14.6 percent and 6.8 percent for the two samples of firms.

13. These values were obtained from the results using alternative parameter experiments.

14. The activation patterns that the hidden-layer neurons assume in response to different input value configurations can be observed in order to try to understand how the network has formed responses. An alternative method consists of causing voluntary "damages" inside the network by deactivating certain connections, by removing entire groups, or by altering the size of its values.

15. The price paid for these performance levels has been the high number of elementary first-level network learning cycles. Consider that with 5,000 cycles there are over four million changes made to the weightings via the backward propagation algorithm.

PART III

BUSINESS FAILURE PREDICTION

10

A NEURAL NETWORK APPROACH TO BANKRUPTCY PREDICTION

Wullianallur Raghupathi, Lawrence L. Schkade, and Bapi S. Raju

INTRODUCTION

The domain of this exploratory research is in financial analysis. Specifically, the research develops and models the bankruptcy prediction process using a neural network approach. The application can assist auditors, individual investors, portfolio managers, bankers, and other investment advisors in making decisions about investments.

Auditors generally verify financial statements of companies to see if they have been prepared according to generally accepted accounting principles and present fairly the financial picture of the company. Interpretation and prediction are left to the user of the statements. However, it is believed that the auditor's responsibility goes beyond mere verification of the statement. The *Statement on Auditing Standards (SAS) 59* deals with the assessment of going-concern status. An entity is assumed to be a going concern if it is expected to continue in existence for the foreseeable future. The auditor has a responsibility to evaluate whether there is substantial doubt about the entity's ability to continue as a going concern for a reasonable period of time, not to exceed one year beyond the date of the financial statement. If the auditor has a doubt about the likelihood of continued existence, possible or potential mitigating factors must be examined before giving a final opinion. The auditor's work in this respect is made difficult by uncertainty and fuzziness in the financial statement information, laws, and guidelines. This necessitates a good decision support system that the auditors can use to make confident predictions about the future status of a company, for example, whether the company will go bankrupt or remain a going concern.[1]

The following section briefly reviews some of the prior research in the domain of bankruptcy prediction.

LITERATURE REVIEW

Much research has been done utilizing financial statement data for bankruptcy prediction with an emphasis on ratio analysis. McKinley et al.[2] state that ratios are the best known and most widely used of financial analysis tools. They allow the analyst to study the relationships among various components and to compare a company's performance to that of similar enterprises. Miller[3] believes that some ratios represent cause and some represent effect. Gibson and Frishkoff[4] caution that ratios will differ across industry groups and according to accounting methods used. For a more detailed discussion on this issue, see Horrigan.[5]

The primary focus has been on using standard statistical techniques in which it appears that the financial ratios are generally valid discriminators between bankrupt and nonbankrupt firms. Previous researchers have represented nonquantitative items by indicator variables or by regressing one variable on others to reflect trends.

The principal tools in this regard have been discriminant analysis, logit analysis, and recursive partitioning. The problem is generally treated as a classification problem.

Collins and Green[6] compare and contrast the three statistical models most frequently used for bankruptcy prediction: multiple discriminant analysis (MDA), linear probability models (LPM), and logistic regression (logit analysis). Multiple discriminant analysis is a statistical technique used to classify an observation into one of two or more a priori groups. In the case of bankruptcy prediction, there are two predefined groups: bankrupt and nonbankrupt firms. Classification is accomplished through development of a discriminant function, which is generally a linear combination of independent variables. The discriminant function is derived in such a way as to minimize the possibility of misclassification. In order for inferences of MDA to be valid, certain assumptions have to be met. In applying MDA, part of the data set is used as an analysis sample to develop the discriminant function. A cutting score is derived to determine group classification for each observation, and the resultant function is then applied to the remainder of the data set (a holdout sample) for validation. A classification matrix is derived for both the analysis sample and holdout sample. This matrix (also called a confusion matrix) shows the number of observations correctly and incorrectly classified. From this, a hit ratio may be computed, indicating the percentage of observations correctly classified.

In logit analysis, the logit model is based on the cumulative logistic probability function. It has been found appropriate in many situations involving a binary dependent variable (e.g., bankrupt or nonbankrupt). In comparing logit analysis to MDA, Collins and Green[6] assert that the logit model appears to produce lower Type 1 errors (classifying as healthy a firm that subsequently fails) but is not significantly better at classification accuracy. Furthermore, they maintain that MDA seems fairly robust to violations of model assumptions. Therefore, unless the cost of Type 1 errors is large, the additional computational effort of the logit model compared to MDA may not be worthwhile.

Recursive partitioning algorithm (RPA) is a computerized nonparametric classification technique based on pattern recognition. The model is in the form of a binary classification tree that assigns objects to predefined groups in such a way as to minimize misclassification costs. Classification accuracy of a function may be determined by the use of a test sample whose correct classification is known. For instance, in a bankruptcy prediction model, the classification tree may be constructed using a portion of the data and tested with the remainder. Or the model may be built with data from one time period and tested with data from a comparable period. Altman[7] tested his discriminant analysis model on a holdout sample of 66 nonbankrupt firms, of which 65 percent had incurred two or three years of losses. Of the firms, 79 percent were correctly classified. Gentry et al.[8] tested two logit models on a sample of 23 financially weak firms (based on a credit-watch list) and obtained accuracy rates of 70 percent and 78 percent).

Harris[1] performed MDA, logit analysis, and RPA tests on a sample of 100 bankrupt and 100 nonbankrupt companies matched by asset size, industry, and year. Each model was analyzed with the entire data set, then with the set split into analysis and holdout samples of equal size. For discriminant analysis, overall classification accuracy was 84.5 percent for the analysis sample of 100 companies (50 bankrupt and 50 nonbankrupt); pooled and nonpooled versions yielded the same overall classification accuracy of 86 percent, while the holdout sample with pooled variance-covariance matrices had an accuracy rate of 85 percent. In logit analysis, overall classification accuracy was 87 percent; for the analysis sample, 95 percent; and for the holdout sample, 78 percent. In RPA using CART (classification and regression trees, software for RPA), classification accuracy was 77 percent for bankrupt firms and 86 percent for nonbankrupt on the full data set; 80 percent and 94 percent for bankrupt and nonbankrupt respectively in the analysis sample; and 76 percent for bankrupt and 90 percent for nonbankrupt for the holdout sample.[1]

Individuals generally rely on auditor judgment and financial ratios for important investment decisions. However, not all variables are known completely, and some others are difficult to characterize precisely. In the following section, we briefly discuss the limitations of the statistical techniques and the potential of a neural network model.

PROBLEM STATEMENT

Developing a robust and reliable model for bankruptcy prediction is important, as it enables investors, auditors, and others to independently evaluate the risk of investment. The task of predicting bankruptcy of a company can be posed as a classification problem: Given a set of classes (here, bankrupt and nonbankrupt) and a set of input data vectors, the task is to assign each input data vector to one of the classes. For this study, the different financial ratios form the set of input data vectors, and the two possible values (bankrupt and nonbankrupt) form the set of possible classes to which the new input belongs.

Conventional statistical approaches are of limited use in deriving an appropriate prediction model in the absence of well-defined domain models.[9] Statistical techniques always require the assumption of a certain functional form for relating dependent variables to independent variables. When the assumed functional form is not correct, the statistical techniques merely confirm that; they do not predict the right functional form. Additionally, quantitative models suffer from the weakness of being sample specific. Generalizations can be made only with caution. A few atypical companies can skew the results. Further, sample variances can be large.

Neural networks do provide a more general framework for determining relationships in the data and do not require the specification of any functional form.

NEURAL NETWORKS

Neural networks are networks of simple processing units called nodes, which interact with each other using weighted connections. There are various ways of connecting them. Each node sums up the activations of all the nodes connected to it. And, depending on the paradigm of choice, they can have different activation functions to transform the input and different error-correcting rules to guide the learning process. Typically, knowledge in neural networks is stored in the set of weights on the interconnections between various nodes. Therefore, the design of a neural network algorithm for a given problem must address three issues: (1) the type of intralayer and interlayer connectivity between different nodes; (2) the activation function for the nodes for transforming the inputs; and (3) an error-correcting algorithm for training.

The network paradigm of choice in this research is the PDP back-propagation (BP) algorithm.[10] In this BP network, the nodes in adjacent layers are fully connected, and there are no intralayer connections. A non-linear activation function (sigmoid) transforms the inputs at each node. The generalized delta rule is used for error correction. Apart from the input and output layers, another layer (called the hidden layer) between the input and output may be needed. Hidden layers can extract higher-level features and facilitate generalization if the input vectors have low-level features of the problem domain or if the input/output relationship is complex. Given a set of input vectors and the desired output for each input vector, the back-propagation learning algorithm can iteratively find a set of weights that will perform the mapping if such a set exists.

In order to verify how well the neural network has learned the underlying domain model, the same set of weights (on the connections) learned during the learning phase must be used to check the accuracy of the predicted outcome. The success of the predictions of the neural network depends on the range of values covered by the input/output vectors. The neural network model helps us in determining the functional mapping between the input/output exemplar sets.

METHODOLOGY

The following sections describe the various steps in the design and experiment phases of the research.

Selection of Variables

Table 10.1 lists the 13 financial ratios used in the current study. This list is selected from ratios proven popular (and useful) in earlier research on bankruptcy prediction and is by no means exhaustive. Table 10.2 gives the generally accepted interpretations of the various ratios selected. Karels and Prakash[11] believe that the large diversity of ratios in use is because of the limited theoretical basis for choosing them. The selected ratios do have a bearing on the going-concern issue.[1] Since the financial ratios used in this research have proven useful in previous studies, it is expected that they will be good discriminators between bankrupt and nonbankrupt firms. These ratios have been used in earlier studies of bankruptcy prediction.[1,7,8,11] In addition to the financial ratios, a trend variable was included showing how many of the three years prior to bankruptcy a company incurred a loss.[1]

Data Collection

Financial statement data was collected for a total of 102 companies. In keeping with the methods of earlier researchers, these companies consist of 51 pairs of bankrupt and nonbankrupt companies of the same industry and approximately the same asset size. The asset size is taken three years prior to bankruptcy to offset any effects of impending failure on this factor.

Table 10.1
Financial Ratios Used

X_1 — Total current assets / Total current liabilities

X_2 — [Cash + STI + net receivables] / Total current liabilities

X_3 — [Income from continuing operations + DDA] / [Total CL + Long-term debt]

X_4 — [Total CL + Long-term debt / Total assets

X_5 — [Total current assets − Total current liabilities] / Total assets

X_6 — Income from continuing operations / Total assets

X_7 — [ICO + Income taxes + Interest expense] / Total assets

X_8 — Net sales / Total assets

X_9 — Retained earnings / Total assets

X_{10} — Total current assets / Net sales

X_{11} — [Total current assets − Total current liabilities] / Net sales

X_{12} — Total current assets / Total assets

X_{13} — [Cash + Short-term investments] / Total assets

Notes:
STI — Short-term investments.
DDA — Depreciation, depletion, amortization.
CL — Current liabilities.
ICO — Income from continuing operations.

Source: C. Harris, "An Expert Decision Support System for Auditor Going Concern Evaluation," Ph.D. diss., University of Texas at Arlington, 1989.

Bankrupt firms were chosen from listings in *The Wall Street Journal Index* for the years 1980 through 1988 and from a list of deleted companies in the *Moody's Industrial Manual*. Utilities, transportation companies, and financial services were excluded because these firms are structurally different and have a different bankruptcy environment. Financial statement information is obtained from COMPUSTAT, *Moody's Industrial Manual*, *Moody's OTC Manual*, annual reports, and 10-K reports for the three years preceding bankruptcy. Data for nonbankrupt companies were obtained from the same sources for the same three-year period as that of the corresponding bankrupt firms.

Table 10.2
Interpretation of Ratios

X_1 — Short-term liquidity
X_2 — Short-term liquidity (more rigorous test)
X_3 — Availability of funds
X_4 — Financial leverage
X_5 — Working capital relative to total capitalization
X_6 — Return on investment
X_7 — Productivity, irrespective of financing
X_8 — Sales-generating ability of assets
X_9 — Cumulative profitability
X_{10} — Inventory turnover
X_{11} — Working capital turnover
X_{12} — Relative liquidity of assets
X_{13} — Cash position

Source: Harris, "An Expert Decision Support System."

Experiment

The experiment consisted of two parts: training and testing. There are 14 input nodes representing the 14 variables and one output node representing the binary classification decision (0 for bankrupt and 1 for non-bankrupt).

Learning. Since the back-propagation algorithm uses the sigmoid activation function for each node with the function values ranging between 0 and 1, the input data need to be normalized. The values for the 14 variables for each company were input into a LOTUS worksheet and normalized using the following formula:

$$Y = (X - X_1) / (X_2 - X_1)$$

where

Y : Normalized value of X.
X : Actual value for each variable.

X_1 : Minimum value for each variable.
X_2 : Maximum value for each variable.

From the total normalized data set of 51 pairs of asset-matched firms (one bankrupt and one nonbankrupt in each pair), 25 pairs were selected at random for the learning phase. Table 10.3 lists the mean and standard deviation of all 14 variables for the 102 companies.

Since there is no standard criterion for selecting the number of hidden layers and hidden nodes, the learning phase involved experimentation with two different neural network configurations. Table 10.4 lists the values

Table 10.3
Statistical Information on the Financial Ratios

		Mean	Standard Deviation
X_1	—	2.047	1.428
X_2	—	1.125	0.879
X_3	—	−0.276	1.954
X_4	—	0.601	0.294
X_5	—	0.176	0.363
X_6	—	−0.14	0.382
X_7	—	−0.08	0.379
X_8	—	1.402	1.016
X_9	—	−0.086	0.859
X_{10}	—	0.553	0.392
X_{11}	—	−0.002	0.941

Table 10.4
Parameters for the Neural Network Model

Upper threshold	:	0.8
Lower threshold	:	0.3
Learning rate	:	0.9
Momentum term	:	0.65

for various parameters kept constant during the training and testing phases. In this experiment, the two different configurations are (1) one hidden layer with 10, 15, and 20 nodes and (2) two hidden layers with 10 and 15 nodes. For each configuration, the training was halted either after 10,000 iterations were run through the training set or when the network had learned all the training examples, whichever occurred earlier.

Testing. Once the neural network was trained with the training exemplars, each of the two configurations was tested with the remaining 52 companies for classification as either bankrupt or nonbankrupt. The learned weights on the connections between nodes were kept constant during the testing phase. For each company, the 14-variable input was fed to the network, and an output (value between 0 and 1) was generated in one pass through the network. Now, based on the upper and lower thresholds used for learning, the output was interpreted as a 0 or a 1 (bankrupt or nonbankrupt).

RESULTS

Figures 10.1 and 10.2 display the six different trends for the change in total average error over the number of iterations in the learning phase for the two configurations with a different number of nodes. Figures 10.3 and 10.4 show the number of examples learned over the number of iterations. As can be seen, the average error decreased and the number learned increased with successive iterations. The different trends do not indicate any noticeable variation in learning capability. Therefore, the decision to select a particular configuration as the more suitable one for prediction was postponed until the testing phase.

Figure 10.5 illustrates the relative performance of the different configurations in terms of the classification accuracy during the testing phase. The configuration with 15 nodes in the first hidden layer and two in the second seems to have the best percentage of correct classifications (86 percent).

Discussion

Though the training phase did not indicate the best configuration, the testing phase seems to suggest that the one with 15 nodes in the first hidden layer and two nodes in the second hidden layer was able to generalize better. This supports the intuition that financial ratios are mere

Figure 10.1

Training with One Hidden Layer (Average Error versus Number of Iterations)

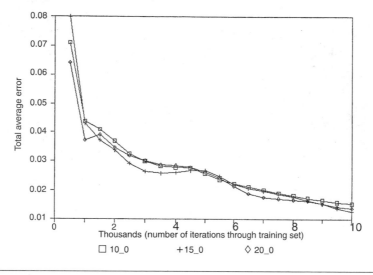

Figure 10.2

Training with Two Hidden Layers (Average Error versus Number of Iterations)

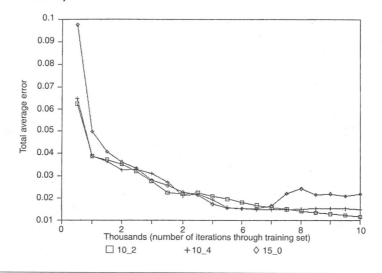

Figure 10.3

Training with One Hidden Layer (Patterns Learned versus Number of Iterations)

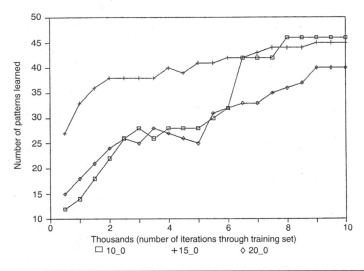

Figure 10.4

Training with Two Hidden Layers (Patterns Learned versus Number of Iterations)

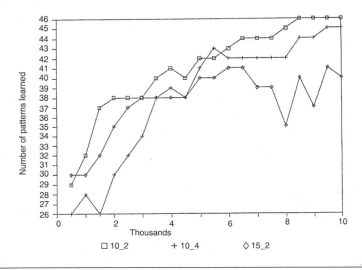

Figure 10.5

Results of Testing Phase

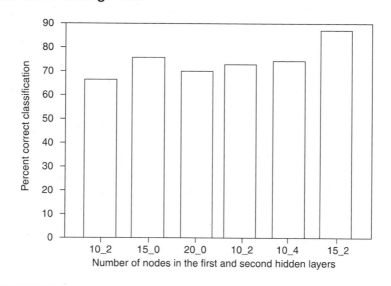

low features representing the dynamics of the bankruptcy prediction prob-lem. The results suggest that the functional mapping between financial ratios and the bankruptcy decision is more complex than can be captured by a one-layered BP network. Various financial ratios may be giving some intermediate features such as immediate financial health of the company, long-term financial health, recent revenue-generating trends, and others. Based on these higher-level features, the network may be arriving at a categorizing decision. Though this is only speculative, the fact that the two-layered network fared better leads to a possible conclusion of hier-archical feature extraction involved before categorization. This means a potential bankruptcy prediction network needs to extract higher-level fea-tures for better generalization.[9]

Assumptions

The financial ratios selected for consideration in this study were based on the previous research in the field of bankruptcy prediction applying standard statistical procedures. The use of these quantitative variables precludes the possible influence of qualitative factors such as litigation, taxes, or other unforeseen situations. Further, the analysis and results are accurate to the extent that the reported data reflect the actual financial condition of the firm.

FUTURE RESEARCH

First, one needs to focus on obtaining a representative data set that encompasses the range of possible values for the financial ratios. Second, more complex configurations need to be considered. Third, the sample size must be increased to accommodate a larger variety of companies in different industries. Fourth, a neural network offers the unique advantage of recognizing the relative importance of the various financial ratios leading to parsimony in selection of variables for bankruptcy prediction. Fifth, in this study, the output reflected either a correct classification or a misclassification. In this regard, we need to address the issue of possible relation between misclassified output values and inconsistencies in the financial ratios. Finally, another concern not addressed in this study that needs to be examined is the possibility of random variation making the categorization more complex. In the future, we intend to test the traditional statistical techniques with the same data for more meaningful comparisons.[12]

CONCLUSION

In this exploratory research, we have examined a neural network application for bankruptcy prediction. Preliminary results indicate that neural networks might provide suitable models for the bankruptcy prediction process. In the long run, a neural network-based decision support system for bankruptcy prediction can be developed to assist auditors and other potentially interested parties.

ENDNOTES

1. C. Harris, "An Expert Decision Support System for Auditor Going Concern Evaluation," Ph.D. diss., University of Texas at Arlington, 1989.

2. J. E. McKinley, R. L. Johnson, G. R. Downey, Jr., C. S. Zimmerman, and M. D. Bloom, *Analyzing Financial Statements* (Washington: American Bankers Association, 1983.)

3. D. E. Miller, *The Meaningful Interpretation of Financial Statements,* rev. ed. (New York: American Management Association, 1972).

4. C. H. Gibson and P. A. Frishkoff, *Financial Statement Analysis: Using Financial Accounting Information,* 3d ed. (Boston: Kent Publishing Company, 1986.)

5. J. O. Horrigan, "A Short History of Financial Ratio Analysis," *The Accounting Review* 43 (April 1968), pp. 284–94.

6. R. A. Collins and R. D. Green, "Statistical Method vor Bankruptcy Forecasting," *Journal of Economics and Business* 32 (1982), pp. 349–54.

7. E. L. Altman, "Financial Ratios, Discriminant Analysis and the Prediction of Corporate Bankruptcy," *The Journal of Finance* 23 (September 1968), pp. 589–609.

8. J. A. Gentry, P. Newbold, and D. T. Whitford, "Classifying Bankrupt Firms with Funds Flow Components," *Journal of Accounting Research* 23 (Spring 1985), pp. 146–60.

9. S. Dutta and S. Shekar, "Bond Ratings: A Non-Conservative Application of Neural Networks," *Proceedings of the ICNN,* 1988, pp. II-443–II-450.

10. D. E. Rumelhart, G. E. Hinton, and R. J. Williams, "Learning Internal Representations by Error Propagation," in *Parallel Distributed Processing: Exploration in the Microstructure of Cognition,* eds. D. E. Rumelhart, and J. L. McClelland (Cambridge, MA: MIT Press, 1986).

11. G. V. Karels and A. J. Prakash, "Multivariate Normality and Forecasting of Business Bankruptcy," *Journal of Business Finance & Accounting* 14 (Winter 1987), pp. 573–93.

12. The neural network simulator used in this study was made available by the character recognition group of the computer science and engineering department of the University of Texas at Arlington. We thank Dr. Carolyn Harris for providing data and other background material in the bankruptcy prediction domain.

11

BANKRUPTCY PREDICTION BY NEURAL NETWORK

Eric Rahimian, Seema Singh,
Thongchai Thammachote, and Rajiv Virmani

BANKRUPTCY AND FINANCIAL DISTRICT ANALYSIS

For the past 22 years, linear discriminant functions have been used to analyze financial data for bankruptcy or financial distress analysis. A pioneer study of bankruptcy analysis was done by Altman in 1968.[1] Altman compared the financial data of 33 manufacturers who filed for bankruptcy with the data of 33 nonbankrupt firms on the basis of similar industry and asset size. Asset size ranged between $1 million and $25 million. He used 22 financial variables to compile five explanatory variables for bankruptcy. These included:

X_1 = Working capital/total assets.
X_2 = Retained earnings/total assets.

Printed with permission of the authors.

X_3 = EBIT/total assets (where EBIT is earnings before interest and tax).

X_4 = MVE/total debt (where MVE is the market value of equity).

X_5 = Sales/total assets.

Altman classified the sample using z-score analysis. The description of z-score is beyond the scope of this study. Z-score computation uses discriminant analysis.[2,3] All firms having a z-score greater than 2.99 fell in the category of nonbankrupt, whereas all firms having a z-score below 1.81 were bankrupt. The area between 1.81 and 2.99 was defined as the zone of "ignorance" or the "gray" area.

Odom and Sharda[4] have recently used the back-propagation neural network model to predict bankruptcy. The purpose of their study was to compare the predictive ability of the neural network and multivariate discriminant analysis model. Many other studies including Deakin,[5] Blum,[6] Moyer,[7] Altman et al.,[8] and Karels and Prakash[9] also have used discriminant analysis of financial data.

This chapter takes advantage of the comparative study of Odom and Sharda.[4] Briefly, three different paradigms of neural networks are utilized. The efficiency (number of cycles and computation time) and predictive capability of these paradigms for bankruptcy prediction are compared with each other as well as with the performance of Odom and Sharda's back-propagation and discriminant analysis.

THEORETICAL COMPARISON OF TRADITIONAL MODELS VERSUS A NEURAL NETWORK MODEL

Discriminant analysis requires certain restrictive assumptions. The distribution of discriminating variables is assumed to be jointly multivariate normal. Karels and Prakash[9] have indicated that the results of discriminant analysis procedure are erroneous when this requirement is violated. Neural networks are not under normality constraints, so if they produce comparable predictive results they are safer to use.

Also, a close relationship exists between two-group discriminant analysis and regression with binary-valued dependent variable (the dummy regression method). Several assumptions such as the normality of the disturbance term U_i and homoscedasticity of variances of the disturbances usually are not satisfied for real-world financial ratios used in discriminant analysis.[10] Hence, the prediction of discriminant analysis or dummy regression analysis should be taken with a grain of salt.

DATA

The data used for this study are the same as the ones used by Odom and Sharda.[4] Our variables are the same financial ratios employed by Altman.[1] We used the sample data that was obtained from Moody's *Industrial Manuals* for 129 firms, where 65 firms went bankrupt during the period 1975 through 1982. Two subsamples were used. The training subsample consisted of 74 firms, 36 nonbankrupt and 38 bankrupt. The testing subsample consisted of 55 firms, 28 nonbankrupt and 27 bankrupt. Using the same data as that of Odom and Sharda made it possible to compare the results of the paradigms of our chapter with the ones of the NeuroShell network and the discriminant analysis of Odom and Sharda.

MODELS FOR BANKRUPTCY PREDICTION

We used three paradigms in our study:
   Back-propagation.

2.   Athena.

3.   Perceptron (like back-propagation but without any hidden layer).

Back-Propagation

Generally, this is a multilayered neural network. It uses the sigmoidal activation (squashing) function:

$$OUT = F(X.W) = F(NET) = 1/(1 + e^{-NET})$$

   (1)

where

W   =   Weight vector w between neuron i in layer k and neuron j in layer $k + 1$.

X   =   The input vector.

OUT =   The final output of a neuron in the output layer.

where range of *OUT* is bounded by (0,1). Other activation functions that are differentiable may also be employed. Back-propagation uses supervised learning. Weights are adjusted to produce desired (target) output. Training pairs consist of input vectors and target output values. As the weights are changed, they perform steepest descent on a surface in weight space whose height at any point in weight space is equal to the error measure. As in the case of perceptron, a learning-rate parameter is used for weight adjustments. In addition, another parameter called momentum is recommended in spaces containing long ravines with sharp curvature across the ravine. The momentum term filters out high curvature and allows weight adjustment steps to be larger. In practice, the best momentum and learning rates are selected in repeated runs of trial and error, where one is trying to optimize the number of cycles (time) and the performance of the model. A bias term also may be introduced for each neuron. This functions the same way as adjusting the threshold of the perceptron.

Stornetta and Huberman[11] have discussed the impact of changing the value of the binary inputs and outputs to a range of [–1/2, +1/2]. They have shown that the convergence time can be reduced by 30 percent to 50 percent. This will modify the output function as follows:

$$OUT = -1/2 \ + \ 1/(1 \ + \ e^{-NET}). \tag{2}$$

Notice that this will reduce the value of output by 0.5.

The network topology used by us is the same as employed by Odom and Sharda and is shown in Figure 11.1. In our application, we learned that normalization of input data to a range of –.5 to +.5 and using the values of –.5 and +.5 instead of 0 and 1 for target output reduced the training time dramatically. Actually, in the best result, the number of cycles was reduced to 95 cycles, which was much smaller than the 191,400 reported by Odom and Sharda. With the ANSim (artificial neural network simulator) package, we ran the original model of Odom and Sharda without such adjustments, and after several days and over 40,000 cycles (ANSim is slower than NeuroShell), it did not converge. Introducing the above modifications allowed us to get much better performance and faster convergence, as is discussed in more detail in comparison of test results below.

It is notable that small learning rates cause slow and inefficient convergence, whereas large learning rates cause paralysis or instability. Network paralysis will occur when weights become very large, producing

Figure 11.1

Back-Propagation Network

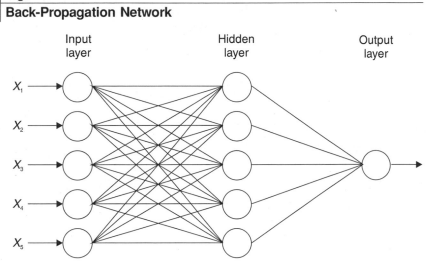

large outputs and small error adjustment signals, which may cause the training to come to a virtual halt.

Athena

Athena is a neural network for pattern classification based on an entropy measure.[12,13] It uses supervised learning. The model uses hyperplanes to partition the object space into groups of convex sets, each of which contains objects of the same class. The net consists of a group of neurons, each of which corresponds to one of the partition's hyperplanes: $P = \{ X \mid X$ is an element of the object space R, and $W'X = T\}$; where X is the input vector, W is the weight vector, and T is the threshold. The weight vector determines the orientation of the hyperplane, and the threshold determines its distance from the origin. The network is formed dynamically, and the training is a one-shot procedure that uses an entropy measure to optimize the partition.

Each hyperplane divides the object space into two regions: the upper half space, P^u, above the hyperplane and the lower half space, P^l, below the hyperplane. For training, each neuron identifies a weight vector and a threshold value, which define a separating hyperplane. As the separation by a neuron is completed and the result is passed to the children neurons, a tree of neurons is built, where the upper half space of a neuron is assigned to the right child, and the lower half space is assigned to the left child neuron. Either way, linearly separable training instances are either completely separated by the hyperplane, or a hyperplane is selected so as to optimize an entropy measure for the quality of the separation. This process continues until each leaf neuron is associated with objects of only one class.

Perceptron

Generally speaking, a single-layer neural network with binary outputs is called a perceptron. Perceptron uses a nonlinear threshold unit:

> If *NET* output $\geq$ Threshold, *OUT* = 1
> Otherwise   *OUT* = 0

Perceptron training occurs through supervised learning. A set of input patterns and target outputs are presented to the network, and the weights applied to inputs are adjusted until the desired output occurs for each input pattern. The input may be binary or continuous.

In this chapter, we have utilized a modified continuous version of the perceptron learning algorithm. The continuous version is called the Δ rule.[14] The perceptron may be summarized as follows:

1. Apply an input pattern, X, and calculate the output.

2. If output is correct, change nothing and go to 1. If output is incorrect, use the Δ rule to adjust the weights. The weight adjustment using the Δ rule in this step is explained as follows:

    $\Delta = T - A$ (where T = target output and A = actual output).
    If $\Delta = 0$, no weight adjustment is required.
    If $\Delta \neq 0$, compute
    $\Delta_i = \alpha \, \Delta \, X_i$ where α is a positive learning rate < 1.
    Notice that Δ may be negative.
    $W_i \, (n + 1) = W_i(n) + \Delta_i$

3. Go to step 1.

In practice, a small value of Δ is acceptable and an exit from the given algorithm can be made if Δ reaches below a predetermined value. In ANSim, the tolerable root mean square error may be set to 0.1, and training is continued until convergence is achieved.[14]

This modified perceptron was realized by using the back-propagation model of ANSim, removing the hidden layer but keeping the values of target output at −.5 and +.5, and using the squashing function of equation (2).

COMPARISON OF TEST RESULTS

By using the same data as the ones used by Odom and Sharda, we are able to directly compare the performance of the paradigms utilized by us with the performance of both discriminant analysis and the back-propagation paradigm used by them.

Two subsamples of the firms were available, one with 74 firms for training the networks and the other with 55 firms for testing the models. The training and testing with Athena were extremely efficient. Because Athena was able to separate the training set with only one hyperplane, it suggested that the bankruptcy prediction problem at hand may be linearly separable. Both training and testing times with Athena were less than one minute, and the number of erroneous predictions was 10 out of 55 — the same number as for Odom and Sharda's back-propagation; normalized back-propagation and number of cycles may be assumed to be one. The testing results of Athena are presented in Tables 11.1 and 11.2, which also give the values of data in the testing subsample.

The back-propagation model with binary target output value as used by Odom and Sharda proved to be extremely slow on our ANSim software using the IBM PC 386. Odom and Sharda used NeuroShell Network release 1.1. Their model, as they confirmed, was tedious and slow in convergence (24 hours and 191,400 cycles). Even this result was obtained by modification of learning rate from 0.6 to 0.1 and change of momentum from 0.9 to 0.8 during the test run.

We chose to normalize the input data to values between −.5 and .5 for our back-propagation training and testing. This model is consistent with the modification of output values from 0 and 1 to −.5 and .5. As anticipated, these modifications produced results that were very encouraging. The lowest training time after such modifications occurred in 14

Table 11.1
Nonbankrupt Firms

WC/TA	RE/TA	EBIT/TA	MVE/TD	S/TA	BR	
.2234	.3931	.1168	1.1371	1.7523	1	
.1725	.3238	.1040	.8847	.5576	1	
.2955	.1959	.2245	1.1606	1.8478	1	
.5542	.4316	.1065	.8375	1.6678	1	
.2489	.4014	.1669	1.4609	7.1658	1	
.3813	.3194	.2044	2.8513	.9851	1	
.4512	.4114	.1146	1.7185	1.5543	1	
.1904	.2011	.1329	.5586	1.6623	1	
.5248	.6437	.2478	6.3501	1.2542	1	
.4058	.4497	.1497	1.1076	1.7428	1	
.2947	.3724	.1104	.9410	1.3568	1	
.4327	.6494	.2996	8.2982	1.2865	1	
.1630	.3555	.0110	.3730	2.8307	1	# @
.5189	.3627	.1015	.9764	.7466	1	
.4792	.3495	.1076	.8105	1.7224	1	
.0669	.2904	.0978	.7659	4.3912	1	
.3449	.1270	−.0083	.1059	.8611	1	*#%&@
.0272	.0503	.0184	.1413	1.2008	1	*#%&@
.6302	.3324	.1524	1.1259	1.5579	1	
.2170	.2507	.0826	.3404	1.9889	1	
.4078	.1316	.1095	.3233	1.8226	1	# % &
.2864	.2823	.1856	2.7709	2.7730	1	
.1841	.3344	.0857	2.1230	2.1686	1	
.0732	.3526	.0587	.2349	1.7432	1	
.0106	.0200	.0226	1.887	1.2274	1	*#%&@
.6398	.1723	.2019	34.5032	1.1388	1	
.3750	.3326	.1290	.9487	1.2529	1	
.2921	.2390	.0673	.3402	.7596	1	

WC / TA   = Working capital / Total assets.
RE / TA   = Retained earnings / Total assets.
EBIT / TA = Earnings before interest and tax / Total assets.
MVE / TD = Market value of equity / Total debt.
S / TA   = Sales / Total assets.
NB   = Nonbankrupt.

*   Misclassified by discriminant analysis.
#   Misclassified by Odom and Sharda model.
%   Misclassified by back-propagation model.
&   Misclassified by perceptron model.
@ Misclassified by Athena model.

Table 11.2
Bankrupt Firms

WC/TA	RE/TA	EBIT/TA	MVE/TD	S/TA	BR	
.0471	.1506	−.0150	.1039	.6253	0	
.2770	−.0417	.0904	.5245	1.9380	0	
.4958	.2199	.0219	.1267	3.0305	0	
.1070	.0787	.0433	.1083	1.2051	0	
.1936	.0778	−.1830	.6531	2.4263	0	
.1611	.0954	.0307	.2113	1.4529	0	
.3732	.3484	−.0139	.3483	1.8223	0	* %
.2653	.2683	.0235	.5118	1.8350	0	* %
−.1599	−.5018	−.0889	.1748	2.1608	0	
.1123	.2288	.0100	.1884	2.7186	0	
.3696	.2917	.0621	.5554	1.7326	0	*#%&@
.2702	.1402	.1668	.2717	2.1121	0	*# &@
.1144	−.0194	.0074	.2940	1.5734	0	
.4044	−.1878	.0768	.2846	1.3489	0	
.2787	.1767	.0305	.1797	5.3003	0	
−.0357	−.9814	−.0031	.3291	2.1088	0	
−.0179	−.2902	.0984	2.2848	2.1803	0	
.4067	.2972	.0454	.5001	2.0631	0	*%&@
.2260	.1620	.0965	.2737	1.9199	0	*
.0780	−.2451	.0627	.0453	.1451	0	
.3422	.2865	.0778	.5300	1.5564	0	*#%&@
.3440	.1725	.1386	.2775	2.0030	0	*#&@
.1756	.1233	.1046	.7468	1.6774	0	*
.1186	.1849	−.0718	.2117	.1376	0	
.3617	.1312	.0413	.3706	2.1890	0	
.1162	.3026	.0863	.9220	.9513	0	*#%&@
.2323	.1095	.1054	.4661	.9193	0	*

WC / TA   = Working capital / Total assets.
RE / TA   = Retained earnings / Total assets.
EBIT / TA = Earnings before interest and tax / Total assets.
MVE / TD   = Market value of equity / Total debt.
S / TA   = Sales / Total assets.
BR   = Bankrupt.

*   Misclassified by discriminant analysis.
#   Misclassified by Odom and Sharda model.
% Misclassified by back-propagation model.
& Misclassified by perceptron model.
@ Misclassified by Athena model.

minutes with the screen display on during the training. This consisted of 95 training cycles only. The learning rate and the momentum term were 0.40 and 0.86, respectively. The accuracy of the prediction remained the same as the test by Odom and Sharda, whereas the training time for our back-propagation paradigm was only about 1 percent of their training time. The number of cycles with other training parameters for the normalized back-propagation paradigm are presented in Table 11.3.

Since the test results of Athena indicated potential linear separability, we removed the hidden layer of the back-propagation network to convert it to a perceptron. The same target output values of –0.5 and 0.5 were used in this model. This modification produced a training time of 17 minutes with 934 cycles, for a learning rate equal to 0.175 and momentum rate of 0.8. A comparative result of performance and efficiency of this modified perceptron is presented in Table 11.4. As this table indicates, the use of a learning rate of 0.20, which is more than 0.175 used in the best output result, increased the number of cycles. The same is true when a learning rate lower than 0.175 is used.

The results of the selected test runs are included in the Appendix.

CONCLUSION

The results of our analysis have indicated that the formulated bankruptcy problem is potentially linearly separable. The best performance was achieved by Athena paradigm (time used was 35 to 45 seconds and the accuracy was the same as other models) (see Table 11.5). The normalization

Table 11.3
Back-Propagation Comparison of Different Parameter Values

Set No.	Learning Rate	Momentum	Number of Cycles
1	0.4	0.86	95 (best case)
2	0.3	0.84	135
3	0.2	0.70	160
4	0.1	0.80	198
5	0.5	0.00	403
6	0.6	0.00	560

Table 11.4
Perceptron Comparison of Different Parameter Values

Set No.	Learning Rate	Momentum	Number of Cycles
1	0.175	0.8	934 (best case)
2	0.15	0.8	1,320
3	0.20	0.8	1,379
4	0.10	0.6	4,423
5	0.225	0.0	3,636

of input data to values between $-.5$ and $.5$ and modification of output target values from 0 and 1 to $-.5$ and $.5$ in the back-propagation model reduced the training time to 14 minutes and number of cycles to 95, an enormous improvement over the regular back-propagation paradigm utilized by Odom and Sharda. As a final conclusion, one may like to assess the importance of the discriminant factors used by comparing the weights assigned to these factors by the Athena paradigm. The weights of the last two variables were negligible (0.0 and -0.0), whereas the weights of X_1, X_2, and X_3 were 0.01, 0.05, and 0.11—an indication of the discriminatory

Table 11.5
Comparison of Different Models

	Training Time	Number of Cycles	# Correct/ # Total
Discriminant analysis test	—	Not available	41/55
Odom and Sharda test	24 hours	191,400	45/55
Athena	35–45 seconds	Not available	45/55
Perceptron	17 minutes	934 with display on	45/55
Back-propagation	14 minutes	95	45/55

power of these variables. Note also that although the weights assigned by the modified perceptron model are much larger (−2.66, 40.28, 29.64, 15.07, −1.27), their predictive powers as indicated by & and @ signs in Tables 11.1 and 11.2 are very similar. Despite the similarity of performance of Athena and the perceptron model, these latter weights are different from the weights of Athena because this perceptron was a back-propagation model without a hidden layer and with a squashing function and used target output values of −.5 to +.5. This makes the meaning of the modified perceptron's weights more difficult to analyze than that of Athena's.

ENDNOTES

1. E. L. Altman, "Financial Ratios, Discriminant Analysis and the Prediction of Corporate Bankruptcy," *Journal of Finance* 23 (1968), p. 596.

2. C. F. Lee, "Financial Analysis and Planning Theory and Applications," (Reading, MA: Addison Wesley, 1985), pp. 97–102.

3. H. D. Platt, *Why Companies Fail* (Lexington, MA: Lexington Books, 1985), pp. 88–91.

4. M. D. Odom and R. Sharda, "A Neural Network for Bankruptcy Prediction," *International Joint Conference on Neural Networks,* vol. II (June 17–21, 1990, San Diego, Calif.), pp. 163–68.

5. E. B. Deakin, "A Discriminant Analysis of Predictors of Business Failure," *Journal of Accounting Research,* Spring 1972, pp. 167–79.

6. M. Blum, "Failing Company Discriminant Analysis," *Journal of Accounting Research,* Spring 1974, pp. 1–25.

7. R. C. Moyer, "Forecasting Financial Failure: A Reexamination," *Financial Management,* Spring 1977, pp. 11–17.

8. E. L. Altman, R. G. Haldeman, and P. Narayanan, "Zeta Analysis," *Journal of Banking and Finance,* June 1977, pp. 29–51.

9. G. V. Karels, and A. Prakash, "Multivariate Normality and Forecasting of Business Bankruptcy," *Journal of Business Finance & Accounting,* Winter 1987, pp. 573–93.

10. D. Gujarati, *Econometrics* (New York: McGraw-Hill, 1978), pp. 312–19.

11. W. S. Stornetta and B. A. Huberman, "An Improved Three Layered Backprop Algorithm," in *Proceedings of the IEEE First International Conference on Neural Networks,* eds. M. Caudill and C. Butler (San Diego, CA: SOS Printing, 1988).

12. C. Koutsougeras and G. Papachristou, "Training of a Neural Network for Pattern Classification Based on an Entropy Measure," *Proceedings of IEEE ICNN*, 1988.

13. C. Koutsougeras and G. Papachristou, "Learning Discrete Mappings—Athena's Approach," IEEE, CH 2636, September 1988, pp. 31–36.

14. P. D. Wasserman, *Neural Computing: Theory and Practice* (New York: Van Nostrand Reinhold, 1989).

APPENDIX

Table 11A.1
The Training Data

NB=1	WC/TA	RE/TA	EBIT/TA	MVE/TD	S/TA
1	.3922	.3778	.1316	1.0911	1.2784
1	.0574	.2783	.1166	1.3441	.2216
1	.1650	.1192	.2035	.8130	1.6702
1	.3073	.6070	.2040	14.4090	.9844
1	.2574	.5334	.1650	8.0734	1.3474
1	.1415	.3868	.0681	.5755	1.0579
1	.3363	.3312	.2157	3.0679	2.0899
1	.3378	.0130	.2366	2.4709	1.2230
1	.4870	.6970	.2994	5.4383	1.7200
1	.4455	.4980	.0952	1.9338	1.7696
1	.4704	.2772	.0964	.4268	1.9317
1	.5804	.3331	.0810	1.1964	1.3572
1	.2073	.3611	.1472	.0417	1.1985
1	.1801	.1635	.0908	.4094	.4566
1	.1778	.3668	.0779	.9742	.5075
1	.2304	.2960	.1225	.4102	3.0809
1	.4328	.5136	.2059	1.9721	1.3194
1	.6674	.4047	.1796	1.0069	1.2968
1	.3255	.5583	.1600	2.2889	1.3146
1	.3684	.3913	.0524	.1658	1.1533
1	.1527	.3344	.0783	.7736	1.5046
1	.4147	.3983	.1532	1.3148	1.3745
1	.1126	.3071	.0839	1.3429	1.5736
1	.0141	.2366	.0905	.5863	1.4651
1	.4135	.3120	.1861	1.1743	1.0319
1	.0140	.2862	.0741	30.6486	1.9606
1	.3735	.4980	.1604	1.8366	2.3793
1	.4934	.3416	.2200	.8144	2.1937
1	.1332	.4077	.0543	1.4921	1.4826
1	.2220	.1797	.1526	.3459	1.7237
1	.3720	.3446	.2124	.8888	1.9241
1	.2776	.2567	.1612	.2968	1.8904
1	.1445	.3808	.1780	1.4796	1.4811
1	.3907	.6482	.1408	3.0489	1.5255
1	.1862	.1687	.1298	.9498	4.9548
1	.1663	.4291	.1133	1.1745	1.6831

NB	= Nonbankrupt.
WC/TA	= Working capital / Total assets.
RE/TA	= Retained earnings / Total assets.
EBIT/TA	= Earnings before interest and tax / Total assets.
MVE/TD	= Market value of equity / Total debt.
S/TA	= Sales / Total assets.

Table 11A.2

The Training Data

BR=0	WC/TA	RE/TA	EBIT/TA	MVE/TD	S/TA
0	.4422	.1379	.0104	.2460	1.2492
0	−.0643	.1094	−.1230	.1725	1.3752
0	.2975	−.3719	−.1390	.9627	2.2774
0	.0478	.0632	−.0016	.4744	1.8928
0	.0718	.0422	.0006	3.2964	2.1331
0	.2689	.1729	.0287	.1224	.9277
0	−.3107	−.8780	−.2969	.1945	1.0493
0	.0766	−.0734	.0076	.1681	1.0789
0	.3899	.0809	.0447	.2186	.9273
0	.0664	−.1266	−.1556	.1471	3.6192
0	.0147	−.1443	−.0498	.1431	6.5145
0	.1321	.0686	.0008	.3544	2.3224
0	.2039	−.0476	.1263	.8965	1.0457
0	.0549	.0592	−.2279	.0913	1.6016
0	−.5359	−.3487	−.0322	.4595	.9191
0	−.0801	−.0835	.0036	.0481	.7730
0	.3294	.0171	.0371	.2877	3.1382
0	.5056	−.1951	.2026	.5380	1.9514
0	.1759	.1343	.0946	.1955	1.9218
0	−.2772	.1619	−.0302	.1225	2.3250
0	.2551	−.3442	−.1108	1.2212	2.2815
0	−.1294	.0085	−.0971	.1764	1.3113
0	.2027	−.1169	−.0261	.5965	.7892
0	−.0901	−.2710	.0014	.1473	2.5064
0	−.3757	−1.6945	−.4504	1.2197	2.2685
0	.3424	−.1104	.0541	1.5052	1.0416
0	.0234	−.0246	.0320	.6406	1.1091
0	.3579	.1515	.0812	.1991	1.4582
0	−.0888	−.0371	.0197	.1931	1.3767
0	.2845	.2038	.0171	.3357	1.3258
0	.0011	−.0631	−.2225	.3891	1.7680
0	.1209	.2823	−.0113	.3157	2.3219
0	.2525	−.1730	−.4861	.1656	1.4441
0	.3181	−.1093	−.0857	.3755	1.9789
0	.1254	.1956	.0079	.2073	1.4890
0	.1777	.0891	.0695	.1924	1.6871
0	.2409	.1660	.0746	.2516	1.8524
0	.2496	.1260	−.2474	.1660	3.0950

BR	= Bankrupt.
WC/TA	= Working capital / Total assets.
RE/TA	= Retained earnings / Total assets.
EBIT/TA	= Earnings before interest and tax / Total assets.
MVE/TD	= Market value of equity / Total debt.
S/TA	= Sales / Total assets.

Table 11A.3

Back-Propagation Network

Number of layers = 3
  layers numbered from 1 (input) to 3 (output)

Layer dimensions:
  layer 1: (1, 5)
  layer 2: (1, 5)
  layer 3: (1, 1)

Cycles trained = 95

Weights initialized from −0.300 to 0.300

Noise = 0.00000, decay = 0.00000

Tolerance = 0.00000

Learning rates for layers:
  layer 2: 0.40000
  layer 3: 0.40000

Momentum terms for layers:
  layer 2: 0.86000
  layer 3: 0.86000

Biases for hidden and output layers:
layer 2 biases:
        0.07636−1.41765   −3.74051   2.887040.31603
layer 3 biases:
        −2.45347

Weight matrices: (to unit I from unit J, J changing fastest)
layer 1 to 2 weights:

−0.29914 −1.12996 −0.94523 −1.05204 0.18254   0.00316 10.80784 9.43302
−0.78687   0.01702 −0.02624 12.85093 9.72821   1.17494 −0.49308 −0.81009
−7.56186 −8.20073 −8.32964   0.94388 0.10122 −1.40891 −1.54195 −1.43610
  0.11747

layer 2 to 3 weights:

−0.58688 5.63501   6.35895 −6.80284 −0.87855

Table 11A.4
Modified Perceptron Network

Number of layer = 2
  layers numbered from 1 (input) to 2 (output)

Layer dimensions:
  layer 1:   (1, 5)
  layer 2:   (1, 1)

Cycles trained = 934

Weights initialized from −0.300 to 0.300

Noise = 0.00000, decay = 0.00000

Tolerance = 0.00000

Learning rates for layers:
  layer 2: 0.17500

Momentum terms for layers:
  layer 2: 0.80000

Biases for hidden and output layers:
layer 2 biases:
  −6.01205

Weight matrices: (to unit I from unit J, J changing fastest)
layer 1 to 2 weights:
  −1.47879   19.58733   29.66311   1.27743   −0.23120

Neural Networks for Bankruptcy Prediction: The Power to Solve Financial Problems

Kevin G. Coleman, Timothy J. Graettinger, and
William F. Lawrence

INTRODUCTION

One cannot pick up a newspaper or tune into a news broadcast without being painfully aware of the rising number of bankruptcies. Within the realm of finance, the FDIC reported that 1,000 banks closed over the past five years. The disaster within the savings and loan industry has been a national issue.

Neural Networks for Bankruptcy Prediction appears courtesy of NeuralWare, Inc., Pittsburgh, PA. This article appeared in *AI Review*, July/August, 1991, pp. 48–50.

Financial institutions are not alone in suffering. As Figure 12.1 shows, commercial and individual bankruptcies are also steadily rising. In 1990 there were about 725,000 filings for Chapter 7 or Chapter 11 bankruptcies. As a natural result, debt associated with bankruptcies is at its largest point in our history.

While bankruptcies pose grave problems for credit institutions, they are also a nightmare for accounting firms. Aside from losing the income from a paying client, accounting firms can share the liability for bankruptcies. Liability was one of the major reasons for the Laventhal liquidation. The state of California sought to have Ernst & Young's accounting license suspended for their role in the collapse of the Lincoln Savings & Loan Association.

Figure 12.1

Rise in Bankruptcy Filings, 1981 through 1989

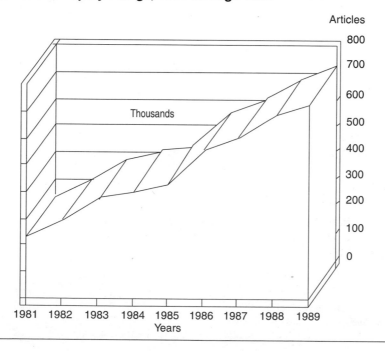

NEURAL NETWORK SOLUTIONS

Clearly the ability to accurately predict if an institution, company, or individual will become bankrupt is of paramount importance. NeuralWare's Applications Development Service and Support (ADSS) group has been involved with a number of successful bankruptcy prediction applications. These applications were built using the NeuralWorks Professional neural network development system. One of the highlights of the NeuralWorks development system is that, after development, NeuralWare Designer Pack can be used to port the network to an ANSI standard "C" module for deployment in a customer's computing system.

Both applications discussed in this chapter used standard back-propagation networks, with the addition of a proprietary error function created by the ADSS staff. The first application was developed for Peat Marwick and was used to predict banks that were certain to fail within a year. The predicted certainty of failure was then given to bank examiners dealing with the bank in question.

The back-propagation network the ADSS engineers developed had 11 inputs, each of which was a ratio developed by Peat Marwick. Figure 12.2 shows an example of one of these ratios. The inputs were connected to a single hidden layer, which in turn was connected to a single node in the output layer. The network output was a single value denoting whether the bank would or would not fail within that calendar year. The network employed the normalized-cumulative-delta learning rule and the

---

Figure 12.2

The Derivation of PRMCAPAS

One of the ratios used as an input to the network developed for Peat Marwick:

Numerator		Total equity capital
	+	Minority interest
	+	Total mandatory conversion into capital
	−	Allowance for losses
Denominator:	−	Total assets and allowances

---

hyperbolic-tangent transfer function, both standard choices within the development system. In fact, with the exception of applying the custom error function, the entire network could be constructed from within a single dialog box in the NeuralWorks Professional II/PLUS development system.

The network was trained on a set of about 1,000 examples, 900 of which were viable banks and 100 of which were banks that had actually gone bankrupt. Training consisted of about 50,000 iterations of the training set.

Peat Marwick[1] has published that the model can predict 50 percent of the population of banks that are viable, and predict failed banks with an accuracy of 99 percent (with an accepted error of 1 percent). If the accepted error is increased to 10 percent, the network can predict both viable and bankrupt banking institutions with an accuracy of 90 percent.

NeuralWare's ADSS has also developed a bankruptcy prediction application for one of the nation's leading credit card institutions. This prediction application is currently used in identifying those credit card holders who have a 100 percent probability of going bankrupt, allowing the institution to take action before this occurs.

NeuralWare isn't the only group that has had success in applying neural computing to bankruptcy prediction. Odom and Sharda,[2] at Oklahoma State University, have compared the prediction capabilities of a back-propagation neural network with a discriminant analysis technique. Using a training set divided into 10 percent bankrupt firms and 90 percent nonbankrupt firms, the neural network was able to predict bankruptcy with an accuracy of 77.78 percent. This was opposed to an accuracy of 59.26 percent produced by discriminant analysis. By changing the ratio of the bankrupt to nonbankrupt firms in the training set to 50 percent each, the bankruptcy predicting accuracy of the neural network improved 81.48 percent. Through techniques developed by the ADSS group, NeuralWare has further improved accuracy over that reported by Odom and Sharda.

WHAT LIES AHEAD?

Figure 12.3 shows a bankruptcy prediction system that incorporates a neural network and an expert system. This hybrid application feeds data from conventional programs (data entry screens, links to external databases,

Figure 12.3

A Hybrid Neural Network and Expert System Bankruptcy Detection Application

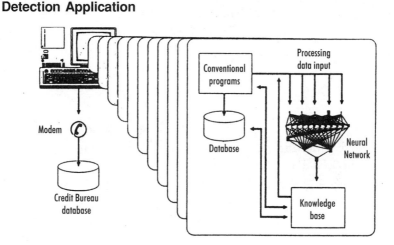

etc.) to both the database and the neural network. The neural network then produces a single output value, which is actually a probability of whether or not the company, institution, or individual will declare bankruptcy. Using the Explain Net function, a unique feature in the NeuralWorks Professional II/PLUS development system, the neural network can also inform the knowledge base about which of the input parameters had the most effect on its prediction.

The expert system can then apply its rule-based decision-making capabilities and recommend remedial actions to improve the financial condition of the company, institution, or individual. It can also recommend a course of action to be taken by its owner—a credit institution or accounting firm. This is a vital capability, as the system is not only able to pinpoint potential problems but also can suggest ways to avoid problems or at least minimize losses.

A fascinating feature of this system is its ability to play "what-if" games to determine the efficacy of remedial action. Because the knowledge base also has access to the conventional programs supplying data to the neural network, it can then vary the parameters that were originally fed into the neural network. By experimenting with changes to the most significant parameters and then checking the resultant probability of bank-ruptcy, the system can actually establish what suggested actions are likely to have the most effect.

Finally, the probability of bankruptcy and the suggested actions are added to the database. The result is a self-contained system that both predicts bankruptcy and advises the credit institution or accounting firm on what to do.

SUMMARY

Neural networks are already having a positive impact on the rising prob-lems of institutional, company, and individual bankruptcies. Combined neural network and expert system applications can take a further step in quelling the problem of bankruptcies, by not only predicting the oc-currence of bankruptcy but by recommending courses of action that have been tested against the neural network model.

ENDNOTES

1. T. B. Bell, G. S. Ribar, and J. R. Verchio, "Neural Nets vs. Logistic Regres-sion: A Comparison of Each Model's Ability to Predict Commercial Bank Failures." Deloitte & Touche/University of Kansas Auditing Symposium, May 1990.

2. M. D. Odom and R. Sharda, "A Neural Network Model for Bankruptcy Prediction," *Proceedings of the IJCNN*, June 1990, pp. II-163–II-168.

13

PREDICTING BANK FAILURES: A NEURAL NETWORK APPROACH

Kar Yan Tam and Melody Y. Kiang

INTRODUCTION

Many managerial decisions involve classifying an observation into one of several groups. A special case of this problem is binary classification, in which the number of groups is limited to two. Extensive literature has been devoted to studying this problem under various contexts, including credit scoring, default prediction, merger and acquisition, and bond rating, just to name a few. The solution to this problem is a discriminant function from the variable space in which observations are defined into a binary set.

© 1992, The Institute of Management Sciences. This article originally appeared in *Management Science* 38, no. 7 (July 1992), pp. 926–47. Reprinted with permission.

Since Fisher's seminal work,[1] numerous methods have been developed for classification purposes. They are typically referred to as multivariate discriminant analysis (hereafter referred to as DA). In general, these methods accept a random sample of observations defined by a chosen set of variables and generate a discriminant function that serves as a classifier. They differ in two major aspects: (1) assumption on group distribution and (2) functional form of the discriminant function. In the current study, we have taken a neural net approach to the binary classification problem and compared it with popular DA methods. Our goal is to identify the potentials and limitations of neural nets as a tool to do discriminant analysis in business research.

The subject of neural nets, once viewed as the theoretical foundation for building artificial intelligent systems in the 1950s and 1960s, was proven to be too limited by Minsky and Papert.[2] Using simple examples, Minsky and Papert showed that only a few functions are guaranteed to be learned by a neural net. In the case of the well-known exclusive or (XOR)[3] function, they showed that the function cannot be learned by a two-layer network; however, recent breakthroughs in neural nets research have overcome some of the limitations cited earlier. For example, Rumelhart, Hinton, and Williams[4] have developed a back-propagation learning algorithm to train a multilayer network that can reproduce the XOR function.

The resurgent interest in neural nets has been manifested in the study of a new class of computation models called the *connectionist models*, which have limited analogy, if any, to their neurophysiology origin.[5] Connectionist systems provide massive parallel processing capabilities that are essential in many domains, such as pattern recognition, concept classification, speech processing, and real-time process control.[6,7] Fault-tolerance is another appealing property that has profound implications in the design and fabrication of integrated circuits. A connectionist system can tolerate minor component failures without impairing the entire system. Existing computers are serial machines based on the Von Neumann architecture proposed some 40 years ago. These machines are designed to execute serial threads of instructions and are vulnerable even to minute component failures. Because our main concern is not in the biological isomorphism of connectionist models nor their implications in computer architecture design, we shall focus on the modeling capability of neural nets as inspired by these computation models. In particular, we shall compare the performance of classification models developed by popular DA methods and by neural nets along the following dimensions: robustness, predictive accuracy, adaptability, and explanatory capability.

The test bed used in our comparative study consists of bank bankruptcy cases reported in the state of Texas. The increasing numbers of commercial bank failures have evolved into an economic crisis that has received much attention in recent years. It is therefore both desirable and warranted to explore new predictive techniques and to provide early warnings to regulatory agencies. Tam and Kiang[8] introduced a neural net approach for bank failure prediction. However, there are methodological problems that limit the generalization of the findings. For instance, not all information about a bank was used, and the final results may be biased by the holdout samples chosen. In this study, we have extended our previous work by incorporating misclassification costs and prior probabilities in the neural net models. We have included additional classification techniques for comparison and have taken a rigorous approach in validating the results.[9]

MULTIVARIATE DISCRIMINANT ANALYSIS

Linear Discriminant Model

Perhaps the most widely used DA method is the one due to Fisher.[1] The Fisher procedure constructs a discriminant function by maximizing the ratio of between-groups and within-groups variances. Classifiers derived from the Fisher procedure are known to be optimal in minimizing the expected costs of misclassifications, provided the following conditions are satisfied:

1. Each group follows a multivariate normal distribution.

2. The covariance matrices of each group are identical.

3. The mean vectors, covariance matrices, prior probabilities, and misclassification costs are known.

In the case of binary classification, the discriminant function is stated as:

$$D(X) = X'\Sigma^{-1}(\mu_1 - \mu_2) - \frac{1}{2}(\mu_1 - \mu_2)^T \Sigma^{-1}(\mu_1 + \mu_2)$$

where μ_1, μ_2, and Σ^{-1} are the mean vectors and inverse of the common covariance matrix, respectively. The threshold value of the decision rule is $\ln(C_{21}\pi_1 / C_{12}\pi_2)$ where C_{12}, C_{21}, π_1, and π_2 are the misclassification costs and prior probabilities of each group. This method yields a linear function relating a set of independent variables to a scoring variable. It represents a hyperplane that divides the variable space into two partitions, with each assigned to a group.

DA minimizes the expected misclassification cost, provided the normality and equal dispersion assumptions are satisfied. Unfortunately, violations of these assumptions occur regularly. It is common that individual variables are not normally distributed.[10] Examples can be found where variables are bounded or assume category values. Transformations, such as taking the natural logarithm, are suggested to approximate normal distribution; however, the transformed variables may be difficult to interpret. If the covariance matrices are different, quadratic instead of linear functions should be employed. Quadratic classifiers may be quite accurate in classifying the training sample, but they do not perform well as linear models in holdout sample tests.[11] Lachenbruch, Sneeringer, and Revo[12] reported a similar conclusion after comparing the two methods under various nonmultivariate normal distributions. Whether the function is linear or quadratic, a fundamental condition that must be satisfied is that the two groups are discrete and identifiable. Situations deviating from this condition can be found where observations of each group form clusters in different regions of the variable space. Depending on the number of clusters in each group, the discriminant functions (linear or quadratic) may incur a high error rate for both the training and holdout sample.

Altman et al.[11] identified four related problems in the use of DA techniques in classification: (1) relative significance of the individual variables, (2) reduction of dimensionality, (3) elimination of insignificant variables, and (4) existence of time series relationships. Recognizing the limitations of linear classifiers, a common practice is to accept the results as if the assumptions had been satisfied.

Logistic Regression

An alternative to the linear DA model is logistic regression. A nonlinear logistic function having the following form is used:

$$Y = \frac{1}{1 + e^{y}}, \qquad y = c_0 + \sum_{i=1}^{n} c_i X_i$$

where X_i, $1 \le i \le n$, represent the set of individual variables, c_i is the coefficient of the ith variable, and Y is the dependent variable. Because Y falls between 0 and 1, it is usually interpreted as the probability of a class outcome. In practice, it has been suggested that the logistic regression approach is often preferred over DA.[13] Harrell and Lee[14] contended that even when all the assumptions of DA hold, a logit model is virtually as efficient as a linear classifier.

k Nearest Neighbor

Distribution-free techniques are applicable under less restrictive conditions regarding the underlying population distribution and data measurement scales. kNN is a nonparametric method for classifying observations into one or several groups based on one or more quantitative variables. It not only relaxes the normality assumption, it also eliminates the functional form required in DA and logistic regression. The group assignment of an observation is decided by the group assignments of its first k nearest neighbor. The distance $d(x, y)$ between any two observations x and y is usually defined by the Mahalanobis distance between x and y. Using the nearest neighbor decision rule, an observation is assigned to the group to which the majority of its k nearest neighbors belong. This method has the merits of better approximating the sample distribution by dividing the variable space into any arbitrary number of decision regions, with the maximum bounded by the total number of observations.

Decision Tree (ID3)

Instead of generating a decision rule in the form of a discriminant function, the ID3 method creates a decision tree that properly classifies the training sample.[15,16,17] This tree induction method has been applied in credit scoring,[18] corporate failures prediction,[19] and stock portfolio construction.[20] Frydman, Altman, and Kao[21] applied a similar technique, called *recursive partitioning*, to generate a discriminant tree. Both ID3 and recursive partitioning employ a nonbacktracking splitting procedure that recursively partitions a set of examples into disjointed subsets. These methods differ in their splitting criteria. The ID3 method intends to maximize the entropy of the split subsets, whereas the recursive partitioning technique is designed to minimize the expected cost of misclassifications.

The five techniques compared in this study can be categorized into two groups: machine learning (neural nets and ID3) and statistical techniques (DA, logit, and kNN). Although previous research has focused mainly on a single method, the mix of techniques employed in this study allows a more comprehensive comparison of the different approaches to the problem.

NEURAL NETWORKS

A neural net consists of a number of interconnected homogeneous processing units. Each unit is a simple computation device. Its behavior can be modeled by simple mathematical functions. A unit i receives input signals from other units, aggregates these signals based on an input function I_i, and generates an output signal based on an output function O_i (sometimes called a transfer function). The output signal is then routed to other units as directed by the topology of the network. Although no assumption is imposed on the form of input/output functions at each node other than to be continuous and differentiable, we will use the following functions as suggested in Rumelhart et al.[5]:

$$I_i = \sum_j w_{ij}O_j + \varphi_i \quad \text{and} \quad O_i = \frac{1}{1 + e^{I_i}}$$

where

I_i = input of unit i.
O_i = output of unit i.
w_{ij} = connection weight between unit i and j.
φ_i = bias of unit i.

Feedforward Networks

The configuration of a neural net is represented by a weighted directed graph (WDG) with nodes representing units and links representing connections. Each link is assigned a numerical value representing the weight of the connection. Variations of the general WDG topology are found in a number of connectionist models.[22,23] A special class of neural nets called feedforward networks is used here.

In a feedforward network, there are three types of processing units: input units, output units, and hidden units. Input units accept signals from the environment and reside in the lowest layer of the network. Output units send signals to the environment and reside in the highest layer. Hidden units are units that do not interact directly with the environment and hence are invisible (i.e., hidden from the environment). Connections within a layer or from a higher layer to a lower are prohibited, but they can skip several layers.

The pattern of connectivity of a feedforward network is described by its weight vector W—weights associated with the connections. It is W that constitutes what a neural net knows and determines how it will respond to any arbitrary input from the environment. A feedforward network with an appropriate W can be used to model the causal relationship between a set of variables. Changing the model is accomplished by modifying the weight associated with each connection.

Back-Propagation Learning Algorithm

It is very difficult to assign an appropriate W for a classification task, especially when there is little information about the population distribution. A general solution is to let the network learn the task by training it with examples.[24] A typical learning algorithm will search through the space of W for a set of weights offering the best fit with the given examples. Notable learning algorithms are the perceptron convergence procedure[25] and the back-propagation algorithm.[4]

The back-propagation learning algorithm, designed to train a feedforward network, overcomes some of perceptron's limitations by making it possible to train a multiple-layer network. It is an effective learning technique that is capable of exploiting the regularities and exceptions in the training sample. A flow chart of the algorithm is shown in Figure 13.1. The back-propagation algorithm consists of two phases: forward-propagation and backward-propagation. Suppose we have s examples, each described by an input vector $X_i = (x_{i1}, x_{i2},...,x_{im})$ and an output vector $D_i = (d_{i1}, d_{i2},...,d_{in})$, $1 \le i \le s$. In forward-propagation, X_i is fed into the input layer, and an output $Y_i = (y_{i1}, y_{i2},...,y_{in})$ is generated on the basis of the current W. The value of Y_i is then compared with the actual (or desired) output D_i by calculating the squared error $(y_{ij} - d_{ij})^2$, $1 \le i \le n$, at each output unit. Output differences are summed up to generate an error function E, defined as:

Figure 13.1

Flowchart of the Back-Propagation Algorithm

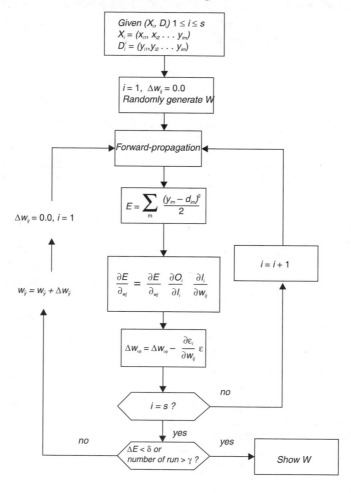

$$E = \sum_{i=1}^{s} \sum_{j=1}^{n} \frac{y_{ij} - d_{ij})^2}{2}$$

The objective is to minimize E by changing W so that all input vectors are correctly mapped to their corresponding output vectors. Thus, the learning process can be cast as a minimization problem with objective function E defined in the space of W.

The second phase performs a gradient descent in the weight space to locate the optimal solution. The direction and magnitude change Δw_{ij} of each w_{ij} can be calculated as:

$$\Delta w_{ij} = -\frac{\partial E}{\partial w_{ij}}\, \varepsilon$$

where $0 < \varepsilon < 1$ is a parameter controlling the convergence rate of the algorithm.

The total squared error calculated in the first phase is propagated back, layer by layer, from the output units to the input units in the second phase. Weight adjustments are determined by the way propagation occurs at each level. Because I_i, O_i, and E are all continuous and differentiable, the value of $\partial E/\partial w_{ij}$ at each level can be calculated by applying the chain rule:

$$\frac{\partial E}{\partial w_{ij}} = \frac{\partial E}{\partial O_i}\frac{\partial O_i}{\partial I_i}\frac{\partial I_i}{\partial w_{ij}}$$

W can be updated in two ways. Either W is updated for each (X_i, D_i) pair, or Δw_{ij} are accumulated and updated after a complete run of all examples. The two phases are executed in each iteration of the back-propagation algorithm until E converges. Although the back-propagation algorithm does not guarantee optimal solution, Rumelhart et al.[5] reported that solutions obtained from the algorithm come close to the optimal ones in their experiments.

BANK BANKRUPTCY PREDICTION

The number of financial distresses in the banking industry has reached a historic high unparalleled since the Great Depression. The number of bankruptcy cases filed under the Federal Deposit Insurance Corporation (FDIC) increased from less than 50 in 1984 to an estimate of over 400 in 1991. To monitor the member banks and to assure their proper compliance with federal regulations, the FDIC has committed substantial efforts to both on-site examinations and off-site surveillance activities. Since the mid-1970s, the FDIC has been operating an "early warning" system that facilitates the rating process by identifying troubled banks and alerting the agency for early inspection.[26] This is accomplished by statistically evaluating the reports filed by each bank on a regular basis. According to West,[27] "performance ratios of banks are compared to some standard or arranged to some sort of statistical cutoff. Banks that 'fail' these ratio tests are singled out for more careful scrutiny."

Given the importance of this subject at both the micro and macro level, numerous models have been developed to predict bank failure. These models employ statistical techniques that include regression analysis,[28] multivariate discriminant analysis,[29,30,31] multivariate probit or logic analysis,[32,33] arctangent regression analysis,[34] and factor-logistic analysis.[27] Although widely practiced, these models have been criticized for their problematic methodologies,[35] and a satisfactory model has yet to be developed.

DATA SAMPLE AND MODEL CONSTRUCTION

Data Sample

The data sample consists of Texas banks that failed in the period 1985–1987.[36] Texas banks were selected for two reasons. First, more than one quarter of the failed banks in 1987 were located in Texas.[37] Not surprisingly, the high bankruptcy rate coincides with the general economic conditions in the Southwestern region, especially in the energy and real estate sectors of the economy. Thus, it is interesting to develop a prediction model specifically tailored to the economic environment in this region. Second, involving banks from the same region, instead of those from other states, increases the sample's homogeneity.

The data sample consists of bank data one year and two years prior to failure. As a control measure, a failed bank was matched with a nonfailed bank in terms of (1) asset size, (2) number of branches, (3) age, and (4) charter status. In each period, 118 banks (59 failed and 59 nonfailed) were selected as the training sample.

Each bank is described by 19 financial ratios that have been used in previous studies. The list of ratios is shown in Table 13.1. The selection of variables followed closely the CAMEL criteria used by the FDIC. CAMEL is an acronym for capital, asset, management, equity, and liquidity, which is generally adopted by all U.S. bank regulatory agencies. An assessor rates a bank according to its scores in each of these five areas, and the composite ratings are taken to reflect the financial conditions of the bank. Rating results provide early warnings to an agency, drawing its attention to those banks that have a high likelihood of failure in the coming one or two years.

Table 13.1
A List of Financial Variables

Name	Description
capas	Capital/Assets
agfas	(Agricultural production & farm loans + Real estate loans secured by farm land)/Net loans & leases
comas	(Commercial and industrial loans)/Net loans & leases
indas	(Loans to individuals)/Net loan & leases
resas	(Real estate loans)/Net loan & leases
pasin	(Total loans 90 days or more past due)/Net loans & leases
nonin	(Total nonaccrual loans & leases)/Net loans & leases
losin	(Provision for loan losses)/Average loans
netln	(Net charge-offs)/Average loans
rtoas	Return on average assets
intdp	(Total interest paid on deposits)/Total deposits
expas	(Total expense)/Total assets
incas	(Net income)/Total assets
infln	(Interests and fees on loans + Income from lease financing rec)/Net loans & losses
incex	(Total income)/Total expense
curas	(Cash + U.S. Treasury & government agency obligations)/Total assets
govas	(Federal funds sold + Securities)/Total assets
llnas	(Total loans & leases)/Total assets
llndp	(Total loans & leases)/Total deposits

The 19 ratios can be grouped into four of these five criteria. The first ratio represents the capital adequacy of the bank; ratios 2–10 measure asset quality; the bank's earnings are captured by ratios 11–15; and liquidity is represented by ratios 16–19. No explicit ratio was used for the management criterion because the quality of management, which is difficult to quantify, will eventually be reflected by the above-mentioned ratios.

Linear Discriminant Model

The Kolmogorov-Smirnov test[38] was performed for each of the 19 financial ratios in the data sample to check if the normal distribution assumption was satisfied. The test indicated that 15 out of 19 ratios were not normally distributed in the one-year period. In the two-year period, only one ratio was shown to be normally distributed. For those ratios that failed the test, the natural logarithm transformation was performed. The Kolmogorov-Smirnov test was then repeated for the transformed ratios. The results showed that 13 out of 19 ratios in the one-year period and 14 out of 19 in the two-year period were still not normally distributed. Because no significant improvement was observed, we decided to use the original ratios to construct the DA models. The DA models were implemented using FORTRAN with embedded IMSL procedure calls.

Logistic Model

Like the DA model, no variable transformation was performed. All 19 variables were used to estimate the logit model for the one- and two-year period.[39] A bank will be classified as a failed bank if the value of the dependent variables is less than 0.5, and as a nonfailed bank otherwise.

kNN Models

Two kNN models, one with $k = 1$ and the other with $k = 3$, were constructed for each period.[40] For $k = 1$, a bank was assigned to the group that contains its nearest neighbor, whereas in $k = 3$, the bank was assigned to the group that contained the majority of its three closest neighbors. Even values of k were not included due to the possibility of a tie.

ID3

The ID3 algorithm was implemented in CommonLisp. A chi-square stopping rule with a significance level of 5 percent was used to reduce the
effects of noisy data. The classification trees generated by using ID3 for
both periods are shown in Figures 13.2a and 13.2b. The *F* and *NF* in
each leaf of the tree denote the number of failed and nonfailed banks,
respectively. The number of variables has been reduced from 19 to 6 in
the one-year period and to 8 in the second-year period. The classification
tree for the former exhibits a more balanced and less complex structure
than the latter, indicating that observations in the two-year period may
intermesh more uniformly than those in the one-year period. In addition,
two-thirds of the variables in the one-year period (nonln, expas, pasln,

Figure 13.2

Classification Trees

a. Classification Trees for One-Year Period

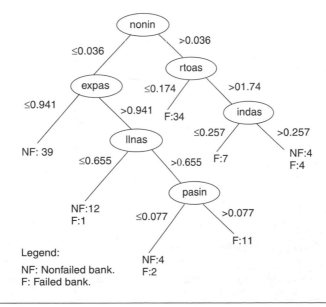

Legend:

NF: Nonfailed bank.
F: Failed bank.

Figure 13.2

(concluded)

b. Classification Tree for Two-Year Period

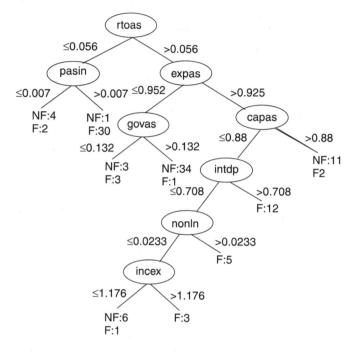

Legend:
NF: Nonfailed bank.
F: Failed bank.

rtoas), representing mainly asset quality and earnings, also appear in the two-year period.

Neural Network Models

We have performed some exploratory experiments to decide on the configuration of the neural nets used in our study. This is a required step because there is yet a formal algorithm to be developed to map a task

Figure 13.3
Network Configurations

a. The Network Configuration of Net_0

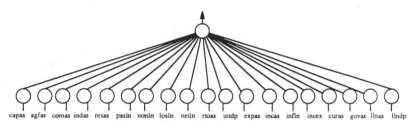

capas agfas comas indas resas pasln nonln losln netln rtoas intdp expas incas infln incex curas govas llnas llndp

b. The Network Configuration of Net_{10}

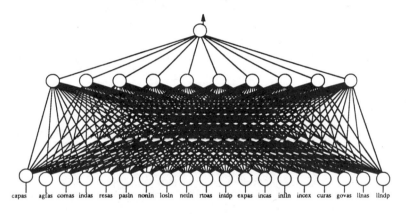

capas agfas comas indas resas pasln nonln losln netln rtoas intdp expas incas infln incex curas govas llnas llndp

to a configuration. We have constructed two-layer and three-layer networks; for three-layer networks, different numbers of hidden units were tried. Finally, two configurations, one with no hidden unit (two-layer) and the other with 10 hidden units (three-layer), were constructed for each period (see Figures 13.3a and 13.3b).

The original back-propagation algorithm does not take into account the prior probabilities of each group and their misclassification costs. To incorporate them into the learning algorithm, the objective function E is generalized to E_w, defined as:

$$E_w = \sum_{i=1}^{2} Z_i \sum_{j=1}^{n_i} \frac{(y_{ij} - d_{ij})^2}{2}$$

where $Z_2 = C_{12}\pi_2$ represents Type I misclassification error, $Z_1 = C_{21}\pi_1$ represents Type II misclassification error, and n_i (i = 1, 2) is the number of examples in group i. The Type I error is defined as the event of assigning an observation to group 1 that should be in group 2, while the Type II error involves assigning an observation to group 2 that should be in group 1. The value of Z_i is treated as the weight of the squared error incurred by each observation. It is clear that the initial objective function E is a special case of E_w by setting $C_{12}\pi_2 = C_{21}\pi_1$. In the current study, we will refer to nonfailed banks as group 1 and failed banks as group 2.

Because we are concerned with dichotomous classification (failure versus nonfailure), only a single output unit is needed. The decision is stated as:

output unit > 0.5 → group 1 (nonfailed banks),

output unit ≤ 0.5 → group 2 (failed banks).

Instead of using $\Delta w_{ij} = -\partial E/\partial w_{ij}\varepsilon$, which may be slow in terms of convergence, we use an accelerated version as shown:

$$\Delta w_{ij}(t) = -\varepsilon \frac{\partial E}{\partial w(t)} + \alpha \Delta w_{ij}(t-1)$$

where $0 \leq \alpha \leq 1$ is an exponential decay factor determining the contribution of the previous gradient descent.

To smooth out drastic changes to W by some outlining examples, we prefer the accumulated weights updating scheme. No prior information is available as to how units should be connected in the three-layer network, so all hidden units are fully connected to the input units.

The back-propagation procedure was implemented in Pascal and run on an EMX machine. Five different sets of weights were generated and five different runs were done for each neural net model. Each run was allocated a maximum of 2,000 iterations. The classification accuracy obtained by each run was ranked by total misclassifications, and the median run was taken as the result.

COMPUTATION RESULTS

The classification accuracy of neural nets is first compared with that of DA, using different prior probabilities and misclassification costs. Two prior probabilities for failed banks (π_2), 0.01 and 0.02, and eight misclassification costs were used. We followed the distribution of misclassification costs used previously by Frydman et al.,[21] where the misclassification cost of nonfailed banks (i.e., C_{21}) is kept to 1, whereas the misclassification costs of failed banks (i.e., C_{12}) are set to 1, 5, 25, 40, 50, 60, 75, and 100. The values of ε, α, and δ are set to 0.7, 0.5, and 0.01, respectively.

Results of this comparison are shown in Tables 13.2–13.5. In Tables 13.2 and 13.3, the Type I and Type II errors of each model are given for each combination of prior probability and misclassification cost. The resubstitution risks for each combination are also calculated and displayed in Tables 13.4–13.5. According to Frydman et al. (1985), the resubstitution risk is the observed expected cost of misclassification, defined as:

$$C_{12}\pi_2\frac{n_2}{N_2} + C_{21}\pi_1\frac{n_1}{N_1},$$

where n_i is the total number of type i misclassifications, and N_i is the sample size of the ith group.

The numbers in Tables 13.2 and 13.3 indicate that neural nets transcend smoothly from minimizing Type I errors to Type II errors as C_{12} increases. On the contrary, there is a sharp transition from $C_{12} = 5$ to $C_{12} = 25$ in DA. The proportion of DA's Type I and Type II errors remains virtually the same as C_{12} increases beyond 25, and its resubstitution risk starts to level off at this value. As shown, DA models are not sensitive to changes in C_{12} and π_2. This can be explained by the fact that the training samples are not normally distributed. There is evidence that nonfailed banks have a multimodal distribution that is particularly apparent in the one-year period. For example, looking at the first and fourth rows in Table 13.2, there is a distinct cluster of 12 to 13 nonfailed banks that fall into the decision region of the failed group. Similarly, a cluster of about 10 nonfailed banks is observed in Table 13.3.

In Table 13.2, there are several occasions where Net_0 and Net_{10} generate inconsistent results. For example, the values of Z_i are known to be identical for both $C_{12} = 100$, $\pi_2 = 0.0,1$ and $C_{12} = 50$, $\pi_2 = 0.02$. One should expect similar results in both cases, but both their number and proportion of

Table 13.2

Misclassification Errors in the Training Sample for Different Misclassification Costs and Prior Probabilities (One-Year Period)

C_{12} =	1			5			25			40			50			60			75			100		
Model	I	II	T	I	II	T	I	II	T	I	II	T	I	II	T	I	II	T	I	II	T	I	II	T
$\pi_2 = 0.01$																							(*)	
DA	8	7	(15)	4	8	(12)	0	11	(11)	0	12	(12)	0	12	(12)	0	12	(12)	0	13	(13)	0	13	(13)
Net0	11	1	(12)	9	1	(10)	8	1	(9)	6	2	(8)	6	3	(9)	4	6	(10)	4	7	(11)	0	8	(8)
Net10	16	0	(16)	11	0	(11)	10	0	(10)	8	0	(8)	5	0	(5)	4	0	(4)	3	0	(3)	0	2	(2)
$\pi_2 = 0.02$													(*)											
DA	6	8	(14)	3	9	(12)	0	12	(12)	0	13	(13)	0	13	(13)	0	14	(14)	0	14	(14)	0	14	(14)
Net0	17	1	(18)	9	2	(11)	8	3	(11)	6	5	(11)	6	5	(11)	0	7	(7)	0	11	(11)	0	15	(15)
Net10	11	0	(11)	10	0	(10)	10	0	(10)	0	6	(6)	0	7	(7)	0	9	(9)	0	10	(10)	0	13	(13)

Notes:
(*) $\pi_2 C_{12} \approx \pi_1 C_{21}$.
I   Number of Type I misclassifications.
II   Number of Type II misclassifications.
T   Total number of misclassifications (in parentheses).

Table 13.3

Misclassification Errors in the Training Sample for Different Misclassification Costs and Prior Probabilities (Two-Year Period)

C_{12} =	1			5			25			40			50			60			75			100		
Model	I	II	T	I	II	T	I	II	T	I	II	T	I	II	T	I	II	T	I	II	T	I	II	T
$\pi_2 = 0.01$																								(*)
DA	34	5	(39)	20	6	(26)	5	8	(13)	5	10	(15)	5	10	(15)	5	10	(15)	5	10	(15)	4	10	(14)
Net0	39	0	(39)	30	0	(30)	17	1	(18)	16	1	(17)	11	2	(13)	12	4	(16)	10	6	(16)	8	6	(14)
Net10	35	0	(35)	19	0	(19)	19	0	(19)	14	2	(16)	12	3	(15)	9	3	(12)	6	5	(11)	5	6	(11)
$\pi_2 = 0.02$															(*)									
DA	27	5	(32)	13	8	(21)	5	10	(15)	5	10	(15)	4	10	(14)	4	10	(14)	3	10	(13)	3	11	(14)
Net0	35	0	(35)	20	0	(20)	16	1	(17)	4	8	(12)	4	8	(12)	4	8	(12)	4	10	(14)	3	13	(16)
Net10	29	0	(29)	13	0	(13)	11	3	(14)	10	4	(14)	3	6	(9)	3	6	(9)	3	6	(9)	0	17	(17)

Notes:
(*) $\pi_2 C_{12} \approx \pi_1 C_{21}$.
I   Number of Type I misclassifications.
II   Number of Type II misclassifications.
T   Total number of misclassifications (in parentheses).

Table 13.4

Resubstitution Risks of the Training Sample (One-Year Period)

Model	$C_{12} =$	1	5	25	40	50	60	75	100
	$\pi_2 = 0.01$								(*)
DA		0.119	0.138	0.185	0.201	0.201	0.201	0.218	0.218
Net_0		0.019	0.024	0.151	0.074	0.101	0.141	0.168	0.134
Net_{10}		0.003	0.009	0.042	0.054	0.042	0.041	0.038	0.034
	$\pi_2 = 0.02$								(*)
DA		0.135	0.155	0.199	0.216	0.216	0.233	0.233	0.233
Net_0		0.022	0.019	0.117	0.158	0.185	0.116	0.183	0.249
Net_{10}		0.004	0.017	0.085	0.100	0.116	0.150	0.166	0.216

Notes:
Resubstitution risk = $\pi_1 C_{21} n_1/N_1 + \pi_2 C_{12} n_2/N_2$ where n_i = total number of type i misclassifications; N_i = sample size of the i th group.

(*) $\pi_2 C_{12} \equiv \pi_1 C_{21}$.

Table 13.5

Resubstitution Risks of the Training Sample (Two-Year Period)

Model	$C_{12} =$	1	5	25	40	50	60	75	100
	$\pi_2 = 0.01$								(*)
DA		0.089	0.118	0.155	0.202	0.210	0.219	0.231	0.236
Net_0		0.007	0.025	0.089	0.125	0.127	0.189	0.228	0.236
Net_{10}		0.006	0.016	0.081	0.128	0.152	0.142	0.160	0.185
	$\pi_2 = 0.02$								(*)
DA		0.092	0.155	0.208	0.234	0.234	0.247	0.242	0.284
Net_0		0.012	0.034	0.152	0.187	0.203	0.214	0.268	0.318
Net_{10}		0.010	0.022	0.143	0.202	0.151	0.161	0.176	0.282

Notes:
Resubstitution risk = $\pi_1 C_{21} n_1/N_1 + \pi_2 C_{12} n_2/N_2$ where n_i = total number of type i misclassifications; N_i = sample size of the i th group.

(*) $\pi_2 C_{12} \cong \pi_1 C_{21}$.

errors are quite different. This is indirectly due to the initial weights assigned to Net_0 and Net_{10}. Because the time a net takes to converge varies according to the starting point, the search may have yet to settle on a local optimum when the program halts, resulting in a different number of misclassification errors. We have rerun the algorithm to validate this argument by lifting the iteration bound in some of these inconsistent cases. Similar results were obtained this time. Rumelhart et al.[5] and many other researchers have mentioned in their work that initial weights are used to break up the symmetry of a net.[41] They do not have a major effect on the final results if sufficient time is allowed for the net to converge. The use of five random weights is designed to average out the discrepancy in convergence periods.

In both periods, Net_0 and Net_{10} dominate DA with lower resubstitution risk across all combinations of π_2 and C_{12}. The results of Tables 13.4 and 13.5 also illustrate that Net_{10} outperforms Net_0 in most cases, with a few exceptions. These exceptions can be explained by the different running times associated with the initial weights and can be eliminated by allowing a net to run to convergence. The better performance of Net_{10} can be explained by the incorporation of hidden units, which provides a better fit with the training sample distribution. The resubstitution risks of Net_{10} and Net_0 are almost identical in the two-year period for small C_{12}. The dominating performance of Net_{10}, however, starts to degrade in the two-year period. The percentage reduction in resubstitution risk over Net_0 decreases from an average of 44 percent in the first period to 16.2 percent in the second period.

Table 13.6 depicts the misclassification rates of each method in predicting the training samples. Because logit, kNN, and ID3 do not account for prior probabilities and misclassification costs, the comparison is made possible by setting approximately $C_{12}\pi_2 \approx C_{21}\pi_1$ in DA and the neural nets.

In the one-year period, Net_{10} outperforms other methods with lower Type I and total misclassification rates. This is followed by logit, ID3, Net_0, DA, 1NN, and 3NN. In the two-year period, DA is the best classifier, scoring the lowest Type II and total misclassification errors. Net_{10} is the second best, which is followed by ID3, Net_0, logit, 1NN, and 3NN.

Misclassification rates based on the training sample are often overestimated and need further validation. The predictive accuracy of each method is validated by a holdout sample. The sample consists of 44 banks (22 failed and 22 nonfailed) and 40 banks (20 failed and 20 nonfailed) in the one- and two-year periods, respectively. Selection is made according

Table 13.6

Misclassification Rates of the Various Models Using the Training Sample

Model	Percentage (%) One-Year Prior			Two-Year Prior		
	I	II	T	I	II	T
DA	0.0	22.0	(11.0)	10.2	1.7	(6.0)
Logit	8.5	6.8	(7.7)	13.6	13.6	(13.6)
INN	37.3	23.7	(30.5)	32.2	32.2	(32.2)
3NN	35.6	25.4	(30.5)	37.3	37.3	(34.8)
ID3	10.2	5.1	(7.7)	13.5	5.1	(9.3)
Net_0	5.0	11.0	(8.0)	10.2	11.9	(11.0)
Net_{10}	0.0	7.6	(3.8)	6.7	10.2	(8.5)

Note:
The Type I and Type II misclassification rates of DA, Net_0, and Net_{10} are based on the average of $(C_{12} = 100, \pi_2 = 0.01)$ and $(C_{12} = 50, \pi_2 = 0.02)$.

to a similar matching procedure for the training sample. To facilitate comparison, the expected costs of misclassification for both Type I and Type II errors are approximately identical (i.e., $C_{12}\pi_2 \approx C_{21}\pi_1$). The validation results of the holdout sample are reported in Table 13.7.

The performance ranking in Table 13.7 is different from that of Table 13.6. In the one-year period, Net_{10} remains the best classifier in terms of fewer Type II and total errors. This is followed by DA, Net_0, logit, ID3, 1NN, and 3NN. To our surprise, logit scores the lowest Type II and total errors in the two-year period. Net_{10} comes next and is followed by Net_0, DA, 3NN, ID3, and 1NN.

The performances of DA and logit are not stable in both tests. In the first test, DA ranks the fifth in the one-year period and becomes the best classifier in the two-year period. In the holdout sample test, DA scores the second lowest misclassification rates but degrades to the fourth place in the two-year period. Logit behaves in a similar way. In the first test, it ranks second to Net_{10} in the first period and drops to the fifth place in the second period. In the validation test, it jumps from the fourth place in the one-year period to the first in the two-year period. The performances of other methods are relatively stable. Although Net_{10} remains high in

Table 13.7

Misclassification Rates of the Various Models Using the Holdout Sample

| | Percentage (%) One-Year Prior | | | Two-Year Prior | | |
Model	I	II	T	I	II	T
DA	18.2	13.6	(15.9)	30.0	5.0	(17.5)
Logit	31.8	4.5	(18.2)	15.0	0.0	(7.5)
INN	40.9	4.6	(22.8)	20.0	25.0	(22.5)
3NN	36.4	9.1	(22.8)	30.0	10.0	(20.0)
ID3	22.7	18.2	(20.5)	40.0	5.0	(22.5)
Net_0	31.8	4.5	(18.2)	20.0	12.6	(16.3)
Net_{10}	18.2	11.4	(14.8)	2.5	20.0	(11.3)

Note:
The Type I and Type II misclassification rates of DA, Net_0, and Net_{10} are based on the average of ($C_{12} = 100$, $\pi_2 = 0.01$) and ($C_{12} = 50$, $\pi_2 = 0.02$).

the ranking list, kNN performs the worst in both tests. Net_0 and ID3 reside in the middle of the list with their positions interchanged in Tables 13.6 and 13.7.

Five out of seven methods in Table 13.7 have lower misclassification rates in predicting bank failures two years ahead. This is contrary to our intuition because the earlier the prediction, the more uncertain it is, and one should expect a higher misclassification rate. It is difficult to conceive that the logit model can reduce more than half of its misclassification errors (18.2 percent in the one-year and 7.5 percent in the two-year period) one year earlier. Furthermore, the ratios of Type I to Type II errors in the holdout sample test are not consistent with those in Table 13.6. The number and ratio of Type I and Type II errors vary widely in both tables. The only explanation is that the holdout sample (probably both training and holdout samples) is not a representative sample of the group distributions.

Depending on the samples chosen, error rates estimated by the holdout sample may be biased. An alternative estimation method is the jackknife method that Lachenbruch[9] has shown to produce unbiased estimates for the probability of misclassification. The method involves holding one example out of the training set and using the estimated discriminant function to predict the extracted example. This is repeated for each example in the training set, and the proportion of misclassifications in each class is reported as its misclassification rate. The training and holdout samples are pooled to form one single training sample, which consists of 162 (81 failed, 81 nonfailed) and 158 (79 failed, 79 nonfailed) examples in the one- and two-year periods, respectively. Descriptive statistics of the training samples are shown in the Appendix. The neural nets are allowed to run until convergence this time.

As shown in Table 13.8, Net_{10} scores the lowest total misclassification rates in both periods. This is followed by Net_0, DA, logit, ID3, 3NN, and 1NN. The relative ranking remains virtually the same in both periods. The only difference is between DA and Net_0, which have their positions interchanged. The performance of logit is not as superior as in the holdout sample test. It ranks in the fourth place behind Net_{10}, Net_0, and DA. 1NN and 3NN remain the worst classifiers after ID3 in both periods. When compared between predictive periods, all methods except 3NN have lower total misclassification rates in the one-year period than in the two-year period. This is consistent with our intuition.

Misclassification rates estimated from both validation tests are compared. The proportions between Type I and Type II errors are less extreme in the jackknife test. For example, in the two-year period, the ratio of

Table 13.8
Misclassification Rates Estimated Using the Jackknife Method

| | Percentage (%) | | | | | |
| | One-Year Prior | | | Two-Year Prior | | |
Model	I	II	T	I	II	T
DA	17.3	11.1	(14.2)	17.3	13.9	(15.6)
Logit	12.3	17.3	(14.8)	15.2	20.3	(17.7)
INN	17.3	38.3	(27.8)	31.6	29.1	(30.4)
3NN	18.5	30.9	(24.7)	19.0	26.6	(22.8)
ID3	21.0	17.3	(19.2)	20.3	25.3	(22.8)
Net_0	8.6	13.5	(11.1)	8.9	25.3	(17.1)
Net_{10}	8.6	12.3	(10.5)	8.9	12.7	(10.8)

Type I and Type II errors changed from 6 to 1.24 in DA and from 0.13 to 1 in Net_{10}. The holdout test overestimates the total misclassification rates of 1NN, 3NN, logit (one-year), and Net_0 (two-year) and underestimate that of DA, Net_{10}, logit (two-year), and Net_0 (one-year). The results of ID3 are quite consistent, although its Type I and Type II error compositions are very different in the two tests. Furthermore, the absolute difference between total misclassification rates estimated by the two tests is relatively small for most methods.

Because the misclassification rates estimated by the jackknife method have been shown to be unbiased, there is evidence that the neural-net approach provides better predictive accuracy than DA methods. We have also eliminated the effects of premature termination of the learning procedure by allowing each net in the jackknife method to run until convergence. As shown in both tests, a net with no hidden unit has a performance similar to a DA, but the incorporation of a layer of hidden units improves considerably its predictive accuracy. This can best be explained by viewing the partitioning structure induced by a DA method. Each method divides the variable space into disjointed partitions in very different ways. For instance, a DA model cuts the space into two partitions with a hyperplane, whereas an ID3 model divides the space into a number of recursive rectangular partitions. The sensitivity of a partitioning structure to the distribution of the training sample varies among methods, resulting in very different misclassification rates. Net_{10}, with the lowest total misclassification rates, offers a structure that best matches the training examples. In fact, it has been shown that a three-layer net can be used as a universal approximate for any continuous function in a multidimensional space. Geometrically, a network is capable of generating nonlinear partitioning structures that very often fit better a given training sample than other DA methods.

DISCUSSION

The neural net approach presented in this paper offers an alternative to existing bankruptcy prediction models. Empirical results show that neural nets offer better predictive accuracy than DA, logit, kNN, and ID3. The original back-propagation algorithm is modified to include prior probabilities and misclassification costs. Depending on the classification tasks, the trade-off between Type I and Type II errors may be very different and needs to be accounted for. It is essential to allow an assessor to state his or her own preference in deciding such a trade-off. For example, the error of misclassifying a failed bank to the nonfailed group (Type I error) is generally accepted to be more severe than the other way. The original function E is generalized to E_w by multiplying each error term by Z_i. It is worthwhile to note that minimizing E_w is not equivalent to minimizing the expected misclassification cost. Although the results in Tables 13.2–13.5 show that the nets do behave in this direction and outperform linear classifiers in minimizing resubstitution risks, more empirical studies are needed to validate this result.

Our comparison is based on a training set with an equal proportion of failed and nonfailed banks. In many cases, the number of defaults constitutes only a small portion of the whole population. The matching process may introduce biases to the model. To avoid this, the entire population should be used as the training set. There are many application domains (for example, handwritten character recognition) for which a neural net is an appropriate choice for identifying a single group from a large set of alternatives. It has been proved that a net with a hidden layer can compute any Boolean function with k variables.[42] It is therefore possible to identify a group out of a total of 2^k cases. As illustrated in the XOR example, this is not possible for a linear DA model.

In terms of explanatory capability, it has been shown that the coefficients of a linear discriminant function convey little information about the relative importance of individual variables. Unlike logit analysis, there is no rigorous statistical test on the significance of individual coefficients. The same criticism is also applicable to kNN and neural nets, the results of which are difficult to interpret. On the other hand, the symbolic approach of ID3 sheds some light on the importance of individual variables. A variable is selected as the splitting variable when it can partition a set of examples into the most homogeneous subgroups. Homogeneity is measured by the weighted entropy of the resulting subgroups. For example, in Figure 13.2a, the root node nonln (nonln > 0.036) correctly identifies 93.22 percent of the nonfailed banks and 76.27 percent of the failed banks; and, in Figure 13.2b, the root node rtoas (rtoas > 0.056) accounts for 91.5 percent of the nonfailed banks and 54.32 percent of the failed banks.

Dimension reduction is another problem associated with existing DA techniques. West[27] extended the logit approach by augmenting it with factor analysis. The factor-logistic method reduces the number of dimensions by transforming the space of initial variables into one composed of important factors that account for a large portion of the variance (for example, 90 percent). Observations are described by their factor scores in the new factor space. The factor scores are then put into a logistic regression model with a dichotomy dependent variable. This combined factor-logistic approach has proven effective in predicting bank bankruptcy; however, the meaning of each factor is subject to interpretation, and the actual number of variables for describing each observation remains the same. In the ID3 approach, Quinlan[17] showed that minimizing the entropy of a decision tree is equivalent to minimizing the expected number of tests to make a decision. Thus, the ID3 method has a built-in mechanism to reduce the dimensions of the variable space. For example, in Figures 13.2a and 13.2b, the number of variables is reduced by 66.67 percent and 57.89 percent in the one-year and two-year periods, respectively. In feed-forward nets, the number of dimensions equals the number of input units.

A neural net allows adaptive adjustment to the predictive model as new examples become available. This is an attractive property, especially when the underlying group distributions are changing. Statistical methods assume old and new examples are equally valid, and the entire training set is used to construct a new model. The batch update is necessary if the distributions do not change. However, in situations where the new sample is drawn from a new distribution, retaining the old examples may result in a predictive model with low accuracy. An important feature of a neural net is that past information is not ignored; instead, its importance will be reduced (or strengthened) incrementally as new examples are fed into the network. In actual implementation, a sliding window scheme is needed to retain part of the old sample and combine it with the new sample to create a new training set. The exact proportion of old sample to be retained depends on the stability of the distribution and the level of noise in the sample.

Although the study reported here is far from sufficient to generate any conclusive statements about the applicability of neural nets in general, it does provide some insights into their potentials and limitations. Based on the comparison reported above, the neural net approach offers a comparative alternative to classification techniques, especially under the following conditions:

1. *Multimodal distribution.* The nonlinear discriminant function represented by a neural net provides a better approximation of the sample

distribution, especially when the latter is multimodal. Many classification tasks have been reported to have a nonlinear relationship between variables. Whitred and Zimmer[43] suggest that loan officers may have a higher prediction accuracy than linear DA models because of their ability to relate variables and loan outcome in a nonlinear manner. In another experiment conducted by Shepanski,[44] it was reported that human judgments are better approximated by a nonlinear function.

2. *Adaptive model adjustment.* The ability to adaptively adjust the model is a virtue of a neural net. This allows the model to respond swiftly to changes in the real world.

3. *Robustness.* The network does not assume any probability distribution or equal dispersion. There is also no rigid restriction on the use of input/output functions other than that they be continuous and differentiable.

Despite the successful applications of neural nets reported recently, their usage is still rather ad hoc. Some of their limitations are summarized here.

Network Topology

There is no formal method to derive a network configuration for a given classification task. Although it was shown that only one hidden layer is enough to approximate any continuous functions,[45,46,47] the number of hidden units can be arbitrarily large. In addition, there is a possibility of overfitting the network. This problem arises when the number of hidden units is relatively large with respect to the size of the training sample.[48] Unless the whole population is used for training, one has to be cautious in selecting the number of hidden units in order to avoid this problem. Currently, deciding how many hidden units to use is part of the modeling process itself.

Computational Efficiency

Training a neural net demands more computation time than the other methods. In the current study, computation time ranges from a few minutes to 3 hours on an EMX minicomputer. One strategy we have employed to reduce computation time is to allocate five different sets of weights and to restrict each run to an acceptable number of iterations. It seems to be an effective strategy in most cases, but inconsistent results are generated occasionally. All statistical methods took at most half a minute on an IBM 3081 mainframe. ID3 required on average 8 minutes on a Mac II microcomputer.

Explanatory Capability

The discriminant capability of a neural net is difficult to express in symbolic form. This may not be a serious drawback if one is concerned primarily with predictive accuracy. However, a neural net is limited if one wants to test the significance of individual inputs. There is no formal method to derive the relative importance of an input from the weights of a neural net.

Continuous improvements are being made in all these directions. Recently, Miller, Todd, and Hedge[49] suggested applying genetic algorithms to the design of network configurations. Genetic algorithms adopt an evolutionary approach in which a pool of networks, called the *population*, is continuously being modified by using genetic operators such as crossover and mutation.[50] Each synthesized network, which corresponds to a possible configuration, is evaluated using the back-propagation algorithm. Genetic algorithms have a built-in bias toward retaining and combining good configurations in the next generation. The evolutionary nature of the algorithm enables the search for good configurations to proceed in a parallel fashion, thus reducing the possibility of trapping in local optimal configuration.

The problem of lengthy computation time is attributed to our implementation, which is basically a simulation that runs on a serial machine. The intrinsic parallel processing capability of a network is not exploited in our study. Progress is underway to implement neural nets on silicon, which will significantly reduce computation time.[51]

Heuristics have been developed to give the modeler some insights into the relative importance of variables with respect to a single example. A method using the partial derivative of the error function has been suggested in Tam and Kiang.[8] In addition, the limited explanatory capability of neural nets can be explained by linking them with fuzzy logic. The latter provides a means of combining symbolic and numeric computations in inference processing. The linkage between neural nets and symbolic reasoning can be established through the membership function of fuzzy logic. The function measures the degree of possibility of a concept as related to a numeric quantity. A neural net can be used to synthesize a membership function by training it with instances of the relation. In our present case, a neural net may represent the membership function of the concept "high likelihood of failure." Such a representation can be easily combined with other symbolic conditions appearing in the rules of an expert system. By using neural nets as front ends in rules definition, one can take advantage of the explanatory capability of expert systems as well as the subsymbolic computational capability offered by neural nets.[52]

CONCLUSION

We have presented a new approach to bank bankruptcy prediction using neural nets. We believe neural nets can be extended to other managerial applications, particularly those involving classification. Furthermore, a neural net may supplement a rule-based expert system in real-time applications. While rule-based expert systems are satisfactory for off-line processing, a neural net-based system offers on-line capabilities. More work needs to be done in prototype development, and actual applications need to be empirically tested before the full potential of neural nets can be asserted.[53]

ENDNOTES

1. R. A. Fisher, "The Use of Multiple Measurements in Taxonomic Problems," *Ann. Eugenics* 7 (1936), pp. 179–88.

2. M. Minsky and S. Papert, *Perceptrons* (Cambridge, MA: MIT Press, 1969).

3. XOR is a binary function that returns true when only one of its inputs is true, and false otherwise.

4. D. E. Rumelhart, G. Hinton, and R. Williams, "Learning Representation by Back-Propagating Errors," *Nature* 323, no. 9 (1986), pp. 533–36.

5. D. E. Rumelhart, J. McClelland, and the PDP Research Group, eds., *Parallel Distributed Processing: Explorations in the Microstructure of Cognition* (Cambridge, MA: Bradford Books, 1986).

6. D. L. Waltz, "Applications of the Connection Machine," *IEEE Computer*, January 1987, pp. 85–97.

7. L. W. Tucker and G. Robertson, "Architecture and Applications of the Connection Machine," *IEEE Computer*, August 1988, pp. 26–38.

8. K. Y. Tam and M. Kiang, "Predicting Bank Failures: A Neural Network Approach," *Applied Artificial Intelligence* 4, no. 4 (1990), pp. 265–82.

9. P. A. Lachenbruch, "An Almost Unbiased Method of Obtaining Confidence Intervals for the Probability of Misclassification in Discriminant Analysis," *Biometrics*, December 1967, pp. 639–45.

10. E. B. Deakin, "Distributions of Financial Accounting Ratios: Some Empirical Evidence," *Accounting Review*, January 1976, pp. 90–96.

11. E. L. Altman, R. A. Eisenbeis, and J. Sinkey, *Applications of Classification Techniques in Business, Banking, and Finance* (Greenwich, CT: JAI Press, 1981).

12. P. A. Lachenbruch, C. Sneeringer, and L. Revo, "Robustness of the Linear and Quadratic Discriminant Function to Certain Types of Non-Normality," *Commun. Statistics* 1 no. 1 (1973), pp. 39–56.

13. S. J. Press and S. Wilson, "Choosing between Logistic Regression and Discriminant Analysis," *Journal of the American Statistical Association* 73 (1978), pp. 699–705.

14. F. E. Harrell and K. L. Lee, "A Comparison of the Discrimination of Discriminant Analysis and Logistic Regression under Multivariate Normality," in *Biostatistics: Statistics in Biomedical, Public Health, and Environmental Sciences*, ed. P. K. Sen (Amsterdam: North Holland, 1985).

15. J. R. Quinlan, "Discovering Rules by Induction from Large Collection of Examples," in *Expert Systems in the Micro Electronic Age*, ed. D. Michie (Edinburgh: Edinburgh University Press, 1979).

16. J. R. Quinlan, "Learning Efficient Classification Procedures and Their Applications to Chess End Games," in *Machine Learning: An Artificial Intelligence Approach*, Vol. I, eds. R. S. Michalski, J. Carbonell, and T. Mitchell (Palo Alto, CA: Tioga Publishing Company, 1983).

17. J. R. Quinlan, "Induction of Decision Trees," *Machine Learning* 1 (1986), pp. 81–106.

18. C. Carter and J. Catlett, "Assessing Credit Card Applications Using Machine Learning," *IEEE Expert*, Fall 1987, pp. 71–79.

19. W. F. Messier and J. Hansen, "Inducing Rules for Expert System Development: An Example Using Default and Bankruptcy Data," *Management Science* 34, no. 12 (1988), pp. 1403–15.

20. K. Y. Tam, M. Kiang, and R. Chi, "Inducing Stock Screening Rules for Portfolio Construction," *Journal Operational Research Society* 49 no. 9, pp. 747–57.

21. H. Frydman, E. Altman, and D. Kao, "Introducing Recursive Partitioning for Financial Classification: The Case of Financial Distress," *Journal of Finance* 40 no. 1 (1985), pp. 269–91.

22. D. S. Broomhead and D. Lowe, "Multivariate Functional Interpolation and Adaptive Networks," *Complex Systems* 2 (1988), pp. 321–55.

23. J. Moody and C. Darken, "Fast Learning in Networks of Locally-Tuned Processing Units," *Neural Computing* 1, no. 2 (1989), pp. 281–94.

24. G. E. Hinton, "Connectionist Learning Procedures," *Artificial Intelligence* 40 (1989), pp. 185–234.

25. F. Rosenblatt, *Principles of Neurodynamics* (New York: Spartan, 1962).

26. Similar early warning systems have been operated in the Office of Comptroller of the Currency (OCC) and the Federal Reserve System (Fed).

27. R. G. West, "A Factor-Analytic Approach to Bank Condition," *Journal of Banking and Finance* 9, no. 2 (1985), pp. 253–66.

28. P. A. Meyer and H. Pifer, "Prediction of Bank Failures," *Journal of Finance* 25 (September 1970), pp. 853–68.

29. E. L. Altman, "Financial Ratios, Discriminant Analysis and the Prediction of Corporate Bankruptcy," *Journal of Finance* 23 no. 3 (1968), pp. 589–609.

30. J. F. Sinkey, "A Multivariate Statistical Analysis of the Characteristics of Problem Banks," *Journal of Finance* 30, no. 1 (1975), pp. 21–36.

31. A. M. Santomero and J. Vinso, "Estimating the Probability of Failure for Commercial Banks and the Banking System," *Journal of Banking and Finance* 1, no. 2 (1977), pp. 185–205.

32. G. A. Hanweck, "Predicting Bank Failures," *Research Papers in Banking and Financial Economics*, Financial Studies Section, Board of Governors of the Federal Research System, Washington, DC, 1977.

33. D. Martin, "Early Warning of Bank Failure, A Logit Regression Approach," *Journal of Banking and Finance* 1, no. 3 (1977), pp. 249–76.

34. L. Korobow and D. Stuhr, "Performance Measurement of Early Warning Models," *Journal of Banking and Finance* 9 (1985), pp. 267–73.

35. R. A. Eisenbeis, "Pitfalls in the Application of Discriminant Analysis in Business, Finance, and Economics," *Journal of Finance* 32 no. 3 (1977), pp. 875–900.

36. *Bank of Texas*, Vols. 1–3, Sheshunoff Information Services Inc., 1987.

37. Federal Deposit Insurance Corporation, 1987 Annual Report.

38. Significance level of the test is 5 percent.

39. Coefficients of the logit model were estimated using SAS LOGIT procedure.

40. The 1NN and 3NN models were constructed using the SAS NEIGHBOR procedure.

41. Usually, values slightly different from zero are used as initial weights to break up the symmetry.

42. J. Denker, D. Schwartz, B. Wittner, S. Solla, R. Howard, L. Jackal, and J. Hopfield, "Large Automatic Learning, Rule Extraction and Generalization," *Complex Systems* 1 (1987), pp. 877–922.

43. G. Whitred and I. Zimmer, "The Implications of Distress Prediction Models for Corporate Lending," *Accounting and Finance* 25 (1985), pp. 1–13.

44. A. Shepanski, "Tests of Theories of Information Processing Behavior in Credit Judgment," *Accounting Review* 58 (1983), pp. 581–99.

45. G. Cybenko, "Approximation by Superpositions of a Sigmoidal Function," *Math, Control, Signals, and Systems* 2 (1989), pp. 303–14.

46. K. Funahashi, "On the Approximate Realization of Continuous Mappings by Neural Networks," *Neural Networks* 2 (1989), pp. 183–92.

47. K. Hornik, M. Stinchcombe, and H. White, "Multilayer Feedforward Networks are Universal Approximators," *Neural Networks* 2 (1989), pp. 359–66.

48. E. B. Baum and D. Haussler, "What Size Net Gives Valid Generalization?," *Neural Comput.* 1 (1989), pp. 151–60.

49. G. F. Miller, P. Todd, and S. Hedge, "Designing Neural Networks Using Genetic Algorithms," *Proceedings of the Third International Conference on Genetic Algorithms*, Morgan Kaufmann, Palo Alto, CA, 1989, pp. 379–84.

50. D. E. Goldberg, *Genetic Algorithms in Search, Optimization, and Machine Learning* (Reading, MA: Addison-Wesley, 1989).

51. C. A. Mead, *Analog VLSI and Neural Systems* (Reading, MA: Addison-Wesley, 1988).

52. B. Kosko, *Neural Networks and Fuzzy Systems* (Englewood Cliffs, NJ: Prentice Hall, 1990).

53. The authors are grateful for the comments and suggestions of the associate editor and the four anonymous reviewers. They would like to thank William Cooper and Patrick Brockett for their valuable comments on an early draft of this chapter.

APPENDIX

Table 13A.1
Descriptive Statistics of Variables (One Year Ahead)

Name	Nonfailed		Failed	
	Mean	St. Dev	Mean	St. Dev.
capas	10.76	5.45	5.53	2.98
agfas	0.09	0.15	0.09	0.15
comas	0.29	0.16	0.35	0.16
indas	0.28	0.16	0.26	0.16
resas	0.36	0.16	0.34	0.16
pasln	0.01	0.01	0.05	0.07
nonln	0.01	0.02	0.08	0.06
losln	1.80	1.92	5.31	3.71
netln	1.45	1.72	4.18	3.51
rtoas	−0.14	2.10	−3.19	2.79
intdp	0.06	0.01	0.07	0.01
expas	0.09	0.02	0.12	0.02
incas	0.00	0.02	−0.04	0.03
infln	0.12	0.03	0.13	0.02
incex	1.11	0.19	1.00	0.17
curas	0.27	0.12	0.20	0.11
govas	0.28	0.15	0.17	0.10
llnas	0.53	0.14	0.67	0.11
llndp	0.61	0.16	0.71	0.18

Table 13A.2

Descriptive Statistics of Variables (Two Years Ahead)

Name	Nonfailed		Failed	
	Mean	St. Dev	Mean	St. Dev.
capas	9.87	4.03	7.87	2.54
agfas	0.08	0.14	0.10	0.16
comas	0.30	0.14	0.36	0.14
indas	0.28	0.15	0.25	0.14
resas	0.35	0.15	0.31	0.15
pasln	0.01	0.01	0.02	0.03
nonln	0.01	0.01	0.04	0.05
losln	1.16	1.15	3.01	2.99
netln	0.81	1.04	2.51	2.78
rtoas	0.69	1.44	−1.44	2.51
intdp	0.06	0.01	0.07	0.01
expas	0.09	0.01	0.11	0.02
incas	0.01	0.01	−0.01	0.03
infln	0.12	0.02	0.13	0.02
incex	1.16	0.12	1.05	0.15
curas	0.25	0.13	0.21	0.09
govas	0.28	0.15	0.17	0.09
llnas	0.55	0.14	0.66	0.10
llndp	0.62	0.17	0.73	0.11

14

NEURAL NETWORKS: A NEW TOOL FOR PREDICTING THRIFT FAILURES

Linda M. Salchenberger, E. Mine Cinar, and Nicholas A. Lash

INTRODUCTION

Recently, there has been considerable interest in the development of artificial neural networks (ANNs) for solving a variety of problems. Neural networks, which are capable of learning relationships from data, represent a class of robust, nonlinear models inspired by the neural architecture of the brain. Theoretical advances, as well as hardware and software innovations, have overcome past deficiencies in implementing machine learning and made neural network methods available to a wide variety of disciplines. Financial applications that require pattern matching, classification, and prediction such as corporate bond rating,[1] credit evaluation, and underwriting[2] have proven to be excellent candidates for this new technology.

This article originally appeared in *Decision Sciences* 23, no. 4 (July/August, 1992), pp. 899–916. Reprinted with permission.

In this chapter, we present a neural network developed to predict the probability of failure for savings and loan associations (S&Ls), using the financial variables that signal an institution's deteriorating financial condition. We compare its performance with a logit model, since logit has frequently been used to discriminate between failed and surviving institutions. For all cases examined, the neural network performs as well or better than logit in classifying institutions as failed or nonfailed.

Even a moderate improvement in the ability to correctly classify insolvent institutions represents a significant contribution, given the magnitude of the current crisis in the thrift industry and the enormous costs of resolution.[3] Early identification of financial decline provides the opportunity for close monitoring of the problem institution and the ability to take immediate corrective actions.

The chapter is organized into four major sections. First, a selected group of past studies of thrift failures is presented. This is followed by a discussion of back-propagation neural networks and the relationship of the back-propagation learning to statistics. Next, we present a back-propagation neural network that uses financial data to predict thrift institution failures. Finally, we evaluate the ability of the neural network to predict thrift failures using a logit model as a performance benchmark.

PAST STUDIES OF THRIFT FAILURES

Past studies of thrift institution failures were typically devoted to either building early warning systems or explaining failures. The discriminatory variables included a set of financial ratios, determined from internal call report data and organized into a CAMEL framework. CAMEL is an acronym for the five major classes of financial data: capital adequacy (C), asset quality (A), management efficiency (M), earnings quality (E), and liquidity (L). Capital adequacy, determined largely by the extent of compliance with regulatory capital requirements, is important not only to absorb losses but also to deter management from taking inordinate risks. Asset quality, measured by the volume and severity of problem loans, is often considered the most critical determinant of an institution's soundness and receives much of the examiners' attention. Other critical factors are the technical competence, leadership ability, and integrity of management. However, assessing management is highly subjective and difficult to capture directly with specific financial ratios. In empirical studies, management efficiency is often evaluated in terms of the ability to control costs and expenditures.[4] Earnings are judged on the basis of level, trend, stability, and source. The final component refers to liquidity and is gauged by the institution's liquid assets and ability to tap funding sources.

A review of past studies of thrift institution failures reveals that multiple discriminant analysis, logit, and probit models are frequently developed to classify institutions as failed or surviving. Altman[5] used a quadratic discriminant model to categorize 212 S&Ls as "serious problem," "moderate problem," and "no problem" using data from 1966 through 1973 (Table 14.1). Barth, Brumbaugh, Sauerhaft, and Wang[6] developed a logit model using semiannual data for 318 closed and 588 solvent institutions for the period 1981 through 1985. Logit was also used by Benston[7] in a study of 178 closed and 712 solvent S&Ls for the years 1981 through 1985. An early warning system based on multiple discriminant analysis was developed by Pantalone and Platt[8] for the S&Ls in the Boston district of the Federal Home Loan Bank System. Recently, a robust multivariate procedure, based on the evaluation of statistical outliers, was developed by Booth, Alam, Ahkam, and Osyk[9] to predict savings and loans failures.

Expert systems have also been used to predict bankruptcy in the thrift and other industries. Elmer and Borowski[10] developed a rule-based expert system to compute an index that was a weighted average of measures of capital, asset quality, earnings, and liquidity. A system that incorporates this index performs as well as statistical models in identifying problem institutions 6 months before failure and achieves greater prediction accuracy in identifying problem institutions 12 and 18 months before failure.

A direct comparison of the performance of the statistical predictor models is difficult for a number of reasons. Each study differs with respect to modeling technique, a priori categories, and classification criteria. However, some common results do emerge from an examination of these past studies. First, predicting thrift institution failure is often formulated as a classification problem in which a group of independent variables are used to predict failure. Second, the relationship between failure or nonfailure and the financial variables is frequently assumed to be nonlinear. Finally, the financial predictor variables may be highly correlated. For classification problems in which the dependent variable is a nonlinear function of correlated independent variables, neural networks provide a promising tool. These observations motivated our decision to develop a neural network to discriminate between surviving and failed institutions.

Table 14.1

Financial Variables Found to Be Significant in Selected Studies

Author	Statistical Technique	Significant Financial Ratios
Altman[5]	MDA	Net worth/Total assets (C) Net operating income/Gross operating income (E) Real estate owned/Total assets (A)
Barth et al.[6]	logit	Net worth/Total assets (C) Interest sensitive funds/Total funds(E) Net income/Total assets (E) Loans/Total assets (L) Liquid assets/Total assets (L)
Benston[7]	logit	Net worth/Total assets (C) Net income/Total assets (E) Change in interest and fee income/ earning assets (E) Change in interest and depositor's dividends/Earning assets (E)
Pantalone and Pratt[8]	MDA	Net Worth/Total assets (C) Cash and securities/Total savings and short-term borrowing (L) Operating expense/Gross operating income (M)

Note: MDA = Multiple discriminant analysis.
            A   = Measure of asset quality.
            C   = Measure of capital adequacy.
            E   = Measure of earnings quality.
            M   = Measure of management efficiency.
            L   = Measure of liquidity.

NEURAL NETWORKS

Inspired by studies of the brain and nervous system, neural networks are composed of neurons, or processing elements and connections, organized in layers. These layers can be structured hierarchically; the first layer is called the input layer, the last layer the output layer, and the interior layers the middle or hidden layers. Feedforward networks map inputs into outputs with signals flowing in one direction only, from the input layer to the output layer. A two-layer neural network consisting of an input layer and an output layer is shown in Figure 14.1. Each connection between neurons has a numerical weight associated with it, which models the influence of an input cell on an output cell. Positive weights indicate reinforcement; negative weights are associated with inhibition. Connection weights are learned by the network through a training process, as examples from a training set are presented repeatedly to the network.

Each processing element has an activation level, specified by continuous or discrete values. If the neuron is in the input layer, its activation level is determined in response to input signals received from the environment. For cells in the middle or output layers, the activation level is computed as a function of the activation levels on the cells connected to it and the associated connection weights. This function is called the transfer function or activation function and may be a linear discriminant function (i.e., a positive signal is output if the value of this function exceeds a threshold level, and 0 otherwise). It may also be a continuous, nondecreasing function. For example, the sigmoidal (logistic) function:

$$f(\theta) = (1 + \exp(-\theta))^{-1} \tag{1}$$

(Figure 14.2), which assigns values between 0 and 1 (or –1 and 1) to inputs, is often used in back-propagation networks.

Figure 14.1

A Two-Layer Neural Network

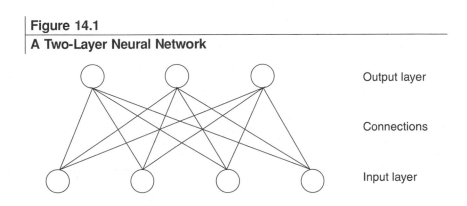

Output layer

Connections

Input layer

While basically an information-processing technology, neural networks differ from traditional modeling techniques in a fundamental way. Parametric statistical models require the developer to specify the nature of the functional relationship between the dependent variable and the independent variables (e.g., linear, logistic). Once an assumption is made about the functional form, optimization techniques are used to determine a set of parameters that minimizes a measure of error. Neural networks with at least one middle layer use the data to develop an internal representation of the relationship between the variables so that a priori assumptions about underlying parameter distributions are not required. As a consequence, better results might be expected with neural networks when the relationship between the variables does not fit the assumed model. Nevertheless, many decisions regarding model parameters and network topology can affect the performance of the network.

Two-layer neural networks do not have the ability to develop internal representations. They map input patterns into similar output patterns. While these networks have proved useful in a variety of applications,

Figure 14.2

Graph of Sigmoidal Function

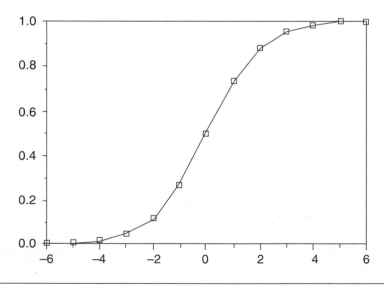

they cannot generalize or perform well on patterns that have never been presented.

Neural networks with hidden layers have the ability to develop internal representations. The middle layer nodes are often characterized as feature detectors, which combine raw observations into higher order features, thus permitting the network to make reasonable generalizations.

A two-layer neural network has an input layer that can be represented by a vector $\mathbf{x} = (x_1, x_2,...,x_n)$ of features and an output layer that can be represented by an output vector $\mathbf{y} = g(\mathbf{x})$. We assume, for the remainder of this discussion, that there is a single output node $y = g(\mathbf{x})$; the connection weights are represented by β_i, $i = 0,...,n$; and we have a linear transfer function. It follows that:

$$y = g(\mathbf{x}) = \Sigma\beta_i x_i. \tag{2}$$

Thus, the familiar linear regression model is similar in form to a two-layer neural network that has a linear transfer function.

In the two-layer perceptron model with a linear discriminant transfer function, neurons are not activated until some threshold level θ_0 is reached, that is:

$$y = F(\Sigma\beta_i x_i) \tag{3}$$

where $F = 1$ when $\Sigma\beta_i x_i > \theta_0$, and 0 otherwise. Since the transfer function F can be any continuous, nondecreasing function, F can represent a cumulative distribution frequency (cdf). When F is the normal cumulative distribution function, $F(\Sigma\beta_i x_i)$ is the conditional expectation of a Bernoulli random variable generated by a probit model. When F is the logistic cdf, $F(\Sigma\beta_i x_i)$ is the conditional expectation generated by the logistic model.[11] Therefore, in a two-layer neural network, the network output function can be compared to the familiar logit and probit regression models.

We now focus attention on multilayered neural networks. Consider a single middle layer, feedforward network with a single output cell, k middle layer nodes, and n input nodes. Any middle layer cell receives the weighted sum of all inputs and a bias term and produces an output signal:

$$m_j = f(\Sigma\omega_{ij} x_i), \quad j = 1,...,k, \ i = 0,...,n, \tag{4}$$

where f is the transfer function, x_i is the ith signal, w_{ij} is the strength of the connection from the ith input neuron to the jth middle layer cell. The activation levels from the middle-layer cells are transferred to the output layer cells in the same way so that the output cell sees the weighted sum of the outputs of the middle layer cells and produces a signal:

$$y = F\left(\sum v_j f\left(\sum w_{ij} x_i\right)\right) = g(x,\theta) \tag{5}$$

where $\mathbf{x}$ is the vector of inputs, and θ is the vector of network weights. We can interpret (5) as a nonlinear regression function that represents a single middle-layer, feedforward neural network.

The ability of multilayer networks to represent nonlinear models has been established through an application of an existence theorem proved by Kolmogorov.[12,13] This theorem has been used to show that, for any feedforward network with a single middle layer, there exists a network output function:

$$g(\mathbf{x},\theta) = \Sigma v_j f \left(\Sigma w_{ij} x_i\right) \tag{6}$$

that can provide an accurate approximation to any function of $(x_1, x_2,...,x_n)$, if the inputs are scaled to be within [0.1]. The number of middle units required by the theorem is $2n + 1$, where n is the number of input nodes, although representations with fewer middle nodes may also exist.[14] The implication of the Kolmogorov theorem is that classification problems that are not linearly separable can be solved with multilayered neural networks.

It is interesting to note that research in neural networks was abandoned for almost 20 years when it was discovered that only linearly separable problems could be solved with two-layer networks. The linear perceptron network, a two-layer network using a linear threshold response function, was proposed by Rosenblatt[15] in the 1950s. While some theoretical limitations of the linear perceptron, including the requirement that data points be linearly separable for perfect classification, were recognized by Rosenblatt, a more complete analysis of its computational limitations was developed by Minsky and Papert.[16] They made extensive use of geometrical arguments to prove that properties like connectedness and parity could not be computed with perceptrons.[17]

Back-Propagation Networks and Learning Rules

Back-propagation is an approach to supervised network learning that permits weights to be learned from experience, based on empirical observations on the object of interest. Training consists of repeatedly presenting the network with examples that can be viewed as input/output vectors. Supervised learning methods require that for each input pattern, an appropriate response or classification of the output be presented to the network during training. These networks cannot learn from an input pattern for which no correct response has been provided.

In an approach to learning that does not require a teacher, no correct response is provided. These unsupervised learning methods take advantage of natural groupings that appear within the data by using a variety of approaches to learning. In the simplest form of competitive learning, an output node with the greatest net input is denoted winner, and its weights are updated, using a learning rule.[18] Adaptive resonance theory (ART) overcomes some of the limitations and instability associated with competitive learning.[19] In self-organizing feature maps, the concept of neighbor is added to competitive learning, and a group of associated nodes responds to an input pattern.[20]

Although the term *back-propagation* can be used to refer to the dynamic feedback of errors propagated backward through a network to adjust the weights, it is also commonly used to describe learning by the generalized delta rule. Rumelhart, Hinton, and Williams[21] described the generalized delta rule with the following three steps. First, the derivative of the square error with respect to the outputs and the target values of the network is computed. The chain rule is applied in the second step to calculate the derivatives of error with respect to outputs and weights within the network. Finally, the weights are updated using:

$$\theta_t = \theta_{t-1} + \alpha \nabla \mathbf{f}(X_t, \theta_{t-1})(Y_t - f(X_t, \theta_{t-1})) \tag{7}$$

$$t = 1, 2, \dots,$$

where α is the learning rate, Y_t is the target, θ_0 is a random set of small initial weights, and $\nabla \mathbf{f}$ is the gradient (vector of partial derivatives with respect to the weights θ). Thus, the learning process updates the current set of weights with a function of the difference between the system's response to an input vector and the associated correct category. The steepest descent algorithm is used where changes are made in the direction of the gradient (i.e., direction of the largest change in the error).

Better results may be achieved by replacing the steepest descent algorithms with response surface methods. Response surface optimization does not require any functional form assumption, in contrast to the specification function required in current methods, and thus represents a future research area that may improve neural network performance.

Under appropriate conditions, the learning rule given in (7) yields weights converging to a vector θ^* that solves:

$$E[\nabla f(X_t,\theta)(Y_t - f(X_t,\theta)] = 0 \qquad (8)$$

where the mathematical expectation is taken with respect to the joint distribution of the random variables X_t, Y_t. A solution θ^* to this equation satisfies the necessary conditions for a local solution to the least squares problem:

$$\min_{\theta} E\left[(Y_t - f(X_t, \theta))^2\right] \qquad (9)$$

A set of weights that solves (7) yields a network output that is mean square optimal for Y_t; it minimizes expected squared error as a prediction for Y_t. Also, the weights θ^* guarantee a network that is a mean square optimal approximation to the conditional expectation $E(Y_t \mid X_t)$. Thus, back-propagation learning is an approach for which convergence to a local optimal set of weights is guaranteed.[14]

The application of the generalized delta rule involves a forward pass through the network during which errors are accumulated by comparing actual outputs with the targets. This is followed by a backward pass during which adjustments in connections weights are made based on the errors, using a recursive rule such as (7).

Back-propagation is a gradient descent method that minimizes the mean squared error of the system by moving down the gradient of the error curve. The error surface is multidimensional and may contain many local minima. As a result, training the network often requires experimentation with starting position, adjusting the weights during training, and modifying various learning parameters. In particular, the learning rate α is usually adjusted downward during training, and a momentum term may be increased to avoid getting stuck in local optima.

A NEURAL NETWORK TO PREDICT THRIFT INSTITUTION FAILURES

A back-propagation neural network that forecasts the probability of failure of thrift institutions has been developed using five financial variables as inputs. Back-propagation learning was selected because it has been successfully used to solve many pattern recognition and classification problems.

Selection of Variables

In past studies, the usual procedure was to select a rather large group of independent variables and reduce that to a smaller group of statistically significant variables. We wished to see how well the neural network would perform, when measured against the best logit model we could formulate. To reduce the dimensionality of the model, we experimented with 29 variables (Table 14.2) and performed stepwise regression that resulted in the identification of five variables. Each variable selected represents one of the CAMEL categories. Although this is a rather small set of variables, we obtained the best results using logit with this group and consequently developed our models with these variables.

The predictor variables representing the categories of capital adequacy, asset quality, management efficiency, earnings, and liquidity were GNWTA (GAAP net worth/total assets), RATA (repossessed assets/total assets), NIGI (net income/gross income), NITA (net income/total assets), and CSTA (cash securities/total assets), respectively.

Since regulators use RAP (regulatory accounting principles) net worth to close institutions, we experimented with models utilizing both GNWTA (GAAP net worth/total assets) and RAPTA (RAP net worth/total assets) as measures of capital adequacy. These variables were highly correlated for all our data sets, and the best prediction rates on the training set were obtained with GNWTA.

Table 14.2

Financial Ratios Tested

Capital	GNWTA*	GAAP net worth/Total assets
	ESTA	Earned surplus/Total assets
	RAPTA	RAP net worth/Total assets
Assets	RETA*	Repossessed assets/Total assets
	RLTA	High risk loans/Total assets
	REOTA	Real estate owned/Total assets
	ORATA	Other risky assets/Total assets
	TLS	Total loans/Savings
	ITA	Direct investments/Total assets
Management	NIGI*	Net income/Gross income
	TEOI	Total operating income/Other income
	OETA	Other expenses/Total assets
	OHAOI	Overhead/Adjusted operating income
Earnings	NITA*	Net income/Total assets
	NIM	Net interest margin
	ROA	Return on assets
Liquidity	CSTA*	Cash + securities/Total assets
	VLTA	Volatile liabilities/Total assets
	LATA	Liquid assets/Total assets
	ADRAP	FHLBB advances/RAP net worth
	ADGAP	FHLBB advances/GAAP net worth
	OBMTF	Other borrowed money/Total funds
	CSSB	Cash + securities/Savings + borrowed money
	BDS	Brokered deposits/Savings
	ADTA	FHLBB advances/Total assets
	ISFTF	Interest-sensitive funds/Total funds
	BFTA	Borrowed funds/Total assets
	IBLEA	Interest-bearing liabilities/Earning assets
Size	LOGTA	Log total assets

Note: GAAP = Generally accepted accounting principles.
         RAP = Regulatory approved principles.
*Used in results reported in Tables 14.3 through 14.5.

The Data Set and Sampling Techniques

The data set consists of financial data on 3,479 S&Ls for the period January 1986 to December 1987. The data are taken from Federal Home Loan Bank board quarterly tapes. The training sets, which were used to generate the logit model and to provide examples to the neural network during its training process, were developed from call report data for June 1986. For the first neural network and logit models, the 100 failures from January 1986 to December 1987 were matched with 100 nonfailed S&Ls, based on geographic location and value of total assets. For each failure, all the surviving institutions located in the same state were identified. Next, the absolute percentage differences in asset size between each failed institution and the survivors in the state were computed. These were ranked, and those that most closely matched the asset size of the failure were included in the appropriate sample.

For testing the predictive capabilities of logit and the neural network, a second sample consisting of call report data for each failed institution 6, 12, and 18 months prior to failure was used. Data were available for 58 failed and 58 surviving institutions 6 months prior to failure, 47 failed and 47 surviving institutions 12 months prior to failure, and 24 failed and 24 surviving institutions 18 months prior to failure.

A third sample was also tested, in which 75 failures were matched with 329 nonfailed institutions. Due to mergers and regulatory actions, data were available for the two-year period for only 75 of the 100 failures. The reasons for diluting this sample with surviving institutions were to develop a larger sample that more closely resembles the true population and to test the robustness of our models with respect to sampling rates.

The Development of the Neural Network

The first step in the development of a neural network model is to select an appropriate neural network paradigm by matching the application requirements with the paradigm capabilities. The application is heteroassociative (i.e., it requires mapping one set of patterns onto a different set). Supervised learning was used since the network would be trained using examples that included the result. For this application, a single, middle-layer, feedforward, back-propagation neural network consisting

Figure 14.3

Neural Network for Predicting Thrift Failures

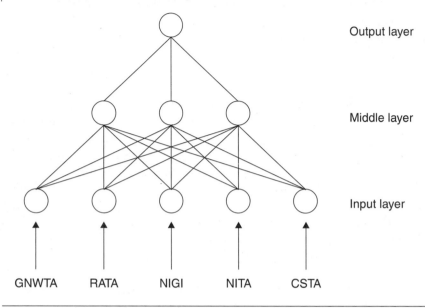

of five input nodes, three middle-layer nodes, and one output node was developed (Figure 14.3). The input nodes represent the financial ratios selected, which measure capital adequacy (C), asset quality (A), management efficiency (M), earnings (E), and liability (L), and the output node is interpreted as the probability that an institution was classified as failed or surviving.

After experimentation with two middle layers did not result in better prediction rates, a single middle layer was adopted. This was consistent with other results with classification problems that demonstrated no improvement with more than one middle layer.[1,2]

Determining the proper number of nodes for the middle layer is more art than science, and experimentation and heuristics assisted in making this choice. Our initial network was constructed with three nodes in the middle layer, based on a rule of thumb that suggests that the number of nodes in the middle layer should be 75 percent of the number of nodes in the input layer. Other models using four and five nodes in the middle layer were also tested. Generally speaking, too many nodes in the middle layer, and hence too many connections, produce a neural network that memorizes the input data and lacks the ability to generalize. Therefore, increasing the number of nodes in the middle layer will improve the network's ability to classify institutions in the training set but will degrade its ability to classify institutions outside the training set. This proved to be true for our application.

The required output layer in this model consists of a single node, which would be interpreted as a classification node, indicating insolvency or solvency of the institution. Initially, we set a threshold of .5 (i.e., if the output value is greater than .5, failure is predicted; otherwise, the institution is classified as surviving). We also used a threshold of .2 to test the sensitivity of the network to changes in this value.

The generalized delta rule was used with the back-propagation of error to transfer values from internal nodes. (For a more detailed explanation of back-propagation learning and the generalized delta rule, see Rumelhart and McClelland.[22]) The sigmoidal function is the activation function specified in this neural network and is used to adjust weights associated with each input node. This is the same transformation employed in logit analysis in which the dependent variable is assumed to be a logistic function of the independent variables and a constant. This function was the best choice for our application since its steepest slope occurs at .5. Therefore, the result of applying the sigmoidal function to a weighted sum of the independent variables will be greatest at the midpoint, and the transfer function will have less effect when an output transferred from the input layer is close to the extreme values (Figure 14.2).

The network was implemented using the software package Neural-Works Explorer running on a 386-based microcomputer with a math co-processor. NeuralWorks Explorer, developed by NeuralWare, Inc., was selected because it can be used to implement over a dozen network paradigms.[23] It allows the user to easily alter learning parameters during training and to view the weights and output values associated with trained networks. Automatic scaling of input parameters and randomization of the training set reduce the development effort. The major limitation encountered when using NeuralWorks Explorer for this application was its inability to support the numerous experiments required to find a satisfactory combination of network architecture and set of learning parameters.

Training the Neural Network

Supervised learning was conducted with training sets consisting of five CAMEL ratios and the corresponding result (failure/surviving) for each S&L. For the input nodes in which the data were not in ratio form, the values were scaled to be within a range of 0 to 1. Automatic scaling is performed by the network software that computes the range of a set of values, and the difference between the input value and the minimum, and then divides the latter by the former. This minimizes the effect of magnitude among the inputs and increases the effectiveness of the learning algorithm. The selection of the examples for the training set focused on quality and the degree to which the data set represented the population. The size of the training set is important since a larger training set may take longer to process computationally but may accelerate the rate of learning and reduce the number of iterations required for convergence.

All the weights in the fully connected network were randomized before training. The learning rate and momentum were set initially at .9 and .6, respectively, the learning rate was adjusted downward, and the momentum was adjusted upward during training to improve performance. The learning rate is a constant of proportionality (see (7)), which determines the effect of past weight changes on the current direction of movement in the weight space. In back-propagation, it is usually set close to 1.0 for early iterations when larger changes take place as the optimum is approached. The learning rate should be set as high as possible, while avoiding oscillation. A momentum term can be added to the back-propagation learning rule (7), and this value is increased as an optimum is approached. This effectively provides the impetus to help the algorithm avoid becoming lodged in local minima. The NeuralWorks software allows the user to adjust these parameters dynamically, to maximize learning.

The training examples were presented to the network in random order to maximize performance and to minimize the introduction of bias. During each iteration, a training vector is presented to the network, the network error is computed, the error is propagated back through the network, and the weights are updated using this new information. In practice, the number of presentations made before the weights are updated is called the epoch size and is under the control of the user. Convergence was achieved after 40,000 iterations when the network errors remained relatively unchanged for subsequent iterations. In NeuralWorks, the user specifies the number of iterations to be performed, and the training process is stopped when an appropriate measure of network error is achieved. The training process can be interrupted at any point in time, and measures of network error can be displayed to assist the user in determining whether to stop or continue.

RESULTS

The performance of the neural network that was trained using 100 failures and 100 surviving institutions from January 1986 to December 1987 is compared to the logit model. The regression coefficients, significant variables, and the log likelihood function for the logit model are given in Table 14.3. Four of the five variables, representing capital adequacy, asset quality, management efficiency, and earnings quality, are significant at the 1 percent error level, as is the log likelihood ratio. The explanatory variables were checked for linear dependence by examining the correlation matrices. None were found to be linear combinations of any others, and this was confirmed by a principal components analysis. Therefore, multicolinearity does not pose a serious problem for this model with these data.[24,25]

For both the logit and the neural network models, we classify the institutions as failed if the output values exceed a cutoff point. While some previous studies set a cutoff point of .5, this overlooks the fact that

---

Table 14.3

Logit Results for Matched Sample

Intercept	−.0103
GNWTA	−55.7485[*]
RETA	28.7573
NIGI	−1.2828[*]
NITA	−79.3499[*]
CSTA	6.4446
Log Likelihood Ratio	−51.000[*]

*Significant at the 1 percent error level.

Table 14.4

Comparison of Logit and the Neural Network January 1986 to December 1987 (Matched Sample)

	All			Failed			Nonfailed		
	Logit		Neural Network	Logit		Neural Network	Logit		Neural Network
Cutoff = 0.5									
Training set	187/200 (93.5%)	$p = .10$*	194/200 (97.0%)	90/100 (90.0%)	$p = .10$*	96/100 (96.0%)	97/100 (97.0%)	$p = .60$	98/100 (98.0%)
Six months before failure	102/116 (87.8%)	$p = .25$	107/116 (92.2%)	56/58 (96.6%)	$p = 1.0$	56/58 (96.6%)	46/58 (79.3%)	$p = .20$	51/58 (87.9%)
Twelve months before failure	79/92 (85.9%)	$p = .15$	85/92 (92.4%)	43/46 (93.5%)	$p = .99$	44/46 (95.6%)	36/46 (78.3%)	$p = .15$	41/46 (89.1%)
Eighteen months before failure	40/48 (83.3%)	$p = .25$	44/48 (91.7%)	18/24 (75.0%)	$p = .10$*	22/24 (91.7%)	22/24 (91.7%)	$p = 1.0$	22/24 (91.7%)
Cutoff = 0.2									
Training set	166/200 (83.0%)	$p = .01$†	186/200 (92.5%)	95/100 (95.0%)	$p = 1.0$	96/100 (96.0%)	71/100 (71.0%)	$p = .001$†	90/100 (90.0%)
Six months before failure	101/116 (87.1%)	$p = .60$	104/116 (89.7%)	56/58 (96.6%)	$p = 1.0$	56/58 (96.6%)	45/58 (77.6%)	$p = .5$	48/58 (82.8%)
Twelve months before failure	79/92 (85.9%)	$p = .15$	85/92 (92.4%)	44/46 (95.7%)	$p = .60$	45/46 (97.8%)	35/46 (76.1%)	$p = .05$*	40/46 (87.0%)
Eighteen months before failure	41/48 (85.4%)	$p = .40$	44/48 (91.7%)	19/24 (79.2%)	$p = .25$	22/24 (91.7%)	22/24 (91.7%)	$p = 1.0$	22/24 (91.7%)

* Significant difference at the 10 percent level.
† Significant difference at the 5 percent level or less.

the costs associated with a Type I error (misclassifying a failed institution) are usually greater than those with a Type II error.[6] Thus, we present the results for cutoff points of .5 and .2 since lowering the cutoff point reduces the probability of committing a Type I error.

Results with the Matched Sample

In Table 14.4, we report the number of institutions correctly classified by each model and the *p*-values from the nonparametric test of equality of proportions.[26] The null hypothesis that the proportion of institutions correctly classified by each method is the same is tested using a nonparametric test since the data is categorical. The chi-square test statistic for equality of *k* proportions is:

$$Q = \sum_{j=1}^{k} \frac{(f_j - n_j p)^2}{n_j p (1 - p)} \qquad (10)$$

where *p* is the proportion of successes, f_j is the observed frequency of success, and n_j is the number of observations.

For the training set data and cutoff points of .5 and .2, each failed and nonfailed institution correctly classified using logit is also correctly classified by the neural network. In addition, the network commits fewer total classification errors for each cutoff point, and the difference is significant at the 10 percent level for a cutoff point of .5. For the 6-, 12-, and 18-month predictions, the number of correct classifications made by the neural network is greater than or equal to those made by logit regardless of the cutoff point. For a cutoff point of .5, significant differences at the 10 percent level were indicated for the predictions made 18 months before failure. There was one institution, a failed S&L, that was correctly classified by logit and incorrectly classified by the neural network.

Differences between the misclassifications for the training set and 18-month forecasts made by the models were observed. Tables were developed to further analyze these misclassifications, with the rows as the misclassified failures and nonfailures made by the logit model and the columns as the misclassifications made by the neural network. We used Cohen's measure of agreement[27] to determine whether the categorizations developed by the models were in agreement. The maximum likelihood estimate of Cohen's K is computed as:

$$K = \frac{N\sum x_{ii} - \sum x_{i+}x_{+i}}{N^2 - \sum x_{i+}x_{+i}}$$

where N = total number of observations, x_{ij} is the observed value in the $(i,j)^{th}$ cell, x_{i+} is the sum of the observed values in row i, and x_{+i} is the sum of the observed values in column i.

Since we observed a large number of cases in which the methods agreed, we computed K for the cases in which the models disagreed, and, using the asymptotic variance,[27] confidence intervals for K were developed. The 95 percent confidence interval for the true value of K was (–.7, .25) for the training set and (–.9, .58) for the 18-month forecasts. Since a value of 1 would indicate perfect agreement, these results lead to the conclusion that there is significant disagreement between the misclassifications made by the models at the 5 percent error level. When combined with the results of the test of equality of proportions, this shows that, for these two samples, the neural network did provide a better forecast of failures.

For the training set, changing the cutoff point had a greater effect on the number of correct classifications made by logit because the neural network assigned fewer output values between .2 and .5. For example, when the cutoff point is changed from .5 to .2, logit correctly classifies 5 more failures, but the total number of nonfailures misclassified increases from 3 to 29. In contrast, the number of nonfailures misclassified by the neural network increases from 2 to 10. Changing the cutoff point had less effect on the prediction set for both models; this may be a consequence of the smaller sample sizes.

Results with Diluted Sample

The results of the logit and neural network models, which included 75 failed and 329 nonfailed institutions, are given in Table 14.5. The coefficients for the logit model, the number of S&Ls correctly classified, and the p-values for the nonparametric test for differences[26] are reported. The variables representing capital adequacy, management efficiency, and earnings quality

Table 14.5

Comparison of Logit and the Neural Network January 1986 to December 1987 (Diluted Sample)

	Correctly Classified S&Ls					
	All		**Failed**		**Nonfailed**	
Cutoff=.5	**Logit**	**Neural Network**	**Logit**	**Neural Network**	**Logit**	**Neural Network**
	381/404	391/404	54/75	64/75	327/329	327/329
	(94.3%)	(96.8%)	(72.0%)	(85.3%)	(99.4%)	(99.4%)
	p=.10		p=.05†		p=1.0	

	373/404	387/404	65/75	68/75	308/329	319/329
Cutoff=.2	(92.3%)	(95.8%)	(86.7%)	(90.7%)	(93.6%)	(96.9%)
	p=.05†		p=.50		p=.05†	

Logit Results

Intercept	−1.0501**
GNWTA	−49.1956**
RETA	11.5391
NIGI	−1.3257**
NITA	−105.8590**
CSTA	−.1824
Log likelihood ratio	−80.6950**

*Significant difference at the 10 percent level.
†Significant difference at the 5 percent level or less.

are statistically significant at the 1 percent level. Logit correctly classifies 54 of 75 failures, and the neural network correctly classifies 64 of 75, with this difference significant at the 5 percent level. The 95 percent confidence interval for the value of K is (.23, .55), indicating mild disagreement on misclassification errors. A significant difference is also observed for the classification of the nonfailed institutions when the cutoff is .2. Also, when the cutoff point changes from .5 to .2, the number of failures misclassified by logit is reduced from 21 to 10, and the number of misclassified nonfailures increases from 2 to 21. The number of failures misclassified by neural network is reduced from 11 to 7, and the number of misclassified nonfailures increases from 2 to 10. As with the matched sample, the neural network is less sensitive to reducing the cutoff point. Finally, each S&L correctly classified by logit was also correctly classified by the neural network.

CONCLUSIONS AND SUGGESTIONS FOR FURTHER RESEARCH

In our study, we evaluated the ability of a neural network to predict thrift institution failures by comparing it with the best logit model we could develop with our data. Since for each data set we examined in our study the neural network has performed as well or better than logit, neural networks may offer a competitive modeling approach for failure prediction. We also observe that, in some cases, when the cutoff point was lowered, the reduction in Type I errors committed was accompanied by greater increases in Type II errors for the logit model than for the neural network. This may be an important result when examiners factor in the cost of committing Type I and Type II errors. An examination of Table 14.5 shows a significant difference between the total number of correct classifications made by the two models when the sample is diluted with healthy institutions, for both cutoff points. Since the diluted sample more closely resembles the total population of thrift institutions, the neural network may yield more consistent results when used with the data sets available to regulators. Finally, our results are consistent with those obtained in other studies[1,2] in which neural network technology is determined to be a promising tool for classification problems. For this application, the three-layer neural network gains some predictive power over logit, which can be viewed as a two-layer model. While model specifications such as the choice of activation function and learning parameters are required in neural network models, benefits may be derived when there is insufficient information available to make assumptions about population distributions.

Several limitations may restrict the use of neural network models for prediction. There is no formal theory for determining optimal network topology; therefore, decisions such as the appropriate number of layers and middle-layer nodes must be determined using experimentation. The development and interpretation of neural network models requires more expertise from the user than traditional statistical models. Training a neural network can be computationally intensive, and the results are sensitive to the selection of learning parameters. Poor results can also occur if the wrong activation function is selected. Finally, back-propagation neural network models seem to be most successful when solving pattern recognition and classification problems; more research is required to determine if there are other types of problems that may be good candidates.

The inability of neural networks to provide explanations of *how* and *why* conclusions may restrict the use of this modeling technique. This is in contrast to expert systems, which can provide explanations to the user about how inferences are made. One approach used to determine the relative importance of individual input variables is to design a special data set that exaggerates the values of the input variables to be tested. The activation levels of hidden nodes and the output nodes are examined as each observation is processed by the network.[28] Another approach that applies nonlinear statistical methods for misspecified models is under investigation.[14] Finally, some hybrid systems have been developed that include an expert system to provide explanations for the behavior of the neural network.[28]

There are many opportunities for conducting research in this area. Neural networks may be extended to other financial applications, particularly those requiring classification, such as credit approval and bond rating. Further investigation into the relationship between the back-propagation network and traditional nonlinear statistical models may yield benefits to both areas of study.

ENDNOTES

1. S. Dutta and S. Shekhar, "Bond-Rating: A Non-Conservative Application of Neural Networks," in *Proceedings of the IEEE International Conference on Neural Networks* 2 (1988), pp. 443–50.

2. E. Collins, S. Ghosh, and C. Scofield, "An Application of a Multiple Neural-Network Learning System to Emulation of Mortgage Underwriting Judgments," *Proceedings of the IEEE International Conference on Neural Networks* 2 (1988), pp. 459–66.

3. E. J. Kane, *The S&L Insurance Mess: How Did It Happen?* (Washington, DC: The Urban Institute, 1989).

4. In some studies of S&Ls, the management component is ignored, resulting in a CAEL framework. See notes 5–7, 10.

5. E. L. Altman, "Predicting Performance in the Savings and Loan Industry," *Journal of Monetary Economics*, 1977, pp. 443–66.

6. J. R. Barth, R. D. Brumbaugh, D. Sauerhaft, and G. H. K. Wang, "Thrift Institution Failures: Estimating the Regulator's Closure Rule," in *Research in Financial Services*, Vol. 1, ed. G. G. Kaufman (Greenwich, CT: JAI Press, 1989).

7. G. J. Benston, "An Analysis of the Causes of Savings and Loans Failures," *Monograph Series in Finance and Economics*, 1986, Series 1985 (4).

8. C. Pantalone and M. Platt, "Predicting Failure of Savings and Loan Associations," *AREUEA Journal* 15, no. 2 (1987), pp. 46–64.

9. D. E. Booth, P. Alam, S. N. Ahkam, and B. Osyk, "A Robust Multivariate Procedure for the Identification of Problem Savings and Loan Institutions," *Decision Sciences* 20 (1989), pp. 320–33.

10. P. Elmer and D. Borowski, "An Expert System Approach to Financial Analysis: The Case of S&L Bankruptcy," *Financial Management* (1988), pp. 66–76.

11. G. S. Maddala, *Limited Dependent and Qualitative Variables in Econometrics* (Cambridge: Cambridge University Press, 1983), pp. 12–41.

12. A. N. Kolmogorov, "On the Representation of Continuous Function of Many Variables by Superposition of Continuous Functions of One Variable and Addition," *Doklady akademii nauk SSSR* 144 (1957), pp. 679–81.

13. ———, "On the Representation of Continuous Function of Many Variables by Superposition of Continuous Functions of One Variable and Addition," *American Mathematical Society Translation* 28 (1963), pp. 55–59.

14. H. White, "Some Asymptotic Results for Learning in Single Hidden Layer Feedforward Network Models," *Journal of the American Statistical Association* 84 (1989), pp. 1003–13.

15. F. Rosenblatt, "The Perceptron: A Probabilistic Model for Information Storage and Organization in the Brain," *Psychological Review* 65 (1958), pp. 386–408.

16. M. Minsky and S. Papert, *Perceptrons* (Cambridge, MA: MIT Press, 1969).

17. For a more complete discussion of the development of the percep-tron by Rosenblatt, and the contributions of Minsky and Papert, see Anderson and Rosenfeld (note 29).

18. D. E. Rumelhart and D. Zipser, "Feature Discovery by Competitive Learning," *Cognitive Science* 9 (1985), pp. 75–112.

19. G. Carpenter and S. Grossberg, "ART2: Self-Organization of Stable Category Recognition Codes for Analog Input Patterns," *Applied Optics* 26 (1987), pp. 4919–46.

20. T. Kohonen, *Self-Organization and Associate Memory* (New York: Springer-Verlag, 1988).

21. D. E. Rumelhart, G. Hinton, and R. Williams, "Learning Internal Representation by Error Propagation," in *Parallel Distributed Processing,* eds. D. E. Rumelhart and J. L. McClelland (Cambridge, MA: MIT Press, 1986), pp. 318–62.

22. D. E. Rumelhart and J. L. McClelland, *Parallel Distributed Processing* (Cambridge, MA: MIT Press, 1986).

23. C. C. Klimasauskas, *NeuralWorks: An Introduction to Neural Computing* (Sewickley, PA: NeuralWare, Inc., 1988).

24. M. D. Intrilligator, *Econometric Models, Techniques, and Applications* (Englewood Cliffs, NJ: Prentice-Hall, 1978), pp. 151–56.

25. J. Kmenta, *Elements of Econometrics* (New York: Macmillan, 1971), pp. 389–91.

26. J. Gibbons, *Nonparametric Methods for Quantitative Analysis* (New York: Holt, Rinehart, & Winston, 1976), pp. 259–62.

27. Y. Bishop, S. Fienberg, and P. Holland, *Discrete Multivariate Analysis* (Cambridge, MA: MIT Press, 1975).

28. M. Caudill and C. Butler, *Naturally Intelligent Systems* (Cambridge, MA: MIT Press, 1990).

29. J. A. Anderson and E. Rosenfeld, *Neurocomputing: Foundations of Research* (Cambridge, MA: MIT Press, 1989).

15

A Study on Using Artificial Neural Networks to Develop an Early-Warning Predictor for Credit Union Financial Distress with Comparison to the Probit Model

Clarence N. W. Tan

I am indebted to Prof. Jeffrey Carmichael for making this study possible and for his invaluable input in developing this paper. I would also like to thank Assoc. Prof. Anthony Hall for his patience, guidance, and assistance in providing the data for the study. I am also grateful to the Reserve Bank of Australia for financial support through their EFRF fund and to the Australian Financial Intsitution Commission for their kind assistance.

INTRODUCTION

Since Beaver's (1966) pioneering work in the late 1960s, there has been considerable interest in using financial ratios to predict financial failure.[1] The great upsurge in interest probably owes most to the seminal work by Altman (1968), in which he combined financial ratios into a single predictor of corporate bankruptcy. One of the main reasons for the popularity of Altman's methodology is that it provides a standard benchmark for comparison of companies in similar industries. It also enables a single indicator of financial strength to be constructed from a company's financial accounts. While the methodology is widely appealing, it does have limitations. As pointed out by Gibson and Frishkoff (1986), ratios can differ greatly across industrial sectors and accounting methods used.[2]

This limitation is probably nowhere more evident than in using financial indicators to predict financial distress among financial institutions. The naturally high leverage of financial institutions means that models developed for the corporate sector are not readily transportable to the financial sector. The approach has nonetheless gained acceptance in the area of financial institutions. Recent examples in Australia include unpublished analyses of financial distress in the nonbank area by Hall and Byron (1992) and McLachlan (1993). Both of these studies use a probit model to deal with the limited dependent variable nature of financial distress data.

This study examines the viability of an alternative methodology for the analysis of financial distress based on artificial neural networks (ANNs). In particular, it focuses on the applicability of ANNs as an early-warning predictor of financial distress among credit unions. The ANN-based model developed in this paper is compared with the probit model results of Hall and Byron. In particular, this study is based on the same data set used by Hall and Byron. This facilitates an unbiased comparison of the two methodologies. The results reported in the paper indicate than the ANN approach is marginally superior to the probit model over the same data set. The paper also considers ways in which the model design can be altered to improve its performance as an early-warning predictor.

Existing Studies: Methodological Issues

Discriminant analysis is one of the most popular techniques used to analyze financial data in the context of financial distress. This method has been described by Jones (1987, p. 143) as "a multivariate technique that assigns a score, z, to each company in a sample, using a combination of independent variables." The analyst then decides on a cutoff z-score based on the sample results; companies below the cutoff are predicted to become bankrupt, and those above the cutoff are predicted to remain healthy. The main appeal of this approach is its ability to reduce a multidimensional problem to a single score. Altman (1968) was the first to use discriminant analysis in predicting bankruptcy. Studies using the discriminant analysis methodology generally find a high level of classification accuracy.[3]

The main criticism of the discriminant analysis method is the restrictive statistical requirements the model poses. For example, the requirement that the independent variables have a multivariate normal distribution is often violated, as when dummy independent variables are used. Further, the score that is produced by the model is of limited use in interpreting the results since it is basically an ordinal ranking. There is also no simple method of determining the statistical significance of the contributions of the various independent variables to the overall score.

Binary choice models (or limited dependent variable techniques) such as probit, tobit, and logit are able to overcome the main problems of discriminant analysis. Martin's paper (1977) of bank failure is the seminal work in the use of binary choice regression techniques in this area.[4]

Martin compared the classification accuracy of a logit regression based on the cumulative logistic function with multiple discriminant analysis in analyzing financial distress among a large number of Federal Reserve supervised banks from 1970 to 1976. He found that while logit and multiple discriminant analysis had similar levels of accuracy, both methods were superior to the linear discriminant model.

In a study of corporate failures, Collins and Green (1982) found that the logit model appeared to produce fewer Type I errors (misclassifying a failed firm as healthy) but that the method was not significantly better than multiple discriminant analysis. They concluded that the additional computational effort required by the logit model may not be justified unless the cost of Type I errors is very large.

The least supportive study of these general methodologies is that by Pacey and Pham (1990), who address three methodological problems in bankruptcy prediction models: (1) the use of choice-based and equally distributed samples in model estimation and validation, (2) arbitrary use of cutoff probabilities, and (3) the assumption of equal costs of errors in predictions. Using both probit and multiple discriminant models to correct for these problems, they found that neither the multiple discriminant model nor the probit model outperformed a naive model that assumed all firms to be nonbankrupt.

The study that is used as the basis for comparison in this paper is that by Hall and Byron. Hall and Byron use a probit model with 13 basic financial ratios to predict financial distress among credit unions in New South Wales. Of the 13 ratios, 4 were found to make a significant contribution to predicting financial distress. The significant ratios were:

RA: Required doubtful debt provision.

RB: Permanent share capital + reserves + overprovision for doubtful debt to total assets (%).

RC: Operating surplus to total assets (%).

RG: Operating expenses to total assets (%).

Their estimated index function was:

$$V = 0.330RA - 0.230RB - 0.671RC + 0.162RG - 1.174 - 0.507Q1 - 0.868Q2 + 0.498Q3$$

where the variables Q1 to Q3 are seasonal dummy variables to capture any seasonal effects in the data.

A conditional probability of financial distress is obtained by referring to the cumulative normal statistical tables. Any credit unions with a conditional probability greater than one were classified by Hall and Byron as being in "distress."

ARTIFICIAL NEURAL NETWORKS

In traditional statistical analysis, the modeler is required to specify the precise relationship between inputs and outputs and any restrictions that may be implied by theory. ANNs differ from conventional techniques in that the analyst is not required to specify the nature of the relationships involved; the analyst simply identifies the inputs and the outputs. The user trains an ANN to "learn" from previous samples of data in much the same way that a teacher would teach a child to recognize shapes, colors, alphabets, and so on. The ANN builds an internal representation of the data that it is shown and by doing so "creates" an internal model that can be used with new data that it has not seen before.

The training process is relatively simple. However, the preprocessing of the data, including the data selection and representation to the ANN and the postprocessing of the outputs (required for interpretation of the output and performance evaluation) require a significant amount of work.[5]

ANN Strengths and Weaknesses

ANNs are easy to construct and deal very well with large amounts of noisy data. They are especially suited to solving nonlinear problems. They work well for problems where domain experts may be unavailable or where there are no known rules. ANNs are also adaptive in nature. This makes them particularly useful in fields such as finance, where the environment is potentially volatile.

They are also very tolerant of noisy and incomplete data sets. In fact, their robustness in storing and processing of data earned them some applications in space exploration by NASA, where fault-tolerant types of equipment are required. This flexibility derives from the fact that information is duplicated many times over in the many complex intricate network connections in ANNs, just as in the human brain. This feature of ANNs is in contrast with the serial computer (or Von Neumann computer, as it is commonly known in computer literature), where if one piece of information is lost, the entire information set is corrupted.

The major weakness of ANNs is the lack of explanation for the models they create. Research is currently being conducted to unravel these complex network structures. Even though ANNs are easy to construct, finding a good ANN structure and processing and postprocessing the data are very time-consuming processes.

Basic Structure of an ANN

The basic structure of an ANN consists of *neurodes*[6] (similar to neurons in the human brain) that are grouped into *layers*.[7] The most common ANN structure consists of an input layer, one or more hidden layers, and an output layer. A modified simple model of an artificial neuron is shown in Figure 15.1.

In the human brain, neurons communicate by sending signals to each other through complex connections. ANNs are based on the same principle in an attempt to simulate the learning process of the human brain via complex algorithms. Every connection has a weight attached, which may have either a positive or a negative value associated with it. Positive weights activate the neurode, while negative weights inhibit it. Figure 15.1 shows a network structure with inputs $(x_1, x_2,....x_i)$ being connected to neurode j with weights $(w_{1j}, w_{2j} ... w_{ij})$ on each connection. The neurode sums all the signals it receives, with each signal being multiplied by its associated weights on the connection.

This output (h_j) is then passed through an activation or a threshold function $g(h)$ that is normally nonlinear to give the final output O_j. The most commonly used function is the sigmoid (logistic function) because of its easily differentiable properties,[8] which is very convenient when the back-propagation algorithm is applied.

The back-propagation ANN is a feedforward neural network structure that takes the input to the network and multiplies it by the weights on the connections between neurons or nodes, summing their products before passing it through a threshold function to produce an output. The back-propagation algorithm works by minimizing the error between the output and the target (actual) through propagating the error back into the network. The weights on each of the connections between the nodes or neurons (processing units) are then changed according to the size of the initial error. The input data are then fed forward again, producing a new output and error. The process is reiterated until an acceptable minimized error is obtained. Each of the neurons uses the sigmoid (logistic) function as its threshold function and is fully connected to nodes on the next layer. Once the error reaches an acceptable value, the training is halted and

Figure 15.1

Modified Simple Model of an Artificial Neuron

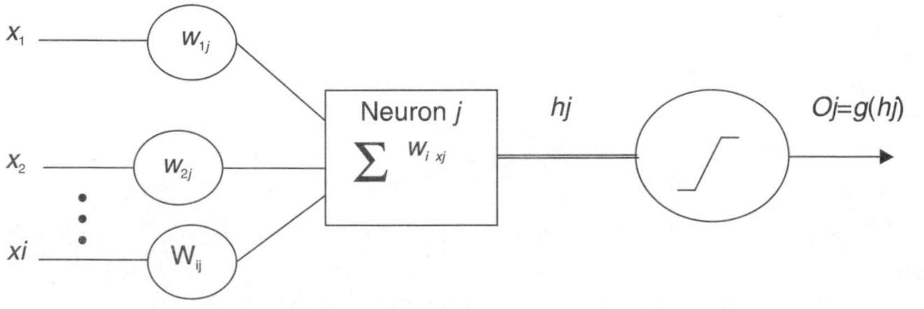

a model or a function that is an internal representation of the output in terms of the inputs is obtained. For a more detailed discussion of the back-propagation model, see Rumelhart et al. (1986).

Constructing the ANN

Setting up an ANN is essentially a four-step procedure. First, the data to be used need to be defined and presented to the ANN as a pattern of input data with the desired outcome or target. Second, the data are categorized as either in the training or validation set. The ANN only uses the training set in its learning process in developing the model. The validation set is used to test the model for its predictive ability. Third, the ANN structure is defined by selecting the number of hidden layers to be constructed and the number of neurons for each hidden layer. Finally, all the ANN parameters are set before starting the training process.

As there are no fixed rules in determining the ANN structure or its parameter values, a large number of ANNs may have to be constructed with different structures and parameters before determining an acceptable model. The trial-and-error process can be tedious, and the experience of the ANN user in constructing the networks is invaluable in the search for a good model.

Determining when the training process needs to be halted is of vital importance in obtaining a good model. If an ANN is overtrained, a curve-fitting problem may occur where the ANN starts to fit itself to the training set instead of creating a generalized model, resulting in poor predictions of the validation data set. On the other hand, if the ANN is not trained long enough, it may settle at a local minimum rather than the global minimum solution, thus generating a suboptimal model. By performing periodic testing of the ANN on the validation set and recording both the results of the training and validation data set results, the number of iterations that produces the best model can be obtained. All that is needed is to reset the ANN and train the network up to that number of iterations.

Applications of ANNs in Predicting Financial Distress

Recently, ANNs have been used in predicting financial distress with a few reported successful applications. Odom and Sharda (1990) found that a back-propagation artificial neural network was superior to a discriminant analysis model in bankruptcy prediction of firms. The accuracy of their model has since been improved upon by Neuralware's applications development service and support (ADSS) group (Coleman et al. 1991) Coleman reported that the ADSS group had successfully developed an ANN-based system to detect bank failures for the accounting firm of KPMG Peat Marwick.[9] In their analysis, they claim an accuracy rate of 90 percent. Salchenberger et al. (1992) showed that an ANN-based model performed as well as or better than the logit model. They also observed that when the cutoff point (probability level) was lowered, the reduction in Type I errors (misclassifying a failed firm as healthy) was accompanied by a greater increase in Type II errors (misclassifying a healthy firm as failed) for the logit model than for the ANN model.

In their survey of savings and loan associations, Tam and Kiang (1992) argue that empirical results have shown that ANNs have better predictive accuracy than discriminant analysis, logit, k nearest neighbor (kNN), and decision tree (ID3) analysis. They further argue that ANNs may be a better alternative to classification techniques under the following conditions:

1. *Multimodal distributions.* Improvement here is due to the ANN's ability to better represent the nonlinear discriminant function. Many classification tasks have been reported to have nonlinear relationships between variables. For example, Whitred and Zimmer (1985) find that the higher prediction accuracy of loan officers to linear discriminant analysis models is due to their ability to relate variables and loan outcomes in a nonlinear manner. Shepanski (1983) also finds that human judgments are better approximated by a nonlinear function.

2. *Adaptive model adjustment.* ANNs have the ability to adapt to the changing environment by adjusting the model, thus allowing the model to respond swiftly to changes.

3. *Robustness.* ANNs make no assumptions of any probability distribution or equal dispersion, nor are there any of the rigid restrictions, such as linearity, found in other models.

In the same ANN framework, this paper discusses a back-propagation model that utilizes financial ratios as input to build a model for predicting financial distress in credit unions in New South Wales, Australia. The back-propagation model was chosen as it had been used quite successfully in bankruptcy prediction tasks (Coleman et al.; Bell et al.; Tam et al.;

Odom et al; and Salchenberger et al.), and tools for implementing it are readily available.

DATA AND TESTING METHODOLOGY

As Hall and Byron note in their paper, defining failure of credit unions in Australia is not a clear-cut process, as many of the failed credit unions are not resolved in bankruptcy. They are mostly resolved by forced mergers, voluntary mergers, or being placed under direction. Since this study uses the same data set as Hall and Byron, the definition of the distress category will be the same as theirs; namely, those credit unions that are placed under direction or placed under notice of direction.

The binary format for the output of the models is 1 for credit unions classified as distressed and 0 for credit unions classified as nondistressed.

The data used in the study are quarterly financial data for 191 New South Wales credit unions from 1989 to 1991. The data were "cleaned" by Hall and Byron to exclude all credit unions with total assets less than $60,000. The total number of observations obtained for the study was 2,144, of which 66 were classified as in distress. The input (independent) variables were financial ratios derived from the financial data used by Hall and Byron.

In-Sample (Training) and Out-of-Sample (Validation) Data Sets

There are two popular methods in validating bankruptcy prediction models. The first method is to separate a single data set into two, using one to build the model and the second to test the model. The second method involves using data from one time period as in-sample data and data from another similar time period as the out-of-sample test set. In this paper, the former method is adopted.

The data set was divided into two separate sets. Data for all quarters of 1989 to 1990 were used as the training set (in-sample data) to build the early warning predictor, while data for all quarters of 1991 were used as the validation set (out-of-sample data). The training sets contained a total of 1,449 observations with 46 credit unions in the distress category. The validation set contained a total of 695 observations, with 20 credit unions classified as in distress.

Input (Independent) Variables

The inputs used in the ANN are the same variables used by Hall and Byron. They are the 13 financial ratios they considered to reflect the stability, profitability, and liquidity of a credit union plus four dummy variables to indicate the quarters in a year. Hall and Byron argued that the quarterly seasonal dummies were needed to adjust for the seasonality in some of the ratios. They also conducted a statistical analysis on the ratios to determine their significance to credit unions in distress.

While Hall and Byron's final model only incorporates 4 of the 13 ratios and three of the four quarterly dummy variables, the ANN model uses all the available information as input. The reason for this is that ANNs are very good at dealing with large, noisy data sets and will, in their learning processes, eliminate inputs that are of little significance because they have little or no weight value on the connections between the input nodes of those variables. The trade-off is that larger networks require larger amounts of training time.

The financial ratios and Hall and Bryon's comments on their significance are reproduced in Table 15.1.

The four dummy variables are as follows:

Q1 = 1 in March quarter and = 0 otherwise.

Q2 = 1 in June quarter and = 0 otherwise.

Q3 = 1 in September quarter and = 0 otherwise.

Q4 = 1 in December quarter and = 0 otherwise.

Therefore, the input layer of the ANN consists of 17 neurodes, with each neurode representing one of the above input variables. The output layer consists of only one output that indicates the status of the credit union. The target that the ANN needs to predict is the binary output of the status of the credit unions, with 1 indicating that the credit union is in distress and 0 indicating that it is in nondistress. The output of the ANN can be any value ranging from 0 to 1 and can be used like a probability distribution.

ANN Topology and Parameter Settings

The pattern of input data was the financial ratios for each quarter of a credit union, and the desired output (target) was the binary status of the credit unions; in other words, distressed or nondistressed. The final

Table 15.1

Financial Ratios

Ratio	Definition	Comments
RA:	Required doubtful debt provision	Distress significantly larger
RB	Permanent share capital + Reserves + Overprovision for doubtful debt to total assets (%)	Distress significantly smaller
RC	Operating surplus to total assets (%)	Distress significantly smaller
RD	Operating surplus to total income (%)	Distress significantly smaller
RE	Required doubtful debt provision to actual doubtful debt provision (%)	Distress significantly smaller
RF	Liquid funds to total assets	Distress significantly smaller
RG	Operating expenses to total assets (%)	Substantial seasonality
RH	Physical assets to total assets (%)	No significant difference
RI	Loans under 5 years to total loans (%)	No significant difference
RJ	Delinquent loans to total loans (%)	Distress significantly larger
RK	Required doubtful debt provision to total loan (%)	Distress significantly larger
RL	Actual doubtful debt provision to total loans (%)	No significant difference
RM	Gross profit margin = Total income − Cost of funds to total income (%)	No significant difference

model consisted of a hidden layer with 5 neurodes, 17 input neurodes, and 1 output neurode. The parameter settings are shown in Table 15.2.

The ANNs constructed in this study used the same set of initial weights. This allowed the results obtained to be replicated. The ANNs

Table 15.2	
Parameter Settings	
Network Parameters	
Learning rate	0.05
Momentum	0.1
Input noise	0
Training tolerance	0.9
Testing tolerance	0.9

were trained in over 25,000 iterations although the best model needed only 3,000 iterations to be fully trained. Further training did not improve results and actually reduced accuracy. This could be due to curve-fitting, as noted earlier, which results from overtraining. This occurs when an ANN starts to specifically model the training set rather than build a general model of the problem at hand.

Many ANNs were constructed with different network topologies and different parameter settings in an attempt to find the best model. The performance of the models was measured by the least number of Type I errors committed rather than the overall accuracy, which is the standard used by most studies, including Hall and Byron's. Type I errors involve the misclassification of financially distressed credit unions as healthy. Type I errors can be very costly to regulators in that they could generate financial crisis or loss of confidence in the regulator. Type II errors involve the misclassification of healthy credit unions as distressed. The cost of Type II errors is mainly that associated with the extra work required in analyzing credit unions with potential problems. Therefore, this paper uses as its criterion for selecting the best model the minimization of Type I errors in the combined training (in-sample) and validation (out-of-sample) data sets.[10]

A brief description of each of the parameters is discussed below.

Learning Rate

The learning rate determines the amount of correction term that is applied to adjust the neurode weights during training. The learning rate of the neural net was tested with (1) adaptive values and (2) fixed values ranging from 0.05 to 0.1. Small values of the learning rate increase learning time but tend to decrease the chance of overshooting the optimal solution. At the same time, they increase the likelihood of getting stuck at local minima. Large values of the learning rate may train the network faster but may result in no learning occurring at all. The adaptive learning rate varies according to the amount of error being generated. The larger the error, the smaller the values and vice versa. Therefore, if the ANN is heading in the right direction toward the optimal solution, it will accelerate. Correspondingly, it will decelerate when it is heading in the wrong direction. Small values were used so as to avoid missing the optimal solution. Adaptive learning proved to be less efficient than small learning rate values in producing accurate predictions.

Momentum

The momentum value determines how much of the previous corrective term should be remembered and carried on in the current training. The larger the momentum value, the more emphasis is placed on the current correction term and the less on previous terms. Momentum serves as a smoothing process that "brakes" the learning process from heading in an undesirable direction.

Input Noise

Random noise is used to perturb the error surface of the neural net to jolt it out of local minima. It also helps the ANN to generalize and prevent curve-fitting. No input noise was used in this study, as good results were obtained without it. It could be that the data set itself may already be noisy.

Training and Testing Tolerances

This is similar to the cutoff point or the level of probability in determining which category a credit union should fall into. A 0.1 cutoff point would be equal to a tolerance of 0.9. This means that any output values that fall within the 90 percent range of the target would be considered correct. Thus, when the target is 1, an output with any value greater than 0.1, indicating that the credit union is in distress, will be classified as correct. The ANN topology can be seen in Figure 15.2.

Figure 15.2

ANN Topology

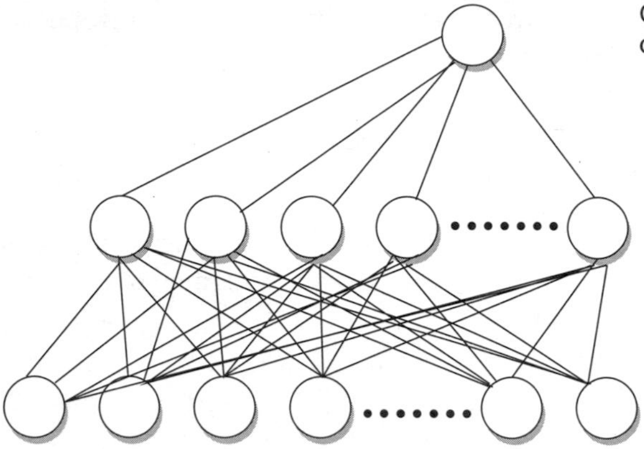

One neurode
output layer

Five neurodes
hidden layer

Seventeen neurodes
input layer

RESULTS

A summary of the overall accuracy of both models' training (in-sample) and validation (out-of-sample) data sets as well as selected credit unions are displayed in a similar fashion to the Hall and Byron's paper so as to allow for a direct comparison of the two models. The full results for all the credit unions (except for credit unions numbered 1058, 1093, 1148, and 1158, which were too small) from both models are in Appendix B.

In Tables 15.3 and 15.4, the Type I errors are highlighted by circles, and the Type II errors are highlighted by boxes. The accuracy of the models was computed by taking the percentage of the total number of correct classifications in both categories from the total number in both categories:

$$Accuracy = \frac{\begin{array}{c}Total\,number\,of \\ distressed\,CUs \\ classified\,as\,distressed\end{array} + \begin{array}{c}Total\,number\,of \\ nondistressed\,CUs \\ classified\,as\,nondistressed\end{array}}{Total\,number\,of\,CUs}$$

Table 15.3

Summary Results of Training Data

□ Type 1 Error: Predicting Credit Unions in Distress as Non-Distressed
○ Type 2 Error: Predicting Credit Unions Not in Distress as Distressed

Probit Model In-Sample Results	Predictions						
	Distress = Pr(Distress)>0.5		Distress = Pr(Distress)>0.25		Distress = Pr(Distress)>0.1		Total
Actual Groups	Nondistress	Distress	Nondistress	Distress	Nondistress	Distress	
Nondistress	1403	⓪	1382	㉑	1294	⑩⑨	1403
Distress	㊲	9	㉑	25	⑬	33	46
Total	1440	9	1403	46	1307	142	1449
Accuracy	97.45%		97.10%		91.58%		

ANN Model In-Sample Results	Predictions						
	Distress = Pr(Distress)>0.5		Distress = Pr(Distress)>0.25		Distress = Pr(Distress)>0.1		Total
Actual Groups	Nondistress	Distress	Nondistress	Distress	Nondistress	Distress	
Nondistress	1399	④	1376	㉗	1258	⑭⑤	1403
Distress	㉒	24	⑮	31	⑩	36	46
Total	1421	28	1391	58	1268	181	1449
Accuracy	98.21%		97.10%		89.30%		

Table 15.4

Summary Results of Validation Data

□ Type 1 Error: Predicting Credit Unions in Distress as Nondistressed
○ Type 2 Error: Predicting Credit Unions Not in Distress as Distressed

Probit Out-of-Sample

Actual Groups	Prediction — Distress = Pr(Distress)>0.1		
	Nondistress	*Distress*	Total
Nondistress	631	(44)	675
Distress	[8]	12	20
Total	639	56	695
Accuracy	92.52%		

ANN Out-of-Sample

Actual Groups	Prediction — Distress = Pr(Distress)>0.1		
	Nondistress	*Distress*	Total
Nondistress	627	(48)	675
Distress	[6]	14	20
Total	633	62	695
Accuracy	92.23%		

Training Set (In-Sample) Discussion

The training set consists of the data for all quarters of 1989 to 1990. The summary results are shown in Table 15.3.

The cutoff point or level of probability that is used to categorize a credit union as in distress was varied to see the effect on the results. It was noted that by decreasing the cutoff point, fewer Type I errors are committed, that is, less misclassification of credit unions that were actually in distress as nondistressed, with the trade-off of more Type II errors being committed, that is, nondistressed credit unions being misclassified as in distress. This holds true for both the probit and the ANN model.

Type I errors were lower in all cases of the ANN model though, at the 0.1 level, the Type II errors committed were marginally higher than the probit model. The ANN model with a cutoff at 0.1 gave the lowest Type I error, committing only 10 misclassification of distressed credit unions as nondistressed while the probit model yielded 13 misclassifications. However, the tradeoff was an increase in Type II errors to 145 misclassifications for the ANN model and 109 for the probit model. The trade-off of improving the Type I errors committed must be weighed against the increase in Type II errors. The optimal cutoff point for the ANN model in terms of the total number of Type I errors committed in both the in-sample and out-of-sample data is 0.1.

Validation Set (Out-of-Sample) Result Comparison

The validation data set is all the quarterly data of 1991. The summary results are shown in Table 15.4.

The ANN model performed better in predicting correctly credit unions that were actually in distress. The Type I error committed by the ANN model is 10 percent lower than the probit model. The Type II error in using the ANN model is a little over half a percent higher than the probit model.

Validation Set (Out-of-Sample) Evaluation

Any output of greater than 0.1 from the ANN model will classify the credit union as in distress; any values less than 0.1 will classify it as nondistressed. The 0.1 cutoff value was chosen from observing the results in the in-sample data. It gave the least number of Type I errors with a marginal increase in Type II errors, as was discussed earlier. The probit model classifies a credit union as in distress if the conditional probability is greater than 0.1

In the tables that follow, the output results of the training set from the ANN model and the fitted conditional probability values of the probit model are shown for all the quarters of 1989 to 1990 as well as 1991 predicted values based on the financial ratios for the 1991 quarters. The actual status (ranging from 1 nondistressed, to 5, distressed) of each credit union is shown together, with the normalized status of 1 being in distress and 0 being nondistressed.

A direct comparison will now be made on the credit unions (except credit union 1148 due to its small size) that were highlighted in the Hall and Byron study.

Credit Unions under Direction/Notice in 1991

The ANN model performed as well as or better than the probit model in most of the cases here. The overall results in terms of percentage correctly predicted could be misleading, as the models in most cases were able to predict a few quarters ahead that a credit union would be in distress. However, in the overall reporting of the predictive accuracy of the models, the early warning signals would have shown up as Type II errors.

Credit Union 1023. This credit union has been under direction since 1989. The ANN model clearly shows that it has not resolved its problems yet and correctly predicts its distress status on all the relevant quarters. The probit model failed to predict it to be in distress in the first two quarters of 1991 although it managed to get the other quarters correctly.

ANN Model					Probit Model		
Identity	Quarter	ANN Output	ANN Predicted	Actual Status	Probit Predicted	Probit Quarter	Probit Probability
1023	8903	0.0622	0	0	0	8903	0.061
1023	8906	0.4895	1	0	1	8906	0.285
1023	8909	0.6929	1	1	1	8909	0.412
1023	8912	0.7401	1	1	1	8912	0.489
1023	9003	0.9468	1	1	1	9003	0.667
1023	9006	0.9850	1	1	1	9006	0.84
1023	9009	0.2813	1	1	1	9009	0.181

1023	9012	0.1250	1	1	1	9012	0.112
1023	9103	0.1635	1	1	0	9103	0.094
1023	9106	0.1235	1	1	0	9106	0.095
1023	9109	0.7649	1	1	1	9109	0.213
1023	9112	0.5606	1	1	1	9112	0.216

Credit Union 1149. None of the models were able to predict correctly that this credit union would be in distress from the third quarter of 1990 to the second quarter of 1991.

ANN Model					Probit Model		
Identity	Quarter	ANN Output	ANN Predicted	Actual Status	Probit Predicted	Probit Quarter	Probit Probability
1149	8903	0.0041	0	0	0	8903	0
1149	8906	0.0004	0	0	0	8906	0
1149	8909	0.0037	0	0	0	8909	0.001
1149	8912	0.0050	0	0	0	8912	0.001
1149	9003	0.0101	0	0	0	9003	0.003
1149	9006	0.0012	0	0	0	9006	0
1149	9009	0.0280	0	1	0	9009	0.003
1149	9012	0.0154	0	1	0	9012	0.001
1149	9103	0.0237	0	1	0	9103	0.001
1149	9106	0.0029	0	1	0	9106	0.001
1149	9109	0.0058	0	0	0	9109	0
1149	9112	0.0067	0	0	0	9112	0

Credit Union 1061. Both models classified this credit union as in distress from late 1990 onwards although it was not put under direction until the first quarter of 1991. The Type II errors committed by both models are not indicative of their usefulness as early predictors of financial distress in this case. This classification problem will be discussed in greater detail in the section titled Further Research.

ANN Model					Probit Model		
Identity	Quarter	ANN Output	ANN Predicted	Actual Status	Probit Predicted	Probit Quarter	Probit Probability
1061	8903	0.0158	0	0	0	8903	0.01
1061	8906	0.0051	0	0	0	8906	0.004
1061	8909	0.0979	0	0	0	8909	0.032

1061	8912	0.0264	0	0	0	8912	0.011
1061	9003	0.0576	0	0	0	9003	0.02
1061	9006	0.0568	0	0	0	9006	0.042
1061	9009	0.1631	1	0	0	9009	0.071
1061	9012	0.1920	1	0	1	9012	0.35
1061	9103	0.4856	1	1	1	9103	0.774

Credit Union 1062. All the models predicted from the outset that this credit union was in distress. However, it was only put under direction in the fourth quarter of 1991. Again, in this case, the Type II errors made by the models are not consistent with their early-warning predictive capability.

ANN Model					Probit Model		
Identity	Quarter	ANN Output	ANN Predicted	Actual Status	Probit Predicted	Probit Quarter	Probit Probability
1062	8903	0.1953	1	0	0	8903	0.089
1062	8906	0.1524	1	0	1	8906	0.128
1062	8909	0.2898	1	0	1	8909	0.137
1062	8912	0.3477	1	0	1	8912	0.198
1062	9003	0.5972	1	0	1	9003	0.246
1062	9006	0.8097	1	0	1	9006	0.459
1062	9009	0.2256	1	0	1	9009	0.116
1062	9012	0.1879	1	0	1	9012	0.117
1062	9103	0.3316	1	0	1	9103	0.207
1062	9106	0.4154	1	0	1	9106	0.195
1062	9109	0.3401	1	0	0	9109	0.085
1062	9112	0.3006	1	1	1	9112	0.151

Credit Union 1078. Both models failed to predict distress in this credit union.

ANN Model					Probit Model		
Identity	Quarter	ANN Output	ANN Predicted	Actual Status	Probit Predicted	Probit Quarter	Probit Probability
1078	8903	0.0139	0	0	0	8903	0
1078	8906	0.0134	0	0	0	8906	0
1078	8909	0.0140	0	0	0	8909	0
1078	8912	0.0137	0	0	0	8912	0

1078	9003	0.0134	0	0	0	9003	0
1078	9006	0.0135	0	0	0	9006	0
1078	9009	0.0136	0	0	0	9009	0
1078	9012	0.0148	0	0	0	9012	0
1078	9103	0.0150	0	1	0	9103	0
1078	9106	0.0185	0	1	0	9106	0.001

Credit Union 1153. The ANN model provided an early warning of distress in the first quarter of 1990 though the warning waned in the second quarter. However, stronger signals were given from the third quarter of 1990 onwards. The probit model predicted distress in the late 1990 but failed to predict the distress in the first quarter of 1991 when the credit union was put under direction.

ANN Model				Probit Model		
Identity	Quarter	ANN Output	ANN Predicted	Actual Status	Probit Predicted	Probit Quarter Probability

Identity	Quarter	ANN Output	ANN Predicted	Actual Status	Probit Predicted	Quarter	Probit Probability
1153	8903	0.0401	0	0	0	8903	0.017
1153	8906	0.0338	0	0	0	8906	0.028
1153	8909	0.0665	0	0	0	8909	0.055
1153	8912	0.0484	0	0	0	8912	0.053
1153	9003	0.1172	1	0	0	9003	0.072
1153	9006	0.0494	0	0	0	9006	0.083
1153	9009	0.1796	1	0	1	9009	0.129
1153	9012	0.1367	1	0	1	9012	0.109
1153	9103	0.1978	1	1	0	9103	0.1
1153	9106	0.9782	1	1	1	9106	0.994
1153	9109	0.6603	1	1	1	9109	0.849
1153	9112	0.3328	1	1	1	9112	0.567

Credit Union 1174. The ANN model committed a Type II error in the first quarter of 1991 though its predictions agreed with the probit predictions of no problems in the other quarters of 1991.

ANN Model				Probit Model		
Identity	Quarter	ANN Output	ANN Predicted	Actual Status	Probit Predicted	Probit Quarter Probability

Identity	Quarter	ANN Output	ANN Predicted	Actual Status	Probit Predicted	Quarter	Probit Probability
1174	8903	0.7985	1	1	1	8903	0.42
1174	8906	0.6926	1	1	1	8906	0.318
1174	8909	0.8491	1	1	1	8909	0.607

1174	8912	0.7088	1	1	1	8912	0.441
1174	9003	0.6450	1	1	1	9003	0.297
1174	9006	0.3613	1	1	1	9006	0.221
1174	9009	0.3089	1	1	1	9009	0.268
1174	9012	0.2415	1	1	1	9012	0.114
1174	9103	0.1501	1	0	0	9103	0.024
1174	9106	0.0409	0	0	0	9106	0.009
1174	9109	0.0936	0	0	0	9109	0.084
1174	9112	0.0787	0	0	0	9112	0.024

Credit Union Transferring in 1991

None of the models seem to be able to predict voluntary transfer. The reason for this could be that the actual status of the voluntary transfer credit unions were classified as nondistressed since they had a status score of 2. If actual status of higher than 1 is used to categorize the credit unions as in distress, the predictive ability of the models on this type of credit unions should improve.

Credit Union 1002. None of the models predicted any problems with this credit union. This credit union was a voluntary transfer in early 1992.

	ANN Model				Probit Model		
Identity	Quarter	ANN Output	ANN Predicted	Actual Status	Probit Predicted	Quarter	Probit Probability
1002	8903	0.0000	0	0	0	8903	0
1002	8906	0.0000	0	0	0	8906	0
1002	8909	0.0000	0	0	0	8909	0
1002	8912	0.0000	0	0	0	8912	0
1002	9003	0.0000	0	0	0	9003	0
1002	9006	0.0000	0	0	0	9006	0
1002	9009	0.0000	0	0	0	9009	0
1002	9012	0.0000	0	0	0	9012	0
1002	9103	0.0000	0	0	0	9103	0
1002	9106	0.0000	0	0	0	9106	0
1002	9109	0.0001	0	0	0	9109	0
1002	9112	0.0001	0	0	0	9112	0

Credit Union 1071. This credit union was a voluntary transfer in the third quarter of 1991. None of the models indicated any problems with it.

ANN Model				Probit Model		
Identity	Quarter	ANN Output	ANN Predicted	Actual Status	Probit Predicted	Probit Quarter	Probit Probability

Identity	Quarter	ANN Output	ANN Predicted	Actual Status	Probit Predicted	Probit Quarter	Probit Probability
1071	8903	0.0171	0	0	0	8903	0
1071	8906	0.0031	0	0	0	8906	0
1071	8909	0.0028	0	0	0	8909	0
1071	8912	0.0018	0	0	0	8912	0
1071	9003	0.0005	0	0	0	9003	0
1071	9006	0.0002	0	0	0	9006	0
1071	9009	0.0005	0	0	0	9009	0
1071	9012	0.0005	0	0	0	9012	0
1071	9103	0.0003	0	0	0	9103	0
1071	9106	0.0002	0	0	0	9106	0

Credit Union 1150. None of the models predicted any problems with this credit union, which subsequently became a voluntary transfer in the second quarter of 1991. The probit model, however, did manage to give a very weak signal in the third quarter of 1990 that the credit union could be in distress.

ANN Model				Probit Model		
Identity	Quarter	ANN Output	ANN Predicted	Actual Status	Probit Predicted	Probit Quarter	Probit Probability

Identity	Quarter	ANN Output	ANN Predicted	Actual Status	Probit Predicted	Probit Quarter	Probit Probability
1150	8903	0.0562	0	0	0	8903	0.008
1150	8906	0.0059	0	0	0	8906	0.011
1150	8909	0.0872	0	0	0	8909	0.056
1150	8912	0.0496	0	0	0	8912	0.059
1150	9003	0.0828	0	0	0	9003	0.063
1150	9006	0.0841	0	0	1	9006	0.113
1150	9009	0.0159	0	0	0	9009	0.019
1150	9012	0.0157	0	0	0	9012	0.019
1150	9103	0.0081	0	0	0	9103	0.008
1150	9106	0.0040	0	0	0	9106	0.008

Credit Union 1190. Again, none of the models gave any indication of problems with this credit union, which was a voluntary transfer in the second quarter of 1991.

ANN Model					Probit Model		
Identity	Quarter	ANN Output	ANN Predicted	Actual Status	Probit Predicted	Probit Quarter	Probit Probability
1190	8903	0.0057	0	0	0	8903	0.008
1190	8906	0.0087	0	0	0	8906	0.027
1190	8909	0.0069	0	0	0	8909	0.011
1190	8912	0.0051	0	0	0	8912	0.01
1190	9003	0.0069	0	0	0	9003	0.011
1190	9006	0.0033	0	0	0	9006	0.016
1190	9009	0.0101	0	0	0	9009	0.011
1190	9012	0.0038	0	0	0	9012	0.005
1190	9103	0.0016	0	0	0	9103	0.002

Credit Unions with Predicted Problems in 1991

Credit Union 1013. This credit union came out of direction in the first quarter of 1991 after being put in direction during 1990. The probit model seems to indicate that the direction may have been lifted too early, which the ANN model seems to agree with except for the last quarter of 1991.

ANN Model					Probit Model		
Identity	Quarter	ANN Output	ANN Predicted	Actual Status	Probit Predicted	Probit Quarter	Probit Probability
1013	8903	0.4031	1	0	1	8903	0.195
1013	8906	0.3883	1	0	1	8906	0.278
1013	8909	0.4678	1	0	1	8909	0.254
1013	8912	0.4810	1	0	1	8912	0.26
1013	9003	0.8718	1	1	1	9003	0.483
1013	9006	0.9742	1	1	1	9006	0.793
1013	9009	0.8493	1	1	1	9009	0.544
1013	9012	0.8532	1	1	1	9012	0.635
1013	9103	0.8979	1	0	1	9103	0.653
1013	9106	0.7730	1	0	1	9106	0.571
1013	9109	0.1377	1	0	1	9109	0.215
1013	9112	0.0775	0	0	0	9112	0.075

Credit Union 1025, Both models seem to indicate problems with this credit union since the first quarter of 1990.

		ANN Model			Probit Model		
Identity	Quarter	ANN Output	ANN Predicted	Actual Status	Probit Predicted	Probit Quarter	Probit Probability
1025	8903	0.0140	0	0	0	8903	0.001
1025	8906	0.0027	0	0	0	8906	0
1025	8909	0.0152	0	0	0	8909	0.007
1025	8912	0.0471	0	0	0	8912	0.01
1025	9003	0.1037	1	0	0	9003	0.018
1025	9006	0.3713	1	0	1	9006	0.138
1025	9009	0.2483	1	0	1	9009	0.14
1025	9012	0.3402	1	0	1	9012	0.262
1025	9103	0.4763	1	0	1	9103	0.281
1025	9106	0.5262	1	0	1	9106	0.266
1025	9109	0.2241	1	0	1	9109	0.167
1025	9112	0.2738	1	0	1	9112	0.175

Credit Union 1044. The ANN model seems to agree with the weak probit model signal that this credit union may have some potential problems.

		ANN Model			Probit Model		
Identity	Quarter	ANN Output	ANN Predicted	Actual Status	Probit Predicted	Probit Quarter	Probit Probability
1044	8903	0.0188	0	0	0	8903	0.004
1044	8906	0.0411	0	0	0	8906	0.038
1044	8909	0.0585	0	0	0	8909	0.029
1044	8912	0.1317	1	0	0	8912	0.041
1044	9003	0.1117	1	0	0	9003	0.026
1044	9006	0.0434	0	0	0	9006	0.051
1044	9009	0.1401	1	0	0	9009	0.07
1044	9012	0.2357	1	0	0	9012	0.095
1044	9103	0.2998	1	0	0	9103	0.096
1044	9106	0.2789	1	0	1	9106	0.142
1044	9109	0.2789	1	0	1	9109	0.117
1044	9112	0.1252	1	0	0	9112	0.076

Credit Union 1052 Both models indicate potential problems with this credit union from the first quarter of 1989.

ANN Model					Probit Model		
Identity	Quarter	ANN Output	ANN Predicted	Actual Status	Probit Predicted	Quarter	Probit Probability
1052	8903	0.3865	1	0	1	8903	0.211
1052	8906	0.4993	1	0	1	8906	0.318
1052	8909	0.1777	1	0	1	8909	0.129
1052	8912	0.1357	1	0	0	8912	0.057
1052	9003	0.1926	1	0	0	9003	0.063
1052	9006	0.5066	1	0	1	9006	0.25
1052	9009	0.1915	1	0	1	9009	0.13
1052	9012	0.4002	1	0	1	9012	0.196
1052	9103	0.6107	1	0	1	9103	0.243
1052	9106	0.7639	1	0	1	9106	0.445
1052	9109	0.4644	1	0	1	9109	0.278
1052	9112	0.3862	1	0	1	9112	0.208

Credit Union 1056. The models are in agreement here concerning potential problems for this credit union.

ANN Model					Probit Model		
Identity	Quarter	ANN Output	ANN Predicted	Actual Status	Probit Predicted	Quarter	Probit Probability
1056	8903	0.2163	1	0	0	8903	0.095
1056	8906	0.0690	0	0	0	8906	0.083
1056	8909	0.0518	0	0	0	8909	0.076
1056	8912	0.2690	1	0	1	8912	0.12
1056	9003	0.1405	1	0	0	9003	0.061
1056	9006	0.2893	1	0	1	9006	0.155
1056	9009	0.1652	1	0	1	9009	0.145
1056	9012	0.2168	1	0	1	9012	0.102
1056	9103	0.5385	1	0	1	9103	0.201
1056	9106	0.6372	1	0	1	9106	0.372
1056	9109	0.2212	1	0	1	9109	0.179
1056	9112	0.2050	1	0	1	9112	0.103

Credit Union 1169. The probit indicated potential problems with this credit union in 1991. Hall and Byron postulated in their paper that the high conditional probabilities may be caused by distinct seasonal patterns in some of the financial ratios of this credit union. The ANN model seems to have captured this seasonal pattern with its output, which seems to predict problems on the third and fourth quarter of every year except for the last two quarters of 1991.

		ANN Model			Probit Model		
Identity	Quarter	ANN Output	ANN Predicted	Actual Status	Probit Predicted	Probit Quarter	Probit Probability
1169	8903	0.0171	0	0	0	8903	0.01
1169	8906	0.0221	0	0	0	8906	0.021
1169	8909	0.3215	1	0	1	8909	0.445
1169	8912	0.2130	1	0	1	8912	0.404
1169	9003	0.0200	0	0	0	9003	0.009
1169	9006	0.0167	0	0	0	9006	0.018
1169	9009	0.1997	1	0	1	9009	0.399
1169	9012	0.2462	1	0	1	9012	0.383
1169	9103	0.0114	0	0	0	9103	0.005
1169	9106	0.0101	0	0	0	9106	0.006
1169	9109	0.0996	0	0	1	9109	0.198
1169	9112	0.0886	0	0	1	9112	0.189

Result Summary of Type I and Type II Errors

The ANN overall Type I error for the entire data set is 16 versus 21 for the probit model out of the 66 distressed credit unions. The Type II error committed by the ANN model over the entire data set is 193 versus 153 for the probit model. The breakdown of Type I and Type II errors for both models in the training and validation sets are shown in Table 15.5.

The ANN model is marginally superior (7.5 percent better) to the probit scores method in terms of the least number of Type I errors committed. The ANN model committed only 1.8 percent more Type II errors. Therefore, there may be a worthwhile trade-off in using the ANN model over the probit model.

CONCLUSION

The ANN model has been demonstrated to perform as well and in some cases better than the probit model as an early warning model for predicting credit unions in distress. The overall accuracy of the ANN model versus

Table 15.5

Type I and Type II Errors

Type of Error	Type I		Type II	
Data Set	ANN Model	Probit Model	ANN Model	Probit Model
Training Set	10	13	145	109
Validation Set	6	8	48	44

the probit model is almost the same, at around 90 percent for the in-sample data and 92 percent for the out-of-sample data.

However, care should be taken in interpreting the accuracy of results. As explained in earlier sections, the Type II errors (predicting a credit union in distress when it is not) may actually be an early warning indicator of problems that do not surface until later quarters. Therefore, the results from the models may actually be better than those reflected in the overall accuracy. A better benchmark would be the model with the least number of Type I errors.

FURTHER RESEARCH

One of the elements that seem to be vital to this type of research but missing from the models in this study is the temporal effect of the independent variables. The temporal effect of the financial data time series was ignored because this study was meant to be a comparison with Hall and Byron's work, which did not utilize any time-dependent variables. They stated in their paper that they found no significance in the one-period change of any of the financial ratios. The models constructed are thus severely restricted in their time horizon forecast, as they are only able to predict financial distress for the quarter that financial ratios are obtained. This seems to be contrary to the objective of creating an early-predictor system.

Future research will concentrate on the time-series component of the financial data, perhaps including new ratios such as growth in assets, liabilities, and so on. ANNs have been applied to many time series problems such as weather forecasting, financial market forecasting (see Tan

1993b; Tsoi, Tan, and Lawrence 1993), EEG to detect mental illness, ECG to predict heart attacks, and so on. Applying ANNs to financial distress prediction from a time-series context should provide better results by potentially providing earlier warnings to financial distress. The data selection will probably be the most vital and time-consuming process. New financial ratios that represent the time-series component of the financial data need to be developed.

Most studies just report the accuracy of the models in terms of percentage correctly classified without regard to the difference in the cost of error, as pointed out by Pacey and Pham (1990). The Type I errors tend to be more serious, as they fail to provide early warning to a credit union that is in financial distress. This could prove to be a very costly affair, as observed in the U.S. S&L failures. The costs of Type II errors are normally restricted to loss of extra labor or resources in auditing or analyzing the credit unions. Therefore, it would be prudent in future studies to use the minimization of Type I error as the objective function of the models. This is assuming that the Type II errors are kept at an acceptable rate.

In this study, the models provided early warning signals in many of the credit unions that eventually were in financial distress but were unjustifiably penalized with Type II errors due to the classification technique that Hall and Byron employed. In their technique, a credit union was classified in distress only after it has been put under direction or under notice of direction. This has a severe effect on ANNs, as they learn through mistakes. Being told that predicting a credit union in distress when the supervisors have not put it under direction or notice of direction is wrong, even though it will actually go into financial distress in the near future. As a result, the ANN will build a suboptimal model that cannot by design provide early warning. This may hold true for the probit model, too. Future studies will reconstruct the data set so that credit unions that failed in n number of quarters will be classified as in potential distress in order to allow for n number of quarters forecast.

The Hall and Byron method of classifying the credit unions also does not allow for voluntary transfers and mergers of credit unions to be built into the models. It may turn out that the voluntary transfers could be a result of potential financial distress in a credit union. Closer examination of those credit unions will need to be conducted to determine if there are any common characteristics that may provide valuable information in predicting financial distress.

The 10 largest conditional probabilities of both models for each quarter of 1991 are provided in Appendix B. The only credit union from the Hall and Byron study that was missing from the table is credit union 1148, which was omitted from this study due to its small size. The Appendix will be used in future research to analyze the relationship of the ratios to the ANN model output.

Since one of the major weaknesses of ANNs is the difficulty in explaining the model, future research will concentrate on studying the interaction of the input variables in relation to the outputs as well as the associated weights of the networks' structures. The ANN parametric effects on the result will be studied in a similar method used by Tan and Wittig (1993) in their parametric study of a stock market prediction model. Different types of artificial neural networks such as the Kohonen type of network will be constructed to see if the results can be improved. The Kohonen network has been used by A.C. Tsoi of the University of Queensland quite successfully in predicting medical claims fraud.

The utilization of genetic algorithms to select the most optimal ANN topology and parameter setting will be explored in future research. Hybrid type of models discussed by Wong and Tan (1994) incorporating ANNs with fuzzy logic and/or expert systems will also be constructed in the future to see if the results can be improved. The benefits of incorporating ANNs with rule- based expert systems as proposed by Tan (1993a) for a trading system will be examined to see if the same concept can be implemented in the context of financial-distress prediction of credit unions.

ENDNOTES

1. See, for example, Beaver (1966); Ohlson (1980); Frydman, Altman, and Kao (1985); Casey and Bartczak (1985); and McKinley et al. (1983), and the works cited in these studies.

2. These cautions are reinforced by Horrigan (1968) and Levy and Sarnat (1988).

3. See, for example, Deakin (1972); Libby (1975ab); Schipper (1977); Altman, Haldeman, and Narayanan (1977); Dambolena and Khoury (1980); Gombola and Ketz (1983); Casey and Bartzak (1985); Gentry, Newbold, and Whitford (1985a); and Sinkey (1975).

4. Other studies that have used binary choice analysis in financial distress prediction include Ohlson (1980); Gentry, Newbold, and Whitford (1985b); Casey and Bartzak (1985); and Zavgren (1985).

5. The old adage of garbage in, garbage out holds especially true for ANN modeling. A well-known case in which an ANN learned the incorrect model involved the identification of a person's sex from a picture of his or her face. The ANN application was trained to identify a person as either male or female by being shown various pictures of faces. At first, researchers thought that the ANN had learnt to differentiate the face of a male person from a female by identifying the visual features of a person's face. However, it was later discovered that the pictures used as input data showed all the male persons' heads nearer to the edge of the top end of the pictures, presumably due to a bias of taller male persons in the data than female persons. The ANN model had therefore learned to differentiate the sex of a person by the distance his or her head is from the top edge of a picture rather than by identifying their visual facial features.

6. There is no standardization of terminology in the artificial neural network field yet although the Institute of Electrical and Electronic Engineers currently has a committee looking into it. The term *neurode* has been used by quite a few major researchers. Other terminology that has been used to describe the artificial neurode includes *processing elements, nodes, neurons, units,* and so on.

7. In some ANN literature, the layers are also called *slabs.*

8. The sigmoid (logistic) function is defined as $O_{pj}{}' = \dfrac{1}{1 + e^{-net_{pj}}}$. In the ANN context, O_{pj} is the output of a neurode j given an input pattern p and net_{pj} is the total input to the ANN. The derivative of the output function to the total input is required to update the weights in the back-propagation algorithm. Thus we have: $\dfrac{\partial O_{pj}}{\partial net_{pj}} = O_{pj}(1 - O_{pj})$, a trivial derivation. For a more detailed discussion on the back-propagation algorithm, see Rumelhart (1986).

9. The results were subsequently published by Bell et al. (1990).

10. Incidentally, the ANN that gave the minimum Type I errors in the in-sample data set also gave the minimum Type I errors for the combined in-sample and the out-of-sample data sets. See Appendix C.

REFERENCES

Altman, E, R. Haldeman, and P. Narayanan, 1977. "Zeta Analysis." *Journal of Banking and Finance,* June, pp. 29–54.

Altman, E., 1968. "Discriminant Analysis and the Prediction of Corporate Bankruptcy." *Journal of Finance,* September, pp. 589–609.

Beaver, W., 1966. "Financial Ratios as Predictors of Failure." *Journal of Accounting Research,* pp. 71–111.

Bell, T.B., G.S. Ribar, and J.R. Verchio, 1990. "Neural Networks vs. Logistic Regression: A Comparison of Each Model's Ability to Predict Commercial Bank Failures." *Deloitte & Touche/University of Kansas Auditing Symposium.*

Coleman, K.G., Timothy J. Graettinger, and William F. Lawrence, 1991. "Neural Networks for Bankruptcy Prediction: The Power to Solve Financial Problems." *AI Review,* July/August, pp. 48–50.

Collins, R.A., and R.D. Green, 1982. "Statistical Methods for Bankruptcy Forecasting." *Journal of Economic and Business* 32, pp. 349–54.

Dambolena, I., and S. Khoury, 1980. "Ratio Stability and Corporate Failure." *Journal of Finance,* September, pp. 1017–26.

Gentry, J., P. Newbold, and D. Whitford, 1985a. "Classifying Bankrupt Firms with Fund Flow Components." *Journal of Accounting Research,* Spring, pp. 146–59.

———, 1985b. "Bankruptcy: If Cash Flow's Not the Bottom Line, What Is?" *Financial Analysts Journal,* September/October, pp. 17–56.

Gibson, C.H., P.A. Frishkoff, 1986. *Financial Statement Analysis: Using Financial Accounting Information* 3rd ed., Boston: Kent Publishing.

Gombola, M., and J. Ketz, 1983. "Note on Cash Flow and Classification Patterns of Financial Ratios." *The Accounting Review,* January, pp. 105–14.

Hall, A.D., and R. Byron, 1992. "An Early Warning Predictor for Credit Union Financial Distress." Unpublished Manuscript for the Australian Financial Institution Commission.

Horrigan, J.O., 1968. "A Short History of Financial Ration Analysis." *The Accounting Review* 43 (April), pp. 284–94.

Jones, F., 1987. "Current Techniques in Bankruptcy Prediction." *Journal of Accounting Literature* 6, pp. 131–64.

Levy, H. and M. Sarnat, 1989. "Caveat Emptor: Limitations of Ratio Analysis." *Principles of Financial Management.* Englewood Cliffs, NJ: Prentice-Hall International, pp. 76–77.

Libby, R., 1975. "Accounting Ratios and the Prediction of Failure: Some Behavioral Evidence." 1975 *Journal of Accounting Research,* Spring, pp. 150–61.

Maclachlan, I., 1993. "Early Warning of Depository Institutions Distress: A Study of Victorian Credit Unions." Unpublished master's thesis. University of Melbourne.

Martin, D., 1977. "Early Warning of Bank Failure—A Logit Regression Approach." *Journal of Banking and Finance* 1, pp. 249–76.

McKinley, J.E., R.L. Johnson, G.R. Downey, Jr., C.S. Zimmerman, and M.D. Bloom, 1983. "Analyzing Financial Statements." *American Bankers Association*, Washington.

Odom, M.D., and Ramesh Sharda, 1990. "A Neural Network Model for Bankruptcy Prediction." *Proceedings of the IEEE International Conference on Neural Networks,* June, pp. II163-II168.

Ohlson, J., 1980. "Financial Ratios and Probabilistic Prediction of Bankruptcy." *Journal of Accounting Research,* Spring, pp. 109–31.

Pacey, J., and T. Pham, 1990. "The Predictiveness of Bankruptcy Models: Methodological Problems and Evidence." *Journal of Management* 15, no. 2 (December), pp. 315–37.

Rumelhart, D.E., G.E. Hinton, and R.J. Williams, 1986. "Learning Internal Representations by Error Propagation." *Parallel Distributed Processing* Vol. I. Cambridge, MA: MIT Press.

Salchenberger, L.M., E.M. Cinar, and N.A. Lash, 1992. "Neural Networks: A New Tool for Predicting Thrift Failures." *Decision Sciences* 23, no. 4 (July/August), pp. 899–916.

Shepanski, A., 1983. "Test of Theories of Information Processing Behavior in Credit Judgment." *Accounting Review* 58, pp. 581–99.

Sinkey, J., "A Multivariate Statistical Analysis of the Characteristics of Problem Banks." *Journal of Finance* 30, no. 1 (March), pp. 21–36.

Tam, K.Y., and M.Y. Kiang, 1992. "Managerial Applications of Neural Networks: The Case of Bank Failure Predictions." *Management Science* 38, no. 7 (July), pp. 926–47.

Tan, C.N.W., 1993a. "Incorporating Artificial Neural Network into a Rule-Based Financial Trading System." *The First New Zealand International Two Stream Conference on Artificial Neural Networks and Expert Systems (ANNES).* University of Otago, Dunedin, New Zealand, November 24–26. IEEE Computer Society Press. ISBN 0-8186-4260-2.

———, "Trading a NYSE Stock with a Simple Artificial Neural Network-Based Financial Trading System," 1993b. *The First New Zealand International Two Stream Conference on Artificial Neural Networks and Expert Systems (ANNES).* University of Otago, Dunedin, New Zealand, November 24–26. IEEE Computer Society Press. ISBN 0-8186-4260-2.

Tan, C.N.W., and G.E. Wittig, 1993. "Parametric Variation Experimentation on a Back- Propagation Stock Price Prediction Model." *The First Australia and New Zealand Intelligent Information System (ANZIIS) Conference.* University of Western Australia, Perth, Australia, December 1–3. IEEE Western Australia Press.

Whitred, G., and I. Zimmer, 1985. "The Implications of Distress Prediction Models for Corporate Lending." *Accounting and Finance* 25, pp. 1–13.

Wong, F., and C. Tan, 1994. "Hybrid Neural, Genetic and Fuzzy Systems." *Trading On The Edge: Neural Genetic and Fuzzy Systems for Chaotic Financial Markets.* New York: John Wiley and Sons, pp. 243–61.

APPENDIX A: THE TEN LARGEST PREDICTED CONDITIONAL PROBABILITIES

The 10 largest conditional probabilities for both the ANN and the probit model are provided in this appendix. Future research will involve analyzing these results with the financial ratios being used.

ANN Model					Probit Model			
Identity	Quarter	Output	Pre-dicted	Actual	Pre-dicted	Quarter	Proba-bility	Identity
1044	9103	0.2998	1	0	1	9103	0.096	1044
1062	9103	0.3316	1	0	0	9103	0.1	1153
1127	9103	0.3588	1	0	1	9103	0.201	1056
1147	9103	0.4613	1	0	1	9103	0.207	1062
1025	9103	0.4763	1	0	1	9103	0.243	1052
1061	9103	0.4856	1	1	1	9103	0.281	1025
1056	9103	0.5385	1	0	1	9103	0.361	1147
1052	9103	0.6107	1	0	1	9103	0.653	1013
1013	9103	0.8979	1	0	1	9103	0.774	1061
1129	9103	0.9979	1	1	1	9103	0.884	1129
1069	9106	0.2863	1	0	1	9106	0.111	1005
1127	9106	0.3052	1	0	1	9106	0.142	1044
1147	9106	0.3344	1	0	1	9106	0.195	1062
1062	9106	0.4154	1	0	1	9106	0.266	1025
1025	9106	0.5262	1	0	1	9106	0.372	1056
1056	9106	0.6372	1	0	1	9106	0.429	1147
1052	9106	0.7639	1	0	1	9106	0.445	1052
1013	9106	0.7730	1	0	1	9106	0.571	1013
1153	9106	0.9782	1	1	1	9106	0.795	1129
1129	9106	0.9957	1	1	1	9106	0.994	1153
1191	9109	0.1845	1	0	1	9109	0.164	1191
1194	9109	0.1855	1	0	1	9109	0.167	1025
1110	9109	0.2157	1	0	1	9109	0.179	1056
1056	9109	0.2212	1	0	1	9109	0.187	1147
1025	9109	0.2241	1	0	1	9109	0.198	1169
1062	9109	0.3401	1	0	1	9109	0.213	1023
1052	9109	0.4644	1	0	1	9109	0.215	1013
1153	9109	0.6603	1	1	1	9109	0.278	1052
1023	9109	0.7649	1	1	1	9109	0.849	1153
1129	9109	0.9993	1	1	1	9109	0.998	1129

ANN Model					Probit Model			
Identity	Quarter	Output	Pre-dicted	Actual	Pre-dicted	Quarter	Proba-bility	Identity
1005	9112	0.1400	1	0	0	9112	0.085	1005
1127	9112	0.1782	1	0	1	9112	0.103	1056
1056	9112	0.2050	1	0	1	9112	0.111	1191
1069	9112	0.2677	1	0	1	9112	0.151	1062
1025	9112	0.2738	1	0	1	9112	0.175	1025
1062	9112	0.3006	1	1	1	9112	0.189	1169
1153	9112	0.3328	1	1	1	9112	0.208	1052
1052	9112	0.3862	1	0	1	9112	0.216	1023
1023	9112	0.5606	1	1	1	9112	0.567	1153
1129	9112	0.9989	1	1	1	9112	0.997	1129

APPENDIX B: IN-SAMPLE AND OUT-OF-SAMPLE RESULTS*

This appendix contains the results of both the models for the 1989 to 1991 quarters of all the credit unions with the exception of credit unions number 1058, 1093, 1148, and 1158. They were excluded entirely since they were not used in the estimation sample of Hall and Byron's study due to their small size. The prediction of the probit model incorporate both the conditional probabilities of the probit scores model. The prediction of the probit model is 1 if the conditional probability of the probit model is greater than 0.1, and 0 if not. The ANN model prediction is 1 if the output from the ANN is greater than 0.1, and 0 if not.

---

* Note: Tables were withheld due to a nondisclosure agreement with the Australian Financial Institution Commission.

APPENDIX C: TRAINING AND TEST SET TYPE I ERROR CHART

Training Set versus Test Set Type I Errors

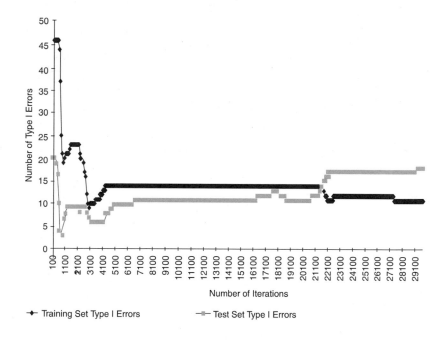

Note:
Model selection based on minimal training set type I errors is the same as minimal training and test set type I errors.

16

Bankruptcy Prediction Using Neural Networks

Rick L. Wilson and Ramesh Sharda

SECTION I. INTRODUCTION

The ability to predict firm bankruptcies has been extensively studied in the accounting literature. Creditors, auditors, stockholders, and senior management all have a vested interest in utilizing and developing a methodology or model that will allow them to monitor the financial performance of a firm via accounting ratios. This "failure analysis" can be helpful in identifying internal problems, in firm evaluation by investors, and as a tool used by auditors to assist them in their job.

Typically, a number of financial ratios are used in a multivariate discriminant analysis approach in an attempt to predict firm bankruptcies.

The authors wish to sincerely thank Marcus Odom and Nik Dalal for their help and assistance in data collection and for their insightful comments on previous drafts of this chapter. Also, the chapter has greatly benefited from comments and suggestions from the anonymous reviewers.

Discriminant analysis is a statistical technique used to construct classification schemes so as to assign previous unclassified observations to the appropriate group [15]. However, it may be a valid technique only under certain restrictive assumptions, including the requirement for the discriminating variables to be jointly distributed according to a multivariate normal distribution. Should this not be the case, results obtained by the discriminant analysis procedure may be erroneous.

Neural networks represents a field of study within the artificial intelligence area where researchers are studying a "biologically inspired" way of processing information. To this point, neural networks have proven to be good at solving some real-world problems, especially in the areas of forecasting and classification decision problems.

The exploratory study presented in this paper contrasts neural network predictive accuracy with that of discriminant analysis for the decision problem of firm bankruptcy prediction. Using a resampling methodological design, a series of experiments was conducted to investigate the effect of the training and testing (holdout) set composition on predictive accuracy. These predictive results were then contrasted with the accuracy obtained by classical discriminant analysis to determine the conditions where neural network models are significantly better predictors.

The major objectives of this paper are as follows: First, we report the results of a comprehensive, statistically sound comparison of discriminant analysis and a neural network model. Second, we utilize in this analysis measures of the validity of any classification technique that have been used extensively in the psychology literature. These measures allow researchers to assess the true value added by a technique. Third, we conclude with a brief conjecture on how neural networks may affect decision support systems.

Our objective is not to examine speed of a new algorithm or to study a new architecture but rather to test a neural network's effectiveness in performing classifications as contrasted with the incumbent techniques. Better algorithms should only improve the performance. In this sense, our results should provide a lower bound of the neural network model's predictive performance in bankruptcy prediction.

Section II briefly reviews bankruptcy prediction and the neural network literature. Section III describes our comparison procedure. Section IV presents the results, while Section V discusses implications of our results for researchers from three areas: bankruptcy prediction, neural networks, and decision support systems.

SECTION II. BRIEF REVIEW OF RELEVANT RESEARCH

Bankruptcy Risk Prediction

In the present days of economic turmoil, it is not surprising that the bankruptcy prediction problem remains of great interest to researchers as well as creditors, shareholders, and auditors. Firm insolvency is a problem throughout the industrialized countries of the world [4]. Creditors have a vested interest in this decision problem in that they wish to identify negative developments of their borrowers. Stockholders hold similar monetary concerns. Auditors, as a normal responsibility, must evaluate the financial position of a client to determine whether or not the firm's operating ability is endangered [3]. Thus, senior management of a firm and the board of directors can attempt to avert the crisis [34]. For all parties, it is essential that an objective opinion on the risk of bankruptcy can be formed as early as possible.

Predicting bankruptcy has been studied extensively in the accounting literature. The first studies were performed to determine whether financial ratios provide useful information [1,5]. There have been many different studies since [5] utilizing financial ratios for bankruptcy prediction, a majority of which use a multivariate discriminant analysis approach [1,2,4,7,12,25,32]. The major evolution in these studies is to identify financial and economic variables that improve predictive performance. Two statistical techniques appear to have been used the most: discriminant analysis and logistic regression [6]. No technique clearly provides substantially better results. We have chosen to study discriminant analysis as a comparative classification technique because of its repeated use in many other problem areas.

Discriminant analysis is a statistical technique used to classify objects into distinct groups on the basis of an object's observed characteristics. Basically, a linear discriminant function that will compute a "score" for an object is developed. This function that is a weighted linear combination of the object's observed values on discriminating characteristics. These weights represent, in essence, the relative importance and impact of the various characteristics. On the basis of its discriminant score, an object is then classified. Often, computer software packages compute the probability of group membership on the basis of this procedure [39].

Multivariate discriminant analysis is subject to a number of restrictive assumptions, including the requirement for the discriminating variables to be jointly multivariate normal. This multivariate normality of the variables is critical to the discriminant analysis procedure; otherwise, results obtained may be erroneous [25]. This theoretical assumption often cannot be realized in practice [4].

Neural Network Applications

Multilayer, feedforward neural networks have been applied to many problem domains in and outside the business field. For instance, neural networks have been successfully trained to determine whether loan applications should be approved [20]. Similarly, neural networks have been shown to predict mortgagee applicant solvency better than mortgage writers [11].

Predicting rating of corporate bonds and attempting to predict their profitability is another area where neural networks have been applied successfully [14,21]. Neural networks outperformed regression analysis and other mathematical modeling tools in predicting bond rating and profitability. The main conclusion reached was that neural networks provided a more general framework for connecting financial information of a firm to the respective bond rating.

Fraud prevention is another area of neural network applications in business. Credit card fraud, a costly and difficult problem faced by banks, was addressed by Chase Manhattan Bank of New York by neural networks [33]. These models were shown to be much more successful than traditional regression analysis. Additionally, neural networks have been used in the validation of bank signatures [19,30]. These networks identified forgeries significantly better than any human "expert."

Several people have tested the applicability of neural networks in financial markets. Collard [10] states that this neural network model for commodity trading would have resulted in significant profits over other trading strategies. Kamijo and Tanigawa [24] used a neural network to chart Tokyo Stock Exchange data. Their findings were that the results of the model would beat a "buy-and-hold" strategy. Additionally, a neural model for predicting percentage change in the S&P 500 five days ahead using a variety of economic indicators has been developed [18]. The authors claim that the model has provided more accurate prediction than alleged experts in the field using the same indicators.

There have been many other applications of neural networks in non-business related fields such as speech recognition, robotics, radar detection, and many others. Additionally, other network paradigms have been useful in solving other types of decision problems. Discussion of these other applications and approaches is beyond the scope of this paper.

Most of the studies that have compared neural networks with statistical techniques report the results on the basis of either a single experiment or in an anecdotal form. There is a need for a thorough comparison using sound statistical procedures. Our study is based on a resampling technique to assess the effectiveness of neural networks on a statistical basis. Further, we borrow some measures from the psychology literature to isolate the value added by a classification technique. We argue that such measures ought to be used in determining alleged superiority of any such model.

SECTION III. METHOD

Financial Ratios and Data Collection

The basic intent of this study is to compare and contrast the predictive performance of classical multivariate discriminant analysis to that of neural networks for firm bankruptcy. The Altman study [1] has been used as the standard of comparison for subsequent bankruptcy classification studies using discriminant analysis. Most follow-up studies have identified several other attributes to improve prediction performance. In this exploratory study, we wanted to see if the neural networks can come close to the traditional techniques. More sophisticated inputs to the neural network model should not worsen its performance. Thus, this could establish a lower bound on neural network performance in bankruptcy prediction. For these reasons, we used the same financial ratios as Altman [1]. These ratios were as follows:

X_1: Working capital/total assets.
X_2: Retained earnings/total assets.
X_3: Earnings before interest and taxes/total assets.
X_4: Market value of equity/total debt.
X_5: Sales/total assets.

The sample from which these ratios were obtained consisted of firms that either were in operation or went bankrupt between 1975 and 1982. The sample, obtained from *Moody's Industrial Manuals*, consisted of a total of 129 firms, 65 of which went bankrupt during the period and 64 nonbankrupt firms matched on industry and year. Data used for the bankrupt firms is from the last financial statements issued before the firms declared bankruptcy. Thus, the prediction of bankruptcy is to be made about one year in advance.

Data Set Generation

In assessing the predictive accuracy of discriminant analysis as compared to neural networks, it is necessary to create two distinct sets of data: a data set to develop the discriminant function (similarly, to train the neural network, often referred to as the training set) and a holdout sample to validate the derived discriminant function (in neural network terminology, the testing set). Because the decision of splitting the original 129 firms could affect the results of the comparison, this study utilizes the concept of Monte Carlo resampling techniques to generate multiple sub-samples from the original firms in order to gain a better measure of predictive accuracy (see [37], for example).

The results of this study could be affected by the proportion of non-bankrupt firms to bankrupt firms in both the training and testing sets. That is, the population of all firms contains a certain proportion of firms on the verge of bankruptcy. A proportion of interest in any population is sometimes referred to as the base rate. The base rate may have an impact on a prediction technique's performance in two ways. First, a technique may not work well when the firms of interest (bankrupt) constitute a very small percentage of the population (low base rate). This would be due to a technique's inability to identify the features necessary for classification.

A second effect of the base rate is in terms of differences in base rates between training samples and testing samples. If a classification model is built using a training sample with a certain base rate, does the model still work when the base rate in the test population is different? This issue is important for one more reason. If a classification model based on a certain base rate works across other proportions, it may be possible to build a model using a higher proportion of cases of interest than actually occur in the population.

To study the effects of this proportion on the predictive performance of the two techniques, we created three proportions (or base rates) for each of the training and testing set compositions. The first factor level (or base rate) was a 50/50 proportion of bankrupt to nonbankrupt cases, the second level was a 80/20 proportion (80 percent nonbankrupt, 20 percent bankrupt), and the third factor level was an approximate 90/10 proportion (approximately 90 percent nonbankrupt; this proportion is not exact due to required round-off to integer number of firms). We do not really know the actual proportion of firms going bankrupt. The 80/20 and 90/10 cases should be close. The 50/50 scenario is utilized to investigate the possibility of a better model by using a high base rate in the training set.

Utilizing a full two-factor design, there were nine different experimental cells, whose composition is indicated in Table 16.1. Within each cell, 20 different training-testing set pairs were generated via Monte Carlo resampling from the original 129 firms. Thus, a total of 180 distinct training

Table 16.1
Number of Observations in Training and Testing Sets

Training Set Composition	Testing Set Composition		
	50%/50%	80%/20%	90%/10% [*]
50%/50%			
Train:	44/44	44/44	44/44
Test:	20/20	20/5	20/2
80%/20%			
Train:	44/11	44/11	44/11
Test:	20/20	20/5	20/2
90%/10% [*]			
Train	44/5	44/5	44/5
Test:	20/20	20/5	20/2

Where for each cell:
Train: (nonbankrupt/bankrupt) firms in training set.
Test: (nonbankrupt/bankrupt) firms in testing set.
[*] Approximately 90%/10% ratio.

and testing data set pairs were generated from the original data. In each case, the training set and test set pairs contained unique firms; that is, no overlap was allowed. This restriction provides a stronger test of a technique's performance.

Implementation of Comparative Methods

SYSTAT [39], a personal computer-based statistical package, was used for discriminant analysis. **SYSTAT** fits the standard multivariate general linear model in performing discriminant analysis and also uses information regarding the prior probability specification of the training set in determining the discriminant function. In this study, the training sets were used to set up initial discriminating functions, which were, in turn, evaluated by the corresponding testing sets. All variables were included in each discriminant analysis conducted in the study. Tests were not undertaken to determine whether the discriminating variables were distributed according to a joint multivariate normal distribution. However, previous research has indicated that neural networks can also perform well in cases of multivariate normal distributions [13]; thus, the distribution of the data used in our study is not a relevant issue in considering robust predictive accuracy.

BRAINMAKER [35], a personal computer-based neural network software package that implements the aforementioned back-propagation training algorithm, was used to construct and test trained neural network models. For each network trained in the study, a structure of 5 input neurons, (one for each financial ratio), 10 hidden neurons, and 2 output neurons (one indicating bankrupt firm, the other indicating nonbankrupt firm) was used. Such a network structure was chosen on the basis of previously espoused heuristic guidelines [8,9,36]. Figure 16.1 illustrates this network.

As training cases are presented to the network, the output neuron values are examined by the training procedure. For instance, consider a bankrupt training case that had its bankrupt output node valued at 0.85 and its nonbankrupt node at 0.17. When training a neural network, a certain amount of variation away from the desired values of 0 and 1 (indicating bankrupt or nonbankrupt) is typically allowed at the output layer when determining whether adjustments should be made in network weights via back-propagation. This allowable variation is referred to as

Figure 16.1

A Typical NN Model for Bankruptcy Prediction

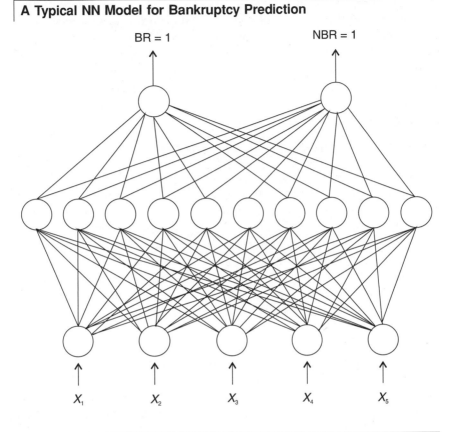

the *training tolerance*. Thus, a training tolerance of .2 would allow the training procedure .2 variation of each output node away from the desired value. Thus, the previous example would satisfy the training tolerance (i.e., 1 − 0.85 0.2, and 0.17 − 0 0.2), and no network weight correction would take place.

In training the networks, a heuristic back-propagation algorithm was used to ensure convergence (all firms in the training set classified correctly). A stringent training tolerance was initially used in training the network (a small value of 0.1) and gradually relaxed until such a point was reached when all training cases satisfied the training tolerance criteria. Then, the training tolerance was incrementally lowered (made more stringent), and the network was trained until convergence occurred at this level. This was repeated until no further reductions of the training tolerance could occur. In all 180 subsamples generated, the neural network models were able to obtain 100 percent classifications of the training set cases. By using a relaxed tolerance, memorization or overtraining should have been avoided.

Dependent Variable: Correct Predictions

The intent of this study was to compare the predictive capability of discriminant analysis and neural networks. Thus, the number that each method correctly predicts in the testing data sets is the chief measure of predictive success. Other measures are described as introduced.

SYSTAT, in using the multivariate general linear model, utilizes Mahalanobis distances [39] to calculate posterior probabilities for each case, indicating the likelihood of group membership for each group. Additionally, prior probabilities were incorporated based upon the composition (base rate) of the training sets. The group with the highest posterior probability, therefore, is used as the discriminant analysis prediction for that case. This is the manner in which correct and incorrect classifications were determined for the discriminant analysis method.

When evaluating the predictive capability of neural networks, a *testing threshold*, similar to training tolerance, is specified. This testing threshold identifies how stringent the allowable variation in output neurons can be when predicting group membership. In this study, a testing threshold of 0.499 was used; thus, if one output neuron exceeded 0.5 (and the other neuron value was), the network classified the case as the corresponding group associated with the first neuron. Cases where double classifications were indicated (both neurons 0.5) were automatically counted as incorrect classifications. It is on this basis that correct and incorrect classifications were determined for the neural network models.

Each data set was evaluated by both discriminant analysis and neural networks. Two different measures of accuracy could be determined: the number of correct classifications that the particular procedure provided on the training set ("learning") and the number of correct classifications that the specific procedure provided on the testing set ("generalization").

SECTION IV. RESULTS

Training Sets—"Learning"

The first results to be presented display the learning performance of the discriminant function and the neural network model. Table 16.2 shows the aggregated percentage of correct classifications of training cases by the two approaches across the three different combinations of training sets. Table 16.2 also distinguishes between the learning accuracy of non-bankrupt and bankrupt training cases.

It is not surprising that the neural network approach outperforms discriminant analysis since the neural network training algorithm employed will not cease until all members of the training set are correctly classified. Thus, on the basis of strictly learning a set of bankrupt and nonbankrupt firms, neural networks appear to have learned more than classical multivariate discriminant analysis.

Testing Sets—"Generalization"

Perhaps a better measure of accuracy comparison between the two techniques is their performance in classifying cases in the holdout samples, or the testing sets. Table 16.3 represents the average percentage of correct

---

Table 16.2

Training Set—Correct Classifications (%) Grouped by Like Composition

Training Set Ratio	Combined Accuracy		Nonbankrupt Cases		Bankrupt Cases	
	NN	DA	NN	DA	NN	DA
50/50	100	88.65	100	94.54	100	82.76
80/20	100	90.33	100	97.69	100	60.91
90/10	100	94.59	100	99.13	100	54.67

NN—neural network.
DA—multivariate discriminant analysis.

Table 16.3

Testing Set—Correct Classification (%) All Cases

Training Set Composition	Testing Set Composition					
	50/50		80/20		90/10	
	NN	DA	NN	DA	NN	DA
50/50	97.5	88.25	95.6	91.8	95.68	93.32
	†		†		*	
	(p < 0.001)		(p = 0.005)		(p = 0.046)	
80/20	82.0	75.875	91.0	89.0	95.68	91.59
	†		†		*	
	(p = 0.002)		(p = 0.126)		(p = 0.001)	
90/10	72.625	72.0	86.25	85.8	94.55	91.81
					†	
	(p = 0.318)		(p = 0.069)		(p = 0.008)	

* Significant at 0.05 level.
† Significant at 0.01 level.

---

classifications (irrespective of type of firm) when utilizing the two different techniques to evaluate the 20 holdout samples for each combination of base rates. When the training sets contained an equal number of bankrupt and nonbankrupt cases, and the testing sets also contained an equal number of the two cases, neural networks correctly classified 97.5 percent of the holdout cases, while multivariate discriminant analysis was correct 88.25 percent of the time. Similarly, when the training sets contained a balanced number of bankrupt and nonbankrupt firms but the testing sets contained 20 percent bankrupt firms, neural networks classified at a 95.6 percent correct rate, while discriminant analysis correctly classified 91.8 percent. Table 16.3 indicates that, in every combination of factor levels, neural networks performed better at generalization than discriminant analysis.

A nonparametric test, the Wilcoxon test for paired observations, was undertaken to assess whether the different correct classification percentages for the two different techniques were significantly different. The critical values of this test are also reported in Table 16.3. Those experimental cells that are statistically significant are highlighted by asterisks. In general, neural networks were statistically significant better predictors of firm bankruptcies in the holdout sample than discriminant analysis.

Tables 16.4 and 16.5 provide a more detailed look at the classification results, breaking down the correct percentages in terms of bankrupt firm predictions and nonbankrupt firm predictions. It is apparent from Table 16.4 that it is in the classification of bankrupt firms that neural networks significantly outperform discriminant analysis. This is important since it is widely accepted in terms of predicting bankrupt firms that it is more costly to classify a failed firm as nonfailing than converse [38].

As with the overall aggregate classification data, the Wilcoxon paired observation test was used to assess the significance of the differences of the two prediction techniques. The critical values of this test are given, and those significant are noted by asterisks. Again, for predicting bankrupt cases, note that neural networks predicted better than discriminant analysis at every factor level combination. For instance, where training and test set composition was equal among the two different classes of firms, neural networks correctly predicted 97.0 percent of the bankrupt firms, while discriminant analysis predicted only 79.75 percent.

Table 16.4

Testing Set—Correct Classification (%) Bankrupt Cases

Train-ing Set Compo-sition	Testing Set Composition					
	50/50		80/20		90/10	
	NN	DA	NN	DA	NN	DA
50/50	97.5	79.75	92.0	82.0	92.5	90.0
	†		†			
	(p < 0.001)		(p = 0.025)		(p = 0.282)	
80/20	62.25	54.25	62.0	54.0	70.0	45.0
	†				†	
	(p = 0.002)		(p = 0.11526)		(p = 0.06)	
90/10	47.00	46.25	49.0	35.0	67.5	45.0
					†	
	(p = 0.439)		(p = 0.022)		(p = 0.036)	

Table 16.5

Testing Set—Correct Classification (%) Nonbankrupt Cases

Training Set Composition	Testing Set Composition					
	50/50		80/20		90/10	
	NN	DA	NN	DA	NN	DA
50/50	98.0	96.75	96.5	94.25	96.0	93.5
	†				†	
	(p < 0.02901)		(p = 0.071)		(p = 0.038)	
80/20	98.75	87.5	98.25	97.75	98.25	92.5
	(p = 0.080)		(p = 0.304)		(p = 0.061)	
90/10	98.25	97.75	98.0	98.5	97.25	96.5
	(p = 0.240)		(p = 0.263)		(p = 0.289)	

* Significant at 0.05 level.
† Significant at 0.01 level.

Similarly, Table 16.5 presents the results for the prediction of nonbankrupt cases by the two techniques. Significance is tested and reported as mentioned previously. Both methods appear to predict nonbankrupt firms quite well, though the neural network model predicts better than discriminant analysis in all but a single combination of factor levels (training set of 90–10, testing set of 80–20), and the difference is negligible and statistically not significant.

Table 16.6 summarizes the prediction classification results for all test sets at each level of the training set base rate and also differentiates between the different categories of firms. From this and the previous tables, it is apparent that neural networks represent a better predictive approach than multivariate discriminant analysis. When considering all 60 cases where a balanced training set was used, the neural network model correctly predicted 95.74 percent of the bankrupt firms and 96.83 percent of the nonbankrupt firms in the holdout samples, as compared to 80.92 percent of bankrupt firms and 94.83 percent of nonbankrupt firms that discriminant analysis predicted. While the percentage of correct classifications of bankrupt firms decreased with the increased imbalance of the training cases, the general trend of neural network prediction superiority remained.

Table 16.6

Training Composition Effect on Classification (%)

Training Set Composition	Bankrupt Cases NN	DA	Nonbankrupt Cases NN	DA	Total Cases NN	DA
50/50	95.74	80.92	96.83	94.83	96.49	90.51
80/20	65.00	53.52	98.42	95.92	88.05	82.76
90/10	48.89	44.07	97.83	97.58	82.64	80.97
Total overall cases					90.56	85.87

Further Assessment of Predictive Capabilities

While the results have clearly shown that neural networks outperformed discriminant analysis in predicting firm bankruptcies, out study must now address whether the neural network prediction results are better than what can be expected by pure chance [22,31]. We will employ tests originally proposed in [29] and further clarified in [22] for studying discriminant analysis classification rates. Because our study uses cross-validation (i.e., testing sets) for measuring classification success and utilizes different base rates for the training and testing set, we will further modify these tests to fit our study.

The underlying concept in comparing a classification or prediction technique to pure chance is to consider what one could do by simply guessing at the predictions. For instance, if the base rate were 50 percent for a two-group problem, guessing would result in, on average, 50 percent correct predictions. Similarly, if the base rate were skewed (80 percent to 20 percent), one could blindly predict with 80 percent accuracy by predicting all cases to belong to the more frequent class [28,29]. It has been shown that to achieve significant levels of predictive validity, the proportion of correct positive predictions (bankrupt firms, in our case) to all positive bankrupt predictions must exceed the base rate of the more frequent class [17,29].

In Table 16.7, this proportion is calculated for both neural networks and discriminant analysis. Thus, when both the training and testing sets

Table 16.7

Percent Predicted as Bankrupt that Were Bankrupt

Training Set Composition	Testing Set Composition					
	50/50		80/20		90/10	
	NN	DA	NN	DA	NN	DA
50/50	98.0	94.9	86.8	78.1	69.8	58.1
80/20	98.0	95.6	89.9	85.7	80.0	37.5
90/10	96.4	95.4	86.0	85.4	71.0	56.3

contained a balanced number of bankrupt and nonbankrupt firms (base rate of 50 percent), a neural network model forecasting a bankrupt firm was correct 98 percent of the time, while discriminant analysis was correct 94.9 percent. Note that neural networks outperformed discriminant analysis irrespective of factor levels (base rates). Also note that, with the exception of measuring prediction with test sets having 90 percent nonbankrupt firms, neural networks also exceeded the base rate of the most frequent class, indicative of good predictive validity.

However, this analysis used the base rates of the testing sets, information not available to the classification technique. Only the base rate of the training set is "learned" by the classification device. Thus, a pure chance technique, exposed to 90 percent nonbankrupt cases in training, would randomly declare 90 percent of testing cases to be nonbankrupt, irrespective of the testing set composition. In further investigating the value added by discriminant analysis and neural networks to the classification problem, our standard normal test statistics will be based on only information known to the classification techniques (base rate of the training sets).

The test statistic utilized will be based upon the proportional chance criterion [22]. This criterion implies that prediction by guessing can achieve a correct rate for each group involved equal to the proportion of that group (base rate) in the training set. Thus, for those training sets with a balanced number of bankrupt and nonbankrupt firms, 50 percent correct predictions could be achieved by chance; while, when there are 90 percent nonbankrupt firms, 90 percent correct predictions of nonbankrupt firms could be achieved by chance. The standard normal test statistic is calculated as:

$$\frac{(O-E) * N^{\frac{1}{2}}}{(E * (N - E))^{\frac{1}{2}}},$$ (1)

where g = groups (bankrupt and nonbankrupt), n_g = number of test cases in group g, b_g = training base rate of group g, o_g = observed correct predictions for group g (refer to Table 16.4), e_g = expected correct predictions for group g by chance ($n_g * b_g$), O = total correct prediction (Σ o_g), E = total correct predictions obtainable by chance (Σ e_g), N = total number of cases (Σ n_g)

Thus, this statistic will indicate whether predictive results obtained by neural networks and discriminant analysis differ greatly from those that can be obtained by chance. Additionally, one can also calculate a similar statistical measure for each separate classification group. Using the same notation as above, the standard normal test statistics for each group (illustrating whether the predictive results obtained by a classification technique significantly differs from chance) is:

$$\frac{(o_g - e_g) * n_g^{\frac{1}{2}}}{(e_g * (n_g - e_g))^{\frac{1}{2}}}.$$ (2)

As Table 16.8 indicates, the predictive validity of neural networks and discriminant analysis is extremely significant. Aggregately, both methods are significantly better than pure chance regardless of the base rate of the training sets. Considering the predictive validity by specific groups, the only nonsignificant result occurs when predicting nonbankrupt firms when the training set base rate is 90 percent, though it is still considerably better than chance. Not surprisingly, as previous results have already shown, neural networks are judged more statistically significant than chance as compared to discriminant analysis in every case.

Another approach useful in assessing a prediction method is determining how much better a classification approach predicts compared to chance assignment. An index useful in such a setting is the improvement-over-chance or reduction-in-error index [22,26]:

$$I = \frac{H_o - H_e}{1 - H_e},$$ (3)

Table 16.8

Predictive Validity of Classifications

Training Set Composition	Bankrupt		Nonbankrupt		Total	
	NN	DA	NN	DA	NN	DA
50/50	2.88	1.86	4.19	4.00	5.19	4.36
	($p = 0.002$)	($p = 0.031$)	($p < 0.001$)	($p < 0.001$)	($p < 0.001$)	($p < 0.001$)
80/20	3.11	2.31	2.06	1.73	2.57	2.33
	($p < 0.001$)	($p = 0.011$)	($p = 0.020$)	($p = 0.042$)	($p = 0.005$)	($p = 0.010$)
90/10	3.89	3.41	1.17	1.13	1.88	1.70
	($p < 0.001$)	($p < 0.001$)	($p = 0.121$)	($p = 0.129$)	($p = 0.030$)	($p = 0.045$)

where H_o is the observed rate of correct predictions and H_e is the correct prediction rate expected by chance. Using the previous notation, H_e is defined as $(\Sigma(b_g * n_g))/N$ for the aggregate case, and b_g for each separate group. The index I represents a reduction-in-error statistic in that 100 * I percent fewer prediction errors result using the classification rule than would be expected by chance.

Table 16.9 provides this calculation for the neural network and discriminant analysis predictions aggregately across firm type, as well as the improvement-over-chance index for both bankrupt and nonbankrupt cases. Thus, when the 50–50 training set is used to train a neural network, the network model provides 92.98 percent fewer classification errors than would occur by blind guessing. Also, as another example, the improvement over chance for the prediction of bankrupt firms with neural networks trained on a balanced training set is 91.48 percent. Also of interest is that even on the 90 percent base rate where neural networks did not indicate significant differences over chance predictions for nonbankrupt cases, the improvement-over-chance percentage is still a relatively high 78.3 percent.

Effect of Training and Testing Set Composition on Generalization

In order to further assess the effect on accuracy of classifications that the factor levels of training and testing set composition have on neural network model predictions, two two-factor ANOVA's were undertaken, one using the percentage of correct classifications of nonbankrupt firms

Table 16.9
Reducton in Error of Classifications

Training Set Composition	Bankrupt		Nonbankrupt		Total	
	NN	DA	NN	DA	NN	DA
50/50	91.5	61.8	93.7	89.7	93.0	81.0
80/20	56.2	41.9	92.1	79.6	69.1	55.4
90/10	43.2	37.8	78.3	75.8	50.2	45.4

as the dependent variable, another utilizing correct predictions of bankrupt firms as the dependent variable. The results of these two ANOVA's are presented in Tables 16.10 and 16.11. Similar analysis was not undertaken for the discriminant analysis results since the neural network approach clearly dominates its performance.

The composition of the training set was significant in determining the neural network prediction accuracy of the bankrupt test cases. This result further reinforces the intuitive thought that to properly train a network (or any model) to recognize two different concepts, utilizing an equal number of examples of each concept is desirable [23].

Table 16.10

ANOVA—Bankrupt Cases

Source	Sum of Squares	DF	Mean Square	F Ratio	P
Train	49246.942	2	24623.471	49.401	0.000
Test	2663.610	2	1331.805	2.672	0.072
Interaction	3397.222	4	349.305	1.704	0.151
Error	85233.750	171	498.443		

R = 0.627 R^2 = 0.394.

Table 16.11

ANOVA—Nonbankrupt Cases

Source	Sum of Squares	DF	Mean Square	F Ratio	P
Train	76.944	2	38.472	3.492	0.033
Test	41.944	2	20.972	1.904	0.152
Interaction	15.556	4	3.889	0.353	0.842
Error	1883.750	171	11.016		

R = 0.258 R^2 = 0.067.

The moderately significant effect of the testing set composition is not as easily explained. Contrasting the different factor levels, only the difference between the 80/20 and 90/10 evaluation sets was significant (p = 0.0286). From Table 16.3, it can be seen that similarly trained networks wee evaluated more favorably when the testing set was composed of 90 percent nonbankrupt cases and 10 percent bankrupt firms. The 80/20 and 50/50 testing sets showed comparable measures of prediction accuracy across different training factor levels. This variation can perhaps be explained by the small number of bankrupt cases found in the holdout samples of factor level 90/10 (two cases). By having such a small number of test cases, the random generation of cases may have led to this experimental finding.

Table 16.11, the ANOVA on the nonbankrupt cases, shows that only the composition of the training set significantly affects neural network predictions. Upon closer contrast analysis among the three different factor levels, the only significant difference between levels is between the 50/50 and 80/20 composition (p = 0.010). In fact, predictive accuracy of networks trained by the 80/20 composition sets provided more accurate results in classifying nonbankrupt cases than the 50/50 training sets.

SECTION V. DISCUSSION

From the results of this experiment, it is apparent that for the bankruptcy prediction problem, neural networks offer a viable alternative approach. With simple data (five variables), neural networks showed extreme promise by correctly predicting as high as a 97 percent accuracy level (when both the training and testing base rates were 50/50). This level is as good as or better than other studies. In every instance, neural networks outperformed discriminant analysis in classification accuracy, especially in the prediction of bankrupt firms, the more difficult and, arguably, the more important classification problem [38]. It stands to reason that neural networks will perform as well as better with the inclusion of more variables in the analysis. Thus, the results of this exploratory study could be considered to offer a lower bound on the predictive accuracy one can expect with a neural network model for bankruptcy prediction. Of course, the results of any study are bound by the limitations of the data and methodology.

Discriminant analysis classification rules often incorporate prior probabilities that account for both the assumed base rate and the costs associated with misclassification errors if different [16,27]. In our comparison study, prior probabilities were calculated from the base rates of the training sets. By using the base rates as the prior probabilities, the discriminant analysis procedure in this study actually incorporates significant unequal misclassification costs (i.e., misclassifying a bankrupt firm is a more costly error) since the true population of bankrupt firms is probably less than the training set base rate. Even so, neural networks continually predicted bankrupt firms more accurately using symmetric costs (testing threshold of 0.499). The major dilemma in utilizing the discriminant analysis model is in estimating the unequal misclassification costs. Future research investigating performance adjustments given explicit values for asymmetric misclassification costs for both discriminant analysis and neural networks may be warranted.

The investigation of the effects of different training and testing set composition on the predictive results lead to further implications for the decision-maker and neural network researcher. Results indicated that the composition of the training set was a significant determinant of neural network predictive accuracy. Basically, it was shown that neural networks provide better understanding and differentiation between two concepts (bankrupt firms and nonbankrupt firms) when an equal number of examples of each concept is used in the learning procedure. This result is not dissimilar to one's intuition and previous results in discriminant analysis [23].

While all prediction errors are undesirable in a specific methodology, it is generally accepted that the incorrect prediction of a bankrupt firm as nonbankrupt is the most costly error. Results have indicated that prediction of the bankrupt firms poses the largest problem to the two different techniques. Neural networks were shown to perform well in predicting both bankrupt firms and nonbankrupt firms when presented with equal numbers of examples in the learning phase. Thus, a more accurate classification model will result when developed with an equal number of instances of each category. Since, in the real world, the decision-maker may not have control over the composition of historical data necessary in the predictive model development, it appears that "smoothing" the distribution of the training set, irrespective of the actual distribution, will provide a better model.

It is true that neural network performance is less impressive as the proportion of nonbankrupt to bankrupt firms diverge. However, neural network models continue to outperform discriminant analysis. If one follows the recommendation of a 50-50 training set, neural network performance does not deteriorate significantly. Bankrupt firms are predicted correctly in the 92–97 percent range, with similar accuracy for nonbankrupt firms, given a balanced training set.

One caution to this approach in developing the training set is also indicated in the experimental results. Significance of testing set composition in bankrupt firm prediction may have indicated overreported accuracy due to the small number of bankrupt firms in the 90–10 test sets. Thus, this study indicates that a potential trade-off exists when creating training and testing sets from the pool of existing problem data. A better predictive neural network model can be created by using a balanced training set; however, if too few of the hard-to-classify or more important cases exist in the cross-validation set, the model performance could be over- or underreported. Either way, this will significantly affect the accuracy of decision-maker confidence in the prediction model.

The results of predicting nonbankrupt cases improved as the imbalance of bankrupt to nonbankrupt firms increased in the training sets. This can be attributed to significantly fewer number of bankrupt firms in the training sets. This phenomenon illustrates that, at the expense of "learning" about bankrupt firms, the network "memorizes" and becomes very good at recognizing (i.e., predicting) nonbankrupt firms. While overall predictive accuracy may remain high, the classification accuracy of bankrupt firms is seriously reduced. Thus, one would be significantly sacrificing the prediction performance of one important category to marginally increase the prediction performance of the other, more easily predicted category. In firm bankruptcy predictions, this is obviously not desirable. Thus, great care must be taken when creating the training and cross-validation sets when developing a neural network prediction model.

From a decision support systems perspective, this study has illustrated that neural networks are a viable model that should be included in the model base of a DSS. Predictive accuracy obtained in this study illustrates the potential of neural networks from a data reduction standpoint. With only five simple ratios, neural networks predicted at a high rate of classification accuracy; thus, these models may provide excellent results with less data requirements than other approaches to the problem.

Discriminant analysis is not the only tool that has been postulated for use in classification problems [13]. However, all other models do have limitations with regard to successful and appropriate use. In the case of discriminant analysis, limitations include the requirement that the variables should be jointly distributed according to a multivariate normal distribution, prior probability specification, and so forth. Neural networks have no such potential restrictive assumptions or requirements; they are more robust prediction techniques. Thus, neural networks offer additional benefits in reducing managerial concern over choosing the appropriate model in the decision support context.

Much additional research needs to be done regarding neural networks for bankruptcy prediction. The effect of network architecture, network training algorithms, and learning paradigms needs to be examined to provide more prescriptive results on implementing a neural network prediction model. As previously mentioned, this exploratory study uses only a small number of variables to achieve its high level of predictive accuracy; other variables should be included in the neural network model [2]. Notable omissions include the size of the firm and time series data (more than just one year's previous financial data), among others. Additionally, using matched firms by industry and year has been postulated to bias results in predicting bankruptcy [40]. Neural networks may or may not be affected by this, but additional research should study this issue.

SECTION VI. CONCLUSION

This chapter has compared the predictive capability of neural networks with that of classical multivariate discriminant analysis within the context of forecasting firm bankruptcies on the basis of a small number of financial ratios. In this study, neural networks clearly outperformed discriminant analysis in prediction accuracy of both bankrupt and nonbankrupt firms under varying training and testing conditions. Additionally, it was shown that neural networks offer a significant improvement in prediction over pure chance and that their use in prediction can reduce errors in this problem domain by as much as 93 percent over chance.

Neural networks, therefore, represent a classification technique that is a robust and promising approach in the prediction of firm stability. While this study is exploratory in nature and has some limitations as noted, it has shown the promise of neural networks through the use of a set of solid statistical analyses that should be utilized as research continues in this area.

REFERENCES

1. Altman, E.I. "Financial Ratios, Discriminant Analysis and the Prediction of Corporate Bankruptcy." *Journal of Finance,* September 1968, pp. 589–609.

2. Altman, E.I., R.G. Haldeman, and P. Narayanan. "Zeta Analysis." *Journal of Banking and Finance,* June 1977, pp. 22–51.

3. Altman, E.I. "Accounting Implications of Failure Prediction Models." *Journal of Accounting, Auditing and Finance,* Fall 1982, pp. 4–19.

4. Baetge, J., M. Huss, and H. Niehaus. "The Use of Statistical Analysis to Identify the Financial Strength of Corporations in Germany." *Studies in Banking and Finance* 7 (1988), pp. 183–96.

5. Beaver, W.H. "Financial Ratios as Predictors of Failure." *Empirical Research in Accounting: Selected Studies,* 1966, pp. 71–111.

6. Bell, T., G. Ribar, and J. Verchio. "Neural Nets vs. Logistic Regression: A Comparison of Each Model's Ability to Predict Commercial Bank Failures." Working paper, Peat Marwick Co., May 1990.

7. Blum, M. "Failing Company Discriminant Analysis." *Journal of Accounting Research,* Spring 1974, pp. 1–25.

8. Caudill, M. "Neural Network Primer: Part III." *AI Expert,* June 1988, pp. 53–59.

9. Caudill, M. "Neural Network Training Tips and Techniques." *AI Expert,* January 1991, pp. 53–59.

10. Collard, J.E. "Commodity Trading with a Neural Net." *Neural Network News* 2, no. 10 (October, 1990).

11. Collins, E., S. Ghosh, and C. Scofield. "An Application of a Multiple Neural Network Learning System to Emulation of Mortgage Underwriting Judgments." Working paper. Nestor, Inc., 1989.

12. Deakin, E.B. "A Discriminant Analysis of Predictors of Business Failures." *Journal of Accounting Research,* Spring 1972, pp. 167–79.

13. Denton, J., M. Hung, and B. Osyk. "A Neural Network Approach to the Classification Problem." *Expert Systems With Applications* 1 (1990), pp. 417–24.

14. Dutta, S. and S. Shekhar. "Bond-Rating: A Non-Conservative Application of Neural Networks." Proceedings of the IEEE International Conference on Neural Networks, San Diego, 1988, pp. 443–50.

15. Eisenbeis, R. and R. Avery. "Discriminant Analysis and Classification Procedures." Lexington MA: Lexington Books, 1972.

16. Eisenbeis, R. "Pitfalls in the Application of Discriminant Analysis in Business, Finance and Accounting." *Journal of Finance*, June 1977, pp. 875–900.

17. Farrington, D.P. and R. Tarling. "Prediction in Criminology." Albany, NY: State University of New York Press, 1985.

18. Fishman, M., D. Barr, and W. Loick. "Using Neural Networks in Market Analysis." *Technical Analysis of Stock and Commodities*, April 1991, pp. 18–25.

19. Francett, B. "Neural Nets Arrive." *Computer Decisions*, January 1989, pp. 58–62.

20. Gallant, S.I. "Connectionist Expert Systems." *Communications of the ACM*, February 1988, pp. 152–69.

21. Goodman, R.M., J.W. Miller, and P. Smyth. "An Information Theoretic Approach to Rule- Based Connectionist Systems." In *Advances in Neural Information Processing Systems* I, ed. D.S. Touretsky. San Mateo, CA: Kaufmann Publishing, 1989, pp. 356–64.

22. Huberty, C.J. "Issues in the Use and Interpretation of Discriminant Analysis." *Psychological Bulletin* 95 (1984), pp. 156–71.

23. Jain, A. and B. Chandrasekaran. "Dimensionality and Sample Size Consideration in Pattern Recognition Practice." In *Handbook of Statistics*, Vol. 2., eds. P. Krishnaiah and L. Kanal. North-Holland, 1982, pp. 835–55.

24. Kamijo, J. and T. Tanigawa. "Stock Price Pattern Recognition: A Recurrent Neural Network Approach." International Joint Conference on Neural Networks, San Diego, June 1990.

25. Karels, G.V. and A. Prakash. "Multivariate Normality and Forecasting of Business Bankruptcy." *Journal of Business Finance and Accounting*, Winter 1987, pp. 573–93.

26. Klecka, W.R. *Discriminant Analysis.* Beverly Hills, CA: Sage Publishing, 1980.

27. Lachenbruch, P. "Discriminant Analysis." New York, NY: Hafner Press, 1975.

28. Meehl, P.E. *Clinical versus Statistical Prediction: A Theoretical Analysis and a Review of the Evidence.* Minneapolis: University of Minnesota Press, 1954.

29. Meehl, P.E. and A. Rosen. "Antecedent Probability and the Efficiency of Psychometric Signs, Patterns or Cutting Scores." *Psychological Bulletin* 52 (1955), pp. 194–216.

30. Mighell, D. "Back-Propagation and its Application to Handwritten Signature Verification." In *Advances in Neural Information Processing Systems* I. ed. D.S. Touretsky. San Mateo, CA: Kaufman Publishing, 1989, pp. 340–47.

31. Morrison, D.G. "On the Interpretation of Discriminant Analysis." *Journal of Marketing Research* 6 (1969), pp. 156–63.

32. Moyer, R.C. "Forecasting Financial Failure: A Reexamination." *Financial Management,* Spring 1977, pp. 11–17.

33. Rochester, J., ed. "New Business Uses for Neurocomputing." I/S Analyzer, February 1990, pp. 1–17.

34. Siegel, J.G. "Warning Signs of Impending Business Failure and Means to Counteract such Prospective Failure." *The National Public Accountant,* April 1981, pp. 9–13.

35. Stanley, J. and E. Bak. *Introduction to Neural Networks.* Sierra Madre, CA: California Scientific Software, 1989.

36. Surkan, A. and J. Singleton. "Neural Networks for Bond Rating Improved by Multiple Hidden Layers." International Joint Conference on Neural Networks. San Diego, June 1990.

37. Teebagy, N. and S. Chatterjee. "Inference in a Binary Response Model with Applications to Data Analysis." *Decision Sciences* 20, no. 2 (1989), pp. 393–403.

38. Watts, R.L. and J.L. Zimmerman. *Positive Accounting Theory.* Englewood Cliffs, NJ: Prentice-Hall, 1986.

39. Wilkinson, L. *SYSTAT: The System for Statistics.* Evanston, IL: SYSTAT, Inc., 1989.

40. Zmijewski, M.E. "Methodological Issues Related to the Estimation of Financial Distress Prediction Models." *Journal of Accounting Research* 22 supplement (1984), pp. 59–82.

PART IV

DEBT RISK ASSESSMENT

17

Bond Rating: A Nonconservative Application of Neural Networks

Soumitra Dutta and Shashi Shekhar

INTRODUCTION

Domains of neural network applications can be classified into two broad categories—recognition and generalization.[1] For both classes, we first train the neural network on a set of input/output pairs (I_1, O_1), (I_2, O_2),...,(I_n, O_n). In recognition problems, the trained network is tested with the input I_j $(1 \leq j \leq n)$ corrupted by noise, as shown in Figure 17.1. The trained network is expected to reproduce the output O_j corresponding to I_j, in spite of the presence of noise. Shape recognition[2] and speech generation[3]

Figure 17.1

Classes of Problems

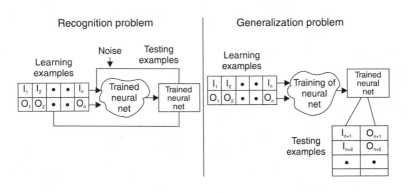

are examples of recognition problems. On the other hand, in *generalization problems*, the trained neural network is tested with input I_{n+1}, which is distinct from the inputs $I_1, I_2,...,I_n$ used for training the network, as shown in Figure 17.1. The network is expected to correctly predict the output O_{n+1} for the input I_{n+1} from the model of the domain it has learned from the training input/output pairs. Typical examples of generalization problems are *classification* (e.g., diagnosis of diseases from symptoms) and *prediction* (e.g., of the future trends in the economy). It should be noted that for classification problems, the various O_is, $1 \leq i \leq n + 1$ may not necessarily be distinct and belong to a finite set of classes, $\{C_1, C_2,...,C_m\}$.

Generalization problems can be further subclassified on the basis of the underlying domain of application as shown in Figure 17.2. Some domains have well-defined domain models (e.g., electrical circuit analysis) while other domains have partially defined domain models (e.g., the diagnosis of diseases from symptoms and laboratory tests). Conventional techniques (e.g., statistical or systems analysis) can be applied to the former domain, and many successful AI applications have been devised for the latter domain (e.g., expert systems such as MYCIN.[4] Yet another important class of problem domains are those that lack a domain model (alternatively termed as nonconservative domains), for example, the problem of assigning ratings to corporate bonds.

Most of the earlier applications of neural networks[2,3] have been to recognition problems. Lately, there have been some applications of neural

Figure 17.2

Recognition and Generalization Problems

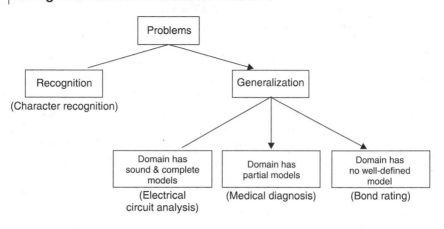

networks to generalization problems in partially defined problem do-mains.[5,6] In this chapter, we explore the application of neural networks in domains lacking a well-defined model or theory. For such nonconservative domains, it is difficult to successfully apply either conventional mathematical techniques or standard AI approaches (e.g., rule-based systems). A neural network may be useful for such domains because it does not require the a priori specification of a functional domain model; rather, it attempts to learn the underlying domain model from the training input/output examples. We choose the ratings of corporate bonds as the practical domain for this study because it is a nonconservative domain of enormous importance in the real world of finance.

THE DOMAIN OF BOND RATING

The *default risk* of a bond is the possibility that the promised coupon and par values of a bond will not be paid. The default risks of the most actively traded bonds are rated by various independent organizations like Standard and Poor's (S&P) and Moody's. Table 17.1 gives some examples of the ratings given by S&P and Moody's. These ratings are used as a metric to reflect the risk of investment in bonds and are also used to define allowable bond purchases by certain investors. For example, the comptroller of currency has stated that bank investments must be of *investment grade*. (Investment grade includes bonds rated in the top four rankings.) These ratings also have a significant effect on the offering yield of a bond issue.

To evaluate a bond's potential for default, rating agencies rely on a committee analysis of various aspects of the issuing company, such as the issuer's *ability* to repay, *willingness* to repay, and *protective* provisions for an issue. It is not known what model, if any, these rating agencies use for rating the various bond issues. The situation is complicated by the fact that all the various aspects analyzed by the ratings committee are not known completely; and some features, such as willingness to repay, are affected by a number of variables that are difficult to characterize precisely. Thus, it is not possible to accurately define a mathematical model that performs the required ratings of bonds. This is the main reason for the poor results yielded by conventional statistical analysis techniques. It is also difficult to develop a rule-based expert system for rating bonds, as very few experts are available, and most knowledge about the process of ratings is confidential. Developing a model for rating bonds is important,

Table 17.1
Definitions of Some Ratings Given by S&P and Moody's

Moody's	S&P	Definition
Aaa	AAA	The highest rating assigned. Capacity to pay interest and principal very strong.
a	AA	Very strong capacity to pay interest and principal. Differ from highest-rated issues only in small degree.
A	A	Strong capacity to repay interest and principal but may be susceptible to adverse changes in economic conditions.
Baa	BBB	Adequate protection to repay interest and principal but more likely to have weakened capacity in periods of adverse economic conditions.

as it enables a financial institution to independently evaluate the default risk of its bond investments.

RATING THE BONDS

The Problem Statement

The task of assigning ratings to the different industrial bond issues can be posed as a *classification* problem: Given a set of classes and a set of input data instances, each described by a suitable set of features, assign each input data instance to one of the classes. For our study, the different bond issues form the set of input data instances, and the various bond ratings (AA, B, etc.) form the set of possible classes to which the input bonds can belong. Each bond instance can be described by a set of features that represent important financial information about the company issuing the bond. Formally, we state the problem as follows:

> Let B represent the space of n bonds, $B_1, B_2,...,B_n$, and R be the set of possible (mutually exclusive) m bond ratings, $R_1, R_2,...,R_m$. Let F represent the k dimensional feature space, $F_1,...,F_k$, describing each of the bonds. Each bond B_i can be considered as a k-tuple ($F1_{Bi}, F2_{Bi},...,Fk_{Bi}$) in the Cartesian space $F_1 \times F_2 \times ... \times F_k$. And rating the bonds involves finding the one to one mapping function f:

$$f : F_1 \times F_2 \times ... \times F_k \rightarrow R$$

The mapping produced by this function f, that is, the ratings assigned to the various bonds, is determined by the rating agencies, but a precise functional form or a mathematical model of this function f is not known. The exact feature space used by the rating agencies is not known, but there is some consensus among researchers in corporate finance on the feature space. Thus an *approximation* to this feature space can be defined. Past researchers have tried to approximate the function f by using various multivariate regression models, with limited success. In this chapter, we attempt to use a neural network for modeling the function f, with the input vector space being given by $F_1 \times F_2 \times ... \times F_k$ and the output vector space being given by R. We choose an input feature space similar to that chosen by past researchers (see below) for their statistical analyses.

Review of Past Research

For determining the ratings of bonds, rating agencies probably use both the financial data of the company and other qualitative factors, such as their subjective judgment concerning the future prospects of the firm. However, researchers in finance have mostly concentrated upon quantifiable historical data for the firm and provisions of the bond issue. The typical financial variables used include proxies for liquidity, debt capacity, debt coverage, size of issue, and so on. They usually take coded bond ratings as an independent variable and use statistical techniques such as regression to get a model of bond ratings.

Horrigan[7] regressed coded ratings with 15 financial ratios. Subject to the magnitudes of cross-correlations, he chose six ratios out of the 15 that had highest correlation with ratings. These were total assets, working capital over sales, net work over total debt, sales over net worth, profit over sales, and subordination. Another regression between the ratings and the new set of variables gave a model. This model was correct for 58 percent of Moody's ratings during the period 1961 through 1964. West[8] has a similar approach, using logarithmic forms of nine variables including earning variability, solvency period, debt-to-equity ratio and outstanding bonds. His model correctly predicted 62 percent of Moody's rating during 1953. Pogue and Soklofsky[9] used a regression model with dichotomous $(0 - 1)$ dependent variables, which represents the probability of group membership in one group of pairs. They ran separate regressions for each pair of successive ratings (e.g., Aaa and aA, Aa and A, A and Baa) with the following independent variables: debt over total capital, income over assets, and income over interest charge. Dummy variables were used for broad industry effects. This approach involved at least $(n - 1)$ regressions for n-rating groups. A bond is assigned to the group in which its probability of occurrence is the highest. This method predicted 8 bonds out of 10 in a holdout sample from the period 1961 through 1966. Pinches and Mingo[10] screened the initial 35 variables via factor analysis and used multiple discriminant analysis to develop the final model. They used the following variables: subordination $(0 - 1)$, years of consecutive dividend, issue size, income over assets, income over interest charge, and debt over assets. Bonds were classified on the probability of group membership. This model predicted roughly 65 percent and 56 percent of the Moody's ratings for holdout samples in the periods 1967 through 1968 and 1969.

Limitations of Regression Models

These approaches (based on multiple regression) have had limited success (approximately 60 percent correctness) in predicting bond ratings, even after considering as many as 35 financial variables and performing a large number of iterative regressions ($n - 1$ iterations for n ratings). This supports our premise that in the absence of well-defined domain models (such as in bond rating) the success of standard mathematical *and/or* statistical techniques is limited. Statistical techniques always require the assumption of a certain functional form for relating dependent variables to independent variables. When the assumed functional form is not correct, the statistical techniques merely confirm that but do not predict the right functional form. Neural networks do provide a more general framework for determining relationships in the data and do not require the specification of any functional form. As shown later, neural networks do perform consistently better than regression.

NEURAL NET MODEL

We use a multilayer network consisting of simple processing elements called "units" that interact with each other using weighted connections. Each unit has a "state" or "activity level" determined by the input received from units in the layer below. The total input, x_j, received by unit j is given by equation $E1$ below, where y_j is the state of the ith unit (which is in a lower layer), w_{ij} is the weight on the connection from the ith to the jth unit, and θ_j is the threshold of the jth unit. The lowest layer contains the input nodes, and an external input vector is supplied to the network by clamping the states of these units. The state of any other unit in the network is a monotonic nonlinear function of its total input, as given by equation $E2$.

$$E1:\ x_j = \sum_i y_i u'_{ji} - \theta_j \qquad E2:\ y_j = \frac{1}{1 + e^{-z_j}}$$

All the network's long-term knowledge about the function it has learned to compute is encoded by the magnitudes of the weights on the connections.

We experimented with two-layered and three-layered networks. In a two-layer network, the input units are directly connected to output units by a set of connections with modifiable weights. Given a set of input vectors and the desired output for each input vector, the back-propagation[11] learning algorithm can iteratively find a set of weights that will perform the mapping, if such a set exists. The two-layered neural network is more powerful than regression due to the nonlinear summation at each unit. This is validated by our results (see below). We also experimented with three-layered networks with hidden nodes that combine the raw observations into higher-order features. The number of input units connected to each hidden unit in a three- (or more) layered network, determines the statistical order of high-order features extracted by the hidden unit.

The choice of the structure of the neural network is very dependent on the application domain of the neural network. If the input vector space consists of extremely low-level features, then we need a larger number of hidden layers to successively extract the higher-order features from the input data. A smaller number of hidden layers suffices if the input data is itself representative of some higher-order features. In our particular study, for reasons of efficiency, many higher-order features were chosen in the input vector space, and thus it was seen that the performance of the neural network did not improve significantly with an increase in the number of hidden layers.

Learning in Neural Nets

We used back-propagation[11] with simultaneous weight adjustments to learn the weights. The learning procedure is briefly described here. The error with a given set of weights is defined by equation $E3$, where y_{jc} is the actual state (weight) of unit j in input/output training example c (in the forward direction), and d_{jc} is its desired state (weight). This allows the network to compute, for each weight, the gradient of output error with respect to that weight. For a hidden unit, j, in layer J, the only way it can affect the error is via its effects on the units, k, in the next layer K. So the derivative of the error $\partial E/\partial y_j$ is given by equation $E4$, where the index c has been suppressed for clarity. The weight is then changed in the direction to reduce the output error. Our neural network simulator uses global optimization for changing the weights

$$E3: \quad E = \frac{1}{2}\sum_{j,c} (y_{j,c} - d_{j,c})^2 \qquad E4: \quad \frac{\partial E}{\partial y_j} = \sum_k \frac{\partial E}{\partial y_k} \frac{dy_k}{dz_k} \frac{\partial I_k}{\partial y_k}$$

simultaneously and avoids the problems of conflicting local weight adjustments.

To verify how well the neural network has learned the underlying domain model, we use the same set of weights (on the connections) learned during the *learning phase* and check the accuracy of the predicted output for a new set of input vectors. We refer to the input vectors used for learning the weights as the *learning sample* and the input vectors used for testing as the *testing sample*. The success of the predictions of the neural network depends upon the range of the domain covered by the learning input/output vectors. Thus, for the case of bond ratings, it is desired that the neural network be shown examples of bonds belonging to all the different rating categories during the learning phase.

Regression Analysis versus Neural Net Models

Regression gives us the parameters of a given functional form but not the correct functional form. The neural network model is helpful for determining the functional form as well as the parameters. It does not require us to guess any functional form but determines the functional form by itself. It tunes the functional form and parameters to fit the learning examples as closely as desired. We can specify both the desired size (number of parameters) of the model (neural network) and the error tolerance for the model. This gives us a more general framework for discovering relationships existing in data. As expected, we found that it consistently outperformed regression methods for predicting bond ratings.

However, we note that the regression models are useful in determining the right set of independent variables, which determine the dependent variable to the largest extent. This is difficult to do with neural networks, as the hidden layers (intermediate layers) of a neural network extract the higher-order features from the input variables to decide the output, so the output is not influenced directly by the inputs. The weights on the connections for a two-layered network can give the relative importance of the input variables, but for any three- or higher-layered network, such a discrimination from the weights on the connections becomes very difficult.

DESIGN OF THE EXPERIMENT

Selection of Variables

Based on the results of Horrigan,[7] and Pinches and Mingo,[10] we selected 10 financial variables for predicting bond ratings. The influence of a variable on the bond rating and ease of availability of data were the primary factors in the selection of the variables. These are listed in Table 17.2 and explained elsewhere (the *Valueline Index* and the *S&P Bond Guide*).

Our first experiment uses all the 10 variables in predicting the bond rating. Then, we used only the first six variables to predict the bond ratings. The correlations of the chosen variables were all small, and hence the chosen variables are independent (as desired).

Data Collection

Bond ratings and values of the financial variables for a set of industrial bonds are taken from the April 1986 issue of the *Valueline Index* and the *S&P Bond Guide*. Bond issues of 47 companies were selected at random, and we used 30 of them to perform the *learning*, that is, to train the neural network (obtain the weights on the different connections) and obtain the regression coefficients. The rest (17) of the bonds were used to test

Table 17.2
Financial Variables Used to Predict Bond Ratings

Variable	Definition
1	Liability/(Cash + assets)
2	Debt proportion
3	Sales/Net worth
4	Profit/Sales
5	Financial strength
6	Earning/Fixed costs
7	Past five-year revenue growth rate
8	Projected next five-year revenue growth rate
9	Working capital/Sales
10	Subjective prospect of company

the neural network and regression performance. All the selected bonds had approximately the same maturity date (1998–2003).

A linear scale was used to convert the ratings of the bonds. We could have used a binary scale to convert the bonds (e.g., bonds rated A = 1; all other bonds = 0), but such a model would not be too accurate as there is a sort of linear relation in the rating of the bonds versus the quality of the bonds (i.e., AAA is the best, and the quality decreases progressively with lower-rated bonds), and this is not captured by the binary model.

Linear Regression Model

We used the Berkeley ISP (the interactive statistical package developed at the University of California, Berkeley) for multiple regression analysis to get a set of regression coefficients and their respective t-statistics. The t-statistics were significant for every regression coefficient. The regression coefficients obtained were then used to predict the ratings of both the learning sample (to see how well the regression model fitted the learning sample) and the testing sample of new bond issues (to see how well the regression coefficients predicted the ratings of the test bonds). The results are summarized in the next section.

Neural Net Model

We experimented with different neural network configurations (two-layered, three-layered, different number of hidden nodes in three-layered neural nets, etc.). The total permissible tolerance was kept constant for different neural network configurations. We compare the performance of the various neural networks against regression analysis and the performances of the various neural network configurations against themselves in the next section. Finally, we repeated all the above experiments with a smaller number of variables (variables 1 through 6 of the 10 variables initially chosen).

RESULTS

Tables 17.3 through 17.6 summarize the results of our experiments. The models were expected to recognize if a given bond belongs to the class of all bonds with an AA rating. This problem naturally classifies the responses of prediction models into four different categories, described by the pairs of columns (actual, predicted) in Table 17.3.

The column "actual" is "accept" if and only if the *given* bond is actually rated AA by S&P. For an ideal model, our test results should only belong to the first and fourth rows of Table 17.3 where the ratings given by S&P and the model coincide. Rows 2 and 3 of Table 17.3 are the undesirable cases and represent false negatives and false positives, respectively. We report the statistics for the learning case and testing cases separately to bring out the important features of our study. In Table 17.4, we list in detail the results of our study of the regression and neural network models for the four possible response classifications described in Table 17.3. High values in the columns under "percent correct prediction" for the response pairs (accept, accept) and (reject, reject) point to a good model while high values for the response pairs (accept, reject) and (reject, accept) point to an inferior model. The values are listed separately for the learning and testing phases for both neural networks and the regression analysis. This helps us to better compare neural networks and regression analysis. For example (from Table 17.4 for 10 variables), during the learning phase, the regression model correctly classified 61.5 percent of AA bonds as AA bonds and 64.8 percent of non-AA bonds as non-AA, using 10 variables. Similarly (also from Table 17.4 for 10 variables), during the testing phase, the neural network model (both the two-layered neural network and the three-layered neural network) correctly classified 83 percent of the AA bonds as AA and 81.9 percent of the non-AA bonds as non-AA, using 10 variables.

Table 17.3
Possible Classifications of Responses

Actual	Prediction	Description
Accept	Accept	S&P rating is AA and rating of model is also AA
Accept	Reject	S&P rating is AA and rating of model is not AA
Reject	Accept	S&P rating is not AA but rating of model is AA
Reject	Reject	S&P rating is not AA and rating of model is also not AA

Table 17.4

Performance of Regression and Neural Network Using 10 and 6 Variables

Phase	Classification		Percent Correct Prediction Using 10 Variables			Percent Correct Prediction Using 6 Variables		
	Actual	Pre-dicted	Regres-sion	Two-Layer N-Net	Three-Layer N-Net	Regres-sion	Two-Layer N-Net	Three-Layer N-Net
Learning	Accept	Accept	61.5	76.9	92.3	61.5	76.9	76.9
	Accept	Reject	38.5	23.1	7.7	38.5	23.1	23.1
	Reject	Accept	29.4	17.6	0.0	35.2	17.6	17.6
	Reject	Reject	64.8	82.3	100.0	64.8	82.3	82.3
Testing	Accept	Accept	50.0	83.3	83.3	50.0	83.3	83.3
	Accept	Reject	50.0	16.7	16.7	50.0	16.7	16.7
	Reject	Accept	27.2	18.1	18.1	27.2	18.1	18.1
	Reject	Reject	72.8	81.9	81.9	72.8	81.9	81.9

INTERPRETATION OF RESULTS

The data of Table 17.4 is condensed into Tables 17.5 and 17.6 for comparison. Table 17.4 condenses the results of the learning phase, and Table 17.6 condenses the results of the testing phase. The percent of entries in Tables 17.5 and 17.6 essentially represent the percent of correctness of prediction of the two models (regression and neural network) and are obtained by computing a weighted average of the corresponding entries in Table 17.4 for the response pairs (accept, accept) and (reject, reject). (The weights being given by the actual number of bonds in the respective categories.) We also list the absolute error as *tot_sq_err* for each model to give an idea of goodness of fit by various models. The *tot_sq_err* gives the sum of the squares of the errors in prediction in all the cases. Note that we converted bond ratings to a number in the range [0,1]. Thus, the total

Table 17.5

Results (Learning)

Number of Variables	Neural Net		Regression
	Two Layers	Three Layers	
6	80%	80%	63.33%
	tot_sq_err = 0.2365	tot_sq_err = 0.1753	tot_sq_err = 1.107
10	80%	92.4%	66.7%
	tot_sq_err = 0.2241	tot_sq_err = 0.0538	tot_sq_err = 0.924

Table 17.6

Results (Testing)

Number of Variables	Neural Net		Regression
	Two Layers	Three Layers	
6	82.4%	76.5%	64.7%
	tot_sq_err = 0.198	tot_sq_err = 0.1939	tot_sq_err = 1.528
10	88.3%	82.4%	64.7%
	tot_sq_err = 0.1638	tot_sq_err = 0.2278	tot_sq_err = 1.643

squared error is given by the sum of the squares of the differences between the numerical values of the actual and predicted bond ratings.

From Tables 17.4 through 17.6 we can draw the following conclusions:

1. Neural networks consistently outperform regression models in predicting bond ratings from the given set of financial ratios. Both in the training and learning samples, the total squared error for regression analysis is about an order of magnitude higher than that for neural networks (see Tables 17.5 and 17.6). Also, the success rate of prediction for neural networks is considerably higher than that for regression

analysis; for example, the success rate during the testing phase for the two-layered neural network (10 variables) is 88.3 percent as compared to 64.7 percent for the regression model.

2. For the different configurations of neural networks, we observe that during the learning phase the total squared error decreases for a neural network with a larger number of layers, but there are no significant differences in results during the testing phase. Given the training sample, we can obtain a better fit (with respect to the training sample) using a larger number of layers in the neural network, but the additional layers do not seem to add to its predictive power, as evidenced during the testing phase. This result can be understood in light of our earlier comments (see Neural Net Model, above) regarding the required number of hidden layers in a neural network. Our input financial features of a bond are relatively high-level abstractions, and thus there is no significant improvement in prediction with an increase in the number of hidden layers.

3. The results obtained during the testing phase by our regression analysis are comparable to those obtained by previous researchers (see Neural Net Model, above). The poor performance of the regression models indicates that the linear multivariate model is inadequate for explaining the rating of bonds. There are substantial gains by applying neural networks to nonconservative domains such as bond rating.

4. It was observed that whenever the neural network model is in error, it is off by at most one rating. In contrast, regression analysis was often off by several ratings. We have not presented details here due to space limitations.

CONCLUSION

Domains of application of neural networks are not limited to recognition problems. They can be applied successfully to generalization problems, where the underlying application domain does not have any models. For nonconservative problem domains, neural networks perform much better than classical mathematical modeling techniques such as regression.[12]

ENDNOTES

1. P. D. Wasserman et al., "Neural Networks, Part 2," *IEEE Expert Magazine* 3, no. 1 (Spring 1988).

2. G. E. Hinton, "Learning to Recognize Shapes in Parallel Networks," in *Proceedings of the Fyssen Conference,* ed. M. Imbert (Oxford: Oxford University Press).

3. T. J. Senjowski et al., "NETtalk: A Parallel Network That Learns to Read Aloud," Baltimore, MD: Johns Hopkins University, EECS Department, Tech. Rep. 86-01.

4. E. H. Shortliffe, *Computer Based Medical Consulations: MYCIN* (New York: Elsevier, 1976).

5. S. I. Gallant, "Connectionist Expert Systems," *Comm. of the ACM* 31, no. 2 (February 1988).

6. H. V. Parunak et al., "Material Handling: A Conservative Domain for Neural Connectivity and Propagation," *Proceedings AAAI Conference,* 1987, pp. 307–11.

7. J. O. Horrigan, "The Determination of Long Term Credit Standing with Financial Ratios," Empirical Research in Accounting: Selected Studies, *Journal of Accounting Research,* 1966.

8. R. R. West, "An Alternative Approach to Predicting Corporate Bond Ratings," *Journal of Accounting Research,* Spring 1970.

9. T. E. Pogue and R. M. Soklofsky, "What is in a Bond Rating?" *Journal of Financial and Quantitative Analysis,* June 1969.

10. G. E. Pinches and K. A. Mingo, "A Multivariate Analysis of Industrial Bond Ratings," *Journal of Finance,* March 1977.

11. D. E. Rumelhart et al., "Learning Internal Representations by Back-propagating Errors," *Nature* 323, pp. 533–36.

12. We would like to thank Professor Andrew Rudd, Business School, University of California at Berkeley, for introducing us to the problem of bond rating and providing valuable insights from time to time. We also thank Rajesh Mehra of the quantitative finance research group, BARRA, for providing data related to several bond issues. We had fruitful discussions about the applicability of neural models in nonconservative domain with

Professor L. A. Zadeh, Computer Science, University of California at Berkeley. We are grateful to Dr. Shabbir Rangwala, Mechanical Engineering, University of California at Berkeley, for his help with the neural network simulator.

18

NEURAL NETWORKS FOR BOND RATING IMPROVED BY MULTIPLE HIDDEN LAYERS

Alvin J. Surkan and J. Clay Singleton

INTRODUCTION

Choosing values for neural network architectural parameters that specify both the number of hidden layers and the number of active elements within those layers is still more an art than a science. Mathematical analysis that might answer such questions is made intractable by the complexity of the interactions among the many dimensions represented in simulated neural networks. Also, each trained network, in an incomprehensibly complex way, is dependent on the initial connection weight values and subsequent chance sequencing of their updating in training with backward-error propagation,[1] which performs optimization through a nondeterministic, hill-climbing procedure. Until there is a better understanding of both the performance of backward-error propagation and the internal representation of problem knowledge over the connection weights, it is vital that alternative internal neural network architectures be explored by experimentation with data that is either real or truly representative of the problems for which neural networks have promise. In practice, this means frequently starting with very small training data sets, which themselves may have errors in patterns or have incorrect labels. For these, one must establish the extent to which the resulting trained networks will generalize so as to classify the test patterns initially set aside from those used in training.

While it is assumed that infrequent labeling errors or even frequent small errors characteristic of patterns occurring in large training sets will have negligible permanent effect on training, it is clear that even one error in labeling a training pattern appearing in a small training set can drastically reduce the trained network's generalization performance. For this reason, when networks are trained to generalize from small training sets, it is necessary to study and filter incorrectly labeled patterns. Censoring may be required, independent of the reason the label is incorrect, that is, erroneous label assignment or the presence of noise contaminating the pattern to such a degree that it, in fact, becomes effectively more representative of a class with a different label.

BOND RATINGS

Many researchers in economics and finance have studied the determinants of bond ratings. The essence of these investigations is to discover a model that mimics the ratings awarded by either of the major rating companies: Moody's or Standard & Poor's. These agencies claim their quality ratings combine analysis of financial variables with expert judgment to produce an estimate of the probability the company will default. Bond ratings also have economic significance, as higher-quality ratings command lower interest rates. Models of bond ratings, therefore, are of great interest to investors, who want to anticipate the rating given a change in company circumstances, and to financial managers, who seek to predict the rating (and accompanying interest rate) of a potential issue. Moody's ranks bonds from Aaa (highest quality) to Aa1, Aa2, Aa3 (medium quality) to A1, A2, A3 (investment grade, but lower quality).

DESCRIPTION OF THE FINANCIAL DATA USED

Bond raters publicly announce they consider leverage, coverage, and profitability as prime determinants of bond issue quality. Peavy and Scott[2] modeled the bonds of 18 Bell Telephone operating companies divested by American Telephone and Telegraph Company (AT&T) in 1982. To construct a model, they surveyed bond rating research and found seven variables related to these three financial characteristics and often highly correlated with bond ratings in previous classification studies (mostly discriminant analysis). They used linear discriminant analysis to estimate their model and correctly classified 10 of the 18 bonds (56.6 percent) into four rating classes (Aa2, Aa3, A1, A2). For this study, similar data (bond ratings and financial variables) were obtained for the same 18 telephone operating companies for the years 1982 through 1988. Specifically, the financial variables were as follows:

1. Debt divided by total capital (LEVERAGE)—a measure of the bondholders' security.

2. Pretax interest expense divided by income (COVERAGE)—a measure of the company's ability to pay bondholders from current income.

3. Return on equity (ROE) or income—a profitability measure.

4. Coefficient of variation of ROE calculated over the past five years (CV of ROE)—an indication of the stability of profitability.

5. Logarithm of the total assets (TA)—a measure of size.

6. Construction costs divided by total cash inflow (FLOW)—a measure of the capacity to fund construction without increased borrowing.

7. Toll revenue ratio calculated as intradivided by inter-LATA (TOLL)—an indication of the effect of divestiture on profitability.

These financial variables should measure quality and, therefore, should be distinguishable by bond rating. A summary comparison of financial data is displayed in Table 18.1. This table gives the means of each of the seven financial variables and shows the distribution of the bonds by rating. The relationship between the rating classes among these variables is not obvious but suggestive of a complex interaction that is consistent with the rating agencies' claim of the need for expert judgment. These relationships may also be more amenable to a neural network than the tra-

Table 18.1

Means of Financial Variables by Bond Ratings for 18 Telephone Operating Companies (1982–1988)

Variable	Aaa	Aa1	Aa2	Aa3	A1	A2	A3
			Bond Rating Symbol				
Leverage	.39	.41	.39	.36	.36	.39	.39
Coverage	4.5	4.48	4.99	5.69	5.02	4.30	4.46
ROE	.25	.14	.14	.15	.12	.14	.15
CV of ROE	.1	.10	.08	.10	.14	.09	.07
TA	14.7	15.75	13.00	14.25	15.15	16.36	16.43
Flow	1.05	.92	1.05	1.05	.85	.74	.83
Toll	1.34	1.08	.82	1.24	1.04	1.01	.90
Frequency	30	23	20	27	10	11	5

ditional linear model. One advantage of the current research is that neural networks are trained with economic (not simulated) data and tested against a classification technique accepted by financial researchers.

CREATION OF NEURAL NETWORK MODELS

Each alternate configuration of an initially untrained PDP-type of layered connection network was emitted by a dynamic network generation program function called GENNET. Its operation requires only a few seconds and is initiated by evoking GENNET with a single vector argument, LL, on its right. The argument LL supplies the layer lengths first for the output, then the sequence of hidden layers, and finally the input. During each such synthesis of an experimental network, all the needed connection arrays and vectors are created. These are all correctly dimensioned to represent the connections and thresholding values for each simulated neuron. Also produced, simultaneously, are the input and activation vectors that supply the input to each successive processing layer and finally to the output. In all experiments, the number of elements in the input and output vectors were fixed at seven and two, respectively. The minimum and maximum number of elements provided in hidden layers ranged from 5 to 15. These would be introduced either all in a single hidden layer or divided between two layers. In experiments using two hidden layers, unequal numbers of elements were tested with trial combinations with the numbers of elements either increasing or decreasing, in the direction input to output.

TRAINING PROCEDURES AND DATA SELECTION AND SEQUENCING

Operation of the back-propagation updating during the training phase is managed in a specialized way tailored for training with small data sets. Besides having a schedule for diminishing the learning rate parameter as training proceeds, it is necessary to decide what useful role, if any, the momentum term should play in the weight update process. Besides this parametric control, the progress of training may be significantly influenced by the selection of the training patterns. Also, training is affected by any errors in the assigned pattern labels and how they are sampled and sequenced.

Unless training data sets are very large, experience suggests that using fewer prototypical training patterns with correct labels as training exemplars is preferable to using slightly larger training sets contaminated by even a very few labeling errors. In the absence of any knowledge of distribution of noise or errors in the pattern, it seems appropriate to provide an equal number of exemplars for representing each distinct output class. When this is made impossible by one or more too-poorly populated classes, the classes with smaller numbers of sample patterns are randomly sampled repeatedly with an increased frequency.

It was found experimentally that intentionally mislabeled real patterns inserted among the correct observed patterns could be identified early during the process of training a neural network. It follows that unless the patterns themselves are contaminated with too much noise, this same process for identifying mislabeled training patterns, soon after beginning training, provides a means of data censoring, which proved beneficial for producing trained networks with improved generalization capabilities. This is especially true when the training set size is rather small.

This staged training improves the data quality by identifying better training data, which is retained for producing the final model. Also, with small training sets, the weight update process is implicitly rather than explicitly batched. This is done by performing a new weight update immediately after every training pattern makes its forward pass through the network. However, complete generations of such training passes are implicitly imposed by random sampling of each class without replacement. This is continued until all training patterns in a class are exhausted. As before, if one class becomes exhausted before others, it may be repeatedly sampled with replacement. Besides imposing this control on the random sampling within classes, an additional data sequencing constraint guarantees that samples representing differing output classes are chosen systematically. This ensures that classes will be randomly sampled repeatedly and without replacement among classes during each indirect training cycle or generation.

EXPERIMENTS ON EFFECTS OF NUMBER AND SIZE OF HIDDEN LAYERS

An APL[3] function GENNET was written and repeatedly used to generate various configurations of layered networks. All had a seven-element input layer that received the financial pattern values and a two-element output layer indicating into which bond class the data were finally mapped from the output of any intervening hidden layers. For these particular experiments, either a single or a pair of hidden layers were present. Usually, the number of intermediate elements was varied from 5 to about 15. When the number of elements was fixed, they were either all in one layer or redistributed among multiple layers.

Single Hidden-Layer Experiments

When there is only a single hidden layer of neurons, its elements are activated by the signals arriving from the input. The activations on that hidden layer are processed by a second layer of processing neurons that finally activate the output. Each additional hidden layer introduced one set of processing neurons, which imposes an additional intermediate representation of the pattern as it is mapped from its input codes to the desired output codes. Experiments with single and multiple layers were performed by a fixed training set and by testing the performance of trained networks with a different number of elements placed either in a single hidden layer or divided between two hidden layers. With a pair of hidden-layer lengths, it is also important to find out how pairs of unequal layer lengths should be sequenced in a mapping network that is optimal with respect to its ability to generalize. Here the word *generalize* is used to mean that the network constructed from the training patterns of presumably correct known class labels are able to predict the correct labels for those patterns that were set aside for testing and not permitted to be used during the training process.

RESULTS OF THE TRAINING AND TESTING EXPERIMENTS

It was found that the length of a single hidden layer could be varied over a relatively wide range (5 to 15) without significantly degrading the classification performance. This performance was measured simply by the number of patterns correctly labeled in the two classes. The results in the first row of Table 18.2 are for the typical sequence of layer lengths 7, 14, 2 proceeding from the input to the output. They are the same or representative of those obtained from the range of single hidden layers trained with the same 20 patterns of bond rating data. From the columns on the right half of Table 18.2, it is seen that the classification accuracy for the set-aside test patterns was 85 percent and 45 percent for classes 1 and 2, respectively. For 40 test samples of classes 1 and 2 combined, an overall performance of 65 percent was obtained. Because in practice all small sets of training samples can be preselected to include only that subset of data patterns that were correctly classified, the meaningful performance measure is the percent correct among only the test patterns. Also, it is of interest to examine the clarity of the network output code signals for those classifications for which the classes appeared incorrect. This is so because the discrepancy could arise from either a misclassification by the network or by humans who originally assigned the bond ratings. Frequently, inconsistency was accompanied by similar or almost equivocal pairs of activations of the two elements of the output layer.

Two Hidden-Layer Model Results

When a variety of networks with two hidden layers were trained on the same 20 dot patterns, they would consistently provide greater accuracy in classifying the test data than did the single hidden-layer network. This was true even when the hidden-layer elements were distributed so that the shortest hidden layer preceded the longer one during the mapping

Chapter 18

Table 18.2

Classification Accuracy Results

Samples	Both Training and Test Patterns			Only the Test Patterns		
Bond Class	1(Aaa)	2 (A1, A2, A3)	1 and 2	1(Aaa)	2 (A1, A2, A3)	1 and 2
Count	30	26	56	20	20	40
7, 14, 2	(27) [90%]	(15) [58%]	(38) [68%]	(17) [85%]	(9) [45%]	(26) [65%]
7, 5, 10, 2	(28) [93%]	(20) [77%]	(48) [86%]	(18) [90%]	(14) [70%]	(32) [80%]
7, 10, 5, 2	(30) [100%]	(21) [81%]	(51) [91%]	(20) [100%]	(15) [75%]	(35) [88%]

Note: Entries give (number) and [percent] correctly classified by trained neural networks with a single pair of transposed hidden layer lengths as given in the leftmost column.

process. In this case, an immediate dimension reduction from 7 to 17 in the first layer suggests that the intrinsic dimension of the data is close to 5 or lower. As expected, when the longer hidden layer of neurons precedes the shorter and the training and test data are fixed for evaluating the action of permuting the hidden-layer length sequences with a constant number of elements, improved performance was obtained when the sequence decreased monotonically in the direction of the output.

The two lower rows of Table 18.2—which contain the layer length sequences {7, 5, 10, 2} and {7, 10, 5, 2}—show marked improvement over the single hidden-layer network in the top row. The {7, 10, 5, 2} architecture correctly classified 100 percent of class 1, 75 percent of class 2, and 88 percent of the test patterns of classes 1 and 2 combined. It is important to explain that only six of the class 2 exemplars were explicitly assigned an A rating. The remaining four were, in fact, patterns chosen from higher-rated bonds assigned to rating category Aa3 adjacent to class 2 and distant from the class 1 exemplars, which were all assigned an Aaa rating.

COMPARISON WITH DISCRIMINANT CLASSIFICATION TECHNIQUES

These experiments show that both single and multiple hidden-layer networks for classifying patterns of a few variables (seven financial features) perform well. The results, however, do not necessarily establish neural networks as superior to simpler techniques, such as discriminant analysis. Discriminant analysis was selected as a benchmark because it has often been applied to bond classification problems. A valid comparison between various alternative hidden-layer configurations of simulated networks and discriminant analysis requires that both methods be applied fairly and to their best advantage. The neural networks classified the test patterns unavailable to it during training. Linear discriminant functions were estimated using the two groups as dependent and the seven financial features as explanatory variables. All 56 observations were used in a hold-one-out approach by iteratively calculating the model over 55 observations and classifying the 56th. Every observation was held out in turn, avoiding the bias of classifying the same observations used to estimate the model. The discriminant analysis may have been given a slight advantage in this comparison, as it was exposed to all the observations during training. Nevertheless, the superior ability of neural networks to classify bonds can be confirmed by comparing the results in Table 18.2 with the discriminant success rates of 40 percent (12 of 30) for group 1, 38 percent (10 of 26) for group 2, and 39 percent (22 of 56) overall. Even the earlier study by Peavy and Scott[2] (over a smaller, more homogeneous sample) only classified 56.6 percent (10 of 18) of the bonds correctly. Although neural networks are more complex than discriminant analysis, these results suggest the neural network may be the more powerful classification technique.

SUMMARY OF EXPERIMENTS WITH SINGLE AND MULTIPLE HIDDEN-LAYER NETWORKS

The results shown in Table 18.2 and mentioned earlier demonstrate that neural networks with either single or pairs of hidden layers can provide 65 percent, 80 percent, and 88 percent correct classification among the collections of 26, 32, and 35 test patterns not used in training each final network. This progression of improvements in classification accuracy corresponded with the reconfiguring from a single hidden layer (with network layer lengths of 7, 14, and 2) to double hidden-layer configurations with layer lengths sandwiched in the sequences {7,5,10,2} or {7,10,5,2}. As expected, a classifier network trained one way and then retrained after swapping its two hidden layers so they were sequenced to decrease, rather than increase, the number of processing elements increased accuracy from 80 percent to 88 percent. At the same time, it is both surprising and not yet understood how the significantly improved classification accuracy was produced even when the pair of hidden layers was reversed so the layer length sequence was {7,5,10,2}. Similar improvement is realized even when the double hidden-layer network has many different redistributions of the two layers, provided the number of simulated neurons is fixed at approximately the number used in a single hidden layer. This leads to the conjecture that redistributing an adequate number of single hidden-layer elements to many optional pairings of hidden layers can produce a significant performance improvement without an unacceptable increase in training time.

GENERAL CONCLUSIONS

Bond rating by trained, layered, neural networks is an increasingly attractive area for the application of learning from limited numbers of examples when there are only a few variables known to be useful as class determinants. Also, this research provides real problems for neural networks to solve and a standard of comparison familiar in the field. The experimental evidence suggests the advantages of multiple hidden layers over a single one. The improvement in classification accuracy from redistributing the neurons from one to a pair of layers can be marked. Significant advantages arise even when the layers are ordered so that a smaller number of neurons receive their inputs directly from the inputs. This suggests that for this bond rating data, the problem of mapping from seven features to two classes may have an inherent dimensionality of five or lower. The mapping of the five elements' (or neurons') output of the first layer down to two layers can be performed first. Then, there is still an advantage from the use of a subsequent hidden layer to provide another representation of useful classification information. There is a hope that some of the intermediate representations may be identified with concepts used by humans to analyze this bond classification problem. Finding such representations with correspondences to familiar higher-level concepts remains a challenge for understanding the internal operation of neural networks.

ENDNOTES

1. D. E. Rumelhart et al., "Learning Internal Representations by Back-Propagating Errors," *Nature* 323 (1986), pp. 533–36.

2. J. W. Peavy III and J. A. Scott, "The AT&T Divestiture: Effects of Rating Changes on Bond Returns," *Journal of Economics and Business* 38 (1986), pp. 255–70.

3. K. E. Iverson, "A Dictionary of APL," I. P. Sharp Associates Limited, 1987. (Also printed in *SIGATL Quote-Quad* 18, September 1987.)

19

RISK ASSESSMENT OF MORTGAGE APPLICATIONS WITH A NEURAL NETWORK SYSTEM: AN UPDATE AS THE TEST PORTFOLIO AGES

Douglas L. Reilly, Edward Collins,
Christopher Scofield, and Sushmito Ghosh

INTRODUCTION

Nestor's multiple neural network technology has been applied to many problems; among them, applications in signal processing for character recognition,[1] in medicine,[2] in vision,[3] industrial inspection,[4,5] diagnostics,[6] and speech recognition.[7] Neural net applications have also been developed in the financial services arena. One particular problem domain that has been under investigation is that of automated decision-making and risk assessment for mortgage insurance underwriting. The application of Nestor's neural net technology to this problem has been previously reported.[8-10] This chapter presents an update to this work, returning to the risk assessment portion of the problem to analyze how well the risk prediction has fared for the mortgage portfolio under study, now that the portfolio has aged.

RISK ASSESSMENT

Mortgage risk assessment begins with mortgage origination. A mortgage originator filters the general population of potential property owners according to a set of simple guidelines on acceptable ranges for such risk measures as the proposed loan-to-value ratio, the ratio of proposed obligations to income, and so on. Fannie Mae and others in the secondary mortgage market publish guidelines that serve to qualify and segregate the home loan applicant pool into risk categories. Some of the higher risk loans are referred for private mortgage insurance. The process of determining whether or not a loan applicant should be accepted for mortgage insurance involves, in effect, a second underwriting. If the applicant exhibits an acceptable level of risk, he or she will be sold insurance. Mortgage insurance applicants are by nature a higher risk group than the general originator and assessed as less-secure cases. Thus, this second-order underwriting performed by the mortgage insurer is bound to be more difficult and prone to greater uncertainty.

The mortgage insurance problem can be divided into two parts. The first problem is that of automating the decision-making process of the underwriters. This can be served by constructing a system that can learn to emulate the decisions that underwriters make on mortgage applications. A system that correctly mimics the judgment of human underwriters on some subset of the loan applications presented to it can have economic benefit as a result of introducing consistency in underwriter judgments and in allowing an underwriting agency to better handle peak workloads. The strategy of applying a neural network approach to this phase of the problem is to capture data that represents loan application information together with the corresponding judgments that an underwriter has made on each application. The pool of data represents judgments from a number of underwriters. The neural net system trains to emulate the decision-making of this collection of experts on the problem.

A different aspect of the problem arises not from the use of the network in automating the human decision-making but rather from the use of the network to improve on the quality of the decisions through its ability to learn to estimate some measure of the risk of a loan applicant's defaulting on his or her mortgage payments. Underwriters for loan originators and private mortgage insurance companies do not perform this task flawlessly. Although these insurance underwriters typically decline approximately 20 percent of the applications they review, of the remaining accepted group, some 20 percent will go delinquent during the course of the loan. Approximately 6 percent will eventually lead to losses as a result of claims. The peak in claims rates occurs some three to five years after the loan is granted. Because any feedback from an incorrect decision occurs some number of years after the decision is made and because of the high turnover rate in underwriter staffing, there is little opportunity to improve on the underwriters' judgments from observations of historical outcomes.

Although the economic payoff of improving the quality of the underwriting decisions can be substantially greater than that of simply automating and replicating their current decision-making trends and practices, the acceptance of the former can require a higher level of commitment and reliance on the technology. It is relatively easy to immediately verify whether or not the system is deciding as the underwriter would decide. From the simple perspective of "trusting the machine," it requires more commitment to accept that the machine, when disagreeing with the underwriter, is actually making the *better* decision about something that might happen three to five years from now.

The neural network that was used for this application is a derivative of an RCE network that has been reported on elsewhere.[11] The RCE network is a three-layer network that has been described extensively.[12–15] Essentially, the network trains by committing cells on its single internal layer that represent prototypical "exemplars" of the pattern classes that it sees in the training set. It automatically selects from the training set the exemplars that are to be stored in memory, storing in its weights the values that define the prototype features. Associated with each prototype cell is a cell threshold, a number that captures the extent to which this prototype's exemplar will participate in the classification of incoming new patterns. This cell threshold represents a region of influence around the prototype in the pattern space.

Data used for the risk assessment study were taken from a collection of some 111,080 home mortgage loans from the period July 1984 to December 1986. The status of the loans was noted as of December 1987, and this served as the classification of "good" and "bad" loans. For the initial study, "bad" was defined as any loan that had gone delinquent at least once in the period from origination through the end of 1987. A total of 758 good applications and 844 bad applications were used for the risk assessment study.

The results of the initial study are shown in Figure 19.1. For a certain percentage of the applications (10 percent), it is possible to predict with 95 percent accuracy the loans which, if granted, would go delinquent in payment. (Delinquency is not the same as default, but it is a necessary precursor.) If the system's decisions are accepted at this throughput (10 percent of applications), then some number of good applications will also be called "bad." Rejecting such loan applicants would amount to turning away good business. Since the cost of replacing this lost business is far less than the cost associated with underwriting loans that go to claim, this 10 percent throughput represents an operating point with a viable economic benefit.

As noted earlier, these results were reported on a portfolio of mortgages whose delinquency/default status was dated as of December 1987. Since

Figure 19.1

Performance of Mortgage Risk Processor

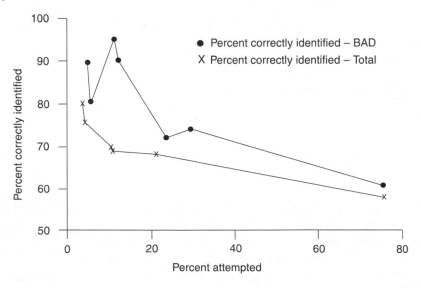

the portfolio represented originations between July 1984 and December 1986, the age of the applications at the time of the study ranged from one to three and one-half years. Updates on the status of this portfolio were provided as of September 1988. Since claims begin to peak in the three- to five-year period after origination, we would expect to see significantly more claims in the updated portfolio. Special attention is paid to those loans that at the time of the initial study had been labeled good but have since gone bad.

Additionally, sensitivity of the model to the size of the training set is important. The collection of a portfolio for training purposes can often have some cost associated with it if all the information that is typically available to underwriters is not available in electronic file format for the neural network to process. Consequently, it can be important to establish some measure of the additional marginal benefit in risk assessment as a function of additional loan examples made available for training. Figure 19.2 shows a learning curve for the neural net risk assessment system as a function of the percentage of the data set trained on.

Figure 19.2

Claims Prediction Learning Curve

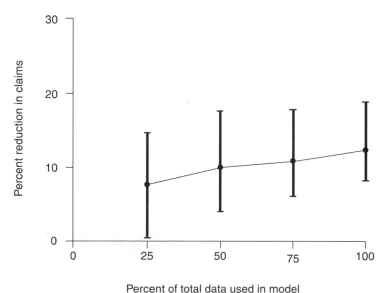

ENDNOTES

1. D. Ward, C. L. Scofield, and D. L. Reilly, "An Application of a Multiple Neural Network with Modifiable Network Topology (GENSEP) to On-Line Character Recognition," *Abstracts of INNS*, Boston, 1988.

2. T. O. Carroll, H. Ved, and D. L. Reilly, "A Neural Network ECG Analysis," *Proceedings of IJCNN* II (June 1989), p. II-575.

3. R. Rimey, P. Gouin, C. Scofield, and D. L. Reilly, "Real-Time 3-D Object Classification Using a Learning System," *Proceedings SPIE Cambridge Symposium on Intelligent Robots and Computer Vision*, October 26–31, 1986.

4. D. L. Reilly, C. Scofield, P. R. Gouin, R. Rimey, E. A. Collins, and S. Ghosh, "An Application of a Multiple Neural Network Learning System to Industrial Part Inspection," *Proceedings of ISA*, October 1988.

5. R. O. Fox, F. Czerniewjewski, F. Fluet, and E. Mitchell, "Neural Network Machine Vision," *Abstracts of INNS* I (1988), p. 438.

6. K. Marko, J. James, J. Dosdall, and J. Murphy, "Automotive Control System Diagnostics Using Neural Nets for Rapid Pattern Classification of Large Data Sets," *Proceedings of IJCNN* II (June 1989), pp. 13–16.

7. P. Zemany, W. Hogan, E. Real, D. P. Morgan, L. Riek, D. L. Reilly, C. L. Scofield, P. Gouin, and F. Hull, "Experiments in Discrete Utterance Recognition Using Neural Networks," *Proceedings of Second Biennial Acoustics Speech and Signal Processing Conference*, May 1989.

8. E. Collins, S. Ghosh, and C. L. Scofield, "An Application of a Multiple Neural Network Learning System to Emulation of Mortgage Underwriting Judgments," *IEEE International Conference on Neural Networks* II, 1988, pp. 459–66.

9. C. Scofield, E. A. Collins, and S. Ghosh, "Prediction of Mortgage Loan Performance with a Multiple Neural Network Learning System," *Abstracts of INNS* I (1988), p. 439.

10. *DARPA Neural Network Survey Study*, AFCEA, November 1988, pp. 429–43.

11. C. L. Scofield, D. L. Reilly, C. Elbaum, and L. N. Cooper, "Pattern Class Degeneracy in an Unrestricted Storage Density Memory," in *Neural Information Processing Systems*, ed. D. Z. Anderson, (New York: American Institute of Physics, 1985), pp. 674–82.

12. D. L. Reilly, L. N. Cooper, and C. Elbaum, "A Neural Model for Category Learning," *Biological Cybernetics* 45 (1982), pp. 35–41.

13. L. N. Cooper, C. Elbaum, and D. L. Reilly, "Self-Organizing General Pattern Class Separator and Identifier," U.S. Patent No. 4,326,259, awarded April 20, 1982.

14. L. N. Cooper, C. Elbaum, D. L. Reilly, and C. L. Scofield, "Parallel, Multi-Unit Adaptive Nonlinear Pattern Class Separator and Identifier," U.S. Patent No. 4,760,604, awarded July 26, 1988.

15. D. L. Reilly, C. Scofield, C. Elbaum, and L. N. Cooper, "Learning System Architectures Composed of Multiple Learning Modules," *IEEE First International Conference on Neural Networks* II, 1987, pp. 495–503.

20

Predicting Consumer Credit Performance: Can Neural Networks Outperform Traditional Statistical Methods?

Leslie Richeson, Raymond A. Zimmermann, and Kevin Gregory Barnett

INTRODUCTION

Artificial neural networks (ANNs) have largely been the province of computer scientists and cognitive researchers whose primary interests lie in design and development. It is only in the past few years, as potential applications of the technology have emerged, that neural networks have caught the attention of the business community and the popular press. The uses of neural networks are numerous and incredibly diverse. Current applications include pattern recognition, optical character recognition, noise filtering, signal processing, product inspection, mechanical diagnosis, statistical analysis, and planning and forecasting.[1]

This paper presents an application of neural networks that is of interest to both the commercial banking industry and the accounting profession. The authors were guided by two objectives. The first objective was to develop a neural network model to predict consumer credit payment performance. The second objective was to compare the predictive accuracy of the neural network model with that of discriminant analysis.

ARTIFICIAL NEURAL NETWORKS

Neural networks are based on the concept of the brain and central nervous system. By simulating the structure of the nervous system, neural networks are designed to crudely mimic human thought processes and methods of learning. This capacity for learning probably represents the most fundamental distinction between neural networks and traditional computing. Hecht-Nelson defined a neural network as "a computing system made up of a number of simple, highly interconnected processing elements, which processes information by its dynamic response to external inputs."[2]

The human brain is made up of billions of densely interconnected neurons. Each neuron is a "simple microprocessing unit which receives and combines signals from many other neurons through input processes (structures) called dendrites."[1] Synapses are links between neurons that transfer signals between neurons through chemical and electrical processes. Learning occurs through changes in the synaptic connections.

Artificial neural networks are greatly simplified models of the central nervous system. Where the brain has billions of neurons, the most sophisticated neural network contains no more than a few hundred equivalent units. There are also far fewer connectors in the ANN than in a biological system.

Figure 20.1 illustrates the structure of a generic neural network. Processing elements (PE) are the equivalent of neurons in an artificial neural network. Neural networks consist of processing elements arranged in layers linked through interconnectors. A processing element will receive information from other processing elements, then process and relay that information to the next PE.

Figure 20.2 shows the basic structure of a processing element. Processing elements do little more than take a weighted sum of inputs and generate an output signal. The transfer function, a mathematical function that relates input to output, determines the rules that decide whether

Figure 20.1

Structure of a Generic Neural Network

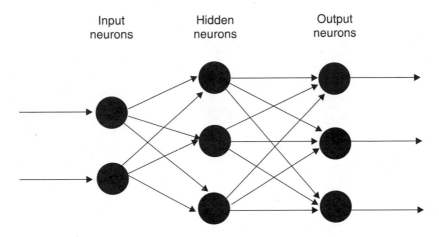

Neurons in a neural network

| Input neurons | Hidden neurons | Output neurons |

Source: Kirrane[3]

the processing element will produce an output signal. Learning rules govern changes in the relative importance of interconnectors to processing elements by continuously adjusting the weight vectors between these elements based on prior inputs. It is the continuous updating and correction of weights that cause the network to learn.

Research Background

Literature discussing the relevant topics being presented is derived from three areas. The first area concerns comparisons of neural network performance with that of traditional statistical methods in financial applications. The second area examines the literature concerning existing neural network applications in the banking industry. And finally, the third area consists of a review of bankruptcy prediction and consumer-oriented models.

Weiss and Kulikowski[4] used four different data sets to compare three learning techniques: machine learning, a statistical method, and neural

Figure 20.2
Basic Structure of a Processing Element

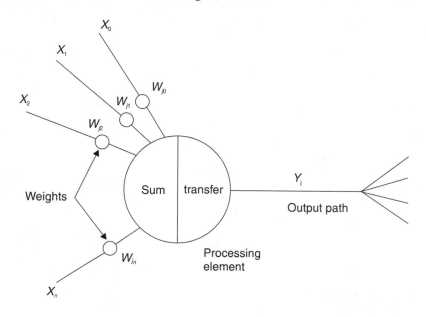

Source: *Neural Computing*[1]

---

networks. They conclude that machine learning slightly outperformed ANNs while ANNS performed better than traditional statistical methods. Other researchers have used ANNs and discriminant analysis in selected financial applications including trading ranges of Treasury bond futures,[5] predicting bond ratings and stock prices,[6] and predicting distressed and healthy firms.[7]

Banks have been one on the leading users of neural network technology for a variety of uses. Mellon Bank Corporation developed a mainframe-based neural network to detect possible cases of credit card fraud. A number of financial institutions and credit card issuers are now using this technology for similar purposes. One credit card issuer reports up to a 50 percent reduction in credit card fraud (Robins, 34–35).[8] A neural network can learn the spending pattern of individual credit card users and then detect suspicious purchasing patterns.[9] Another fruitful area is the development of sophisticated credit-scoring models that attempt to predict future credit performance based on payment histories. The most well-known of these models is the Fair-Isaac model developed by the TRW credit agency. While the use of credit-scoring models is becoming more widespread, their results to date have been mixed because the models rely strictly on past payment performance.[8] Incorporating variables such as income, debt payments, credit history, and demographic characteristics appear to increase their potential for success. Jensen developed a model using income levels, debt payment, and credit history, among other variables.[10]

Credit payment performance and bankruptcy prediction are problems similar in nature. Two of the more common business bankruptcy prediction models are the Altman Z model[11] and the Beaver model,[12] which use selected financial ratios to predict the likelihood of bankruptcy. A less widely studied topic is the development of models that predict consumer credit behavior. One possible explanation for this lack of research is that academic researchers seldom have access to private credit information. Financial information for a publicly traded company is more readily available for developing models of firm bankruptcy prediction. However, two studies have been conducted that predict consumer credit behavior. One was by Jensen[10] and was discussed above. In the other, Clark and McDonald[13] obtained access to the database of a large consumer credit bureau and were able to develop a consumer credit behavior model. There were 23 financial and credit history variables available for use in this study. However, the credit bureau would not disclose to the researchers what the actual variables were, as they were considered proprietary information that could not be disclosed in an academic journal.

There are several advantages in using a mathematically derived credit-scoring model for evaluating credit decisions. Beares notes that the advantages of the credit-scoring approach include (1) increased management control, (2) reduced loan-processing costs, (3) increased legal defensibility, (4) easier training for new lenders, and (5) facilitation of data gathering.[14]

RESEARCH METHODOLOGY

Stein identifies three phases of data preparation for neural network models: data specification and collection, data inspection, and data preprocessing.[15] These issues are considered first, followed by a discussion of the design of the neural network for the prediction of consumer payment performance and network training and testing.

Data Specification

In this phase, the variables relevant to evaluating the performance of consumer loans are identified. Before the development of quantitative models describing the variables that explain consumer credit behavior, bankers developed their own heuristics or rules of thumb to predict the likelihood of credit default based on the five Cs of credit: character, capacity, capital, collateral, and conditions. Bankers and bank regulators consider the presence of these factors essential to making sound consumer credit decisions.

The research model consists of five independent variables, three of which were taken directly from the bank's standard credit application. These variables are the applicant's length of residency (RESTIM), time on the job (JOBTIM), and home ownership (HMEOWN). The applicant's credit history (CREDHIS) is assessed from a review of the borrower's personal credit bureau. The fifth variable was the borrower's debt-to-income ratio (DEBTINC). Information for this variable is derived from both the loan application and credit bureau.

In summary, the independent variables were selected based on two factors. First, variables were chosen that were perceived as significant in the credit-approval process. Most banking scholars, practitioners, and regulators recognize the importance of the five selected variables. Residency, time on the job, and home ownership are measures of stability. These factors, along with credit history, help the banker evaluate the borrower's character and creditworthiness. The debt-to-income ratio is a proxy indicator of cash flow that measure's the borrower's capacity to service his or her obligations as they come due. Second, the information had to be readily retrievable from the credit files. The selected variables are standard items required on most loan applications. Each of the variables chosen for this study were acquired from the reviewed credit files.

Data Collection and Inspection

There is a balance between having enough data and having good data. Lawrence and Andriola recommend a minimum of 100 examples, with 1,000 examples providing better results.[16] A sample of 300 consumer loans was obtained from a local financial institution for purposes of developing the network. Of these, 75 were in default and 225 were paying as agreed. This percentage of defaults (25 percent) is much higher than the actual loss experience of most financial institutions. Most banks typically would have no more than one default for every 100 performing loans. A high percentage of nonperforming loans was used to give the network the opportunity to recognize the characteristics of nonperforming loans.

The data inspection process involves analyzing the data to ensure its usefulness. Much of the data inspection for this project occurred during data collection. In addition, before the data can be used in a neural network, it must be preprocessed by transforming it into a format that can be read by the neural net software. The number of years was rounded for RESTIM and JOBTIM. Retired and unemployed individuals were assigned zero years for time on the job. There were only about three such responses for the entire data set.

The home ownership variable was coded 10 for a yes response and 01 for a no response. A satisfactory credit history from the credit bureau was similarly coded. To qualify for a satisfactory credit history, the applicant had to be current on all credit accounts as of the date of the credit bureau. There could be no delinquency history of greater than 60 days past due, and there could be no indication of prior bankruptcy, judgments, or collection accounts on other debts. The debt-to-income ratio was entered as a percentage to four significant digits. An example would be .372 to indicate a debt-to-income ratio of 37.2 percent. The dependent variable identified the loan as either a performing or nonperforming loan that was charged-off by the bank for lack of payment or due to bankruptcy of the borrower. A loan that was paying as agreed was coded 10 while a nonperforming loan was coded 01.

Network Design

In constructing a neural network model, a number of design factors must be considered. These considerations include the choice of model type (e.g., feedforward or feedbackward), the number of processing elements in each layer, the number of hidden layers, the transfer function and the learning rule. An illustration of the model for this study is presented in Figure 20.3.

The network used in this study is based on a back-propagation design, a common model for neural network applications. Back-propagation in-

Figure 20.3

An Illustration of Model A

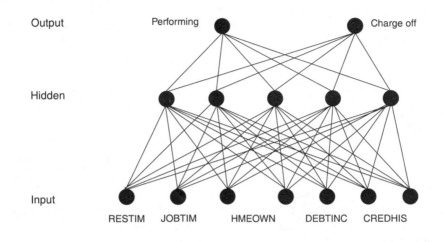

volves two distinct phases. Inputs proceed through the network in the forward pass and generate an output. The difference between the actual and desired output creates an error signal in the backward pass. The error signal is propagated back through the network to teach responses to more closely match the desired output in subsequent iterations.[17]

Hidden layers link the input layer to the output layer. Their function is to discern the patterns within the data, which allows the model to generate predictions. Too few hidden layers tend to require more training iterations and reduce accuracy while too many hidden layers tend towards memorization of the data rather than finding patterns.[2] There are different opinions regarding the appropriate numbers of hidden layers.[18–20] Models using one, two, and three hidden layers were tested.

Several recommendations exist regarding the determination of the number of processing elements in the hidden layer(s). One is a complex formula suggested by the developers of NeuralWare (Zurada, p. 20).[21] Another is recommended by Salchenberger et al.,[19] whereby the number of hidden layer nodes is at least 75 percent of the number of input layer processing elements. Based on this rule, the model incorporated five processing elements in each hidden layer.

Figure 20.4

Sigmoid Function

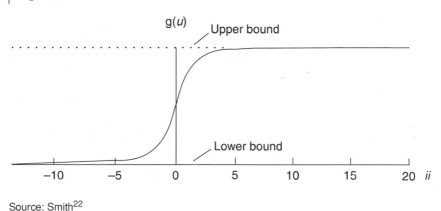

Source: Smith[22]

The transfer function refers to the mathematical method of transform-ing the data. It is the component of a processing element through which the sum is passed to create a net output. Two of the more common transfer functions are the sigmoid function and the hyperbolic tangent function. Models were developed using both. The sigmoid function is shown in Figure 20.4.

A neural network requires a learning rule for updating weight vectors. The delta rule was used to modify the weights, thereby reducing the difference between the desired output and the actual output (i.e., the root mean square error) of a processing element in the models tested.

Network Training and Testing

To assure the integrity of testing, data were partitioned into a training set and a testing set (Hart, 223).[23] The training file consisted of 200 loans while the testing file consisted of 100 loan examples. It is generally desirable to devote as much data to the training file as possible to provide the neural network with more examples from which to learn. The training file consisted of 148 performing loans and 52 nonperforming loans while the testing file included 77 performing loans and 23 loans in default.

Table 20.1

Seven Neural Network Models

Model	Transfer Function	Number of Layers
A	Sigmoid	1
B	Sigmoid	2
C	Sigmoid	3
D	Hyperbolic tangent	1
E	Hyperbolic tangent	2
F	Hyperbolic tangent	3
Training set	Hyperbolic tangent	3

Seven separate models were processed (see Table 20.1). The transfer function and number of hidden layers were varied in each of the models. A model was also tested using the original training data to see how well it could predict the data on which it trained.

Each training session used 25,000 iterations. According to Raghupathi et al.,[20] average error rates tend to decrease and learning capacity increases with successive iterations. The software developer recommends using up to 50,000 iterations before looking at other parameters.[21] More iterations may produce better results but require longer running time, and eventually a point of diminishing returns is reached. The 25,000 iterations represented a good compromise between model development time and model accuracy.

In the initial training and testing phases, models were developed using many of the default parameters in the NeuralWare software. Generally, these default settings failed to produce a model that provided satisfactory results. One problem with back-propagation models is that they sometimes become stuck in a local minimum, and learning ceases. A useful analogy to illustrate the learning process of neural networks is to compare it to a ball rolling downhill. If sufficient momentum is not maintained, the ball will get stuck in small valleys. It can happen that a neural network stops learning because it cannot overcome a "local minimum." Several adjustments can be made to the networks to ensure that learning will continue. These adjustments are similar to providing alternate paths for the ball to allow it to roll all the way downhill. One such adjustment involved increasing the epoch size to two hundred (the number of loans in the training set) to improve learning performance.[21] An epoch is the number of sets of training data presented to the network between weight updates. Also, the convergence threshold was increased from the default setting of 0.0001 to 0.05. This threshold value is used by the network's error instruments as a juncture where the network ceases to learn. Increasing this value tends to help the network learn on "noisy" data where high error rates in the data could cause the network to stop learning at a lower threshold value. In addition, Using Nworks[21] recommends adjusting the learning coefficients to reduce network learning time. The learning coefficients provide a means of updating weights in the multilayer network. When learning rates are too large, the network may never converge. Smaller rates tend to be more stable. In this study, learning coefficients were lowered in all hidden layers and the output layer. Learn counts were also decreased. Initial learning coefficients were held constant through a certain number of iterations determined by the learn count. A reduction in the learn count caused a more rapid change in the learning coefficients.

Implementing changes recommended by the software developer (e.g., changing learning coefficients or convergence thresholds) does not guarantee improved learning or model performance. Changing these parameters does provide a basis for possible enhancement of the network. For further reading on setting and changing parameters, see Vogl et al.[24] Another methodology suggested by Hoptroff[25] and by Curram and Mingers[26] recommends using an independent validation set for training purposes so as to remove the need for fine-tuning the network size and to lessen the required iterations.

RESULTS AND INTERPRETATIONS

Neural Net Results

Model results are listed in Table 20.2. All of the models in the study were able to distinguish performing loans from nonperforming loans. The overall prediction rate of the six models ranged from 76–82 percent. Model E, using two hidden layers and the hyperbolic tangent transfer function, showed the highest overall success rate by correctly predicting 82 of the 100 test loans.

All of the models had a much better rate in correctly predicting performing loans than in determining loans in default. As can be seen in Table 20.2, the models correctly predicted performing credits at a rate

Table 20.2

Neural Network Model Results

Model	Correct Performing (total=77)		Correct Nonperforming (total=23)		Total Correct	
A	67	87.1%	12	52.2%	79	79.9%
B	70	90.7%	11	47.9%	81	81.0%
C	72	93.5%	9	39.2%	81	81.0%
D	74	96.1%	7	30.5%	81	81.0%
E	72	93.5%	10	43.5%	82	82.0%
F	60	77.9%	16	69.9%	76	76.0%
TS*	144	97.3%	15	28.9%	159	79.5%

* Training set: total performing = 148, total nonperforming = 52.

ranging from 87.1 percent to 96.1 percent. The models were considerably less successful in assessing charged-off credits, with ranges from 30.5 percent to 69.6 percent.

It is interesting to note the model only had a predictive accuracy rate of 80 percent when it was tested using the original training data. The model run on the training set was much better at predicting performing loans (97.3 percent) than at evaluating loans in default (28.9 percent).

Discriminant Analysis Results

Linear discriminant analysis was performed on the data set. This statistical tool is useful for predicting categories for dependent variables. Discriminant analysis differs from other statistical methods in that the dependent variable is discrete or categorical rather than continuous. Ragsdale and Stam[27] document a wide array of business uses of discriminant analysis (DA), including the credit-granting decision, bankruptcy prediction, and other accounting/auditing uses. Discriminant analysis is a widely known and used statistical method. For a more in-depth review of discriminant analysis, see Dillon and Goldstein.[28]

Table 20.3

Discriminant Analysis Test Results

Data	Correct Predictions for Performing Loans		Correct Predictions for Nonperforming Loans		Total Correct Predictions	
Test data[*]	50	64.9%	17	73.9%	67	67.0%
Training data[†]	117	49.1%	38	73.1%	155	77.5%

[*] Test data: Total Performing = 77; Total Charge Off = 23.
[†] Training data: Total Performing = 148; Total Charge Off = 52.

In this project, DA classified the dependent variable as either a performing or a nonperforming loan. A summary of the discriminant analysis results is presented in Table 20.3. As with the neural network models, discriminant analysis models were run using both the testing and training data. Usually better results are obtained when a model is tested on the same data it was trained with. Contrary to usual expectations, better results were obtained using the testing data for testing than using the training data for testing. It is also interesting that the discriminant analysis model using the test data better predicted charge-off loan relationships (73.9 percent) than the performing loans (64.9 percent).

Interpretations

The overall prediction rate of 82 percent for the best neural network model was higher than the overall predictive accuracy produced with discriminant analysis (67 percent). Neural network performance in predicting credits that pay as agreed was significantly above that of discriminant analysis (91 percent for ANNs versus 65 percent for DA). However, except for Model F, the neural networks showed considerably less success than discriminant analysis in determining potential charge-off relationships. Most of the neural network models appeared to be taking a "guess" on these credits. Discriminant analysis appears to be better suited to discerning the factors that indicate a potential problem loan.

Table 20.4

Data on Misclassified Nonperforming Loans

Years on Job	Years in Residence	Home Ownership	Debt/Income	Satisfactory Bureau Report
29	6	Yes	18.7%	No
20	30	Yes	34.2%	Yes
6	26	Yes	59.1%	No
3	13	Yes	44.3%	Yes
7	4	No	39.8%	No
2	7	No	37.2%	Yes
2	3	Yes	54.9%	No
10	0	Yes	37.8%	No
15	0	No	28.4%	No
15	2	Yes	21.9%	No

The neural network models appeared to have problems in classifying many of the same credits. In other words, the models consistently classified a number of charge-off loans as performing. A review of the data for 10 of these misclassified charge-off loans is presented in Table 20.4. Although most of these loans contained "red flags" to suggest the possibility of a nonperforming loan, the models categorized each of the loans as performing. Seven of the 10 borrowers had an unsatisfactory credit rating. Six of the 10 borrowers had marginal-to-high debt/income ratios. Loan number two is perhaps the only loan that looks as though it would be satisfactory. While the majority of these loans would appear to be marginal or unacceptable prospects, it is possible that the network trained on enough performing loans with similar data to classify them as performing.

SUMMARY OF FINDINGS AND CONCLUSIONS

As noted earlier, the objectives of this study were twofold: to develop a neural network to predict consumer credit payment performance and to compare the predictive accuracy of the neural network model with that of discriminant analysis.

Seven different models were developed, including one model run on the training data. Overall prediction accuracy ranged from 76–82 percent. The two-hidden-layer, hyperbolic tangent model yielded the best results. The neural network model run on the training data correctly identified about 80 percent of the loans on this data. All of the models except Model F were much better at predicting performing loans than in evaluating loans in default.

Although the overall prediction rate was slightly higher for neural networks than for discriminant analysis, the models achieved less success in correctly evaluating potential default credits. In many respects, the correct evaluation of nonperforming borrowers is a more important barometer of model success for financial institutions than is the correct prediction of paying credits. Failure to identify potential default relationships can have a more severe impact on bank profitability due to the potential loss of principal involved. High loss rates can also cause a financial institution to come under increased scrutiny from bank regulators and can even threaten its survival.

A financial institution or auditor may wish to run data sets on both neural network and discriminant analysis models to incorporate the benefits of both applications. Financial institutions might also consider the use of other statistical methods such as logit regression or random effects logit. Leonard reports a 92 percent prediction rate for logit regression versus 87 percent for discriminant analysis in evaluating whether commercial loans are accepted or declined.[29]

Although neural network and discriminant analysis models have potential commercial applications, it is important to note that this technology will not supplant human judgment in the credit-decision process. The overall success rates of these models does not approach that of most successful lenders. However, these models do have a use as a decision tool in assisting a lender in evaluating potential borrowers. Neural network models help the loan officer function more efficiently by prescreening and eliminating unqualified applicants. The models can also assist the bank manager or auditor in evaluating how well the bank is adhering to its own credit standards. The technology will be most effective when combined with seasoned professional judgment rather than as a replacement for that judgment.

It is a certainty that neural network technology will have a greater impact on our lives in future years. Undoubtedly, financial institutions and accounts will make greater use of the technology as its benefits are realized. It will become increasingly important that financial professionals gain a familiarity with neural networks to take advantage of their benefits and to properly evaluate the impact of this technology on their business and that of their customers.

ENDNOTES

1. *Neural Computing (NeuralWorks Professional II/Plus and NeuralWorks Explorer)*. Pittsburgh: NeuralWare, Inc., 1991.

2. M. Caudill, *Neural Network Primer*, reprinted from issues of *AI Expert*, 1990.

3. D.E. Kirrane, "Machine Learning," *Training and Development Journal*, December, 1990, pp. 24–29.

4. S.M. Weiss and C.A. Kulikowski, *Computer Systems That Learn: Classification and Prediction Methods from Statistics, Neural Nets, Machine Learning and Expert Systems*, California: Morgan Kaufmann Publishers, 1991.

5. W. Walker and M. Devaney. "Enhanching Performance," *Pensions and Investments*, May 3, 1993, pp. 33–35.

6. Y. Yoon, G. Swales, Jr. and T. Margavio, "A Comparison of Discriminate Analysis versus Neural Networks." *Journal of Operational Research Society* 44, no. 1 (1993), pp. 51–60.

7. P.K. Coats and F.L. Fant, "A Neural Network Approach to Forecasting Financial Distress," *Journal of Business Forecasting*, Winter 1991–1992, pp. 9–12.

8. G. Robins, "Credit Scoring: Can Retailers Benefit from Neural Networks?" *Stores*, April 1993, pp. 34–35.

9. A. Classe, "Little Grey Cells," *Accountancy*, May 1993, pp. 67–69.

10. H.L. Jensen, "Using Neural Networks for Credit Scoring," *Managerial Finance*, 1992, pp. 15–26.

11. E.I. Altman, "Financial Ratios, Discriminant Analysis and the Prediction of Corporate Bankruptcy," *Journal of Finance* 23 (1968), pp. 589–609.

12. W.H. Beaver, "Financial Ratios as Predictors of Failure," *Empirical Research in Accounting: Selected Studies, 1996.* Supplement to *The Journal of Accounting Research 4 (1966), pp. 71–111.*

13. Clark and McDonald

14. P.R. Beares, *Consumer Lending*. Washington, DC: American Bankers Association, 1992.

15. R. Stein, "Selecting Data for Neural Networks," *AI Expert*, February 1993, pp. 42–47.

16. J. Lawrence and P. Andriola, "Three-Step Method Evaluates Neural Networks for Your Application." *EDN*, August 6, 1992, pp. 93–100.

17. C.T. Hsieh, "Some Potential Applications of Artificial Neural Systems in Financial Management," *Journal of System Management*, April 1993, pp. 12–15.

18. J. Villiers and E. Barnard, "Backpropagation Neural Nets with One and Two Hidden Layers," *IEEE Transactions on Neural Networks*, January 1992, pp. 136–41.

19. L.M. Salchenberger, E.M. Cinar, and N.A. Lash, "Neural Networks: A New Tool for Predicting Thrift Failures," *Decision Sciences*, July/August 1992, pp. 899–916.

20. W. Raghupathi, L. Schkade, and B.S. Raju, "A Neural Network Application for Bankruptcy Prediction," *IEEE*, 1991, pp. 147–55.

21. J. Zurada, *Introduction to Artificial Neural Systems*. St. Paul, MN: West Publishing Company, 1992.

22. M. Smith, *Neural Networks for Statistical Modeling*. New York: Van Norstrand Reinhold, 1993.

23. A. Hart, "Using Networks for Classification Tasks—Some Experiments on Datasets and Practical Advice," *Journal of the Operational Research Society* 43, no. 3 (1992), pp. 215–26.

24. T.P. Vogl, J.K. Mangis, A.K. Rigler, W.T. Zink, and D.L. Alkon, "Accelerating the Convergence of the Back-Propagation Method," *Biological Cybernetics* 59, 1988, pp. 257–63.

25. R.G. Hoptroff, "The Principles and Practice of Time Series Forecasting and Business Modeling Using Neural Nets," *Neural Computing and Applications* 2 (1993), pp. 59–66.

26. S.P. Curram and J. Mingers, "Neural Networks, Decision Tree Induction and Discriminant Analysis: An Empirical Comparison," *Journal of the Operational Research Society* 45, no. 4 (1994), pp. 440–50.

27. C.T. Ragsdale and A. Stam, "Introducing Discriminant Analysis to the Business Statistics Curriculum," *Decision Sciences*, February 1992, pp. 724–45.

28. W.R. Dillon and M. Goldstein, *Multivariate Analysis: Methods and Applications*. New York: John Wiley, 1984.

29. K.J. Leonard, "Who's Keeping Score? A Credit Scoring Model for Commercial Loan Applications," *Business Credit*, November/December 1993, pp. 8–12.

21

USING NEURAL NETWORKS FOR CREDIT SCORING

Herbert L. Jensen

The development of a credit-scoring model typically costs between $50,000 and $100,000.[1] Yet, 82 percent of banks using expert systems employ them for credit scoring in commercial, consumer, and mortgage loans.[2] The three major credit reporting bureaus in the U.S.—Trans Union, TRW, and CBI—all now market bankruptcy scores as part of their reporting services.

Usually, the model has to be quite complex because institutional lending rules may not be well-enunciated and because different criteria are applied by different lenders.[3] Both the type of loan and the requirements of the lending institution must be considered. In one case, more than 2,000 rules were built into an expert system to aid in the evaluation of commercial loans.

> On one hand, expert system technology has proven highly successful in solving problems where the rules for decision making are clear and the information is reliable. On the other hand, neural network software is now acknowledged as a viable means for reaching

conclusions in situations where explicit decision rules are obscure (or even nonexistent) and information is partially correct.[4]

Neural networks are parallel processors designed after the neural structure of the brain. They are good at pattern recognition but poor at computational tasks. Their main uses, then, are in tasks such as association, evaluation, and pattern recognition. "Predictions of behavior and analysis of large amounts of data are also good applications, such as stock market forecasting and consumer loan analysis."[5]

Two recent studies have shown the applicability of neural network technology to the credit-granting process. The first article demonstrated how an expert system linked to a neural network might be used to predict the outcome of a loan based on 13 variables obtainable from applicant data found on commercial credit reports.[6] This mainframe-based system could identify the input variables having the greatest impact on the loan decision, thus providing the rationale for the decision. Whether or not the model is operational is unknown, as the article only showed two examples of actual loan classifications without presenting any statistics on classification accuracy.

Again in the second article, no data was presented: only the system's design was described.[7] This is a personal computer-based model, which integrates an expert system with a neural network. It uses four financial ratios (quick ratio, debt to net worth, sales to receivables, and pretax profit to net worth) to evaluate a small business's probability of obtaining a loan. According to the author, the analysis of financial data seems quite amenable to neural network reasoning.

CREDIT SCORING

After 20 years of trying to get lenders to understand credit scoring, credit risk prediction using numerical formulas has been increasingly relied upon in the last decade. The concepts, principles, and procedures for developing and implementing a credit-scoring model had been fully developed by the early-1970s.[8] Lending institutions, however, resisted credit-scoring systems because of a reluctance to replace the expertise of loan officers, the known error rates for existing mathematical formulae, and the absence of credit management schooled in quantitative techniques.[9] Some also felt that the credit-granting process was not amenable to an objective, nonpersonal, approach.

> [T]he loan collectability problem is essentially a heuristic classification problem. The objective is to classify a loan, using relatively subjective evaluation criteria rather than scientific process.[10]

Nonetheless, the traditional judgmental procedures used by a loan officer in evaluating a loan application suffer from being inherently subjective, dependent on the officer's past experience and considering the evidence sequentially rather than simultaneously. They are also costly and time-consuming as well as divorced from the grim reality of collection procedures.[11] Lenders' desire for reduced delinquency rates and for greater control over credit policies eventually led them to experiment with credit scoring. They found that credit scoring provided (1) lower processing costs, (2) improved credit control, (3) racially and ethnically nondiscriminatory lending, (4) ease in adjusting credit standards, and (5) faster loan approval decisions.[12] An unexpected consequence was that lending institutions experienced an increase in the number of customers without a corresponding increase in delinquency rates.

The credit application has historically been the prime source of information on the applicant's characteristics. Credit-scoring schemes are developed by using historical loan data to identify the applicant characteristics given on the loan application that significantly differ between paid-off loans and charged-off loans. Consumers form relatively large homogeneous populations, and consumer loans tend to be relatively uniform as to size, terms, collateral, and payment.[13] Indicators of "bad debts" and "good debts" do, however, vary with geographical locations, consumer types, and loan terms.

> The primary purpose of a credit scoring system is to develop an indicator which will help to distinguish between good and undesirable accounts and which relies on statistical techniques rather than subjective judgement.[14]

Selected applicant characteristics are then used as independent variables in a discriminant or multivariate regression analysis that establishes the weights or scores for each characteristic. "The shape, depth, and availability of data play an important role in developing a credit-scoring model."[15] Generally, a large, random sample of known good and bad accounts is used to develop the model based on the actual applicant characteristics at the time the loan was made. These statistical techniques require fairly large samples of good and bad loans to ensure reasonably high predictive accuracy. One typical study of 600 loan applications achieved a 73.7 percent correct classification using an eight-variable formula derived with stepwise regression.[16] Most institutions set cutoff points for automatic acceptance and automatic rejection. "The definition of cutoff levels is quite complex because the scores of good and bad loans usually overlap."[17] The nether region between these two scores is sometimes left to the judgment of a loan officer.

Table 21.1 shows a typical scorecard from the California-based The Fair, Issac Companies. It employees the same sort of applicant characteristics found useful in the United States.[18] This particular rating card, however, was devised for a leading British bank. Successful credit applicants score 200 and over; those who total less have their applications rejected.

Table 21.1

Where You Stand in the Credit Jungle

Own/ Rent	Owns 45	Rents 18	All Other 24		
Years with employer	Under 1 year 15	1–2 years 22	3–9 years 26	10–12 years 29	13 years 36
Credit cards	Card 19	No card 0			
Store account	Yes 36	No 0			
Bank account	Check & savings 50	Current 31	Deposit 32	No account 5	
Occupation	Professional 29	Office staff 25	Production 15	Sales 22	All other 15
Previous account	Unsatisfactory 0	New 55	Satisfactory 87		
Credit bureau	No file 15	Derogatory –33	Satisfactory 24	Three satisfactory 30	

Source: David Bowe, "Secret Scoreboard Reveals How Much You Can Borrow," *Today* [U.K.], August 16, 1989, p. 21.

NEURAL NETWORKS

All neural networks consist of layers of interconnected neurons. A simple neural network has three layers of neurons: input, hidden, and output. The hidden layer forms an internal symbol set to represent concepts. Multiple hidden layers are used to increase the generalization abilities of the network. With the data for this study, the network converged to a solution state faster with two layers than with one.

Neurons process inputs and produce outputs. A connection is the unique line of communication between a sending and a receiving neuron. The connection strength or weight at the input of a neuron controls the strength of the incoming signal. The transfer function defines how the inputs received by a neuron are output. A sigmoid function seems most typical.

> Unlike expert systems, neural networks do not require the user to specify a number of "if–then" rules. The network only requires specific examples of input values along with the corresponding output values. The network determines rules that work for the specific examples.[19]

Interconnected layers of neurons result in a neural network. Through the connection strengths between layers, the network is capable of learning and storing associations. Modifications of connection strengths establish new associations in a manner that emulate rule-like behavior. Connection strengths are modified in response to training sets—lists of facts correctly matching input and outputs.

Back-propagation is a supervised learning scheme wherein feedback of local error signals through the network is used to adjust neurons' connection strengths. Numerical values representing the input half of the fact are presented to the neurons in the input layer of the network. The resulting values produced by the neurons in the network's output layer are compared to the values for the output half of the fact. If they agree, no action is taken. If they differ, the connection strengths in the network are modified to decrease the error.

This process is repeated for every fact in a training set, and the entire training set is run through the network over again until the network produces the correct output for every fact. Training a neural network thus consists of repeatedly presenting related input–output sets so the back-propogation algorithm can incrementally adjust the connection weights for each neuron. The extent to which pattern-matching capacity is developed depends on the size and variety of the training set used.

> Artificial neural networks can modify their behavior in response to their environment. Shown a set of inputs (perhaps with desired outputs), they self-adjust to produce consistent responses. Once trained, a network's response can be, to a degree, insensitive to minor variations in its input. This ability to see through noise and distortion to the pattern that lies within is vital to pattern recognition in the real world.[20]

CREDIT-EVALUATING NETWORKS

The data for this study consists of applicant data identical to that in Table 21.1 on 125 loans. The outcomes of those loans were classified as either delinquent, charged-off, or paid-off. Loans were classified as delinquent if payments had ever been 90 days or more overdue but the loan had eventually been paid in full. Table 21.2 gives the distribution of the applicants' characteristics among the criteria used by the credit-scoring scheme.

The task here is to predict the loan outcomes shown by credit scores in Table 21.3 using a neural network. While the data in this sample can be evaluated using the credit-scoring scheme, there is insufficient data to develop a credit scoring scheme. Moreover, the delinquency rate is only 9.6 percent and the charged-off rate is only 11.2 percent, so the number of loans in these categories would be insufficient to develop a credit-scoring scheme.

This study tackles these two data limitations by building a neural network model using a DOS-based software package called BrainMaker.[21] The authors describe it as "a fully automated non-linear multidimensional regression analysis tool."[22] Practically speaking, it is easy to use, reasonably powerful, and very inexpensive.

The model was straightforward to build. Each of the applicant characteristics given in Table 21.1 was input symbolically. For example, the first input from each loan was one of the three English words: *own, rent,* or *other.* Overall, 24 such descriptors were used. This meant that the neural network's input layer needed 24 neurons.

Table 21.2

Distribution of Characteristics among Applicants

Own/ Rent	Owns 50	Rents 62	All Other 13		
Years with employer	Under 1 year 16	1–2 years 26	3–9 years 31	10–12 years 25	13 years 27
Credit cards	Card 79	No card 46			
Store account	Yes 91	No 34			
Bank account	Check & Savings 9	Current 31	Deposit 32	No account 33	
Occupation	Profes- sional 22	Office staff 29	Production 35	Sales 28	All other 11
Previous account	Unsatis- factory 7	New 37	Satisfactory 81		
Credit bureau	No file 18	Derogatory 28	Satisfactory 46	Three satisfactory 33	

There were three possible outcomes (delinquent, charged-off, or paid-off), so the network's output layer consisted of three neurons. The actual output from the network were 0 to 1 ratings for the three alternatives. All of the outputs for this sample were clearcut, but the network is capable of giving fuzzy set evaluations. This would occur if the output for one loan application were a series of values like 0.32 delinquent, 0.16 charged-off, 0.43 paid-off. This would indicate that this particular case was not similar to those used in the network's training set.

A rule of thumb states that the hidden layer should have half as many neurons as the input and output layers combined. Consequently, this network used two hidden layers with 14 neurons each. Experimentation showed that the network trained faster with two hidden layers than with a single hidden layer.

Table 21.3

Credit Scores and Actual Loan Outcomes

Credit Score	Total Number	Delinquent	Charged-Off	Paid-Off
260 & over	36	1	0	35
220–259	32	2	1	29
180–219	30	4	2	24
179 & under	27	5	11	11
Totals	125	12	14	99

Table 21.4

Neural Network Trained on 75 Applications

	Network		
Sample = 50	Delinquent	Charged-Off	Paid-Off
Paid-off	4	4	35
Delinquent	0	1	1
Charged-off	2	2	1

TEST RESULTS

Once the network was built, it was subjected to two training trials. In the first trial, the data was arranged in random order and the first 75 applications were used to train the network. The remaining 50 applications were then evaluated using the trained network. These results are shown in Table 21.4.

As can be seen in Table 21.4, the network was unable to identify the delinquent loans, incorrectly classified 71.4 percent of the charged-off loans but correctly classified 94.5 percent of the paid-off loans. If delinquent and charged-off are considered as a single "bad" category, then the network misclassified 10 out of the 50 applications in the sample, for an 80 percent success rate. Stated otherwise, the network classified 16 percent of the applications as good when they were bad and classified 4 percent of the applications as bad when they were good. In short, the network favors approving loan applications.

The results of applying the credit-scoring scheme of Table 21.1 to this same sample of 50 loan applications are given in Table 21.5. The credit-scoring scheme misclassified 13 out of the 50 loan applications, yielding a 74 percent success rate. The credit-scoring scheme, however, is more conservative than the neural network in granting credit. Using credit scoring, 8 percent of the applications would have been approved when they were bad loans, and 18 percent of the applications would have been rejected even though they were good loans.

In order to judge the effect of greater diversity in the training set on the network's evaluative ability, the available data was redistributed. In the second trial, the data was rearranged in different random order and the first 100 applications were used to train the network. The remaining 25 applications were then evaluated using the trained network. These results are shown in Table 21.6.

Table 21.5

Classification by Credit Scoring

Sample = 50	Delinquent	Charged-Off	Paid-Off
Accept	4	0	28
Reject	3	6	9

Table 21.6

Neural Network Trained on 100 Applications

	Network		
Sample = 25	Delinquent	Charged-Off	Paid-Off
Paid-off	2	1	18
Delinquent	0	0	2
Charged-off	1	0	1

Table 21.7

Classification by Credit Scoring

Sample = 25	Delinquent	Charged-Off	Paid-Off
Accept	0	0	15
Reject	3	1	6

As can be seen in Table 21.6, the network misclassified 6 of the 25 applications in the sample, for a 76 percent success rate. Classifications of good loans as bad and of bad loans as good were equal, at 12 percent each. The credit-scoring scheme for this sample of 25 applications, as shown in Table 21.7, also misclassified 6 of the 25 applications. In this case, the entire 24 percent misclassification error arose from rejecting good loans.

In summary, the results of this study strongly indicate that building a neural network capable of analyzing the creditworthiness of loan applicants is quite practical and can be done quite easily. The neural network used here was trained on no more than 100 loan applications yet achieved a 75–80 percent success rate. The BrainMaker software used here now retails for $195 U.S. and runs on any IBM-compatible machine. One day's work by an operator familiar with the software package was required to build, train, and test the network. Except for showing a greater bias toward approving weak loan applications, the neural network's loan classification rate was identical to that achieved using a commercial credit-scoring scheme.

ENDNOTES

1. Walter Alexander. "What's the Score?" *ABA Banking Journal,* August 1989, p. 59.

2. Donna M. Thompson and John S. Martin. "Expert Systems in Banking: A Strategy for Success." *PC AI,* May/June 1990, p. 32.

3. Don Baker. "Analyzing Financial Health." *PC AI,* May/June 1990, p. 26.

4. *Ibid.,* p. 24.

5. Mark Lawrence. "BrainMaker from California Scientific Software." *PC AI*, May/June 1990, p. 36.

6. HNC, Inc. "KnowledgeNet." *PC AI*, September/October 1990, pp. 40–43.

7. Baker, pp. 27, 62–64.

8. See Yair E. Orgler. *Analytical Methods in Loan Evaluation* (Lexington, MA: D.C. Health and Company, 1975), Chapter 3.

9. *Ibid.*, p. 51.

10. Gary S. Ribar. "Development of an Audit Expert System." *Expert Systems Review for Business & Accounting*, June 1988, p. 4.

11. Orgler, *Analytical Methods in Loan Evaluation*, p. 33.

12. Frank P. Johnson and Richard D. Johnson. *Commercial Bank Management* (Chicago: Dryden Press, 1985) p. 229.

13. Yair E. Orgler. "A Credit Scoring Model for Commercial Loans," In *Management Science in Banking*. Eds. Kalman J. Cohen and Stephen E. Gibson (Boston: Warren, Gorham & Lamont, 1978), pp. 324–25.

14. Barry J. Savery. "Numerical Point Systems in Credit Screening," In *Developments in Financial Management*. Eds. Thomas W. McRae and Richard Dobbins (Bradford, UK: MCB Publications, 1977), p 40.

15. Orgler, *Analytical Methods in Loan Evaluation*, p. 37.

16. Vincent P. Apilado, Don C. Warner, and Joel J. Dauten. "Evaluative Techniques in Consumer Finance—Experimental Results and Policy Implications for Financial Institutions," *Journal of Financial and Quantitative Analysis*, March 1974, pp. 275–83.

17. Orgler, *Analytical Methods in Loan Evaluation*, p. 45.

18. Robert A. Morris. "Credit Analysis: An O.R. Approach." In *Innovations in Bank Management*, ed. Paul F. Jessup (New York: Holt, Rinehart and Winston, 1969), p. 307.

19. Charles W. Engel and Margaret Cran. "Pattern Classification: A Neural Network Competes with Humans," *PC AI*, May/June 1990, p. 20.

20. Philip D. Wassermann. *Neural Computing: Theory and Practice* (New York: Van Nostrand Reinhold, 1989), p. 2.

21. Available from California Scientific Software, 10141 Evening Star Drive #6, Grass Valley, CA 95945. (916) 477-7481.

22. Lawrence, p. 36.

REFERENCES

Alexander, Walter. "What's the Score?" *ABA Banking Journal,* August 1989, pp. 58, 59, 62, and 63.

Apilado, Vincent P., Don C. Warner, and Joel J. Dauten. "Evaluative Techniques in Consumer Finance—Experimental Results and Policy Implications for Financial Institutions." *Journal of Financial and Quantitative Analysis,* March 1974, pp. 275–83.

Baker, Don. "Analyzing Financial Health." *PC AI,* May/June 1990, pp. 24–27, 62–64.

Engel, Charles W. and Margaret Cran. "Pattern Classification: A Neural Network Competes with Humans." *PC AI,* May/June 1990, pp. 20–23, 61.

HNC, Inc. "Knowledge Net." *PC AI,* September/October 1990, pp. 40–43.

Johnson, Frank P. and Richard D. Johnson. *Commercial Bank Management* (Chicago: Dryden Press, 1985).

Lawrence, Mark. "BrainMaker from California Scientific Software." *PC AI,* May/June 1990, pp. 34–37, 59.

Morris, Robert A. "Credit Analysis: An O.R. Approach." In *Innovations in Bank Management*, ed. Paul F. Jessup (New York: Holt, Rinehart and Winston, 1969), pp. 300–310.

Orgler, Yair E. *Analytical Methods in Loan Evaluation* (Lexington, MA: D.C. Heath and Company, 1975).

"A Credit Scoring Model for Commercial Loans." In *Management Science in Banking*, eds. Kalman J. Cohen and Stephen E. Gibson (Boston: Warren, Gorham & Lamont, 1978), pp. 323–34.

Ribar, Gary S. "Development of an Audit Expert System." *Expert Systems Review for Business & Accounting,* June 1988, pp. 3–8.

Rowe, David. "Secret Scoreboard Reveals How Much You Can Borrow." *Today* [UK], August 16, 1989, p. 21.

Savery, Barry J. "Numerical Point Systems in Credit Screening." In *Developments in Financial Management*, eds. Thomas W. McRae and

Richard Dobbins (Bradford, UK: MCB Publications, 1977), pp. 36–50.

Thompson, Donna M. and John S. Martin. "Expert Systems in Banking: A Strategy for Success." *PC AI*, May/June 1990, pp. 28, 30, 32–33.

Wasserman, Philip D. *Neural Computing: Theory and Practice* (New York: Van Nostrand Reinhold, 1989).

Weingartner, H. Martin. "Concepts and Utilization of Credit-Scoring Techniques." In *Innovations in Bank Management*, ed. Paul F. Jessup (New York: Holt, Rinehart and Winston, 1969), pp. 311–15.

PART V

STOCK MARKET APPLICATIONS

22

ECONOMIC PREDICTION USING NEURAL NETWORKS: THE CASE OF IBM DAILY STOCK RETURNS

Halbert White

INTRODUCTION

The value of neural network modeling techniques in performing complicated pattern recognition and nonlinear forecasting tasks has now been demonstrated across an impressive spectrum of applications. Two particularly interesting recent examples are those of Lapedes and Farber, who apply neural networks to decoding genetic protein sequences[1] and demonstrate that neural networks are capable of decoding deterministic chaos.[2] Given these successes, it is natural to ask whether such techniques can

---

be of use in extracting nonlinear regularities from economic time series. Not surprisingly, especially strong interest attaches to the possibility of decoding previously undetected regularities in asset price movements, such as the minute-to-minute or day-to-day fluctuations of common stock prices. Such regularities, if found, could be the key to great wealth.

Against the optimistic hope that neural network methods can unlock the mysteries of the stock market, is the pessimistic received wisdom (at least among academics) of the "efficient markets hypothesis." In its simplest form, this hypothesis asserts that asset prices follow a random walk.[3] That is, apart from a possible constant expected appreciation (a risk-free return plus a premium for holding a risky asset), the movement of an asset's price is completely unpredictable from publicly available information such as the price and volume history for the asset itself or that of any other asset. (Note that predictability from publicly unavailable [insider] information is not ruled out.) The justification for the absence of predictability is akin to the reason that there are so few $100 bills lying on the ground. Apart from the fact that they are not often dropped, they tend to be picked up very rapidly. The same is held to be true of predictable profit opportunities in asset markets: They are exploited as soon as they arise. In the case of a strongly expected price increase, market participants go long (buy), driving up the price to its expected level, thus quickly wiping out the profit opportunity that existed only moments ago. Given the human and financial resources devoted to the attempt to detect and exploit such opportunities, the efficient markets hypothesis is indeed an attractive one. It also appears to be one of the few well-documented empirical successes of modern economic theory. Numerous studies have found little evidence against the simple efficient markets hypothesis just described, although mixed results have been obtained using some of its more sophisticated variants.[3-6]

Despite the strength of the simple efficient markets hypothesis, it is still only a theory, and any theory can be refuted with appropriate evidence. It may be that techniques capable of finding such evidence have not yet been applied. Furthermore, the theory is realistically mitigated by bounded rationality arguments.[7,8] Such arguments hold that humans are inherently limited in their ability to process information so that efficiency can hold only to the limits of human information processing. If a new technology (such as neural network methods) suddenly becomes available for processing available information, then profit opportunities may arise for the possessor of that technology. The technology effectively allows creation of a form of inside information. However, the efficient markets hypothesis implies that as the new technology becomes publicly available, these advantages will dwindle rapidly and ultimately disappear.

In view of the relative novelty of neural network methods and the implications of bounded rationality, it is at least conceivable that previously undetected regularities exist in historical asset price data and that such regularities may yet persist. The purpose of this chapter is to illustrate how the search for such regularities using neural network methods might proceed, using the case of IBM daily common stock returns as an example. The necessity of dealing with the salient features of economic time series highlights the role to be played by methods of statistical inference and also requires modifications of neural network learning methods that may prove useful in general contexts.

DATA, MODELS, METHODS, AND RESULTS

The target variable of interest in the present study is r_t, the one-day rate of return to holding IBM common stock on day t, as reported in the Center for Research in Security Price's security price data file ("the CRSP file"). The one-day return is defined as $r_t = (p_t - p_{t-1} + d_t)/p_{t-1}$, where p_t is the closing price on day t and d_t is the dividend paid on day t. The one-day return, r_t, is also adjusted for stock splits, if any. Of the available 5,000 days of return data, we select a sample of 1,000 days for training purposes, together with samples of 500 days before and after the training period, which we use for evaluating whatever knowledge our networks have acquired. The training sample covers trading days during the period 1974:II through 1978:I. The evaluation periods cover 1972:II through 1974:I and 1978:II through 1980:I. The training set is depicted in Figure 22.1.

Stated formally, the simple efficient markets hypothesis asserts that $E(r_t \mid I_{t-1}) = r^*$, where $E(r_t \mid I_{t-1})$ denotes the conditional expectation of r_t given publicly available information at time $t-1$, I_{t-1} (formally I_{t-1} is the σ-field generated by publicly available information), and r^* is a constant (which may be unknown) consisting of the risk-free return plus a risk premium. Because I_{t-1} includes the previous IBM price history, the force of the simple efficient markets hypothesis is that this history is of no use in forecasting r_t.

In the economics literature, a standard way of testing this form of the efficient markets hypothesis begins by embedding it as a special case in a linear autoregressive model for asset returns of the form:

Figure 22.1

Training Set

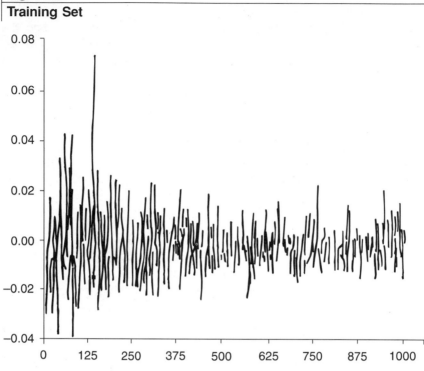

$$r_t = w_0 + w_1 r_{t-1} + \ldots + w_p r_{t-p} + \varepsilon_t \,, \; t = 1, 2, \ldots,$$

where $w = (w_0, w_1, \ldots, w_p)'$ is an unknown column vector of weights, p is a positive integer determining the order of the autoregression, and ε_t is a stochastic error assumed to be such that $E(\varepsilon_t \mid I_{t-1}) = 0$.

The efficient markets hypothesis implies the restriction that $w_1 = \ldots = w_p = 0$. Thus, any empirical evidence that $w_1 \neq 0$ or $w_2 \neq 0 \ldots$ or $w_p \neq 0$ is evidence against the efficient markets hypothesis. On the other hand, empirical evidence that $w_1 = \ldots = w_p = 0$, while not refuting the efficient markets hypothesis, does not confirm it; numerous instances of deterministic nonlinear processes with no linear structure whatsoever are now well known.[9,10] The finding that $w_1 = \ldots = w_p = 0$ is consistent with either the efficient markets hypothesis or the presence of linearly undetectable nonlinear regularities.

An equivalent implication of the simple efficient markets hypothesis that will primarily concern us here is that $var\ r_t = var\ \varepsilon_t$, where var denotes the variance of the indicated random variable. Equivalently, $R^2 \equiv 1 - var\ \varepsilon_t / var\ r_t = 0$ under the simple efficient market hypothesis. Thus, empirical evidence that $R^2 \neq 0$ is evidence against the simple efficient markets hypothesis, while empirical evidence that $R^2 = 0$ is consistent with either the efficient markets hypothesis or the existence of nonlinear structure.

Thus, as a first step, we examine the empirical evidence against the simple efficient markets hypothesis using the linear model posited above. The linear autoregressive model of order p ($AR(p)$ model) corresponds to a very simple two-layer linear feedforward network. Given inputs r_{t-1}, ..., r_{t-p}, the network output is given as $\hat{r}_t = \hat{w}_0 + \hat{w}_1 r_{t-1} + ... + \hat{w}_p r_{t-p}$, where $\hat{w}_0, \hat{w}_1, ..., \hat{w}_p$ are the network weights arrived at by a suitable learning procedure. Our interest then attaches to an empirical estimate of R^2, computed in the standard way[11] as $R^2 \equiv 1 - \hat{var}\ \varepsilon_t / \hat{var}\ r_t$, where:

$$\hat{var}\ \varepsilon_t \equiv n^{-1} \sum_{t=1}^{n} (r_t - \hat{r}_t)^2$$

$$\hat{var}\ r_t \equiv n^{-1} \sum_{t-1}^{n} (r_t - \bar{r})^2$$

$$\bar{r} \equiv n^{-1} \sum_{t=1}^{n} r_t$$

and n is the number of training observations. Here $n = 1{,}000$.

These quantities are readily determined once we have arrived at suitable values for the network weights. A variety of learning procedures is available. A common learning method for linear networks is the delta method:

$$\underline{w}_{t+1} = \underline{w}_t - \eta\ \underline{x}'_t (r_t - \underline{x}_t \underline{w}_t) \quad t = 1, ..., 1{,}000$$

where $\underline{w}_t$ is the $(p + 1) \times 1$ weight vector after presentation of $t - 1$ target/input pairs, η is the learning rate, and $\underline{x}_t$ is the $1 \times (p + 1)$ vector of inputs $\underline{x}_t = (1, r_{t-1}, ..., r_{t-p})$. A major defect of this method is that because of the constant learning rate and the presence of a random component

ε_t in r_t, this method will never converge to a useful set of weight values but is doomed to wander eternally in the netherworld of suboptimality.

A theoretical solution to this problem lies in allowing η to depend on t. As shown by White,[12,13] an optimal choice is $\eta \propto t^{-1}$. Nevertheless, this method yields very slow convergence. A very satisfactory computational solution is to dispense with recursive learning methods altogether and simply apply the method of ordinary least squares (OLS). This gives weights by solving the problem:

$$\min_{\underline{w}} \sum_{t=1}^{n} (r_t - \underline{x_t}\,\underline{w})^2$$

The solution is given analytically as:

$$\underline{w} = (X'X)^{-1}X'r$$

where X is the $1,000 \times (p+1)$ matrix with rows $\underline{x_t}$, r is the $1,000 \times 1$ vector with elements r_t, and the -1 superscript denotes matrix inversion.

Network learning by OLS is unlikely as a biological mechanism; however, our interest is not on learning per se, but on the results of learning. We are interested in the performance of "mature" networks. Furthermore, White[12,13] proves that as $n \to \infty$ both OLS and the delta method with $\eta \propto t^{-1}$ converge stochastically to identical limits. Thus, nothing is lost and much computational effort is saved by using OLS.

When OLS is applied to the linear network with $p = 5$, we obtain $\hat{R}^2 = .0079$. By construction, $\hat{R}^2$ must lie between zero and one. The fact that $\hat{R}^2$ is so low suggests little evidence against the simple efficient markets hypothesis. In fact, under some statistical regularity conditions, $n\hat{R}^2$ is distributed approximately as χ^2_p when $w_1 = ... = w_p = 0$. In our case, $n\hat{R}^2 = 7.9$, so we have evidence against $w_1 = ... = w_p = 0$ at less than the 10 percent level, which is below usual levels considered to be statistically significant. The plot of $\hat{r}_t$ also reveals the virtual absence of any relation between $\hat{r}_t$ and r_t (see Figure 22.2).

Thus, standard methods yield standard conclusions, although nonlinear regularities are not ruled out. To investigate the possibility that neural network methods can detect nonlinear regularities inconsistent with the simple efficient markets hypothesis, we trained a three-layer feed-

Figure 22.2

Training Set

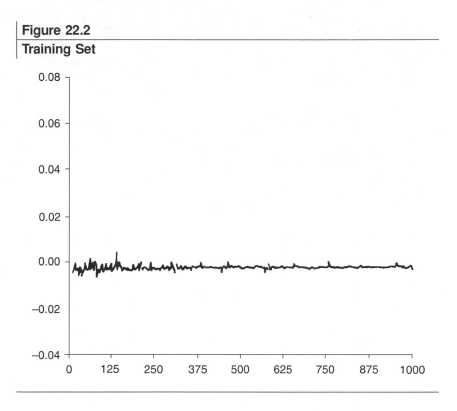

forward network with the same five inputs and five hidden units over the same training period. The choice of five hidden units is not entirely ad hoc, as it represents a compromise between the necessity to include enough hidden units so that at least simple nonlinear regularities can be detected by the network (Lapedes and Farber[2] detected the deterministic chaos of the logistic map using five hidden units with the squashing functions; we use logistic squashes, but performance in that case at least is comparable, even with only three or even two hidden units) and the necessity to avoid including so many hidden units that the network is capable of "memorizing" the entire training sequence. It is our view that this latter requirement is extremely important if one wishes to obtain a network that has any hope at all of being able to generalize adequately in an environment in which the output is not some exact function of the input but that exhibits random variation around some average value determined by the inputs. Recent results in the statistics literature for the method of sieves[14,15] suggest that with a fixed number of inputs and outputs, the number of hidden units should grow only as some small power of the number of training observations. Overelaborate networks are capable of data-mining as enthusiastically as any young graduate student.

The network architecture used in the present exercise is the standard single hidden-layer architecture, with inputs x_t passed to a hidden layer (with full interconnections) and then with hidden layer activations passed to the output unit. Our analysis was conducted with and without a logistic squash at the output; results were comparable, so we discuss the results without an output squash.

The output of this network is given by:

$$\tilde{r}_t = \hat{\beta}_o + \sum_{j=1}^{5} \psi(x_t \hat{\gamma}_j)\hat{\beta}_j \equiv f(x_t, \hat{\theta})$$

where $(\hat{\beta}_o, \hat{\beta}_1, ..., \hat{\beta}_5)$ are a bias and weights from the hidden units to the output and $\hat{\gamma} \equiv (\hat{\gamma}_1, ..., \hat{\gamma}_5)$ are weights from the input units, both after a suitable training procedure; and ψ is the logistic squashing function. The function f summarizes the dependence of the output on the input x_t and the vector of all connection strengths $\hat{\theta}$.

As with the preceding linear network, the efficient markets hypothesis implies that $\tilde{R}^2 \equiv 1 - \hat{var}\,\tilde{\varepsilon}_t / \hat{var}\, r_t$ should be approximately zero, where now $\hat{var}\,\tilde{\varepsilon}_t \equiv n^{-1}\sum_{t=1}^{n}(r_t - \tilde{r}_t)^2$ and $\hat{var}\, r_t = n^{-1}\sum_{t=1}^{n}(r_t - \bar{r})^2$ as before. This result will be associated with values for $\hat{\beta}_1, ..., \hat{\beta}_5$ close to zero, and random values for $\hat{\gamma}_j$. A value for $\tilde{R}^2$ close to zero will reflect the inability of the network to extract nonlinear regularities from the training set.

As with the linear network, a variety of training procedures is available. One popular method is the method of back-propagation.[16,17] In our notation, it can be represented as:

$$\theta_{t+1} = \theta_t - \eta_t \nabla_\theta f(x_t, \theta_t)'(r_t - f(x_t, \theta_t))$$

where θ_t is the vector of all connection strengths after $t - 1$ training observations have been presented, η_t is the learning rate (now explicitly dependent on t), ∇_θ represents the gradient with respect to θ (a row vector), and the other notation is as before.

Back-propagation shares the drawbacks of the delta method previously discussed. With η_t a constant, it fails to converge, while with $\eta_t \propto t^{-1}$, it converges (in theory) to a local minimum. Unfortunately, the random components of r_t renders convergence extremely difficult to obtain in practice. In fact, running on an IBM RT at well over 4 MIPS, convergence was not achieved after 36 hours of computation.

Rather quick convergence was obtained using a variant of the method of nonlinear least squares described in White.[18] The method of nonlinear least squares (NLS) uses standard iterative numerical methods such as Newton-Raphson and Davidson-Fletcher-Powell[19] to solve the problem:

$$\min_{\underline{\theta}} \sum_{t=1}^{n} (r_t - f(\underline{x}_i, \underline{\theta}))^2$$

Under general conditions, both NLS and back-propagation with $\eta_t \propto t^{-1}$ converge stochastically to the same limit, as shown by White.[12,13]

Our nonlinear least-squares method yields connection strengths $\hat{\theta}$ that imply $\tilde{R}^2 = .175$. At least superficially, this is a surprisingly good fit, apparently inconsistent with the efficient markets hypothesis and consistent with the presence of nonlinear regularities. Furthermore, the plot of fitted $(\tilde{r}_t)$ values shows some very impressive hits (see Figure 22.3).

If for the moment we imagine that $\hat{\gamma}$ is given and not the result of an optimization procedure, then $n\tilde{R}^2 = 175$ is χ_5^2 under the simple efficient markets hypothesis, a highly significant result by any standards. Unfortunately, $\hat{\gamma}$ is the result of an optimization procedure, not given a priori. For this reason, $n\tilde{R}^2$ is in fact not χ_5^2; indeed, its distribution is a complicated nonstandard distribution. The present situation is similar to that considered by Davies[20,21] in which certain parameters (γ here) are not identified under the null hypothesis. A theory applicable in the present context has not yet been developed and constitutes an important area for further research.

Given the unknown distribution for $n\tilde{R}^2$, we must be cautious in claiming that the simple efficient markets hypothesis has been statistically refuted. We need further evidence. One way to obtain this evidence is to conduct out-of-sample forecasting experiments. Under the efficient markets hypothesis, the out-of-sample correlation between r_t and $\tilde{r}_t$ (or $\hat{r}_t$) where $\tilde{r}_t$ ($\hat{r}_t$) is computed using weights determined during the training (sample)

Figure 22.3
Training Set

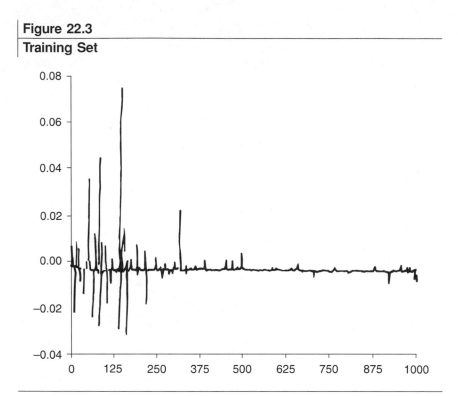

period and inputs from the evaluation (out-of-sample) period, should be close to zero. If, contrary to the simple efficient markets hypothesis, our three-layer network has detected nonlinear structure, we should observe significant positive correlation between r_t and $\tilde{r}_t$.

This exercise was carried out for a postsample period of 500 days and a presample period of 500 days. For the postsample period, we observe a correlation of –.0699; for the presample period, it is .0751. (For comparison, the linear model gives postsample correlation of –.207 and presample correlation of .0996.) Such results do not constitute convincing statistical evidence against the efficient markets hypothesis. The in-sample (training period) results are now seen to be overoptimistic, being either the result of overfitting (random fluctuations recognized incorrectly as nonlinearities) or of learning evanescent features (features that are indeed present during the training period but that subsequently disappear). In either case, the implication is the same: The present neural network is not a money machine.

CONCLUDING REMARKS

Although some might be disappointed by the failure of the simple network considered here to find evidence against the simple efficient markets hypothesis, the present exercise suggests some valuable insights: (1) Finding evidence against efficient markets with such simple networks is not going to be easy; (2) even simple networks are capable of misleadingly overfitting an asset price series with as many as 1,000 observations; (3) on the positive side, such simple networks are capable of extremely rich dynamic behavior, as evidenced by time-series plots of $\tilde{r}_t$ (Figure 22.3).

The present exercise yields practical benefits by fostering the development of computationally efficient methods for obtaining mature networks.[18] It also highlights the role to be played by statistical inference in evaluating the performance of neural network models and in fact suggests some interesting new statistical problems (finding the distribution of $n\tilde{R}^2$). Solution of the latter problem will yield statistical methods for deciding on the inclusion or exclusion of additional hidden units to a given network.

Of course, the scope of the present exercise is very limited; indeed, it is intended primarily as a vehicle for presenting the relevant issues in a relatively uncomplicated setting and for illustrating relevant approaches. Expanding the scope of the search for evidence against the efficient markets hypothesis is a high priority. This can be done by elaborating the network to allow additional inputs (e.g., volume, other stock prices and volume, leading indicators, macroeconomic data, etc.) and by permitting recurrent connections of the sort discussed by Jordan.[22] Any of these elaborations must be supported with massive infusions of data for the training period: The more connections, the greater the danger of overfitting. There may also be useful insights gained by permitting additional network outputs, for example, returns over several different horizons (two-day, three-day, etc.) or prices of other assets over several different horizons, as well as by using within—rather than between—day data.

Another important limitation of the present exercise is that the optimization methods used here are essentially local. Although the final weight values were determined as giving the best performance over a range of different starting values for our iterations, there is no guarantee that a global maximum was found. A global optimization method such as simulated annealing or the genetic algorithm would be preferable.

Finally, it is extremely important to point out that while the method of least squares (equivalently, back-propagation) is adequate for testing the efficient markets hypothesis, it is not necessarily the method that one should use if interest attaches to building a network for market trading purposes. Such networks should be evaluated and trained using profit and loss in dollars from generated trades, not squared forecast error. Learning methods for this criterion are under development by the author.

ENDNOTES

1. A. Lapedes and R. Farber, "Genetic Data Base Analysis with Neural Nets," paper presented to the IEEE Conference on Neural Information Processing System—Natural and Synthetic, 1987.

2. A. Lapedes and R. Farber, "Nonlinear Signal Processing Using Neural Networks," paper presented to the IEEE Conference on Neural Information Processing System—Natural and Synthetic, 1987.

3. B. G. Malkiel, *A Random Walk Down Wall Street* (New York: Norton, 1985).

4. R. T. Baillie, "Econometric Tests of Rationality and Market Efficiency," working paper, Michigan State University Department of Economics.

5. A. Lo and A. C. MacKinley, "Stock Market Prices Do Not Follow Random Walks: Evidence from a Simple Specification Test," *Review of Financial Studies*, 1988.

6. R. J. Shiller, "The Use of Volatility Measures in Assessing Market Efficiency," *Journal of Finance* 36 (1981), pp. 291–304.

7. H. Simon, "A Behavioral Model of Rational Choice," *Quarterly Journal of Economics* 69 (1955), pp. 99–118.

8. H. Simon, *Models of Bounded Rationality* (Cambridge, MA: MIT Press, 1982).

9. H. Sakai and H. Tokumaru, "Autocorrelations of a Certain Chaos," *IEEE Transactions on Acoustics, Speech and Signal Processing* ASSP-28, 1980, pp. 588–90.

10. J. P. Eckmann and D. Ruelle, "Ergodic Theory of Chaos and Strange Attractors," *Review of Modern Physics* 57 (1985), pp. 617–56.

11. H. Theil, *Principles of Econometrics* (New York: Wiley, 1971).

12. H. White, "Some Asymptotic Results for Learning in Single Hidden Layer Feedfoward Network Models," discussion paper 87–13, UCSD Department of Economics, 1987.

13. H. White, "Some Asymptotic Results for Back-Propagation," *Proceedings of the First Annual IEEE Conference on Neural Networks*, 1987.

14. U. Grenander, *Abstract Inference* (New York: Wiley, 1981).

15. S. Geman and C. H. Hwang, "Nonparametric Maximum Likelihood Estimation by the Method of Sieves," *Annals of Statistics* 70 (1982), pp. 401–14.

16. D. B. Parker, "Learning Logic," Office of Technology Licensing, Stanford University, 1982, Invention Report, S81-64, File 1.

17. D. E. Rumelhart, G. E. Hinton, and R. J. Williams, "Learning Internal Representation by Error Propagation," in *Parallel Distributed Processing: Explorations in the Microstructures of Cognition*, vol. 1, eds. D. E. Rumelhart and J. L. McClelland (Cambridge, MA: MIT Press, 1986), pp. 318–62.

18. H. White, "A Performance Comparison for Some On-Line and Off-Line Learning Methods for Single Hidden Layer Feedforward Nets," discussion paper, UCSD Department of Economics, 1988.

19. J. E. Dennis, *Numerical Methods for Unconstrained Optimization and Nonlinear Equations* (Englewood Cliffs, NJ: Prentice Hall, 1983).

20. R. B. Davies, "Hypothesis Testing When a Nuisance Parameter Is Present Only Under the Alternative," *Biometrika* 64 (1977), pp. 247–54.

21. R. B. Davies, "Hypothesis Testing When a Nuisance Parameter Is Present Only Under the Alternative," *Biometrika* 74 (1987), pp. 33–43.

22. M. Jordan, "Serial Order: A Parallel Distributed Processing Approach," UCSD Institute of Cognitive Science Report 86-04, 1986.

23

PREDICTING STOCK PRICE PERFORMANCE: A NEURAL NETWORK APPROACH

Youngohc Yoon and George Swales

INTRODUCTION

The prediction of stock price performance involves the interaction of many variables, making prediction very difficult and complex. Many analysts and investors use financial statement data to assist in projecting future stock price trends. Qualitative information, while not as easily interpreted, may also have an effect on investment value. Both quantitative and qualitative variables help form the basis of investor stock price expectations and, hence, influence investment decision-making.

The multivariate analytical techniques using both quantitative and qualitative variables have been used repeatedly in finance and investments.

© January 1991, IEEE. Reprinted with permission from *Proceedings of the IEEE 24th Annual International Conference of Systems Sciences*, pp.156–62.

However, the performance of multivariate analytical techniques is often less than conclusive and needs to be improved for more accurately forecasting stock price performance.

The neural network (NN) method has demonstrated its capability of addressing problems with a great deal of complexity. The neural network method may be able to enhance an investor's forecasting ability. However, comparatively few applications[1-3] using the neural network have been attempted in finance.

The purpose of this chapter is to apply the neural network approach to a dynamic and complex problem in a business environment and to investigate its ability to predict stock price performance. It also illustrates the methodology of applying this approach and compares its predictive power with that of multiple discriminant analysis (MDA) methods.

LITERATURE REVIEW

Discriminant analysis techniques are used to classify a set of independent variables into two or more mutually exclusive categories. It involves finding a linear combination of independent variables that reflect large differences in group means. The technique can be used for description as well as prediction.

Multivariate analytical techniques have repeatedly been used in finance. Applications are found in corporate finance, banking, and investments. Credit scoring of loan applications to estimate the probability of consumer or corporate default and bond rating analysis are examples of discriminant analysis applications in the finance discipline.

Perhaps the best known, seminal work in the field of multiple discriminant analysis methodology applied to finance was conducted by Edward I. Altman.[4] Altman's use of multiple discriminant analytical techniques focused on predicting corporate bankruptcy. After several early attempts, he settled on a discriminant model that contained five financial ratios used as independent variables. The model could reasonably predict corporate bankruptcy for up to two years in the future. Subsequent development and refinement of the model increased the two-year accuracy level and obtained a 70 percent accuracy rate for up to five years in the future.[5] A drawback of this linear approach is that it classifies some firms as likely to go bankrupt when in actuality they do not.

Since Altman's original work, there have been numerous attempts by researchers to modify and enhance his MDA model. Some of the results have been successful, while others have not. Gentry, Newbold, and Whitford[6] found that adding cash-based-funds flow components to Altman's model provided superior results in predicting financial failure. They also concluded that cash outflow components were more closely related than cash inflow components to corporate failure.

Meyer and Pifer's method of predicting corporate bankruptcy utilized the same financial ratios as were found in Altman's model, but added financial data from more than one period prior to failure to determine a time trend. Collins[7] tested both models, using credit union financial data, and concluded that this approach adds little, if anything, to Altman's model.

Altman and Spivack[8] compared the value line relative financial strength system and the zeta bankruptcy classification methods of predicting corporate bankruptcy. Their findings reveal that, although significant methodological differences do exist, a high correlation between the methods is evident, and that bond systems' scores correlate well with published bond ratings.

Pinches and Mingo[9] and others utilized the MDA concept to classify industrial bonds into multiple categories, using multiple independent variables. Most of these attempts have utilized quantitative financial variables to construct the model with reasonably good predictive results.

Direct applications of the use of the MDA technique to enhance corporate performance are found in the literature. An example is given by La Fleur Corporation, who, finding financial ruin at their doorstep, worked Altman's model backwards to turn the company around.[10]

While most of the development of MDA techniques involves the use of quantitative financial data, other approaches using qualitative assessments have been used in finance. Forecasting how a firm's stock will perform in equity markets, using qualitative variables found in the firm's annual report to the stockholders, has recently been attempted. McConnell, Haslem, and Gibson,[11] and Swales[12] have found that qualitative data can provide additional information to forecast stock price performance.

As indicated above, using qualitative information to supplement an investor's forecasting ability in equity markets is beneficial. This type of information is often overlooked by investors, perhaps due to its subjective, not readily interpreted, form. While these techniques are valuable, other methods using nonlinear approaches may further enhance forecasting ability.

RESEARCH QUESTION

The studies mentioned above have generally indicated that multiple discriminant analysis, as used in the finance discipline, can be a valuable
tool to the decision-maker. It has also been recognized that qualitative
information can enhance an investor's stock price forecasting ability.

Given the above factors, can nonlinear methods significantly enhance
an MDA model's stock price predictive power? Specifically, how does
multiple discriminant analysis compare with the neural network approach
in forecasting stock price performance? Additionally, can the use of neural
network methods enhance the results of a recently published study, which
used multiple discriminant analysis to assess the investor's ability to forecast
stock price performance? These questions are addressed below.

DESCRIPTION OF THE DATA

As mentioned earlier, qualitative variables can provide an often neglected
source of valuable information to the investor. Two independent research
groups presented the results of the multiple discriminant analysis method,
which used qualitative information found in the firm's annual report to the
stockholder.[11,12] The study conducted by Swales serves as the basis for the
application of the neural network approach, which this chapter addresses.

The data used in this study were gathered from two information
sources frequently used by investors: "The Fortune 500" and *Business
Week*'s "Top 1000."[13,14] These sources provide total return (dividends and
stock price appreciation) and market valuation data, respectively, for widely
followed companies. A stock's total return and market valuation are used
by investors and financial analysts as performance measures.

For this experiment, two separate sets of data were gathered. From
the Fortune 500 firms, five industries that offered investors the highest
total returns in each year were selected; the sample consisted of 58 companies. The 10 industries that were reported by *Business Week* to have
the highest market valuations provided the data for the second set; 40
firms were included in this sample. It was felt that, if differences across
the firms could be found among the top industries, then more pronounced
differences were likely to exist in industries further down the line.

We classified the *Fortune* set of companies into two groups according
to their total return. Group 1 provided investors with the highest total
returns in their respective industries; Group 2 provided the lowest returns

in their industries. We classified the *Business Week* set of 40 companies in each of 10 industries into two groups. Again, Group 1 consisted of those firms with the highest market valuations for their industries; Group 2 consisted of those firms with the lowest market valuations for their industries.

For each company in the study, the president's letter to stockholders from the annual report for the period immediately prior to the group selection year was studied. A qualitative content analysis technique was used to classify and tally recurring themes identified by similar words or phrases. An examination of presidents' letters to stockholders identified nine recurring themes commonly addressed in discussion of the future. These themes included reference to confidence, economic factors outside the firm's control, growth, strategic plans, new products, anticipated losses, anticipated gains, long-term optimism, and short-term optimism.

Each letter was read for content and references to the themes noted above. The frequency and percentage of each letter devoted to these themes was then recorded. When the letter did not contain a specific, direct reference to one of the themes, a subjective judgment was made by the researcher as to which, if any, theme should be credited with the phrase or statement. In those instances when reference was not made to a theme(s) in the letter, the data set reflected this finding. The frequency data set was then used for both MDA techniques and NN methods to predict stock price performance.

Content analysis techniques have been widely used in the social sciences.[15] Financial researchers have also applied these techniques to analyze narrative components of financial reports.[11,12,16,17] Refer to McConnell[11] and Swales[12] for further details of the content analysis technique used to analyze the presidents' letters to stockholders.

NEURAL NETWORK MODEL

Design of the Network

The neural network model is structured in a four-layered network, as shown in Figure 23.1: an input layer, two hidden layers, and an output layer. An input unit has excitatory (positive) or inhibitory (negative) connections to a hidden unit in the hidden layer, and a hidden unit has connections to an output unit in the output layer. Therefore, an input unit in this network structure has indirect connections to an output unit.

Figure 23.1

Four-Layered Network

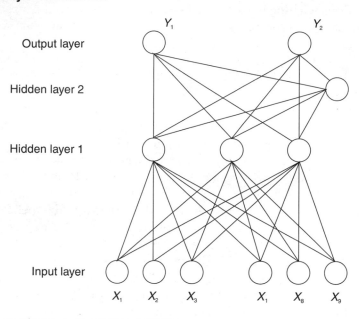

Output layer

Hidden layer 2

Hidden layer 1

Input layer

Y_1 Y_2

X_1 X_2 X_3 X_1 X_8 X_9

Input for the network was a list of nine variables: confidence, economic factors outside the firm's control, growth, strategic gains, new products, anticipated loss, anticipated gain, long-term optimism, and short-term optimism. Output was a classification of two patterns: a firm whose stock price performed well and a firm whose stock price performed poorly. In a network, each input parameter is represented in an input unit. Therefore, the network has the nine input units in the input layer and the two output units in the output layer. The number of hidden units necessary to accurately predict the stock price performance was determined empirically.

The network for the prediction of stock price performance uses the following nine input ($X_1 - X_9$) and two output ($Y_1 - Y_2$) parameters.

Input Parameters

X_1: Confidence

X_2: Economic factor

Output Parameters

Y_1: Well-performing firms

Y_2: Poorly performing firms

Input Parameters	Output Parameters
X_3: Growth	
X_4: Strategic plans	
X_5: New products	
X_6: Anticipated loss	
X_7: Anticipated gains	
X_8: Long-term optimism	
X_9: Short-term optimism	

Learning Process

Once a network structure was developed, a set of initial weights was assigned at random. Then, the back-propagation learning algorithm (BPLA)[18] was used with the *Fortune* set to estimate the weights of the feedforward network. In this algorithm, the input vector with nine input values was assigned as the activation vector of an input layer, propagating forward to the upper layer as the product of weights on the interconnections and the activation values. A sigmoid function in equation (1) was used to compute the activation value of a unit, A_j, on the upper layer:

$$A_j^{(L)} = \cfrac{1}{1 + Exp\left(\sum_{i=0}^{n} W_{ji} A_i^{(L-1)} - \theta_j^{(L)}\right)}$$

(1)

If the upper layer is not an output layer, its activation vector propagates forward to the higher layer in a network in the same manner. The superscripts L and $L - 1$ represent an upper and lower layer, respectively. If the upper layer is an output layer, an activation value of each output unit is compared to the desired one, and the error is measured according to:

$$E = \frac{1}{2} \sum_{j=0}^{n} (D_j - A_j)^2$$

(2)

The learning algorithm iteratively modifies the set of weights in order to reduce this error. Thus, BPLA is a gradient descent algorithm in which weights in the network are iteratively modified to minimize the overall mean square error between desired and actual output values for all output units over all input patterns. The amount the weights are to be adjusted for each input pattern is determined by the derivative of the error function in equation (2) with respect to the weight as follows:

$$\Delta W_{ji} \propto -\frac{\partial E}{\partial W_{ji}}$$
(3)

This derivative yields the error signal:

$$\delta_j = (D_j - A_j)A_j(1 - A_j)$$
(4)

for an output unit, and:

$$\delta_j = A_j(1 - A_j)\sum_{k=0}^{n} \delta_k W_{kj}$$
(5)

for hidden units.

Finally, the connection weight between the jth unit in the Lth layer and the ith unit in the $L - 1$st layer is modified according to:

$$\Delta W_{ji} = \alpha \delta_j^{(L)} A_i^{(L-1)}$$
(6)

where δ_j is defined above. A_i is the activation values of the ith unit, and α is the learning rate, which is used to control the speed of the training process. For further details and discussions of BPLA, see Rumelhart.[18] In this experiment, the initial training data consisted of 58 cases in the *Fortune* set. A small learning rate of $\alpha = 0.1$ was used. The experiment was conducted on a VAX 11/750 using the C programming language.

RESULTS

The performance of the trained network was tested with the *Business Week* set, which contains 40 cases. In the first experiment, the effect of varying the number of hidden units in a four-layered network was tested. The result of this experiment is represented in Figure 23.2. In a four-layered

Figure 23.2

Effect on Performance of Varying the Number of Hidden Units in a Four-Layered Network

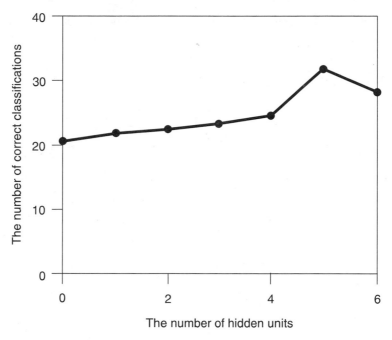

network, performance improved as the number of hidden units increased up to a certain point. This supports previous findings on the importance of the hidden layer for the different applications.[19,20] The best performance was achieved by a network with four hidden units on the first hidden layer and one hidden unit on the second hidden layer. Increasing the number of hidden units beyond this point produced no further improvement but impaired the network's performance.

The performance of the NN model was also compared with that of MDA. Table 23.1 summarizes the result of this experiment. The report includes the performance of MDA and four-layered network on a training data set, as well as a testing data set, to demonstrate the important aspects of this study. The value indicates that MDA resulted in a 74 percent mean posterior membership probability for the training set: 21 of the 29 companies

Table 23.1

Performance of the MDA and Four-Layered Network on the Training and Testing Data

Models	Training Data, Percent			Testing Data, Percent		
	Group 1	Group 2	Mean	Group 1	Group 2	Mean
MDA	72	76	74	70	60	65
Four-layer	86	96	91	90	65	77.5

were correctly classified into Group 1, while 22 of the 29 companies were correctly classified into Group 2. However, during the testing phase, the model yielded only an overall 65 percent success rate for the testing data set: 14 and 12 of the 20 companies were correctly classified into Group 1 and 2, respectively.

The four-layered network correctly classified 91 percent of the mean training data and appropriately predicted 77.5 percent of the mean testing data: 18 of 20 companies were correctly classified into Group 1, whereas 13 of 20 companies were correctly classified into Group 2. During the training phase, the MDA model provided better predictive capability for firms in the lower performance category than for firms in the higher performance category. However, during the testing phase, all models demonstrated better predictive capability for firms in the higher performance category.

This study shows that the mean success rate during the testing phase for the four-layered network was 77.5 percent as compared with 65 percent for the MDA technique. This result shows that a NN method significantly enhanced the MDA model's stock price predictive power. Dutta and Shekhar[1] also reported better performance in rating bonds by the NN approach than by the regression method. The higher performance of the four-layered NN model indicates that this nonlinear technique with hidden units in the network was a more appropriate method to use to forecast stock price performance than the multiple discriminant analysis method.

However, the NN approach demonstrates a limitation. In general, MDA is useful for both descriptions and predictions, since it can explain the characteristics of each group and the significance of each input parameter. In the NN model, it is a difficult task to analyze the characteristics of each group and the importance of input parameters in a NN model due to the hidden units employed in the network. The hidden unit is useful to extract the high-order mapping function between output and input; however, it makes separating the contribution of each input parameter to the output value very difficult.

CONCLUDING REMARKS

The study demonstrated that the neural network approach is capable of learning a function that maps input to output and encoding it in the magnitudes of the weights in the network's connection. The number of hidden units employed in the network contributed to its viability. The increase in the number of hidden units resulted in higher performance up to a certain point. However, additional hidden units beyond the point impaired the model's performance. Comparison of the NN technique with the MDA approach indicated that the NN approach can significantly improve the predictability of stock price performance.

While some limitations of this approach were noted, it is evident that its use can improve an investor's decision-making capability. Further research into the application of neural network techniques, using both quantitative and qualitative data, is suggested and encouraged.

ENDNOTES

1. S. Dutta and S. Shekhar, "Bond Rating: A Non-Conservative Application of Neural Networks," *Proceedings of the IEEE International Conference on Neural Networks* 2 (1988), pp. 443–50.

2. K. Kamijo and T. Tanigawa, "Stock Price Pattern Recognition: A Recurrent Network Approach," *Proceedings of the International Joint Conference on Neural Networks* 1 (1990), pp. 215–22.

3. T. Kimoto, K. Asakawa, M. Yoda, and M. Takeoka, "Stock Market Prediction System with Modular Neural Networks," *Proceedings of the International Joint Conference on Neural Networks* 1 (1990), pp. 1–6.

4. E. L. Altman, "Financial Ratios, Discriminant Analysis and the Prediction of Corporate Bankruptcy," *The Journal of Finance*, September 1968, pp. 589–609.

5. E. L. Altman, R. G. Haldeman, and P. Narayanan, "Zeta Analysis: A New Model to Identify Bankruptcy Risk of Corporations," *Journal of Banking and Finance*, June 1977, pp. 29–54.

6. J. A. Gentry, P. Newbold, and D. T. Whitford, "Predicting Bankruptcy: If Cash Flow's Not the Bottom Line, What Is?" *Financial Analysts Journal*, September–October 1985, pp. 47–56.

7. R. A. Collins, "An Empirical Comparison of Bankruptcy Prediction Models," *Financial Management*, Summer 1980, pp. 52–56.

8. E. L. Altman and J. Spivack, "Predicting Bankruptcy: The Value Line Relative Financial Strength System vs. the Zeta Bankruptcy Classification Approach," *Financial Analysts Journal*, November-December 1983, pp. 60–67.

9. G. E. Pinches and K. A. Mingo, "A Multivariate Analysis of Industrial Bond Ratings," *Journal of Finance*, March 1977, pp. 1–8.

10. M. Ball, "Z Factor: Rescue by the Numbers," *Inc.*, December 1980, pp. 45–48.

11. D. McConnell, J. A. Haslem, and V. R. Gibson, "The President's Letter to Stockholders: A New Look," *Financial Analysts Journal*, September-October 1986, pp. 66–70.

12 G. S. Swales, Jr., "Another Look at the President's Letter to Stockholders," *Financial Analysts Journal*, March–April 1988, pp. 71–73.

13. "The Fortune 500," *Fortune*, April 30, 1984; April 29, 1985; April 28, 1986.

14. "The Top 1000: America's Most Valuable Companies," *Business Week*, April 18, 1986.

15. B. Berlson, "Content Analysis in Communication Research" (New York: Hafner Publishing Company, 1971).

16. E. H. Bowman, "Content Analysis of Annual Reports for Corporation Strategy and Risk," *Interfaces*, January/February 1984, pp. 61–71.

17. K. B. Frazier, R. W. Ingram, and B. M. Tennyson, "A Methodology for the Analysis of Narrative Accounting Disclosures," *Journal of Accounting Research*, Spring 1984, pp. 318–31.

18. D. E. Rumelhart, G. E. Hinton, and R. J. Williams, "Learning Internal Representations by Error Propagation," in *Parallel Distributed Processing: Exploration in the Microstructure of Cognition*, eds. D. E. Rumelhart and J. L. McClelland. Cambridge, MA: MIT Press, pp. 318–62.

19. R. P. Gorman and T. J. Sejnowski, "Analysis of Hidden Units in a Layered Network Trained to Classify Sonar Targets," *Neural Networks* 1 (1988), pp. 75–89.

20. Y. Yoon, R. W. Brobst, P. R. Bergstresser, and L. L. Peterson, "A Desktop Neural Network for Dermatology Diagnosis," *Journal of Neural Network Computing* 1 (Summer 1989), pp. 43–52.

24

STOCK MARKET PREDICTION SYSTEM WITH MODULAR NEURAL NETWORKS

Takashi Kimoto, Kazuo Asakawa,
Morio Yoda, and Masakazu Takeoka

INTRODUCTION

Modeling functions of neural networks are being applied to a widely expanding range of applications in addition to the traditional areas such as pattern recognition and control. Its nonlinear learning and smooth interpolation capabilities give the neural network an edge over standard computers and expert systems for solving certain problems.

Accurate stock market prediction is one such problem. Several mathematical models have been developed, but the results have been disappointing. We chose this application as a means to check whether neural networks could produce a successful model in which their generalization capabilities could be used for stock market prediction.

Fujitsu and Nikko Securities are working together to develop a TOPIX buying and selling prediction system. The input consists of several technical and economic indexes. In our system, several modular neural networks learned the relationships between the past technical and economic indexes and the timing for when to buy and sell. A prediction system made up of modular neural networks was found to be accurate. Simulation of buying and selling stocks using the prediction system showed an excellent profit. Stock price fluctuation factors could be extracted by analyzing the networks.

ARCHITECTURE

System Overview

The prediction system is made up of several neural networks that learned the relationships between various technical and economical indexes and the timing for when to buy and sell stocks. The goal is to predict the best time to buy and sell for one month in the future.

TOPIX is a weighted average of market prices of all stocks listed on the First Section of the Tokyo Stock Exchange. It is weighted by the number of stocks issued for each company. Its use is similar to the Dow-Jones average.

Figure 24.1 shows the basic architecture of the prediction system. It converts the technical indexes and economic indexes into a space pattern to input to the neural networks. The timing for when to buy and sell is a weighted sum of the weekly returns. The input indexes and teaching data are discussed in detail below.

Network Architecture

Network Model. Figure 24.2 shows the basic network architecture used for the prediction system. It consists of three layers: the input layer, the hidden layer, and the output layer. The three layers are completely connected to form a hierarchical network.

Each unit in the network receives input from low-level units and performs weighted addition to determine the output. A standard sigmoid function is used as the output function. The output is analog in the [0,1] section.

Figure 24.1
Basic Architecture of Prediction System

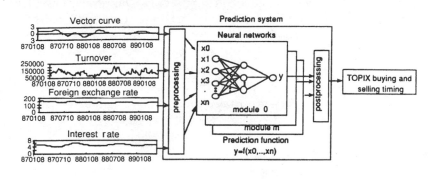

Figure 24.2
Neural Network Model

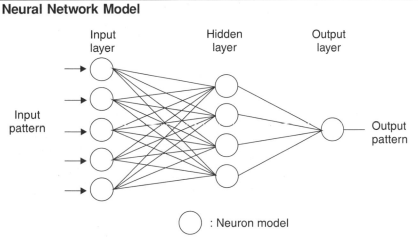

High-Speed Learning Algorithm. The error back-propagation method proposed by Rumelhart[1] is a representative learning rule for hierarchical networks. For high-speed learning with a large volume of data, we developed a new high-speed learning method called supplementary learning.[2]

Supplementary learning, based on error back-propagation, automatically schedules pattern presentation and changes learning constants.

In supplementary learning, the weights are updated according to the sum of the error signals after presentation of all learning data. Before learning, tolerances are defined for all output units. During learning, errors are back-propagated only for the learning data for which the errors of output units exceed the tolerance. Pattern presentation is automatically scheduled. This can reduce the amount of calculation for error back-propagation.

As learning progresses, learning data for which tolerances are exceeded are reduced. This also reduces the calculation load because of the decreased amount of data that needs error back-propagation. High-speed learning is thus available even with a large amount of data.

Supplementary learning allows the automatic change of learning constants, depending on the amount of learning data. As the amount of learning data changes and learning progresses, the learning constants are automatically updated. This eliminates the need for changing learning parameters depending on the amount of learning data.

With supplementary learning, the weight factor is updated as follows:

$$\Delta w(t) = (\varepsilon / \text{learning \_ patterns})\, \partial E / \partial W + \alpha \Delta w(t-1)$$

where

    ε: learning rate.
    α: momentum.
    learning _ patterns: number of learning data items that require
      error back-propagation.

The value of ε is divided by the number of learning data items that actually require error back-propagation. The required learning rate is automatically reduced when the amount of learning data increases. This allows use of the constants ε regardless of the amount of data.

As learning progresses, the amount of remaining learning data decreases. This automatically increases the learning rate. Using this automatic control function of the learning constants means that there is no need to change the constants ($\varepsilon = 4.0$, $\alpha = 0.8$) throughout simulation and that high-speed learning can be achieved by supplementary learning.

Learning Data

Data Selection. We believe stock prices are determined by time-space patterns of economic indexes such as foreign exchange rates and interest rates and of technical indexes such as vector curves and turnover. The prediction system uses a moving average of weekly average data of each index for minimizing influence due to random walk. Table 24.1 lists some of the technical and economic indexes used. The time–space patterns of the indexes were converted into space patterns. The converted indexes are analog values in the [0,1] section.

Teaching Data. The timing for when to buy and sell is indicated as an analog value in the [0,1] section in one output unit. The timing for when to buy and sell used as teaching data is weighted sum of weekly returns. When the TOPIX weekly return is r_i, teaching data $r_N(t)$ is defined as:

$$r_t = \ln \left(\text{TOPIX}(t) / \text{TOPIX} \ (t-1) \right)$$

TOPIX (*t*): TOPIX average at week *t*

$$r_N(t) = \sum_i \varphi^i \, r_{t+i}$$

φ : *Weight*

Preprocessing

Input indexes converted into space patterns and teaching data are often remarkably irregular. Such data is preprocessed by log or error functions to make them as regular as possible. It is then processed by a normalization function that normalizes the [0,1] section, correcting for the irregular data distribution.

Table 24.1

Input Indexes

1. Vector curve
2. Turnover
3. Interest rate
4. Foreign exchange rate
5. New York Dow-Jones average
6. Others

Learning Control

In the TOPIX prediction system, we developed new learning control. The system automatically controls learning iterations by referring to test data errors, thereby preventing overlearning. The learning control allows two-thirds of data in the learning period to be learned and uses the rest as test data in the prediction system. The test data is evaluation data for which only forward processing is done during learning, to calculate an error but not to back-propagate it.

Our learning control is done in two steps. In the first step, learning is done for 5,000 iterations, and errors against test data are recorded. In the second step, the number of learning iterations where learning in the first step suggests a minimum error against the test data is determined, and relearning is done that number of iterations. This prevents overlearning and acquires a prediction model involving learning a moderate number of times. In the second step, learning is done for at least 1,000 iterations.

Moving Simulation

For prediction of an economic system, such as stock prices, in which the prediction rules are changing continuously, learning and prediction must follow the changes.

We developed a prediction method called moving simulation. In this system, prediction is done by simulation while moving the objective learning and prediction periods. The moving simulation predicts as follows.

As shown in Figure 24.3, the system learns data for the past m months, then predicts for the next l months. The system advances while repeating this.

RESULT OF SIMULATIONS

Prediction Simulation

We verified the accuracy of the prediction system by simulating prediction of the timing for when to buy and sell. We used historical data of stock prices, technical indexes, and economic indexes.

The TOPIX prediction system improves its prediction accuracy by averaging prediction results of modular networks that learn for different learning data items. Four independent modular networks learn for four

Figure 24.3
Moving Simulation

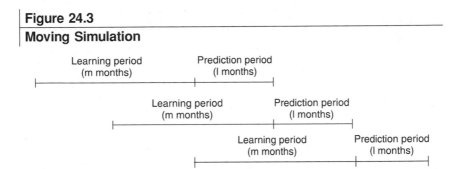

types of different learning data. Moving simulation is used with L as one month. The average of prediction outputs from these networks became the prediction output from the system. Prediction was thus repeated by moving simulation for each month to verify accuracy. Prediction was done for 33 months, from January 1987 to September 1989.

Table 24.2 shows the correlation coefficient between the predictions and teaching data and those of individual networks and the prediction system. The prediction system uses the average of the predictions of each network. Thus, the prediction system could obtain a greater correlation coefficient for teaching data than could be obtained with neural network prediction.

Simulation for Buying and Selling Simulation

To verify the effectiveness of the prediction system, a simulation of buying and selling of stock was done. Buying and selling according to the prediction system made a greater profit than the buying and holding.

Buying and selling was simulated by the one-point buying and selling strategy, so performance could be clearly evaluated. One-point buying and selling means that all available money is used to buy stocks and means all stocks held are sold at single points in time. In the prediction system, an output of 0.5 or more indicates buy, and an output less than an 0.5 indicates sell. Signals are intensified as they get close to 0 or 1.

The buying and selling simulation considered "buy" to be an output above some threshold and "sell" to be below some threshold. Figure 24.4 shows an example of the simulation results. In the upper diagram, the buy-and-hold performance (that is, the actual TOPIX) is shown as dotted

Table 24.2

Correlation Coefficient

Network 1	0.435
Network 2	0.458
Network 3	0.414
Network 4	0.457
System	0.527

Figure 24.4

Performance of the Prediction System

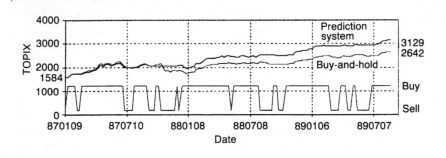

lines, while the prediction system's performance is shown as solid lines. The TOPIX index of January 1987 was considered as 1.00; it was 1.67 by buy-and-hold at the end of September 1989. It was 1.98 by the buying and selling operation according to the prediction system. Use of the system showed an excellent profit.

ANALYSIS

Comparison with Multiple Regression Analysis

The timing for when to buy and sell stocks is not linear, so statistical methods are not effective for creating a model. We compared modeling with the neural network and with multiple regression analysis. Weekly learning data from January 1985 to September 1989 was used for modeling. Since the objectives of this test were comparison of learning capabilities and internal analysis of the network after learning, the network learned 100,000 iterations.

The hierarchical network that had five units of hidden layers learned the relationships between various economic and technical indexes and the timing for when to buy and sell. The neural network learned the data well enough to show a very high correlation coefficient; the multiple regression analysis showed a lower correlation coefficient. This shows our method is more effective in this case. Table 24.3 shows the correlation coefficient produced by each method. The neural network produced a much higher correlation coefficient than multiple regression

Extraction of Rule

The neural network that learned from January 1985 to September 1989 was analyzed to extract information on stock prices stored during that period.

Cluster analysis is often used to analyze internal representation of a hierarchical neural network.[3,4] In 1987, stock prices fluctuated greatly. The hidden layer outputs were analyzed to cluster learning data. The cluster analysis was applied to the output values in the [0,1] sections of the five units of hidden layers. Clustering was done with an intercluster distance determined as Euclidian, and the clusters were integrated hierarchically by the complete linkage method. Figure 24.5 shows the cluster analysis

Table 24.3
Comparison of Multiple Regression Analysis and Neural Network

	Correlation Coefficient with Teaching Data
Multiple regression analysis	0.543
Neural network	0.991

Figure 24.5
Cluster Analysis Results from 1987

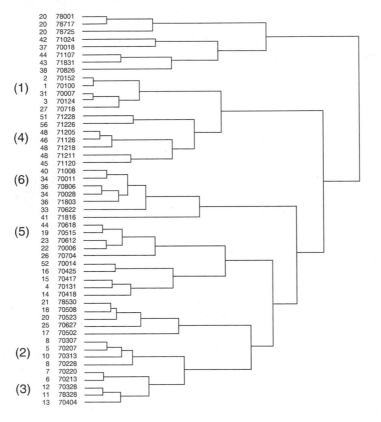

results of the hidden layers in 1987. It indicates that bull, bear, and stable markets each generate different clusters.

From cluster analysis, characteristics common to data that belong to individual clusters were extracted by analyzing the learning data. Figure 24.6 shows the relationships between TOPIX weekly data and six types of clusters in 1987.

This chapter analyzes the factors for the representative bull (clusters (2) and (3)) and bear (cluster [6]) markets in 1987 as follows.

Figure 24.6

TOPIX in 1987

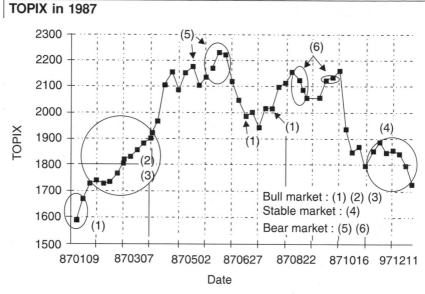

Data (2) and (3) belong to different clusters but have similar characteristics. Figure 24.7 shows learning data corresponding to clusters (2)
and (3). The horizontal axis shows some of the indexes of the neural
network. The vertical axis show the value of each index. For example,
the New York Dow-Jones average is low when it is close to 0 and is
high when close to 1.

This diagram suggests that the vector curve in the bull market during
February to the beginning of April in 1987 was high enough to indicate
a high-price zone. At the same time, however, the high turnover kept
the market going up. Also, the low interest rates and high New York
Dow-Jones average helped push up stock prices.

Figure 24.8 shows the learning data corresponding to (6) in Figure
24.6. It is obvious that the high interest rate pulled prices down.

Part of the learning data in 1987 was analyzed. It was proved that
the causes of stock price fluctuation could be analyzed by extracting the
characteristics common to the learning data in the clusters obtained by
cluster analysis of the neural network.

Figure 24.7

Input Indexes for Bull Market (2) (3)

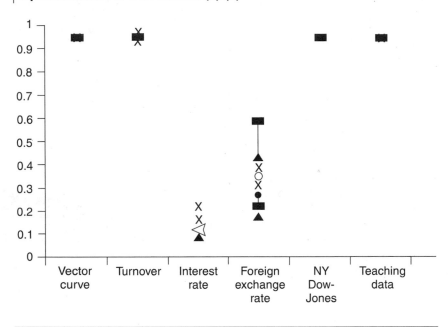

FURTHER RESEARCH

The following subjects will be studied.

❖ Using the system for actual stock trading.

> The current prediction system uses future returns to generate teaching data. A system in which teaching data is generated in combination with a statistical method must be developed.

❖ Adaptation of network model that has regressive connection and self-looping.

> The current prediction system requires much simulation to determine moving average. Automatic learning of individual sections requires building up a prediction system consisting of network models to fit to time-space processing.

Figure 24.8

Learning Data in Bear Market (6)

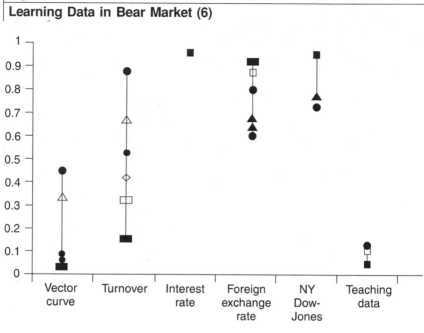

SUMMARY

This chapter has discussed a prediction system that advises the timing for when to buy and sell stocks. The prediction system made an excellent profit in a simulation exercise. The internal representation also was discussed, and the rules of stock price fluctuation were extracted by cluster analysis.

For developing the prediction system, Nikko Securities offered investment technology and know-how of the stock market and Fujitsu offered its neural network technology. Fujitsu and Nikko Securities are proceeding further to build up more accurate economic prediction systems.

ENDNOTES

1. D. E. Rumelhart et al., *Parallel Distributed Processing*, vol. 1. Cambridge, MA.: MIT Press, 1986.

2. R. Masuoka et al., "A Study on Supplementary Learning Algorithm in Back Propagation," *JSAI*, 1989, pp. 213–17.

3. T. J. Sejnowski and C. R. Rosenberg, "Parallel Networks that Learn to Pronounce English Text," *Complex Systems* 1 (1987).

4. R. Paul Gorman and T. J. Sejnowski, "Analysis of Hidden Units in a Layered Network Trained to Classify Sonar Targets," *Neural Networks* 1, no. 1 (1988), pp. 75–90.

25

TWO MULTILAYER PERCEPTRON TRAINING STRATEGIES FOR LOW-FREQUENCY S&P 500 PREDICTION

Ypke Hiemstra and Christian Haefke

SECTION I. INTRODUCTION

Finance research suggests that monthly, quarterly, and annual excess returns are to some extent predictable assuming a linear model specification. Only marginal attention has been paid to possible nonlinearities in the return generating process. Renshaw (1993) investigates the impact of a number of variables on the annual return of the S&P Composite Stock Index, and claims significant nonlinearity. This chapter compares ordinary least squares regression (OLS) with two MLP training strategies to predict the quarterly excess return on the S&P500. The motivation to consider multilayer perceptrons (MLPs) to model the return-generating process is their universal approximation capability (Hornik, Stinchcombe, White 1989), and MLPs are robust estimators when distributions are non-Gaussian (Lippmann 1987). Hiemstra (1996) trains MLPs by back-propagation, varying the number of hidden nodes and applying early stopping (Weigend et al. 1990). We extend this classical approach by considering an alternative way to train MLPs and by including a formal test of whether the mean squared errors of the various models differ significantly. The additional strategy that we consider seeks to minimize the in-sample error of MLPs with varying numbers of hidden nodes, using the Polak-Ribière conjugated gradient (PRCG) algorithm and selects an MLP of particular complexity using an estimate of prediction risk.

In Section II, we discuss excess return prediction and input selection. Section III discusses the generation of out-of-sample predictions. Section IV discusses the two MLP training strategies. Section V presents the MLP results and compares them to OLS. Section VI presents a sensitivity analysis, and Section VII discusses the results of a tactical asset-allocation policy based upon the MLP and OLS predictions. Section VIII contains the conclusions.

SECTION II. PREDICTING EXCESS RETURNS

Evidence has been accumulated that a significant part of the variation in stock market returns can be predicted using information known at the time of prediction, (e.g., Campbell 1987; Fama and French 1989; Ferson and Harvey 1991; and Pesaran and Timmermann 1994. These studies invariably apply linear modeling, with a limited number of independent variables. In particular, evidence has been accumulated that ex ante information on inflation, interest rates, the business cycle, and valuation measures such as the dividend yield, can be used to predict monthly, quarterly, and annual excess returns.

This study focuses on quarterly excess returns. The linear model we use as a benchmark can be found in Hiemstra (1996). The model uses four inputs: dividend yield (YSP), short-term interest rate (SIR), inflation rate based on the consumer price index (CPI), and the change in the 12-month moving average of the industrial production index (DIP). YSP and SIR are instantaneously available, and so the latest observations prior to the forecasted period were used to predict, that is, the values at the

Table 25.1

Regression Statistics

Regression Statistics for OLS

Multiple R	0.45
R^2	0.20
Adjusted R^2	0.16
Standard error	7.58
Observation	93

Table 25.2

Coefficients of Linear Model

	Coefficients	Standard Error	t-Statistic
Intercept	−2.87	3.43	−0.84
YSP_{t-1}	4.43	1.26	3.52
CPI_{t-2}	−1.00	0.39	−2.54
SIR_{t-1}	−0.76	0.37	−2.03
DIP_{t-2}	−6.78	2.12	−3.20

end of the preceding month. Macroeconomic information is available typically on a monthly basis with a lag of some 20 days, and so DIP and CPI were used with a two-month lag. The data set consists of 93 quarterly observations covering the period 1970–1993 of YSP_{t-1}, DIP_{t-2}, SIR_{t-1}, and CPI_{t-2}. The desired output is the S&P 500 quarterly excess return, defined as total return (price movement plus dividends related to the initial investment) minus the risk-free rate of return, the three-month T-bill rate.

Tables 25.1 and 25.2 present the in-sample OLS results on the entire data set. The R^2 has a satisfactory value for predictions at this frequency, and all coefficients pass the test for significance at the 95 percent level. The signs of the coefficients correspond to the findings of other studies, YSP having a positive coefficient, and the other variables having a negative coefficient.

SECTION III. GENERATING OUT-OF-SAMPLE PREDICTIONS

Given the small sample size at the quarterly frequency and the noisy character of the data, it is crucial to produce sufficient out-of-sample results to reliably estimate generalization. Pesaran and Timmermann (1994) apply a recursive approach to predicting excess returns, in which case all data available at time t is used to forecast the excess return at time $t+1$. Cross-validation and bootstrapping are examples of resampling techniques (see, for example, Weiss and Kulikowski 1991). Cross-validation uses all data for testing, and consumes considerably fewer resources than recursive prediction or bootstrapping. We apply 10-fold cross-validation to estimate generalization. The 10 test sets were combined to form out-of-sample estimations on the entire data set.

SECTION IV. ESTIMATING THE MULTILAYER PERCEPTRONS

The MLP architecture we use is the standard MLP architecture for non-linear regression (Haykin 1994), with bias weights and one hidden layer. The hidden units have *tanh* activation functions; the output unit has a linear activation function. Inputs were normalized to have mean zero and unit variance.

The motivation to use back-propagation is to stop training before the in-sample minimum on the error function is reached (early stopping), based on the assumption that in the initial stages of learning the MLP picks up the most overt and accessible patterns (Thornton 1992). The iterative character of back-propagation makes it possible to stop learning if at a certain stage in the learning process the MLP starts fitting noise, which may be well before the error function reaches its minimum on the training set. Weigend et al. (1990) suggest setting part of the training data apart, introducing a cross-validation set in addition to the train and test sets, and stopping training at the point where the error function on the cross-validation set has its minimum. True generalization is estimated by the performance on the original test set. To apply early stopping, it is necessary to select the number of hidden nodes in advance. The sample size is a constraint on the number of weights in order to produce reliable training. A rule of thumb is that there should be at least five training examples for each weight (Klimasauskas 1996). Hiemstra (1993,1996) proposes an MLP with two hidden neurons for quarterly excess return prediction.

On the other hand, White (1991) points out that overtraining and overfitting should be separated. "In the statistical context there is no such thing as overtraining, because the closer one gets to $\hat{\Theta}_n$ the better." $\hat{\Theta}_n$ denotes the estimator for the true parameter vector Θ_n of the underlying process. So, given an MLP of some complexity, the goal is to find the global minimum of the error function, and from the set of alternative algorithms (e.g., back-propagation, second-order algorithms, genetic algorithms, see, for example, Sarle 1994) any algorithm that efficiently minimizes in-sample error is applicable. Overfitting occurs in cases where there are too many free parameters in the MLP; while a network with too few hidden units has no capacity for satisfactory internal representation and will be unable to learn properly. To select the network with the right complexity, we apply *sequential network construction* (SNC) (Moody and Utans 1994). We start out with 1 hidden unit and estimate the MLP. Then a hidden unit is added, and the MLP is retrained. This is repeated until the hidden layer has a particular maximum number of nodes. The fit of each MLP is evaluated using an estimator of its prediction risk (i.e., the expected out-of-sample performance). We estimate prediction risk for each MLP using the Schwartz Information Coefficient (SIC) (Schwartz 1978; Rissanen 1978, 1980, 1987), which produces very conservative models and which can be used for nonlinear and ARCH models (Granger, King and White 1992). The SIC of model λ is computed as follows:

$$SIC_\lambda = \log MSE + \frac{P}{N} \log N \qquad (1)$$

with MSE being the mean squared error, N the number of observations and P the number of parameters.[1] For each of the 10 cross-validation sets, we estimated MLPs using PRCG,[2] selecting the appropriate complexity through SIC (Swanson and White 1992).

SECTION V. EVALUATION AND COMPARISON OF OUT-OF-SAMPLE RESULTS[3]

Table 25.3 compares the SIC-optimal complexity approach with the results for back-propagation using two hidden neurons (BPN2) and OLS as reported by Hiemstra (1996). The error rate refers to the ratio of incorrect

Table 25.3

Comparison of Out-of-Sample Results of the Three Approaches

	SIC-Optimal MLP	BPN2	OLS
MSE	77.882	64.662	65.64
NMSE	1.145[†]	0.951[†]	0.965[†]
R^2	0.085	0.084	0.07
Theil coefficient	0.664	0.551	0.559
Correlation	0.292[*]	0.29[*]	0.265[*]
Mean	2.531	1.887	1.95
Error rate	0.387	0.419	0.43
Business value	35.534	53.298	29.306

[*] Significantly different from 0 at the 95% confidence level.
[†] Not significantly different from 1 at the 95% confidence level.

sign predictions to all predictions. Business value calculates the sum of the excess returns for those occasions that the predicted excess return is negative and indicates the benefits obtained by implementing during the period covered by the data (93 quarters), a timing strategy that exits the stock market when the expected excess return is negative. R^2 is computed as the squared correlation of the predicted and the actual values. Theil's coefficient of inequality considers the case of a no-change forecast and has a value of less than one if the forecast outperforms a no-change forecast (Theil 1966). The MLP models outperform OLS in terms of correlation, error rate, and business value. The poor results on MSE and normalized MSE (NMSE) of the SIC-optimal MLP are explained by the high mean of the predictions of this model.

An F-test was performed to test whether the variances of the residuals of two alternative models are significantly different from each other. If so, one model outperforms the other because a larger variance of residuals is inferior. Assuming under the H_0 that the variances of the residuals are equal,[4] the F-test statistic reduces to:

$$F = \frac{MSE_1}{MSE_2} \quad (2)$$

where F follows an F-distribution with $(N-P_1)$, $(N-P_2)$ degrees of freedom, N denoting the number of observations and P_λ the number of parameters. The F-test did not reject the null hypotheses of identical MSEs.

SECTION VI. SENSITIVITY ANALYSIS AND MODEL VISUALIZATION

Sensitivity analysis reveals the qualitative behavior of the MLP models. Figures 25.1 and 25.2 illustrate the behavior of the BPN2 model. Figure 25.1 shows a shaded plane in the input space, with DIP being fixed at its average value, and the other inputs along the axes. The shading of the plane indicates the excess return prediction; lighter shading means a higher predicted excess return.

Figure 25.1

A shaded plane in the input space

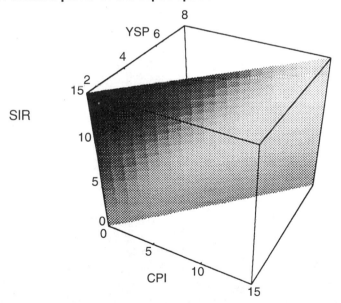

Lighter shading means higher expected excess return.

Figure 25.2

Four 3-D Contour Plots for Increasing YSP Showing the Decision Surface in Input Space that Represents an Expected Excess Return of 0

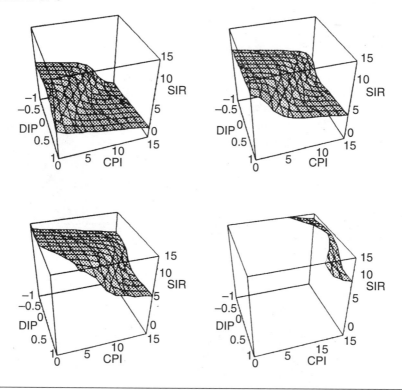

Figure 25.2 shows four 3-D contour plots. The 3-D contour plot shows the decision surface in the input space, with YSP fixed at a particular value and the other inputs along the axes, that represents a predicted excess return of 0. YSP increases from the top left figure to the bottom right figure. This graphic represents the impact of the macroeconomic investment conditions. On-screen animations of figures 25.1 and 25.2 (varying the fixed input in time) comprehensively visualize the behavior of the BPN2 and SIC-optimal MLP model. The graphics demonstrate significant, but not extreme, nonlinearity.

SECTION VII. ASSET ALLOCATION

Figure 25.3 compares the performance of asset-allocation strategies using the three models. The top panel of Figure 25.3 shows policy-efficient frontiers. A policy efficient frontier (Hiemstra 1996) represents the annualized ex post risk-return properties of a particular tactical investment policy for those strategic portfolios that, given the policy, produced the highest return for the respective risk exposures. The investment policies shown operate on a strategic portfolio consisting of stocks and bonds and exit the stock market when the excess return prediction is negative. The policies were tested on the period 1976–1993 (net of trading costs), the Shearson-Lehman Aggregate Bond Index representing bond returns. The bottom line indicates the results of a buy-and-hold policy, a 100 percent bonds portfolio located at the low end, and a 100 percent stocks portfolio located at the high end. The line in between shows the results of a tactical policy using OLS predictions. The solid upper line and the dashed line show the results using the predictions of the SIC-optimal MLP and BPN2, respectively. The latter two lines basically collapse, reflecting a striking similarity in the two MLP models from this point of view.

Figure 25.3 shows that active management has a dramatic payoff. For a particular risk exposure, an OLS-based policy can add well over 100 basis points annually, and both MLPs can generate a similar additional return on top of that. The bottom panel shows the relative value over time of an initial investment in 1976 when the three policies operate on a strategic portfolio of 100 percent stocks.

SECTION VIII. CONCLUSION

The MLP models that we estimated improve over OLS in terms of correlation and error rate. We did not find indications for strong nonlinearities, as OLS captures most of the predictability demonstrated by the MLPs. Also, on the basis of the F-test we cannot reject the H_0 that the out-of-sample MSEs of the two MLP models and OLS are equal. The sensitivity analysis confirmed moderate nonlinearity. However, in terms of added value when applying a straightforward tactical asset allocation policy, the differences are very significant. The SIC-optimal MLP results are particularly compelling, since this model reflects a purely formal approach to MLP estimation that lets the data determine MLP size.

Figure 25.3

Comparison of Performances Using Models

The top panel shows policy efficient frontiers, the bottom panel the relative value of a 1976 investment when adopting a strategic stock weight of 1 (net of trading costs). In both cases, buy-and-hold is the bottom line; the line above buy-and-hold represents OLS results. The solid upper line and the dashed line show the results using the predictions of the SIC-optimal MLP and BPN2, respectively.

Annualized return

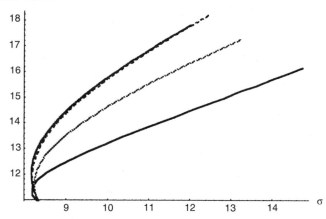

Relative value

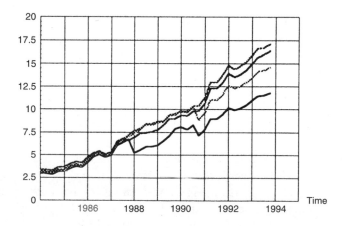

REFERENCES

Campbell, J.Y., 1987. "Stock Returns and the Term Structure." *Journal of Financial Economics* 18, pp. 373–99.

Fama, E. and K. French, 1989. "Business Conditions and Expected Stock Returns." *Journal of Financial Economics* 25, pp. 23–50.

Ferson, W.E. and C.R. Harvey, 1991. "Sources of Predictability in Portfolio Returns". *Financial Analysts Journal*, May-June, pp. 49–56.

Granger, C.W.J., M.L. King, and H. White, 1995. "Comments on Testing Economic Theories and the Use of Model Selection Criteria." *Journal of Econometrics* 67, pp. 173–87.

Haykin, S., 1994. *Neural Networks.* New York: MacMillan

Hiemstra, Y., 1993. "A Neural Net to Predict Quarterly Stock Market Excess Returns Using Business Cycle Turning Points." *Proceedings of The First International Workshop on Neural Networks in the Capital Markets.* London Business School.

Hiemstra, Y., 1996. "Linear Regression versus Backpropagation Networks to Predict Quarterly Stock Market Excess Returns." *Computational Economics.* forthcoming.

Hiemstra, Y. and C. Haefke, 1995. "Predicting Quarterly Excess Returns: Two Multilayer Perceptron Training Strategies." *Proceedings of The Third International Conference on Artificial Intelligence Applications on Wall Street.* Gaithersburg: Software Engineering Press, pp. 212–17.

Hornik, K., M. Stinchcombe, and H. White, 1989. "Multilayer Feedforward Networks are Universal Approximators." *Neural Networks* 2, pp. 359–66.

Klimasauskas, C., 1996. "Applying Neural Networks" (see Chapter 3 of this book).

Lippmann, R.P., 1987. "An Introduction to Computing with Neural Nets." *IEEE ASSP Magazine*, April, pp. 4–22.

Moody, J., 1992. "The *Effective* Number of Parameters: An Analysis of Generalization and Regularization in Nonlinear Learning Systems". *Advances in Neural Information Processing Systems 4.* San Mateo: Morgan Kaufman.

Moody, J. and J. Utans, 1994. "Architecture Selection Strategies for Neural Networks: Application to Corporate Bond Rating Prediction." In *Neural Networks in the Capital Markets*. ed. A.N. Refenes. London: Wiley & Sons.

Pesaran, M.H. and A. Timmermann, 1994. "Forecasting Stock Returns." *Journal of Forecasting* 13, pp. 335–67.

Renshaw, E., 1993. "Modeling the Stock Market for Forecasting Purposes." *Journal of Portfolio Management* 20, no. 1, pp. 76–81.

Rissanen, J., 1978. "Modelling by Shortest Data Description." *Automatica* 14, pp. 465–71.

Rissanen, 1980. "Consistent Order-Estimates of Autoregressive Processes by Shortest Description of Data." In *Analysis and Optimization of Stochastic Systems*. eds. O. Jacobs, M. Davis, M. Dempster, C. Harris, and P. Parks. New York: Academic Press, pp. 451–61.

Rissanen, J., 1987. "Stochastic Complexity and the MDL Principle." *Econ. Rev.* 6, pp. 85–102.

Sarle, W.S., 1994. "Neural Network Implementation in SAS Software." *Proceedings of the Nineteenth Annual SAS Users Group International Conference . SAS* Institute, Cary, NC .

Schwartz, G., 1978. "Estimating the Dimension of a Model." *Ann. Statist.* 6, pp. 461–64.

Swanson, N. and H. White, 1995. "A Model Selection Approach to Assessing the Information in the Term Structure Using Linear Models and Artificial Neural Networks." *Journal of Business and Economics Statistics* 13, pp. 265–75.

Theil, H., 1966. *Applied Economic Forecasting*. Amsterdam: North Holland Publishing Company.

Thornton, C.J., 1992. *Techniques in Computational Learning*. London: Chapman and Hall.

Weigend, A.S., B.A. Huberman, and D.E. Rumelhart, 1990. "Predicting the Future: a Connectionist Approach." *International Journal of Neural Systems* 1, no. 3, pp. 193–209.

Weigend, A.S. and B. LeBaron, 1994. "Evaluating Neural Network Predictors by Bootstrapping." *CU-CS-725-94.* University of Colorado

Weiss, S. and C. Kulikowski, 1991. *Computer Systems That Learn*. Palo Alto: Morgan Kaufman.

White, H., 1991. "Parametric Statistical Estimation with Artificial Neural Networks." *Department of Economics and Institute for Neural Computation, University of California,* San Diego.

ENDNOTES

1. We used the number of weights; an alternative is Moodys *effective* number of parameters (Moody 1992).

2. Every single MLP was estimated using the PRCG algorithm, as provided by Gauss. This is a local optimization algorithm, and so training was repeated five times. The MLP with lowest in-sample error was selected.

3. We thank Gerhard Ruenstler, Institute for Advanced Studies, for his helpful comments on this section.

4. A t-test confirmed that the mean of the residuals is not significantly different from zero at the 95 percent confidence level.

26

USING ARTIFICIAL NEURAL NETWORKS TO PICK STOCKS

Lawrence Kryzanowski, Michael Galler, and David W. Wright

According to Elton and Gruber, portfolio managers are generally stock pickers and only occasionally market timers.[1] As stock pickers, their task is to pick (avoid) those stocks that are unlikely to out-perform (under-perform) other stocks of comparable risk. Although computer expert systems have been applied to stock picking, such programs are driven by fixed rules that require continual review and refinement as economic conditions evolve. Each refinement requires reprogramming the system, which is time-consuming and costly.

Artificial neural networks (ANNs) relearn relationships automatically from new examples as conditions change. Their popularity has risen as the cost of computing technology has declined. Many investment firms in North America are currently experimenting with ANNs for financial applications such as stock picking.[2] Because of the proprietary nature of these systems, detailed accounts of applications have yet to appear in the literature.[3]

Reprinted, with permission, from the *Financial Analysts Journal*, July/August 1993. Copyright 1993, Association for Investment Management and Research, Charlottesville, VA. All rights reserved.

When picking a company using either a top-down or bottom-up approach, portfolio managers attribute much importance to the company's financial track record. Demonstrated ability to manage social and economic shocks may enhance a company's risk-adjusted return prospects, which should favorably affect the company's stock price.

Much contradictory evidence exists regarding the use of current information to predict stock price movements (returns). Fama notes that there is "no lack of old evidence that short-horizon returns are predictable from other variables."[4] These variables include historical earnings-to-price (E/P) ratios or their inverse (P/E) ratios.[5] These and other variables (factors) have been used in multifactor models to screen securities.[6] As current information about the economic environment can also play a significant role in the future health of a company, multifactor screening models may be augmented with macroeconomic variables that are priced sources of risk in the stock market.[7]

This chapter examines the ability of an ANN using historical and current accounting and macroeconomic data to discriminate between stocks providing superior future returns and those providing inferior future returns. The ANN application discussed uses the pattern classification algorithm of the Boltzmann machine (BM), which employs a technique of stochastic optimization called simulated annealing.[8] The ANN learns the relationship between a company's stock return one year in the future and the most recent four years of financial data on the company and its industry, as well as data on seven macroeconomic factors.

This research represents an initial step in the development of a model that can accurately classify a company's stock price as being likely to either rise or fall over the coming year (or some other future period). The speed of such a system should greatly shorten the time needed to screen companies. This should increase the number of companies a portfolio manager or financial analyst can evaluate over a given period. Also, the availability of such a system should lower the minimum level of sophistication required for new analysts.

ARTIFICIAL NEURAL NETWORKS

The traditional method for solving complex problems using computing technology is to use an expert system (ES). Such a system is inappropriate for certain tasks, such as financial analysis, where a constantly changing rule base requires costly programming and maintenance. Also, for financial analysis, enormous time and effort is required to extract the knowledge base from human experts and to translate it into a complete program rule set.[9]

There are two primary differences between artificial neural networks (ANNs) and expert systems.[10] First, because automated procedures are employed in programming ANNs, the learning process is rapid. Since ANNs learn by observing data from previous experiences, interviews of experts are not necessary. Second, the parallel nature of network computing allows ANNs to solve a problem even if some of its neurons make mistakes. An ANN is able to form judgments or achieve stable configuration patterns, even if it is given "fuzzy" or incomplete information.

An ANN is designed to mimic the knowledge-acquisition and organization skills of the human brain. It contains a large number of interconnected nodes (the neurons), whose output states are determined by the inputs from each of its neighbors. A network is "taught" by presenting it with a set of sample data as inputs and by varying the "weighting factors" in the algorithm that determines the corresponding output states. An ANN not only accumulates, stores, and recognizes patterns of knowledge based on experience, but it also constantly retrains as the environment of examples evolves.

A large number of examples are generally required to train networks. However, this limitation can be overcome by careful data collection. Another limitation of an ANN is that it is difficult to trace the step-by-step logic it uses to arrive at the outputs from the inputs provided. A system user must generally rely on the output as a gauge of the system's consistency and reliability.[11] But practitioners are, after all, in the same state when it comes to most business decisions, which cannot be fully explained by tracing the process and weighting factors used in arriving at a particular conclusion.

Although potential applications for ANNs are numerous, reports on the results of actual applications are sparse.[12] Wong, Wang, Goh, and Quek use inputs similar to those used in this article to predict security returns.[13] Their ANN is augmented by an expert system that contains a rule base of 32 company rules. Swales and Yoon use content analysis and ANN technology to differentiate between stocks that perform well and those that perform poorly.[14] Their model performs significantly better than a linear multiple discriminant analysis approach.

Glossary

Artificial Neural Network (ANN). A computer or computer program consisting of a set of simple parallel units or "neurons" with connections between them. The neurons change state (for example, switch on or off) according to some simple function of the inputs received and the weights associated with their connections. In an ANN, knowledge is embodied in the connection weights. An ANN can be used to compute a function by forcing the input units into a given state and observing the state of the output neurons.

Back-Propagation. The error back-propagation rule is a two-pass weight-learning algorithm for neural networks. Error is first estimated during a forward pass through the network, then the measured error is propagated backward through the network while connection weights are adjusted to reduce the error.

Boltzmann Machine (BM). A kind of ANN that uses simulated annealing to set the states of the neurons during both the weight-learning and function-computing stages of its operation.

Expert System. A computer program that uses a set of rules and facts and a procedure for making inferences or deductions in order to simulate the problem-solving abilities of a human expert.

Simulated Annealing. A discrete optimization method that uses a gradually decreasing amount of random noise while searching some problem space for a globally optimal solution.

The Boltzmann Machine

At least two supervised learning methods have been used successfully by complex neural networks. In both back-propagation and the Boltzmann machine (BM), knowledge is induced by automatic means using training data. The BM used here applies a technique of randomized optimization called *simulated annealing.*[15]

This pattern classifier is based on a weak constraint-satisfaction network that uses a learning set, a verification set, and a test set. During the learning phase, the BM observes the relationship between inputs and their resulting outcomes. The learning set allows the BM to develop (or "learn") the relationships between inputs and outcomes. The BM increases the weightings of those particular inputs that are most often present when a particular outcome occurs. The BM might discover, for example, that companies with high returns experience an increase in their return-on-common equity (RCE) ratios. The BM would then increase the importance given to the RCE ratio when classifying the security returns (or prices) of other companies. During the training phase, these learned relationships are periodically verified against a second subset of companies, the verification set. The prediction accuracy of these outcomes helps the ANN decide when to end the training in order to maximize generalizability.

During the test phase, the BM is fed only inputs from a test data set. Using previously learned relationships, the BM attempts to predict outcomes (say, security returns). Comparing these predictions with the classifications of actual returns measures the accuracy of the BM.

RAW DATA AND DATA MANIPULATION

The primary data include the annual income statements and balance sheets of 120 publicly traded companies.[16] All publicly available financial statements for these companies over the six-year period 1984–89 are used. The companies represent 49 of the industry classifications used by Dun & Bradstreet (D&B). Table 26.1 presents cross-sectional profiles of the total revenues, net incomes, and total assets for the sample. Table 26.2 summarizes the distribution of the fiscal year-ends by month.

Five industry ratios (gross profit margin, current ratio, net profit margin, return on equity, and total debt-to-equity ratio) are used as benchmarks for analyzing each company. The annual (calendar year-end) industry averages for each of the five financial ratios are obtained from D&B's publication, *Key Business Ratios*, and from *Statistics Canada*. The industry averages are related to financial data for the current year for companies with a fiscal year-end between July and December, inclusive, and to financial data for the following year for companies with a fiscal year-end between January and June.

Table 26.1

Revenues, Income, and Assets, 1989 ($millions)

	Total Revenues	Net Incomes	Total Assets
Maximum	14,864.3	898.5	28,791.8
First quartile	144.8	5.5	101.5
Second quartile	53.1	1.8	40.7
Third quartile	23.8	0.4	17.6
Minimum	3.0	−17.0	3.7

Table 26.2

Distribution of Fiscal Year-Ends

Year-End	Number
Jan. 31	12
Feb. 28	7
Mar. 31	8
Apr. 30	3
May 31	3
June 30	8
July 31	5
Aug. 31	9
Sep. 30	10
Oct. 31	9
Nov. 30	5
Dec. 31	41
Total	120

Feature Extraction

For each firm, we analyzed the trends of the 14 financial ratios listed in Table 26.3 over three fixed, overlapping four-year periods, 1984–87, 1985–88, and 1986–89.[17] Five of these ratios describe profitability, four

Table 26.3
Financial Ratios

Profitability

Gross margin[*]	=	(Sales - Cost of sales)/Sales
Net profit margin[*]	=	Net income/Sales
Total asset turnover	=	Sales/Total assets
Fixed asset turnover	=	Sales/Fixed assets
Return on total assets	=	Net profits after taxes/Total assets
Return on equity[*]	=	Net profits after taxes/Shareholders' equity

Debt

Debt ratio	=	Total liabilities/Total assets
Debt-to-equity ratio[*]	=	Total liabilities/Shareholders' equity
Interest coverage ratio	=	Earnings before interest and taxes/Annual interest expense
Long-term debt ratio	=	Long-term debt/Total assets

Liquidity and Activity

Current ratio[*]	=	Total current assets/Total current liabilities
Quick ratio	=	(Total current assets − Inventories)/Total current liabilities
Accounts receivable turnover[†]	=	Sales/Average accounts receivable
Accounts payable turnover[†]	=	Sales/Average accounts payable

[*] Industry benchmarks available.
[†] Uses data for current year if previous year's data are unavailable.

describe debt, and five describe liquidity and activity. The mean, variance, and trend calculations require four years of data. These horizontal (general trend) analyses use the t-values for the slopes of the OLS regressions and the relative ratios of current-to-mean financial ratios for each of the

14 financial ratios for each four-year period. This results in the extraction of 28 (2 × 14) features for each case.

For each company, we also compared five of these ratios with the respective industry benchmarks. These vertical analyses consist of two types of evaluations. The first compares the relative performance of each of the five firm-to-industry ratios for each of the four years. This results in the extraction of a further 20 (5 × 4) features for each case. The second compares the relative volatility of each of the five ratios for the firm with the volatility of its respective industry ratio over each four-year period. This results in another five features for each case.

For the macroeconomic variables, we used month-end levels of seven factors over the period January 1980 through September 1991, collected from *Statistics Canada* and the Bank of Canada *Review*. The factors are industrial production, gross domestic product, the McLeod Young Weir corporate long bond index, the 90-day Treasury bill rate, the government of Canada long bond index, the consumer price index, and the Montreal Exchange (ME) 25 index. We matched the five year-over-year percentage changes for each macroeconomic factor to each firm's five fiscal year-ends. This results in the extraction of another 35 (7 × 5) features for each case.

The stock prices, obtained from the Reuters stock price database and the ME stock tables, consist of the closing stock price at the end of the third month after each fiscal year-end of each company for the time period March 1986 through September 1991, inclusive. Cash dividends and stock splits are included. The future return one year hence is calculated using the closing monthly price three months after the most recent fiscal year-end, the closing monthly price one year hence, and the cash dividends to be paid over the one-year future period.

An input pattern for each firm for each four-year period thus consists of 88 factors or data points (i.e., 28 + 20 + 5 + 35). The corresponding output pattern consists of a single data point (i.e., the representation of each firm's return in the future year).

Building Input and Output Vectors

Theoretically, a BM can accept all the previously described continuous data as inputs. Unfortunately, a BM requires several thousand examples to extract a generalization from a continuous data set. The data are therefore simplified (made discrete) before being used to train the BM.

We machine coded each feature point in the input vector, using a front-end computer program with a three-bit combination of zeros or ones representing one of its three discrete states. The possible three-bit combinations are <100>, <010>, and (001>. To illustrate, the front-end computer program codes the measure "trend of each financial ratio" as upward <100>, stable <010>, or downward <001>, based on a comparison of the adjusted t-values with the lower and upper cutoff values of –1 and +1, respectively. The adjusted t-values are obtained by dividing unadjusted values by the critical (positive) t-value at the 95 percent level.

The front-end computer program codes the annual performance of each macroeconomic variable over the past five years as good <100>, average <010>, or bad <001>, based on a comparison of its year-over-year percentage changes with the variable's empirically derived distribution of changes for the 129-month period January 1981 to September 1991. If a change falls into the top, middle, or bottom of the empirically derived distribution, it is converted to <100>, <010>, or <001>, respectively. The vector for each macroeconomic factor for each company consists of binary data points coinciding with the company's five fiscal year-ends.

The output vector is similarly coded as a two- or three-bit combination to represent one of the two or three discrete stock return classifications for the subsequent one-year period. Specifically, each return in the two-bit output vector is coded as <10> or <01> for positive or negative return performance, respectively. Each result in the three-bit output vector is coded <100>, <010>, or <001> for positive, neutral, or negative return performance, respectively. For the three discrete performance classes, the distribution of returns is arbitrarily divided into three equally likely partitions, corresponding to lower and upper return cutoff values of –22 percent and 13 percent, respectively.

As noted earlier, each training pattern consists of 88 input data points and one output data point. Since each point is converted to a three-bit binary vector, a 267-bit binary vector representation is used for each training case. The BM thus needs 264 input cells and three output cells.

EMPIRICAL DESIGN

The input and output vectors for a given number of cases are required to train the BM. From this set (or sample) of training cases, the BM learns the *a posteriori* probabilities of the outputs.

The output vectors are used as a feedback mechanism to adjust the neural connection weightings so as to improve the BM's predictive accuracy. Based on conventional practice designed to ensure maximum generalizability, the chosen weightings are the best of three runs for a given experiment. Because the network performs a stochastic optimization, each run yields slightly different weightings.

Only the input vectors of a holdout (or test) sample are used by the BM to classify performance. The BM-classified outputs are compared with the classification of actual outputs to determine the classification accuracy of the BM and to evaluate the "true" performance of the learning phase.

When two adjacent output cells have their states switched on, the BM provides a "split decision" rather than an arbitrary clear choice ("call"). If all output cells are switched on, the network makes "no decision" ("call") for the test case.

Twenty-five of the 256 cases available to train, verify, and test the BM were rejected by the front-end computer program that prepared the input vectors because of insufficient data. The final sample thus consists of 231 cases. Table 26.4 summarizes the division of the two- and three-category output classifications by training, verifying, and testing subsets.

Two tests are conducted. The first measures the accuracy of the BM in predicting whether a stock's return is positive or negative over the next year. For this two-category output classification, the training, verifying, and testing subsets consist of 40, 42, and 149 vectors (one for each case), respectively (see Table 26.4). The training and verifying vectors are selected so that they contain a balanced number of input vectors (i.e., the same number of positive and negative outputs).

The second measures the accuracy of the BM in three-category output classification (i.e., positive, neutral, and negative). From Table 26.4, the training and verifying subsets consist of 39 and 42 vectors, respectively. The testing subset consists of 149 vectors, which are not balanced by output category.

RESULTS

When the BM undertakes a two-category output classification of the 149 test cases, an accuracy rating significantly higher than 50 percent (i.e., the level achievable by chance) is required if the BM's predictions are to be potentially valuable. Table 26.5 shows that the BM achieves a 66.4

Table 26.4

Division of Output Classifications

Output Classification	Division of Cases			Total
	Training	Verifying	Testing	
a. Two-Category Output Classification				
Positive	20	21	24	65
Negative	20	21	125	166
Total	40	42	149	231
b. Three-Category Output Classification				
Positive	13	14	17	44
Neutral	13	14	47	74
Negative	13	14	85	112
Total	39	42	149	230

percent overall accuracy in predicting whether a stock's return will be positive or negative over the coming year. In 11 cases, the BM did not make any call (i.e., could not decide on the expected outcome). Judging the BM only on the cases for which it made a decision (described herein as "clear calls") results in an accuracy level of 71.7 percent. The BM displays a lower level of accuracy for cases with negative outcomes, and for cases in 1989. These differences are significant at the 1 percent level.[18]

Table 26.6 profiles the errors by year. Like the errors of real-life stock pickers, the 39 ANN cases are not confined to any one time period or any particular return range. However, they are somewhat more predominant for negative cases in 1989. At the extremes are the 150 percent return for which the BM had predicted a negative return and the –73 percent return for which the BM had predicted a positive return. In contrast, the BM accurately predicted cases with returns of only 1 percent, 3 percent, –4 percent and –5 percent.

In the second test, the BM undertook a three-category output classification for the same 149 cases. The results, summarized in Table 26.8, show the BM again outperformed chance with an overall accuracy rate of 45.6 percent. As is evident from Table 26.7, the 79 error cases are drawn from all categories and years. The largest proportion of the errors occurs

Table 26.5

Results for Positive/Negative Classification

Class	(a) Number Tested	(b) No Decision	(c) Clear Calls (a − b)	(d) Accurate calls	(e) Errors	(f) No-Decision Rate (b/a)	(g) Total Accuracy Rate (d/a)	(h) Total Error Rate (e/a)	(i) Called Accuracy Rate (d/c)	(j) Called Error Rate (e/c)
Positive	24	3	21	16	5	12.5%	66.7%	20.8%	76.2%	23.8%
Negative	125	8	117	83	34	6.4%	66.4%	27.2%	70.9%	29.1%
Total	149	11	138	99	39	7.4%	66.4%	26.2%	71.7%	28.3%
1987	16*	0	16	12	4	0.0%	75.0%	25.0%	75.0%	25.0%
1988	72	1	71	57	14	1.4%	79.2%	19.4%	80.3%	19.7%
1989	61	10	51	30	21	16.4%	49.2%	34.4%	58.8%	41.2%
Total	149	11	138	99	39	7.4%	66.4%	26.2%	71.7%	28.3%

*Number of positive cases for 1987, 1988, and 1989 are 2, 3, and 19, respectively.

536

Table 26.6

Analysis of Error Cases

Year	% Return One Year Forward			
	Maximum	Minimum	Average	Median
a. Two–Category Output Classification				
1987	150	−36	28	0
1988	41	−73	−22	−14
1989	52	−60	−20	−17
b. Three–Category Output Classification				
1987	150	−66	1	−13
1988	5	−73	−21	−11
1989	95	−62	−16	−15

Table 26.8

Analysis of Returns Wrongly Classified as Neutral

	BM Assignment			
	Negative Class	Positive Class	No Decision	Total
Actually negative	16	22	1	39
Actually positive	1	6	0	7
Total	17	28	1	46

for the BM's prediction of neutral returns. Table 26.8 shows that, of the 47 cases defined as neutral, the BM improperly classified 46 as being either positive or negative. Of these "mistakes," 22 were assigned ratings appropriate to their actual two-category outcomes, while 22 were assigned a positive rating when the actual two-category outcome was negative.

Table 26.7

Results for Positive/Neutral/Negative Classification

Class	(a) Number Tested	(b) No Decision	(c) Clear Calls (a – b)	(d) Accurate calls	(e) Errors	(f) No Decision Rate (b/a)	(g) Total Accuracy Rate(d/a)	(h) Total Error Rate (e/a)	(i) Called Accuracy Rate (d/c)	(j) Called Error Rate (e/c)
Positive	17	0	17	13	4	0.0%	76.5%	23.5%	76.5%	23.5%
Neutral	47	1	46	0	46	2.1%	0.0%	97.9%	0.0%	100.0%
Negative	85	1	84	55	29	1.2%	64.7%	34.1%	65.5%	34.5%
Total	149	2	147	68	79	1.3%	45.6%	53.0%	46.3%	53.7%
1987	16[*]	1	15	5	10	6.3%	31.3%	62.5%	33.3%	66.7%
1988	72	0	72	41	31	0.0%	56.9%	43.1%	56.9%	43.1%
1989	61	1	60	22	38	1.6%	36.1%	62.3%	36.7%	63.3%
Total	149	2	147	68	79	1.3%	45.6%	53.0%	46.3%	53.7%

[*] Number of positive cases for 1987, 1988, and 1989 are 1, 1, and 15, respectively. Number of neutral cases for 1987, 1988, and 1989 are 7, 20, and 20, respectively.

Thus, while the first test produced 39 errors, the second corrected 10 of these but made 50 new errors. The 11 no-call cases in the first test resulted in nine incorrect and two correct calls in the second test. The second test resulted in only two (new) no-decisions.

CONCLUDING REMARKS

As a pattern classifier, the BM appears to have potential for stock picking based on a modest number of learning examples. Superior precision based on greater learning is presumably achievable if a greater number of learning cases are used. However, the reported results may be unique to the limited sample of smaller companies and the relatively short time period (three years) studied here. The literature suggests that smaller companies are more likely to experience delayed stock responses to new information. Whether an actively managed portfolio using a BM can outperform a passive portfolio remains a question for future testing.

Future research should explore the effectiveness of using a BM for stock picking for a greater number of examples covering a longer time frame and a wider range of firm sizes. This should be done for various future time horizons using additional features such as the number of shares outstanding, market capitalization, and analysts' earnings expectations.[19]

ENDNOTES

1. E. J. Elton and M. J. Gruber, *Modern Portfolio Theory and Investment Analysis* (New York: John Wiley & Sons, 1991), p. 561.

2. J. C. Smith, "A Neural Network—Could it Work for You?" *Financial Executive,* May–June 1990.

3. In contrast, the literature on the financial application of expert systems in finance is more extensive. See the Autumn 1988 issue of *Financial Management* and the May 1990 issue of *AI Expert.*

4. E. F. Fama, "Efficient Capital Markets: II," *Journal of Finance,* December 1991, p. 1582.

5. See, for example, W. S. Bauman and R. Dowen, "Growth Projections and Common Stock Returns," *Financial Analysts Journal,* July/August 1988; L.

C. Bhandari, "Debt/Equity Ratio and Expected Common Stock Returns: Empirical Evidence," *Journal of Finance,* June 1988; and R. G. Ibbotson, "On the Cheap," *Financial Analysts Journal,* September/October 1989.

6. See, for example, R. J. Dowen and W. S. Bauman, "A Fundamental Multifactor Asset Pricing Model," *Financial Analysts Journal,* July/August 1986; M. R. Reinganum, "The Anatomy of a Stock Market Winner," *Financial Analysts Journal,* March/April 1988; and R. C. Jones, "Designing Factor Models for Different Types of Stock: What's Good for the Goose Ain't Always Good for the Gander," *Financial Analysts Journal,* March/April 1990.

7. For example, N. F. Chen, R. Roll, and S. A. Ross ("Economic Forces and the Stock Market," *Journal of Business* 59 (1986), pp. 383–403) find that innovations in five macroeconomic variables (the spread between long and short-term interest rates, expected inflation, and industrial production and the spread between high- and low-grade bonds) are significantly priced risks in the U.S. market for the 1953–83 period. L. Kryzanowski and H. Zhang ("Economic Forces and Seasonality in Security Returns," *Review of Quantitative Finance and Accounting* 2 (1992), pp. 227–44) find that lagged industrial production, lagged gross domestic product, term structure, unexpected inflation, and the risk premium have significantly priced risk premiums in the Canadian equity market over the 1956–88 period.

8. Attempts to use automatic learning in finance concentrate on credit-scoring problems. See, for example, C. Carter and J. Catlett, "Assessing Credit Card Applications Using Machine Learning," *IEEE Expert,* Fall 1987; and M. J. Shaw and J. A. Gentry, "Using an Expert System with Inductive Learning to evaluate Business Loans," *Financial Management,* Autumn 1988.

9. One of the few descriptions for one method for extracting a knowledge base for financial analysis from an experienced analyst is given in M. J. Bouwman, "Human Diagnostic Reasoning by Computer: An Illustration from Financial Analysis," *Management Science,* June 1983.

10. S. Maital, "Brainy Computers," *Across the Board,* June 1990.

11. D. Hawley, J.D. Johnson, and D. Raina, "Artificial Neural Systems: A New Tool for Financial Decision-Making," *Financial Analysts Journal,* November/December 1990.

12. The Growth America Fund of Fidelity Investments Canada Ltd. supposedly uses a neural network to identify buy and sell timing opportunities. Over $600,000 is spent annually on databases to provide information for the NN. The fund achieved a 44 percent growth rate in 1991, which was the fourth best fund performance among approximately 500 funds sold in Canada. (See E. Roseman, "Research Keeps Growth America in High

Fidelity," *Globe and Mail,* March 28, 1992.) One investment firm that uses an NN to predict prices of stock index futures claims to be correct 85 percent of the time. (See L. Belsie, "A Computer That Can Think," *Financial Times,* June 10, 1991.)

13. F. S. Wong, P. Z. Wang, T. H. Goh, and B. K. Quek, "Fuzzy Neural Systems for Stock Selection," *Financial Analysts Journal,* January/February 1992.

14. G. S. Swales, Jr., and Y. Yoon, "Applying Artificial Neural Networks to Investment Analysis," *Financial Analysts Journal,* September/October 1992.

15. S. E. Fahlam, G.E. Hinton, and T. J. Sejnowsky, "Massively Parallel Architecture for AI: NETL, Thistle, and Boltzmann Machines," *Proceedings of the National Conference on Artificial Intelligence, AAAI-83* (1983); and S. Kirpatrick, C. D. Gelatt, Jr., and M. P. Vecchi, "Optimization by Simulated Annealing," *Science* 220 (1983), pp. 671–80.

16. All the companies issued stock under the Quebec Stock Savings Plan (QSSP).

17. Seven ratios are sufficient to describe the financial health of a company. See K. H. Chen and T. A. Shimerda, "An Empirical Analysis of Useful Financial Ratios," *Financial Management,* Spring 1981; and G. E. Pinches, A. A. Eubank, K.A. Mingo, and K. Caruthers, "The Hierarchical Classification of Financial Ratios," *Journal of Business Research,* October 1975.

18. The chi-square value of 16.446 is greater than the critical value of 9.210, for an alpha of 0.01 with two degrees of freedom. Therefore, the differences are significant.

19. Financial support for our research was provided by Fonds pour la formation de chercheurs et l'aide a la recherche (FCAR), Shell Research Grant, and the Social Sciences and Humanities Research Council of Canada (SSHRC). The authors thank R. De Mori for his helpful comments.

TESTABILITY OF THE ARBITRAGE PRICING THEORY BY NEURAL NETWORKS

Hamid Ahmadi

INTRODUCTION

The arbitrage pricing theory (APT) offers an alternative to the traditional asset pricing model in finance. It is an important study in evaluating and understanding the nature of asset pricing. This theory has given researchers great insight into asset prices, and it has provided the organized framework for much current research in finance. While the promise is great, this promise has not yet been achieved. In almost all of the published papers, a statistical methodology called "factor analysis" is used to test or estimate the APT model. And the major shortcoming of this procedure is that it

---

identifies neither the number nor the definition of the factors that influence the assets. This study offers a unique solution to this problem. It uses a simple back-propagation neural network with the generalized delta rule to learn the interaction of the market factors and securities return. This technique helps us to investigate the effect of several variables on one another simultaneously without being plagued with uncertainty of probability distributions of each variable.

ARBITRAGE PRICING THEORY

Arbitrage pricing theory is based on the law of one price. The law of one price says that the same good cannot sell at different prices. If the same good sells at different prices, arbitrageurs will buy the good where it is cheap and simultaneously sell the good wherever its price is higher. Arbitrageurs will continue this activity until the different prices for the good are all equal. Equivalently, the law of one price says that securities with identical risks must have the same expected rate of return. More specifically, one of the fundamental theorems of APT says that assets with the same stochastic behavior must have the same expected returns.

THE MODEL

APT assumes that the rate of return on any security is a linear function of k factors.

$$R_i = E_i + b_{i1}F_1 + b_{i2}F_2 + \ldots + b_{ik}F_k + e_i \tag{1}$$

where

   R_i = Rate of return on the ith asset
   E_i = Expected return on the ith asset
   F_j = jth factor (or communality) common to the returns of all
        assets under consideration.
        $j = 1 \ldots k$. This factor has a mathematical expectation of
        zero ($E[F_j] = 0$).
   b_{ij} = Sensitivity of the ith asset's return to the jth factor
   e_i = Random zero mean error term for the ith asset

To make equation (1) more concrete, it is easy to think of several factors that might affect stock returns. Consider, for example, that the first factor in this equation is the rate of change in stock market (change in Standard & Poor's stock market index), the second factor is the change in GNP, the third is change in inflation rates, and so on.

The b_{ij} coefficient in equation (1) is a measure of *risk*—it indicates how sensitive the ith asset is to the jth factor. For instance, in the above example, b_{i1} indicates how sensitive the ith asset is to the stock market; incidentally, the sensitivity of a security with respect to the stock market is called "beta" or "beta risk."

An arbitrage opportunity exists if one can form a portfolio with no risk and at no cost with a positive return. An arbitrage opportunity is expressed more formally in equations (2) through (4) below.

$$\sum x_i = 0 \qquad (2)$$

The x_i is the weight (or the dollar amount) invested in ith asset. In order to form an arbitrage portfolio with no change in wealth, the usual course of action would be to sell some assets and use the proceeds to buy others.

Secondly, if there are n assets in the arbitrage portfolio, we will choose x_i's in such a way that portfolio has no risk. The following condition eliminates all risk:

$$\sum x_i b_{ij} = 0 \qquad \text{for each factor } j \ (j = 1 \ldots k) \qquad (3)$$

The rate of return of this n asset portfolio is:

$$R_p = \sum x_i R_i \qquad (4)$$

The arbitrage opportunity exists if (R_p), the return of the above portfolio, is positive. At equilibrium, all portfolios that satisfy the condition of no wealth and having no risk must have no return on average.

To see how the equilibrium condition is constructed, let us write Equation (4) and substitute for R_i from equation (1):

$$R_p = \sum x_i E_i + \sum x_i b_{i1} F_1 + \sum x_i b_{i2} F_2 + .. + \sum x_i b_{ik} F_k + \sum x_i e_i \qquad (5)$$

Because the error terms, e_i, are independent, the law of large numbers guarantees that a weighted average of many of them will approach zero in the limit as n becomes large. Since the arbitrage portfolio has no risk or according to equation (3), $\sum x_i b_{ij} = 0$, therefore equation (5) becomes:

$$R_p = \sum x_i E_i \tag{6}$$

If the return on the arbitrage portfolio is positive, then arbitrage opportunity exists. Such an opportunity is impossible if the market is to be in equilibrium, and the return on arbitrage portfolios must be zero. In other words:

$$R_p = \sum x_i E_i = 0 \tag{7}$$

Suppose we rewrite equations (2), (3), and (7):

$$\left(\sum x_i\right) \times 1 = 0 \tag{2}$$

$$\sum x_i b_{ij} = 0 \qquad \text{for each factor } j \ (j = 1 \ldots k) \tag{3}$$

$$\sum x_i E_i = 0 \tag{7}$$

The above three equations are really statements in linear algebra. Any vector that is orthogonal to the constant vector (equation [2]), and to each of the coefficient vectors (equation [3]), has to be orthogonal to the 'E_i' vector. The vectors E_i, 1, and b_{ij} are in the same vector space, and E_i is spanned by 1 and b_{ij}. In other words, there must exist a set of $k + 1$ coefficients, $\lambda_0, \lambda_1, \lambda_2, \ldots , \lambda_k$ such that:

$$E_i = \lambda_0 + \lambda_1 b_{i1} + \lambda_2 b_{i2} + \ldots + \lambda_k b_{ik} \tag{8}$$

Recall that the b_{ij} represent the sensitivity of the return on the ith asset to the jth factor.

In the context of the APT, it is impossible to construct two different portfolios, both having the same risk, with two different expected returns. equation (8) shows the general APT model, and the following equation shows the specific APT model that can be derived from the numerical values in Table 27.1.

$$E_i = 5 + 14b_{i1} + 2b_{i2} \qquad (9)$$

Any three points, like E_i, b_{i1}, b_{i2}, for example, define a plane in geometry. equation (9) is a formula for a specific three-dimensional plane that is an asset pricing model for three assets in Table 27.1. Figure 27.1 illustrates the APT plane of equation (9). In equilibrium, the risks and return of every asset should conform to the APT model of equation (8).

Table 27.1
APT Example

Asset (i)	Expected return (%)	b_{i1}	b_{i2}
A	16	.5	2.0
B	15	.5	1.5
C	28	1.5	1.0

Figure 27.1
Arbitrage Pricing Plane for Two Factors

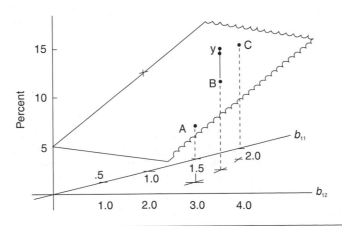

TECHNIQUES OF ESTIMATING LAMBDAS

To test or estimate the APT model, a statistical methodology called factor analysis is used. Factor analysis is a technique of statistical analysis with which most financial analysts were unfamiliar in 1976, when Stephen A. Ross's seminal article[1] introducing APT was published. Today, many empirical tests of the APT have been published. The dominant approach in testing APT still follows the initial empirical work published by Stephen Ross and Richard Roll.[2]

In their work, the factor analysis algorithm analyzes time-series data of 'T' periods rate of return over a cross-section of 'N' different assets and statistically extracts those factors that affect the returns. Factor analysis produces or extracts its own explanatory variables, called *factors* from the matrix of return below:

$$
\begin{vmatrix}
r_{1,1} & r_{1,2} & r_{1,3} & \ldots & \ldots & r_{1,T} \\
r_{2,1} & r_{2,2} & r_{2,3} & \ldots & \ldots & r_{2,T} \\
& & & & \cdot & \\
& & & \cdot & & \\
& & \cdot & & & \\
r_{N,1} & r_{N,2} & r_{N,3} & \ldots & \ldots & r_{N,T}
\end{vmatrix}
$$

where $r_{N,T}$ is the return of the Nth asset at time period T. The purpose of factor analysis is to reduce the 'N by T' matrix of returns to a smaller 'K by T' matrix that explains all or most of the variation in the matrix of returns. The K factors $(K < N)$ extracted by factor analysis have factor scores for each factor at each time period. For instance, $F_{K,T}$ represents the factor score for the Kth factor in time period T in the matrix below.

$$
\begin{vmatrix}
F_{1,1} & F_{1,2} & F_{1,3} & \ldots & \ldots & F_{1,T} \\
F_{2,1} & F_{2,2} & F_{2,3} & \ldots & \ldots & F_{2,T} \\
& & & & \cdot & \\
F_{K,1} & F_{K,2} & F_{K,3} & \ldots & \ldots & F_{K,T}
\end{vmatrix}
$$

The factor scores in the matrix above are used as the independent variables in equation (1) to estimate the b_{ij} coefficients for every asset. For instance, the estimated coefficients for the first asset are derived from the following T equations $(t = 1,...T)$:

$$R_{1,t} = E_1 + b_{1,1} F_{1,t} + b_{1,2} F_{2,t} + \dots + b_{1,K} F_{K,t} + e_1, \tag{10}t$$

This process is repeated for all N assets. Therefore, we have N estimates for every coefficient, as shown in the matrix below.

$$
\begin{vmatrix}
b_{1,1} & b_{1,2} & b_{1,3} \dots \dots \dots b_{1,K} \\
b_{2,1} & b_{2,2} & b_{2,3} \dots \dots \dots b_{2,K} \\
& \cdot & \\
& \cdot & \\
& \cdot & \\
b_{N,1} & b_{N,2} & b_{N,3} \dots \dots b_{N,K}
\end{vmatrix}
$$

Using the above estimates, the following APT equation is employed to estimate the APT "factor risk premiums," denoted λ_j, $(j = 1, \dots k)$:

$$E_i = \lambda_0 + \lambda_1 b_{i1} + \lambda_2 b_{i2} + \dots + \lambda_k b_{ik} \tag{8}$$

This regression was actually run by Ross and Roll in order to see whether or not the estimated λs are statistically significant. Ross and Roll employed factor analytic techniques to analyze 1,260 NYSE stocks randomly divided into 42 groups containing 30 stocks each, for 2,619 time periods. They repeated the above estimation 42 times to find the number of significant factors in each group. Their results show that 37 of the 42 groups had at least one statistically significant factor (at the 95 percent level of confidence). For 24 of the 42 groups, at least two factors were significant. In general, the results suggest that two or possibly even three risk factors exist that systematically influence common stock returns.

PROBLEMS WITH APT EMPIRICAL TESTS

The major problems with APT are essentially problems with factor analysis, not problems with the APT model. The usefulness of an APT model cannot be differentiated from the methodology used to estimate it. The theory may well be correct, but if it cannot be implemented or estimated in a meaningful sense, then, while it remains useful as a way of thinking, it cannot be used as part of the investment process. Apart from its economic and financial problems (many signs on the factor loadings have no logical meaning), we here just concentrate on the statistical problems in testing the APT model.

First, one problem inherent in any empirical application of factor analysis is that the statistical procedure is not capable of testing rigorously specified hypotheses. Factor analysis is a "flexible procedure"; it is capable of accidentally furnishing support for models that are illogical and/or erroneous because sampling errors may influence the results.

A second problem, and a detrimental one, is that the ability of the factor analysis to specify factors to explain the securities' returns is highly dependent on the sample. Thus, for example, each of the 42 groups of 30 stocks used by Ross and Roll could conceivably contain *different* factors. In order words, if two significant factors were found in each of the 42 groups, for instance, this finding might actually represent as many as 84; (2 × 42 = 84) *different* factors or as few as two factors or any number between 2 and 84. Thus, the principal disadvantage of this procedure is that it identifies neither the number nor the definition of the factors that influence the security returns.

SOLVING THE APT PROBLEM WITH NEURAL NETWORKS

In statistics, methods to estimate trends or recognize patterns are actually optimization methods. They all seek to minimize error. In addition to employing optimization techniques, in neural networks we also look at the whole pattern rather than sequentially looking at one feature at a time. However, the operation is generally presented as a mapping from one set of vectors to another set of vectors:

$$\{\text{vector space } v\} \rightarrow [\,W\,] \rightarrow \{\text{vector space } u\}, \text{ or } u = Wv$$

This says that for each input vector v, the network searches for a weight-matrix W such that it produces vector u, whose components are very close to the output units. The process can be viewed as a search for a matrix W that when applied to a pattern v, yields an output u.

A typical neural network can be presented schematically in the form of an array of multiples and summing junctions. In a network with no hidden layer, inputs are connected to the output by a link such that the input to the output node is the sum of all the appropriately weighted inputs. In this work, a feedforward net similar to Rumelhart, Hinton,

Figure 27.2

Feedforward Net

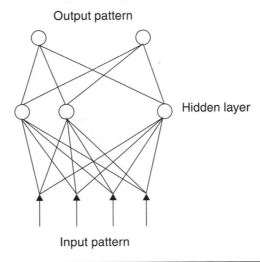

Output pattern

Hidden layer

Input pattern

and Williams,[3] illustrated in Figure 27.2, has been found to be an effective system for learning risk factors of APT from a body of time-series examples.

Again, the network used in this study is—like the Rumelhart, Hinton, and Williams study—made up of sets of nodes arranged in layers. The outputs of nodes in one layer are transmitted to nodes in another layer through links that amplify, attenuate, or inhibit such outputs through weighting factors. Each node is activated in accordance with the input, the activation function, and the bias of the node.

The net input to a node in layer j is:

$$net_j = \sum w_{ji} x_i$$

where x_i is the ith input, and the output of node j is:

$$y = f(net_j)$$

where f is the activation function, and (Φ) is the bias.

$$y = f(net_j) = \frac{1}{1 + e^{-(net + \Phi)}}$$

In this study, the NeuralWare Professional II software has been used. The learning rules employed here are the generalized delta rule in a back-propagation schedule. The net is presented schematically in Figure 27.3. The inputs are the rate of returns of assets and also several factors that generally are believed to have an effect on stock returns have been added to the inputs. These are the rate of change in the stock market, the change in GNP, the unemployment rate, and the inflation rate. The inputs are normalized such that they are scaled to fall between the values 0 and 1. In the learning process, there were 3,000, 5,000, 8,000, and 10,000 presentations of data to the network. After testing the network, there was not a significant improvement after 5,000 times. The success of the system did depend on the number of hidden layers. At this time, it is not known why two hidden layers were the best choice. One hidden layer did not produce a better system, but more than two hidden layers definitely reduces the effectiveness of the network. Consequently, there are two hidden layers; one is capturing the effect of other stocks on a particular asset. The other hidden layer is designed to capture macroeconomic factors. Therefore, every asset at the output layer is influenced by other assets, market factors, and macroeconomic factors.

Figure 27.3

Back-Propagation Network

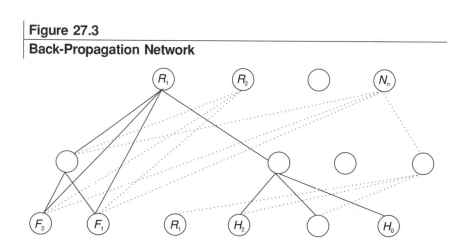

Applying neural nets with hidden processing elements to the APT problem eliminates all the shortcomings of the factor analysis mentioned above. This system is distribution free; that is, we do not need to know the probability distribution of the rate of returns. Additionally, this system is not concerned with the number of factors. The researcher can add as many factors as desired, and the network learns that some factors are not relevant to this problem.

Figure 27.4
Alternative Representation

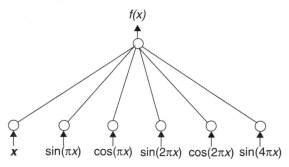

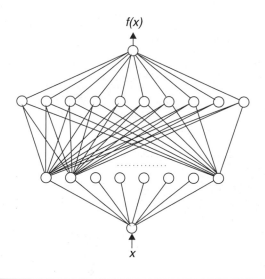

OTHER NEURAL NET POSSIBILITIES

Economists and financial analysts, at this point, are very much concerned about the meaning of the "weights" in a trained network. They would like to relate them to slope, sensitivity, and rate of change or marginal effects. Interpreting these weights in finance is not an easy task, especially when the network has several hidden layers. The only solution to this problem is to create a functional-link network. This system is suggested by Klassen and Pao[4] and has been tested by Pao.[5] This network actually eliminates the effect of hidden layers and makes the interpretation easier and, according to Pao, "improves the rate of learning," too. In this model, each input vector is acted on by the functional link to yield input-related values.

Pao suggests, "the net effect is to map the input pattern into a larger pattern space. We associate and represent each component x with the quantities $x, x^2, x^3,.....$ or with $x, \sin \pi x, \cos \pi x, \sin 2\, \pi x, \cos 2\, \pi x$, and so on, depending on the set of functions that we deem to be appropriate. No intrinsically new ad hoc information is introduced, but the representation is enhanced." This concept is shown schematically in Figure 27.4.

ENDNOTES

1. S. Ross, "The Arbitrage Pricing Theory of Capital Asset Pricing," *Journal of Economic Theory*, December 1976, pp. 344–60.

2. R. Roll and S. Ross, "An Empirical Investigation of the Arbitrage Pricing Theory," *Journal of Finance* 35 (December 1980), pp. 1073–1103.

3. D. E. Rumelhart, G. E. Hinton, and R. J. Williams, "Learning Internal Representations by Error Propagation," in *Parallel Distributed Processing*. Cambridge, MA: MIT Press, pp. 318–62.

4. M. S. Klassen and Y. H. Pao, "Characteristics of the Functional Link Net: A Higher Order Delta Rule Net," *IEEE Proceedings of the Second Annual International Conference on Neural Networks*, 1988.

5. Y. H. Pao, *Adaptive Pattern Recognition and Neural Networks* (Reading, MA: Addison-Wesley, 1989).

28

ARTIFICIAL NEURAL NETWORK MODELS FOR PRICING INITIAL PUBLIC OFFERINGS

Bharat A. Jain and Barin N. Nag

INTRODUCTION

This study has been designed as an integration between the established technology of artificial neural networks (ANNs) and the equally well-known problem of pricing initial public offerings (IPOs). An IPO is the first public stock offering of a company that might have been operating, but not in the public domain. As a result, asset valuations are based on incomplete and imperfect information. The valuation problem is further complicated by the fact that prices depend on several complex and often interrelated variables whose relationships are unclear. These conditions make it particularly difficult to establish the specific parametric form of the underlying asset price dynamics or obtain an analytical expression. Misspecification of the stochastic process of the price dynamics will lead to systematic pricing errors. Such applications lend themselves to being modeled nonparametrically. ANNs have been used extensively, and successfully, for modeling nonlinear statistical relations nonparametrically in a wide variety of decision-making applications. These applications present conditions where more conventional models and mathematical decision tools tend to perform poorly. More reliable results have been documented from decision-making using human intelligence, in particular in the use of human characteristics such as pattern recognition, pattern matching, and pattern classification [14] [26]. ANN models simulate these same human characteristics operationally as suggested by brain theory. In a manner similar to intelligent and associative reasoning, an ANN model can recognize existing patterns in data and help support decisions on this basis.

In recent times, research literature has shown considerable interest in the development of ANNs for improving the quality of decisions in financial applications, especially in situations that are predictive in nature and are based upon pattern matching and classification. Successful applications of neural networks have been reported in a wide variety of financial applications, including corporate bond rating [4], credit evaluation and underwriting [3], bankruptcy prediction [25], and prediction of savings and loan association failures [23]. These successes can be partly attributed to the specific characteristics of financial decision problems that lend themselves to ANN work. For instance, ANNs require extensive data sets to be sufficiently trained, and financial applications are usually characterized by an abundance of historical data. At the same time, financial decisions often involve in some way people, environment, and vagaries of economic conditions. Inevitably, noise and irregularities in the relationships arise that introduce errors in conventional parametric models. The nature of neural network memory, however, leads to a reasonable network response even when presented with incomplete, noisy, or previously unseen inputs.

In this chapter, we attempt to price IPOs using a data-driven, neural network approach. The IPO pricing problem is somewhat similar to that of pricing new and unique products where there is little or no information on market demand, product acceptance, competitive response, or prior experience to guide the decision process. Companies going public and their investment bankers are faced with the decision of pricing the stock for the initial offering. A primary consideration in arriving at an issue price is the assessment of the net present value of future cash flows. Other considerations such as market/demand conditions, industry structure, product uniqueness, and competitive response are important additional inputs in the pricing decision. Once the issue price is selected, the firm is committed to selling the entire offering to the public at this fixed price. The market price of the firm is established when trading commences in the secondary market on completion of the IPO. If the post-issue market price turns out to be significantly above/below the IPO issue price, losses in the form of underpricing/overpricing are incurred by the firm/investors. Thus, it is critical that issuing firms and their investment bankers price IPOs as closely as possible to the unobservable post-IPO market price.

Despite the need to accurately price new issues, a vast body of empirical evidence suggests that IPOs, on average, are significantly underpriced. Several studies suggest that the average IPO underpricing exceeds 15 percent [2], [9], [10], [11], [12], [18], [19], and [20]. Such high levels of IPO underpricing result in staggering losses to issuers. For instance, *Business Week* reports that within the United States, IPO firms sold close to $100 billion of equity during 1990–1993 [24]. Assuming an average underpricing of 15 percent indicates that these issuers incurred a $15 billion loss of capital due to mispricing. Overall, if the underpricing problem persists, firms planning to go public will find it optimal to seek alternative sources of capital or forego their positive net present value (NPV) projects. A decline in the IPO market can result in a capital crunch leading to problems of underinvestment, slow growth, high unemployment, and loss of prosperity. Thus, there is a compelling economic argument to identify decision tools that have the potential to improve the accuracy of pricing IPOs. Due to the size of the new issues market, even a moderate reduction in the level of underpricing represents a significant economic contribution.

We construct neural network models to price IPOs using a large sample of 552 new issues. The inputs to the network include primary economic variables that potentially influence IPO stock prices. The output of the network is the post-IPO market price. Consistent with [1], [9], [10], [11], [12], [18], [19], and [20] we define the post-IPO market price as the closing bid price established at the end of the first day of trading in the aftermarket. The price distribution over the sample cases generated by the neural network models are compared with the actual post-issue market price distribution to detect statistically significant differences. The economic benefits of the neural network models are evaluated by examining their ability to reduce the average level of underpricing. The results provide evidence of substantial economic gains with the neural network models.

For instance, the best neural network model provides an 8 percent reduction in the average underpricing on a holdout test data set. Similar results are documented for networks with different node configurations of the hidden layer. The results hold both for the training and test data set, thereby establishing the generalizability and robustness of the results.

The rest of this chapter is organized as follows. First, the IPO pricing problem is discussed. This is followed by network construction details and a discussion of the performance evaluation criteria. A discussion of the main empirical results follows. The last section provides a summary and conclusion.

THE PROBLEM OF PRICING INITIAL PUBLIC OFFERINGS

The pricing of new securities by issuing firms or their investment bankers is a complex and difficult decision problem. The value of the firm is the present value of future cash flows from tangible and intangible assets. While it is a relatively easier task to value tangible assets, arriving at a value for intangible assets such as future growth opportunities is considerably more complicated since it involves forecasting future cash flows and estimating firm-specific risk. This requires an in-depth analysis of the industry structure, market conditions, and competitive positioning of the firm both at present and in the near future. At the firm level, factors such as the quality and experience of management, product uniqueness, board composition, risk factors, incentive structure, and financial performance need to be carefully evaluated. The final price is determined after a thorough analysis of all the above information. Since the evaluation of these issues is subjective, there is often considerable disagreement between the issuing firm and their investment bankers on their respective assessments of the issue price at which the firm can be sold. A major reason for differences in opinion are due to conflicting objectives. The issuing firm would like to maximize IPO proceeds. On the other hand, while the investment bankers share this objective, they would also like to ensure that the offer is fully subscribed and their regular customers are satisfied that the issue price represents fair value. Usually, extensive negotiations and discussions are involved during the process of establishing a final issue price that both parties can agree on.

However, the accuracy of this final issue price is known only after the IPO, when market prices are established. The relevant benchmark for comparison is the closing bid price established at the end of the first day of trading in the aftermarket [1], [9], [10], [11], [12], [18], [19], and [20]. When this post-issue market price deviates from the IPO issue price, direct or indirect costs are imposed on the issuers in the form of underpricing or overpricing. Underpricing represents a direct cost to the firm in terms of lost revenue. On the other hand, overpricing results in a wealth loss to investors and indirectly imposes costs on the firm in the form of lawsuits, lost reputation capital, and higher costs of raising capital in the future.

The substantial economic inefficiency incurred as a result of mispricing IPOs can be seen from the case of Microsoft Corporation, which went public in 1986 in what is considered a highly successful offering due to huge investor demand and subsequent superior investment performance [16]. However, Microsoft and their investment bankers apparently left a considerable sum of money on the table. After extensive negotiations between the firm and their investment bankers, the issue was priced at $21 per share and sold to the public. As it turned out, this price considerably underestimated the value that investors associated with the company. At the end of the first day of trading, Microsoft shares were selling at $27.50 per share, effectively suggesting that the firm and their investment bankers had underpriced the issue by over 30 percent. As a result of underestimating market prices, Microsoft incurred an 18 million dollar capital loss in a total offering of 61 million dollars. Thus, it is imperative that issuers and their investment bankers are able to accurately gauge the price investors associate with a new issue to avoid such huge losses due to mispricing.

Empirical evidence, however, suggests that issuing firms and their investment bankers consistently underestimate the value of their assets, leading to widespread underpricing. Several researchers have documented that, on average, IPOs are significantly underpriced. For instance, Ibbotson, Sindelar, and Ritter [10] document an average underpricing of 16.38 percent in a large sample of 8800 IPOs issued between 1960 and 1987. Other studies suggest similar numbers. Table 28.1 shows the average underpricing documented by various researchers using U.S. data. Further, Ibbotson and Ritter [11] find that the IPO underpricing phenomena is not just a U.S. capital market phenomena and occurs in practically every country where an active stock market exists.

It is apparent that IPOs are systematically mispriced, leading to a significant loss of capital for issuers worldwide. The economic consequences of mispricing IPOs are likely to become even more serious with

Table 28.1

Empirical Evidence on the Problem of Underpricing

Study	Sample Size	Sample Period	Mean Underpricing (%)
Ibbotson [9]	120	1960–1974	11.40
Ritter [20]	664	1977–1982	14.80
Ibbotson, Sindelar, and Ritter [10]	8800	1960–1987	16.38
Muscarella and Vetsuypens [18]	1184	1983–1987	7.60
Carter and Manaster [2]	501	1979–1983	16.79
James [13]	520	1980–1983	8.00
Jain [12]	1960	1980–1988	12.17

the boom in the new issues market within the United States and the movement towards privatization and market economies in several Central European and Asian countries. As a result of these trends, several hundred billion dollars of equity from new issues are likely to be released in the world markets. If the underpricing problem persists, the economic losses are likely to assume staggering proportions. Consequently, decision tools that even marginally improve the accuracy of pricing IPOs have the potential to provide substantial economic benefits.

Prior attempts at estimating the determinants of IPO underpricing have produced models with very low explanatory power. These studies have used conventional parametric modeling techniques such as ordinary least squares (OLS) or weighted least squares (WLS) regressions to estimate the determinants of underpricing [1], [2], [12], and [20]. The results suggest that underpricing is negatively related to the size of the offering, managerial ownership retention, and the reputation of the investment banker, and positively related to the risk of the firm. A problem with these studies, however, is their low explanatory power. For instance Beatty and Ritter[1] report R^2 of only 7 percent when underpricing is regressed against log IPO offer size and a proxy for the risk of the firm. Further, no more than 10 percent of the cross-sectional variation in underpricing can be explained by various proxies for uncertainty [18]. The low explanatory power of these models limit their use in providing decision-makers with means to accurately price new issues.

It is not surprising, however, that parametric statistical models provide such limited success in accurately pricing IPOs. Parametric models require the assumption of a specific functional form of the relationship between the variables. The pricing of IPOs involves the interaction of many variables whose relationships are often ill-defined or unclear, and hence it is difficult if not impossible to specify the exact functional form of the relationship between variables. Further, since parametric models are based on certain strong assumptions, they are highly sensitive to specification errors. On the other hand, neural network based methods differ fundamentally from traditional parametric techniques and provide a promising alternative to model the IPO pricing problem. Unlike parametric statistical models, neural networks do not need to, a priori, specify the functional relationship between the dependent variable and the independent variables. They do not need to assume lognormality or sample path continuity, and hence are robust to specification errors. Neural networks scan the data to develop an internal representation of the relationship between the variables. This makes them more adaptive and responsive to structural changes in the data-generating process. Finally, neural networks are better equipped to handle situations involving large number of input variables, noisy data sets and correlated variables, which are usually present in most financial applications, including that of pricing IPOs.

THE NEURAL NETWORK MODEL

This section describes the neural network models constructed to price IPOs. The inputs to the network are primary economic variables that potentially influence the market price of the firm. Information on these variables is usually provided in the initial prospectuses supplied to regulators and potential investors prior to the offering. The output of the network is the post-issue market price.

Data Description

The sample consists of 552 IPOs issued between 1980 and 1990 and are identified from *Going Public: The IPO Reporter* [6]. The sample is randomly split into two sets of equal size to form the training and test data sets.

The network is initially trained on the training data set. Subsequently, its performance is evaluated on the holdout test sample.

The network is trained with 11 input variables representing a broad spectrum of financial indicators usually used by investors in valuing assets of firms going public. The variables RANK, LSIZE, and ALPHA represent the reputation of the investment banker, the log of gross proceeds raised at the IPO, and the extent of ownership retained by the original entrepreneurs in the post-IPO firm, respectively. SALES represents the inverse of the sales in millions of dollars in the year prior to the IPO and has often been used as a proxy for the risk of the firm [1], [19]. Prior studies have suggested that the above variables are important determinants of IPO underpricing. For instance, [1], [2], [12], and [20] suggest that RANK, LSIZE, and ALPHA are negatively related to underpricing, while proxies of risk such as the standard deviation of aftermarket returns or 1/sales are positively related. In addition to these four variables, seven additional financial variables are included as inputs to the network. The variables CAPEA and CAPES represent capital expenditure over assets and capital expenditure over sales in the fiscal year prior to the IPO. Profitability measures are represented by OPRA, OPRS, OPCFA, and OPCFS, which are the operating return over assets, operating return over sales, operating cash flow over assets, and operating cash flow over sales, respectively (all measured in the fiscal year prior to the IPO). The variable ATU represents the asset turnover.

Table 28.2 provides a list of the input variables and their descriptive statistics. In Table 28.3, a correlation matrix is provided. As expected, there is evidence of significant correlation among some of the 11 variables. For instance, the correlation between LSIZE and SALES is 0.75 and is statistically significant at =0.01 level. Other variables that are highly correlated include CAPEA with CAPES, OPRA with OPRS, OPRA with OPCFS, OPCFS with CAPES, and OPCFS with OPRS. The correlations between other input variables, however, are generally insignificant.

Training the Neural Network

The ANN model development involves selecting design parameters such as the number of hidden layers, the number of nodes in the hidden layer, the number of training cycles, epoch size, initial and final learning rate, and momentum terms. These are important decisions in modeling the network and can significantly affect the performance of the system. Un-

Table 28.2

Distribution of Input Variables Provided to the Neural Network for Pricing IPOs

Input Variables	Mean (Median)	$Q1(Q3)$
Size of issue (SIZE) M$	27.69(12.60)	6.90(24.00)
Underwriter reputation (RANK)	6.24(7.00)	5.00(8.00)
Fraction of firm sold at IPO (ALPHA)%	28.65(26.60)	21.10(34.40)
1/sales prior to IPO (SALES)M$	77.45(23.52)	10.34(55.14)
Operating return on assets (OPRA)%	22.53(22.11)	14.06(30.85)
Operating return on sales (OPRS)%	15.45(14.29)	8.25(21.49)
Capital expenditure/assets (CAPEA)%	12.73(8.24)	3.98(16.92)
Asset turnover (ATU)%	1.72(1.54)	1.08(2.14)
Operating cash flow/assets (OPCFA)%	26.04(11.00)	0.00(0.21)
Operating cash flow/sales (OPCFS)%	4.40(7.00)	0.00(14.00)
Capital expenditure/sales (CAPES)%	11.05(5.00)	3.00(12.00)

fortunately, in the area of selecting model parameters and network topology, there are very few theoretical foundations. However, several heuristic guidelines have been developed that seem to perform well. For example, Salchenberger, Cinar, and Lash [23] suggest that the number of nodes in the hidden layer should be 75 percent of the number of input nodes. Further, some literature suggests that while at least one hidden layer is a must, there is little to be gained by adding multiple hidden layers [4], [5], and [23]. In our analyses, we experimented with the number

Table 28.3

Correlation Matrix

	RANK	LSIZE	ALPHA	CAPEA	SALES	OPRA	OPCFA	OPCFS	CAPES	OPRS	ATU
RANK	1.00	0.17	-0.11	0.05	0.13	0.04	-0.02	-0.01	0.08	0.08	-0.15
LSIZE	0.17	1.00	0.17	-0.05	0.75*	-0.06	-0.01	-0.03	0.01	0.05	-0.11
ALPHA	-0.11	0.17	1.00	-0.10	0.05	0.01	0.03	0.05	-0.12*	-0.06	0.14
CAPEA	0.05	-0.05	-0.10	1.00	-0.09	0.05	-0.02	-0.53*	0.74*	0.08	-0.10
SALES	0.13	0.75*	0.05	-0.09	1.00	-0.09	-0.01	0.05*	-0.06	0.04	-0.03
OPRA	0.04	-0.06	0.01	0.05	-0.09	1.00	0.05	0.56*	-0.13	0.60*	0.31
OPCFA	-0.02	-0.01	0.03	-0.02	-0.01	0.05	1.00	0.05	-0.04	0.02	0.03
OPCFS	-0.01	-0.03	0.05	-0.53	0.08	0.56	0.05	1.00	-0.65*	0.61*	0.10
CAPES	0.08	0.01	-0.12	0.74*	-0.06	-0.13	-0.04	-0.65	1.00	0.19	-0.37
OPRS	0.08	0.05	-0.06	0.08	0.04	0.60	0.02	0.61	0.19	1.00	-0.25
ATU	-0.15	-0.11	0.14	-0.10	-0.03	0.31	0.03	0.10	-0.37	-0.25	1.00

* Significant at the 0.01 level.

of hidden layers, number of nodes in the hidden layer, learning rate, momentum, and the number of times examples are presented before the weights are updated (epoch size).

The final basic architecture of the network developed is shown in Figure 28.1. The system is a feedforward back-propogation neural network with 11 input nodes, a single hidden layer with k nodes, and a univariate output node that provides estimates of the post-issue market price of the stock. The choice of a single hidden layer was straightforward since experimentation revealed no significant improvement in performance with two or more hidden layers. This finding is consistent with Dutta and Shekhar [4] and Salchenberger, Cinar, and Lash [23], who also find no significant improvement with more than one middle layer. However, the choice of the number of nodes in the hidden layer presented a more difficult task due to conflicting outcomes. For instance, a larger number of hidden layer nodes is likely to improve the fit on the training set but may not be generalizable to other data sets. To determine the effect of changing the number of hidden layer nodes, results are presented for several alternative choices tested both on the training and holdout test data set.

Figure 28.1

A Neural Network for Pricing IPOs with One Hidden Layer (one output variable—market price)

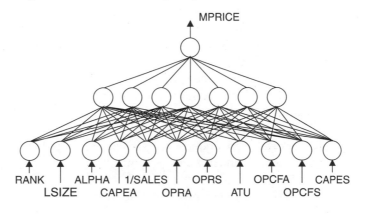

A tanh transfer function and the generalized delta rule are used with the back-propogation of error. An initial set of random weights is generated, and gaussian noise is assumed at the input stage. An initial learning rate of 0.40 and a momentum term of 0.40 are selected. For better tracking of error surface, they are progressively reduced to 0.05 and 0.05, respectively. The 276 observations from the training data set are presented randomly to the network. After experimentation, we settled on an epoch size of 16, which seemed to provide the best results. Training is terminated after 40,000 iterations, when the error stabilizes and further training does not lead to any additional improvements.

Performance-Evaluation Methodology

The objective of this study is to construct network models to estimate the market price of IPOs conditional on firm-specific inputs. The analysis is based on three different price distributions. From the sample of IPOs, the distributions of the post-issue market price (defined as the market price established at the end of the first day of trading after the IPO) and the IPO issue price set by issuers/underwriters are known. As a result of underpricing by issuers and their investment bankers, these two distributions are significantly different. The third price distribution is the neural network-generated estimate of the post-issue market prices. Thus, the accuracy of the neural network model depends on its ability to generate a price distribution that does not deviate significantly from the actual post-issue market price distribution.

The price distribution over the sample cases generated by the network model (henceforth referred to as network generated price) is compared with the post-issue market price distribution and the distribution of IPO issue price to detect significant differences. We test the null hypothesis of no difference in the mean (median) post-issue market price and the network-generated price. The significance tests are based on the parametric t-test and the nonparametric Wilcoxon's signed rank test.

To estimate the economic gains provided by the network model, the mean neural network-based underpricing is compared with the actual underpricing. The actual underpricing is computed as follows:

$$\text{Actual } underpricing = (P_m - P_0 / P_0 \tag{1}$$

where P_m is the post-issue market price and P_o is the IPO issue price set by the issuers/investment bankers. In a similar fashion, the under-pricing that would occur as a result of using the neural network to price IPOs is computed as follows:

$$\text{Neural net based underpricing} = (P_m - P_{nm})/P_{nm}, \qquad (2)$$

where P_{nm} is the network generated price and P_m is the actual post-issue market price of the stock. The null hypothesis of no difference in the mean underpricing between the network-based and actual underpricing is tested using the t-test. Evidence of superior performance by the network models is established if the network-based underpricing is significantly lower than the actual underpricing.

Initially, all of the above tests are performed on the training data set. Subsequently, to establish generalizability, the comparisons are repeated on a holdout test data set. Finally, to provide the decision-maker with the ability to conduct sensitivity analyses, a test statistic is computed to measure the relative importance of each input variable on the output variable. This allows the decision-maker a certain level of confidence in the prediction of the models and also the ability to evaluate the performance of pruned networks containing only those input variables that have a strong association with the output variable.

RESULTS

Training Data Set

In Table 28.4, the results on the training data set are provided. In Table 28.4a, the distributions of the network-generated market price, post-issue market price, and IPO issue price are compared. The results with neural networks are reported for configurations of 4, 6, 7, 9, and 12 hidden layer nodes. The mean (median) post-issue market price for the 276 IPOs in the training set is $13.38 ($13.00). The mean (median) IPO issue price is $12.67 ($12.00) and is significantly lower (at =0.01 level) than the mean (median) post-issue market price. These figures are consistent with the findings of earlier studies, which provide strong evidence to suggest that issuers/investment bankers significantly underestimate the post-issue

Table 28.4

Results on Training Set

a. Comparison of Pricing Distribution

Description	Mean	Median	Standard Deviation	$H_0{:}Z(p)^{*}$
Post-IPO mkt Price $	13.38	13.00	5.74	—
Actual IPO Selling price	12.67	12.00	5.35	$2.83^{a}(0.005)$
NN price (4)[†]	13.45	12.64	5.35	0.56(0.575)
NN price (6)	13.39	12.44	5.23	0.02(0.98)
NN price (7)	13.36	12.48	5.32	−0.28(0.774)
NN price (9)	13.28	12.33	5.24	−0.83(0.40)
NN price (12)	13.53	12.63	5.28	0.95(0.34)

b. Comparison between NN Based and Actual Underpricing

Description	Mean	Median	Standard Deviation	$H_0{:}Z(p)^{‡}$
Actual underpricing	8.40^{a}	1.40^{a}	56.10	—
NN undpr (4)	−0.59	$−2.41^{b}$	12.56	$2.73^{a}(0.006)$
NN undpr (6)	−0.28	$−2.00^{b}$	13.03	$2.61^{a}(0.009)$
NN undpr (7)	0.28	$−1.63^{c}$	12.79	$2.51^{a}(0.015)$
NN undpr (9)	0.76	−0.77	13.06	$2.37^{b}(0.0183)$
NN undpr (12)	−1.21	$−3.08^{a}$	12.74	$2.99^{a}(0.0030)$

[a,b,c] Significantly different from zero at the 0.01, 0.05, and 0.10 level, respectively.
[*] Test of the null hypothesis that the price distribution is not significantly different from the post-issue market price distribution.
[†] The numbers in parenthesis represent hidden-layer nodes.
[‡] Test of the null hypothesis that the mean network-based underpricing is not significantly different from that of the actual underpricing.

market price of new issues. The results in Table 28.4a, however, suggest that the network models provide a significant improvement in the accuracy of pricing IPOs. For instance, the mean (median) network-generated market price using a four-hidden-node configuration is $13.45 ($12.64) and is not significantly different from the mean (median) post-issue market price. Further, the superior performance of the network models are robust to the choice of number of hidden layer nodes. The variation in the mean network generated price for the various hidden-layer configurations evaluated in this study are marginal, ranging from a low $13.28 for a 9-node network to a high of $13.53 for a 12-node network. In all instances, the network-generated market price distributions are not significantly different from that of the post-issue market price.

In Table 28.4b, the economic benefits of using the neural network models to price IPOs are evaluated by comparing the actual underpricing with the network-based underpricing. The mean actual underpricing for the sample of 276 firms in the training set is 8.40 percent (significantly different from zero at $\alpha=0.01$ level). The mean neural net based underpricing for the same training sample is –0.59 percent (not significantly different from zero) for the 4-node network. The null hypothesis of no difference in mean actual and network-based underpricing is rejected at $\alpha=0.01$ level. Thus, the network model provides substantial gains in the form of reduced underpricing. Further, the ability of the network models to reduce the level of underpricing is robust to the choice of number of hidden layer nodes. The mean network-based underpricing ranges from a low of –1.21 percent for the 12 node network to a high of 0.76 percent for the 9-layer network. In all instances, the mean network-based underpricing is not significantly different from zero. Further, in all instances, the null hypothesis of no difference in mean actual and network-based underpricing is rejected at $\alpha=0.01$ level.

The above results suggest that pricing IPOs with the neural network models increases economic efficiency in the form of reduced underpricing costs. However, prior to making any definitive assertions on the value of using neural networks to price IPOs, it is important to establish the generalizability of the results. To address this issue, we repeat the analysis by analyzing the performance of the network models constructed with data from the training set on a separate holdout test data set.

Table 28.5

Results on Test Data Set

a. Comparison of Pricing Distribution

Description	Mean	Median	Standard Deviation	$H_0\!:\!Z(p)$[*]
Post-IPO mkt Price $	13.94	13.00	6.05	—
Actual IPO Selling price	12.52	12.00	4.49	$-4.39^a(0.001)$
NN price (4)[†]	13.49	12.36	5.20	$-2.98^a(0.003)$
NN price (6)	13.27	12.13	4.99	$-4.45^a(0.001)$
NN price (7)	13.34	12.18	5.13	$-3.83^a(0.001)$
NN price (9)	13.26	12.13	4.98	$-4.46^a(0.001)$
NN price (12)	13.58	12.48	5.03	$-2.82^a(0.005)$

b. Comparison between NN Based and Actual Underpricing

Description	Mean	Median	Standard Deviation	$H_0\!:\!Z(p)$[‡]
Actual underpricing	10.45^a	3.50^a	18.81	—
NN undpr (4)	3.11^a	-2.03^b	17.06	$5.21^a(0.001)$
NN undpr (6)	-4.40^a	-0.45	17.26	$4.78^a(0.001)$
NN undpr (7)	4.12^a	-1.06^c	17.38	$9.61^a(0.001)$
NN undpr (9)	4.40^a	-0.45	17.25	$5.74^a(0.001)$
NN undpr (12)	2.43^a	-2.50^b	16.92	$6.53^a(0.001)$

[a,b,c] Significantly different from zero at the 0.01, 0.05, and 0.10 levels, respectively.
[*] Test of the null hypothesis that the price distribution is not significantly different from the post-issue market price distribution.
[†] The numbers in parenthesis represent hidden-layer nodes.
[‡] Test of the null hypothesis that the mean network-based underpricing is not significantly different from that of the actual underpricing.

Test Data Set

The results of the analysis with the holdout test data set are reported in Table 28.5. In Table 28.5a, the distributions of the network generated market price, post-issue market price, and IPO issue price are compared. The mean (median) post-IPO market price for the 276 IPOs in the test dataset is $13.94 ($13.00) while the mean (median) IPO issue price is $12.52 ($12.00) and is significantly lower than the post-issue market price at =0.01 level. The mean (median) network-generated market price ranges from a low $13.26 ($12.13) for a 9-node network to a high of $13.58 ($12.48) for a 12-node network. In all instances, the network-generated market price distribution lies in between the IPO issue price and the post-issue market price distribution. Further, the distribution of network-generated market prices are significantly higher than the IPO issue price distribution, thereby providing consistent evidence to suggest that the neural network models improve upon the performance of issuers/investment bankers in pricing IPOs. However, the results are somewhat weaker than the training data set since the distributions of network-generated market prices are significantly lower than the post-issue market price distribution, which is indicative of the network models somewhat underestimating the market price of IPOs.

In Table 28.5b, the mean network-based and actual underpricing are compared. The mean actual underpricing for the 276 IPOs in the test sample is 10.45 percent and is significantly different from zero at =0.01 level. The network-based underpricing ranges from a low -4.40 percent for a six-node network, to a high of 4.40 percent for a nine-node network. The best results are obtained with the 12-node neural network with a mean underpricing of 2.43 percent. Further, in all instances, the null hypothesis of no difference in mean actual and network-based underpricing is rejected at α=0.01 level.

Thus, the results provide consistent evidence to suggest that the network models outperform issuers/investment bankers in pricing IPOs. The results hold both with the training and a holdout test data set. To get an approximate idea of the extent of the economic benefits of using neural network models, we examine the aggregate cost savings as a result of their superior performance in pricing IPOs. The mean actual underpricing of 8.40 percent for the 276 firms in the training data set results in an aggregate loss of 507 million dollars due to mispricing. Using a four-node network to price these 276 IPOs in the training set results in reducing the aggregate underpricing costs to $28.04 million. Similarly,the mean actual underpricing of 10.45 percent for the 276 firms in the test data set results in an aggregate loss of $571 million. Using a four-node network to price these IPOs in the test set results in reducing the aggregate underpricing costs to $84.13 million. Examining the performance of networks with different nodes in the hidden layer provides evidence of similar substantial reductions in aggregate underpricing costs. As a result, both the economic benefits as well as the generalizability of using neural networks to price IPOs is established.

Interpretation of Relative Strength of Input Variables

Unlike traditional statistical modeling techniques, neural networks do not directly provide information regarding the importance of each input variable on the output variable. However, for any real decision-making application, it is essential that the decision-maker has a certain degree of comfort both with the construction of the model and its predictions. One way to achieve such comfort levels is to establish whether the model and its predictions make intuitive sense through sensitivity analysis. However, in an ANN with hidden layers, it is difficult to evaluate the importance of each independent variable on the output layer since the input is indirectly connected to the output through hidden units. To overcome this limitation of neural network models, Yoon, Swales, and Margavio [27] propose a methodology to profile the impact of each input variable. For a network with one hidden layer, this methodology involves computing a test statistic of the form:

$$RS_{ji} = \Sigma(W_{ki}U_{jk}) \, / \, (\Sigma\text{ABS}\, \{\Sigma(W_{ki}U_{jk})\}), \tag{3}$$

where RS_{ji} is the relative strength between the ith input and the jth output variables, W_{ki} is the weight between the kth hidden unit and the ith input unit, and U_{jk} is the weight between the jth output unit and the kth hidden unit.

We use the above methodology to compute the relative strength of each input unit on the output variable using a 12-hidden-layer node neural network as an example. The results are reported in Table 28.6a. The variable LSIZE has by far the highest relative strength with a value of 0.28. The next five variables in order of the absolute value of their relative strengths are SALES, ALPHA, CAPES, CAPEA, and RANK. The remaining

Table 28.6

Sensitivity Analysis and Reduced Variables Analyses

a. Relative Strength of Input Variables

Input Variable	Relative Strength	Input Variable	Relative Strength
RANK	0.0173	OPRS	−0.0028
LSIZE	0.2833	ATU	−0.0093
ALPHA	0.0420	OPCFA	−0.0022
CAPEA	−0.0255	OPCFS	−0.0128
SALES	−0.0438	CAPES	−0.0280
OPRA	0.0132		

b. Reduced Variable Trials on Training Set

Input Variables (four-hidden–layer node network)	Mean Underpricing
RANK, LSIZE, ALPHA, CAPEA, SALES, CAPES	−2.72[a]
RANK, LSIZE, ALPHA, SALES	−3.80[a]
ALPHA, CAPEA, SALES, CAPES, −3.59[a]	

c. Reduced Variable Trials on Test Data Set

RANK, LSIZE, ALPHA, CAPEA, SALES, CAPES	7.01[a]
LSIZE, RANK, ALPHA, SALES	4.63[a]
ALPHA, CAPEA, SALES, CAPEA	5.30[a]

[a] Significantly different from zero at the 0.01 level.

input variables, however, are weakly associated with the output by virtue of their low relative scores (either positive or negative). Consistent with prior studies, the relative strengths suggest that LSIZE, RISK, ALPHA, and SALES are strongly associated with the output variable [1], [2], [12], and [20].

We also attempt to evaluate the performance of pruned networks utilizing a reduced set of input variables that are strongly associated with the output. This approach is similar to factor analysis or stepwise regression in parametric models. The results with the training data set using a four-node network are reported in Table 28.6b. It can be seen that the performance of the pruned networks are inferior to a four-node full network reported in Table 28.4 (both trained on the same dataset). For instance, the four-node full network provides an average underpricing of -0.59 (not significantly different from zero) compared to an average underpricing of –2.72 (significantly different from zero at $\alpha=0.01$ level) for the pruned network containing the six input variables with the highest relative strengths. In Table 28.6c, the performance of the pruned networks with four-hidden layer nodes on the holdout test dataset are reported. Once again, there is clear evidence that the pruned networks underperform the full network, all else being equal. In results not reported here, we repeat the analyses with different combinations of input variables and different nodes in the hidden layer. While the results are not always consistent, there is a general pattern to indicate that the full network outperforms the pruned networks, especially on the holdout test data set.

The above methodology provides a means to determine the relative impact of input variables on the output variable. This procedure provides the decision-maker with the option of conducting sensitivity analysis with regard to selection of input variables to include in the network model. However, the process of pruning the networks must be approached cautiously. Sometimes the removal of a few input variables with low relative strengths can have a dramatic negative impact on the performance of the network due to interactions between input variables [15]. Further, a major advantage of neural networks is their ability to find relationships among seemingly unrelated variables. Thus, while network pruning can provide some useful insights, in general, the benefits of adopting it are far from certain and likely to vary with different applications.

CONCLUSIONS

Private companies/entrepreneurs that seek to go public by selling equity are faced with the complex task of pricing the issue. Since the value of the firm is the sum of its assets in place and the present value of its growth opportunities, there is considerable uncertainty in estimating the price. The true market price is known only after the company goes public and its stock starts to trade in the market. If issuers/investment bankers underestimate this post-issue market price, they incur significant losses in the form of underpricing. Prior research has established that IPO firms incur substantial underpricing costs as a result of their inability to accurately price the issue.

A major obstacle in pricing IPOs is the difficulty in specifying the stochastic path of the price process. Previous studies that modeled the IPO underpricing problem with parametric models were plagued with the problem of low explanatory power. In this paper, an alternative neural network-based approach to price IPOs is evaluated. This method has the advantage of not requiring some fairly restrictive assumptions imposed by parametric models. The pricing performance of the network models are compared with the actual IPO issue prices and actual post-issue market prices. We find that the neural network models improve the accuracy of pricing IPOs and thereby provide substantial economic benefits in the form of reduced underpricing costs.The generalizability of the results are established by evaluating the performance both on a training and holdout test data set. Sensitivity analyses with respect to the input variables are also conducted.

The promising results with neural networks in this study lead us to believe that they can be extended to other important financial decision-making applications, particularly those where parametric pricing formulas are unavailable. Applications that come to mind include pricing derivatives such as warrants, put and call options, futures and forward contracts, and hybrid securities. Neural networks also have the potential to address classification and prediction problems such as new venture performance, identification of takeover and acquisition targets, and design of trading systems. Evaluating the performance of neural networks in addressing these problems are likely to provide fruitful research opportunities. [Received: October 5, 1994. Accepted: June 1, 1995.]

ENDNOTES

[1] Beatty, R., and J.R. Ritter. Investment Banking Reputation and the Underpricing of Initial Public Offerings. *Journal of Financial Economics* 1 (1986), pp. 213–32.

[2] Carter, R.B., and S. Manaster. Initial Public Offerings and Underwriter Reputation. *Journal of Finance* 45 (1990), pp. 1045–67.

[3] Collins, E., S. Ghosh, and C. Scofield. An Application of a Multiple Neural Network Learning System to Emulation of Mortgage Underwriting Judgments. *Proceedings of the IEEE International Conference on Neural Networks* 2, (1988), pp. 459–66.

[4] Dutta, S., and S. Shekhar. Bond-rating: A Non-Conservative Application of Neural Networks. In *Proceedings of the IEEE International Conference on Neural Networks* 2 (1988), pp. 443–50.

[5] Fletcher, D., and E. Goss. Forecasting with Neural Networks: An Application Using Bankruptcy Data. *Information and Management* 24 (1993), pp. 159–67.

[6] *Going Public: The IPO Reporter.* Philadelphia, PA: Howard & Co.

[7] Hecht-Nielsen, R. *Neurocomputing.* Reading, MA: Addison-Wesley, 1989.

[8] Hutchinson, J.M., A.W. Lo, and T.A. Poggio. Nonparametric Approach to Pricing and Hedging Derivative Securities via Learning Networks. *Journal of Finance* 49 (1994), pp. 851–89.

[9] Ibbotson, R.G. Price Performance of Common Stock New Issues. *Journal of Finance* 2 (1975) pp. 235–72.

[10] Ibbotson, R.G., J.L. Sindelar, and J.R. Ritter. Initial Public Offerings. *Journal of Applied Corporate Finance* 1 (1988), pp. 37–45.

[11] Ibbotson, R.G., and J.R. Ritter. Initial Public Offerings. *North Holland Handbook of Operations Research and Management Science: Finance*, 1994.

[12] Jain, B. The Underpricing of 'Unit' Initial Public Offerings. *Quarterly Review of Economics and Finance* 3 (1994), pp. 309–32.

[13] James, C. Relationship Specific Assets and the Pricing of Underwriter Services. *Journal of Finance* 47 (1992), pp. 1865–85.

[14] Kamijo, K., and T. Tanigawa. Stock Price Pattern Recognition: A Recurrent Neural Network Approach, *Proceedings of the International Joint Conference on Neural Networks* 1 (1992), pp. 215–21.

[15] Klimasauskas, C.C. *NeuralWorks*[TM] *An Introduction to Neural Computing* Sewickley, PA: NeuralWare, Inc, 1988.

[16] Lipman, F.D. *Going Public.* Rocklin, CA: Prima Publishing, 1993.

[17] Minsky, M., and S. Papert. *Perceptrons.* Cambridge, MA: MIT Press, 1969.

[18] Muscarella, C.J., and M.R. Vetsuypens. Firm Age, Uncertainty and Ipo Underpricing: Some New Empirical Evidence. Southern Methodist University Working Paper, 1990.

[19] Ritter, J.R. The 'Hot Issue' Market of 1980, *Journal of Business* 32 (1984), pp. 215–40.

[20] ———. The Costs of Going Ppublic, *Journal of Financial Economics* 19 (1987), pp. 269–81.

[21] Rosenblatt, F. The Perceptron: A Probablistic Model for Information Storage and Organization in the Brain, *Psychological Review*, 65 (1958), pp. 386–408.

[22] Rumelhart, D.E., G.E. Hinton, and R.J. Williams. Learning Internal Representations by Error Propogation. *Parallel distributed processing*, eds. D.E. Rumelhart and J.L. McClelland. Cambridge, MA: MIT Press, 1986, pp. 318–62.

[23] Salchenberger, L.M., E.M. Cinar, and N.A. Lash. Neural Networks: A New Tool for Predicting Thrift Failures, *Decision Sciences* 23 (1992), pp. 899–916.

[24] Spiro, L.N., M. Schroeder, and P.L. Zweig. Beware the IPO Market, *Business Week*, April 4, 1994, pp. 84–90.

[25] Tam, K.Y., and M.Y. Kiang. Managerial Applications of Neural Networks: The Case of Bank Failure Predictions, *Management Science* 38, no. 7 (1992), pp. 926–47.

[26] Wang, D. Pattern recognition: Neural Networks in Perspective, *IEEE Expert*, August 1993, pp. 52–60.

[27] Yoon, Y., G. Swales, and T.M. Margavio. A Comparison of Discriminant Analysis versus Artificial Neural Networks, *Journal of Operational Research Society* 44 (1993), pp. 51–60.

PART VI

OTHER SECURITY MARKET APPLICATIONS

A COMMODITY TRADING MODEL BASED ON A NEURAL NETWORK-EXPERT SYSTEM HYBRID

Karl Bergerson and Donald C. Wunsch II

Neural networks apply to problems that have proven difficult if not impossible to solve by programming a computer with algorithms. Problems such as predicting the market fall into this category because solving them involves the recognition of patterns—even patterns that are vaguely defined, buried in noise, or otherwise difficult to decompose into the neat steps of an algorithm.

It is not necessary to solve the mysteries of human intelligence to make a useful system. Even the smallest insects have pattern processing, learning, and other capabilities that elude even the most powerful supercomputers. It is not surprising, then, that some insights in the field of neural networks have led to impressive gains in the capabilities of software-based trading.

Like several others who have tried market prediction with neural networks, we have used the back-propagation network,[1] with some parameters selected experimentally, as discussed below. However, we expended the majority of our efforts in providing good training data, which we believe sets our work apart. We wanted to control precisely what the network learned about market prediction, preferring that it only attempt to make a trade when the chances for profit were high. Therefore, it was not desirable to train the network purely on historical data, expecting it to predict gains and losses under all possible conditions. Instead, we used a human expert to implicitly define patterns, using hindsight, that an intelligent system might have been able to use for an accurate prediction. Desired outputs were found by a combination of observing the behavior of technical indices that normally precede a certain kind of market behavior and by observing the actual market behavior in retrospect. Thus, the network learned to give signals based on data that looked favorable to a human expert but was tempered by the requirement that anything considered a "good example" must also be accompanied by a profitable history. The network also received a number of "bad examples," that is, examples where the indices looked good or borderline good but were not borne out by historical data and therefore deserved an output indicating an unfavorable condition.

In contrast to merely pumping a neural network with massive amounts of historical data, our method was extremely labor-intensive. Figure 29.1 shows four technical indicators plotted against the daily Standard & Poor's 500 Index (S&P 500). The boxes show that the human expert felt that the patterns were clear enough to indicate that a "sell" decision could be made, and the triangles are where the human expert chose a "buy" decision. These points, chosen manually, were given as training examples to the network, together with technical data from the recently preceding days. The process demanded many hours of expert time and careful consideration of each potential pattern in the data. These figures cover the period of September 19, 1980, to January 2, 1981. The triangles and boxes were chosen manually by the expert, and it took him about three hours to do this example. The total amount of data used for training covered approximately nine years.

Figure 29.1

Buying ▲ and Selling ■ Decisions

a. Moving Average of Price—Normal

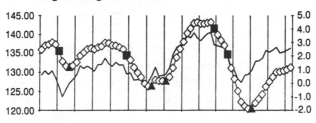

b. Moving Average of Price—Fast

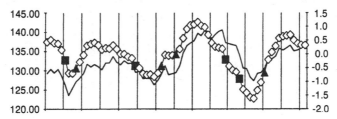

c. Moving Average of Advance Decline Line—Normal

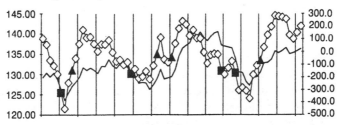

d. Moving Average of Advance Decline Line—Fast

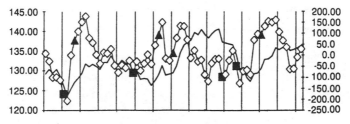

Solid line = S&P 500

The selection of parameters for the neural architecture also involved some extra effort. Two issues that were addressed experimentally were the number of hidden units to use and the amount of training to provide. The number of hidden units was determined by pruning. We began with a full layer of 54 hidden units, the same as the number of input units. After training had stabilized, we removed those units whose weights were smallest, and retrained. In this way, we corrected for any possibility of overfitting the training data. The amount of training to provide was also monitored. We did this by comparing the error on the test data to the error on the training data. When these were the same, we did no further training. Note, however, that the test data we used for the performance figures that we show includes data that were never seen by the network, even in this implicit manner.

It is very important to note that this hybrid approach offers strong advantages over either rule-based or unaided neural network approaches. Rule-based approaches are lacking in the flexibility to easily deal with the recognition of poorly defined patterns. Unaided neural networks are better at pattern recognition (in a theoretical sense) than they are at doing things that are naturally well-handled by rules, such as risk management. It is possible to make a theoretically excellent market prediction system using neural networks alone, but it is the combination of this capability with a rule-based system that makes a useful real-world investment system. Our system uses a risk-management rule that governs where stop-loss points are put to control losses when an incorrect prediction is made. Furthermore, these stops need to be increased when a trade goes well so that one knows when to take profits. Also, certain extreme values of indicators are known to be a sign of extreme volatility in the market, making predictions more uncertain. These are best tracked by rules. The rule-based system thus has veto power over the neural networks' signals but does not generate signals on its own. It is the synergy of the rule-based and neural system that permits the design of such an attractive reward-to-risk-ratio trading model. The reward-to-risk ratio for our system's performance to date is shown in Table 29.1.

Figure 29.2 shows the results of a rule-based daily trading system that has been augmented by a neural network market predictor.[2] The neural network was trained on data from 1980 to 1988 and then ran with an initial investment of $10,000 from January 4, 1989, to January 25, 1991. The final account value was $76,034, which represents a growth of 660

Table 29.1

Hybrid System Performance

	Long	Short	All
Win ratio (%)	58.33	91.67	75.00
Reward/risk	5.82	3.81	4.81
Number of trades	12.00	12.00	24.00
Average gain points	6.10	4.06	5.08
Maximum loss points	1.54	1.39	1.54
Average loss points	0.45	0.12	0.28
Average duration	9.42	2.17	5.79
Maximum drawdown	1.04	0.90	1.04
Average drawdown	0.32	0.16	0.24

Report dates: 89/01/04 through 91/01/29. Slippage: 0.50 [$250].

percent over 25 months. The maximum drawdown was for the period from September 15, 1989, to September 25, 1989. During this period, the account went from a value of $32,954 to $32,187, a 2.3 percent loss. The program easily recovered from this in a single successful trade. The reason for this resilient property is a conservative risk-management rule that limits the amount of losses that will be tolerated but allows maximal advantage of profit-making opportunities. It should be noted that these are theoretical gains although we have been trading the system successfully with real dollars since August 1990.

Our point that learning can enhance the performance of trading systems is now clear. This enhancement is beyond that attainable with rule-based or neural network systems alone. The key issue is to move beyond mere theoretical prediction to profitability. As Figure 29.2 makes clear, that move has been made. The key technical insight that led to this achievement is that the neural network can be used as a knowledge acquisition tool, and when that tool is used with some real-world risk management expertise, the result is impressive. It is not a magic solution; in fact, it involved more hard work and more demands on the expert's time than traditional knowledge engineering approaches. The results, though, seem to justify the difficulty of the approach.

Figure 29.2

Plot of Neural System Performance versus the S&P 500

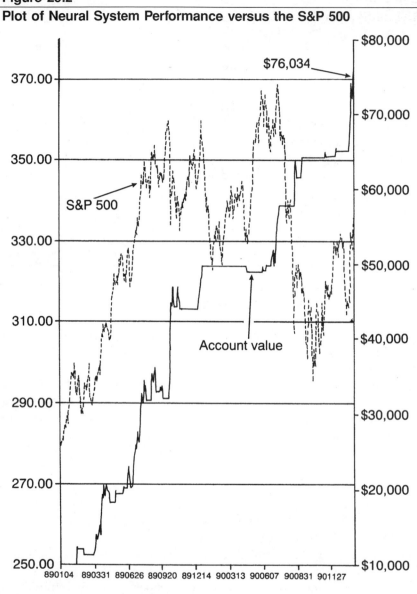

ENDNOTES

1. D. E. Rumelhart, G. E. Hinton, and J. R. Williams, "Learning Internal Representations by Error Propagation," in *Parallel Distributed Processing*, vol. 1 (Cambridge, MA: MIT Press, 1986).

2. Neural$ from Neural Trading Company.

30

COMMODITY TRADING WITH A THREE YEAR OLD

J. E. Collard

INTRODUCTION

This chapter reports on continuing work to train the ANN to recognize a long/short (buy/sell) pattern for the live cattle commodity futures market. The back-propagation of errors algorithm was used to encode the relationship between a long or short position in the live cattle commodity futures market (the desired output) and fundamental variables plus technical variables into an artificial neural network (ANN). Trained on three years of past data, the ANN is able to correctly predict long or short market positions for 178 trading days in 1991, yielding a profit of $1,547.50. If the account started with $3,000, this would represent a return of 52 percent for the 178 trading days or an annualized return of 81 percent.

Printed with permission of the author, acknowledging support from Gerber Inc., Schwieterman Inc., and Martingale Research Corp.

NETWORK ARCHITECTURE

The ANN 044 was a simple feedforward, single hidden-layer network with no input units (inputs were prescaled), 30 hidden units, and one output unit.

TRAINING PROCEDURE

Back-Propagation of Errors Algorithm

The ANN was trained using the well-known ANN training algorithm called back-propagation of errors with the following optional features:

1. Use of a minimum slope term in the derivative of the activation function.

2. Momentum of .9.[1]

3. Weights changed once each epoch (data pass).[2]

DATA

The training data set for 044 consisted of 789 trading days in 1988, 1989, 1990, and 1991. Each trading day had associated with it a 37-component pattern vector consisting of 18 fundamental indicators, plus six market technical variables (open, high, low, close, open interest, and volume) for that trading day, six market technical variables for the previous trading day, six market technical variables for the two-days-previous trading day, and finally, the target or TEACHER's long/short decision. The trained model was then traded in 1991 from April 11 through December 19, or 178 trading days.

TRAINING RESULTS

Figure 30.1 shows the extent to which network 044 was trained on the 789 trading days in the training data set. The network has not been able to correctly encode the long/short position for 11 trading days in the training data set. Figure 30.2 shows that the resulting profit steps are relatively unchanged despite these 11 days of disagreement.

Figure 30.1

Trained Network 044

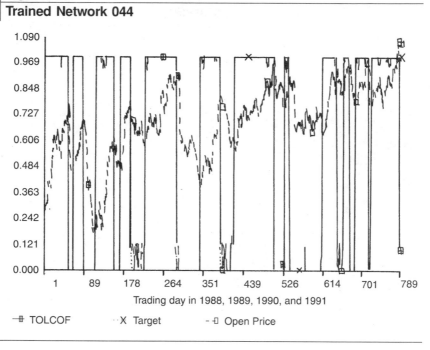

Trading day in 1988, 1989, 1990, and 1991

—⊞ TOLCOF   ··X Target   - ⊡ Open Price

Figure 30.3 plots the profit and loss for the model during the training period as it exists on paper only. Each time a round turn (RT) is completed, the current paper profit or loss is recognized as real profit or loss, and the curve goes to zero. As can be seen from the plot, the largest paper profit during the training period is $4,976, and the largest paper loss for the period is $120.

TRADING RESULTS

Table 30.1 shows the actual trading performance of network 044 for 178 trading days in 1991.

Figures 30.4 and 30.5 show the actual long/short positions for network 044 for 178 trading days in 1991 and the profit step function for network 044 resulting from these positions.

Figure 30.2
Profit Step Function for Trained Network 044

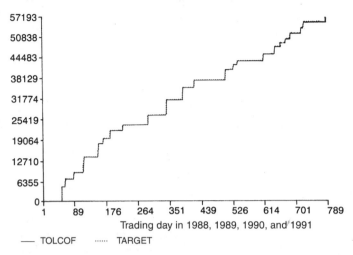

Trading day in 1988, 1989, 1990, and 1991

—— TOLCOF   ⋯⋯ TARGET

Figure 30.3
Paper Profit for Trained Network

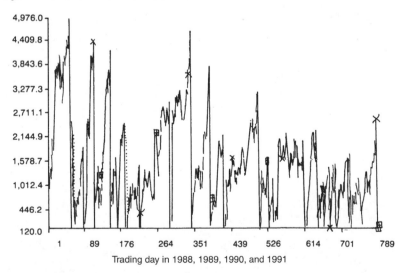

Trading day in 1988, 1989, 1990, and 1991

---⊟- TOLCOF   ⋯⋯✗ Target

Figure 30.4

044's Long/Short Positions in 1991

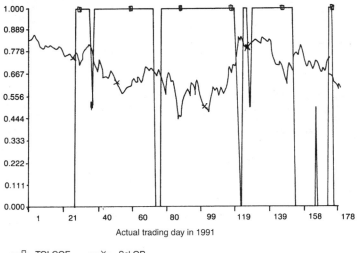

Actual trading day in 1991

--□- TOLCOF   ····✕·· Scl OP

Figure 30.5

Profit Step Function for 1991

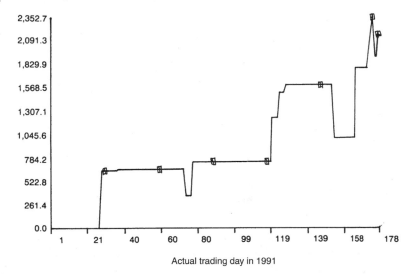

Actual trading day in 1991

OTHER RESULTS

Results for 16 trained networks are summarized in Tables 30.1 and 30.2.

ENDNOTES

1. D. E. Rumelhart and J. McClelland, *Parallel Distributed Processing* (Cambridge, MA: MIT Press, 1986).

2. Y. H. Pao, *Adaptive Pattern Recognition and Neural Networks* (Reading, MA: Addison-Wesley, 1989).

Table 30.1

Actual Trading Results

Date	Price	Position	Profit	Cumulative Profit	Balance
4-11-91	77.18	SELL,1 – SHORT	$0.00	$0.00	$3,000.00
5-20-91	75.38	BUY,2 – LONG	$648.30	$648.30	$3,648.30
6-03-91	75.60	SELL,1 – OUT	$18.30	$666.60	$3,666.60
6-03-91	73.65	BUY,1 – LONG	$0.00	$666.60	$3,666.60
7-23-91	73.10	SELL,2 – SHORT	($291.74)	$374.86	$3,374.86
7-29-91	71.98*	BUY,2 – LONG	$378.26	$753.12	$3,753.12
8-01-91	70.65*	SELL,1 – LONG*	($601.74)†	$151.38	$3,151.38†
8-01-91	73.40	BUY,1 – LONG	$0.00	$151.38	$3,151.38
9-27-91	74.88	SELL,1 – OUT	$488.26	$639.64	$3,639.64
10-01-91	76.85	SELL,1 – SHORT	$0.00	$639.64	$3,639.64
10-03-91	76.00	BUY,2 – LONG	$268.26	$907.90	$3,907.90
10-08-91	76.40	SELL,1 – OUT	$88.26	$996.16	$3,996.16
10-10-91	76.78	BUY,1 – LONG	$0.00	$996.16	$3,996.16
11-13-91	75.50	SELL,2 – SHORT	($581.74)	$414.42	$3,414.42
12-02-91	73.40	BUY,1 – OUT	$768.26	$1,182.68	$4,182.68
12-02-91	74.43	SELL,1 – SHORT	$0.00	$1,182.68	$4,182.68
12-12-91	72.83	BUY,2 – LONG	$568.30	$1,750.98	$4,750.98
12-17-91	71.70	SELL,2 – SHORT	($431.74)	$1,319.24	$4,319.24
12-19-91	70.95	BUY,1 – OUT	$228.26	$1,547.50	$4,547.50

* The trade on this date was necessitated by human error in not buying the second contract on the 29th of July (the previous trade) in October live cattle instead of August live cattle. This is contrary to the agreed-upon procedure and required a rollover trade two days later, which cost the account $601.74. The model did not recommend a change in position on August 1, 1991.

† Without this error, the profit would have been $2148.24 on 12 round turns (RTs). The profit step function in Figure 30.5 does not include this error.

595

Table 30.2

Study Results

	#	Size/In	Training		Test	
			Data	Profit/RTs	Data	Profit/RTs
Target	>>		253-'88	$25,296/10	205-'89	$14,596/ 6
	009	10-1/24	253-'88	$24,173/14	205-'89	$ 7,272/ 6
	010	6-1/24	105-'88	$17,534/13	253-'88	80 percent
Target	>>		251-'88	$24,819/10	205-'89	$14,596/ 6
	011	10-1/36	251-'88	$23,370/14	205-'89	$ 7,272/ 6
	012	13-1/36	251-'88	$22,965/12	205-'89	$ 6,554/14
	013	16-1/36	251-'88	$22,495/12	205-'89	$10,301/19
Target	>>		253-'88	$25,232/ 9	252-'89	$16,576/ 7
Target	>>		251-'88	$23,360/19	252-'89	$25,184/19
	022	11-1/18*	235-'88	$24,368/15	252-'89	$ 5,936/ 4
	023	16-1/24*	235-'88	$25,008/11	252-'89	$ 8,688/ 9
	024	16-1/24	485-'8889	$49,936/27	85-90	$ 6,848/11
Target	>>		485-'8889	$49,712/29	85-90	$ 7,840/ 7
	025	23-1/36	252-'89	$25,184/19	235-'88	$ 2,752/ 6
Target	>>		252-'89	$ 5,472/23	235-'88	$25,232/ 9
	026	16-1/24	252-'89	$ 7,520/19		$ 4,368/ 3
	027	16-1/24	250-'89	$16,944/ 7		$ 5,248/ 6
Target	>>		250-'89	$16,944/ 7	57-'90	$(1,376)/ 6
	028	16-1/36	250-'89	$ 7,824/29	57-'90	$ (4,80)/ 9
	029	10-1/36			57-'90	5 made
	032	11-1/36	6 mo-'8889		Next mo.	$ 1,446/ 1
Target	>>		737-88-90	$41,449/22	52-'91	$ 536/ 8
	043	31-1/36	737-88-90	$38,823/32	52-'91	$13,498/ 6
Target	>>		789-88-91	$57,471/22	178-'91 *S	$(1,169)/23
	044	31-1/36	789-88-91	$57,257/29	178-'91 *A	$ 2,148/12

* = Pass-through connections *S = Simulated trades, *A = Actual trades.
#, = The numerical designation of the network.
Size/in, = The hidden-output layer dimensions/the number of inputs to the network.
Data, = The number of days and year of the data set.
Profit RTs, = The profit computed for the data and how many round turns (RTs) to generate that profit.

TRADING EQUITY INDEX FUTURES WITH A NEURAL NETWORK

A Machine Learning-Enhanced Trading Strategy

Robert R. Trippi and Duane DeSieno

Neural network technology, which has been receiving increasing attention in the investment community, represents a radically different form of computation from the conventional algorithmic model. Neural networks consist of multiple simple processors arranged in a communicative network, each programmed to perform one identical, elementary processing task.

This technology is especially suited for simulating intelligence in pattern detection, association, and classification activities. Such problems arise frequently in areas such as credit assessment, security investment, and financial forecasting, so it is not surprising that after the Department of

Defense, which in 1989 embarked on a five-year, multimillion dollar program for neural network research, financial services organizations have been the principal sponsors of research in neural network applications.

We describe here a specific neural network-based day trading system for Standard & Poor's (S&P) 500 index futures contracts that has, in ex ante evaluation, outperformed passive investment in the index. This system, which is fairly representative of a neural network-based trading strategy implementation, also demonstrates how performance can be enhanced by integrating neural networks with conventional rule-based expert system techniques (e.g., see Lee, Trippi, Chu, and Kim 1990; and Trippi 1990).

BACKGROUND

Neural networks have proven effective in automating both routine and ad hoc financial analysis tasks (Chithelin 1989). Neural network-based decision aids have been developed for such applications as the following:

- ❖ Credit authorization screening.

- ❖ Mortgage risk assessment.

- ❖ Project management and bidding strategy.

- ❖ Economic prediction.

- ❖ Risk rating of exchange-traded fixed-income investments.

- ❖ Detection of regularities in security price movements.

- ❖ Portfolio selection/diversification.

Other potential financial applications meriting further research, development, and evaluation include:

- ❖ Simulation of market behavior.

- ❖ Index construction.

- ❖ Identification of explanatory economic factors.

- ❖ "Mining" of financial and economic databases.

Of greatest import to portfolio managers are neural network-based systems that can assist directly with risk assessment, asset selection, and timing decisions. Representative of such systems are those that have been built to perform the following tasks:

- ❖ Generate improved risk ratings of bonds (Dutta and Shekhar 1988; Surkan and Singleton 1991; and Collins, Ghosh, and Scofield 1988).

- ❖ Search for regularities in the price movements of an individual stock (White 1988).

- ❖ Classify multiple stocks as to upside potential using fundamental and general economic data (Yoon and Swales 1991).

- ❖ Recognize a specific price pattern, such as the Japanese "candlestick" triangle (Kamijo and Tanigawa 1990).

- ❖ Determine optimal buy-and-sell timing for an equity index (Kimoto, Asakawa, Yoda, and Takeoka 1990).

- ❖ Drive a trading strategy for a nonfinancial commodity index (Collard 1991).

HOW NEURAL NETWORKS LEARN

An individual processor within a neural network, simulated by specialized software for this purpose, is referred to as a *processing element*, or PE. Each has one output but more than one input. Outputs of one PE become inputs to other PEs or outputs of the network.

In most neural network paradigms, the actual processing that takes place within each PE is relatively simple: taking a weighted sum of the inputs and calculating an output value that is a function of that sum, as follows:

$$x_j = T(\textstyle\sum_i w_{ij} x_i)$$

where x_j is the output of processing element j, T is a *transfer* or *activation function*, and w_{ij} is the weighting coefficient of the interconnect link between processing elements i and j. The most commonly used transfer functions are variations of the S-shaped sigmoid:

$$(1-e^{-u})^{-1}$$

Other functions, including Z-shaped and threshold detectors, can be used in some applications. The PE's local memory stores interconnect weights and parameters used by its transfer function. When many processors are linked, a neural network is created.

Learning in a neural network takes place through incremental changes in interconnect weight coefficients as examples are run through the system during the training phase. For example, under the *delta learning rule*, the change in output PE interconnect weight Δw_{ij} is made proportional to the difference between the desired output o_j and the actual output x_j:

$$\Delta w_{ij} = k(o_j - x_j) \, x_i \, (x_j(1 - x_j))$$

where k is a constant that determines the learning rate, and x_i is the level of the input to PE j from PE i. The delta rule is somewhat analogous to gradient or path of steepest descent optimization, as the changes made lead to local improvement only. There are about a half-dozen different learning rules in common use.

The learning rules that can be employed depend to some extent on the pattern of interconnections among the PEs. There are about 20 different network configurations, of which a dozen are commonly employed. In most of these, individual networks are combined in layers. Usually, there is an input layer, an output layer, and one or more intermediate or hidden layers.

A TRADING SYSTEM FOR S&P 500 FUTURES

The S&P 500 trading system consists of several trained neural networks plus a set of rules for combining network results to generate a composite recommendation for the current day's position. The trading strategy is time-invariant; that is, whatever trades are executed occur at a fixed time during the trading day. Specifically, the system enters the market 15 minutes after the opening and unwinds its positions 25 minutes before the close of trading for that day unless a stop has previously been hit.

The general network architecture is a feedforward network such as that shown in Figure 31.1, where the lines indicate *connections* along which processing element outputs are transferred to the inputs of other processing elements.

Inputs to the network are primarily technical variables for the two-week period prior to the trading day. This differs substantially from the inputs used in the Collard (1991) commodity trading system, which are

Figure 31.1

Basic Neural Network Feedforward Model

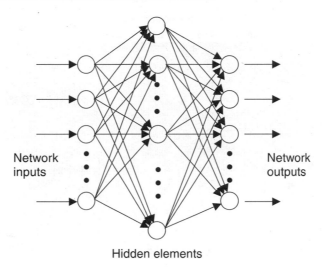

Hidden elements

mostly exogenous or fundamental. Inputs include open, high, low, and close price information, plus several statistics derived from past price data, including recent volatility. The only real-time information used from the current trading day are the opening price and the price 15 minutes after the market opening.

The output from each network is a long or short recommendation. A trailing stop controls losses and protects gains. For initial evaluation of the system, a constant 2.5 point stop is used. The optimal stop size appears to be a function of market volume, with smaller stops performing best when volume is light.

The system is designed to be run overnight to generate an input–output decision map for the next day for each network, such as that in Figure 31.2. To exploit possible synergy among networks, six differently configured networks, labeled Net 1 through Net 6, are trained using the same historical data. Figure 31.3 shows a typical daily decision map for a composite trading decision rule set that combines the outputs of several networks. Both exhibits, with short recommendations represented by darker regions, show complex nonlinearity of decision map partitions.

Figure 31.2

Typical Net 2 Decision Map

Change from open

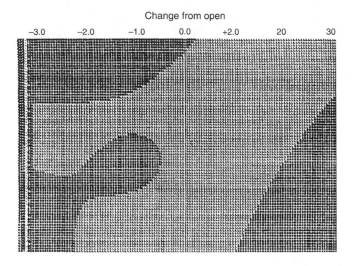

Figure 31.3

Typical Composite Rule Set Decision Map

Change from open

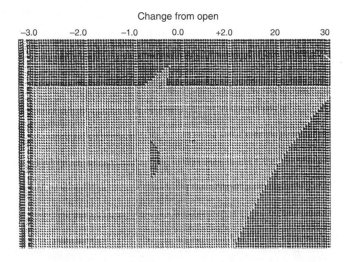

TRAINING INDIVIDUAL NETWORKS

In training the networks, price data from the front (generally most actively traded) contract are employed. The training period spans 1,168 days, from January 1986 to June 1990. This is not an exceptionally large training set compared to those used in other neural network applications.

The minimum training set size required for typical classification tasks has been estimated by Baum and Haussler (1989) to be N/I, where N is the number of weights in the network and I is the fraction of test examples incorrectly classified. With a target 10 percent error level, the network would thus have no more than 116 weights, which is far too few for a problem of this complexity. Thus, with the data available, we were willing to accept a network performance on training data with a higher error level as well as some sensitivity to the initial weights.

The test period covers 106 days from December 20, 1990, through May 31, 1991. With the exception of Net 1, the only differences in the trained networks are their initial randomly generated starting weights and the length of training. Net 1 has a slightly different input configuration, excluding the current index price as an input.

The performance of the individual networks is summarized in Table 31.1. Trades of a single contract were assumed to be executed every day. Maximum drawdown and a $5,000 margin were used to calculate the geometric mean return on investment over the test period, and a round-turn commission of $60 was charged to each transaction. As mentioned above, to minimize the uncertainties of slippage, for the purposes of system evaluation we assume transactions are executed at a certain time of day rather than at a specific price.

Net 6 represents a special case created to examine the effects of overtraining or overfitting. This network was deliberately overtrained, enabling it to achieve a relatively low 10 percent error rate on the training data. This ex post optimized network would have generated nearly twice the net gain over the training period in comparison to the other networks. As indicated in Table 31.1, however, its ex ante performance over the subsequent test period was worse than the other networks. Nevertheless, the network proved to be of value as a tie-breaker in the composite trading strategy.

Table 31.1

Performance of Individual Networks

Net-work	No. of Gains	No. of Losses	% Gains	Average Gain	Average Loss	No. of Stops	Maximum Draw Down	Total Gain	Expected Value	%ROI
Net 1	49	57	46.2	1320.10	786.31	67	8195.00	19865.00	187.41	150.5
Net 2	56	50	52.8	1261.43	803.00	64	8620.00	30490.00	287.64	223.9
Net 3	51	55	48.1	1303.24	786.82	62	4985.00	23190.00	218.77	232.2
Net 4	54	52	50.9	1241.85	836.92	61	7830.00	23540.00	222.08	183.5
Net 5	54	52	50.9	121.48	804.23	63	9880.00	24140.00	227.74	162.2
Net 6	48	58	45.3	1194.17	851.81	69	14485.00	7915.00	74.67	40.6

GENERATION OF COMPOSITE TRADING DECISION RULES

In the system developed by Kimoto et al. (1990) for prediction of the TOPIX index, several different networks are trained and their outputs averaged in order to achieve a higher correlation with the training data. For our trading system, the outputs of individual networks are combined through the use of logical (Boolean) operators to produce a set of composite rules. This process is called *rule synthesis*.

There are two possible benefits from rule synthesis. First, using the outputs of more than one network makes it easier to recognize days when there is genuine ambiguity, and therefore it is best not to trade. Second, by combining rules, it may be possible to generate a composite decision rule set that is more consistently profitable than even the best of the individual networks.

On a typical day, a number of networks will agree in their recommendations. For example, Net 1 through Net 5 were in agreement for 30 of the test days. If a trade had been made only on those days, the expected value of the trade would have been $549, which is 1.9 times the expected value of simply using the best individual net. If trading could take place only when all networks were in agreement, however, it would have occurred only 26 percent of the time, so the gain over the period would have been limited to just $16,470.

The composite rule-generation procedure examines the results of all possible combinations of networks on trading days where no rule yet applies. If the expected value of trades resulting from applying one or more of these newly synthesized rules is greater than that of the best individual network (in this case Net 2), the best rule is added to the current rule set. This process is continued until there are no more days left unexamined, or the rules become very complex (exceeding five logical operations).

Table 31.2 shows the first rule set that was developed, Composite 1, which includes Net 1 through Net 5 and is designed to be scanned sequentially. Table 31.3 shows the performance of the individual rules on the days that they applied, or "fired." The performance of a composite trading system using these rules in combination exceeds that of the best single network (Net 2) by 21 percent. The combined system trades 84 out of 106 days or 79 percent of the time.

Using the rule synthesis procedure above, we examined whether Net 6 could in any way improve the composite system performance. This

Table 31.2

Rules for Combining Outputs of Networks

Composite 1

Rule 1: If all nets agree, make the indicated trade.

Rule 2: If Net 1 and Net 2 agree and one of Net 3, Net 4, or Net 5 disagrees, follow Net 1.

Rule 3: If Net 1 and Net 2 agree and two out of Net 3, Net 4, or Net 5 disagree, follow Net 1.

Rule 4: If Net 1 and Net 2 agree and the others disagree, follow Net 3.

Rule 5: If Net 2 and Net 3 agree and the others disagree do not trade.

Rule 6: If Net 1 and Net 2 disagree and the others have the same decision, do not trade.

Rule 7: If rules 1 through 6 do not apply, follow Net 2.

Composite 2

Rule 1: If all nets agree, make the indicated trade.

Rule 2: If Net 1 and Net 2 agree and one of Net 3, Net 4, or Net 5 disagrees, follow Net 1.

Rule 3: If Net 1 and Net 2 agree and two out of Net 3, Net 4, or Net 5 disagree, follow Net 1.

Rule 4: If Net 1 and Net 2 agree and the others disagree, follow Net 3.

Rule 5a: If Net 2 and Net 3 agree and the others disagree, do the opposite of Net 6.

Rule 6a: If rules 1 through 5 do not apply, follow Net 6.

---

resulted in the rule set Composite 2, also shown in Table 31.2, where rules 5, 6, and 7 are replaced with the new rules 5a and 6a. This rule set trades every day and has a per-trade expected value of $460 and cumulated gain of $48,750 over the initial test period.

It should be noted that the use of any data to determine the choice of network, setting of parameters, length of training, or use of networks in

Table 31.3

Performance of Rules 1–7

Rule	No. of Days Fired	Expected Value	Gain	Cumulative Gain
1	30	549.00	16470.00	16470.00
2	20	388.75	7775.00	24245.00
3	12	606.67	7280.00	31525.00
4	7	665.00	4655.00	36180.00
5	8	—	—	36180.00
6	12	—	—	36180.00
7	17	41.17	700.00	36880.00

combination redefines that data as training data and makes it inappropriate for use in further testing. Thus, although the composite decision rule set performed better than did individual rules, it did so over a period that had been used previously to generate the individual network weights. Therefore, it was necessary to test the composite rules further using newer data.

EVALUATING THE COMPOSITE DECISION RULE SET

In testing any index trading strategy, it is desirable to determine whether it outperforms both the index and a purely random trading strategy applied to the index over the same time period. Our approach to the former as to regress account gain/loss against time for the Composite 2 rule set and to compare the results with a regression on the index. Both will have just a single free parameter, slope, because initial gain or loss at the beginning of the test period is zero. The slope can be interpreted as the expected value of a single trade when exactly one trade is made per day.

Figure 31.4 shows the regression lines for the S&P 500 and Composite 2 (labeled system value), the latter with its 99 percent confidence limits on either side. The expected gain is $317.06 per day, which is significantly

Figure 31.4

S&P 500 versus Composite 2 System Performance

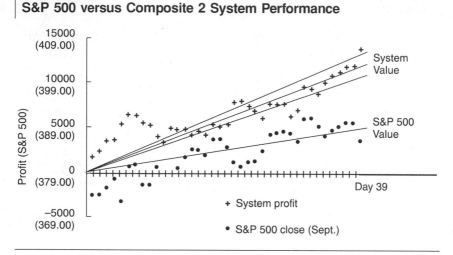

different at the 99 percent confidence level from the $139.06 per-day index trend over this time period.

Using the Composite 2 rule set, both actual and simulated trades of the September S&P 500 contract were made over the period from June 24 through August 16, 1991, showing a cumulative gain of $14,247. For the 39 days that trading took place, there were gains on 24 days, or 61.5 percent of the time. The average gain was $961.23, and the average loss was $588.15. Note that the S&P 500 index value does not include commissions, while an $81.49 actual commission per contract was deducted in evaluating the Composite 2 rule set.

To determine performance relative to a random trading strategy, we simulated 100,000 sequences of intraday positions over the same period. The percentage of sequences that would have outperformed the Composite 2 rule set can be interpreted as the probability of Composite 2's performance being achievable by randomly going long or short.

The frequency distribution of the simulation run outcomes appears in Figure 31.5. The probability of the random trading strategy meeting or exceeding the Composite 2 rule set performance is 0.01. In other words, we are 99 percent confident that Composite 2 will outperform randomly generated long- and short-day positions.

Figure 31.5

Gain/Loss from 100,000 Randomly Generated Intraday Index Trading Sequences (Composite 2 = $14,200)

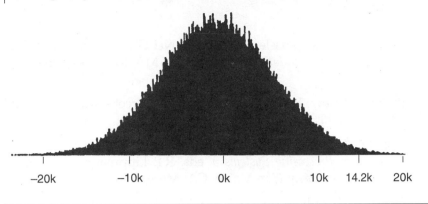

SUMMARY AND CONCLUSIONS

This article has reviewed uses of neural networks in investment management and outlined a specific neural network-based intraday trading system for S&P 500 futures contracts. This system, which combines several trained neural networks, appears to outperform each of its individual networks and the index. As a point of reference, the best network in Collard's (1991) system produced a gain of $10,301 over a year of trading, while our best composite synthesized rule set system achieved a gain of $14,247 in just eight weeks. With an expected return of $317 per day, the potential annual return is $60,000 per contract.

The system is deliberately limited to trading at specified times during each trading day to facilitate performance evaluation. It is likely that performance in actual trading would be improved by varying the timing of the trades. It should be noted also that trading was forced every day for the same reason. In normal use, when significant news events impact the market, trades could be suspended until the market stabilizes.

Further development of neural network-driven trading systems will likely follow two general directions. The first is to apply existing successful system designs to other types of assets. The second direction is to attempt to improve such systems by designing the networks to operate "on-line" in real time. We expect production versions of such systems to be commonplace within the next few years.

REFERENCES

Baum, E.B., and D. Haussler. "What Size Net Gives Valid Generalization." *Neural Computation* 1. Cambridge, MA: MIT Press, 1989, pp. 151–60.

Chithelin, I. "New Technology Learns Wall Street's Mindset." *Wall Street Computer Review*, June 1989, pp. 19–21.

Collard, J.E. "A B-P ANN Commodity Trader." In *Advances in Neural Information Processing Systems 3*, eds. R.P. Lippmann, J.E. Moody, and D.S. Touretzky (San Mateo, CA: Morgan Kaufmann, 1991).

Collins, E., S. Ghosh, and C. Scofield. "An Application of a Multiple Neural Network Learning System to Emulation of Mortgage Underwriting Judgments." *Proceedings of the IEEE International Conference on Neural Networks*, July 1988, pp. II-459–66.

Dutta, S., and S. Shekhar. "Bond Rating: A Non-Conservative Application of Neural Networks." *Proceedings of the IEEE International Conference on Neural Networks*, July 1988, pp. II-443–50.

Kamijo, K., and T. Tanigawa. "Stock Price Pattern Recognition: A Recurrent Neural Network Approach." *Proceedings of the International Joint Conference on Neural Networks*, vol. I. San Diego: IEEE Network Council, 1990, pp. 215–21.

Kimoto, T., K. Asakawa, M. Yoda, and M. Takeoka. "Stock Market Prediction System with Modular Neural Networks." *Proceedings of the International Joint Conference on Neural Networks*, vol. I San Diego, IEEE Network Council, 1990, pp. 1–6.

Lee, J.K.; R.R. Trippi; S. Chu; and H. Kim. "K-Folio: Integrating the Markowitz Model with a Knowledge-Based System." *Journal of Portfolio Management* 16 (Fall 1990), pp. 89–93.

Surkan, A., and J. Singleton. "Neural Networks for Bond Rating Improved by Multiple Hidden Layers." *Proceedings of the IEEE International Conference on Neural Networks, July 1991, pp. II-157–62.*

Trippi, R. "Intelligent Systems for Investment Decision Making." In *Managing Institutional Assets*, ed. F. Fabozzi. New York: Harper & Row, 1990.

Trippi, R., and E. Turban. *Neural Networks in Finance and Investment: Applying Artificial Intelligence to Improve Real-World Performance.* Chicago: Probus Publishing, 1992.

White, H. "Economic Prediction Using Neural Networks: The Case of IBM Daily Stock Returns," *Proceedings of the IEEE International Conference on Neural Networks*, July 1988, pp. II-451–58.

Yoon, Y., and G. Swales. "Predicting Stock Price Performance: A Neural Network Approach." *Proceedings of the 24th Annual Hawaii International Conference on Systems Sciences*, vol. IV. Hawaii: IEEE Computer Society Press, 1991, pp. 156–62.

ENDNOTES

1. These and other papers on the use of neural networks in investment management may be found in Trippi and Turban (1992).

2. As the return variances are almost identical, it was unnecessary to consider differential risk levels explicitly. This is to be expected, as in the long run a time-invariant intraday trading strategy such as this would tend to produce a return variance identical to that of the index itself, whether intraday positions are always long, always short, or randomly long and short.

32

NEURAL NETWORKS FOR PREDICTING OPTIONS VOLATILITY

Mary Malliaris and Linda Salchenberger

INTRODUCTION

The desire to forecast volatility of financial markets has motivated a large body of research during the past decade (Engle and Rothschild 1992). Volatility is a measure of price movement often used to ascertain risk. Relationships between volatility and numerous other variables have been studied in an attempt to understand the underlying process so that accurate predictions can be made. The ability to accurately forecast volatility gives the trader a significant advantage in determining options premiums.

Both researchers and traders use two estimates of option volatility: the historical volatility and the implied volatility. It is almost routinely reported in various publications of exchanges that these two series differ, but no significantly better forecasting model of volatility has emerged. The purpose of this research is to compare these two existing methods of predicting volatility for S&P 100 options with a new approach that uses neural networks. Neural networks, which have been shown to effectively model nonlinear relationships, prove to be a superior approach to predicting options volatility in all cases tested and can be used to develop monthly forecasts.

CALCULATING HISTORICAL AND IMPLIED VOLATILITIES

In their seminal work on pricing options, Black and Scholes (1973) assumed that the price of the underlying asset follows an Itô process:

$$dS/S = \mu dt + \sigma dZ \tag{1}$$

where dS/S denotes the rate of return, μ is the instantaneous expected rate of return, σ is the expected instantaneous volatility, and Z is a standardized Wiener process or dZ is a continuous-time random walk. To simplify their analysis, Black and Scholes assumed that both μ and σ were constants, and, by using an elegant arbitrage argument, they derived their call option pricing model. Their formula expresses the call price C, as a function of five inputs:

$$C = C(S, X, t, \sigma, r) \tag{2}$$

where S is the current price of the underlying asset, X is the exercise or strike price, T is the time from now to expiration of the option, σ is the expected instantaneous volatility, and r is the riskless short-term rate of interest.

Observe that the μ of equation (1) does not appear in (2). The mathematical derivation of the call-option pricing formula as shown in Malliaris (1982) shows that arbitrage requires that the per-unit of risk excess returns between two appropriately designed portfolios must be equal. Making the necessary substitutions in this arbitrage relationship, the term containing μ drops out. With μ now out of the picture and with four of the five remaining variables directly observable, an estimate of the asset's volatility σ in (2) becomes the focal point of attention for both theorists and traders.

There are two main approaches to estimating and predicting the non-constant σ: the historical approach and the implied volatility approach. The historical approach is the simplest because tomorrow's volatility σ_{t+1} is an estimate obtained from a sample, of a given size, of past prices of the underlying asset. Suppose that the sample size is n and let:

$$S_{t-n+1}, \ldots , S_{t-1}, S_t$$

denote daily historical prices for the underlying asset. To get an estimate for σ_{t+1}, first compute daily returns, r_{t-i}, $i=0$, ..., $n-2$, where $r_{t-i} = \ln(S_{t-i}) - \ln(S_{t-i-1})$.

For a sample of n historical prices, we obtain $(n-1)$ rates of daily return. The annualized standard deviation of these rates of return is defined as the historical volatility and can be used as an estimate of σ_{t+1}. The nearby historical volatility uses 30 days of data, the middle historical volatility uses 45, and the distant historical volatility has 60 daily prices.

An obvious problem with the historical approach is that it assumes that future volatility will not change and that history will exactly repeat itself. Markets, however, are forward looking. Numerous illustrations can be presented to show that historical volatility does not always anticipate future volatility and that a better estimate comes from the Black–Scholes option pricing model itself (Choi and Wohar 1992).

Simply stated, supporters of implied volatility claim that tomorrow's volatility σ_{t+1} can only be estimated during trading tomorrow, that is, in real time. As option prices are being formed by supply and demand considerations, each trader assesses the asset's volatility prior to making his or her bid or ask prices and, accepting the consensus price of a call as a true market price reflecting the corporate opinions of the trading participants, one solves the Black–Scholes model for the volatility that yields the observed call price. When volatility is calculated in this way, it is called the "implied volatility," with the adjective "implied" referring to the volatility estimate obtained from the Black–Scholes pricing formula. Unlike historical volatility, which is backwards looking to past returns, the implied volatility is forward looking to the stock's future returns from now to the time of the expiration of the option. This implied volatility technique has become the standard method of estimating volatility at the moment of trading

NEURAL NETWORKS FOR PREDICTION

While there are dozens of network paradigms, the back-propagation network has frequently been applied to classification, prediction, and pattern-recognition problems. Financial applications of neural networks include underwriting (Collins, Ghosh, and Scofield 1988), bond rating (Dutta and Shekhar 1988), predicting thrift institution failure (Salchenberger, Cinar, and Lash 1992), and estimating option prices (Malliaris and Salchenberger 1993). The term *back-propagation* technically refers to the method used to train the network, although it is commonly used to characterize the network architecture. For details of this method, see Rumelhart and McClelland (1986). Currently, a number of variations on this method exist that overcome some of its limitations.

DATA AND METHODOLOGY

Data have been collected for the most successful options market: the S&P 100 (OEX), traded at the Chicago Board Options Exchange. Daily closing call and put prices and the associated exercise prices closest to at-the-month, S&P 100 Index prices, call volume, put volume, call open interest, and put open interest were collected from *The Wall Street Journal* for calendar year 1992.

Three estimates for the historical volatilities using Index price samples of sizes 30, 45, and 60 were computed for each trading day in 1992. We also used the Black–Scholes model to calculate implied volatilities for the closest at-the-money call for three contracts: those expiring in the current month, those expiring one month away, and those expiring two months away (nearby, middle, and distant, respectively). Thus, we have approximately 250 observations for six series of volatilities for use in our study.

Comparisons were made between the nearby historical, implied, and network volatility estimates. Because the neural network must have sufficient previous data in order to generalize, these estimates were developed using each method for June 22 through December 30, 1992. Trading cycles were used as the prediction periods, with each trading cycle ending on the third Friday of the month.

A COMPARISON OF HISTORICAL AND IMPLIED VOLATILITY ESTIMATES

The historical and implied volatility for the nearby contract are graphed together in Figure 32.1 for June 22 through December 30, 1992. As can be observed, the historical estimate significantly underestimates the volatility used by most traders, that is, the implied volatility. Since the historical volatility is an average based on returns from 30 preceding days, it is not surprising that the estimate smooths out the peaks, giving a value for each day that is less variable and thus less sensitive to daily market fluctuations. The implied volatility for any given day uses only trading information from that day, not a previous time period, to generate a value. Thus, the implied volatility is more reflective of market changes.

Figure 32.1

Historical and Implied Volatilities

June 22 through December 30, 1992

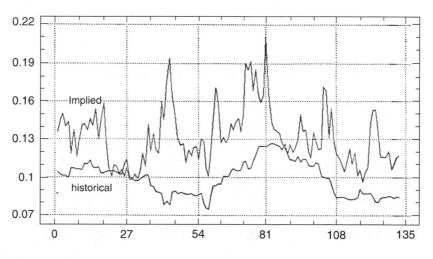

The average MAD (mean absolute deviation) and MSE (mean squared error) for the entire forecasting period, from June 22 through December 30 were 0.0331 and 0.0016. The proportion of times the historical volatility correctly predicted that the implied volatility would increase or decrease are shown in the last column of Table 32.1. An overall average of the number of times a change was correctly indicated is .4439, that is, a little less than half of the time.

DEVELOPMENT OF THE NEURAL NETWORKS

To develop a neural network that is capable of generalizing a relationship between inputs and outputs, the training set selected must contain a sufficient number of examples that are representative of the process being modeled. Therefore, the neural network models developed to predict volatility were trained with data sets from historical data from January 1 through July 18 and used to make predictions for six trading cycles beginning with the period July 20 through August 21 and ending with the period November 23 through December 31. All prior historical data was used when predicting the volatility for the next trading period. Predicting the volatility for the next cycle is a rather rigorous test of the forecasting capabilities of the network since we are asking it to predict volatility for up to 30 days in the future.

There is no well-defined theory to assist with the selection of input variables, and, generally, one of two heuristic methods is employed. One

Table 32.1

A Comparison of Historical and Implied Volatilities

Dates of Forecast	MAD	MSE	Correct Directions
June 22–Jul 19	.0318	.0012	8/19 = .421
July 20–Aug 21	.0292	.0019	11/25 = .440
Aug 24–Sep 18	.0406	.0018	12/18 = .667
Sep 21–Oct 16	.0479	.0027	7/20 = .350
Oct 19–Nov 20	.0213	.0008	14/25 = .560
Nov 23–Dec 18	.0334	.0014	8/18 = .444
Dec 21–Dec 30	.0294	.0009	2/6 = .333

approach is to include all the variables in the network and perform an analysis of the connection weights or a sensitivity analysis to determine which may be eliminated without reducing predictive accuracy. An alternative is to begin with a small number of variables and add to new variables that improve network performance. In this research, the latter was used, and variables were selected using existing financial theory, sensitivity analysis, and correlation analysis. Thus, a number of preliminary models were developed to determine which input variables of the group available in the data set would best predict volatility.

The first models were developed with variables representing volatility lagged from three to seven periods to determine an appropriate set of lag variables. Next, other networks were developed and trained to determine which variables were the best predictors of volatility. The final models include the following 13 variables: change in closing price, days to expiration, change in open put volume, the sum of the at-the-money strike price and market price of the option for both calls and puts for the current trading period and the next trading period, daily closing volatility for the current period, daily closing volatility for next trading period, and four lagged volatility variables. By including both the time-dependent path of volatility and related contemporaneous variables in our model, we obtained better predictions.

The back-propagation network developed to predict volatility has 13 input nodes representing the independent variables used for prediction, one middle layer consisting of 9 middle nodes, and an output node representing the volatility. The cumulative delta rule for training was selected, with an epoch size of 16, a decreasing learning rate initially set at 0.9, and an increasing momentum, initially set at 0.2. The networks were trained using Neuralworks Professional II software from Neuralware.

A COMPARISON OF THE NEURAL NETWORK AND IMPLIED VOLATILITY ESTIMATES

Using historical volatility as a benchmark, we evaluated the performance of the neural network by measuring mean absolute deviation, mean squared error, and the number of times the direction of the volatility (up or down) was corrected predicted. These results are shown in Figure 32.2 and Table 32.2, where comparisons are made between the volatility forecasted by the network and tomorrow's implied volatility. The overall MAD

Figure 32.2

Network and Implied Volatilities

June 22 through December 30, 1992

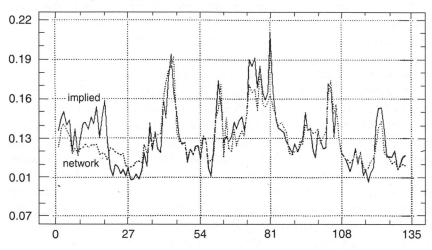

Table 32.2

Neural Network and Implied Volatilities

Dates of Forecast	MAD	MSE	Correct Directions
Jun 22–Jul 19	.0148	.0003	16/19 = .842
July 20–Aug 21	.0107	.0002	16/25 = .640
Aug 24–Sep 18	.0056	.0001	13/18 = .722
Sep 21–Oct 16	.0127	.0003	19/20 = .950
Oct 19–Nov 20	.0059	.0001	20/25 = .800
Nov 23–Dec 18	.0068	.0001	15/18 = .833
Dec 21–Dec 30	.0039	.0000	5/6 = .833

for the entire period was .0116, and the MSE was .0001 as compared to 0.0331 and 0.0016, when the historical was compared to the implied volatility. Furthermore, for each forecasting period, the MAD and MSE were considerably lower (see Tables 32.1 and 32.2). In each of the time periods, the proportion of correct predictions of direction made by the neural network was greater than that of historical volatility. The overall proportion of correct direction predictions was 0.794, as compared to .4439 for the historical volatility estimate. This is not surprising since historical volatility smoothes out the estimate because it is an average of 30 values. The correlation between the implied volatility and the volatility predicted by the network is 0.85, as compared with 0.31 for the historical volatility, at the 5 percent level of significance.

DISCUSSION

The results of this comparative study of neural networks and conventional methods for forecasting volatility are encouraging. Because historical estimates are traditionally poor predictors, traders have been forced to rely on formulas such as Black–Scholes, which can be solved implicitly for the real-time volatility. But these models are difficult to use and limited since they can only provide estimates that are valid at that current time. Furthermore, they fail to incorporate knowledge of the history of volatility. The neural network model, on the other hand, employs both short-term historical data and contemporaneous variables to forecast future implied volatility.

The neural network approach has two advantages that make it more useable as a forecasting tool. First, predictions can be made for a full trading cycle, thus avoiding the problems associated with the need for real-time calculations. Second, and more importantly, the network forecasts, in the cases we tested, were very accurate estimates of the volatility preferred by traders.

The limitations of neural networks as financial modeling tools are well documented. Unlike the more familiar analytical models, a trained neural network does not provide information about the underlying model structure. It is often viewed as a black box since there are no theory-based methods available to interpret and analyze network parameters. Neural networks lack systematic procedures for developing network architecture, selecting training and testing sets, and setting network parameters and thus are difficult to develop. Explicit knowledge of the phenomenon being predicted is required to assist in variable selection.

There are several ways to extend this research. While the performance of these networks in forecasting volatility is superior to the use of historical volatility, improvement may be possible through experimentation with other variables and network architectures. In this chapter, we report results for predicting nearby volatility. However, networks for predicting middle and distant volatility have been developed, using different variables and different network architectures.

REFERENCES

Black, F., and M. Scholes. The Pricing of Options and Corporate Liabilities. *Journal of Political Economy* 81(1973) pp. 637–54.

Choi, J.S., and M. E. Wohar. Implied Volatility in Options Markets and Conditional Heteroscedasticity in Stock Markets. *The Financial Review* 27, no. 4 (1992) pp. 503–30. Collins, E., S. Ghosh, and C. Scofield. An Application of a Multiple Neural-Network Learning System to Emulation of Mortgage Underwriting Judgments. *Proc. of the IEEE International Conference on Neural Networks*, 1988, pp. 459–66.

Dutta,]S., and S. Shekhar. Bond-rating: A Non-Conservative Application of Neural Networks. *Proc. of the IEEE International Conference on Neural Networks*, 1988, pp. 142–50.

Engle, R.F., and M. Rothschild. Statistical Models for Financial Volatility. *Journal of Econometrics* 52 (1992) pp. 1–4.

Malliaris, A.G. *Stochastic Methods in Economics and Finance*. Amsterdam: North Holland Publishing Company, 1982.

Malliaris, M.E., and L. Salchenberger. Beating the Best: A Neural Network Challenges the Black–Scholes Formula. *Proc. of the Ninth Conference on Artificial Intelligence for Applications*. Los Alamitos, CA: IEEE Computer Society Press, 1993, pp. 445–49.

Rumelhart, D.E., and J. L. McClelland. *Parallel Distributed Processing*. Cambridge, MA: MIT Press, 1986.

Salchenberger, L., E. M. Cinar, and N. Lash. Neural Networks: A New Tool for Predicting Thrift Failures. *Decision Sciences* 23, no. 4 (1992), pp. 899–916.

33

A NONPARAMETRIC APPROACH TO PRICING AND HEDGING DERIVATIVE SECURITIES VIA LEARNING NETWORKS

James M. Hutchinson, Andrew W. Lo, and Tomaso Poggio

This article reports research done within the Massachusetts Institute of Technology Artificial Intelligence Laboratory and the Sloan School of Management's Laboratory for Financial Engineering. We thank Harrison Hong and Terence Lim for excellent research assistance, and Petr Adamek, Federico Girosi, Chung-Ming Kuan, Barbara Jansen, Blake LeBaron, and seminar participants at the DAIS Conference, the Harvard Business School, and the American Finance Association for helpful comments and discussion. Hutchinson and Poggio gratefully acknowledge the support of an ARPA AASERT grant administered under the Office of Naval Research contract N00014-92-J-1879. Additional support was provided by the Office of Naval Research under contract N00014-93-1-0385, by a grant from the National Science Foundation under contract ASC-9217041 (this award includes funds from ARPA provided under the HPCC program), by the Laboratory for Financial Engineering, and by Siemens AG. A portion of this research was conducted during Lo's tenure as an Alfred P. Sloan Research Fellow.

Much of the success and growth of the market for options and other derivative securities may be traced to the seminal articles by Black and Scholes (1973) and Merton (1973), in which closed-form option pricing formulas were obtained through a dynamic hedging argument and a no-arbitrage condition. The celebrated Black–Scholes and Merton pricing formulas have now been generalized, extended, and applied to such a vast array of securities and contexts that it is virtually impossible to provide an exhaustive catalog. Moreover, while closed-form expressions are not available in many of these generalizations and extensions, pricing formulas may still be obtained numerically.

In each case, the derivation of the pricing formula via the hedging/no-arbitrage approach, either analytically or numerically, depends intimately on the particular parametric form of the underlying asset's price dynamics $S(t)$. A misspecification of the stochastic process for $S(t)$ will lead to systematic pricing and hedging errors for derivative securities linked to $S(t)$. Therefore, the success or failure of the traditional approach to pricing and hedging derivative securities, which we call a *parametric* pricing method, is closely tied to the ability to capture the dynamics of the underlying asset's price process.

In this chapter, we propose an alternative data-driven method for pricing and hedging derivative securities, a *nonparametric* pricing method, in which the data is allowed to determine both the dynamics of $S(t)$ and its relation to the prices of derivative securities with minimal assumptions on $S(t)$ and the derivative pricing model. We take as inputs the primary economic variables that influence the derivative's price, for example, current fundamental asset price, strike price, time-to-maturity, and so on, and we define the derivative price to be the output into which the learning network maps the inputs. When properly trained, the network "becomes" the derivative pricing formula, which may be used in the same way that formulas obtained from the parametric pricing method are used: for pricing, delta-hedging, simulation exercises, and so on.

These network-based models have several important advantages over the more traditional parametric models. First, since they do not rely on restrictive parametric assumptions such as lognormality or sample-path continuity, they are robust to the specification errors that plague parametric models. Second, they are adaptive and respond to structural changes in the data-generating processes in ways that parametric models cannot. Finally, they are flexible enough to encompass a wide range of derivative securities and fundamental asset price dynamics, yet they are relatively simple to implement.

Of course, all these advantages do not come without some cost: The nonparametric pricing method is highly data-intensive, requiring large quantities of historical prices to obtain a sufficiently well-trained network. Therefore, such an approach would be inappropriate for thinly traded derivatives, or newly created derivatives that have no similar counterparts among existing securities.[1] Also, if the fundamental asset's price dynamics are well-understood and an analytical expression for the derivative's price is available under these dynamics, the parametric formula will almost always dominate the network formula in pricing and hedging accuracy. Nevertheless, these conditions occur rarely enough that there may still be great practical value in constructing derivative pricing formulas by learning networks.

In Section I, we provide a brief review of learning networks and related statistical methods. To illustrate the promise of learning networks in derivative pricing applications, in Section II we report the results of several Monte Carlo simulation experiments in which radial basis function (RBF) networks "discover" the Black–Scholes formula when trained on Black–Scholes call option prices. Moreover, the RBF network pricing formula performs as well as the Black–Scholes formula in delta-hedging a hypothetical option and, in some cases, performs even better (because of the discreteness error in the Black–Scholes case arising from delta-hedging daily instead of continuously). To gauge the practical relevance of our nonparametric pricing method, in Section III we apply the RBF pricing model to daily call option prices on S&P 500 futures from 1987 to 1991 and compare its pricing and delta-hedging performance to the naive Black–Scholes model. We find that in many cases the network pricing formula outperforms the Black–Scholes model. We suggest several directions for future research and conclude in Section IV.

SECTION I. LEARNING NETWORKS: A BRIEF REVIEW

Over the past 15 years, a number of techniques have been developed for modeling nonlinear statistical relations nonparametrically. In particular, projection pursuit regression, multilayer perceptrons (often called back-propagation networks[2]), and radial basis functions are three popular examples of such techniques. Although originally developed in different contexts for seemingly different purposes, these techniques may all be viewed as nonparametric methods for performing nonlinear regressions. Following Barron and Barron (1988), we call this general class of methods *learning networks* to emphasize this unifying view and acknowledge their common history. In the following sections, we shall provide a brief review of their specification and properties. Readers already familiar with these techniques may wish to proceed immediately to the Monte Carlo simulation experiments of Section II.

A. Standard Formulations

In this section, we describe the standard formulations of the learning networks to be used in this article. For expositional simplicity, we shall focus our attention on the problem of mapping multiple input variables into a univariate output variable, much like regression analysis, although the multivariate-output case is a straightforward extension.

Given the well-known trade-offs between degrees of freedom and approximation error in general statistical inference, we shall also consider the number of parameters implied by each model so that we can make comparisons between them on a roughly equal footing. Note, however, that the number of free parameters is a crude measure of the complexity of nonlinear models, and more refined measures may be available, for example, the nonlinear generalizations of the influence matrix in Wahba (1990).

A common way to visualize the structure of these networks is to draw them as a graph showing the connections between inputs, nonlinear "hidden" units, and outputs (see Figure 33.1).

A.1. Radial Basis Functions

RBFs were first used to solve the *interpolation* problem—fitting a curve exactly through a set of points (see Powell 1987 for a review). More recently, the RBF formulation has been extended by several researchers to perform the more general task of approximation (see Broomhead and Lowe 1988; Moody and Darken 1989; and Poggio and Girosi 1990). In particular, Poggio and Girosi (1990) show how RBFs can be derived from the classical regularization problem in which some unknown function $y = f(\vec{x})$ is to be approximated given a sparse dataset $(\vec{x_t}, y_t)$ and some smoothness con-

---

Figure 33.1

Structure of the Learning Networks Used in this Chapter

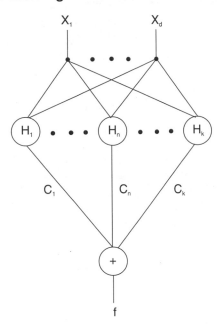

---

straints. In terms of our multiple-regression analogy, the d-dimensional vector, $\vec{x_t}$, may be considered the "independent" or "explanatory" variables, y_t the "dependent" variables, and $f(\cdot)$ the (possibly) nonlinear function that is the conditional expectation of y_t given $\vec{x_t}$, hence:

$$y_t = f(\vec{x_t}) + \varepsilon_t, \quad E[\varepsilon_t \,|\, \vec{x_t}] = 0. \tag{1}$$

The regularization (or "nonparametric estimation") problem may then be viewed as the minimization of the following objective functional:

$$H(\hat{f}) \equiv \sum_{t=1}^{T} \left(||\hat{y_t} - \hat{f}(\vec{x_t})||^2 + \lambda\, ||P\hat{f}(\vec{x_t})||^2 \right) \tag{2}$$

where $||\cdot||$ is some vector norm and P is a differential operator. The first term of the sum in equation (2) is simply the distance between the approximation $\hat{f}(\vec{x_t})$ and the observation y_t, the second term is a penalty function that is a decreasing function of the smoothness of $\hat{f}(\cdot)$, and λ controls the trade-off between smoothness and fit.

In its most general form, and under certain conditions (see, for example, Poggio and Girosi (1990)), the solution to equation (2) is given by the following expression:

$$\hat{f}(\vec{x}) = \sum_{i=1}^{k} c_i h_i(\| \vec{x} - \vec{z_i} \|) + p(\vec{x}) \tag{3}$$

where $\vec{z_i}$ are d-dimensional vector prototypes or "centers" $\{c_i\}$ are scalar coefficients, $\{h_i\}$ are scalar functions, $p(\cdot)$ is a polynomial, and k is typically much less than the number of observations T in the sample. Such approximants have been termed "hyperbasis functions" by Poggio and Girosi (1990) and are closely related to splines, smoothers such as kernel estimators, and other nonparametric estimators.[3]

For our current purposes, we shall take the vector norm to be a weighted Euclidean norm defined by a $(d \times d)$ weighting matrix W, and the polynomial term shall be taken to be just the linear and constant terms, yielding the following specification for $\hat{f}(\cdot)$:

$$\hat{f}(\vec{x}) = \sum_{i=1}^{k} c_i h_i\left((\vec{x} - \vec{z_i})' W'W(\vec{x} - \vec{z_t}) \right) + \alpha_0 + \vec{\alpha}'_1 \vec{x} \tag{4}$$

where α_0 and $\vec{\alpha_1}$ are the coefficients of the polynomial $p(\cdot)$. Micchelli (1986) shows that a large class of basis functions $h_i(\cdot)$ are appropriate, but the most common choices for basis functions $h(x)$ are Gaussians e^{-x/σ^2} and multiquadrics $\sqrt{x + \sigma^2}$.

Networks of this type can generate any real-valued output, but in applications where we have some a priori knowledge of the range of the desired outputs, it is computationally more efficient to apply some nonlinear transfer function to the outputs to reflect that knowledge. This will be the case in our application to derivative pricing models, in which some of the RBF networks will be augmented with an "output sigmoid," which maps the range $(-\infty, \infty)$ into the fixed range $(0, 1)$. In particular, the augmented network will be of the form $g(\hat{f}(\vec{x}))$ where $g(u) = 1/(1 + e^{-u})$.

For a given set of inputs, $\{\vec{x_t}\}$, and outputs, $\{y_t\}$, RBF approximation amounts to estimating the parameters of the RBF network: the $d(d + 1)/2$ unique entries of the matrix $W'W$, the dk elements of the centers $\{\vec{z_i}\}$, and the $d + k + 1$ coefficients α_0, α_1, and $\{c_i\}$. Thus the total number of parameters that must be estimated for d-dimensional inputs and k centers is $dk + (d^2/2) + (3d/2) + k + 1$.

A.2. Multilayer Perceptrons

Multilayer perceptrons (MLPs), arguably the most popular type of "neural network," are the general category of methods that derive their original inspiration from simple models of biological nervous systems. They were developed independently by Parker (1985) and Rumelhart, Hinton, and Williams (1986) and popularized by the latter. Following the notation of Section I.A.1, a general formulation of MLPs with univariate outputs may be written as follows:

$$f(\vec{x}) = h\left(\sum_{i=1}^{k} \delta_i h\left(\beta_{0i} + \vec{\beta}'_{1i} \, \vec{x} \right) + \delta_0 \right) \tag{5}$$

where $h(\cdot)$ is typically taken to be a smooth, monotonically increasing function such as the "sigmoid" function $1/(1 + e^{-x})$, $\{d_i\}$ and $\vec{\beta}$ are coefficients, and k is the number of "hidden units." The specification equation (5) is generally termed an MLP with "one hidden layer" because the basic "sigmoid-of-a-dot-product" equation is nested once—the nesting may, of course, be repeated arbitrarily many times, hence the term "multilayer" perceptron. Unlike the RBF formulation, the nonlinear function h in the MLP formulation is usually fixed for the entire network.

For a given set of inputs $\{\vec{x_t}\}$ and outputs $\{y_t\}$, fitting an MLP model amounts to estimating the $(d + 1)k$ parameters $\{\beta_{0i}\}$ and $\{\vec{\beta}_{1i}\}$, and the $k + 1$ parameters $\{\delta_i\}$, for a total of $(d + 2)k + 1$ parameters.

A.3. Projection Pursuit Regression

Projection pursuit is a method that emerged from the statistics community for analyzing high-dimensional datasets by looking at their low-dimensional projections. Friedman and Stuetzle (1981) developed a version for the nonlinear regression problem called projection pursuit regression (PPR). Similar to MLPs, PPR models are composed of projections of the data, that is, dot products of the data with estimated coefficients, but, unlike MLPs, they also estimate the nonlinear combining functions from the data. Following the notation of Section I.A.1, the formulation for a PPR with univariate outputs can be written as

$$\hat{f}(\vec{x}) = \sum_{i=1}^{k} \delta_i h_i\left(\vec{\beta}'_{i}\,\vec{x}\right) + \delta_0 \tag{6}$$

where the functions $h_i(\cdot)$ are estimated from the data (typically with a smoother), the $\{\delta_i\}$ and β are coefficients, and k is the number of projections. Note that δ_0 is commonly taken to be the sample mean of the outputs y.

In counting the number of parameters that PPR models require, a difficulty arises in how to treat its use of smoothers in estimating the inner h functions. A naive approach is to count each smoothing estimator as a single parameter, its bandwidth. In this case, the total number of parameters is dk projections indices, k linear coefficients, and k smoothing bandwidths, for a total of $(d + 2)k$ parameters. However, a more refined method of counting the degrees of freedom, for example, Wahba (1990), may yield a slightly different count.

B. Network Properties

Although the various learning network techniques originated from a variety of backgrounds, with implications and characteristics that are not yet fully understood, some common and well-established properties are worth noting.

B.1. Approximation

All of the above learning networks have been shown to possess some form of *universal approximation* property. For example, Huber (1985) and Jones (1987) prove that with sufficiently many terms, any square-integrable function can be approximated arbitrarily well by PPR. Cybenko (1988) and Hornik (1989) demonstrate that one-hidden-layer MLPs can represent to arbitrary precision most classes of linear and nonlinear continuous functions with bounded inputs and outputs. Finally, Girosi and Poggio (1990) show that RBFs can approximate arbitrarily well any continuous function on a compact domain. In a related vein, Girosi and Poggio (1990) also show that RBFs have the "best" approximation property—there is always a choice for the parameters that is better than any other possible choice—a property that is not shared by MLPs.

B.2. Error Convergence

The universal approximation results, however, say nothing about how easy it is to find those good approximations or how computationally efficient they are. In particular, does the number of data points we will need to estimate the parameters of a network grow exponentially with its size (the so-called "curse of dimensionality")? Recent results show that this is not necessarily true *if we are willing to restrict the complexity of the function we wish to model.* For example, Barron (1991) derives bounds on the rate of convergence of the approximation error in MLPs based on the number of examples, given assumptions about the smoothness of the function being approximated. Chen (1991) obtains similar results for PPR. Girosi and Anzellotti (1992) derive bounds on convergence in RBFs using somewhat more natural assumptions about the smoothness of the function being approximated. Niyogi and Girosi (1994) extend this result for the estimation problem and derive a bound on the "generalization error" of RBFs, the error an RBF network will make on unseen data.

The importance and centrality of generalization error bounds to the process of data-driven modeling is worth noting. In particular, these bounds show that for a fixed number of data points the generalization error that we can expect from a network first decreases as the network complexity—number of parameters—increases, then after a certain point the error *increases* (see Figure 33.2). For the financial modeling problems considered in this article, the data set size is, to some extent, fixed, and thus these results indicate that there will be an optimal number of parameters to use for that size of data set.

Other interesting estimation properties have been investigated for PPR in particular. Diaconis and Shahshahani (1984) provide necessary and sufficient conditions for functions to be represented *exactly* using PPR. Donoho and Johnstone (1989) demonstrate the duality between PPR and kernel regression in two dimensions and show that PPR is more parsimonious for modeling functions with angular smoothness.

Figure 33.2

Generalization Error $E(N,n)$ for a Gaussian RBF Network as a Function of the Number of Data Points N and the Number of Network Parameters n

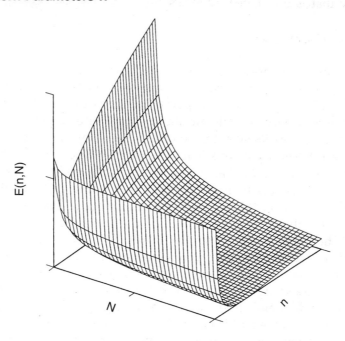

Reprinted with permission from Niyogi and Girosi (1994).

B.3. Model Specification

A key question for most approximation techniques, and in particular for neural network-like schemes, concerns the type and the complexity of the model or the network to be used for a specific problem. Different approaches and different network architectures correspond to different choices of the space of approximating functions. A specific choice implies a specific assumption about the nature of the nonlinear relation to be approximated. For example, Girosi, Jones, and Poggio (1993) have show that different assumptions about smoothness of the function to be approximated lead to different approximation schemes, such as different types of radial basis functions, as well as different kinds of splines and ridge approximators. Certain classes of smoothness assumptions in the different variables even lead to multilayer perceptron architectures. The number of basis functions, and in general the number of network parameters, is a related and difficult issue. Even if one type of architecture can be chosen based on prior knowledge about the smoothness to be expected in a specific problem, the question about the appropriate complexity of the architecture remains, that is, the number of parameters. A general answer does not yet exist and is unlikely to be discovered any time soon. The standard approach to the problem relies on cross-validation techniques and their variations (Wahba 1990). A related, more fundamental approach—called structural risk minimization—has been developed by Vapnik (1982).

B.4. Parameter Estimation Methods

In our discussion above, we have focused primarily on the specification of $\hat{f}(\cdot)$ for each method, but of course a critical concern is how each of the model's parameters is to be estimated. To some extent, the estimation issue may be divorced from the specification issue. Indeed, there is a large body of literature concerned solely with the estimation of network parameters. Much of this literature shows that the speed and accuracy of the estimation process depends on the kind of derivative information used, whether all parameters are estimated simultaneously or sequentially, and whether all the data is used at once in a "batch" mode or sequentially in an "on-line" mode. In Hutchinson (1993), estimation techniques for RBF networks are more fully explored.

However, a rigorous comparison of estimation methods is not the primary goal of our article; rather, our objective is to see if *any* method can yield useful results. As such, we have adopted the most common estimation schemes for our use of the other types of learning networks. In particular we adopt Levenberg–Marquardt for batch mode estimation of the RBF networks, gradient descent (with momentum) for on-line mode estimation of the MLP networks, and the Friedman and Stuetzle algorithm for PPR (which uses a Newton method to compute the projection directions and the "supersmoother" for finding the nonlinear functions h).

Although it is not pursued here, readers interested in exploring the trade-offs between on-line and batch-mode estimation are encouraged to consult the "stochastic approximation" literature (see Robbins and Monro 1951; Ljung and Soderstrom 1986; and Widrow and Stearns 1985). In general, it is not known why on-line methods used with neural network techniques often seem to perform better than batch methods on large-scale, nonconvex problems. It seems difficult to extract any general conclusions from the diverse body of literature reporting the use of different on-line and batch techniques across many disparate applications.

B.5. Equivalence of Different Learning Networks

There is another reason we do not focus on the merits of one type of learning network over another: Recent theoretical developments suggest there are significant connections between many of these networks. For example, Maruyama, Girosi, and Poggio (1991) show an equivalence between MLP networks with normalized inputs and RBF networks. Girosi, Jones, and Poggio (1993) prove that a wide class of approximation schemes can be derived from regularizational theory, including RBF networks and some forms of PPR and MLP networks. Nevertheless, we expect each formulation to be more efficient at approximating some functions than others, and, as argued by Ng and Lippman (1991), the practical differences in using each method, for example, in running time or memory used, may be more important than model accuracy.

SECTION II. LEARNING THE BLACK–SCHOLES FORMULA

Given the power and flexibility of learning networks to approximate complex nonlinear relations, a natural application is to derivative securities whose pricing formulas are highly nonlinear even when they are available in closed form. In particular, we pose the following challenge: If option prices were truly determined by the Black–Scholes formula exactly, can learning networks "learn" the Black–Scholes formula? In more standard statistical jargon: Can the Black–Scholes formula be estimated nonparametrically via learning networks with a sufficient degree of accuracy to be of practical use?

In this section, we face this challenge by performing Monte Carlo simulation experiments in which various learning networks are trained on artificially generated Black–Scholes option prices and are then compared to the Black–Scholes formula both analytically and in out-of-sample hedging experiments to see how close they come. Even with training sets of only six months of daily data, learning-network pricing formulas can approximate the Black–Scholes formula with remarkable accuracy.

While the accuracy of the learning network *prices* is obviously of great interest, this alone is not sufficient to ensure the practical relevance of our nonparametric approach. In particular, the ability to *hedge* an option position is as important since the very existence of an arbitrage-based pricing formula is predicted on the ability to replicate the option through a dynamic hedging strategy. This additional constraint motivates the regularization techniques and, in particular, the RBF networks used in this study. Specifically, delta-hedging strategies require an accurate approximation of the derivative of the underlying pricing formula, and the need for accurate approximations of derivatives leads directly to the smoothness constraint imposed by regularization techniques such as RBF networks.[4] Of course, whether or not the delta-hedging errors are sufficiently small in practice is an empirical matter, and we shall investigate these errors explicitly in our simulation experiments and empirical application described below.

The accuracy we desire cannot be achieved without placing some structure on the function to be approximated. For example, we begin by asserting that the option pricing formula $f(\cdot)$ is smooth in all its arguments and that its arguments are the stock price $S(t)$, the strike price X, and the time to maturity $T - t$. In fact, we know that the Black–Scholes formula also depends on the risk-free rate of interest r and the volatility σ of the underlying asset's continuously compounded returns, for example,

$$C(t) = S(t)\Phi(d_1) - Xe^{-r(T-t)}\Phi(d_2),\qquad(7)$$

where

$$d_1 = \frac{\ln(S(t)/X) + (r + \sigma^2/2)(T - t)}{\sigma\sqrt{T - t}}, \quad d_2 = d_1 - \sigma\sqrt{T - t}$$

and $\Phi(\cdot)$ is the standard normal cumulative distribution function. However, if r and σ are fixed throughout the network's training sample, as we shall assume, then the dependence of the option's price on these two quantities cannot be identified by *any* nonparametric estimator of $f(\cdot)$ in the way that equation (7) does.[5] Of course, if interest rates and volatility vary through time as they do in practice, learning networks can readily capture their impact on option prices explicitly.

One further simplification we employ is to assume that the statistical distribution of the underlying asset's return is independent of the level of the stock price $S(t)$, hence by Theorem 8.9 of Merton (1990, Chapter 8), the option pricing formula $f(\cdot)$ is homogeneous of degree one in both $S(t)$ and X so that we need only estimate $f(S(t)/X,1,T-t)$. By requiring only two rather than three inputs to our learning networks, we may be lessening the number of data points required for learning, but it should also be possible to relax these assumptions and use all three inputs.

We can now outline the components of our Monte Carlo simulation experiments, which consists of two phases: training and testing. The training phase entails generating sample paths of stock and option prices on which the learning networks are "trained"; that is, the network parameters are fitted to each sample path so as to minimize a quadratic loss function. This yields a network pricing formula, which is then "tested" on newly simulated sample paths of stock and option prices; that is, various performance measures are calculated for the network pricing formula using the test past.

To obtain a measure of success of the "average" network pricing formula, we repeat the training phase for many independent option/stock price sample paths, apply each network formula to the *same* test path, and average the performance measures across training paths. To obtain a measure of the "average success" of any given network pricing formula, we do the reverse: For a single training path, we apply the resulting network pricing formula on many independent option/stock price test paths and average the performance measures across *test* paths.

Since we conduct multiple training-path and test-path simulations, our simulation design is best visualized as a matrix of results: Each row corresponds to a separate and independent training path, each column corresponds to a separate and independent test path, and each cell contains the performance measures for a network trained on a particular training path and applied to a particular test path. Therefore, the "average success" of a given network may be viewed as an average of the performance measures across the columns of a given row, and the performance of the "average network" on a given test path may be viewed as an average of the performance measures across the rows of a given column. Although these two averages obviously are closely related, they do address different aspects of the performance of learning networks, and the results of each must be interpreted with the appropriate motivation in mind.

A. Calibrating the Simulations

In the first phase of our Monte Carlo simulation experiment—the training phase—we simulate a two-year sample of daily stock prices and create a cross-section of options each day according to the rules used by the Chicago Board Options Exchange (CBOE) with prices given by the Black–Scholes formula. We refer to this two-year sample of stock and (multiple) option prices as a single "training-path," since the network is trained on this sample.

We assume that the underlying asset for our simulation experiments is a "typical" New York Stock Exchange stock, with an initial price $S(0)$ of $50, an annual continuously compounded expected rate of return % of 10 percent, and an annual volatility σ of 20 percent. Under the Black–Scholes assumption of a geometric Brownian motion:

$$dS(t) = \mu S(t)\,dt + \sigma S(t)\,dW(t) \tag{8}$$

and taking the number of days per year to be 253, we draw 506 pseudorandom variates Z_t from the distribution $N(\mu/253, \sigma^2/253)$ to obtain two years of daily continuously compounded returns, which are converted to prices with the usual relations:

$$S(t) = S(0)\exp(\sum_{i=1}^{t} Z_i), t \geq 0.$$

Given a simulated training path $\{S(t)\}$ of daily stock prices, we construct a corresponding path of option prices according to the rules of the CBOE for introducing options on stocks. Since a thorough description of these rules is unnecessary for our purposes, we summarize only the most salient features here.[6] At any one time, CBOE stock options outstanding on a particular stock have four unique expiration dates: the current month, the next month, and the following two expirations from a quarterly schedule. The CBOE sets strike prices at multiples of $5 for stock prices in the $25 to $200 range, into which all of our simulated prices fall. When options expire and a new expiration date is introduced, the two strike prices closest to the current stock prices are used. If the

Figure 33.3

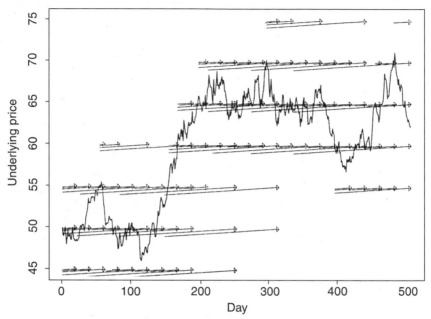

See the text for parameters.

Dashed line represents the stock price, while the *arrows* represent the options on the stock. The y-coordinate of the tip of the arrow indicates the strike price (*arrows* are slanted to make different introduction and expiration dates visible).

current price is very close to one of those strike prices—within $1 in our simulations—a third strike price is used to better bracket the current price. If the stock price moves outside of the current strike-price range, another strike price is generally added for all expiration dates to bracket that price.[7] We assume that all of the options generated according to these rules are traded every day, although in practice, far-from-the-money and long-dated options are very often illiquid.

A typical training path is shown in Figure 33.3. We can also plot the training path of a three-dimensional surface if we normalize stock and option prices by the appropriate strike price and consider the option price as a function of the form $f(S/X, 1, T - t)$ (see Figure 33.4). Because of the options generated for a particular sample path are a function of

Figure 33.4

Simulated Call Option Prices Normalized by Strike Price and Plotted versus Stock Price and Time to Expiration

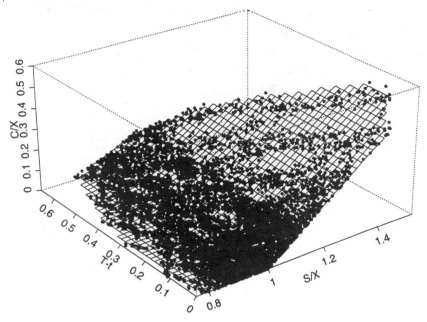

Points represent daily observations. Note that the denser sampling of points close to expiration is due to the CBOE strategy of always having options that expire in the current and next month.

the (random) stock price path, the size of this data matrix (in terms of number of options and total number of data points) varies across sample paths. For our training set, the number of options per sample path range from 71 to 91, with an average of 81. The total number of data points range from 5,227 to 6,847, with an average of 6,001.

B. Training Network Pricing Formulas

Now we are set to estimate or train pricing formulas of the form of $f(S/X,1,T - T)$ on the simulated training paths, using two "inputs": $S(t)/X$ and $T - t$. For comparison, we first estimate two simple linear models estimated

---

Table 33.1

Regression Summaries for Typical Linear Models

	Coefficient	Standard Error	t-Statistic	p-Value
a. Single Linear Model[*]				
Intercept	−0.6417	0.0028	−231.4133	0
S/X	0.6886	0.0027	259.4616	0
T − t	0.0688	0.0018	38.5834	0
b. "In-the-Money" Linear Model[†]				
Intercept	−0.9333	0.0012	−763.6280	0
S/X	0.9415	0.0011	875.0123	0
T − t	0.0858	0.0006	150.6208	0
c. "Out-of-the-Money" Linear Model[‡]				
Intercept	−0.1733	0.0022	−80.3638	0
S/X	0.1882	0.0023	80.6965	0
T − t	0.0728	0.0007	108.2335	0

[*] Residual standard error = 0.027, R^2 = 0.9098, N = 6782, $F_{2,6666}$-statistic = 34184.97, p-value = 0.
[†] Residual standard error = 0.0062, R^2 = 0.9955, N = 3489, $F_{2,6666}$-statistic = 385583.4, p-value = 0.
[‡] Residual standard error = 0.007, R^2 = 0.8557, N = 3293, $F_{2,6666}$-statistic = 9753.782, p-value = 0.

---

using ordinary least squares (OLS). The first model is a linear regression of the option price on $S(t)/X$ and $T - t$. The second is a pair of linear regressions, one for options currently in the money, and another for those currently out of the money. Typical estimates of these models are shown in Table 33.1.

Although these linear models fit quite well, the R^2s well above 80 percent, they have particularly naive implications for delta-hedging strategies. In particular, delta-hedging with the first linear model would amount to purchasing a certain number of shares of stock in the beginning (0.6886 in the example in Table 33.1) and holding them until expiration, regardless of stock price movements during the option's life. The second linear model improves on this slightly by switching between hedging with a large number (0.9415 in Table 33.1b) and a small number of shares (0.1882 in Table 33.1c), depending on whether the current stock price is less than or greater than the strike price.

The nonlinear models obtained from learning networks, on the other hand, yield estimates of option prices and deltas that are difficult to distinguish visually from the true Black–Scholes values. An example of the estimates and errors for an RBF network is shown in Figure 33.5, which was estimated from the same data as the linear models from Table 33.1. The estimated equation for the particular RBF network is:

$$
\widehat{C/X} = -0.06 \sqrt{ \left[\begin{matrix} S/X - 1.35 \\ T-t-0.45 \end{matrix} \right]' \left[\begin{matrix} 59.79 & -0.03 \\ -0.03 & 10.24 \end{matrix} \right] \left[\begin{matrix} S/X - 1.35 \\ T-t-0.45 \end{matrix} \right] } + 2.55
$$

$$
-0.03 \sqrt{ \left[\begin{matrix} S/X - 1.18 \\ T-t-0.24 \end{matrix} \right]' \left[\begin{matrix} 59.79 & -0.03 \\ -0.03 & 10.24 \end{matrix} \right] \left[\begin{matrix} S/X - 1.18 \\ T-t-0.24 \end{matrix} \right] } + 1.97
$$

$$
+0.03 \sqrt{ \left[\begin{matrix} S/X - 0.98 \\ T-t+0.20 \end{matrix} \right]' \left[\begin{matrix} 59.79 & -0.03 \\ -0.03 & 10.24 \end{matrix} \right] \left[\begin{matrix} S/X - 0.98 \\ T-t-0.20 \end{matrix} \right] } + 0.00
$$

$$
+0.10 \sqrt{ \left[\begin{matrix} S/X - 1.05 \\ T-t+0.10 \end{matrix} \right]' \left[\begin{matrix} 59.79 & -0.03 \\ -0.03 & 10.24 \end{matrix} \right] \left[\begin{matrix} S/X - 1.05 \\ T-t-0.10 \end{matrix} \right] } + 1.62
$$

$$
+0.14 S/X - 0.24(T-t) - 0.01. \tag{9}
$$

Observe from equation (9) that the centers in the RBF model are not constrained to lie within the range of the inputs, and in fact do not in the third and fourth centers in our example. The largest errors in these networks tend to occur at the kink-point for options at the money at expiration and also along the boundary of the sample points.

PPR and MLP networks of similar complexity generate similar response surfaces, although, as we shall see in the next section, each method has its own area of the input space that it models slightly more accurately than the others.

Figure 33.5

Typical Behavior of Four Nonlinear Term RBF Models

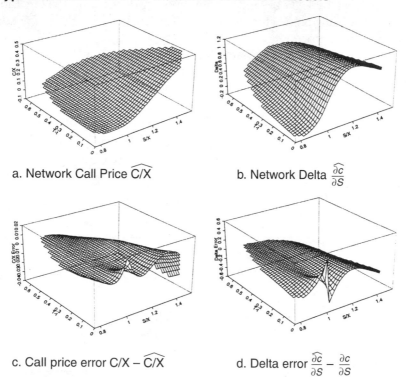

a. Network Call Price $\widehat{C/X}$

b. Network Delta $\dfrac{\widehat{\partial c}}{\partial S}$

c. Call price error $C/X - \widehat{C/X}$

d. Delta error $\dfrac{\widehat{\partial c}}{\partial S} - \dfrac{\partial c}{\partial S}$

Our choice of model complexity is not arbitrary and in fact is motivated by our desire to minimize error and maximize "fit" for out-of-sample data. In this regard, a critical issue in specifying learning networks is how many nonlinear terms—"hidden units," basis functions, projections, and so on—to use in the approximation. Following the discussion in Section I.B.2, for actual market data we might expect an optimal number of parameters that minimizes out-of-sample error. But in the simulations of this section, the data are noise-free (in the sense that there is a deterministic formula generating the outputs from the inputs), and hence we are interested primarily in how quickly adding more parameters reduces the error. Preliminary out-of-sample tests with independent sample paths have indicated diminishing returns beyond four nonlinear terms (as measured by the percentage of variance explained), and thus we adopt this specification for all the learning networks considered in this article.[8] In the next sections we will assess how well we have done in meeting our goal of minimizing out-of-sample error.

C. Performance Measures

Our learning networks estimate the option prices $\widehat{C/X}$; thus, our first performance measure is simple the usual coefficient of determination, R^2, of those estimated values compared with the true option prices C/X, computed for the out-of-sample data.

However, the R^2 measure is not ideal for telling us the practical value of any improvement in pricing accuracy that the learning networks might give us. A more meaningful measure of performance for a given option pricing formula is the "tracking error" of various replicating portfolios designed to delta-hedge an option position, using the formula in question to calculate the hedge ratios or deltas. In particular, suppose at date 0 we sell one call option and undertake the usual dynamic trading strategy in stocks and bonds to hedge this call during its life. If we have correctly identified the option pricing model, and if we can costlessly and continuously hedge, then at expiration the combined value of our stock and bond positions should exactly offset the value of the call. The difference between the terminal value of the call and the terminal combined value of the stock and bond positions may then serve as a measure of the accuracy of our network approximation. Of course, since it is impossible to hedge continuously in practice, there will always be some tracking error due to discreteness, and therefore we shall compare the RBF tracking error with the tracking error of discrete delta-hedging under the exact Black–Scholes formula.

More formally, denote by $V(t)$ the dollar value of our replicating portfolio at date t and let:

$$V(t) = V_S(t) + V_B(t) + V_C(t) \tag{10}$$

where $V_S(t)$ is the dollar value of stocks, $V_B(t)$ is the dollar value of bonds, and $V_C(t)$ is the dollar value of call options held in the portfolio at date t. The initial composition of this portfolio at date 0 is assumed to be:

$$V_S(0) = S(0)\Delta_{RBF}(0), \quad \Delta_{RBF}(0) \equiv \frac{\partial F_{RBF}(0)}{\partial S} \tag{11}$$

$$V_C(0) = -F_{BS}(0) \tag{12}$$

$$V_B(0) = -(V_S(0) + V_C(0) \tag{13}$$

where $F_{BS}(\cdot)$ is the Black–Scholes call option pricing formula and $F_{RBF}(\cdot)$ is its RBF approximation. The portfolio positions in equations (11) to (13) represent the sale of one call option at date 0, priced according to the theoretical Black–Scholes formula $F_{BS}(0)$, and the simultaneous purchase of $\Delta_{RBF}(0)$ shares of stock at price $S(0)$, where $\Delta_{RBF}(0)$ is the derivative of the RBF approximation $F_{RBF}(0)$, with respect to the stock price.[9] Since the stock purchase is wholly financed by the combination of riskless borrowing and proceeds from the sale of the call option, the initial value of the replicating portfolio is identically zero, and thus:

$$V(0) = V_S(0) + V_B(0) + V_C(0) = 0.$$

Prior to expiration, and at discrete and regular intervals of length τ (which we take to be one day in our simulations), the stock and bond positions in the replicating portfolio will be rebalanced so as to satisfy the following relations:

$$V_S(t) = S(t)\Delta_{RBF}(t), \quad \Delta_{RBF}(t) \equiv \frac{\partial F_{RBF}(t)}{\partial S} \tag{14}$$

$$V_B(t) = e^{r\tau}V_B(t-\tau) - S(t)(\Delta_{RBF}(t) - \Delta_{RBF}(t-\tau)) \tag{15}$$

where $t = k\,\tau \leq T$ for some integer k. The tracking error of the replicating portfolio is then defined to be the value of the replicating portfolio $V(T)$ at expiration date T. From this, we obtain the following performance measure:

$$\xi \equiv e^{-rT}E[\,|V(T)|\,]. \tag{16}$$

The quantity ξ is simply the present value of the expected absolute tracking error of the replicating portfolio. Although, for more complex options portfolios ξ may not be the most relevant criterion, nevertheless ξ does provide some information about the accuracy of our option pricing formula.[10]

A third measure of performance may be defined by combining the information contained in the expected tracking error with the variance of the tracking error. In particular, we define the "prediction error" η as:

$$\eta \equiv e^{-rT}\sqrt{E^2[V(T)] + \text{Var}[V(T)]} \tag{17}$$

which is the present value of the square root of the sum of the squared expected tracking error and its variance. The inclusion of the variance of $V(T)$ is significant; the expected tracking error of a delta-hedging strategy might be zero, but the strategy is a poor one if the variance of the tracking error were large. We shall use all three measures, R^2, ξ, and η, in our performance analysis below.

D. Testing Network Pricing Formulas

To assess the quality of the RBF pricing formula obtained from each training path, we simulate an independent six-month sample of daily stock prices—a "test path"—and use the trained network to delta-hedge various options (individually, not as a portfolio) introduced at the *start* of the test path. By simulating many independent test paths, 500 in our case, and averaging the absolute tracking errors over these paths, we can obtain estimates $\hat{\xi}$ and $\hat{\eta}$ of the expected absolute tracking error ξ and the prediction error η for each of the 10 network pricing formulas. The performance of the network delta-hedging strategy may then be compared to the performance of a delta-hedging strategy using the Black–Scholes formula.

D.1. Out-of-Sample R^2 Comparisons

As a preliminary check of out-of-sample performance, we observe that the pricing errors of the direct model outputs $\widehat{C/X}$ are typically quite small for all of the networks examined, with out-of-sample R^2's of 99 percent and above for the "average" network (except for the single linear model). These results are presented in Table 33.2. From the minimum R^2 values, it is also evident that not all types of networks yield *consistently*

Table 33.2

Out-of-Sample R^2 Values (in Percent) for the Learning Networks, Summarized across All Training and Out-of-Sample Test Sets

	Linear-1	Linear-2	RBF	PPR	MLP	B–S
Minimum	14.72	94.34	98.58	55.23	76.60	100.00
Mean	83.40	99.27	99.95	99.08	99.48	100.00
Maximum	95.57	99.82	99.99	100.00	99.96	100.00

Note: Linear-1 refers to the single-regression model of the data; Linear-2 refers to the two-regression model, one for in-the-money options and one for out-of-the-money options; RBF refers to a radial-basis-function network with four multiquadric centers and an output sigmoid; PPR refers to a projection pursuit regression with four projections; and MLP refers to a multilayer perceptron with a single hidden layer containing four units. B-S indicates Black–Scholes model.

good results, perhaps because of the stochastic nature of the respective estimation processes.

D.2. Tracking Error Comparisons

Table 33.3 reports selected raw simulation results for a call option with three months to expiration and a strike price X of $50. In each row, the absolute tracking errors for delta-hedging this option are reported for the network pricing formula trained on a single training path, the entries in each column corresponding to a different test path for which the absolute tracking error is calculated. For example, the training path no. 1/test path no. 200-entry 0.2719 is the absolute tracking error for delta-hedging this three-month, $50-strike option over test path no. 200, using the network pricing formula trained on training path no. 1.

For comparison, over the same test path, the absolute tacking error for a delta-hedging strategy using the Black–Scholes formula is 0.3461, reported in the bottom row. The fact that the RBF network pricing formula can yield a smaller delta-hedging error than the Black–Scholes formula may seem counterintuitive. After all, the Black–Scholes formula is indeed the correct pricing formula in the context of our simulations. The source of this apparent paradox lies in the fact that we are delta-hedging *discretely* (once a day), whereas the Black–Scholes formula is based on a continuously ad-

Table 33.3

Simulations of Absolute Delta-Hedging Errors for RBF Networks for an At-the-Money Call Option with $X = 50$, $T - t = 3$ Months, and a Black–Scholes Price of $2.2867

	Test No. 100	Test No. 200	Test No. 300	Test No. 400	Test No. 500
Train no. 1	0.6968	0.2719	0.1154	0.0018	0.5870
Train no. 2	0.6536	0.2667	0.0882	0.0903	0.5523
Train no. 3	0.6832	0.2622	0.0698	0.0370	0.5534
Train no. 4	0.7175	0.2682	0.0955	0.0155	0.5918
Train no. 5	0.6938	0.2767	0.1055	0.0229	0.5993
Train no. 6	0.6755	0.2692	0.1085	0.0083	0.5600
Train no. 7	0.6971	0.2690	0.1104	0.0054	0.5809
Train no. 8	0.7075	0.2717	0.1087	0.0022	0.5859
Train no. 9	0.6571	0.2652	0.1016	0.0013	0.5389
Train no. 10	0.7105	0.2706	0.1135	0.0038	0.5913
B–S	0.0125	0.3461	0.0059	0.0677	0.0492

Note: The current stock price $S(0)$ is assumed to be $50. The last row displays the same errors for the Black–Scholes formula. "Train" indicates training path; "Test" indicates testing path; "B–S" indicates Black–Scholes formula.

---

justed delta-hedging strategy. Therefore, even the Black–Scholes formula will exhibit some tracking error when applied to Black–Scholes prices at discrete time intervals. In such cases, an RBF pricing formula may well be more accurate since it is trained directly on the discretely sampled data and is not based on a continuous-time approximation.

Of course, other columns in Table 33.3 show that Black–Scholes can perform significantly better than the RBF formula (for example, compare the training path no. 1/test path no. 100-entry of 0.6968 with the Black–Scholes value of 0.0125). Moreover, as the delta-hedging interval shrinks, the Black–Scholes formula will become increasingly more accurate and, in the limit, will have no tracking error whatsoever. However, since such a limit is empirically unattainable for a variety of institutional reasons, the benefits of network pricing formulas may be quite significant.

Table 33.4

Fraction of 500 Test Sets in which the Absolute Delta-Hedging Error was Lower than Black–Scholes for an At-the-Money Call Option with $X = 50$, $T - t = 3$ Months, and a Black–Scholes Price of $2.2867

	Linear-1	Linear-2	RBF	PPR	MLP
Train no. 1	0.062	0.102	0.354	0.362	0.260
	(0.011)	(0.014)	(0.021)	(0.021)	(0.020)
Train no. 2	0.048	0.112	0.340	0.390	0.264
	(0.010)	(0.014)	(0.021)	(0.022)	(0.020)
Train no. 3	0.088	0.108	0.380	0.350	0.268
	(0.013)	(0.014)	(0.022)	(0.021)	(0.020)
Train no. 4	0.084	0.098	0.370	0.340	0.254
	(0.012)	(0.013)	(0.022)	(0.021)	(0.019)
Train no. 5	0.062	0.100	0.358	0.360	0.278
	(0.011)	(0.013)	(0.021)	(0.021)	(0.020)
Train no. 6	0.056	0.108	0.364	0.378	0.274
	(0.010)	(0.014)	(0.022)	(0.022)	(0.020)
Train no. 7	0.084	0.102	0.368	0.362	0.272
	(0.012)	(0.014)	(0.022)	(0.021)	(0.020)
Train no. 8	0.080	0.104	0.358	0.328	0.262
	(0.012)	(0.014)	(0.021)	(0.021)	(0.020)
Train no. 9	0.066	0.104	0.368	0.374	0.272
	(0.011)	(0.014)	(0.022)	(0.022)	(0.020)
Train no. 10	0.080	0.104	0.354	0.382	0.280
	(0.012)	(0.014)	(0.021)	(0.022)	(0.020)

Note: Standard errors are given in parentheses. The current stock price $S(0)$ is assumed to be $50. "Train" indicates training path.

For a more complete comparison of RBF networks and the Black–Scholes formula across all 500 test paths, Table 33.4 reports the fraction of test paths for which each of the ten RBF network exhibit *lower* absolute tracking error than the Black–Scholes formula. Similar comparisons are also performed for the single-regression model ("Linear-1"), the two-re-

Table 33.5

Fraction of 500 Test Sets

RBF	$X = 40$	$X = 45$	$X = 50$	$X = 55$	$X = 60$
$T - t = 1$					
Mean	0.001	0.120	0.278	0.266	0.032
(SE)	(0.000)	(0.005)	(0.006)	(0.006)	(0.003)
Minimum	0.000	0.108	0.270	0.176	0.022
Maximum	0.002	0.140	0.284	0.332	0.040
$T - t = 3$					
Mean	0.072	0.296	0.361	0.269	0.254
(SE)	(0.004)	(0.006)	(0.007)	(0.006)	(0.006)
Minimum	0.054	0.242	0.340	0.248	0.170
Maximum	0.084	0.336	0.380	0.322	0.336
$T - t = 6$					
Mean	0.164	0.263	0.316	0.243	0.304
(SE)	(0.005)	(0.006)	(0.007)	(0.006)	(0.007)
Minimum	0.120	0.220	0.298	0.234	0.276
Maximum	0.200	0.310	0.324	0.258	0.320

Note: The absolute delta-hedging error using a radial basis function (RBF) network with four multiquadric centers and an output sigmoid is lower than the Black–Scholes delta-hedging error for call options with strike price X and time-to-maturity $T - t$ months on a nondividend-paying stock currently priced at $50. Within each section, the top entry of each column is the average of this fraction across the 10 training paths, the second entry (in parentheses) is the standard error of that average, and the third and fourth entries are the minimum and maximum across the 10 training paths. SE indicates standard error.

gression model ("Linear-2"), a projection pursuit regression ("PPR") with four projections, and a multilayer perceptron ("MLP") with one hidden layer containing four units.

The third column of entries in Table 33.4 shows that in approximately 36 percent of the 500 test paths, RBF networks have lower tracking error than the Black–Scholes formula. For this particular option, RBF networks and PPR networks have quite similar performance, and both are superior

Table 33.6

Fraction of 500 Test Sets

MLP	$X = 40$	$X = 45$	$X = 50$	$X = 55$	$X = 60$
$T - t = 1$					
Mean	0.000	0.046	0.238	0.125	0.019
(SE)	(0.000)	(0.003)	(0.006)	(0.005)	(0.002)
Minimum	0.000	0.034	0.228	0.110	0.008
Maximum	0.000	0.066	0.246	0.132	0.028
$T - t = 3$					
Mean	0.022	0.174	0.268	0.354	0.280
(SE)	(0.002)	(0.005)	(0.006)	(0.007)	(0.006)
Minimum	0.004	0.130	0.254	0.324	0.216
Maximum	0.040	0.220	0.280	0.386	0.384
$T - t = 6$					
Mean	0.030	0.187	0.252	0.330	0.253
(SE)	(0.002)	(0.006)	(0.006)	(0.007)	(0.006)
Minimum	0.004	0.152	0.204	0.298	0.216
Maximum	0.074	0.212	0.302	0.354	0.274

Note: The absolute delta-hedging error using a multilayer perceptron (MLP) network with a single hidden layer containing four units is lower than the Black–Scholes delta-hedging error for call options with strike price X and time-to-maturity $T - t$ months on a nondividend-paying stock currently priced at \$50. See Table 33.5 for details. SE indicates standard error.

to the three other pricing models; the next closest competitor is the MLP, which outperforms the Black–Scholes formula for approximately 26 percent of the test paths.

Of course, tracking errors tend to vary with the terms of the option, such as its time-to-maturity and strike price. To gauge the accuracy of the RBF and other pricing models across these terms, we report in Tables 33.5–33.9 the fraction of test paths for which each of the four pricing models outperforms Black–Scholes for strike prices $X = 40, 45, 50, 55,$ and 60, and times-to-maturity $T - t = 1, 3,$ and 6 months.

Table 33.7

Fraction of 500 Test Sets

PPR	X = 40	X = 45	X = 50	X = 55	X = 60
$T - t = 1$					
Mean	0.000	0.165	0.316	0.303	0.024
(SE)	(0.000)	(0.005)	(0.007)	(0.006)	(0.002)
Minimum	0.000	0.118	0.272	0.208	0.006
Maximum	0.002	0.198	0.394	0.364	0.052
$T - t = 3$					
Mean	0.060	0.282	0.363	0.325	0.177
(SE)	(0.003)	(0.006)	(0.007)	(0.007)	(0.005)
Minimum	0.006	0.202	0.328	0.244	0.076
Maximum	0.126	0.344	0.390	0.420	0.286
$T - t = 6$					
Mean	0.125	0.287	0.315	0.293	0.197
(SE)	(0.005)	(0.006)	(0.007)	(0.006)	(0.006)
Minimum	0.020	0.190	0.290	0.234	0.116
Maximum	0.202	0.346	0.352	0.358	0.286

Note: The absolute delta-hedging error using a projection pursuit regression (PPR) network with four projections is lower than the Black–Scholes delta-hedging error for call options with strike price X and time-to-maturity $T - t$ months on a nondividend-paying stock currently priced at $50. See Table 33.5 for details. SE indicates standard error.

Table 33.5 shows that the average RBF network—averaged over the 10 training paths—performs reasonably well for near-the-money options at all three maturities, outperforming Black–Scholes between 12 and 36 percent of the time for options with strike prices between $45 and $55. As the maturity increases, the performance of the average RBF network improves for deep-out-of-the-money options as well, outperforming Black–Scholes for 30 percent of the test paths for the call with a strike price of $60.

Tables 33.6 and 33.7 provide similar comparisons for the average MLP and PPR networks, respectively—averaged over the same training paths

Table 33.8

Fraction of 500 Test Sets

Linear-1	$X = 40$	$X = 45$	$X = 50$	$X = 55$	$X = 60$
$T - t = 1$					
Mean	0.000	0.020	0.103	0.016	0.002
(SE)	(0.000)	(0.002)	(0.004)	(0.002)	(0.001)
Minimum	0.000	0.012	0.068	0.010	0.002
Maximum	0.000	0.032	0.124	0.026	0.002
$T - t = 3$					
Mean	0.003	0.029	0.071	0.018	0.007
(SE)	(0.001)	(0.002)	(0.004)	(0.002)	(0.001)
Minimum	0.000	0.016	0.048	0.010	0.006
Maximum	0.010	0.060	0.088	0.032	0.012
$T - t = 6$					
Mean	0.012	0.035	0.039	0.037	0.019
(SE)	(0.002)	(0.003)	(0.003)	(0.003)	(0.002)
Minimum	0.010	0.026	0.024	0.034	0.010
Maximum	0.016	0.046	0.050	0.042	0.026

Note: The absolute delta-hedging error using a single-regression model is lower than the Black–Scholes delta-hedging error for call options with strike price X and time-to-maturity $T - t$ months on a nondividend-paying stock currently priced at $50. See Table 33.5 for details. SE indicates standard error.

as the RBF model—with similar results: good performance for near-the-money options at all maturities and good performance for deep-out-of-the-money options at longer maturities.

Not surprisingly, Tables 33.8 and 33.9 show that the linear models exhibit considerably weaker performance than either of the network models, with fractions of outperforming test paths between 0.0 and 10.3 percent for the single-regression model and between 0.0 and 14.6 percent for the two-regression model. However, these results do offer one important insight: Even simple linear models can sometimes, al-

Table 33.9

Fraction of 500 Test Sets

Linear-2	X = 40	X = 45	X = 50	X = 55	X = 60
T − t = 1					
Mean	0.000	0.080	0.146	0.068	0.004
(SE)	(0.000)	(0.004)	(0.005)	(0.004)	(0.001)
Minimum	0.000	0.060	0.128	0.058	0.004
Maximum	0.000	0.090	0.170	0.092	0.004
T − t = 3					
Mean	0.018	0.107	0.104	0.095	0.033
(SE)	(0.002)	(0.004)	(0.004)	(0.004)	(0.003)
Minimum	0.010	0.088	0.098	0.080	0.020
Maximum	0.024	0.116	0.112	0.112	0.052
T − t = 6					
Mean	0.045	0.082	0.072	0.082	0.059
(SE)	(0.003)	(0.004)	(0.004)	(0.004)	(0.003)
Minimum	0.032	0.074	0.056	0.068	0.038
Maximum	0.054	0.090	0.080	0.096	0.072

Note: The absolute delta-hedging error using a two-regression model is lower than the Black–Scholes delta-hedging error for call options with strike price X and time-to-maturity $T − t$ months on a nondividend-paying stock currently priced at $50. See Table 33.5 for details. SE indicates standard error.

beit rarely, outperform the Black–Scholes model when delta-hedging is performed on a daily frequency.

Finally it is important to note that network pricing formulas should be monitored carefully for *extrapolation*. Because the networks are trained on a sampling of points covering a specific region of input space, it should not be surprising that they may not perform as well on points outside of this region. For example, Figure 33.6 illustrates that the worst tracking error for RBF networks in our simulations occurred for test data that was well outside of the range of the training data.

Figure 33.6

Input Points in the Training Set and Test Set for the RBF Network with the Largest Error Measure ξ

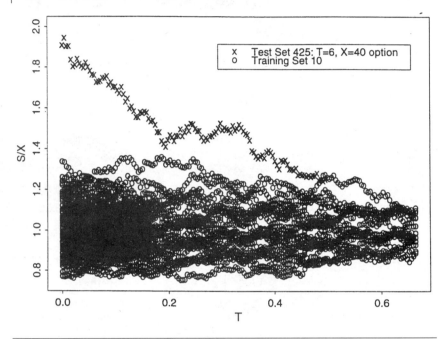

| x | Test Set 425: T=6, X=40 option |
| o | Training Set 10 |

Table 33.10

Estimated Prediction Errors for the Absolute Tracking Error of a Delta-Hedging Strategy Using the Black–Scholes (B–S) Formula

B–S	$X = 40$	$X = 45$	$X = 50$	$X = 55$	$X = 60$
$T - t = 1$	0.001	0.069	0.217	0.116	0.007
$T - t = 3$	0.043	0.146	0.213	0.155	0.098
$T - t = 6$	0.088	0.157	0.208	0.211	0.147

Note: These are for call options with strike price X and time-to-maturity $T - t$ months on a nondividend-paying stock currently priced at $50, estimated across 500 independent test paths. Since the Black–Scholes parameters are assumed to be known, not estimated, these errors do not vary across training paths.

Table 33.11

Estimated Prediction Errors for the Absolute Tracking Error of a Delta-Hedging Strategy Using a Radial Basis Function (RBF) Network with Four Multiquadric Centers and an Output Sigmoid

RBF	$X = 40$	$X = 45$	$X = 50$	$X = 55$	$X = 60$
$T - t = 1$					
Mean	0.044	0.164	0.310	0.157	0.039
(SE)	(0.003)	(0.002)	(0.002)	(0.001)	(0.001)
Minimum	0.031	0.150	0.298	0.152	0.035
Maximum	0.059	0.172	0.316	0.163	0.045
$T - t = 3$					
Mean	0.142	0.215	0.296	0.257	0.155
(SE)	(0.008)	(0.002)	(0.001)	(0.001)	(0.001)
Minimum	0.113	0.208	0.291	0.249	0.152
Maximum	0.177	0.225	0.299	0.263	0.161
$T - t = 6$					
Mean	0.286	0.271	0.309	0.340	0.214
(SE)	(0.011)	(0.006)	(0.002)	(0.002)	(0.001)
Minimum	0.236	0.243	0.299	0.329	0.207
Maximum	0.334	0.300	0.315	0.347	0.224

Note: These are for call options with strike price X and time-to-maturity $T - t$ months on a nondividend-paying stock currently priced at $50, estimated across 500 independent test paths. Within each section, the top entry of each column is the average of the estimated prediction error across the 10 training paths, the second entry (in parentheses) is the standard error of that average, and the third and fourth entries are the minimum and maximum across the training paths. SE indicates standard error.

D.3. Prediction Error Comparisons

To complete our performance analysis of the networking option pricing formulas, we compare the estimated prediction errors, $\hat{\eta}$, of the network delta-hedging strategies to those of the Black–Scholes formula. Recall from equation (17) that the prediction error combines the expectation and vari-

Table 33.12

Estimated Prediction Errors for the Absolute Tracking Error of a Delta-Hedging Strategy Using a Multilayer Perceptron (MLP) Network with a Single Hidden Layer Containing Four Units

MLP	$X = 40$	$X = 45$	$X = 50$	$X = 55$	$X = 60$
$T - t = 1$					
Mean	0.214	0.264	0.389	0.209	0.060
(SE)	(0.024)	(0.008)	(0.006)	(0.004)	(0.002)
Minimum	0.124	0.228	0.365	0.194	0.050
Maximum	0.386	0.314	0.429	0.234	0.075
$T - t = 3$					
Mean	0.690	0.323	0.336	0.285	0.178
(SE)	(0.118)	(0.016)	(0.003)	(0.004)	(0.002)
Minimum	0.271	0.261	0.356	0.270	0.171
Maximum	1.477	0.417	0.388	0.308	0.194
$T - t = 6$					
Mean	1.187	0.733	0.400	0.356	0.264
(SE)	(0.174)	(0.087)	(0.007)	(0.004)	(0.002)
Minimum	0.538	0.425	0.373	0.344	0.255
Maximum	2.377	1.352	0.448	0.377	0.274

Note: These are for call options with strike price X and time-to-maturity $T - t$ months on a nondividend-paying stock currently priced at $50, estimated across 500 independent test paths. See Table 33.11 for further details. SE indicates standard error.

ance of the absolute tracking error; hence, the estimated prediction error is calculated with the sample mean and sample variance of $|V(T)|$, taken over the 500 test paths. The benchmarks for comparison are the estimated prediction errors for the Black–Scholes delta-hedging strategy, given in Table 33.10.

Once again, we see from Table 33.10 that delta-hedging with the Black–Scholes formula at discrete intervals does not yield a perfect hedge. The

Table 33.13

Estimated Prediction Errors for the Absolute Tracking Error of a Delta-Hedging Strategy Using a Projection Pursuit Regression (PPR) Network with Four Projections

PPR	$X = 40$	$X = 45$	$X = 50$	$X = 55$	$X = 60$
$T - t = 1$					
Mean	0.198	0.121	0.271	0.147	0.081
(SE)	(0.094)	(0.005)	(0.006)	(0.004)	(0.024)
Minimum	0.028	0.101	0.245	0.131	0.028
Maximum	0.991	0.144	0.301	0.167	0.261
$T - t = 3$					
Mean	1.180	0.275	0.276	0.238	0.247
(SE)	(0.299)	(0.056)	(0.006)	(0.011)	(0.046)
Minimum	0.134	0.174	0.254	0.202	0.136
Maximum	3.113	0.759	0.309	0.320	0.555
$T - t = 6$					
Mean	2.140	1.056	0.383	0.367	0.443
(SE)	(0.383)	(0.201)	(0.045)	(0.029)	(0.074)
Minimum	0.511	0.246	0.259	0.268	0.224
Maximum	4.337	2.325	0.719	0.589	0.931

Note: These are for call options with strike price X and time-to-maturity $T - t$ months on a nondividend-paying stock currently priced at $50, estimated across 500 independent test paths. See Table 33.11 for further details. SE indicates standard error.

estimated prediction errors are all strictly positive and are larger for options near the money and with longer times to maturity.

However, under the prediction error performance measure, the Black–Scholes formula is superior to all of the learning network approaches for this simulated data (see Tables 33.11–33.15). For example, these tables show that the average RBF network has larger estimated prediction errors than the Black–Scholes formula for all option types (although RBF net-

Table 33.14

Estimated Prediction Errors for the Absolute Tracking Error of a Delta-Hedging Strategy Using a Single-Regression Model

Linear-1	$X = 40$	$X = 45$	$X = 50$	$X = 55$	$X = 60$
$T - t = 1$					
Mean	1.047	0.967	0.911	1.672	1.879
(SE)	(0.096)	(0.091)	(0.036)	(0.091)	(0.098)
Minimum	0.561	0.507	0.813	1.251	1.425
Maximum	1.492	1.393	1.132	2.135	2.375
$T - t = 3$					
Mean	1.849	1.486	1.697	2.624	3.015
(SE)	(0.172)	(0.117)	(0.049)	(0.153)	(0.163)
Minimum	0.983	0.959	1.580	1.936	2.260
Maximum	2.649	2.091	2.013	3.411	3.845
$T - t = 6$					
Mean	2.276	2.124	2.170	2.910	3.780
(SE)	(0.213)	(0.149)	(0.073)	(0.173)	(0.214)
Minimum	1.208	1.495	2.000	2.170	2.805
Maximum	3.275	2.926	2.629	3.821	4.879

Note: These are for call options with strike price X and time-to-maturity $T - t$ months on a nondividend-paying stock currently priced at \$50, estimated across 500 independent test paths. SE indicates standard error. See Table 33.11 for further details.

works have smaller errors than the other learning network types) and that the linear models are significantly worse than the others.[11] We also note that the pattern of errors is somewhat different for each learning network, indicating that each may have its own area of dominance.

Overall, we are encouraged by the ease with which the learning networks achieved error levels similar to those of the Black–Scholes formula, and on a problem posed in the latter's favor. We suspect that the learning-network approach will be a promising alternative for pricing and hedging derivatives where there is uncertainty about the specification of the asset-return process.

Table 33.15

Estimate Prediction Errors for the Absolute Tracking Error of a Delta-Hedging Strategy Using a Two-Regression Model

Linear-2	$X = 40$	$X = 45$	$X = 50$	$X = 55$	$X = 60$
$T - t = 1$					
Mean	0.212	0.207	0.724	0.455	0.518
(SE)	(0.018)	(0.013)	(0.011)	(0.034)	(0.045)
Minimum	0.154	0.168	0.681	0.335	0.344
Maximum	0.340	0.304	0.776	0.628	0.739
$T - t = 3$					
Mean	0.371	0.555	1.054	0.836	0.790
(SE)	(0.029)	(0.003)	(0.013)	(0.024)	(0.067)
Minimum	0.277	0.539	0.995	0.767	0.539
Maximum	0.586	0.566	1.118	0.972	1.130
$T - t = 6$					
Mean	0.500	0.955	1.544	1.454	1.042
(SE)	(0.027)	(0.008)	(0.022)	(0.019)	(0.055)
Minimum	0.412	0.909	1.452	1.373	0.880
Maximum	0.709	0.988	1.650	1.563	1.342

Note: These are for call options with strike price X and time-to-maturity $T - t$ months on a nondividend-paying stock currently priced at $50, estimated across 500 independent test paths. SE indicates standard error. See Table 33.11 for further details.

SECTION III. AN APPLICATION TO S&P 500 FUTURES OPTIONS

In Section II, we have shown that learning networks can efficiently approximate the Black–Scholes pricing formula if the data is generated by it, and this provides some hope that our nonparametric approach may be useful in practice. After all, if there is some uncertainty about the parametric assumptions of a typical derivative pricing model, it should come as no surprise that a *nonparametric* model can improve pricing and hedging performance. To

Figure 33.7

Overlay of S&P 500 Futures Prices for All Contracts Active from January 1987 to December 1991

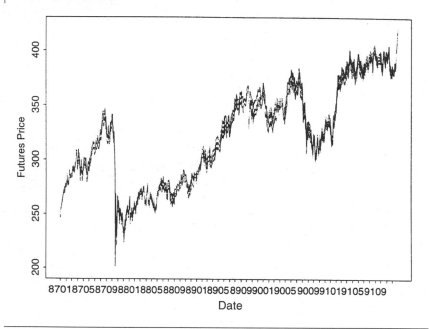

gauge the practical relevance of learning networks in at least one context, we apply it to the pricing and hedging of S&P 500 futures options and compare it to the Black–Scholes model applied to the same data. Despite the fact that the Black–Scholes model is generally not used in its original form in practice, we focus on it here because it is still a widely used benchmark model and because it serves as an example of a parametric model whose assumptions are questionable in the context of this data.

A. The Data and Experimental Setup

The data for our empirical analysis are daily closing prices of S&P 500 futures and futures options for the five-year period from January 1987 to December 1991. Futures prices over this period are shown in Figure

Figure 33.8

S&P 500 Futures and Futures Options Active from July through December 1989

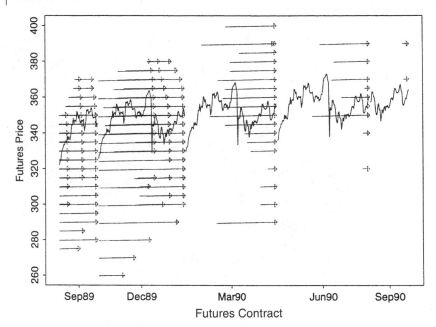

Note: The *dashed line* represents futures price, and the *arrows* represent the options on the future. The y-coordinate of the tip of the arrow indicates the strike price (*arrows* are slanted to make different introduction and expiration dates visible).

33.7. There were 24 different futures contract and 998 futures call options active during this period.[12] The futures contracts have quarterly expirations, and on a typical day 40 to 50 call options based on four different futures contracts were traded.

Our specification is similar to that given in Section II. A for the simulated data. We divide the S&P 500 data into 10 nonoverlapping six-month subperiods for training and testing the learning networks. Six-month subperiods were chosen to match approximately the number of data points in each training path with those of our simulations in Section II. Data for the second half of 1989 is shown in Figures 33.8 and 33.9. Notable

Figure 33.9

July through December 1989 S&P 500 Futures Call Option Prices, Normalized by Strike Price and Plotted versus Stock Price and Time to Expiration

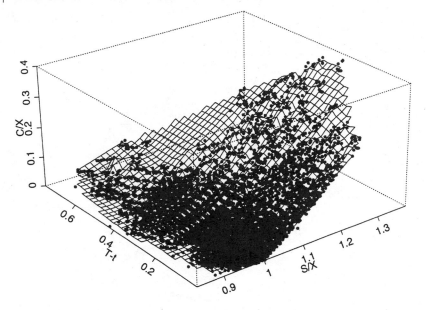

Note: Points represent daily observations. Note the bumpiness of the surface and the irregular sampling away from the money.

differences between this data and the simulated data of Section II are the presence of "noise" in the real data and the irregular trading activity of the options, especially for near-term, out-of-the-money options.

For the S&P 500 data, the number of futures call options per subperiod ranged from 70 to 179, with an average of 137. The total number of data points per subperiod ranged from 4,454 to 8,301, with an average of 6,246. To limit the effects of nonstationarities and to avoid data-snooping, we trained a separate learning network on each of the first nine subperiods and tested those networks only on the data from the immediately following subperiod. We also considered the last seven test paths separately, that is, data from July 1988 to December 1991, to assess the influence of the October 1987 crash on our results.

Figure 33.10

Black–Scholes Parameters Estimated from S&P 500 Data

a. Risk-free rate $\hat{r}$

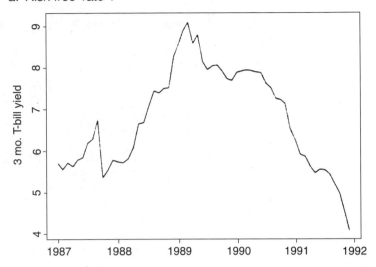

b. Volatility $\hat{\sigma}$

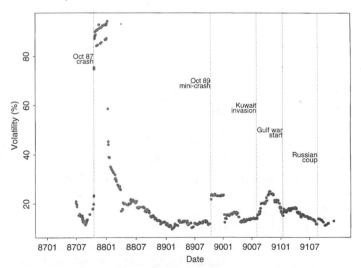

Note: See text for details: Values for $\hat{\sigma}$ fall between 9.63 and 94.39 percent, with a median of 16.49 percent.

Table 33.16

Delta-Hedging Prediction Error for the Out-of-Sample S&P 500 Data from July 1988 to December 1991

	Linear-1	Linear-2	RBF	PPR	MLP	B-S	$\overline{C}(0)$
Short-term							
In-the-money	6.70	4.92	5.04	4.52	4.94	4.42	24.26
Near-the-money	8.70	4.12	3.49	3.37	3.42	2.76	8.04
Out-of-the-money	8.38	2.71	2.17	2.31	1.63	1.59	1.00
Medium-term							
In-the-money	9.48	6.41	6.70	6.53	5.62	5.93	35.88
Near-the-money	8.82	6.93	4.18	5.02	4.54	5.31	10.62
Out-of-the-money	11.27	4.69	2.53	2.73	2.32	2.55	2.74
Long-term							
In-the-money	8.23	6.14	7.24	11.40	5.60	7.58	39.27
Near-the-money	8.55	8.58	6.37	5.55	5.17	6.18	16.14
Out-of-the-money	12.13	7.35	3.54	5.39	4.36	5.02	6.86

Note: Data excludes the subperiods directly influenced by the October 1987 crash, averaged across all training/test sets. RBF indicates radio basis function; PPR indicates projection pursuit regression; MLP indicates multilayer perceptrons; and B–S indicates Black–Scholes formula.

B. Estimating Black–Scholes Prices

Estimating and comparing models on the S&P 500 data will proceed much as it did in Section II for the linear and learning-network models. However, the Black–Scholes parameters r and σ must be estimated when using actual market data. From a theoretical perspective, the Black–Scholes model assumes that both of these parameters are constant over time, and thus we might be tempted to estimate them using all available past data. Few practitioners adopt this approach, however, due to substantial empirical evidence of nonstationarities in interest rates and asset-return distributions. A common compromise is to estimate the parameters using only a window

---

Table 33.17

Delta-Hedging Prediction Error for the Out-of-Sample S&P 500 Data from July 1987 to July 1988

	Linear-1	Linear-2	RBF	PPR	MLP	B-S	$\overline{C}(0)$
Short-term							
In-the-money	10.61	8.80	7.27	9.23	9.12	3.94	20.18
Near-the-money	16.30	12.73	7.77	7.48	8.08	9.09	10.76
Out-of-the-money	23.76	8.48	7.43	5.51	5.34	10.53	5.44
Medium-term							
In-the-money	9.18	11.17	7.13	12.57	13.90	16.00	36.05
Near-the-money	24.48	13.36	7.59	5.65	5.11	6.12	12.98
Out-of-the-money	34.31	14.80	12.30	9.44	9.64	13.46	7.45
Long-term							
In-the-money	24.97	22.37	13.84	23.75	27.13	30.36	28.08
Near-the-money	35.06	12.93	10.78	10.11	12.27	16.03	16.98
Out-of-the-money	29.07	14.05	9.50	8.59	8.10	10.86	10.26

Note: Data for the subperiods directly influenced by the October 1987 crash, averaged across all training test sets. RBF indicates radial basis function; PPR indicates projection pursuit regression; MLP indicates multilayer perceptron; and B–S indicates Black–Scholes formula.

---

of the most recent data. We follow this latter approach for the S&P 500 data. Specifically, we estimate the Black–Scholes volatility, σ, for a given S&P 500 futures contract using

$$\hat{\sigma} = s/\sqrt{60} \qquad (18)$$

where s is the standard deviation of the 60 most recent continuously compounded daily returns of the contract. We approximate the risk-free rate r for each futures option as the yield of the three-month Treasury bill on the close of the month before the initial activity in that option (see Figure 33.10).

Table 33.18

Out-of-Sample R^2 Values (in Percent) for the Learning Networks, Summarized across the Nine Out-of-Sample S&P 500 Futures Options Test Sets

	Linear-1	Linear-2	RBF	PPR	MLP	B–S
Minimum	7.85	82.63	81.33	92.26	92.28	37.41
Mean	75.57	95.54	93.26	96.56	95.53	84.76
Maximum	95.74	99.44	98.41	99.54	98.98	99.22

Note: RBF indicates radial basis function; PPR indicates projection pursuit regression; MLP indicates multilayer perceptron; and B–S indicates Black–Scholes formula.

Table 33.19

Fraction of Out-of-Sample Test Set S&P 500 Futures Options

	Linear-1	Linear-2	RBF	PPR	MLP
July-December 1987	0.160	0.377	0.506	0.593	0.580
January-June 1988	0.189	0.357	0.476	0.497	0.538
July-December 1988	0.122	0.341	0.382	0.358	0.301
January-June 1989	0.221	0.405	0.534	0.550	0.481
July-December 1989	0.355	0.428	0.529	0.609	0.543
January-June 1990	0.329	0.423	0.557	0.550	0.631
July-December 1990	0.230	0.425	0.540	0.569	0.649
January-June 1991	0.296	0.419	0.497	0.346	0.313
July-December 1991	0.248	0.337	0.218	0.327	0.317

Note: The absolute delta-hedging error for each learning network was lower than the Black–Scholes delta-hedging error, shown for each test period. RBF indicates radial basis function; PPR indicates projection pursuit regression; and MLP indicates multilayer perceptrons.

C. Out-of-Sample Pricing and Hedging

In this section, we present the out-of-sample results of fitting the various models to the S&P 500 data. Based on our experience with the simulated data, we chose learning networks with four nonlinear terms as a good

Table 33.20

Paired *t*-Test Comparing Relative Magnitudes of Absolute Hedging Error, Using Results from All S&P 500 Test Sets from July 1987 to December 1991

Pair	*t*-Statistic	*p*-Value
Linear-1 vs. B–S	−15.1265	1.0000
Linear-2 vs. B–S	−5.7662	1.0000
RBF vs. B–S	2.1098	0.0175
PPR vs. B–S	2.0564	0.02
MLP vs. B–S	3.7818	0.0001

Note: The degrees of freedom for each test were 1299 (but see comments in the text concerning dependence). RBF indicates radial basis function; PPR indicates projection pursuit regression; MLP indicates multilayer perceptrons; and B–S indicates Black–Scholes formula.

compromise between accuracy and complexity, although it may be worth reexamining this trade-off on actual S&P 500 data.[13]

The out-of-sample data tests show some evidence that the learning networks outperform the naive Black–Scholes model on this data. This is hardly surprising, given the fact that many of the assumptions of the Black–Scholes formula are violated by the data, for example, geometric Brownian motion, constant volatility, frictionless markets, and so on.

As with the simulated-data-trained learning networks, the performance of each of the actual-data-trained networks varied over the input space. To see how the performance varies in particular, we divide each dimension of the input space into three regimes: long-, medium-, and short-term regimes for the time-to-expiration $(T - t)$ input, and in-, near-, and out-of-the-money regimes for the stock-price/strike-price (S/X) input. Specifically, breakpoints of 2 and 5 months for the $(T - t)$ input and 0.97 and 1.03 for the S/X input were chosen to yield approximately the same number of data points in each of the 9 paired categories. The delta-hedging prediction errors, broken down by these maturity/richness groups, are shown in Tables 33.16 and 33.17. Interestingly, results from the subperiods influenced by the October 1987 crash still yield lower prediction errors for the learning networks than for the Black–Scholes model, except for near-term in-the-money options.

For completeness we also show the out-of-sample R^2s (see Table 33.18) and the absolute hedging error comparison (see Table 33.19) as we did in Section II. D for the synthetic data. Table 33.18, for instance, shows that the average out-of-sample R^2 of roughly 85 percent for the estimated Black–Scholes model is somewhat worse than that of the other network models. Note, however, that, unlike the case for our synthetic data, the options in the S&P 500 data set are *not* independent, and thus we must look at these results with caution. Furthermore, we only have one test set for each trained network, and thus for the hedging error comparison in Table 33.19 we show these results broken down by test period instead of the summary statistics shown in Section II. D.2. Nonetheless, this table shows that the learning networks exhibit less hedging error than the estimated Black–Scholes formula in a substantial fraction of the options tested—up to 65 percent of the options tested against the MLP network for the July to December 1990 testing period.

From these results, it is difficult to infer which network type performs best in general. Hypothesis tests concerning the relative sizes of hedging error are difficult to formulate precisely because of the statistical dependence on the option-price paths. Focusing on a single nonoverlapping sequence of options would solve the dependence problem but would throw out 98 percent of the available options. Instead, we present a less formal test on all of the data, but caution the reader not to give it undue weight. Since we have hedging errors for each option and learning network, we can use a paired *t*-test to compare the Black–Scholes model absolute hedging error on each option with the network's absolute hedging error on the same option. The null hypothesis is that the average difference of the two hedging errors is zero, and the (one-sided) alternative hypothesis is that the difference is positive; that is, the learning-network hedging error is smaller. Results of this simple test show evidence that all three learning networks outperform the Black–Scholes model, while the linear models do not (see Table 33.20).

It is also interesting to compare the computing time required to estimate these models, although no effort was made to optimize our code, and we did not attempt to optimize the estimation method for each type of learning network. With these qualifications in mind, we find that second-order methods are preferable for our application. For example, the MLP network gradient descent equations were updated for 10,000 iterations, requiring roughly 300 minutes per network on a multiuser SUN

SPARCstation II, while the Levenberg-Marquardt method for the RBF networks used form 10 to 80 iterations and took roughly seven minutes per network. Similarly, the PPR networks (with a Newton method at the core) took roughly 120 minutes per network.

SECTION IV. CONCLUSIONS

Although parametric derivative pricing formulas are preferred when they are available, our results show that nonparametric learning-network alternatives can be useful substitutes when parametric methods fail. While our findings are promising, we cannot yet claim that our approach will be successful in general: For simplicity, our simulations have focused only on the Black–Scholes model, and our application has focused only on a single instrument and time period, S&P 500 futures options for 1987 to 1991. In particular, there are a host of parametric derivative pricing models, as well as many practical extensions of these models that may improve their performance on any particular data set. We hope to provide a more comprehensive analysis of these alternatives in the near future.

However, we do believe there is reason to be cautiously optimistic about our general approach, with a number of promising directions for future research. Perhaps the most pressing item on this agenda is the specification of additional inputs, inputs that are not readily captured by parametric models such as the return on the market, general market volatility, and other measures of business conditions. A related issue is the incorporation of the predictability of the underlying asset's return and cross-predictability among several correlated assets (see Lo and Wang 1993 for a parametric example). This may involve the construction of a factor model of the underlying assets's return and volatility processes.

Other research directions are motivated by the need for proper statistical inference in the specification of learning networks. First, we require some method of matching the network architecture—number of nonlinear units, number of centers, type of basis functions, and so on—to the specific dataset at hand in some optimal (and, preferably, automatic) fashion.

Second, the relation between sample size and approximation error should be explored, either analytically or through additional Monte Carlo simulation experiments. Perhaps some data-dependent metric can be constructed, such as the model prediction error, that can provide real-time estimates of approximation errors in much the same way that standard errors may be obtained for typical statistical estimators.

And finally, the need for better performance measures is clear. While typical measures of goodness-of-fit such as R^2 do offer some guidance for model selection, they are only incomplete measures of performance. Moreover, the notion of degrees of freedom is no longer well-defined for nonlinear models, and this has implications for all statistical measures of fit.

REFERENCES

Barron, A.R. 1991. Universal Approximation Bounds for Superpositions of a Sigmoidal Function. Technical Report 58. Department of Statistics, University of Illinois at Urbana-Champaign.

————, and R.L. Barron. 1988. Statistical Learning Networks: A Unifying View. In *20th Symposium on the Interface: Computing Science and Statistics*. eds. E. Wegman, D. Gantz, and J. Miller. Reston, VA: American Statistical Association, pp. 192–203.

Black, F. and N. Scholes. 1973. The Pricing of Options and Corporate Liabilities. *Journal of Political Economy* 81, pp. 637–59.

Broomhead, D.S., and D. Lowe. 1988. Multivariable Functional Interpolation and Adaptive Networks. *Complex Systems* 2, pp. 321–55.

Chen, H. 1991. Estimation of a Projection-Pursuit Type Regression Model. *Annals of Statistics* 19, pp. 142–57.

Cybenko, G. 1988. Approximation by Superpositions of a Sigmoidal Function. Technical Report 856. University of Illinois, Department of Electrical and Computer Engineering.

Diaconis, P. and M. Shahshahani. 1984. On Nonlinear Functions of Linear Combinations. *SIAM Journal of Scientific and Statistical Computing* 5, pp. 175–91.

Donoho, D.L. and I. Johnstone. 1989. Projection-Based Approximation and a Duality with Kernel Methods. *Annals of Statistics* 17, pp. 58–106.

Friedman, J.H. and W. Stuetzle. 1981. Projection Pursuit Regression. *Journal of the American Statistical Association* 76, pp. 817–23.

Gallant, A. and H. White. 1992. On Learning the Derivatives of an Unknown Mapping with Multilayer Feedforward Networks. *Neural Networks* 5, pp. 128–38.

Girosi, F. and G. Anzellotti. 1992. Rates of Convergence of Approximation by Translates, Artificial Intelligence Memo 1288. Massachusetts Institute of Technology, Artificial Intelligence Laboratory.

Girosi, F., M. Jones, and T. Poggio. 1993. Priors, Stabilizers and Basis Functions: From Regularization to Radial, Tensor and Additive Splines, Artificial Intelligence Memo 1430. Massachusetts Institute of Technology, Artificial Intelligence Laboratory.

Girosi, F. and T. Poggio. 1990. Networks and the Best Approximation Property. *Biological Cybernetics* 63, pp. 169–76.

Hornik, K. 1989. Multilayer Feedforward Networks Are Universal Approximators. *Neural Networks* 2, pp. 359–66.

———, M. Stinchcombe, and H. White. 1990. Universal Approximation of an Unknown Mapping and Its Derivatives. *Neural Networks* 3, pp. 551–60.

Huber, P.J. 1985. Projection Pursuit. *Annals of Statistics* 13, pp. 435–525.

Hull, J.C. 1993. *Options, Futures, and Other Derivative Securities,* 2nd ed. Englewood Cliffs, NJ: Prentice-Hall.

Hutchinson, J.M. 1993. A Radial Basis Function Approach to Financial Time Series Analysis. Technical Report 1457. Artificial Intelligence Laboratory, Massachusetts Institute of Technology.

Jones, L.K. 1987. On a Conjecture of Huber Concerning the Convergence of Projection Pursuit Regression. *Annals of Statistics* 15, pp. 880–882.

Ljung, L. and T. Söderstrom. 1986. *Theory and Practice of Recursive Identification.* Cambridge, MA: MIT Press.

Lo, A. and J. Wang. 1993. Implementing Option Pricing Models When Asset Returns Are Predictable. Research Program in Computational

Finance Working paper RPCF-1001-93. Sloan School of Management, Massachusetts Institute of Technology.

Maruyama, M., F. Girosi, and T. Poggio. 1991. A Connection between GRBF and MLP. Artificial Intelligence Memo 1291. Massachusetts Institute of Technology, Artificial Intelligence Laboratory.

Merton, R. 1973. Rational Theory of Option Pricing. *Bell Journal of Economics and Management Science* 4, pp. 141–83.

Micchelli, Charles A. 1986. Interpolation of Scattered Data: Distance Matrices and Conditionally Positive Definite Functions. *Constructive Approximation* 2, pp. 11–22.

Moody, J. and C. Darken. 1989. Fast Learning in Networks of Locally Tuned Processing Units. *Neural Computation* 1, pp. 281–94.

Ng, K. and R. Lippman. 1991. A Comparative Study of the Practical Characteristics of Neural Network and Conventional Pattern Classifiers. In *Advances in Neural Information Processing Systems* 3. Eds. R. Lippman, J. Moody, and D. Touretsky. San Mateo, CA: Morgan-Kaufman.

Niyogi, P. and F. Girosi. 1994. On the Relationship between Generalization Error, Hypothesis Complexity, and Sample Complexity for Radial Basis Functions. Artificial Intelligence Memo 1467. Artificial Intelligence Laboratory, Massachusetts Institute of Technology.

Parker, D.B. 1985. Learning logic. Technical Report 47. Center for Computational Research in Economics and Managmeent Science, Massachusetts Institute of Technology.

Poggio, T. and F. Girosi. 1990. Networks for Approximation and Learning. *Proceedings of IEEE* 78, pp. 1481–97.

Powell, M.J.D. 1987. Radial Basis Functions for Multivariable Interpolation: A Review. In *Algorithms for Approximation*. eds. J.C. Mason and M.G. Cox. Oxford: Clarendon Press, pp. 143–67.

Reinsch, C.H. 1967. Smoothing by Spline Functions. *Numerische Mathematik* 10, pp. 177–83.

Robbins H. and S. Monro. 1951. A Stochastic Approximation Model. *Annals of Mathematical Statistics* 22, pp. 400–07.

Rumelhart, D.E., G.E. Hinton, and R.J. Williams. 1986. Learning Internal Representation by Error Propagation. In *Parallel Distributed Processing: Explorations in the Microstructure of Cognition, Volume 1: Foundations*. eds. D.E. Rumelhart and J.L. McClelland. Cambridge, MA: MIT Press, Chapter 8.

Vapnik, V.N. 1982. *Estimation of Dependences Based on Empirical Data* Berlin: Springer-Verlag.

Wahba, G. 1990. Spline Models for Observational Data. In *Regional Conference Series in Applied Mathematics*. Philadelphia: SIAM Press.

Widrow, B., and S.D. Stearns. 1985. *Adaptive Signal Processing*. Englewood Cliffs, NJ: Prentice-Hall.

ENDNOTES

1. However, since newly created derivatives can often be replicated by a combination of existing derivatives, this is not as much of a limitation as it may seem at first.

2. More accurately, the term *back-propagation* is now typically used to refer to the particular gradient descent method of estimating parameters, while the term *multilayer perceptron* is used to refer to specific functional form described below.

3. To economize on terminology, in this article we use the term *radial basis functions* to encompass both the interpolation techniques used by Powell and its subsequent generalizations.

4. In fact, it is well known that the problem of numerical differentiation is ill-posed. The classical approach (Rheinsch 1967) is to regularize it by finding a sufficiently smooth function that solves the variational problem in equation (2). As we discussed earlier, RBF networks, as well as splines and several forms of MLP networks, follow directly from the regularization approach and are therefore expected to approximate not only the pricing formula but also its derivatives, provided the basis function corresponding to a smoothness prior is of a sufficient degree (see Poggio and Girosi 1990—in particular, the Gaussian is certainly sufficiently smooth for our problem). A special case of this general argument is the result of Gallant and White (1992) and Hornik, Stinchcombe, and White (1990), who show that single-hidden-layer MLP networks can approximate the derivative of an arbitrary nonlinear mapping arbitrarily well as the number of hidden units increases.

5. This is one sense in which analytical pricing formulas for derivative securities are preferred whenever available.

6. See Hull (1993) for more details.

7. In our simulations, this was not done for options with less than one week to expiration.

8. Four nonlinear terms corresponds to approximately 20 parameters in total.

9. Note that for the RBF and MLP learning networks, Δ can be computed *analytically* by taking the derivative of the network approximation. For PPR, however, the use of a smoother for estimating the nonlinear functions, h, forces a numerical approximation of Δ, which we accomplish with a first-order finite difference with an increment ∂S of size $1/1000$ of the range of S.

10. In particular, other statistics of the sample path $\{V(t)\}$, for the entire portfolio may be of more concern, such as its maximum and minimum, and the interaction between $\{V(t)\}$ and other asset returns.

11. We caution the reader from drawing too strong a conclusion from the ordering of the RBF, MLP, and PPR results, however, due to the sensitivity of these nonparametric techniques to the "tuning" of their specifications, for example, the number of hidden nodes, network architecture, the choice of basis function, and so on. In particular, the superiority of the RBF network results may be due to the fact that we have had more experience in tuning their specification.

12. For simplicity, we focus only on call options in our analysis.

13. A sample reuse technique such as cross-validation would be appropriate in this context for choosing the number of nonlinear terms.

34

A MODEL-SELECTION APPROACH TO ASSESSING THE INFORMATION IN THE TERM STRUCTURE USING LINEAR MODELS AND ARTIFICIAL NEURAL NETWORKS

Norman R. Swanson and Halbert White

An issue of continuing interest in the finance literature is the extent to which forward interest rates are useful as predictors of future spot rates. Fama's (1984) work represents a milestone in examining this issue, providing evi-

We are grateful to Frederic S. Mishkin for providing the data used here and for discussions with Robert F. Engle, Scott Gilbert, Pu Shen, and Ross M. Starr. Financial support was provided by Social Sciences and Humanities Research Council of Canada Award 753-91-0416 and by National Science Foundation Grants SES-8921382 and SES-9209023.

dence that forward rates do indeed contain information about future spot rates. Mishkin (1988) refined and updated Fama's analysis by conducting tests of the hypothesis that forward rates have predictive content using econometric techniques that properly take account of heteroscedasticity and serial correlation, neglected by Fama, by using a somewhat more general method for obtaining interest rates from the term structure, and by making use of data available subsequent to Fama's. Mishkin also found evidence that forward rates help predict future spot rates.

In this chapter, we examine this issue from a *model-selection* perspective to shed some additional light rather than from a classical hypothesis-testing perspective such as that of Mishkin (1988). Specifically, we address the question: Given an array of alternative models for forecasting future spot rates and appropriate forecasting-based model-selection criteria, does the model selected by this procedure make use of forward rates? If so, we have additional direct evidence of the usefulness of forward rates in predicting future spot rates. If not, we have direct evidence to the contrary. We consider not only linear models, as did Mishkin (1988), but also a class of flexible nonlinear functional forms called artificial neural networks. The reported results provide additional support for the hypothesis that forward rates are indeed useful and suggest that the class of nonlinear models that is considered may also prove useful for forecasting interest rates. More specifically, we find that the premium of the forward rate over the spot rate helps to predict the sign of future changes in the interest rate.

We adopt the model-selection perspective as a complement to the more traditional hypothesis-testing approach for a variety of reasons, while noting that the two methods are not completely dissimilar (e.g., when in-sample model-selection criteria are used). Our first reason is the fact that model selection permits us to focus directly on the issue at hand: out-of-sample forecasting performance. Next is the advantage that the model-selection approach does not require specification of a correct model for its valid application as does the traditional hypothesis-testing approach. Another desirable feature of the model-selection approach is that, if properly designed, the probability of selecting the truly best model approaches 1 as the sample size increases, in contrast to the traditional practice of fixing a test size and rejecting the null hypothesis at that fixed size regardless of sample size, thus ensuring that Type I errors (wrongly rejecting the null hypothesis) will always occur with nonvanishing probability no matter how many data are available.

A limitation of the model-selection approach is that it can sometimes be difficult to assess the Type I error associated with testing the implicit model-selection hypothesis that two models under consideration truly perform equally well based on observed differences in realized model-selection criteria. The procedure we implement will have this defect; however, this is a defect of the same order as using a traditional test whose size is known only asymptotically. In the model-selection case, the size is also known only asymptotically, but it is known to be 0, a consequence of the fact that the truly best model is selected with probability approaching one, as discussed previously. Nevertheless, the distinction between the model-selection approach and the traditional hypothesis-testing approach should not be overemphasized. For example, the comparison of two nested models using a sample-based complexity-penalized likelihood criterion (such as the Schwarz information criterion [SIC]) amounts to a likelihood ratio test with the significance level being determined by the penalty term associated with the information criterion.

A final conceptual motivation for using the model-selection approach is that it can be used in conjunction with traditional hypothesis-testing procedures. As recently discussed by Pötscher (1991), once a model is selected by a procedure that yields the truly best model with probability approaching 1, one can test hypotheses about the parameters of the truly best model in the usual way without adverse asymptotic consequences for the size of the test. Of course, if one does not impose the belief that the model selected is correctly specified, one must be careful to appropriately interpret the hypothesis being tested; for example, that the role of forward rates in the best model among those tested is nil, rather than that forward rates do not aid whatsoever in forecasting future spot rates. Due to the statistical complexity of the relatively computationally simple procedures considered here, we shall not engage in such hypothesis-testing exercises but leave development of the necessary distributions to other work. The reasons for this statistical complexity will become apparent later. We mention this final motivation so that the reader does not carry away the impression that we are proposing a substitute for traditional hypothesis testing. In fact, we are proposing a logically prior complement for cases in which the two methods cannot be equated to one another.

By adopting this model-selection perspective, we believe that we contribute not only to the discussion of the usefulness of forward rates as a predictor of future spot rates but also to the methodology of examining this and similar issues. One dimension of this contribution is that we consider a variety of model-selection criteria, including the SIC, together with three out-of-sample criteria: forecast mean squared error, forecast direction accuracy, and forecast-based trading-rule profitability. Contributions are also attempted in several other related, interesting directions. Specifically, we examine the usefulness of a class of novel nonlinear prediction models called *artificial neural networks* (e.g., Kuan and White 1994), and we examine the issue of appropriate window sizes for rolling-window-based prediction methods.

The rest of the article is organized as follows. Section I discusses the data, and Section II discusses the models considered in this study. Section III describes our estimation methods and the model-selection criteria examined here. Section IV discusses the results for statistical performance measures, and Section V discusses the results for profitability performance measures. Section VI contains a summary and concluding remarks.

SECTION I. THE DATA

We use data graciously provided by Frederic S. Mishkin, as used in his study (1988). Two objects are of interest, $R_{t+\tau}$, the one-month spot rate observed at time $t + \tau - 1$, and $F_{\tau,t}$, the forward rate for month $t + \tau$ observed at time t. (This notation is similar to that of Fama 1984 and Mishkin 1988.) As described by Mishkin (1988, p. 309), end-of-month U.S. Treasury-bill rate data were obtained from the Center for Research on Security Prices at the University of Chicago. The one-month bill is defined as having a maturity of 30.4 days, the two-month bill 60.8 days, and so on, up to the six-month bill with a maturity of 182.5 days. For each defined maturity, the interest rate was interpolated linearly from the two bills that were closest to the defined maturity. As pointed out by an anonymous referee, it should be noted that the Mishkin data that are used here do not make use of actual transactions-price data, as was done by Fama (1984), because the interest rates are interpolated from the two bills that are closest to the defined maturity. Thus, although the Mishkin data have the advantage that the term-structure slope around the desired maturity is constant rather than 0 and is thus less restrictive, using actual transactions-price data is more suitable when the focus is on predicting future premiums in the market. For this reason, the discussion of the most *profitable* regression model given a specific trading strategy (Section

V) should be thought of as methodological and not as suggesting that the results will hold when dealing with actual prices in the market.

SECTION II. THE MODELS

Linear Models

Mishkin (1988) considered the following two models estimated by Fama:

$$R_{t+\tau} - R_{t+1} = \alpha + \beta(F_{\tau,t} - R_{t+1}) + v_{t+\tau-1} \tag{1}$$

and

$$R_{t+\tau} - R_{t+\tau-1} = \alpha + \beta(F_{\tau,t} - F_{\tau-1,t}) + v_{t+\tau-1}. \tag{2}$$

In these models, it is of interest to test whether β_0, the "true" value of β, is 0. If so, the forward rate is unimportant (linearly) in predicting future spot rates. If not, forward rates contain useful predictive information. As Fama (1984) discussed, the null hypothesis ($\beta_0 = 0$) occurs when risk premiums in forward rates obliterate the predictive relationship that would occur in the absence of these premiums. Fama (1976) and Shiller, Campbell, and Schoenholtz (1983) found no evidence against the null, but Fama (1984) and Mishkin (1988) did find evidence against the null.

   In this study, we consider these models as special cases of a fairly broad array of forecasting models. We refer to models with dependent variables $R_{t+\tau} - R_{t+1}$ as Case 1 and models with dependent variables $R_{t+\tau} - R_{t+\tau-1}$ as Case 2.)

   For Case 1, we consider linear models containing the following regressors: a constant, lags of $F_{\tau,t} - R_{t+1}$ from orders 0 to 2, and lags of $R_{t+\tau} - R_{t+1}$ from "observable order" 1 to 3. By a lag of "observable order" 1, we mean the first lag of $R_{t+\tau} - R_{t+1}$, observable at time t; that is, $R_{t+1} - R_{t+1-\tau}$ and so on for observable lag orders 2 and 3. We separately consider models with a constant only, a constant and lags of $F_{\tau,t} - R_{t+1}$, a constant and observable lags of $R_{t+\tau} - R_{t+1}$, and a constant, lags of $F_{\tau,t} - R_{t+1}$, and observable lags of $R_{t+\tau} - R_{t+1}$. The number of lags included was dictated by the necessity of keeping the total number of regressions to a manageable number while still exploring a range of plausible possibilities.

Table 34.1 provides a summary of the regressors included in the Case 1 regressions. The linear regressions are Models 1.0 through 1.16. Note that Model 1.0 is the simple random-walk model [i.e., (1) with α and β both constrained to 0], but Model 1.2 coincides with (1). The models differ primarily in the number of included lags. Table 34.1 also references two models (1.17 and 1.18), which we shall discuss later.

For Case 2, we consider linear models containing the following regressors: a constant, lags of $F_{\tau,t} - F_{\tau-1,t}$ from orders 0 to 2, and lags of $R_{t+\tau} - R_{t+\tau-1}$ from observable order 1 to 3. As in Case 1, we consider separately models with a constant only, a constant and lags of $F_{\tau,t} - F_{\tau-1,t}$, a constant and observable lags of $R_{t+\tau} - R_{t+\tau-1}$, and a constant, lags of $F_{\tau,t} - F_{\tau-1,t}$, and observable lags of $R_{t+\tau} - R_{t+\tau-1}$. Table 34.1 provides a summary of the regressors included in the Case 2 regressions, with linear regressions designated as Models 2.0 through 2.16. Also referenced are Models 2.17 and 2.18, which will be discussed later. Model 2.2 coincides with the preceding Equation (2), but Model 2.0 is again the random walk ($\alpha = \beta = 0$).

Nonlinear Models

Cognitive scientists have proposed a class of flexible nonlinear models inspired by certain features of the way the brain processes information. (A good introduction to the cognitive science literature is that of Rumelhart and McClelland 1986.) Because of their biological inspiration, these models are referred to as *artificial neural network models* or simply *artificial neural networks* (ANN's). Because of their flexibility and simplicity and because of demonstrated successes in a variety of empirical applications in which linear models fail to perform well (see White 1989 and Kuan and White 1994 for some specifics), ANN's have become the focus of considerable attention as a possible vehicle for forecasting financial variables. Among recent applications are those of White (1988); Dutta and Shekhar (1988); Moody and Utans (1991); Dorsey, Johnson, and van Boening (1991); Dropsy (1992); and Kuan and Liu (1992). See also the recent book by Trippi and Turban (1993).

For those interested in a detailed discussion of ANN's and their econometric applicability, we refer to Kuan and White (1994). For present purposes, it suffices to treat these models as a potentially interesting black

Table 34.1

Included Regressors for Case 1 and 2 Regressions

| Model # | Number of Lags Included, p | | | | | | | Hidden Units |
| | Dependent | | | Exogenous | | | | |
	0	1	2	1	2	3	4	
c.0								
c.1								
c.2	X							
c.3	X	X						
c.4	X	X	X					
c.5				X				
c.6				X	X			
c.7				X	X	X		
c.8	X			X				
c.9	X			X	X			
c.10	X			X	X	X		
c.11	X	X		X				
c.12	X	X		X	X			
c.13	X	X		X	X	X		
c.14	X	X	X	X				
c.15	X	X	X	X	X			
c.16	X	X	X	X	X	X		
c.17	X	X	X	X	X	X	X	
c.18	X	X	X	X	X	X	X	X

Note: The c in Model # corresponds to Case 1 and Case 2, so that Model 1.0 is model 0 for Case 1, and Model 2.0 is model 0 for Case 2, for example. For Cases 1 and 2, the dependent variables are $R_{t+\tau} - R_{t+1}$ and $R_{t+\tau} - R_{t+\tau-1}$, respectively. The exogenous variables are lags of $F_{\tau,t} - R_{t+1}$ and $F_{\tau,t} - F_{\tau-1,t}$, respectively. For Models 1.18 and 2.18, up to four hidden units are included as regressors. All regressions include an intercept, except for Models 1.0 and 2.0. Case 1: $R_{t+\tau} - R_{t+1} = a_1 + \sum_i \alpha_{1,i} (F_{\tau,t-i} - R_{t+1-i}) + \sum_i \beta_{1,i} (R_{i+\tau-i} - R_{t+1-i}) + u_{1,t}$; Case 2: $R_{t+\tau} - R_{t+\tau-1} = a_2 + \sum_i \alpha_{2,} (F_{\tau,t-i} - F_{\tau-1,t-i}) + \sum_i \beta_{2,i} (R_{t+\tau-i} - R_{t+\tau-1-i}) + u_{2,t}$

box, delivering a specific class of nonlinear regression models. In particular, the ANN nonlinear regression models considered here have the form

$$f(x,\theta) = \tilde{x}'\,\alpha + \sum_{j=1}^{q} G(\tilde{x}'\,\gamma_j)\beta_j, \qquad (3)$$

where $\tilde{x}$ is a (column) vector of explanatory variables, $\tilde{x} = (1, x')'$ augments x by the inclusion of a constant term, $\theta = (\alpha', \beta', \gamma')'$, $\beta = (\beta_1, ..., \beta_q)'$, $\gamma = (\gamma', ..., \gamma_q)'$, q is a given integer, and G is a given nonlinear function—in our case, the logistic cumulative distribution function (cdf) $G(z) = 1/(1 + \exp(-z))$.

A network interpretation of (3) is as follows: *Input units* send signals $x_0(=1)$, x_1, ..., x_r over *connections* that amplify or attenuate the signals by a factor *(weight)* γ_{ji}, $i = 0, ..., r$, $j = 1, ..., q$. The signals arriving at *intermediate* or *hidden* units are first summed (resulting in $\tilde{x}'\,\gamma_j$) and then converted to a *hidden-unit activation* $G(\tilde{x}'\,\gamma_j)$ by the operation of the *hidden-unit activation function* G. The next layer operates similarly, with hidden activations sent over connections to the *output unit*. As before, signals are attenuated or amplified by weights β_j and summed. In addition, signals are sent directly from input to output over connections with weights α. A nonlinear activation transformation at the output is also possible, but we avoid it here for simplicity.

In network terminology, $f(x,\theta)$ is the *network output activation* of a *hidden-layer feedforward network* with *inputs* x and *network weights* θ. The parameters γ_j are called *input to hidden-unit weights*, and the parameters β_j are called *hidden-to output-unit weights*. The parameters are called *input-to-output-unit weights*.

Hornik, Stinchcombe, and White (1989, 1990) (among others; see also Carroll and Dickinson 1989; Cybenko 1989; Funahashi 1989) showed that functions of the form (3) are capable of approximating arbitrary functions of x arbitrarily well, given q sufficiently large and a suitable choice of θ. This *universal approximation* property is one reason for the successful application of ANN's. In fact, White (1990) established that ANN models can be used to perform nonparametric regression, consistently estimating any unknown square integrable conditional expectation function.

Here we apply Model (3) to the problem of forecasting $R_{t+\tau} - R_{t+1}$ (Case 1) or $R_{t+\tau} - R_{t+\tau-1}$ (Case 2) using explanatory variables x corresponding to all the variables considered in the linear forecasting models described previously and with $q = 4$. Note that, when $\beta_1 = \beta_2 = \beta_3 = \beta_4 = 0$, we have Models 1.16 and 2.16 as a special case. Inclusion of the nonlinear terms $G(x'\gamma_j)$ should enhance forecasting ability if overfitting is properly avoided.

These *nonlinear* ANN's appear in Table 34.1 as Models 1.18 and 2.18. We also consider a final *linear* model, designated as Model 1.17 or 2.17, in which no hidden units are included, but for which the *linear* regressors are selected *stepwise* (with regressors added one at a time as in the ANN models; see Sec. 3). Due to constraints in the manner in which inputs can be specified for consideration in our software, it was necessary to permit a fourth observed lag of the dependent variable to be available to the Models 1.17, 1.18, 2.17, and 2.18, for selection. In no case was the fourth lag selected, however, so that although the possible presence of this variable is indicated in Table 34.1, its inclusion in fact had no impact on the relative forecasting performance of our models.

SECTION III. ESTIMATION AND MODEL-SELECTION PROCEDURES

The parameters of Models 1.0–1.16 and 2.0–2.16 are estimated by the method of least squares. Because of the possibility that the underlying relation between forward and future spot rates is evolving through time, however, we estimate parameters using only a finite *window* of past data rather than all previously available data. Window sizes of 42, 60, 78, and 96 months are used for our regressions.

To evaluate the *linear* regression models and the various window widths, a sequence of out-of-sample one-step-ahead forecast errors is generated by performing the regression over a given window terminating at observation T, say, and then computing the error in forecasting $R_{T+\tau+1} - R_{T+2}$ (Case 1) or $R_{T+\tau+1} - R_{T+\tau}$ (Case 2), using data available at time $T + 1$ and the coefficients estimated using data in the window terminating at time T. Each time the window rolls forward one period, a new out-of-sample residual is generated, simulating true out-of-sample predictions and prediction errors made in real time by this process. For our study, the smallest value for T corresponds to February of 1979, and the largest to June of 1986. We therefore have a sequence of 89 out-of-sample one-step forecast errors with which to evaluate our models. This period was selected to cover the most recent Federal Reserve policy regimes observable in the data (occurring in October 1979 and October 1982) while still obtaining a computationally manageable out-of-sample period.

By simulating forecasts in real time, we obtain measures of forecasting performance analogous to those recently discussed by Diebold and Rudebusch (1991). Our procedure differs from theirs in that (1) they used a growing data window with fixed first observation because they were not concerned with tracking a possibly evolving system, and (2) they focused on the effects of using unrevised instead of revised leading indicators in real-time simulations for predicting economic upturns and downturns. Because we focus on financial market data that is accurately available in real time, we have no need to worry about revision effects.

Four measures of out-of-sample model/window performance are computed in this article. The first is the *forecast mean squared error* (FMSE) for the 89 one-step forecast errors for each model and window, and for each horizon $\tau = 2, ..., 6$. Using this measure, we can precisely address the question "Does the model/window combination with the smallest FMSE include the forward rate?" If so, we have direct and specific evidence of the value of forward rates in predicting future spot rates. The out-of-sample forecast R^2 is also calculated, where:

$$R^2 = 1 - \text{FMSE}/S_\gamma^2, \tag{4}$$

and S_γ^2 is the sample variance of the dependent variable in the out-of-sample period. Of note is that (4) can take negative values because the FMSE can exceed S_γ^2 out-of-sample.

The second measure of forecast performance that is calculated is how well a given forecasting procedure identifies the *direction* of change in the spot rate, regardless of whether the *value* of the change is closely approximated. To examine this aspect of forecast performance, we calculate the *confusion matrix* of the model/window combination. A hypothetical confusion matrix is:

		Actual	
		Up	Down
Predicted	Up	36	15
	Down	12	26

(5)

The columns in (5) correspond to *actual* spot-rate moves, up or down, and the rows correspond to *predicted* spot-rate moves. In this way, the diagonal cells correspond to correct directional predictions, and off-diagonal cells correspond to incorrect predictions. We measure overall performance in terms of the model's *confusion rate*, the sum of the off-diagonal elements, divided by the sum of all elements. Because (5) is simply a 2×2 contingency table, the hypothesis that a given model/window combination is of no value in forecasting the direction of spot-rate changes can be expressed as the hypothesis of independence between the actual and predicted directions. Methods for testing the independence hypothesis in the context of forecasting the direction of asset price movements were given by Henriksson and Merton (HM 1981). Based on the hypergeometric distribution, the p values delivered by HM's method require for their validity the independence of the directional forecast from the magnitude of the asset price change. We present the HM p values. As with the FMSE, a finding that the least confused model contains the forward rate is direct evidence that forward rates are useful predictors of the direction of spot-rate changes.

As a third measure of the relevance of forward rates in predicting future spot rates, it is determined whether profitable trading strategies can be devised that make use of forward-rate information. Although mean-variance values for the trading strategy are calculated, note that a relevant question is whether the investment is on the conditional mean-variance frontier at each point in time. Unfortunately, resolving this question is beyond the scope of the present work. Because of the nature of the forecasts involved, the profitability analysis can be conducted only for Case 1 models. Further discussion of this performance measure is given in Section V.

A drawback of the use of out-of-sample-based model-selection procedures is that they can be quite computationally intensive. Much less demanding procedures that use only in-sample information can be based on a variety of complexity-penalized likelihood measures. Among those most commonly used are the Akaike information criterion (AIC) (1973, 1974) and the Schwarz information criterion (SIC) (Sawa 1978; Schwarz 1978). These information criteria add a complexity *penalty* to the usual sample log-likelihood, and the model that optimizes this *penalized* log-likelihood is preferred. Because the SIC delivers the most conservative models (i.e., least complex) and because the SIC has been found to perform well in selecting forecasting models in other contexts (e.g., see Engle and Brown 1986), we examine its behavior in the present context as a final measure of forecast performance. Two questions are of interest: First, taking the SIC at face value as a reasonable model-selection criterion, does the SIC-selected model contain the forward rate? Second, what sort of guide is the in-sample SIC to out-of-sample performance? The first question is directed to our main issue of interest. The second question is of nearly equal importance, however, for if the relatively straightforward SIC reliably identifies the model that performs best according to one of our out-of-sample criteria, we may use SIC as a welcome computational shortcut.

For a model with p parameters estimated on a window of size n, the SIC is:

$$SIC = \log s^2 + p(\log n)/n, \tag{6}$$

where s^2 is the regression mean squared error. The first term is a goodness-of-fit measure, and the second is the complexity penalty. We report the *mean* of the 89 values for the SIC, called MSIC, for given model/window combinations.

So far, no mention has been made of how the ANN models are estimated. It is to this issue that we now turn. In estimating the ANN Models 1.18 and 2.18, it is inappropriate to simply fit the network parameters with $q = 4$ hidden units by least squares because the resulting network typically will have more parameters than observations, achieving a perfect or nearly perfect fit in sample, with disastrous performance out-of-sample. To enforce a parsimonious fit, the ANN models were estimated by a process of forward stepwise (nonlinear) least squares regression, using the SIC to determine included regressors and the appropriate value for q. Specifically, a forward stepwise linear regression is performed first, with regressors added one at a time until no additional regressor can be added to improve the SIC. The linear regression coefficients are thereafter fixed. Next, a single hidden unit is added (i.e., q is set to 1), and regressors are selected one by one for *connection* to the first hidden unit, until the SIC can no longer be improved. Then a second hidden unit is added and the process repeated, until four hidden units have been tried or the SIC for q hidden units exceeds that for $q-1$ hidden units. This ANN model-selection procedure is begun anew each time the data window moves forward one period. A different set of regressors and a different number of hidden units connected to different inputs may therefore be chosen at each point in time. We thus simulate a fairly sophisticated real-time ANN forecasting implementation. We should expect the ANN models to have SIC values superior to (i.e., smaller than) those of the linear models because the ANN model can choose any of the linear models as a special case.

Interestingly, even this fairly conservative procedure did not entirely eliminate the tendency for the neural-network model to overfit, as evidenced by occasional totally wild one-step forecasts from network models that fit very nicely in-sample. Accordingly, we impose a simple "insanity filter" on the network forecasts: If a one-step-ahead predicted change exceeds the maximum change observed during the estimation window, the forecast from Model 1.1 (or Model 2.1)—which includes only a constant—is used instead. Thus, we substitute ignorance for craziness. The performance of the ANN models and the linear forward stepwise regression models (Models 1.17 and 2.17) are evaluated in the same way as Models 1.0–1.16 and 2.0–2.16. For each, we calculate the FMSE averaged over the 89 out-of-sample observations, the out-of-sample R^2, the confusion matrix, confusion rate, and HM p values, and we perform a profitability analysis.

SECTION IV. THE RESULTS FOR STATISTICAL PERFORMANCE MEASURES

To aid in the discussion of the results, a list of the acronyms follows:

ANN—nonlinear model: artificial neural network.

SIC—Schwarz information criterion: SIC = $\log s^2 + p(\log n)/n$.

MSIC—mean Schwarz information criterion.

FMSE—forecast mean squared error; average of 89 one-step forecasts.

HM p value—p value for Henriksson–Merton test of the hypothesis that forward rates predict direction of spot change.

Window—number of observations used, until $t - 1$, for regressions.

Models 1.1–1.18—Case 1 models with dependent variable $R_{t+\tau} - R_{t+1}$.

Models 2.1–2.18—Case 2 models with dependent variable $R_{t+\tau} - R_{t+\tau-1}$.

The results for Case 1 are summarized in Table 34.2, and those for Case 2 are in Table 34.3. In each case, several fairly clear-cut conclusions emerge. Note that in both tables statistical *ties* sometimes occur. For the sake of brevity, though, this information has not been included, and the best models with the *smallest* window size and *fewest* parameters are reported. More detailed results are available by request from the authors.

Table 34.2

Summary of Best Models by Selection Criterion—Case 1

τ	Selection Criterion	Best Model			ANN (Model 1.18)		Constant Only (Model 1.1)	
		Model	Window	Value	Window	Value	Window	Value
2	MSIC	1.18	60	-.17	60	-.17	96	.15
2	FMSE (R²)	1.2	96	1.51	42	1.97	96	1.65
2	Confusion rate (HM p value)	1.10	78	.30 (.084) (.00) [36 15 / 12 26]	42	.37 (<0) (.01) [30 15 / 18 26]	60	.46 (0.000) (.39) [34 27 / 14 14]
3	MSIC	1.18	42	.65	42	.65	96	.79
3	FMSE (R²)	1.10	78	3.02	96	4.55	96	3.32
3	Confusion rate (HM p value)	1.10	60	.33 (.000) (.00) [33 14 / 15 27]	78	.42 (0.090) (.01) [33 22 / 15 29]	60	.43 (<0) (.17) [36 26 / 12 15]
4	MSIC	1.18	78	1.00	78	1.00	96	1.16
4	FMSE (R²)	1.10	42	4.22	60	5.95	96	4.93
4	Confusion rate (HM p value)	1.18	60	.33 (.142) (.00) [31 15 / 14 28]	60	.33 (<0) (.00) [31 15 / 14 28]	60	.45 (<0) (.23) [33 28 / 12 16]
5	MSIC	1.18	42	1.08	42	1.08	96	1.34
5	FMSE (R²)	1.10	96	5.30	96	6.64	96	5.97
5	Confusion rate (HM p value)	1.16	60	.36 (.110) (.01) [29 18 / 14 28]	60	.36 (<0) (.00) [35 24 / 8 22]	42	.40 (<0) (.05) [27 20 / 16 26]
6	MSIC	1.18	42	1.01	42	1.01	96	1.44
6	FMSE (R²)	1.5	96	6.03	96	6.63	96	6.44
6	Confusion rate (HM p value)	1.3	78	.34 (.062) (.00) [36 20 / 10 23]	60	.40 (<0) (.06) [35 25 / 11 18]	42	.37 (<0) (.01) [30 17 / 16 26]

Note: All models except 1.5 contain the current and/or lagged forward rate. The matrices shown in square brackets are confusion matrices (diagonal cells correspond to correct directional predictions, and off-diagonal cells correspond to incorrect predictions). Model 1.18 is the flexible nonlinear form (artificial neural network). The *best model* is chosen by finding the optimal model by selection criterion. For example, for τ = 2, Model 1.18 has the lowest MSIC among all regression models considered. The R^2 value is calculated as $R^2 = 1 - FMSE/S_y^2$, where FMSE is the forecast mean squared error of the 89 out-of-sample, one-step-ahead forecasts and S_y^2 is the sample variance of the dependent variable in the out-of-sample period. The HM p values are based on the null hypothesis that a given model is of no value in predicting the direction of spot-interest-rate changes. Case 1: $R_{t+\tau} - R_{t+1} = a_1 + \sum_i \alpha_{1,i}(F_{\tau,t-i} - R_{t+1-i} - R_{t+1-i}) + \sum_i \beta_{1,i}(R_{t+\tau-i} - R_{t+1-i}) + u_{1,t}$.

Table 34.3

Summary of Best Models by Selection Criterion—Case 2

τ	Selection Criterion	Model	Best Model Window	Best Model Value	ANN (Model 1.18) Window	ANN (Model 1.18) Value	Constant Only (Model 1.1) Window	Constant Only (Model 1.1) Value
3	MSIC	2.17	42	-.22	42	-.15	96	.15
3	FMSE (R^2)	2.1	96	1.65	96	1.98	96	1.65
3	Confusion rate (HM p value)	2.18	42	.41 (.07) (.000) [43 31 / 5 10]	42	.41 (.39) (<0) [43 31 / 5 10]	60	.46 (.07) (.000) [34 27 / 14 14]
4	MSIC	2.17	96	-.06	42	.10	96	.15
4	FMSE (R^2)	2.1	96	1.65	60	1.79	96	1.65
4	Confusion rate (HM p value)	2.7	96	.38 (.03) (.000) [40 26 / 8 15]	60	.44 (.23) (<0) [35 26 / 13 15]	60	.46 (.39) (.000) [34 27 / 14 14]
5	MSIC	2.18	42	-.22	42	-.22	96	.15
5	FMSE (R^2)	2.1	96	1.65	96	1.81	96	1.65
5	Confusion rate (HM p value)	2.3	60	.40 (.07) (.000) [34 22 / 14 19]	78	.51 (.76) (<0) [33 30^j / 15 11^j]	60	.46 (.39) (.000) [34 27 / 14 14]
6	MSIC	2.17	96	.00	96	.19	96	.15
6	FMSE (R^2)	2.1	96	1.65	78	1.86	96	1.65
6	Confusion rate (HM p value)	2.5	60	.39 (.05) (.000) [36 23 / 12 18]	60	.47 (.47) (<0) [33 27 / 15 14]	60	.46 (.39) (.000) [34 27 / 14 14]

Note: All models except 2.1, 2.5, and 2.7 contain the current and/or lagged forward rate. The matrices shown in square brackets are confusion matrices (diagonal cells correspond to correct directional predictions, and off-diagonal cells correspond to incorrect predictions). Model 2.18 is the flexible nonlinear form (artificial neural network). The *best model* is chosen by finding the optimal model by selection criterion. For example, for τ = 3, Model 2.17 has the lowest MSIC among all regression models considered. The R^2 value is calculated as $R^2 = 1 - FMSE/S_Y^2$, where FMSE is the forecast mean squared error of the 89 out-of-sample, one-step-ahead forecasts and S_Y^2 is the sample variance of the dependent variable in the out-of-sample period. The HM p values are based on the null hypothesis that a given model is of no value in predicting the direction of spot-interest-rate changes. Case 2: $R_{t+\tau} - R_{t+\tau-1} = a_2 + \sum_i \alpha_{2,i}(F_{\tau,t-i} - F_{\tau-1,t-i}) + \sum_i \beta_{2,i}(R_{t+\tau-i} - R_{t+\tau-1-i}) + u_{2,t}$

In Case 1, our main question of interest is answered affirmatively. For the period 3/79 through 7/86, the forward rate is valuable in predicting future spot rates in that it appears in the model with the best FMSE for all but horizon $\tau = 6$ and in the model exhibiting the least confusion, for all time horizons, $\tau = 2, ..., 6$. In fact, for the shortest horizon, $\tau = 2$, the FMSE-best model is the simplest model including the forward-spot differential, Model 1.2 (corresponding to Eq. (1)), with maximum window size of 96 observations. For other horizons, more complex models are FMSE-best. Model 1.10, which adds three observable lags of the dependent variable to the simple Model 1.2, is FMSE-best at horizon $\tau = 3, 4, 5$. At $\tau = 6$, however, forward rates no longer enter the FMSE-best model (Model 1.5), which contains only a single observable lag of the dependent variable. A notable feature of our results is the fairly impressive out-of-sample R^2's obtained for each of the FMSE-best models. These range from a low of .062 for $\tau = 6$ to a high of .142 for $\tau = 4$. In each case, a window size of 96 observations is among the FMSE-best, but smaller window sizes also deliver identical performance for horizons $\tau = 3$ and $\tau = 4$. In fact, for $\tau = 4$, window sizes of 42, 60, and 96 deliver identical FMSE performance, suggestive of a mild degree of time instability.

Not surprisingly, the FMSE-best models are *not* generally the least confused (based on the HM p value) because forecast errors for individual observations can simultaneously be small in magnitude and associated with a prediction of the wrong sign. This is especially likely in prediction of small changes in spot rates. In all cases, the least confused model includes the forward-spot differential. Model 1.10 appears at least confused at $\tau = 2$ and $\tau = 3$, and Model 1.18 (the nonlinear ANN model) appears as least confused at horizons $\tau = 4$ and 5. Model 1.3 is least confused for $\tau = 6$. Model 1.13 matches the performance of Model 1.10 at $\tau = 2$, and Model 1.16 matches the performance of Model 1.18 at $\tau = 5$. In each case, the HM p values are rather low, suggesting that correct directional prediction is not simply due to chance. In fact, the least confused models are correctly predicting the direction of spot rate change approximately two-thirds of the time or better. The window widths for the least confused model are, in all but one case, smaller than the maximum size of 96. This is more strongly suggestive of time instability in the underlying process than the results for the FMSE. We cannot, however, rule out the possibility that an estimation technique targeted directly on forecasting the direction of change (e.g., logit) would lead to out-of-sample confusion optimized by choosing the largest window sizes. We leave such analysis for future research.

As a final statistical performance measure, we consider the relation between the models identified as best in Table 34.2 using the (in-sample) MSIC and those identified as best by the out-of-sample FMSE, or the confusion criterion. As should be expected, the MSIC-best model is in each case the ANN model (Model 1.18) because these models are arrived at by minimizing the SIC in each window. In no case, however, does the ANN model deliver best out-of-sample FMSE performance. Instead, the ANN model delivers least confused directional prediction at horizons $\tau = 4$ and 5. This is interesting because it suggests that (at least in the present context) the MSIC cannot be used as a reliable shortcut to identifying models that will perform optimally out of sample. In network jargon, the MSIC-best model is not necessarily the model that "generalizes" best when presented with data not included in the "training set." Instead, it is necessary to do the appropriate out-of-sample analysis to find the best model when using nonlinear ANN's. Because of the combinatorial nature of this analysis for neural networks with hidden units, we defer this to subsequent work.

We note that the SIC is widely believed to select very parsimonious models and that such models usually "win" forecasting competitions. Our results suggest that, at least in the present case, the SIC is not selecting sufficiently parsimonious models. Because the SIC imposes the most severe penalty among the various alternatives (AIC, Hannan–Quinn, etc.), use of other such criteria would likely give worse-performing results. Out-of-sample analysis remains the only recourse.

Table 34.2 also provides summary statistics for models other than those deemed as best, using the performance measures. In particular, Table 34.2 contains results for Models 1.1 and 1.18, to provide background against which to compare the best models and to provide additional insight into how well the least (Model 1.1) and most (Model 1.18) complex models perform. Recall that Model 1.1 contains only a constant term and so implements a random walk with drift. The R^2's for these models are effectively 0. For $\tau = 1, 2, 3, 4, 5$, however, the nonlinear ANN model is no more confused than the best model (based on a p value of .05). Thus, there is some evidence that the nonlinear models can help to predict the direction of change of the spot rate.

The results for the Case 2 regressions are less emphatic in their evidence for the value of the forward rate in predicting future changes in spot rates. For these regressions, the best FMSE at all horizons is achieved for the model containing only a constant (Model 2.1). (Note that only horizons $\tau = 3, ..., 6$ are reported because horizon $\tau = 2$ coincides with Case 1.) For the confusion measures, forward rates do appear in the least confused models at three of the four horizons. The ANN model is the least confused model for $\tau = 3$, with the least confusion achieved by differing models (Models 2.7, 2.3, 2.5, and 2.9) for other horizons. In all cases, the best confusion rates are worse than those seen in Case 1. Nevertheless, the least confused models achieve statistical significance at the 10 percent level or better according to the HM p values, at all four horizons, with correct directional predictions approximately 60 percent of the time. Again, the SIC does not identify either the FMSE- or confusion-best model, out-of-sample. Note that for all horizons (except $\tau = 5$), the SIC best neural network on average contains zero hidden units. In this sense, Model 2.17 dominates Model 2.18 in Case 2.

SECTION V. RESULTS FOR PROFITABILITY PERFORMANCE MEASURES

Let $\Delta_{\tau 1} \equiv R_{t+\tau} - R_{t+1}$ be the change in the spot rate (the dependent variable for the Case 1 regressions), and for a given model/window combination, let $\hat{\Delta}_{\tau T+1}$ denote the first out-of-sample predicted change in spot rates from a window terminating at time T. A forecast of the future spot rate is then given by:

$$\hat{R}_{T+1+\tau} = \hat{\Delta}_{\tau T+1} + R_{T+2}. \tag{7}$$

A simple "straddle" or "spread" trading strategy can be based on (7). Specifically, sell the horizon τ forward instrument short if:

$$\hat{R}_{T+1+\tau} > \tau F_{\tau,T+1} - (\tau - 1)F_{\tau-1,T+1}, \quad \tau = 2, ..., 6. \tag{8}$$

With the proceeds from the short sale, buy the $\tau -1$-horizon forward instrument and when it matures use the proceeds to purchase the spot instrument. If

$$\hat{R}_{T+1+\tau} < \tau F_{\tau,T+1} - (\tau - 1)F_{\tau-1,T+1}, \quad \tau = 2, ..., 6, \tag{9}$$

undertake the reverse strategy. For simplicity, we assume a standard contract of size $1 MM = $1,000,000. The profit (negative profit represents loss) for such a transaction is given by

$$\Pi_{\tau,T+1} \equiv \$1MM(e^{[\tau F \tau_{T+1} - (\tau - 1)F(\tau - 1)_{T+1}]} - e^{-R_{T+1+\tau}} - T_{\tau,T+1}, \qquad (10)$$

where $T_{\tau,T+1}$ is the total transactions cost associated with the spread. This cost includes both commissions and the effects of the bid–ask spreads. To avoid complexities associated with bid–ask spreads and with the effects of investor characteristics on commission costs, we consider a range of fixed values for $T_{\tau,T+1}$, chosen to represent plausible possibilities for average total transactions costs. A simple measure of model/window performance is then given by the sum (undiscounted) of profits over the 89 out-of-sample observation periods.

Conditional on the realized history of asset prices, this profit measure is dependent on the particular realized pattern of correct directional predictions. This dependence can be removed under appropriate conditions by Monte Carlo simulation. To avoid having our conclusions adversely affected by dependence on a particular pattern of correct predictions, we report the results of a relevant Monte Carlo simulation. We follow an approach to trading-rule evaluation given by Leitch and Tanner (1991) and Dorfman and McIntosh (1992). The idea is that if a trading system gives a correct signal (i.e., one profitable apart from transactions costs) $d \times 100$ percent of the time ($0 \le d \le 1$) and if correctness of a given signal is independent of correctness of prior signals and also independent of the magnitude of profit, one can simulate the probability distribution of trading-system profits conditional on a realized price series of length n by repeatedly drawing length n sequences of iid signals correct $d \times 100\%$ of the time and computing the empirical distribution of the resulting profits over many replications.

In our case, our signals are "correct" if

$$(\hat{R}_{T+\tau+1} + (\tau - 1)F_{\tau - 1,T+1} - \tau F_{\tau,T+1})$$

$$\times (R_{T+\tau+1} + (\tau - 1)F_{\tau - 1,T+1} - \tau F_{\tau,T+1}) > 0. \qquad (11)$$

The number of times this occurs divided by 89 gives our value for d. For each horizon, we identify the model/window combination giving the highest value for d. These are reported in Table 34.4. Generally, d is never less than .82, with $d = .90$ for $\tau = 2$. This rather good performance was pleasantly surprising to us. To investigate whether this performance is consistent with pure luck, we again compute the HM p values associated with the confusion matrices. We reject the null hypothesis of independence in all cases rather decisively.

Table 34.4

Best *d* Value Model by Window and Horizon

Horizon	Best Model	Window	Confusion Matrix	HM *p* Value	*d* Value
$\tau = 2$	1.18	42	$\begin{bmatrix} 3 & 1 \\ 8 & 76 \end{bmatrix}$	.01	.90
$\tau = 3$	1.15	60	$\begin{bmatrix} 4 & 3 \\ 10 & 72 \end{bmatrix}$	.01	.85
$\tau = 4$	1.6	60	$\begin{bmatrix} 11 & 4 \\ 9 & 65 \end{bmatrix}$	.00	.85
$\tau = 5$	1.8	60	$\begin{bmatrix} 8 & 1 \\ 10 & 70 \end{bmatrix}$	.00	.88
$\tau = 6$	1.6	96	$\begin{bmatrix} 8 & 3 \\ 13 & 65 \end{bmatrix}$	.00	.82

Note: Models 1.18, 1.15, and 1.8 contain the current and/or lagged forward rate. The matrices shown in square brackets are confusion matrices (diagonal cells correspond to correct directional predictions, and off-diagonal cells correspond to incorrect predictions). The *d* values are based on the number of times that $(\hat{R}_{T+\tau+1} + (\tau - 1) F_{\tau-1, T+1} - \tau F_{\tau,T+1}) (R_{T+\tau+1} + (\tau - 1) F_{\tau-1,T+1} - \tau F_{\tau,T+1}) > 0$, divided by the out–of–sample size, 89. Thus, the trading system gives a correct signal (one profitable apart from transactions costs) $d \times 100$ percent of the time. The HM *p* values are based on the null hypothesis that a given model is of no value in predicting the direction of spot–interest–rate changes. Case 1: $R_{t+\tau} - R_{t+1} = a_1 + \Sigma_i \alpha_{1,i} (F_{\tau,t-i} - R_{t+1-i}) + \Sigma_i \beta_{1,i} (R_{t+\tau-i} - R_{t+1-i}) + u_{1,t}$.

Of particular interest is the fact that in three of the five horizons, $\tau = 2$, 3, and 5, forward rates or their lags enter the best model. This provides additional evidence of the value of forward rates in predicting future spot rates. We note that in no case does the *d*-best model correspond to the confusion-best model for $R_{t+\tau} - R_{t+1}$ and that there is no necessary correspondence. The fact that the *d*-best model for $\tau = 2$ is the ANN model, with the highest observed value for *d*, and that the ANN is nearly *d*-best in all other cases (not shown in the table) is also of interest.

Next, we investigate whether signal correctness is independent of prior signal correctness. For this, we construct a sequence of Bernoulli random variables equal to 1 for a correct signal and 0 otherwise. We then perform a standard runs test (e.g., Mendenhall, Wackerly, and Scheaffer 1990) on the observed sequence for the d-best model at each horizon. The null hypothesis of independence is decisively rejected for all horizons. These results are available from the authors, by request. Because lack of independence could presumably be used to improve a trading system, profit computations such as those reported here, which are based on independence, will be *conservative*.

As a final check on the relevance of the simulation framework, we investigated whether profit magnitude is independent of signal correctness by regressing $|\hat{R}_{T+1+\tau} + (\tau - 1) F_{\tau-1,T+1} - \tau F_{\tau,T+1}|$ on a constant and a signal correctness dummy variable, D_{T+1}. Under the null hypothesis of independence, the coefficient on the dummy variable should be 0. Marginally significant results appear at $\tau = 5$ and $\tau = 6$ with p values of .045 and .06, respectively. Results otherwise are far from significance at conventional levels. These results are available, by request.

Thus, Dorfman and McIntosh's (1992) simulation method for approximating the probability distribution of trading-system profits for a system correct $d \times 100$ percent of the time should give some reasonably informative benchmarks. Our results, reported in Table 34.5, are based on 10,000 replications. Results are reported for total transactions cost levels of from $0 to $1,250, in increments of $250 per spread. Analysis of bid–ask spreads by Shen (1992) suggested that average costs of $250 may be realistic for large institutional investors. Only the first moments are shown in Table 34.5. The simulated variances of the profits shown in the table are very small, in all cases below $20. As pointed out by an anonymous referee, it might also be useful to consider variances that are simulated by taking the average of the variance of profits for each of the 10,000 trials. In this case, the mean should also be the average of the *average* of each trial (i.e., the average profit per monthly transaction). Thus, because the experimental forecast horizon is 89 months long, the mean profit reported by us is 89 times as big as the mean profit that results from the suggested *alternative* method for reporting the simulation results. In this case, however, the variances estimated are still three orders of magnitude less than the mean. To illustrate the difference between the two methods for calculating the mean and variance of profits accruing from the trading strategy, (12) shows the mean and corresponding variance of profits that are reported here, while (13) does likewise for the alternative reporting strategy. With $n = 10,000$, we have the following equations.

Table 34.5

Mean Profit Analysis by Horizon—in Dollars

	Expected Profit by τ and Model				
Transactions Costs (T)	$\tau = 2$; 1.18	$\tau = 3$ Model 1.15	$\tau = 4$ Model 1.6	$\tau = 5$ Model 1.8	$\tau = 6$ Model 1.6
0	66,580	76,210	87,210	118,160	101,710
250	44,260	53,960	64,960	95,910	79,450
500	22,010	31,710	42,710	73,660	57,200
750	−240	9,460	20,460	51,410	34,950
1,000	−22,480	−12,780	−1,780	29,170	12,710
1,250	−44,730	−35,040	−24,040	6,920	−9,540

Note: Best models are chosen by d value, as listed in Table 34.4. The trading strategy entails risk, so no arbitrage is detected, and a proper financial evaluation entails consideration of not only mean profit (or return) but also risk, which is not considered here. The tracing strategy assumes a standard contract of size $1MM, and follows equations (7)–(10), where the profit for a single transaction is given by $\Pi_{\tau,T+1} \equiv \$1\text{MM}(e^{[\tau F_{\tau,T+1} - (\tau-1)F_{\tau-1,T+1}]} - e^{-R_{T+1+\tau}}) - T_{\tau,T+1}$, where $T_{\tau,T+1}$ is the simulations. Numerical values are based on 10,000 simulations.
Case 1: $R_{t+\tau} - R_{t+1} = \alpha_1 + \sum_i \alpha_{1,i}(F_{\tau,t-1} - R_{t+1-i}) + \sum_i \beta_{1,i}(R_{t+\tau-i} - R_{t+1-i}) + u_{1,t}$.

$$\text{mean}(\overline{\Pi})_t = \frac{1}{n}\sum_{i=1}^{n}\left[\sum_{j=1}^{89}\pi_{i,j}\right]$$

$$\text{var}(\overline{\Pi})_1 = \frac{1}{n}\sum_{i=1}^{n}\left(\sum_{i=1}^{89}\pi_{i,j} - \left[\frac{1}{n}\sum_{i=1}^{n}\sum_{j=1}^{89}\pi_{i,j}\right]\right)^2 \tag{12}$$

and

$$\text{mean}(\overline{\Pi})_2 = \frac{1}{n}\sum_{i=1}^{n}\left[\frac{1}{89}\sum_{j=1}^{89}\pi_{i,j}\right]$$

$$\text{var}(\overline{\Pi})_2 = \frac{1}{n}\sum_{i=1}^{n}\left[\frac{1}{89}\sum_{i=1}^{89}\left(\pi_{i,j} - \frac{1}{89}\sum_{j=1}^{89}\pi_{i,j}\right)^2\right] \tag{13}$$

The story that emerges from the simulated profits reported in Table 34.5 is coherent and rather interesting. Positive profits occur at all horizons with total transactions costs per spread of up to $500, with positive profits persisting to the $1,250 level at $\tau = 5$. The standard deviation of profit is quite small, relative to the typical magnitude of the average. Although this suggests that potentially profitable information may be publicly available and in particular in forward rates for horizons $\tau = 2, 3$, and 5, caution and lack of a proper mean-variance frontier analysis dictate that further detailed analysis should be carried out before the approach described here is used to trade debt instruments. Nevertheless, the rather good performance in predicting directions of rate movements could well be valuable to market makers and primary dealers.

SECTION VI. SUMMARY AND CONCLUDING REMARKS

We have used a model-selection approach based on out-of-sample forecasting performance to investigate the extent to which forward-interest rates are useful as predictors of future spot rates. We offer the following conclusions. First, for our out-of-sample period, the best Case 1 model contains forward rates in four out of five horizons, based on a forecast mean squared error performance measure, and five out of five horizons when chosen using a confusion performance measure. The best models from a trading-profitability standpoint contain the forward rate for three of the five horizons. Forward rates are thus useful in predicting future changes in spot rates, to this extent. Second, windows of observations of less than maximal size occasionally appear as FMSE optimal, generally appear as confusion optimal, and often appear as d-best (providing the *best* trading rule signal), suggesting instability in the relationships of interest. Third, the in-sample SIC does not appear to be a reliable guide to out-of-sample performance, so it fails to offer a convenient shortcut to true out-of-sample performance measures for selecting models and for configuring nonlinear ANN models. Finally, ANN models appear to be promising for use in this forecasting context, and further refinement and application of ANN methods is warranted.

The work reported here is merely a starting point. A wide variety of further questions present themselves for subsequent research, both theoretical and empirical. On the theoretical side, it is of interest to establish the statistical properties of the model-selection procedures followed here.

Of particular interest is obtaining asymptotic distributions for a test that the true rolling-window root mean squared error of two models is equal, based on the realized difference in FMSE's.

Interesting empirical projects include conducting a similar analysis using even larger windows, adding post-1986 data to the sample, extending the out-of-sample period in both directions, adding additional interesting predictor variables, using robust regression methods and/or regression methods based on maximizing in-sample excess returns, using out-of-sample criteria to configure ANN models, and investigating the performance of alternatives to ANN models such as multivariate adaptive regression splines (Friedman 1988). All of these projects we leave to future work.

REFERENCES

Akaike, H. 1973. "Information Theory and an Extension of the Maximum Likelihood Principle". In *2nd International Symposium on Information Theory*. eds. B. N. Petrov and F. Csaki. Budapest: Akademiai Kiado, pp. 267–81.

———. 1974. "A New Look at the Statistical Model Identification." *IEEE Transactions on Automatic Control*, AC-19, pp. 716–23.

Carroll, S. M. and B.W. Dickinson. 1989. "Construction of Neural Nets Using the Radon Transform." In *Proceedings of the International Joint Conference on Neural Networks. Washington, DC*. New York: IEEE Press, pp. 607–11.

Cybenko, G. 1989. "Approximation by Superpositions of a Sigmoid Function," *Mathematics of Control Signals and Systems* 2, pp. 303–14.

Diebold, F. X. and G.D. Rudebusch. 1991. "Forecasting Output With the Composite Leading Index: A Real Time Analysis." *Journal of the American Statistical Association* 86, pp. 603–10.

Dorfman, J.H. and C.S. McIntosh. 1992. "Using Economic Criteria for Forecast Valuation and Evaluation." Mimeo. University of Georgia, Dept. of Agricultural Economics.

Dorsey, R.E., J.D. Johnson, and M.V. van Boening. 1994. "The Use of Artificial Neural Networks for Estimation of Decision Surfaces in First Price Sealed Bid Auctions." In *New Directions in Computational Economics*. eds. W. W. Cooper and A. Whinston. Boston: Kluwer, pp. 19–40.

Dropsy, V. 1992. "Exchange Rates and Neural Networks." Working Paper 1–92. California State University, Fullerton, Dept. of Economics.

Dutta, S. and S. Shekhar. 1988. "Bond Rating: A Non-conservative Application of Neural Networks." In *Proceedings of the IEEE International Conference on Neural Networks. San Diego.* New York: IEEE Press, pp. 443–50.

Engle, R. F. and S.J. Brown. 1986. "Model Selection for Forecasting." *Applied Mathematics and Computation* 20, pp. 313–27.

Fama, E.F. 1976. "Forward Rates as Predictors of Future Spot Rates." *Journal of Financial Economics* 3, pp. 361–77.

———. 1984. "The Information in the Term Structure." *Journal of Financial Economics* 13, pp. 509–28.

Friedman, J. 1988. "Fitting Functions to Noisy Data in High Dimensions." In *Computing Science and Statistics: Proceedings of the Twentieth Symposium on the Interface.* eds. E.J. Wegman, D.T. Gantz, and J.J. Miller. Alexandria VA: American Statistical Association, pp. 13–43.

Funahashi, K. 1989. "On the Approximate Realization of Continuous Mappings by Neural Networks." *Neural Networks* 2, pp. 183–192.

Henriksson, R.D. and R.C. Merton. 1981. "On Market Timing and Investment Performance. II. Statistical Procedures for Evaluating Forecasting Skills." *Journal of Business* 54, pp. 513–533.

Hornik, K., M. Stinchcombe, and H. White. 1989. "Multilayer Feed-forward Networks Are Universal Approximators." *Neural Networks* 2, pp. 359–366.

———. 1990. "Universal Approximation of an Unknown Mapping and its Derivatives Using Multilayer Feedforward Networks." *Neural Networks* 3, pp. 551–560.

Kuan, C.M. and T. Liu. 1992. "Forecasting Exchange Rates Using Feedforward and Recurrent Neural Networks." Faculty Working Paper 92-0128, University of Illinois at Urbana-Champaign, Bureau of Economic and Business Research.

Kuan, C.M. and H. White. 1994. "Artificial Neural Networks: An Econometric Perspective." *Econometric Reviews* 13, pp. 1–91.

Leitch, G. and J.E. Tanner. 1991. "Economic Forecast Evaluation: Profits Versus the Conventional Error Measures." *American Economic Review* 81, pp. 580–590.

Mendenhall, W., D.D. Wackerly, and R.L. Scheaffer. 1990. *Mathematical Statistics With Applications.* Boston: PWS-Kent.

Mishkin, F.S. 1988. "The Information in the Term Structure: Some Further Results." *Journal of Applied Econometrics* 3, pp. 307–714.

Moody, J. and J. Utans. 1991. "Principled Architecture Selection for Neural Networks: Applications to Corporate Bond Rating Predictions." In *Advances in Neural Information Processing Systems 4.* eds. J.E. Moody, S.J. Hanson, and R.P. Lippmann. San Mateo: Morgan Kaufman, pp. 683–690.

Pötscher, B.M. 1991. "Effects of Model Selection on Inference." *Econometric Theory* 7, pp. 163–185.

Rumelhart, D.E. and J.L. McClelland. 1986. *Parallel Distributed Processing: Explorations in the Microstructures of Cognition.* Cambridge, MA: MIT Press.

Sawa, T. 1978. "Information Criteria for Discriminating Among Alternative Regression Models." *Econometrica* 46, pp. 1273–1292.

Schwarz, G. 1978. "Estimating the Dimension of a Model." *The Annals of Statistics* 6, pp. 461–464.

Shen, P. 1992. "Determination of Bid–Ask Spreads in the Government Security Market: Theory and Empirical Tests." Unpublished dissertation. University of California, San Diego, Dept. of Economics.

Shiller, R.J., J.Y. Campbell, and K.L. Schoenholtz. 1983. "Forward Rates and Future Policy: Interpreting the Term Structure of Interest Rates." *Brookings Papers on Economic Activity* 1, pp. 173–217.

Trippi, R. and E Turban. 1993. *Neural Networks in Finance and Investing.* Chicago: Probus.

White, H. 1988. "Economic Prediction Using Neural Networks: The Case of IBM Daily Stock Returns." In *Proceedings of the IEEE International Conference on Neural Networks, San Diego.* New York: IEEE Press, pp. 451–458.

———. 1989. "Learning in Artificial Neural Networks: A Statistical Perspective." *Neural Computation* 1, pp. 425–464.

———. 1990. "Connectionist Nonparametric Regression: Multilayer Feedforward Networks Can Learn Arbitrary Mappings." *Neural Networks* 3, pp. 535–549.

PART VII

NEURAL NETWORK APPROACHES TO FINANCIAL FORECASTING

PERFORMANCE OF NEURAL NETWORKS IN MANAGERIAL FORECASTING

Won Chul Jhee and Jae Kyu Lee

INTRODUCTION

In recent years, there has been considerable interest in artificial neural networks (ANN). ANNs have been applied to a wide range of information-processing activities, such as associative memory, pattern classification, pattern clustering, and function approximation and prediction (Pao 1988). In this paper, we describe two different ANN approaches for univariate time-series analysis using multi-layered perceptrons (MLP). One

We would like to thank the editor-in-chief of *Intelligent Systems in Accounting, Finance, and Management* and three anonymous reviewers for their helpful comments on this paper and suggestions for our ongoing research. The research reported here was partly supported by KOSEF (Korea Science and Engineering Foundation) under Grant 921–1100–016–1.

is a pattern classifier to automate the identification stage of the well-known statistical forecasting model. The other is to replace the whole forecasting process by the ANN as a function approximator. The purpose of this research is thus to compare performances of the two approaches so that we can select the better one for managerial forecasting.

Time-series analysis describes the processes or phenomena by which a mathematical model generates a sequence of observations that can be extrapolated into the future, assuming that the processes are stable and the observations show a high degree of correlation. Autoregressive moving average (ARMA) and its variants such as exponential smoothing are typical examples of such mathematical models. On the other hand, ANN can be used as an alternative to conventional mathematical models since ANN can be universal approximators (Hornik et al, 1989).

In the pioneering work of Lapedes and Farber (1987), the feedforward MLP was trained with the time series that was generated by a prespecified equation. Lapedes and Farber showed that for a chaotic time series, the MLP outperformed the conventional linear and polynomial predictive methods in forecasting accuracy. Apparently, MLP learns in its hidden layers to approximate the underlying process that generates such a series. Although the MLP has demonstrated an impressive ability in approximating functions and forecasting, we must address some difficulties in adopting the ANN approach for managerial forecasting:

1. *Limited number of observations.* For the training of the MLP, Lapedes and Farber used 500 input/output pairs. This is a considerable amount of data, but there are many cases in which a large number of historical observations would be unavailable in the managerial environment (Vandale 1983).

2. *Noisy environment.* The early ANN applications used noise-free and computer- generated time series. However, the time series from the real-world business environment often has high levels of noise from unknown sources, and the underlying process that generates the series is usually unknown. Further empirical work of the type done by White (1988) and Weigend et al. (1990) is still necessary to use the ANN as an alternative to conventional forecasting methods.

3. *Size of the network.* There are few rules or guidelines on how to determine the size of the ANN in terms of the number of processing elements or weights to obtain reliable forecasts from a specific time series.

Researchers have tried to find the proper size by simulating various sizes of the ANN. This process is very time-consuming, and it is apt to result in poor forecasting performance because of the *overfitting* problem that results from limited length of noisy data.

To cope with these difficulties, we adopted two directions for the ANN approach as depicted in Figures 35.1b and c. The first is to automate the human judgmental identification stage of ARMA modeling, The second is to replace the whole prediction process by the ANN approach, as did Lapedes and Farber.

In the fist ANN approach, the MLP is used as a pattern classifier of some statistical information to automate the ARMA model identification. An ARMA (p,q) model for a stationary time series $\{z(t),\ t \varepsilon T\}$ is expressed by:

$$z(t) = \phi_1 z(t-1) + \ldots + \phi_p z(t-p)$$
$$+ a(t) - \theta_1 a(t-1) - \ldots - \theta_q a(t-q)$$

where $\{a(t)\}$ consists of normally distributed independent random variables from $N(0,o^2)$, and ϕ's and θ's are autoregressive (AR) and moving average (MA) parameters to be estimated, respectively. ARMA modeling is one of the most widely used tools for managerial forecasting and remains a benchmark method for creating linear models of time-series data because of its theoretical elaborateness and accuracy in short-term forecasting. ARMA models are built through the iterative steps, as shown in Figure 35.1a. Among the modeling steps, the model identification that determines the order p of the AR process and the order q of the MA process is crucial to represent time series adequately because when a time series includes heavy noise, the modeler tends to be prodigal in using the parameters, in spite of the principle of parsimony (Box and Jenkins 1976). In this step, expert judgment should be properly exercised in interpreting some of the statistical information such as the autocorrelation function (ACF) and the partial autocorrelation function (PACF) (Box and Jenkins 1976), and the extended sample autocorrelation function (ESACF) (Tsay and Tiao 1984). Therefore, we attempted to reduce or eliminate trial and error in the procedure of Figure 35.1a by adopting the MLP as a pattern-classification network that substitutes for the human judgment in the ARMA model identification. The role of ANN is to select the order (p,q) by class-

Figure 35.1

ARMA Modeling Procedure and Suggested ANN Approaches

a. Traditional ARMA Model Building Procedure

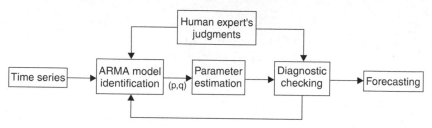

b. Automating the Identification Step by Adopting the ANN

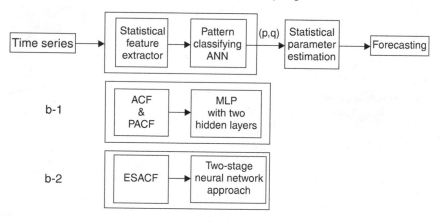

c. Time Series Modeling and Prediction with an ANN

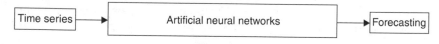

---

ifying patterns in the given statistical features as shown in Figure 35.1b. Thus the following research issues are explored:

1. When we use ACF and PACF as inputs to the pattern-classification network, what is the performance of the ANN method for the ARMA model identification?

2. When we use ESACF instead of ACF and PACF, what is the performance of the ANN method for identification?

3. What is the comparative performance resulting from the above two statistical features?

By automating the identification stage of the ARMA modeling, the whole process of modeling and estimation can be entirely automated. It is very important to apply full automation to situations that have a large number of time series such as production-inventory systems.

In the second approach, as shown in Figure 35.1c, ANN is used as a modeling tool that can effectively capture the sequence of actions taken by the time-series-generating process. Lapedes and Farber (1987) showed that the MLP can predict the future values of time series through nonlinear interpolation of past values. When the MLP is used as a fitting function of the time series that has noise, it seems that the larger size of MLP performs better. However, although time series can be fitted arbitrarily well by the large size of the MLP, it does not necessarily lead to optimal prediction. As in the case of ARMA modeling, it is important to employ a modest size of MLP to prevent the overfitting problem. This requires us to find the minimal structure of the MLP for the time series; therefore, the following research issues are explored:

1. To alleviate the overfitting problem what are possible alternative structures of MLP?

2. What are the comparative performance differences among the alternative structures of the MLP? Can the MLP outperform the ARMA model in forecasting accuracy?

To proceed with the MLP as a function approximation and forecasting tool, first, we tested the performance of the various sizes of MLP using real time series that were already fitted by ARMA models in the literature. Next, we adopted two alternative structures of the MLP to achieve better forecasting accuracy. One structure aims to find the minimal networks by eliminating unnecessary processing elements or weights from the learned MLP to improve the generalization power. The other structure is Elman's (1988) recurrent network, which uses the feedback connections in the MLP. Finally, we tested the prediction performances of those two alternatives in comparison with those of the ARMA models.

ARMA MODEL IDENTIFICATION WITH MULTILAYERED PERCEPTRONS

Statistical Feature Extractors

In order to automate the ARMA model-identification step using the MLP as a pattern classifier, we needed to select the feature extractor that produces input values for the classifier from the time series. We adopted two types of feature extractors: the ACF/PACF and the ESACF.

Although Box and Jenkins (1976) suggested a comprehensive method for the ARMA models, researchers in the field have still tried to reduce the difficulties inherent in the method to enhance its applicability. First, a family of model-identification schemes emphasizes reproducing the variance—covariance structure of the time series in question. These approaches require investigating the statistical patterns such as the ACF and PACF or their transformations. Since the ACF and the PACF in the Box–Jenkins method cannot provide sufficient information to identify an appropriate model, researchers have tried to develop new and simpler statistics that can effectively replace the role of the ACF and the PACF in the identification stage (Benguin et al. 1980; Gray et al. 1978; Tsay and Tiao 1984; Woodward and Gray 1981). Second, some researchers depend on the search strategies and the goodness-of-fit criterion. A systematic search through reasonable combinations of AR and MA orders is believed to produce the best choice of model. However, this scheme involves the estimation of the AR and MA coefficients at each step, the calculation of goodness-of-fit statistics, and comparison with previous steps over all choices or orders (Akaike 1974; Pandit and Wu 1980; Parzen 1983; Schwarz 1976). Finally, the other group developed an approach to automate ARMA modeling where the Box–Jenkins method and Akaike Information Criterion are integrated (Hill and Woodworth 1980; Kang et al. 1982; Wheelwright and Makridakis 1985).

Figure 35.2 shows the behavior of the sample ACFs and PACFs in cases of a pure model AR(2) and a mixed model ARMA(1, 2). The PACF values of the AR(2) model drop abruptly to zero after time lag 2, but neither the ACF nor the PACF pattern of the ARMA(1, 2) model shows this cutoff behavior. Therefore, the modeler may have difficulties in handling mixed classes and may be confused by the distorted patterns due to noise.

Figure 35.2

Sample ACF and PACF Patterns

a. ARMA(2,0): $\phi_1 = 0.9$, $\phi_2 = -0.75$, $\sigma_a^2 = 1$.

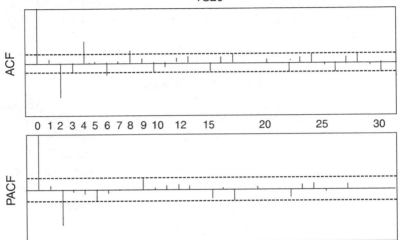

TS20

b. ARMA(1,2): $\phi_1 = 0.7$, $\theta_1 = 0.8$, $\theta_2 = -0.5$, $\sigma_a^2 = 1$.

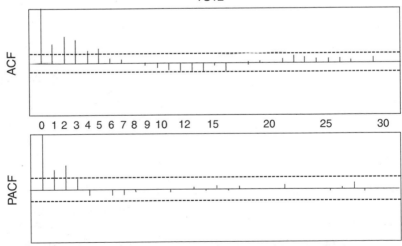

TS12

The ESACF approach (Tsay and Tiao 1984) is a result of such efforts that improve the information values of the ACF and the PACF and is known to be a very powerful approach to ARMA model identification. Figure 35.3a shows a theoretical ESACF pattern of the ARMA(1, 1) without any noise, which is converted into binary values for the purpose of pattern classification. The modeler has only to find the vertex of the triangle of 1's. However, this task may not be so simple if noise exists in cases such as the example in Figure 35.3b. The noise makes it difficult to select the right vertex. This leads us to conclude that an automated judgment aid for the human analyzer is essential.

Thus, our purpose was to design ANN classifiers that receive noisy statistical patterns as inputs and classify them into the ARMA(p,q) model. Figure 35.4 shows an example of the pattern-classification network (PCN), which is trained by a back-propagation algorithm (Rumelhart et al. 1986; Werbos 1988). The reason for starting the study with the ACF and the PACF is to test whether the ANN classifier can extract useful information from such basic features (Jhee et al. 1990). However, the ACF and the PACF play a limited role in automating the identification step because the Box–Jenkins method requires the integration filter to handle the non-stationary time series. In other words, only the ACF and the PACF obtained from the stationary series are meaningful in examining the cutoff phenomenon that gives important information in specifying the orders of ARMA models. However, in the ESACF approach, we need not be concerned about the order of differencing. Therefore, the ESACF is adopted as a second feature extractor, which can increase the possibility of automatic ARMA modeling (Lee and Jhee 1992). In the remainder of this section, the performance of ANN classifiers in ARMA model identification will be reported, together with the comparative experiment between two feature extractors.

Identification with ACF and PACF

Design of Pattern-Classification Network

In the Box–Jenkins method, the ACF pattern provides information about the order q of MA and the PACF pattern about the order p of AR. This dichotomous property of the method suggested to us that the PCN in this ANN method can be separated into two networks: ACF and PACF. Therefore, the final decision can be made by combining the outputs of

Figure 35.3

Examples of ESACF Patterns from the ARMA(1,1) Model

a. The prototype pattern of the converted ESACF table for ARMA(1,1).

AR \ MA	0	1	2	3	4	5	6	7	8	9
0	0	0	0	0	0	0	0	0	0	0
1	0	1	1	1	1	1	1	1	1	1
2	0	0	1	1	1	1	1	1	1	1
3	0	0	0	1	1	1	1	1	1	1
4	0	0	0	0	1	1	1	1	1	1
5	0	0	0	0	0	1	1	1	1	1
6	0	0	0	0	0	0	1	1	1	1
7	0	0	0	0	0	0	0	1	1	1
8	0	0	0	0	0	0	0	0	1	1
9	0	0	0	0	0	0	0	0	0	1

b. The converted ESACF table from Series A in Box and Jenkins (1976).

AR \ MA	0	1	2	3	4	5	6	7	8	9
0	0	0	0	0	0	0	0	0	0	0
1	0	1	1	1	1	1	0	1	1	1
2	0	0	1	1	1	1	0	1	1	1
3	0	1	1	1	1	1	0	1	1	1
4	0	1	1	1	1	1	1	1	1	1
5	0	0	0	1	0	1	1	1	1	1
6	0	0	0	1	0	1	1	1	1	1
7	0	1	1	0	0	1	0	1	1	1
8	0	1	1	0	0	1	1	1	1	1
9	0	1	1	0	1	0	1	1	1	1

Figure 35.4

Pattern Classification with ESACF and MLP

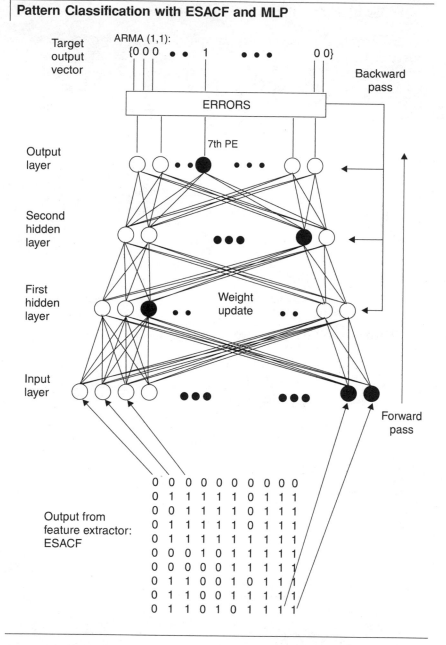

ACF and PACF networks, each representing the appropriate order q of the MA process and p of the AR process, respectively.

The structures of ACF and PACF networks are similar to that in Figure 35.4. Since we were to inspect the first 30-sample ACF and PACF values obtained from time series, the input layers of ACF and PACF networks each had 30 processing elements (PEs). The output layer had three PEs, each denoting the order of 0, 1, and 2 because we only considered up to ARMA (2, 2). We used 60 PEs and sine activation functions in the first hidden layer so that the MLP could decompose a mode and discover any important frequency components of the behaviors of ACF and PACF. To abstract smoothly the information stored in the first hidden layer into the output layer, we used the smaller number of PEs in the second hidden layer and sigmoid activation functions in the second hidden layer and output layer.

Training Data

To prepare the training data, we generated the time series with the parameters that satisfy both stationarity and invertibility conditions of ARMA models (Box and Jenkins 1976). The ACF and PACF were then calculated to be inputted to the PCNs. To select parameters that generate the ACF and PACF patterns that can train the network with the most generalized classification power, we calculated the admissible region of each ARMA model and chose a set of parameters that can effectively cover the region when linked together. Since the ACF and PACF patterns, computed from the simulated time series with these parameters, are expected to represent all the characteristics of the patterns that can be obtained using other parameters within the admissible region, we call our training strategy *maximal region covering* (MRC). The two training sets consisted of 202 ACF and PACF patterns, of which the desired outputs were the orders of MA and AR process, respectively (Jhee et al. 1992).

Test and Discussions

When we tested the PCNs with 54 time series that were also generated using the parameters within the admissible regions, the best performance (83.3 percent classification accuracy) was achieved by the PCNs, which had 30 PEs in the second hidden layer. As the number of PEs in the second hidden layer was varied from 0 to 35, the overall performance of the learned networks fell to between 63.5 percent and 83.3 percent classification accuracy, which is not sufficient for automation of the Box–Jenkins method. A possible explanation is that the noise and inherent complexity in the ACF and PACF patterns disturbed the MLP in identifying the correct orders of the ARMA model. However, in spite of these difficulties, the fact that average classification accuracy reached about 80 percent shows the possibility of applying the ANN approach to overcome the drawbacks of the Box–Jenkins method.

Identification with ESACF

Design of Pattern-Classification Network

We adopted the ESACF as the second feature extractor to increase the possibility of automating the ARMA model identification. Since we used the 10×10 ESACF table, we arranged corresponding 100-input PEs. We considered the maximum orders of $p = 5$ and $q = 5$ and arranged 35-output PEs; that is, $(p+1)(q+1)-1$ PEs, if ARMA (p,q) is a model of the highest order under consideration. The pattern-classification network had 70 and 50 PEs in the first and second hidden layers, respectively, with the sigmoid activation function (Lee and Jhee 1992).

Training Data

To make the PCN robust to the input noise, we added noise to the ESACF prototype patterns, such as in Figure 35.3a by randomly inverting binary values and generating four training data sets, each of which had ESACF patterns with different noise levels, such as 0 percent, 10 percent, 20 percent, and 30 percent. The first set had 35 prototype patterns without noise. The second had 210 patterns, which consisted of the first set and 175 patterns of 10 percent noise. The third set had 385 patterns, which comprised the second set and 175 patterns of 20 percent noise. The fourth set had 560 patterns, which consisted of the third set and 175 patterns of 30 percent noise. By using these four data sets, we can examine the impact of noise in ESACF patterns on classification performance.

Test of Pattern-Classification Network

We prepared 15 test sets, each of 210 test patterns. Since a test set consisted of three noise levels (10 percent, 20 percent, 30 percent), each test set could be divided into three subsets, which had 70 patterns of different noise levels, respectively. Composing the training and test sets according to noise level helped in analyzing the effect of noise on the performance of the PCN.

Table 35.1 summarizes the averaged classification performance of the PCN that learned from each training set. As shown in the fifth column of the table, first, we can observe that the designed MLP as a PCN suffered in classifying the test patterns at a higher noise level, although the PCN could learn from noisy training patterns. Our second observation was that when the PCN was trained with the fourth training set of a 30 percent noise level, the performance did not improve in comparison with the results from the third training set. The training sets with too high a noise level did not help us improve the performance of the PCN. From these observations, we conclude that it is necessary to devise an approach that can reduce the noise in the ESACF test patterns before pattern classification. This led us to introduce a noise-filtering stage to achieve a higher ARMA model identification accuracy by the PCN.

Table 35.1

Average Classification Accuracy of PCN for Each Test Subset as a Function of Training Sets

Noise Level in Test Subset (%)	Noise Level in Training Sets (%)				One-Way ANOVA Test: $F(3,56)$
	1st (0)	2nd (10)	3rd (20)	4th (30)	
10	94.95	96.86	95.81	96.10	1.50
	(2.80)*	(2.40)	(2.24)	(2.11)	$p=0.224$[†]
20	75.05	78.86	84.10	83.04	20.85
	(3.25)	(4.43)	(2.75)	(2.90)	$p=0.001$
30	55.33	58.29	65.05	65.72	15.01
	(4.15)	(5.88)	(4.72)	(5.11)	$p<0.001$
Average over all subsets	75.11	78.00	81.65	81.71	23.50
	(2.01)	(3.06)	(2.10)	(2.52)	$p<0.001$

[*]Standard deviation.
[†]F-probability.

Noise-Filtering Network

To implement this, we used a two-stage neural network approach by adopting a noise filtering network (NFN) as a preprocessor the PCN. The role of the NFN is to filter noises in the ESACF patterns and to recover patterns that are as clean as the triangular prototype patterns, as shown in Figure 35.3a.

In designing the NFN, we utilized the fact that a theoretical prototype pattern of ESACF without noise exists. This means that noisy ESACF patterns can be mapped with their corresponding prototype patterns as target outputs. Therefore the MLP used as a NFN had the same number of PEs in the input and output layers, as shown in Figure 35.5. In the NFN, we used only one hidden layer whose number of PEs was smaller than those in the input/output layers. The reduction in the hidden PE number will reduce the noise by abstracting the essential information about the triangular region in the input pattern and restoring it in the output layer. This process will recover the ESACF pattern that is closer to its prototype. To trace the effect of the number of hidden PEs, we examined four cases: 55, 60, 65, and 70 hidden PEs.

When we analyzed the performance of the NFN with 65 hidden PEs that produced the best result, the input noises of 10 percent, 20 percent, and 30 percent were significantly reduced to 0.67 percent, 2.11 percent, and 5.62 percent, respectively. This noise-filtering effect may result from the fact that our NFN was trained to remember only ESACF prototypes. To validate the use of the two-stage neural network approach, we tested the performance of PCN with the noise-filtered patterns by the NFN. Figure 35.6 shows the average performances of the PCN for the total test patterns (solid lines) and 30 percent noise-level test patterns (dotted lines) for each test set. We can observe that the performance of the PCN with the NFN is far superior to that of the PCN without the NFN. This performance gap becomes even larger for a 30 percent noise level. For total test patterns, the PCN with the NFN showed 89.05 percent average classification accuracy, as shown in Table 35.2.

Comparative Experiment between Two Feature Extractors

To understand the effect of the feature extractor, we applied the two-stage approach to the time-series data used earlier. When the PCN with the NFN learned from the ESACF patterns obtained from the simulated time

Figure 35.5

The Structure of the Noise-Filtering Network

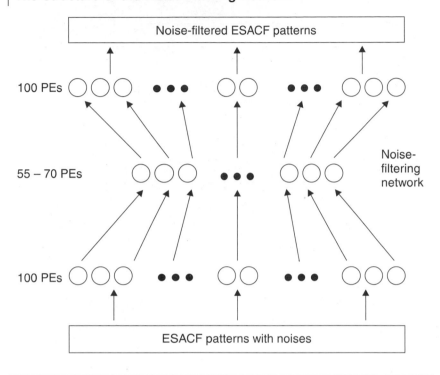

series, only three out of 54 test patterns indicated the incorrect ARMA order, attaining 94.4 percent classification accuracy, while the experiment with the ACF and the PACF showed 83.3 percent accuracy. This performance improvement can be explained as follows. To achieve better ANN classification performance, one can, if possible, use many feature extractors so that all the possible combinations of characteristics of input patterns are explicitly represented (Sejnowski and Kienker 1986). In this sense, it can be shown that the adoption of ESACF as a feature extractor increases the possibility of automating the ARMA modeling procedure because the ESACF table is the collection of many ACFs, each derived under different assumptions about the underlying process of the time series.

   To measure the contribution of the noise-filtering stage in the two-stage approach, we trained the PCN without the NFN and tested the perform-

Figure 35.6

The Effect of the Noise-Filtering Network with 65 Hidden PEs

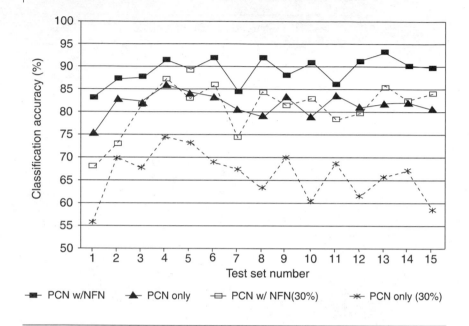

ance with the same data set. The learned PCN showed 87.0 percent classification accuracy. Thus, the net effect of noise filtering was 7.4 percent, while the effect of feature extractor was 3.7 percent. The reason for the significant impact of noise filtering is that the ESACF test patterns in this comparative experiment had 24.5 percent noise level on average.

In summary, the ESACF has better features for pattern classification than the ACF and PACF, but the classification of noisy ESACF patterns is not an easy task even if we use a powerful classifier such as ANN. To cope with this difficulty, we adopted the NFN as a preprocessor to improve the performance of the PCN. The two-stage neural network approach can increase the possibility of automating the ARMA modeling procedure, and human experts can at least reduce trial and error in their modeling by using the output of our approach as a starting point.

We have so far described the ANN approach in which MLPs were used as a pattern classifier for the ARMA model identification. In the

Table 35.2

Average Classification Performance Accuracy of PCN with NFN of 65 Hidden PEs as a Function of Training Sets

Noise Level in Test Subset (%)	Noise Level in Training Sets (%)				One-Way ANOVA Test: F(3,56)
	1st (0)	2nd (10)	3rd (20)	4th (30)	
10	96.48	97.81	97.71	96.67	1.76
	(2.14)*	(1.15)	(1.36)	(2.74)	$p=0.166$†
20	74.00	84.95	90.48	89.71	45.13
	(5.98)	(3.72)	(3.12)	(3.50)	$p<0.001$
30	52.09	62.57	68.86	80.76	60.35
	(5.37)	(6.56)	(5.77)	(5.32)	$p<0.001$
Average over all subsets	74.19	81.78	85.68	89.05	57.29
	(3.64)	(3.10)	(2.88)	(2.97)	$p<0.001$

* Standard deviation.
† F-probability.

next section, MLPs will be used as a fitting function from which the future values of time series are directly predicted.

TIME-SERIES FORECASTING WITH MULTILAYERED PERCEPTRONS

Basic Architecture

To specify a model for short-term time-series forecasting, three factors need to be determined, as follows:

1. Choose a lag space for the time series $\{z(t), t \in T\}$: the time-series-generating process can be modeled by expressing the value $z(t)$ as a function of its previous p values:

$$z(t) = f(\text{past } values)$$

$$= \begin{cases} \Re^p \to \Re^1 \\ \{z(t-1), z(t-2), ..., z(t-p)\} \to z(t) \end{cases}$$

2. Choose a fitting function that can characterize the behavior of the series. Linear, polynomial, and sigmoid functions are typical examples.

3. Choose a cost function that evaluates the adequacy of fit. The cost function reflects the assumption about measurement errors and statistics of the original data.

Given the lag space, fitting function, and cost function, the aim of time-series forecasting is to obtain forecasts using the parameters of a fitting function that can minimize the cost function. According to the approach of Lapedes and Farber (1987), the above statement can be easily reinterpreted in terms of the MLP, as shown in Figure 35.7. The lag space corresponds to the number of input PEs of a MLP, and the fitting function corresponds to the neural network model with the given activation functions and network structure. Assuming the Gaussian white-noise process for the errors, the cost function is usually measured by the total residual variance or the sum of the squared errors for a set of observations as follows:

$$\sum_{t \in T} (\text{target}(t) - \text{prediction }(t))^2 = \sum_{t \in T} (z(t) - \hat{z}(t))^2$$

where $z(t)$ is the observed value at time t and $\hat{z}(t)$ is the fitted value, which is the output of the MLP for time t. This type of cost function can be minimized by the back-propagation algorithm without any modification.

To prepare the training data set, the sliding-window technique is used. The window size is the same as the lag space of the MLP's input data. By sliding the window from the beginning to the end of the time series, the necessary input data set can be selected. The ANNs with this technique are commonly referred to as time-delay neural networks in the literature (Waibel et al. 1989).

The use of the sigmoid activation function means that the MLP can show the nonlinear behavior in the surface, while the ARMA models,

Figure 35.7

The Architecture of the MLP with One Hidden Layer as a Fitting Function for a Time Series

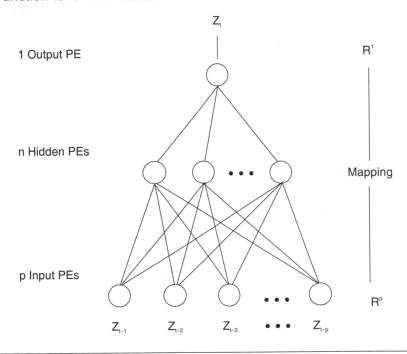

mentioned in previous sections, are linear systems. Therefore, a time series can be better fitted by the MLP. This assertion can be supported by recent research that proved the MLP can be more effectively used instead of multiple regression (Hornik et al. 1989; White 1989; Weigend et al. 1990). However, too many free parameters, which refer to the oversized MLP in terms of weights or connections, will allow the MLP to fit the time series very closely but will not necessarily lead to optimal prediction. If we consider the fact that the MA process is theoretically expressed by the infinite number of AR processes (Box and Jenkins 1976), we must be cautious in choosing the size of input vector for a MLP when the time series does not follow the pure AR process.

Minimal Networks

Since it is important to prevent the MLP from memorizing unnecessary noise in time series, we should use the smallest possible number of parameters for an adequate representation of time series, in the same way that the principle of parsimony plays an important role in ARMA modeling. To solve the overfitting problem, we explored two possible methods which give the MLP a modest parameterization through weight elimination.

The first technique is called *optimal brain damage*, which reduces the size of a learned MLP by selectively deleting weights that seem to have no effect on the generalization power of the MLP (Le Cun et al. 1990). However, this method inevitably involves iterative procedures to choose a reasonable structure of good generalization power. Furthermore, a human analyzer should determine the limiting value of weights to be deleted in each cycle.

The second technique is called *weight-decay*, which uses a cost function with an extra term for network complexity. The cost function can be minimized within the framework of the back-propagation algorithm (Hanson and Pratt 1989; Chauvin 1990). The idea begins with a sufficiently large network for the given problem, with an extra cost attached for each connection weight. Thus the cost function in the weight-decay method is the sum of the following two terms:

$$\sum_{t \in T} (\text{target}(t) - \text{prediction}(t))^2 + \lambda \sum_{i,j} \frac{w_{i,j}^2}{1 + w_{i,j}^2}$$

The first term is the standard sum of squared errors over the set of training data, while the second is the cost for each weight in the network. The parameter λ represents the relative importance of an extra cost term with respect to the standard cost term that determines the fitting performance of the network. If a given performance on the training set can be obtained with fewer weights, the cost function will encourage the reduction and eventually eliminate as many weights as possible. The behavior of the extra cost term and its derivative as a function of the size of weight are shown in Figure 35.8. The derivative of the cost function for the weights is nonmonotonic, and it shows a strong differential effect on small weights, pushing them toward zero, while the large and near-zero weight values are not significantly affected.

Figure 35.8

The Cost of a Weight and Its Derivative in the Weight-Decay Method

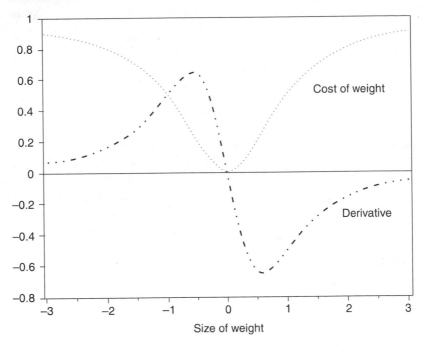

The weight-decay method has two drawbacks: The learning process slows down significantly, and fine-tuning of the learning parameters is required to avoid catastrophic effects in forecasting performance. However, unlike the optimal brain-damage technique, this method does not require human intervention in finding the minimal network for a specific time series. Therefore, we adopted the weight-decay method with the following preconditions:

1. Choose a sufficiently large size of the MLP.

2. Train the MLP with a standard cost function until the MLP learns sufficiently from the time series.

3. Train the learned MLP with an extra complexity term until the error begins to increase.

4.   After deleting the weights of near-zero values, slightly train the MLP once again with a standard cost function for performance tuning.

Deleting a weight can be achieved by freezing it to zero. According to our experiments, it became apparent that the coefficient λ to the complexity term should be set to an extremely small value, such as 0.001, for our test data sets.

Recurrent Neural Networks

The weight-decay method usually requires a considerable amount of input space because the initial network must be sufficiently large. Large input space implies that the MLP learns unnecessary noise in a time series. Therefore, as an alternative for minimal networks, we adopted a recurrent network suggested by Elman (1988). The recurrent network is a restricted extension of feedforward MLP that can be trained by the backpropagation algorithm.

Figure 35.9 shows the recurrent network with a context vector. The activations in the hidden PEs at time $t-1$ are copied into the context vector, which is the input to the network for time t. This is equivalent to having the hidden PEs completely and recurrently connected, and back-propagating one step in time along the recurrent connections. Therefore, the reaction of the network to the new input is a function of both the new input and the preceding context. What is stored in the context vector at any given time is a compressed trace of all preceding inputs, and this compressed trace influences the manner in which the network reacts to each succeeding input.

The above characteristic of the context vector agrees with the basic assumption of time-series analysis and is very helpful, especially when the fitted ARMA model for a time series includes a MA process. Since the MA process can be represented by an infinite order of AR process, we may use a very large size of MLP in order to retain the history of all past data. However, smaller window size data can be used with a context vector, resulting in a small network and thus reducing the overfitting problem.

Learning the Time Series

As mentioned above, the three types of MLPs—the basic MLP, the minimal network with the weight-decay method, and the recurrent network—are trained with each of the three well-known time series that have served

Figure 35.9

The Architecture of Elman's Recurrent Network

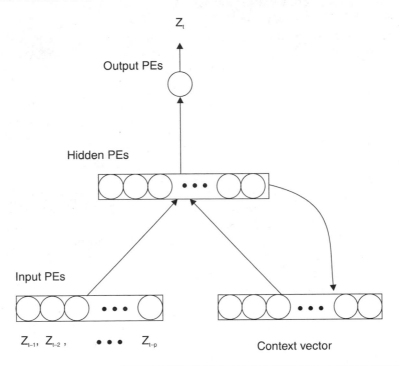

as benchmarks in the forecasting literature. The series are fitted with two pure ARMA models and one mixed ARMA model (Box and Jenkins 1976; Pandit and Wu 1980) and are as follows:

Case 1. Annual Wolf sunspot numbers from 1749 through 1924. This series consists of 176 observations and follows the pure AR(2) process.

Case 2. Daily IBM common stock closing prices from 17 May 1961 through 2 November 1962. This series consists of 369 observations. The first differenced series is fitted as the pure MA(1) model.

Case 3. Chemical process concentration readings. This series consists of 197 observations and follows the mixed ARMA(1, 1) process.

and are Before training the MLPs, we linearly compressed each data set into (0.1, 0.9) by dividing the raw data by the difference between the maximum and minimum values in the data. To validate the performance of the learned MLPs, we split the entire data set into two: a *training set* that was used for determining the values of weights and a *prediction set* that acted as future values to estimate the expected performance in the future. We used the last 10 observations of each time series as the prediction set.

We utilized various sizes of window on each time series to determine the proper input lag space based on the forecasting accuracy. All the MLPs were trained with the learning rate $\eta = 0.1$ and the momentum term $\alpha = 0.9$ in the back-propagation learning process. However, the momentum term was not used in the weight-elimination process of the weight-decay method. During the performance tuning, $\eta = 0.01$ and $\alpha = 0.9$ were used. This uniform application of learning parameters, however, may worsen the performance of the MLP. Figure 35.10 shows the convergence behaviors of some selected structures of MLP for the IBM stock price data.

The residual sum of squares (SSE) gives an indication of how well a model fits the data, but it is difficult to interpret the SSE in isolation as an absolute measure. What is needed is a simple yardstick that enables us to assess the relative size of the SSE. The coefficient of determination, R^2, is always presented to measure the goodness of fit. However, there is no general agreement as to which yardstick should be used in time-series analysis. According to Harvey's suggestion (1984), which is based on the random walk theory, a better measure for time-series data can be obtained by replacing the observation with their first differences:

$$R_D^2 = 1 - SSE / \sum_{t=2}^{T} (\Delta z(t) - \overline{\Delta z})$$

where $\overline{\Delta z}$ is the mean of the first differenced series. We adopted both R^2 and R_D^2 as a measure of goodness of fit. The training results are summarized in Tables 35.3–35.5, together with the test results on the prediction data sets to compare the performances of various structures of MLPs.

Test and Discussions

During the training of each MLP, we tested the forecasting performance at each 1000 epochs. In Tables 35.3–35.5, the number of epochs in the column of training results represents when the learned MLP showed the

Figure 35.10

Convergence Behaviors of the MLPs that Learn from IBM Stock Price Data

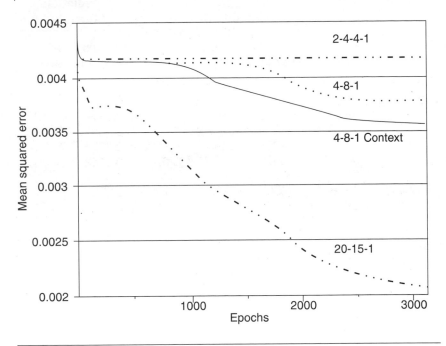

best performance in a given network structure. The results with the weight-decay method were obtained by applying the method to the learned MLP, which showed the better performance among the network structures of "one hidden layer." We used two measures of forecasting performance. One is the mean absolute percentage errors (MAPE); the other is the relative variance, defined as the average sum of the squared error divided by the variance of the prediction set. These measures are used to compare the forecasting results from MLPs with those of ARMA models.

As shown in Table 35.3, the MLPs outperform the ARMA model when the time series follows the pure AR process. For the Wolf sunspot numbers, even the MLPs without the weight-decay method produced better fits and prediction results than the AR(2) process. However, when the time series includes the MA process, the results

Table 35.3

Training and Test Results of Case I

Network Structure		Epochs	R^2	R_D^2	Relative Variance	MAPE
			Training Results		Prediction Results	
Two hidden layers	2–4–4–1	1000	0.8456	0.6119	0.4274	0.1996
One hidden layer	8–6–1	3000	0.8986	0.7292	0.3319	0.2125
	12–8–1	3000	0.9342	0.8240	0.2882	0.1797
	20–15–1	4000	0.9747	0.9326	0.3237	0.1722
	4–8–1	5000	0.8781	0.6747	0.3142	0.1950
Weight-decay	12–8–1	(4500)	0.8951	0.7200	0.2733	0.1619
	20–15–1	(5500)	0.9308	0.8152	0.3103	0.1741
Recurrent network	2–3–1	1000	0.8543	0.6111	0.3419	0.1840
	4–6–1	2000	0.9010	0.7357	0.1985	0.1534
	4–8–1	4000	0.9207	0.7883	0.2645	0.1476
ARMA(2,0)		—	0.8035	0.5107	0.4797	0.4782

are less conclusive. The weight-decay method worsened the performance for IBM stock price data, as shown in Table 35.4, although it slightly improved the performance of the MLP for the data of chemical process concentration readings, as shown in Table 35.5. The recurrent network performed very well for all the three time series. However, with only three data sets tested, more empirical tests are necessary to establish a formal guideline in selecting the correct network architecture. In this section we addressed only the issue of the ANN architecture, but there are other subjects that deserve future research, as the forecasting performance of the ANN will also depend on training methods, amount of training data, and the characteristics of time series such as seasonality, heteroskedasticity, or non-Gaussian errors.

Table 35.4

Training and Test Results of Case II

Network Structure		Training Results			Prediction Results	
	Epochs	R^2	R_D^2	Relative Variance	MAPE
Two hidden layers	2–4–4–1	4000	0.9804	−0.469	1.4357	0.0509
One hidden layer	8–6–1	3000	0.9877	−0.002	0.9433	0.0350
	12–8–1	5000	0.9936	0.0328	0.6872	0.0266
	20–15–1	4000	0.9974	0.0847	0.5250	0.0213
	4–8–1	5000	0.9908	−0.185	1.0556	0.0439
Weight-decay	12–8–1	(6500)	0.8048	0.0151	0.6958	0.0277
	20–15–1	(5500)	0.8546	0.0824	0.4503	0.0248
Recurrent network	2–4–1	3000	0.9943	0.2111	0.3798	0.0185
	4–8–1	5000	0.9934	0.1869	0.4147	0.0199
ARMA(0,1)		—	0.9925	0.0192	0.4315	0.0216

CONCLUSIONS

We developed two ANN approaches to analyze the univariate time series and empirically proved the effectiveness of the approaches. In the first approach, the MLP was used as a pattern classifier to automate the ARMA model-identification step. By using the MLP, we can quickly identify the ARMA models from a time series under consideration and can obtain forecasts using well-established estimation procedures whose functions can be found in statistical packages such as SPSS, SAS, or IMSL. The ANN approach ensures that a time series can be fitted with the appropriate ARMA model with approximately a 90 percent confidence level if the noise-filtering network is used.

Second, MLP is used as a fitting function to predict the future value of a time series. Based on the accuracy of the one-step-ahead forecasts, we compared the performance of three alternative network architectures:

Table 35.5

Training and Test Results of Case III

Network Structure		Epochs	R^2	R_D^2	Relative Variance	MAPE
			Training Results		Prediction Results	
Two hidden layers	2–4–4–1	3000	0.8448	0.5369	0.3733	0.0231
One hidden layer	12–8–1	4000	0.9712	0.8458	0.2378	0.0154
	20–15–1	5000	0.9801	0.9184	0.2107	0.0163
	4–8–1	5000	0.8970	0.6708	0.3142	0.0225
Weight–decay	12–8–1	(5500)	0.9451	0.8276	0.2357	0.0174
	20–15–1	(6500)	0.9387	0.7744	0.2723	0.0205
Recurrent network	2–4–1	3000	0.9524	0.9223	0.2232	0.0148
	4–8–1	3000	0.9663	0.9460	0.1907	0.0141
ARMA(1,1)		—	0.9392	0.9293	0.2415	0.0169

the ordinary MLP, the minimal network with the weight-decay method, and Elman's recurrent network. Although all three approaches needed iterative training and validation to select the best lag space as input and the number of hidden PEs, the recurrent networks with the context vector performed best in the cases of noisy time series. The result is an indication that the context vector can alleviate the overfitting problem. In order to increase the possibility of obtaining reliable forecasts, we are currently trying to discover whether the result of ARMA model identification can be used as a starting point for selecting the window size of recurrent networks.

REFERENCES

Akaike, H. 1974. A New Look at the Statistical Model Identification. *IEEE Transactions on Automatic Control*, AC-19. pp. 716–23.

Benguin, J. M., C. Gourieroux, and A. Monfort. 1980. Identification of a Mixed Autoregressive Moving Average Process: The Corner Method. In *Time Series*. ed. O.D. Anderson. Amsterdam: North Holland, pp. 423–36.

Box, G. E. P., and G.M. Jenkins. 1976. *Time Series Analysis—Forecasting and Control*. San Francisco: Holden-Day.

Chauvin, Y. 1989. A Backpropagation Algorithm with Optimal Use of Hidden Units. In *Advances in Neural Network Information Processing Systems*, Vol. 1. San Mateo, CA: Morgan Kaufmann, pp. 519–526.

Elman, J. L. 1988. *Finding Structure in Time*. Technical Report, CRL #8801. Center for Research in Language. University of California, San Diego.

Gorman, R. P., and T.J. Sejnowski. 1988. Analysis of Hidden Units in a Layered Network Trained to Classify Sonar Targets. *Neural Networks* 1, pp. 75–89.

Gray, H. L., A.G. Kelly, and D.D. McIntire. 1978. A New Approach to ARMA Modeling. *Communications in Statistics* B, no. 7, pp. 1–77.

Hanson S. J., and L.Y. Pratt. 1989. Some Comparison of Constraints for Minimal Network Construction with Backpropagation. In *Advances in Neural Network Information Processing Systems*, Vol. 1. San Mateo, CA: Morgan Kaufmann, pp. 177–85.

Harvey, A. C. 1984. A Unified View of Statistical Forecasting Procedures. *Journal of Forecasting* 3, pp. 245–75.

Hill, G. W., and D. Woodworth. 1980. Automatic Box–Jenkins Forecasting. *Journal of Operational Research Society* 31, pp. 413–22.

Hornik, K., M. Stinchcombe, and H. White. 1989. Multilayer Feedforward Networks Are Universal Approximators. *Neural Networks* 2, pp. 359–66.

Jhee, W. C., J.K. Lee, and K.C. Lee. 1992. A Neural Network Approach for the Identification of Box–Jenkins Model. *Network: Computation in Neural Systems* 3, no. 3, pp. 323–37.

Kang, C. A., D.D. Bedworth, and D.A. Rollier. 1982. Automatic Identification of ARIMA Time Series. *IIE Transactions* 14, pp. 156–66.

Lapedes, A., and R. Farber. 1987. *Nonlinear Signal Processing Using Neural Networks: Prediction and System Modeling*. Los Almos National Laboratory Report La-ur-87-2662.

Le Cun, Y., J.S. Denker, and S.A. Solla. 1990. Optimal Brain Damage. In *Advances in Neural Network Information Processing Systems*, Vol. 2. San Mateo, CA: Morgan Kaufmann, pp. 598–605.

Lee, J. K., and W.C. Jhee. 1992. A Two-Stage Neural Network Approach for ARMA Model Identification with ESACF. *Decision Support Systems*.

Lippmann, R. P. 1987. An Introduction to Computing with Neural Nets. *IEEE ASSP Magazine* 4, pp. 4–22.

Pandit, S. M. and S.M. Wu. 1980. *Time Series and Forecasting with Applications*. New York: John Wiley.

Pao, Y. H. 1988. *Pattern Recognition and Neural Networks*. Reading, MA: Addison-Wesley.

Parzen, E. 1982. ARARMA Models for Time Series Analysis and Forecasting. *Journal of Forecasting* 1, pp. 67–82.

Rumelhart, D. E., G.E. Hinton, and R.J. Williams. 1986. Learning Internal Representations by Error Propagation. In *Parallel Distributed Processing: Explorations in the Microstructure of Cognition*, Vol. I: *Foundations*. eds. D.E. Rumelhart and J.L. McClelland. Cambridge, MA: MIT Press.

Schwarz, G. 1978. Estimating the Dimension of a Model. *The Annals of Statistics* 6, no. 2, pp. 461–4.

Sejnowski, T. J., and P.K. Kienker. 1986. Learning Symmetry Groups with Hidden Units: Beyond the Perceptron. *Physica* 22D, pp. 260–75.

Tsay, R. S., and G.C. Tiao. 1984. Consistent Estimates of Autoregressive Parameters and Extended Sample Autocorrelation Function for Stationary and Nonstationary ARMA Models. *Journal of American Statistical Association* 79, pp. 84–96.

Vandale, W. 1983. *Applied Time Series and Box–Jenkins Models*. New York: Academic Press.

Waibel, A., T. Hanazawa, G. Hinton, K. Shikano, and K. Lang. 1989. Phoneme Recognition Using Time-Delay Neural Networks. *IEEE Transactions on ASSP* 37, no. 3, pp. 328–39.

Werbos, P. J. 1988. Generalization of Backpropagation with Application to a Recurrent Gas Market Model. *Neural Networks* 1, no. 4, pp. 339–56.

Weigend, A. S., D.E. Rumelhart, and B.A. Huberman. 1990. Back-Propagation, Weight-Elimination and Time Series Prediction. In *Connectionist Models:* Proceeding of the 1990 Summer School. eds. D.S. Touretzsky, J.L. Elman, and T.J. Sejnowski, pp. 105–16.

Wheelwright, S. C., and S. Makridakis. 1985. *Forecasting Methods for Management.* New York: John Wiley.

White, H. 1988. Economic Prediction Using Neural Networks: The Case of IBM Daily Stock Returns. *IEEE 2nd International Conference on Neural Networks*, Vol. 2. San Diego, California, pp. 451–58.

Woodward, W. A., and H.L. Gray. 1981. On the Relationship between S-Array and the Box–Jenkins Method of ARMA Model Identification. *Journal of American Statistical Association* 76, pp. 579–87.

36

NEURAL NETWORK MODELS AS AN ALTERNATIVE TO REGRESSION

Leorey Marquez, Tim Hill, Reginald Worthley, and William Remus

INTRODUCTION

Linear statistical models are well established and useful tools in quantitative analysis. A survey by Ledbetter and Cox[1] ranks regression analysis as the most popular of all quantitative methods used in business and finance.

Artificial neural network (ANN) models provide a viable alternative to classical regression models. According to Wasserman, these models can learn from experience, can generalize and "see through" noise and distortion, and can abstract essential characteristics in the presence of irrelevant data. According to Lippman,[2] these models provide a high degree of robustness and fault tolerance. In addition, artificial neural network

© 1991, IEEE. A modified version of a paper is reprinted with permission from *Proceedings of the IEEE 24th Annual Hawaii International Conference on Systems Sciences*, vol. VI, pp. 129–35.

models can find the right transformations for variables,[3] detect weak linear relationships, and deal with outliers.

In spite of the popularity of neural networks, these assertions have not been tested. In this chapter, we report a study that filled this void. Our general approach was to generate data representing common functional forms encountered in regression modeling and then to compare neural networks to regression models using that data.

EXPERIMENTAL DESIGN

The purpose of the experiment described below is to evaluate the performance neural networks in estimating simple functional forms. To perform this kind of research, social scientists advocate testing alternative models side by side in critical experiments.[4] There is precedent for this kind of study using neural networks,[5,6] and in statistics.[7-9] Thus, our experiment is a side-by-side comparison of two competing methods: neural networks and regression.

To be able to generalize to many settings, the estimates were compared in 27 different conditions. The study examines three functional forms, three noise levels, and three common sample sizes for the data set as described below. Since the true underlying functional form is often unknown, we also examined the performance of misspecified regression models with the true model and neural networks. We chose the most logical misspecifications as would be predicted by the ladder of reexpression; this technique is described in more detail in Exhibit 26.1. The details of this simulation study will be described below.

The performance of the regression models and neural network models were evaluated across the three functional forms commonly encountered in regression analysis. These are the linear model ($Y = B_0 + B_1 \times X + e$), the logarithmic model ($Y = B_0 + B_1 \times \log(X) + e$), and the reciprocal model ($Y = B_0 + B_1/X + e$). These will be termed the true functional form, or true model.

For each true model, 100 samples of n (x,y) pairs each (to be used for model estimation) were generated. Each sample of n (x,y) pairs was used to compute the parameters for the three regression estimates, one based on the true model and the others based on the nearest models on the ladder of reexpression. The last two models represent "close" but misspecified regression estimates of the true model. The same data were

Exhibit 36.1

The Ladder of Re-Expression

Mosteller and Tukey[10] introduced the concept of a ladder of reexpressions as a tool to straighten out simple curves. The basic notion starts with the observation that most simple curves can be represented by a relation of the form $Y = X^p$. When p takes on the values such as 3, 2, 1, –1, – 2, and – 3, a series of curves appears as a ladderlike formation.

Given a set of points from an unknown curve, the idea is to move up and down the ladder searching for the expression that will transform the points into a straight line. For example, given a set of data points based on the relation $Y = X^2$ ($p = 2$), the correct model to use would be $Y = B_0 + B_1 \times X^2 + e$. However, since this correct model is not usually known, estimates based on other models might be used. It would be expected that the model $Y = B_0 + B_1 \times X + e$ ($p = 1$) would provide better estimates than $Y = B_0 + B_1/X + e$ ($p = -1$) since the first lies closer to the true relation in the ladder than the second model.

Since the value $p = 0$ leads to a constant, Mosteller and Tukey use the symbol # instead of 0; it represents $Y = \log(X)$. This was an important addition since the logarithm transformation is widely used. In this scheme, the series can be thought of as coming from the $\int X^{(p-1)} dX$. For positive values of X, the curves are monotonically increasing and concave upward for $p > 1$, straight for $p = 1$, and monotonically decreasing and concave downward for $p < 1$.

In this simulation study, we generated data based on the linear ($p = 1$), log ($p = $#), and reciprocal ($p = -1$) functional forms. When displayed using the ladder of reexpressions, there would be three curves in the middle. If we also added the two curves adjacent to each functional form, we would also have two "close" misspecifications of a true functional form. Since the p values of the true functional forms are 1, #, and –1, the additional adjacent curves needed are 2 and –2. The five models and their corresponding values of p in the ladder of reexpression are summarized as follows:

P	Model		Description
2	$Y = B_0 + B_1 \times X^2$	$+ e$	Squared model
–1	$Y = B_0 + B_1/X$	$+ e$	Reciprocal model
#	$Y = B_0 + B_1 \times \log(X)$	$+ e$	Log model
–1	$Y = B_0 + B_1/X$	$+ e$	Log model
–2	$Y = B_0 + B_1/X^2$	$+ e$	Squared-Reciprocal model

also used to generate the neural network estimates. The true, misspecified, and neural network models were then evaluated using an additional 100 data pairs set generated for testing the model.

In this study, we varied the size of the error. Three different R^2 values were used; these were 0.30, 0.60, and 0.90. These three values represent weak, medium, and strong relationships. We also varied the sample size (n) used to derive the regression models and train the neural network; we used samples of size 15, 30, or 60. These sample sizes were chosen to represent the small, medium, and large samples that characterize most regression studies. The number of replications and the sample sizes are consistent with the numbers used in the prior simulation studies.[7-9]

As noted earlier, the models were evaluated in terms of their forecasting accuracy using a test sample of 100. Our measure of performance was that most commonly used by forecasters: the mean absolute percentage error (MAPE). To compare across the conditions, the paired t-test was used. Given Wasserman's assertion that neural networks were able to see through noise and distortion and to perform data transformations automatically, we would expect the neural networks to perform as well as the true regression model in each condition.

ESTIMATING THE NEURAL NETWORKS

An important part of the above experiment was the proper estimation of the regression and neural networks. The regression analysis was straightforward, but the neural network estimation was more complex. In this section, we will detail the latter process.

The neural networks are based on the back-propagation learning algorithm.[11,12] These models were obtained using the Rumelhart and McClelland[11] software written in C.

We experimented with many parameter values but ultimately settled on the Rumelhart and McClelland defaults since other parameter combinations gave little or no improvement. The only parameter that was modified was momentum. We used a momentum value of 0.8 instead of the default of 0.9 since preliminary tests showed that this value resulted in a slightly improved overall performance.

Back-propagation will minimize the least-squared error if (1) the model does not get trapped in a local optimal, and (2) there are an adequate number of nodes in the hidden layer. To assure that the error is minimized, it is customary to build neural networks with one hidden layer and keep doubling the number of nodes until the error is no longer reduced.[13] In the preliminary tests, we experimented with networks containing 3, 6, 12, and 24 nodes in the single hidden layer. We found the improvement in error after six nodes insignificant, while the processing speed and convergence rate were significantly worse.

The neural network weights were adjusted following the presentation of each (x,y) pattern. Convergence was within 800 training periods or epochs. The neural network estimates used the structure 1-6-1; that is, one input node, six nodes in the hidden layer, and one output node. It is worth noting that the CPU time required by the regression models was in seconds whereas the neural network models required tens of minutes.

THE RESULTS OF THE SIMULATION

Tables 36.1 to 36.3 present the performance of the estimates of each of the three true models; the measure of performance is mean absolute percentage errors (MAPE). Each table gives the results for the nine possible combinations of sample sizes and R^2 values for one of the true models.

Table 36.1 shows the results of the simulation study when the true model was linear. The results include the performance of the linear model, the performance of the two nearest misspecified models on the ladder of reexpression (the log and squared models), and the neural networks. In general, the neural networks fit this true model well; the maximum difference in MAPE was 2 percent, and the median difference in MAPE .62 percent. However, the difference in MAPE was lowest for small sample sizes and low noise where there were no significant differences. Overall, the misspecified models also fit the data well. At their worst, the neural networks seemed to perform as well as the misspecified models.

Table 36.2 shows the results of the simulation study when the true model was logarithmic. The results include the performance of the true logarithmic model, the performance of the two nearest misspecified models on the ladder of reexpression (the reciprocal and linear models), and the neural networks. In general, the neural networks fit this true model well; the maximum difference in MAPE was 4 percent, and the median difference in MAPE was .58 percent. However, the difference in MAPE was lowest for small sample sizes and low noise. In all cases, the misspecified models did not fit the data as well as the neural networks.

Table 36.1

MAPE Paired Difference t-test for Model 1 (Linear)

H0: delta MAPE $\leq$ 0   vs.   H1: delta MAPE > 0
* z(.05) = 1.645   **z(.01) = 2.33   Test sample = 100

Training Sample	True Model: Alternate Model:	Linear Quadratic	Linear Log	Linear ANN
n = 15	R-square = .30			
	MAPE (true model)	15.68	15.68	15.68
	MAPE (alt. model)	15.74	15.82	15.38
	Mean diff.	0.06	0.14	−0.30
	Std. dev. of diff.	0.26	0.26	1.55
	Paired t-value	2.44 **	5.34 **	−1.93
	R-square = .60			
	MAPE (true model)	11.66	11.66	11.66
	MAPE (alt. model)	11.80	11.95	11.70
	Mean diff.	0.14	0.29	0.04
	Std. dev. of diff.	0.29	0.30	1.33
	Paired t-value	4.84 **	9.75 **	0.32
	R-square = .90			
	MAPE (true model)	5.59	5.59	5.59
	MAPE (alt. model)	6.12	6.16	7.98
	Mean diff.	0.52	0.57	2.39
	Std. dev. of diff.	0.40	0.52	2.13
	Paired t-value	13.21 **	10.89 **	11.24 **
n = 30	R-square = .30			
	MAPE (true model)	14.44	14.44	14.44
	MAPE (alt. model)	14.29	14.70	14.83
	Mean diff.	−0.15	0.26	0.39
	Std. dev. of diff.	0.14	0.16	0.70
	Paired t-value	−10.55	15.87 **	5.50 **
	R-square = .60			
	MAPE (true model)	11.59	11.59	11.59
	MAPE (alt. model)	11.73	11.63	12.49
	Mean diff.	0.14	0.04	0.89
	Std. dev. of diff.	0.12	0.18	0.59
	Paired t-value	11.54 **	2.29 *	15.26 **

Table 36.1

(concluded)

Training Sample	True Model: Alternate Model:	Linear Quadratic	Linear Log	Linear ANN
	R-square = .90			
	MAPE (ture model)	5.70	5.70	5.70
	MAPE (alt. model)	6.44	6.31	6.90
	Mean diff.	0.74	0.61	1.20
	Std. dev. of diff.	0.18	0.32	0.41
	Paired t-value	40.89 **	19.31 **	29.29 **
n = 60	R-square = .30			
	Mape (true model)	13.87	13.87	18.87
	MAPE (alt. model)	14.19	13.69	14.34
.	Mean diff	0.32	−0.18	0.46
	Std. dev. of diff.	0.09	0.14	0.34
	Paired t-value	36.84 **	−12.78	13.60 **
	R-square - .60			
	MAPE (true model)	10.26	10.25	10.25
	MAPE (alt. model)	10.71	10.50	10.87
	Mean diff.	0.46	0.25	0.62
	Std. dev. of diff.	0.16	0.22	0.29
	Paired t-value	29.03 **	11.10 **	21.67 **
	R-square .90			
	MAPE (true model)	5.20	5.20	5.20
	MAPE (alt. model)	5.68	5.67	5.97
	Mean diff.	0.48	0.47	0.76
	Std. dev. of diff.	0.11	0.27	0.37
	Paired t-value	41.77 **	17.36 **	20.55 **

Table 36.3 shows the results of the simulation study when the true model was reciprocal. The results include the performance of the true reciprocal model, the performance of the two nearest misspecified models on the ladder of reexpression (the reciprocal of the square of X and log models), and the neural networks. In general, again the neural networks fit this true model well; the maximum difference in MAPE was 3 percent, and the median difference in MAPE was .48 percent. The difference in

Table 36.2

MAPE Paired Difference t-test for Model 2 (Log)

H0: delta MAPE ≤ 0   vs.   H1: delta MAPE > 0
* z(.05) = 1.645   **z(.01) = 2.33   Test sample = 100

Training Sample	True Model: Alternate Model:	Log Linear	Log Reciprocal	Log ANN
n = 15	R-square = .30			
	MAPE (true model)	15.68	15.68	15.68
	MAPE (alt. model)	17.49	17.38	15.60
	Mean diff.	1.82	1.70	−0.08
	Std. dev. of diff.	2.24	1.20	1.73
	Paired t-value	8.11 **	14.13 **	−0.45
	R-square = .60			
	MAPE (true model)	11.66	11.66	11.66
	MAPE (alt. model)	14.89	14.96	12.24
	Mean diff.	3.23	3.31	0.58
	Std. dev. of diff.	1.96	1.56	1.38
	Paired t-value	16.44 **	21.24 **	4.22 **
	R-square = .90			
	MAPE (true model)	5.59	5.59	5.59
	MAPE (alt. model)	11.72	11.61	9.72
	Mean diff.	6.13	6.02	4.13
	Std. dev. of diff.	1.59	2.65	2.21
	Paired t-value	38.60 **	22.74 **	18.67 **
n = 30	R-square = .30			
	MAPE (true model)	14.44	14.44	14.44
	MAPE (alt. model)	14.70	15.94	14.12
	Mean diff.	0.26	1.50	−0.32
	Std. dev. of diff.	0.68	0.65	0.46
	Paired t-value	3.85 **	23.15 **	−6.90
	R-square = .60			
	MAPE (true model)	11.59	11.59	11.59
	MAPE (alt. model)	14.08	13.78	12.11
	Mean diff.	2.48	2.19	0.52
	Std. dev. of diff.	0.81	1.44	0.39
	Paired t-value	30.64 **	15.24 **	13.24 **

Table 36.2

(concluded)

Training Sample	True Model: Alternate Model:	Log Linear	Log Reciprocal	Log ANN
	R-square = .90			
	MAPE (true model)	5.70	5.70	5.70
	MAPE (alt. model)	11.35	12.24	7.83
	Mean diff.	5.66	6.54	2.13
	Std. dev. of diff.	0.79	2.07	0.62
	Paired t-value	71.24 **	31.63 **	34.16 **
$n = 60$	R-square = .30			
	MAPE (true model)	13.87	13.87	13.87
	MAPE (alt. model)	16.00	15.06	14.57
	Mean diff.	2.13	1.19	0.70
	Std. dev. of diff.	0.46	0.64	0.40
	Paired t-value	45.95 **	18.49 **	17.39 **
	R-square = .60			
	MAPE (true model)	10.25	10.25	10.25
	MAPE (alt. model)	13.86	13.36	11.10
	Mean diff.	3.61	3.11	0.85
	Std. dev. of diff.	0.70	0.74	0.38
	Paired t-value	51.79 **	42.29 **	22.19 **
	R-square = .90			
	MAPE (true model)	5.20	5.20	5.20
	MAPE (alt. model)	10.59	9.76	5.76
	Mean diff.	5.39	4.56	0.56
	Std. dev. of diff.	0.70	1.18	0.29
	Paired t-value	77.13 **	38.46 **	19.17 **

MAPE was lowest for small sample size and low noise. In all cases, the misspecified models fit the data better than the neural networks although all performed well.

Table 36.3

MAPE Paired Difference t-test for Model 3 (Reciprocal)

H0: delta MAPE $\leq$ 0   vs.   H1: delta MAPE > 0
* z(.05) = 1.645   **z(.01) = 2.33   Test sample = 100

Training Sample	True Model: Alternate Model:	Reciprocal Log	Reciprocal Sq-Recip	Reciprocal ANN
$n = 15$	R-square = .30			
	MAPE (true model)	15.68	15.68	15.68
	MAPE (alt. model)	15.82	15.74	15.67
	Mean diff.	0.14	0.06	−0.01
	Std. dev. of diff.	0.26	0.26	1.67
	Paired t-value	5.34 **	2.44 **	− 0.04
	R-square = .60			
	MAPE (true model)	11.66	11.66	11.66
	MAPE (alt. model)	11.95	11.80	12.20
	Mean diff.	0.29	0.14	0.54
	Std. dev. of diff.	0.30	0.29	1.71
	Paired t-value	9.75 **	4.84 **	3.15 **
	R-square = .90			
	MAPE (true model)	5.59	5.59	5.59
	MAPE (alt. model)	6.16	6.12	8.75
	Mean diff.	0.57	0.52	3.15
	Std. dev. of diff.	0.52	0.40	2.53
	Paired t-value	10.89 **	13.21 **	12.45 **
$n = 30$	R-square = .30			
	MAPE (true model)	14.44	14.44	14.44
	MAPE (alt. model)	14.70	14.29	14.76
	Mean diff.	0.26	−0.15	0.32
	Std. dev. of diff.	0.16	0.14	0.71
	Paired t-value	15.87 **	−10.55	4.47 **
	R-square = .60			
	MAPE (true model)	11.59	11.59	11.59
	MAPE (alt. model)	11.63	11.73	12.43
	Mean diff.	0.04	0.14	0.84
	Std. dev. of diff.	0.18	0.12	0.55
	Paired t-value	2.29 *	11.54 **	15.33 **

Table 36.3

(concluded)

Training Sample	True Model: Alternate Model:	Reciprocal Log	Reciprocal Sq-Recip	Reciprocal ANN
	R-square = .90			
	MAPE (true model)	5.70	5.70	5.70
	MAPE (alt. model)	6.31	6.44	7.15
	Mean diff.	0.61	0.74	1.45
	Std. dev. of diff.	0.32	0.18	0.45
	Paired t-value	19.31 **	40.89 **	32.26 **
n = 60	*R*-square = .30			
	MAPE (true model)	13.87	13.87	13.87
	MAPE (alt. model)	13.69	14.19	14.28
	Mean diff.	−0.18	0.32	0.41
	Std. dev. of diff.	0.14	0.09	0.36
	Paired t-value	−12.78	36.84 **	11.36 **
	R-square = .60			
	MAPE (true model)	10.25	10.25	10.25
	MAPE (alt. model)	10.50	10.71	10.74
	Mean diff.	0.25	0.46	0.49
	Std. dev. of diff.	0.22	0.16	0.21
	Paired t-value	11.10 **	29.03 **	23.21 **
	R-square = .90			
	MAPE (true model)	5.20	5.20	5.20
	MAPE (alt. model)	5.67	5.68	6.00
	Mean diff.	0.47	0.48	0.80
	Std. dev. of diff.	0.27	0.11	0.34
	Paired t-value	17.36 **	41.77 **	23.34 **

DISCUSSION

The overall MAPEs for the neural network models were very good. Also, the median differences in MAPE between the neural networks and true models were generally around .6 percent. Even when there were statistically significant differences between the true and neural network model, these differences may not have held any practical significance. The level of MAPE encountered is considered excellent in most real-world situations. In some of the cases (usually low sample size and low noise), the t-test indicated that the neural network estimates did not differ significantly from the true model.

It is clear from this experiment that the nature of the true functional form is an important consideration in the use of neural network models. It was shown that the neural network model estimated the linear model best. However, neural networks were comparatively successful when compared with misspecifications of the log model but not with the reciprocal model. This means that one cannot just build a neural network model and expect it always to perform best.

The size of the samples used specified the amount of data available in defining the underlying relationship, while the magnitude of the R^2 value described the amount of error or noise in the data. These two variables specified the level at which the underlying relationship is defined by the data. The results show that the neural network models perform reasonably close to the true model when the relationship is not sufficiently defined.

This study only considered linear models, log models, and reciprocal models in the role of the true model. Other important transformation relationships need to be tested. Also combinations of these transformations will have to be examined. The R^2 value used in this study is one way of introducing noise into the model. It would be interesting to examine the impact of outlying or highly influential data on these models. Other considerations worthy of examination include the effects of multicollinearity and heteroschedasticity on neural networks.

This study has shown that neural network models possess considerable potential as an alternative to regression models. Within the limitations of this study, neural network models have been shown to be especially useful in modeling data that do not strongly exhibit underlying relationships between the variables. The study also showed that a neural network's capacity to continuously learn and self-transform as the true relationship becomes more defined depends to some extent on the underlying relationship.

The potential offered by neural network models is tempered by several basic problems. Guidelines are needed to deal with the enormous number of choices and decisions the model builder has to make. Without these guidelines, the procedure for selecting the structure of a neural network will continue to be essentially a trial-and-error process. The selection of the training parameters also remains a trial-and-error process. Even the trial-and-error process itself can be done interactively or in batch mode. It is hoped that more systematic guidelines will be developed soon.

This situation can be viewed both as a blessing and a misfortune. On one hand, it gives the researcher a wide array of model parameters and properties for fine-tuning of the model. On the other hand, there exists the danger that finding the "best" model may turn out to be a laborious undertaking.

ENDNOTES

1. W. Ledbetter and J. Cox, "Are OR Techniques Being Used?" *Industrial Engineering* 9, no. 2 (1977), pp. 19–21.

2. R. P. Lippman, "An Introduction to Computing with Neural Nets," *IEEE ASSP Magazine*, April 1987, pp. 4–22.

3. D. Connor, "Data Transformation Explains the Basics of Neural Networks," *EDN*, May 12, 1988, pp. 138–44.

4. R. M. Hogarth, "Generalizations in Decision Research: The Role of Formal Models," University of Chicago, Graduate School of Business, 1986.

5. D. H. Fisher and K. B. McKusick, "An Empirical Comparison of ID3 and Back-Propagation," *Proceedings of International Joint Conference on Artificial Intelligence*, 1989, pp. 788–93.

6. S. M. Weiss and I. Kapouleas, "An Empirical Comparison of Pattern Recognition, Neural Nets, and Machine Learning Classification Methods," *Proceedings of International Joint Conference on Artificial Intelligence*, 1989, pp. 781–87.

7. A. Mitra and R. F. Ling, "A Monte Carlo Comparison of Some Ridge and Other Biased Estimators," *Journal of Statistics, Computation and Simulation* 9 (1979), pp. 195–215.

8. H. Paarsch, "A Monte Carlo Comparison of Estimators for Censored Regression Models," *Journal of Econometrics* 24 (1984), pp. 197–213.

9. B. Pendleton, I. Newman, and R. Marshall, "A Monte Carlo Approach to Correlational Spuriousness and Ratio Variables," *Journal of Statistics, Computation and Simulation* 18 (1983), pp. 93–124.

10. F. Mosteller and J. Tukey, *Data Analysis and Regression: A Second Course in Statistics*. Reading, MA: Addison-Wesley, 1977, pp. 79–84.

11. D. E. Rumelhart and J. McClelland, *Parallel Distributed Processing*. Cambridge, MA.: MIT Press, 1986.

12. R. Hecht-Nielsen, "Theory of the Backpropagation Neural Network," *Proceedings of International Conference on Neural Networks* 1 (1989), pp. 593–605.

13. O. Ersoy, Tutorial at Hawaii International Conference on Systems Sciences, January 1990.

37

A Connectionist Approach to Time Series Prediction: An Empirical Test

Ramesh Sharda and Rajendra B. Patil

INTRODUCTION

Forecasting has been mentioned as one of the most promising applications of artificial neural networks. The autoassociative memory of certain neural network models can be tapped in prediction problems. Smolensky (1986) specifies a dynamic feedforward network in the following way:

$$u_i\,(t+1) = F\left[\sum_k W_{ki}\,G(u_k(t))\right]$$

where $u_i(t)$ is the activation of unit i at time t, F is a nonlinear sigmoid transfer function, G is a nonlinear threshold function, and W_{ki} is the con-

This article appeared in the *Journal of Intelligent Manufacturing,* published by Chapman and Hall, 1992. Reprinted with permission.

nection strength or weight from unit k to unit i. This relationship can, in principle at least, be used for predicting future values of variables.

Several authors have attempted to apply this idea for forecasting a time series. Werbos[1] states that he laid the foundations for use of back-propagation in forecasting in his doctoral dissertation.[2] In his chapter,[1] he describes an application of back-propagation to locate sources of forecast uncertainty in a recurrent gas market model.

Lapedes and Farber[3] used a multilayered perceptron to predict the values of a nonlinear dynamic system with chaotic behavior. They illustrated the method by selecting two common topics in signal processing—prediction and system modeling—and showed that the nonlinear applications can be handled extremely well by using nonlinear neural networks. They reported that neural networks gave superior prediction for their dynamic system.

Sutton[4] introduces a class of incremental learning procedures specialized for prediction; that is, for using experience with an incompletely known system to predict its future behavior. Whereas conventional prediction-learning methods assign credit by the difference between predicted and actual results, the method used by the author assigns credit by the difference between temporally successive predictions. The author also proves the convergence and optimality for special cases, relates them to supervised-learning methods, and claims that the temporal-difference method requires less memory and less peak computation than conventional methods and produces more accurate predictions. He argues that most problems to which supervised learning is now applied are really prediction problems of some sort, to which temporal-difference methods can be applied to advantage.

Fozzard et al.[5] discuss a neural nets-based expert system for solar flare forecasting and claim that its performance is superior to human experts. Tang et al.[6] discuss the results of a test of the performance of neural networks and conventional methods in forecasting time series. The authors experimented with three time series of different complexities using different feedforward, back-propagation models and the Box–Jenkins model. Their experiments demonstrated that for time series with long memory, both methods produced comparable results. However, for series with short memory, neural networks outperform the Box-Jenkins model. The authors conclude that neural networks are robust, parsimonious in their data requirements, and provide good long-term forecasting. All of these results are based on comparison of the techniques using three time series.

However, the experiences with neural networks in forecasting are not all positive. Fishwick,[7] for example, reports that the forecasting ability of neural networks was inferior to simple linear regression and surface response methods. There are some trade magazine articles about use of neural networks in stock price forecasting, but no concrete descriptions can be found (perhaps for confidentiality reasons). Even when the use of neural networks in forecasting has been shown to be positive, it is usually based on test data sets from a particular problem domain.

Sharda and Patil[8] reported the results of an empirical test of neural networks, which show that neural networks may be used for time series forecasting, at least for a single-period forecasting problem. The authors tested and compared a sample of 75 data series containing annual, quarterly, and monthly observations using neural network models and traditional Box–Jenkins forecasting models. The simple neural network models tested on 75 data series could forecast about as well as an automatic Box–Jenkins ARIMA modeling system. Each method outperformed the other in about half of the tests. These tests were based on one particular set of learning parameters and one architecture.

This chapter also reports results of a forecasting competition between a neural network model and a traditional forecasting technique, Box–Jenkins forecasting. Several data series from a comprehensive forecasting competition were analyzed using a neural network model and the Box–Jenkins time series forecasting techniques. The data series came from a variety of sources. This chapter reports the performance of a neural network model using several different learning parameters. Further, it compares the forecasting ability of a neural net model and the Box–Jenkins technique in forecasting multiple horizons ahead. Previous research has not studied the issue of single-step versus multiple-step-ahead forecasting with neural networks.

DATA, METHODS, AND MODELS

Data

The time series were selected from the famous M-Competition to compare the performance of various forecasting techniques.[9] Out of 1,001 series collected, only 111 series were analyzed in the M-Competition using Box–Jenkins methodology. This was done because the Box–Jenkins approach requires an analyst's intervention and is thus quite time-consuming. Pack and Downing[10] examined this 111 series subset and concluded that several series were not appropriate for forecasting using the Box–Jenkins technique. Sharda and Patil[8] took a sample of 75 series from this 111 series set after considering Pack and Downing's recommendations. The tests reported here are based on the full 111 series. Of course, the comparisons between Box–Jenkins technique and the neural network can only be made using the subset where both techniques were able to build a model. Our test set contains 13 annual, 20 quarterly, and 68 monthly series. In Table 37.1, series numbers ≤ 112 are annual, series numbers 382 and > 112 are quarterly, and the rest are monthly.

Method

One hundred and eleven data sets were analyzed using the following approach. For each data set, $n - k$ observations were used to build the forecast model (to train the network), and then the model (the trained neural network) was used to forecast the future k values, where $k = 6$, 8, and 18 for annual, quarterly, and monthly series, respectively. These values are well established for such comparisons in the forecasting literature. The generated forecasts were compared with the actual values for the k periods, and mean absolute percent error (MAPE) was computed for each series. We also computed the absolute percent error by forecast horizon for monthly series.

Models

Box–Jenkins Method. This approach to time series forecasting is well known and has been applied in practice.[11] It is considered to be a sophisticated approach to forecasting but is quite complex to use. Essentially, the analyst examines both the auto and partial autocorrelations and identifies models of the form:

$$\varphi(B)\Phi(B^s)\nabla^d\nabla_s^D(Z_t - c) = \theta(B)\Theta(B^s)a_t$$

where

B is the back-shift operator (i.e., $Bx_t = x_{t-1}$).
$\nabla = 1 - B$; s = seasonality, a_t = white noise.

$\varphi(B)$ and $\Phi(B^s)$ are nonseasonal and seasonal autoregressive polynomials, respectively.

$\theta(B)$ and $\Theta(B^s)$ are nonseasonal and seasonal moving average polynomials, respectively.

Z_t = series (transformed if necessary) to be modeled.

After identification of several candidate models, the analyst can iterate through the process of estimation and diagnostic checking. Once the final model has been selected, the forecasting process can begin.

The process of model identification, estimation, and diagnostics-checking has been automated and is available in the form of a forecasting expert system. The performance of such an automatic "expert" system has been reported to be comparable to real experts.[12] For our tests, we used such an automatic Box–Jenkins modeling expert system, AUTOBOX.[13] This program can take a data set and iterate through the model identification, estimation, and diagnostics process to develop the best model. The series were run in AUTOBOX using its default setting with no intervention detection.

Neural Network Model. A back-propagation rule was used to train a multilayered perceptron network. We used one hidden layer. The number of neurons in the input, hidden layers, and output was based on an input test to be described shortly.

Different architectures, with increasing numbers of hidden-layer neurons, were trained over different values of learning parameters to find the optimal learning parameters first and then find the optimal architecture for a given class of data series. MAPE and Me-APE (median absolute percent error) were used as the measure of performance. Nine combinations of three learning rates (0.1, 0.5, 0.9) and three momentum values (0.1, 0.5, 0.9) were tried.

Ten data series were trained over different architectures and learning parameter sets, and the optimal learning parameters and architecture were found. These parameters were then taken to model remaining data series. All the models discussed above were nonlinear neural network models. Each hidden neuron and output neuron had a nonlinear sigmoidal transfer function.

The neural network software used for this test was the popular PDP software.[14] This program requires that the data be normalized. The data series were normalized by row. While normalizing the file, two different data files were created: training file and testing file. The format of these two files was the same as the unnormalized data file, except each number was now normalized using the minimum and maximum value over the corresponding complete pattern. Each pattern had different minimum and maximum values. While normalizing, the output was written to two different files. The number of patterns written to training file and testing file were:

# of test patterns = 18, 8, 6 for monthly, quarterly, and yearly data series, respectively

# of training patterns = Total patterns – # of test patterns

The normalizing technique over the testing file was slightly different than for the training file. In the training file, the minimum and maximum was found over each complete pattern (input and output part), and each number in the pattern (input and output) was normalized using:

Normalized number = (Number – Min) / (Max – Min)

Note that maximum and minimum values are over all numbers of the input and output part of each training pattern, and each pattern was normalized by its own minimum and maximum values. In the case of the test file, the maximum and minimum values were only over the input part of the testing patterns because the output part of the pattern is not supposed to be known but is needed in the pattern for calculating the pattern error and total sum of squares error (tss) while testing. The same formula was used for the normalization of the test file. The maximum and minimum values were saved only over the test file for denormalization purpose.

Once the above described preprocessing was done, the neural network model was trained with learning rate = 0.1 and momentum = 0.1. These values were found to be optimal from the tests. Maximum cycles trained were 1,000. Training was stopped if total sum of squares error reached 0.04 before training reached 1,000 cycles. If a series converged in less than 1,000 cycles, the total sum of squares error over all the training patterns was less than 0.04. The same seed was used in all our tests to initialize the network in order to facilitate the best comparison of their performances.

Once a network was trained, the test file was tested over the network, and the activation values of output neurons were logged into a file and denormalized using the normalization parameters saved during normalization of test file. The log file was the forecast generated by the trained network using the test file.

RESULTS AND DISCUSSION

Table 37.1 exhibits the MAPEs of AUTOBOX and the neural network approach. These are the averages of absolute percent errors over all forecasting horizons for each series. It shows that the simple (training algorithm) neural network approach performed as well as a forecast expert system. The mean of the MAPEs for neural nets model is slightly less than that for the Box–Jenkins modeling system. However, due to a large standard deviation, the difference is insignificant. A pairwise means test also indicates the same result. Forecasts using AUTOBOX resulted in lower MAPEs for 22 series, and thus the neural network model was able to do better in the other 50 series. However, the large standard deviations still make these differences insignificant.

When the series are grouped on the basis of periodicity, the MAPEs are still insignificantly different between the two approaches. This suggests that the periodicity of the series being modeled does not affect a technique's performance. It was quite interesting, at least for us, that the neural network model was able to incorporate seasonality automatically, just as AUTOBOX is able to do.

Figure 37.1 shows a graphic comparison of MAPEs of the 43 monthly series included in Table 37.1. This chart indicates that the pattern of MAPEs for both approaches is quite similar.

These results are quite encouraging for the proponents of neural networks as a forecasting tool. Obviously, this work needs to be replicated to assess the full potentiality of neural networks for forecasting. Possible use of other neural network architectures and more sophisticated training algorithms may improve the results.

Different Parameter Effects

One of the objectives here was to examine the effect of different architectural and learning parameters on the performance of neural networks over time series modeling. This test was carried out with monthly data. Different values of learning rate and momentum were used to train a 12-12-1, 12-12-2, 12-12-4, 12-12-6, 12-12-8, 12-12-12 architecture, generating forecasts over 1, 2, 4, 6, 8, and 12 periods ahead, respectively. These architectures were trained over nine different combinations of learning rate (0.1, 0.5, 0.9) and momentum (0.1, 0.5, 0.9) values. Observations over this test gave the optimal learning parameters. These optimal learning parameters were

Table 37.1

MAPE Comparison of Box–Jenkins (AUTOBOX) and Neural Network Performance as Forecasting Experts

Series	AUTOBOX	NN-PDP	Series	AUTOBOX	NN-PDP
SER4	23.53	6.43	SER499	13.50	10.02
SER13	6.58	2.59	SER508	16.11	5.89
SER31	18.07	0.55	SER526	9.95	14.75
SER40	10.16	1.03	SER544	2.72	3.98
SER49	24.77	7.65	SER571	5.57	5.82
SER58	72.57	1.34	SER580	3.03	3.28
SER85	37.00	0.29	SER589	9.66	8.20
SER112	4.55	0.10	SER598	23.49	6.36
SER184	20.61	6.92	SER616	7.22	4.62
SER193	44.43	32.52	SER634	13.70	18.67
SER202	21.51	3.95	SER643	18.92	20.29
SER211	26.31	36.03	SER652	15.23	15.54
SER220	37.10	47.59	SER661	19.80	20.52
SER229	42.19	4.19	SER670	28.39	30.27
SER238	14.22	4.79	SER679	20.42	40.01
SER265	21.15	5.52	SER688	12.86	11.12
SER292	12.67	13.94	SER697	4.13	3.63
SER301	2.91	2.25	SER706	20.11	9.66
SER310	4.46	2.90	SER715	61.31	83.83
SER319	14.30	4.39	SER724	17.43	22.44
SER328	8.02	3.14	SER733	14.21	21.52
SER337	8.52	3.86	SER742	5.00	2.05
SER346	20.23	11.15	SER751	5.19	8.17
SER355	4.75	3.92	SER760	7.75	8.05
SER364	3.73	1.25	SER787	3.17	1.87
SER382	32.78	18.25	SER796	17.68	15.96
SER400	14.14	11.42	SER805	7.93	1.18
SER409	42.80	32.09	SER823	1.29	0.65
SER418	19.23	27.37	SER832	7.96	1.29
SER427	9.89	8.53	SER877	3.73	3.38
SER436	7.09	1.85	SER904	3.88	3.22
SER445	25.71	12.87	SER913	58.53	48.90
SER454	8.48	6.85	SER922	26.35	5.22
SER463	6.19	19.95	SER958	13.67	11.36
SER472	19.21	20.76	SER967	38.74	20.68
SER481	32.36	31.00	Mean	15.94	14.67
SER490	7.90	8.71	Stdev	15.18	15.39

Figure 37.1

MAPEs for Monthly Series

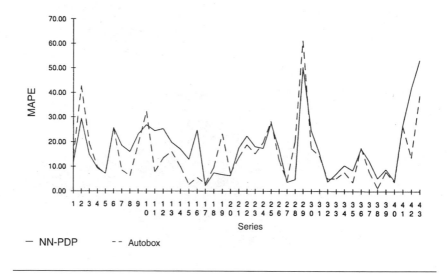

— NN-PDP   -- Autobox

then used to train remaining monthly data series over different architectures as 12-6-1, 12-12-1, 12-18-1, 12-24-1, to observe the effect of different number of hidden neurons. The architecture that performed well in average analysis was then considered as the optimal architecture. The optimal architecture was carried out only over a one-step forecast.

Figure 37.2 shows the average $n + 1$ forecast error with different network architectures. These results are over ser400 and ser409 data series. It is interesting to observe the effect of increasing the number of output neurons. It is observed that, as the number of output neurons was increased from 1 to 12, the $n + 1$ (single step) forecast improved. Figure 37.2 also shows the effect of different learning parameters on the network performance. It is seen that the learning parameters with learning rate = 0.1 and momentum = 0.1 gave the best results. The performance was poor whenever the momentum value was high. Again, the optimal parameters were learning rate = 0.1 and momentum = 0.1.

Optimal learning parameters found in the above test were then used to train the remaining set of data series to find the optimal architectures. This test was carried out only for the single-step forecast. On average

Figure 37.2

Effect of Learning Parameters and Architecture

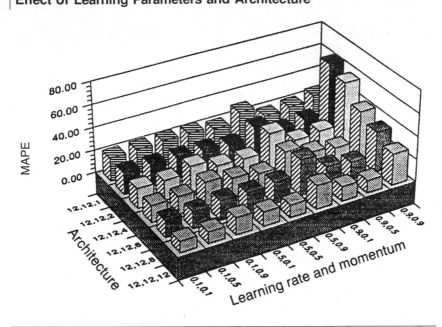

analysis, 12-12-1 appeared to be the best architecture. This architectural parameter (equal number of input and hidden neurons) was then used in further tests.

Multiple Horizon Forecasting

We analyzed 43 monthly series further using AUTOBOX and the neural approach. As before, 18 observations were held back. Remaining data were used to build a model, and forecasts were made at one origin so that the performance of a technique can be evaluated in terms of forecasting multiple horizons. AUTOBOX was used in its default mode. The neural network model was a simple 12-12-18 network. Table 37.2 gives the average absolute percent error for the 43 series at each forecasting horizon. Figure 37.3 depicts these same results graphically. It is apparent that AUTOBOX had a lower MAPE than the neural network models at most of the forecasting horizons. However, the MAPE for neural networks is more stable than for AUTOBOX. Again, the closeness of errors between these two approaches suggests that the neural network models should be investigated further.

CONCLUSIONS AND FUTURE RESEARCH DIRECTIONS

Neural networks provide a promising alternative approach to time series forecasting. The neural network's ability to forecast in a fuzzy sense is more appropriate than the other forecasting methods. Our present study was limited to univariate forecasting, but it is expected that neural networks may be used for multivariate forecasting also. For time series with long

Table 37.2

MAPEs of AUTOBOX and NN Model at Various Horizons (43 Series)

LAG	AUTOBOX	NN-PDP
1	10.75	15.35
2	18.19	14.97
3	10.31	15.17
4	14.00	15.49
5	13.32	16.30
6	16.79	17.16
7	15.17	17.30
8	11.53	17.21
9	16.53	17.22
10	12.57	17.75
11	12.72	17.36
12	13.41	17.10
13	16.48	18.57
14	28.45	19.60
15	14.84	19.12
16	14.61	19.08
17	14.34	19.46
18	17.78	19.36
Average	15.10	17.42

Figure 37.3

Mean APE by Forecasting Horizon (43 Monthly Series)

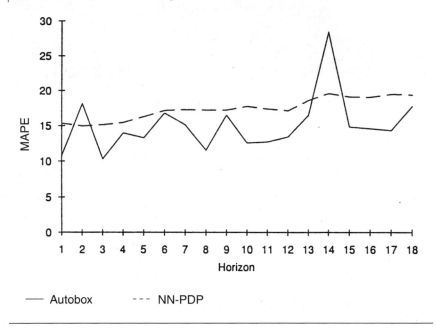

— Autobox   - - - NN-PDP

memory, both Box–Jenkins models and neural networks perform well, with Box–Jenkins models slightly better for short-term forecasting. With short memory, neural networks outperform Box–Jenkins.[6] By approximating the underlying mapping of the time series, a neural network provides robust forecasting in cases of irregular time series. Neural networks can be trained to approximate the underlying mapping of time series albeit the accuracy of approximation depends on a number of factors such as the neural network structure, learning method, and training procedure. Without a hidden layer, the linear neural network model is functionally similar to a Box–Jenkins ARIMA model.

The neural network structure and the training procedure have great impact on its forecasting performance. This fact is evident from the present work that we are doing. The learning algorithms used in our study are by no means the best. We believe that there is still much room for improvement in neural network forecasting.

ENDNOTES

1. P. Werbos, "Generalization of Backpropagation with Application to Recurrent Gas Market Model," *Neural Networks* 1 (1988), pp. 339–56.

2. P. Werbos, "Beyond Regression: New Tools for Prediction and Analysis in the Behavioral Sciences," Harvard University, Ph.D. thesis, 1974.

3. A. Lapedes and R. Farber, "Nonlinear Signal Processing Using Neural Networks: Prediction and System Modeling," Los Alamos National Lab Technical Report LA-UR-87-2261, July 1987.

4. R. S. Sutton, "Learning to Predict by the Methods of Temporal Differences," *Machine Learning* 3 (1988), pp. 9–44.

5. R. Fozzard, G. Bradshaw, and L. Ceci, "A Connectionist Expert System for Solar Flare Forecasting," in *Advances in Neural Information Processing Systems I*, ed. D. S. Touretzky. Morgan Kaufmann Publishers, Inc., 1989, pp. 264–71.

6. Z. Tang, C. de Almedia, and P. A. Fishwick, "Time Series Forecasting Using Neural Networks vs. Box-Jenkins Methodology," International Workshop on Neural Networks, Auburn, AL, February 2–4, 1990.

7. P. Fishwick, "Neural Network Models in Simulation: A Comparison with Traditional Modeling Approaches," *Proceedings of Winter Simulation Conference*, Washington, DC, 1989, pp. 702–10.

8. R. Sharda, and R. Patil, "Neural Networks as Forecasting Experts: An Empirical Test," International Joint Conference on Neural Networks, IJCNN-WASH-DC, vol. II, January 15-19, 1990, pp. 491–94.

9. S. Makridakis et al., "The Accuracy of Extrapolation (Time Series) Methods: Results of a Forecasting Competition," *Journal of Forecasting* 1 (1982), pp. 111–53.

10. D. J. Pack and D. J. Downing, "Why Didn't Box–Jenkins Win (Again)?" *Proceedings, Third International Symposium on Forecasting*, Philadelphia, 1983.

11. G. E. P. Box and G. M. Jenkins, "Time Series Analysis: Forecasting and Control." San Francisco: Holden-Day, 1976.

12. R. Sharda and T. Ireland, "An Empirical Test of Automatic Forecasting Systems," ORSA/TIMS Meeting, New Orleans, May 1987.

13. AUTOBOX, *Software User Manual* (Hatboro, PA: Automatic Forecasting Systems, 1988).

14. J. McClelland and D. E. Rumelhart, *Exploration in Parallel Distributed Processing: A Handbook of Models, Programs and Exercises.* Cambridge, MA: MIT Press, 1988.

TIME SERIES PREDICTION USING MINIMALLY STRUCTURED NEURAL NETWORKS: AN EMPIRICAL TEST

Won Chul Jhee and Michael J. Shaw

INTRODUCTION

Artificial neural networks (ANN) have been advocated as an alternative to conventional tools for time series prediction, after Lapedes and Farber (1987) reported that MLP trained by the back-propagation algorithm are better at predicting by orders of magnitude than conventional forecasting methods. For example, there is an argument that well-designed ANN-based forecasting systems proclaim the opening of a new era in the evolution of forecasting and decision support systems. The works of Werbos

A large part of this work was carried out while Professor Jhee was visiting the Beckman Institute, University of Illinois at Urbana-Champaign, whose kind hospitality is gratefully acknowledged. He is also grateful to Korea Science and Engineering Foundation (KOSEF) and Hong Ik University, who supported his visit.

(1988), Weigend et al. (1990, 1991), Tang et al. (1991), Sharda and Patil (1992), Foster et al. (1992), and Hoptroff (1993) support this argument. However, White (1988), Fishwick (1989), and Ripley (1993) reported that standard statistical procedures will often be at least as effective as neural networks when a fair comparison is made. Observing those inconsistent research results from the analyses of socioeconomic data sets, Chatfield (1993) commented that ANN will be able to outperform standard forecasting procedures for at least certain types of situations, but there is little systematic evidence of this as yet. Thus, the purpose of this paper is to provide such evidence using well-known real world data such as M-Competition Data.

Since the success of forecasting methods depends heavily on the properties of the time series to which the methods are applied, especially when the methods are univariate analyses, we first need to address the basic properties of time series from socioeconomic systems. First, most of the series have very limited number of observations. Since the socioeconomic systems are changing their structures and compositions, the addition of data obtained from much earlier observation are often irrelevant or even harmful to the analysis. Furthermore, one cannot generate extra data as needed because they do not allow experiments. Therefore, there are at most 200 observations or so, and it is not unusual that there are under 50 observations. Second, the time series are often contaminated by noise from unknown sources and suffer from high level of measurement errors. This noise and error is not merely added to the series but become embedded in the series. Consequently, there is no reason to believe that the noise follows independent and identically distribute Gaussian random process. Finally, most of the observed series do not satisfy the assumption of stationarity on which most time series analyses rely. There is frequently a clear trend and/or seasonality—that is, long memory—in the mean process, and the fluctuations in variance are also often observed. Therefore, differencing and log transformation should be applied through intensive data analysis to transform the data into stationary series. The above three facts partly explain why different analysts have different forecasting results on the same time series and why simple linear models such as exponential smoothing or the combination of their forecasts are preferred to more complicated methods for practitioners and even M-Competitions.

However, some researchers argue that a significant portion of real-time series are generated by nonlinear processes and that they can benefit from the recent developments in nonlinear modeling (Tong 1990; De Gooijer

& Kumar 1992). Nevertheless, nonlinear models with many parameters are so extremely flexible that they bear the risk of overfitting the time series. That is, the model that provides the best fit to past data does not necessarily provide the best forecasts, especially if there is noise involved in the series or changes in the generating process. For reasons of conservatism, statisticians have tended to severely restrict the number of free parameters by tolerating some bad results due to underfitting. Since ANN models are at the heart of nonlinear modeling, appropriate parameterization is indispensable to good forecasting performance of ANN. In this sense, the minimally structured neural networks in this paper means that MLP have the proper number of connection weights, which are equivalent to the number of parameters in nonlinear models. To restrict the size of MLP, special attention was paid to determining the number of input units because the moderate size of input space enables MLP to capture the essential features in a time series without being disturbed by noise. ARIMA model identification results were used as valuable information in determining MLP structures, and our approach was tested using the M-Competition data.

DATA AND METHODS

Makridakis et al. (1982, 1993) collected time series from the real world and held the competitions to determine empirically the post-sample accuracy of various univariate methods. Although the results of forecasting competitions are somewhat controversial, the 1001 series provided by the M1-Competition enables us to test a number of interesting questions on forecasting methods. Out of original database, the 111 series, which consists of 20 annual, 23 quarterly and 68 monthly series, has often been investigated in the previous comparative studies (Sharda and Patil 1992). This subset of M1-Competition Data was analyzed in this paper to answer the question of whether the MLP can be an expert under the socioeconomic forecasting environments.

At the time of the first competition, the most recent observations of each series were held out by Makridakis. The numbers of holdout samples were 6, 8, and 18 for annual, quarterly, and monthly series, respectively. Forecasting models were fitted to the remaining observations of each series and then used to obtain its prediction values, which were compared with the holdout sample values. The performance or error measure was mean absolute percentage error (MAPE) over the forecasting horizons. This evaluation scheme was adopted without any modifications in our comparative analysis between ARIMA models and minimally structured neural networks.

AUTOREGRESSIVE MOVING AVERAGE MODELS

ARMA models have been served as a benchmark model for creating linear models because of their theoretical elaborateness and accuracy in short-term forecasting. For time series to be modeled $\{Z_t, t \in 7\}$, transformed if necessary, the general class of ARMA (p,q) model has the following form:

$$\Phi(B)Z_t = C + \Theta(B)a_t$$

where $\Phi(B) = U(B) \, \phi(B) = 1 - \Phi_1 B - \Phi_2 B^2 - \cdots - \Phi_p B^p$, $U(B) = 1 - U_1 B - \cdots - U_d B^d$, $\phi(B) = 1 - \phi_1 B - \cdots - \phi_{p-d} B^{p-d}$, $\Theta(B) = 1 - \theta_1 B - \cdots - \theta_q B^q$, $BZ_t = Z_{t-1}$, C is a constant, and $\{a_t\}$ is a gaussian white noise process. Note that if $U(B) = (1 - B)^d$ then the ARMA (p,q) model can be expressed as ARIMA (p–d,d,q) in the Box–Jenkins approach, which is the most popular ARMA modeling method. Among the iterative modeling steps in Figure 38.1, the model identification step which determines the order of p and q is crucial to representing the time series adequately because the resulting model performs poorly if the modeler is prodigal in using the parameters. Therefore, the principle of parsimony is an im-

Figure 38.1

ARMA Modeling Procedure

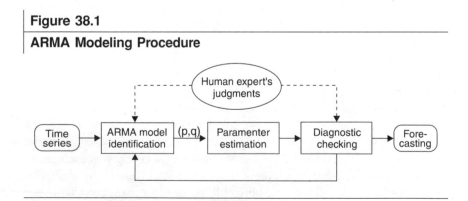

portant modeling philosophy (Box and Jenkins 1976). The identification step requires an intensive data analysis where expert judgment must be exercised to interpret some statistics, such as ACF and PACF, AIC, and so on. Because of the difficulties involved in the model identification step, there have been efforts to automate the modeling procedure (for details, refer to Jhee and Lee 1993). An outgrowth of such efforts is AUTOBOX™ 3.0, whose performance is comparable to human experts. This commercially available software was adopted to secure the objectivity of our comparative analysis. The 111 series of M1-Competition Data was analyzed under the default setting of AUTOBOX™ 3.0, which means the intervention option was not used.

MINIMALLY STRUCTURED NEURAL NETWORKS

Determining MLP Structures

To predict the future values of time series, the iterative one-step ahead forecasting procedure was adopted using the following relationship:

$$\hat{Z}_{t+1} = f\,(Z_t, Z_{t-1}, \cdots), \cdots, \ \hat{Z}_{t+r} = f(\,\hat{Z}_{t+r-1}, \hat{Z}_{t+r-2}, \cdots, \hat{Z}_{t+1}, Z_t, Z_{t-1}, \cdots\,)$$

where $\left\{\hat{Z}_{t+r}, r \in L\right\}$ are the estimated values for the future observations in forecast horizon L. The function f that is fitted for the past observations will be used to predict one point into the future and simply iterate itself on its own outputs and the past data to predict further into the forecast horizon. In our analysis, this approximation function f was replaced by a multilayered feedforward perceptron that has one output unit and one hidden layer. Therefore, the remaining issue is how to choose right number of hidden and input units because the size of MLP greatly affects the forecasting performance.

The fact that MLP can be universal approximators (Hornik et al. 1989) does not mean that the structures of MLP can be arbitrarily chosen. The MLP of large size might promise to extract more information from data, but such MLP also tends to mistake noise for information. As a result, they make more serious errors and rarely yield the gain they promised. This erroneous behavior of MLP tends to be easily magnified in the univariate time series analysis with a limited number of observations. Although there has been some research on the optimal design of MLP structures, it is still largely an art to determine the optimal number of hidden units. Furthermore, we can hardly find any research results that reported the impacts of input spaces on the forecasting performance of MLP.

Since the learning paradigm of ANN is learning by examples, an exploratory data analysis before preparing training examples is recommended to increase the performance of learned ANN. This is why we use the results of ARMA model identification, which involves an intensive correlation analysis among data points. In doing so, the starting point is the observation that an ARMA (p,q) process can be put in state space form by defining a state vector of length m = max (p,q + 1) (Harvey 1984). Therefore, if the order of time series was identified as ARMA (p,q), we used m as the input space and also as the number of hidden units.

Preliminary Experiment

Before applying our idea to the whole data sets, we tested our idea with five time series from the 111 M-competition Data. One of the purposes here is to examine the effects of varying numbers of input and hidden units. Figures 38.2–38.4 present the typical illustration of our results, which were obtained using the S184 series (Figure 38.2) that follows ARIMA(1,4,4) in terms of Box–Jenkins or ARMA(5,4). Figures 38.3–38.4 show the effects of input spaces. When we applied our stopping rule (see the next section for details), the MLP of five input units gave the least MAPE that were measured over the holdout samples and beat the AUTOBOX™ v.3.0, of which MAPE is represented by straight line in Figure 38.3a. We observe that the large input spaces do more harm than good in predicting the future values, even though they brought better fitting results in terms of R^2, on the past observations. During these preliminary experiments, we traced the performance of each MLP structure as the learning of MLP proceeded and recorded when the MLP showed the best prediction results. Figure 38.3b shows that five input units are also best for the series S184. This result may not be always the case. However, we could obtain similar results from the other four time series. Figure 38.4 shows the effects of hidden units when we used 5 and 12 input units. As we expected, the least MAPE's were obtained when we used the same numbers of hidden units as the numbers of input units. Thus, we were very encouraged to utilize the ARMA model identification results in determining the MLP structures. With these favorable experi-

Figure 38.2

Time Series S184

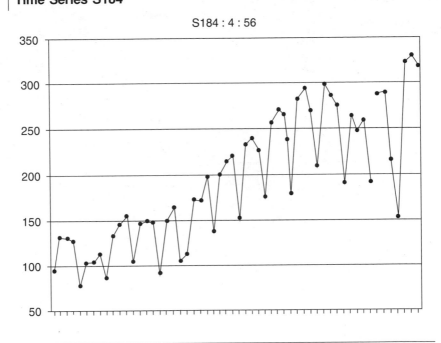

S184 : 4 : 56

mental results, we analyzed the 111 series of M-Competition Data according to the following training procedure.

Training Procedure

To train MLP on each time series using the back-propagation algorithm, we first adopted the stopping rule as follows: Training was terminated if the mean squared error reached 0.0001 before 5,000 training epochs, which was the allowed maximum epochs. This is a very simple rule, but the philosophy behind our stopping rule is "Let MLP learn sufficiently from the given data." Our stopping rule appears to have the risk that MLP overfits the given series, but the risk is not serious as we constrain the size of MLP. If we consider the actual forecasting situations where the future values are not known a prior, our approach can be an easily

Figure 38.3

Effects of Input Spaces

a. S184: By stopping rule

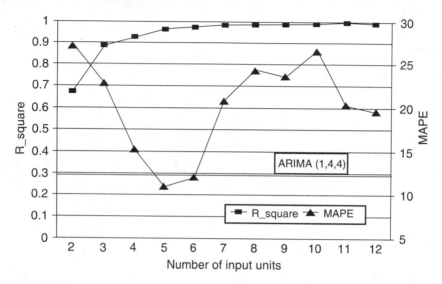

b. S184: Best performance

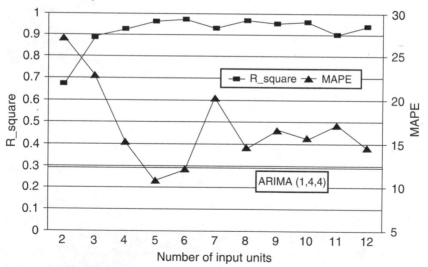

Figure 38.4

Effects of Hidden Units

a. S184: Input PEs = 5

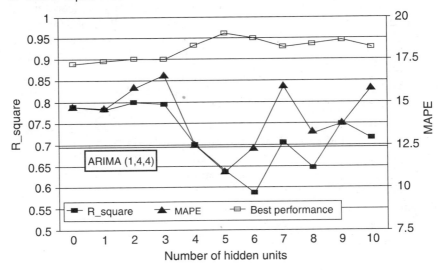

b. S184: Input PEs = 12

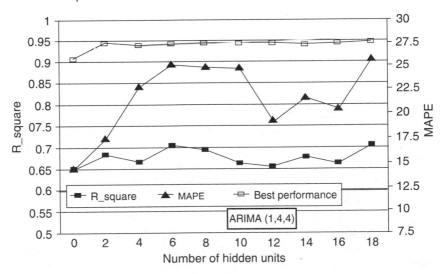

applicable and sound stopping rule. Before the time series were fed into MLP as training data, each series was linearly transformed into the range between 0.1 and 0.9. We did not consider differencing or deseasonalizing to remove nonstationarity from the time series.

During the preliminary experiments, we also determined learning parameters using 12 time series that were selected equally from four categories. We classified time series into four categories according to time series characteristics, that is, trend and seasonality. Four combinations of learning rates and coefficients to momentum term, (0.1, 0), (0.1, 0.1), (0.1, 0.9), and (0.3, 0.5), were tried, and the use of (0.1, 0.1) gave slightly better prediction results. We also tested the weight-updating interval. In addition to updating connection weights pattern by pattern, we tried two cumulative methods: One updated the weights every five input presentations, and the other updated only once during each epoch. Updating the weights at each input presentation outperformed the cumulative methods. Once the MLP learned from time series, the degree of fitness to training data was measured using R^2, and then the learned MLP was tested over the holdout samples of the series. The outputs of the MLP were converted into their original scale, and MAPE was computed to measure the prediction ability.

EXPERIMENT RESULTS

Over the 111 series the minimally structured MLP outperformed ARIMA models in terms of both fitting and forecasting abilities. The pairwise t-tests indicate that performance differences were statistically significant. Some critics on the M-Competition argue that several series in the 111 series are not suitable for forecasting with ARIMA models (Pack and Downing 1983). So, we further analyzed the forecasting results from only 72 series as Sharda and Patil (1992) did. Table 38.1 exhibits the number of series on which MLP performed better than ARIMA and vice versa. Over this reduced data set, the performance differences were also significant. However, the results are grouped according to observation intervals. It is noteworthy that MLP did not perform as well on monthly series as they did on yearly or quarterly series. This observation is against our expectation because most of monthly series have more data points than others. Therefore, we rearranged the reduced data set into three categories according to the number of observations. The first category included series having less than 30 data points, and the series in the third category

Table 38.1

Comparative Prediction Performance Classified by Observation Intervals (unit: no. of series)

Observation Intervals	Yearly	Quarterly	Monthly	Total
MSNN	7	16	30	53
AUTOBOX 3.0	1	2	16	19
Total	8	18	46	72

Figure 38.5

AUTOBOX v3.0 versus Neural Networks—our analysis (MAPE)

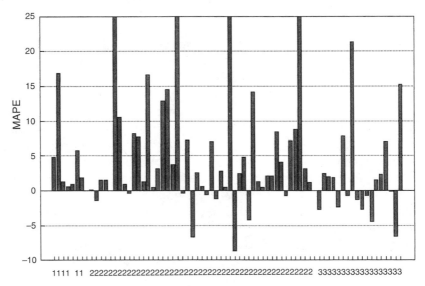

Number of observations

The number of observations(NOB) in each category is:
(1) $NOB < 30$, (2) $30 \leq NOB < 100$, and (3) $100 < NOB$.
$\Delta MAPE = MAPE$ of AUTOBOX $-$ MAPE of NN.

Table 38.2

Comparative Prediction Performance Classified by the Series
Characteristics (unit: no. of series)

Charac- teristics	None	Trend	Seasonality	T + S	Total
MSNN	5	25	15	8	53
AUTOBOX 3.0	1	3	9	6	19
Total	6	28	24	14	72

contained more than 100 data points. We subtracted MAPE's of MLP from those of AUTOBOX™ 3.0. As shown in Figure 38.5, the performances of two methods were not discriminable in the case of the third category. This analysis confirms the above observations.

To explain this phenomenon, we classified the series into four categories according to the characteristics of time series: whether the series has trend or seasonality. Table 38.2 shows that when the series has the seasonality component, MLP did not perform relatively well. This analysis provides us with a cue. In M-Competition Data, the series that have more than 100 data points are all monthly series. If they have seasonality components simultaneously in AR and differencing orders, the MLP in our approach will have large input spaces and overfit the time series to yield poor forecasting performance. At this point, readers need to remember that we did not adopt any data transformations that make the nonstationary series into stationary one. If we use deseasonalized series, the overfitting problems in monthly series will be greatly reduced. At any rate, the minimally structured neural networks outperform ARIMA models.

CONCLUSIONS

Our experiment provides evidence that artificial neural networks are a promising alternative to conventional forecasting methods. We determined the structure of multilayered feedforward perceptrons using the ARMA model identification results and demonstrated that our design works well for noisy time series of limited number of observations. The approach outlined in this chapter can be used as a basis for automating the ANN forecasting procedure. Our experiment also reveals that exploratory data analyses are greatly useful in obtaining better forecasts from MLP.

REFERENCES

AFA Inc. 1991. AUTOBOX™ 3.0 User's Manual. Hatboro, PA.

Box, G. E. P. and G.M. Jenkins. 1976. *Time Series Analysis—Forecasting and Control*. San Francisco: Holden-Day.

De Gooijer, J. G. and K. Kumar. 1992. "Some Recent Developments in Non-Linear Time Series Modelling, Testing, and Forecasting." *International Journal of Forecasting* 8, pp. 135–56.

Foster, W. R., F. Collopy, and L.H. Ungar. 1992. "Neural Network Forecasting of Short Noisy Time Series." *Computers and Chemical Engineering* 16, no. 4, pp. 293–97.

Harvey, A. C. 1984. "A Unified View of Statistical Forecasting Procedures." *Journal of Forecasting* 3, pp. 245–75.

Jhee, W. C. and J.K. Lee. 1993. "Performance of Neural Networks in Managerial Forecasting." *Intelligent Systems in Accounting, Finance and Management* 2, pp. 55–71.

Lapedes, A. S. and R.M. Farber. 1987. "Nonlinear Signal Processing Using Neural Networks: Prediction and System Modeling." Los Alamos National Laboratory Technical Report, LA- UR-87-2662.

Makridakis et al. 1982. "The Accuracy of Extrapolation (Time Series) Methods: Results of a Forecasting Competition." *Journal of Forecasting* 1, pp. 111–53.

Makridakis et al. 1993. "The M2-Competition: A Real-Time Judgmentally Based Forecasting Study." *International Journal of Forecasting* 9, pp. 5–22.

Rumelhart D. and J. McClelland. eds. 1987. *Parallel Distributed Processing: Explorations in the Microstructure of Cognition*. Cambridge, MA: MIT.

Sharda, R. and R.B. Patil. 1992. "A Connectionist Approach to Time Series Prediction: An Empirical Test." *Journal of Intelligent Manufacturing*.

Tang, Z., C. Almeida, and P. Fishwick. 1991. "Time Series Forecasting Using Neural Networks vs. Box–Jenkins Methodology." *Simulation* 57, no. 5, pp. 303–10.

Tong, H. 1990. *Non-Linear Time Series: A Dynamical System Approach*. Oxford University Press.

Weigend, A. S., D.E. Rumelhart, and B.A. Huberman. 1990. "Back-Propagation, Weight-Elimination and Time Series Prediction." In *Connectionist Models: Proc. of the 1990 Summer School*. eds. Touretzski et al. pp. 105–16.

Werbos, P. 1989. "Generalization of Back-Propagation with Application to Recurrent Gas Market Model." *Neural Networks* 1 pp. 339–56.

White, H. 1988. "Economic Prediction Using Neural Networks: The Case of IBM Daily Stock Returns." *IJCNN* II pp. 451–II458.

39

CONSTRUCTIVE LEARNING AND ITS APPLICATION TO CURRENCY EXCHANGE RATE FORECASTING

A. N. Refenes

INTRODUCTION

Forecasting the behavior of a given system follows two distinct approaches. The first and most powerful approach depends on exact knowledge of the laws that underlie a given phenomenon. When this knowledge is expressed in terms of precise equations, which can in principle be solved, it is possible to predict the future behavior of a system once the initial conditions are completely specified. The main problem with this approach is that the knowledge of the rules governing the behavior of the system are not readily available. This is particularly true for most macroeconomic

Printed with permission of the author.

problems. One possible source of this weakness is parameter instability, but it is more likely that the cause is lack of nonlinearities in the models.

A second, albeit less powerful, method for prediction relies on the discovery of strong empirical regularities in observations of the system. There are problems, however, with the latter approach. Regularities are not always evident and are often masked by noise. There are phenomena that seem random, without apparent periodicities, although recurrent in a generic sense.

Several researchers have attempted to use feedforward neural networks[1,2] to predict future values of time series by extracting knowledge from the past. One common approach is to use time-space patterns of economic indexes, such as interest rates, to relate the changes in one time series to other phenomena in the economy. Others believe that currency exchange rates embody all the knowledge that is necessary to predict future behavior. The underlying assumption in this approach is that any changes in economic policy and/or other indexes are ultimately reflected in the currency exchange rate, for example, through direct central bank interventions.

Neural network architectures have drawn considerable attention in recent years because of their interesting learning abilities. However, two main problems are associated with the use of fixed-geometry networks and back-propagation in nontrivial applications:

1. *Convergence.* Back-propagation performs learning by steepest descent in weight space and may be trapped in local minima. The classification may not be learned, and the learning can be extremely slow.

2. *Network configuration.* A main problem is that a priori no realistic estimate can be made of the number of hidden units required to learn the classification. For good generalization, the network must be sufficiently large to learn the problem but also necessarily small to generalize well. Network design is currently something of a "black art" and depends heavily on manual experimentation and fine-tuning of the learning parameters. The aim here is to develop learning procedures that will achieve optimum network configuration.

Recently, several methods have been proposed that attempt to get around the problems of slow convergence and dynamic network construction. They include Cascade Correlation,[3] the Tiling algorithm,[4] the Neural Decision tree,[5] the Upstart Algorithm,[6] and others. In some of these techniques, the hidden units are constructed in layers one by one as they are needed. By showing that at least one unit in each layer makes fewer mistakes than a corresponding unit in the earlier layer, eventual convergence to zero errors is guaranteed. Other techniques operate in the opposite direction by pruning the network and removing "redundant" connections.

The above techniques differ in complexity, convergence speed, and most importantly, in their generalization performance. Although most, but not all, methods will guarantee that the network learns the classification, no realistic statement can be made about their generalization performance. For example, the upstart algorithm shows a rate of generalization between 50 percent and 70 percent,[6] which is unrealistic for most real-life applications.

This chapter describes and evaluates a procedure for constructing and training multilayered perceptrons by adding units to the network dynamically during training. Units are added as they are needed. By showing that the newly added unit makes fewer mistakes than before, and by training the unit not to disturb the earlier dynamics, eventual convergence to zero errors is guaranteed. By training each unit to solve a simpler problem than the entire network, faster convergence is achieved.

The CLS+ procedure is a development from earlier work[7] and is designed to perform well with continuous-valued networks.

BASIC NOTIONS

Constructive techniques are based on the principle that the hidden units of a network are constructed incrementally, one by one as they are needed. The basic building block for constructive techniques is a *linear classifier*. A linear classifier is defined as a simple node with a set of input weights w_i, a set of output weights w_o, and a simple learning rule (Figure 39.1a). The components, $< v_1,...,v_n >$, of an input vector V are mapped into a new vector, V^*, whose components, V_j^*, are computed according to the following rule:

$$V_j^* = w_{oj} f\left(\sum_{i=0}^{n} w_i v_i\right) \qquad (1)$$

A linear classifier can be trained to maximize (or minimize) the correlation (or error) between its outputs and some arbitrary quantity. Constructive

Figure 39.1a, b, c

Generic Algorithm for Constructive Learning

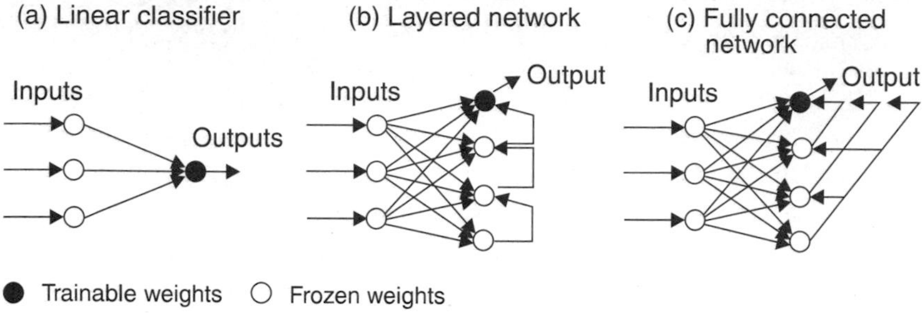

(a) Linear classifier   (b) Layered network   (c) Fully connected
                                                                 network

● Trainable weights   ○ Frozen weights

1. Construct a good (preferably optimal) set of weights for a linear classifier L_1. This is always possible and can be achieved using any of the gradient descent training algorithms (i.e., back-propagation, quickprop, etc.). If all (or the maximum number possible) of the training examples are correctly classified, exit. Otherwise, freeze the weights for L_1.

2. Construct a good (preferably optimal) set of weights for linear classifier L_{i+1} having inputs from the training examples and from linear classifier L_i. Depending on the training technique, it can be shown that D_{i+1} can correctly classify a greater number of training examples than D_i. Freeze the coefficients for D_{i+1}.

3. Repeat from step 2 a finite number of times until all, or the maximum number possible, of training examples are correctly classified.

learning starts with a fixed architecture. By showing that the addition of a new *linear classifier* produces fewer errors than the earlier architecture, eventual convergence to zero errors is guaranteed. An obvious way to use linear classifiers of this type is as mechanisms for correcting errors that the earlier network is making. This can be done by training the linear classifier to further minimize the error or to maximize the correlation between its output and the error that a specific node in the network is making. In this way, the classifier will develop corrective weights in its output connections. Once added into the network, the weights of the linear classifier are frozen, and the procedure is repeated. Linear classifiers can be connected to the network in at least two ways.

First, they can be inserted between the last hidden node and the output units (Figure 39.1b). Secondly, they can be inserted in the same way but connected to all the hidden units (Figure 39.1c). In the simple case where the linear classifier produces binary values, it is called a linear discriminant.

Figure 39.1 shows a linear classifier and two ways of constructing networks with one output unit, by repeatedly extending the output until convergence is achieved. In this case, the construction of L_i is achieved by training to minimize the error between the desired output and the classifier's actual output.

The convergence, generalization, and scalability properties of these techniques depend on the type of linear classifier used, the way in which its weights are calculated (i.e., learning rule), the type of subclassification it is asked to learn, and finally, the way in which it is inserted in the network.

Suppose we are given a training set to be learned. Each input vector $i^{(r)}$ of N continuous values has an associated target $t^{(d)}$. Each unit has a "state" or "activity level" that is determined by the input received from the other units in the network. Information is processed locally in each unit by computing a dot product between its input vector and its weight vector (x_i):

$$x_i = f\left(\sum_{j=0}^{n} y_j w_{ji}\right) \tag{2}$$

This weighted sum, x_i, which is called the "total input" of unit i, is then passed through a squashing function to produce the state of unit i denoted by f. We consider the family of squashing functions $F_n = \{f = f(x, k, T, c) \mid x, k \in R; T, c \in R - \{0\}\}$, which are defined by (3):

$$f(x) = k + \frac{c}{1 + e^{Tx}} \tag{3}$$

Note that for suitable values of k, c, T, the typical sigmoid, hyperbolic tangent, and similar are obtained. In this chapter, we shall use $k = A$, $C = -2A$, and $T = 2S$ to obtain the symmetric scaled hyperbolic tangent function:

$$f(x) = A \tanh S(x) = A \frac{e^{Sx} - e^{-Sx}}{e^{Sx} + e^{-Sx}}$$

$$= A\,\frac{e^{2Sx}-1}{e^{2Sx}+1} = A - \frac{2\,A}{1+e^{2Sx}} \tag{4}$$

where A is the amplitude of the function and S determines its slope at the origin, and the entire squashing function is an odd function with horizontal asymptotes $+A$ and $-A$. Symmetric functions are believed to yield faster convergence, although the learning can become extremely slow if the weights are too small.[8] The cause of this problem is that the origin of the weight space is a stable point for the learning dynamics, and although it is a saddle point, it is attractive in almost all directions. For our simulations, we use parameter values similar to Le Cun's with $A = 1.7159$ and $S = \frac{2}{3}$. With this choice of parameters, the equalities $f(1) = 1$, and $(-1) = -1$ are satisfied. The rationale behind this is that the overall gain of the squashing transformation is around 1 in normal operating conditions, and the interpretation of the state of the network is simplified. Moreover, the absolute value of the second derivative of f is a maximum at $+1$ and -1, which improves the convergence at the end of the learning session.

Before training, the weights are initialized with random values. Training the network to produce a desired output vector $o^{(r)}$ when presented with an input pattern $i^{(r)}$ involves testing the network to see if the actual output vector $a^{(r)}$ is in agreement with the desired output, $d^{(r)}$ and then adding a new hidden unit to correct the residual error. The new unit, and only it, is then trained to recognize those patterns for which the network was in error. The basic idea is that a hidden unit is constructed with the purpose of correcting the mistakes at the output layer. If we are considering binary valued networks, an output unit O_i can make two types of error[6,7]:

wrongly ON $a^{(r)}i = 1$ but $d^{(r)}i = 0$

wrongly OFF $a^{(r)}i = 0$ but $d^{(r)}i = 1$

Consider patterns for which O_i is wrongly ON: O_i could be corrected by a large negative weight from a new hidden unit in the hidden layer, say h_i. The new hidden unit h_i is active and has an inhibitory effect for those vectors for which O_i is wrongly ON. For the remaining patterns, h_i remains silent. Likewise, when O_i is wrongly OFF it could be corrected by a sufficiently large positive weight. Again, h_i has an excitatory effect only for those vectors.

For networks with continuous output, the CLS+ procedure uses a generalization of the above described in the next section.

THE CLS+ PROCEDURE

Overview

The CLS+ procedure is illustrated in Figure 39.2. It begins with some N inputs and M outputs and at least one hidden unit. The number of inputs and outputs is dictated by the problem and by the I/O representation. Every input is connected to the unit in the hidden layer, which is in turn connected to every unit in the output layer.

We add hidden units to the network one by one. Like cascade correlation,[3] each hidden unit receives a connection from each of the networks input and also from the last (but not all) hidden unit. The hidden unit's weights are frozen after the unit is added to the network.

The learning is on-line, and the algorithm begins with only a single, fully connected hidden unit with randomized connection strengths. The learning algorithm proceeds as shown in the following steps.

Step 1. Feedforward test for training vector t_i. If the output o_r makes an error then add a new unit h_k. Connect h_k to the output unit o^r with a connection strength that corrects the error. The connection strength w_{hk} can be calculated analytically as follows. Prior to adding the new unit h_k, the output at o^r is given by:

$$o^r = f\left(\sum_{i=0}^{k-1} w_{h_{i,o}} v_{h_{i,o}}\right) = t^d i \pm \varepsilon \tag{5}$$

where $\varepsilon = |o^r - t^r d|$. After adding $h_{k,0}$ the error at o^r will be eliminated. Thus:

$$o^r = f\left(\sum_{i=0}^{k-1} w_{h_{i,o}} v_{h_{i,o}} + w_{h_k} v_{h_k}\right) = t^d i \tag{6}$$

Figure 39.2

The Constructive Learning Procedure

The network grows sideways; new units are added to correct the mistakes at the output and are then trained to remain silent for those patterns for which there are other feature detectors.

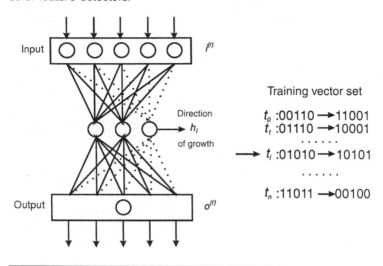

Training vector set

t_o :00110 →11001
t_1 :01110 →10001
. . . . . .
→ t_i :01010→10101
. . . . . .
t_n :11011 →00100

Using (4) we expand (6), and solving for $w_{h_k} v_{h_k}$ we obtain:

$$w_{h_k} v_{h_k} = \frac{\log_e \left(\dfrac{2A}{A - t^d i} - 1 \right) - 2S \sum\limits_{i=0}^{k-1} W_{h_{i,o}} V_{h_{i,o}}}{2S} \tag{7}$$

There are two unknowns in (7): the weight for h_k and its value. If we fix the value that h_k has to produce for pattern t_i, we can compute the weight and vice versa.

Step 2. Connect the newly added unit h_k to all the input units and to h_{k-1}. The connection's strength must be such that the unit recognizes the current vector t_i and none of the previous vectors, $t_o, t_1,...t_{i-1}$ so that the cognitive properties of the network are not disturbed. This is achieved by gradient descent learning.

The main point to note here is the method of training the new units. The current unit is trained using the current pattern and all the patterns that appear before the current pattern in the training set. The new unit is trained such that it will be active for the current pattern but be inactive for all the patterns that appear before the current pattern in the training set. The patterns that appear after the current pattern in the training set are not taken into consideration. It is possible that different patterns appearing after the current patterns in the training set may activate the current unit. This is done to increase the generalization capabilities of the network. The rules for training the newly added unit are summarized in Figure 39.3.

The procedure now moves to the next pattern in the training set. In practice, t_i is not selected sequentially, but on the basis of a largest-error condition. Exactly the same procedure that is used for training pattern t_i is used to train pattern t_{i+1}. This carries on until the algorithm has been through all the training patterns in the training set.

Convergence of the CLS+ Procedure

The convergence result follows immediately from the training method because the error at the output units has been corrected, so the newly added hidden unit is given an easier problem to solve than the output unit. The proof consists of two parts.

Part 1. In Part 1, we prove that after we have added a new unit h_i in the hidden layer, we will always have fewer errors than before.

Proof. Assume we have a training set with n patterns. The CLS+ algorithm goes through the training set a pattern at a time.

Before we add a new unit h_i to the hidden layer, we correctly recognize all the patterns that appear before the ith pattern in the training set, that is, $t_0 \rightarrow t_{i-1}$ patterns recognized correctly.

At this point, t_i and all the patterns that appear after t_i in the training set have not been learned by the network. So inputting any patterns from t_i to t_n will make an error.

At t_i the total error is:

$$E = e_r(t_i) + \dots + e_r(t_n) = \sum_{j=i}^{n} e_r(t_j). \qquad (8)$$

Figure 39.3

Rules for Training a Hidden Unit to Correct the Mistakes Made for Pattern t_i

The unit is trained to produce $0 < |v_k| < A$ for the current pattern, and a zero on all the previous patterns. In practice, t_i is not selected sequentially but on the basis of a largest-error condition.

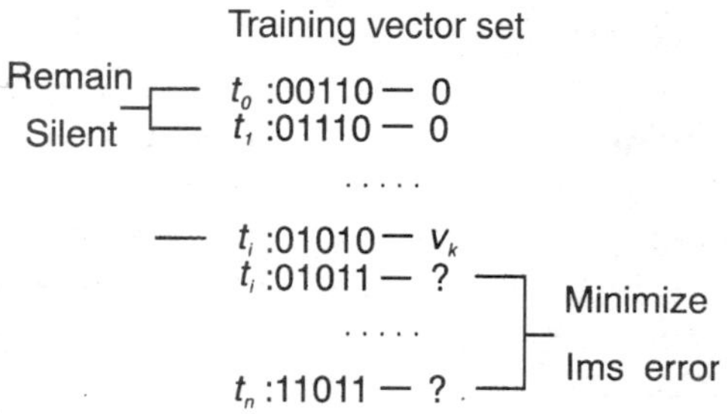

Training vector set

Remain ⌐ t_0 :00110 — 0
Silent ⌊ t_1 :01110 — 0

. . . . .

— t_i :01010 — v_k
t_i :01011 — ? ⌐ Minimize
. . . . .
t_n :11011 — ? ⌊ lms error

by adding the new unit h_i, the error term $e_r(t_i)$ has been eliminated. The total error is now given by:

$$E' = |\sum_{j=i+1}^{n} e_r(t_j)| < |\sum_{j=i}^{n} e_r(t_j)|. \tag{9}$$

By adding unit h_i, we have reduced the total error. Therefore the algorithm converges.

Part 2. In Part 2, we need to show that the new unit h_i will always learn the following conditions simultaneously:

1. *To be active at pattern t_i.* This condition is required so that the new unit h_i can become a feature detector. The output of the unit will then excite the corrective weights.

2. *To be inactive at patterns t_0, ..., t_{i-1}.* This condition is necessary due to the fact that all the previous patterns are already recognized correctly and this should not be disturbed.

This is a linearly separable problem and can be learned by the delta rule,[9] provided that the training data set does not contain a malicious (one-to-many) training vector.

Generalization of the CLS+ Procedure

Neural networks are interesting because of their learning properties— the ability to perform well on all patterns taken from a given distribution after having seen only a subset of them. The generalization properties of the CLS+ procedure depend solely on the way in which hidden units are trained. For the purposes of convergence, it is necessary to train a hidden unit at t_i to acquire the inhibitory and excitatory behavior described earlier. As long as conditions 1 and 2 above are obeyed, we could train the hidden unit in several ways.

If the hidden unit were trained to recognize only pattern t_i and no other patterns, convergence could still be possible (in fact, it is much faster). However, because each unit could only recognize a specific vector, the overall network would not be able to recognize anything outside the training set. The minimal conditions for a lower bound on generalization are as shown:

1. Unit h_i must be trained to be active at pattern t_i.

2. Unit h_i must be trained to be inactive at patterns $t_0, ..., i-1$.

3. Unit h_i must be active for at least one other pattern in $t_{i+1}, ..., t_n$.

Any arbitrary pattern would suffice, but the higher the correlation of the unit's behavior to the regularities within the training set, the higher the probability of good generalization. Such behavior can be achieved by increasing the sophistication of h_i. There are several ways of doing so. Figure 39.4 shows a construction in which h_i is composed of three subsidiary units: A, B, C.

In this construction, the tasks of the subsidiary units are defined as follows:

❖   A is a linear discriminant. It is connected to all input units and to the previous hidden unit h_{i-1}. A is trained to produce the desired output for pattern t_i and 0 for all other patterns.

Figure 39.4

Hidden Unit Construction

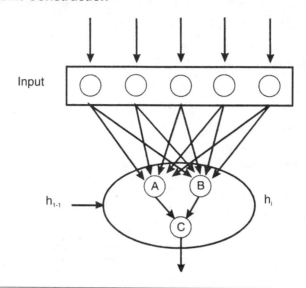

❖ B is a similarity approximator. It is connected in the same way as A but it is trained to minimize the least square error between its output and the desired output for pattern t_{i+1}, ..., t_n.

❖ C is an arbitrator unit. It is connected to both A and B and sees the output of previous A_j, j ε {0, ..., i}. When A is active, C inhibits B and simply passes on the output of A. The connection strength between C and the output is calculated as in (7). When A_j is inactive, C inhibits B and simply passes on the output of A (o^A), suitably adjusted to cancel the effect of W_h by a simple division:

$$o^c = \frac{o^A}{w_{h_i}}$$ (10)

The rationale behind this method of construction has a simple geometric interpretation. Here, an analogy is made between learning and curve-fitting. There are two problems in curve-fitting: finding the *order* of the polynomial and finding the *coefficients* of the polynomial once the order has been established. For example, given a certain data set, one first decides that the curve is second order and thus has the form $ax^2 + bx + c$, and then computes, somehow, the values for a, b, c, for example, to minimize the sum of squared differences between required and predicted $f(x_i)$ for x_i in the training set. Once the coefficients are computed, the value of $f(x_i)$ can be calculated for any x_i, including those not present in the training data set. Orders smaller than the appropriate ones risk not leading to good approximation even for the points in the data set.

On the other hand, choosing a larger order implies fitting a high-order polynomial to the low-order data. Although one hopes that the high order terms will have zero coefficients to cancel their effect, this is not the case in practice. Typically, it leads to perfect fit to points in the data set, but very bad $f(x_i)$ values may be computed for the x_i not in the training data—the system will not generalize well. Similarly, a network having a structure simpler than necessary cannot give good approximations even to patterns in the training set. A structure more complicated than necessary "overfits" in that it leads to good fit for the training set but poor performance on unseen patterns.

By adding units to correct the output for the patterns with the largest errors, the CLS+ procedure has the effect of increasing the order of the polynomial approximator, and by recomputing the connection strengths of the newly added hidden unit, the procedure makes a better approximation to the values of the coefficients. Because only part of the network is retrained, the degrees of freedom in exploring the search space are reduced dramatically.

In our work so far and in the simulation results reported here, hidden units were trained using the construction in Figure 39.4.

EXPERIMENTAL SETUP AND SIMULATION RESULTS

Network Architecture

The network architecture at the input and output levels is largely determined by the application. A common method of identifying regularities within a data set contaminated by noise is *windowing* (Figure 39.5).

The basic idea is to use two windows W^i and W^0 of fixed sizes, n and m, respectively, to look into the data set. For a given window size,

Figure 39.5

Windowing: Looking for Hidden Correlations and Regularities in Time Series

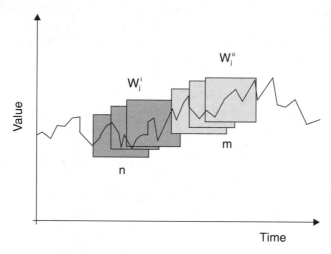

the assumption is that the sequence of values $W^i_0, ... W^i_n$ is somehow related to the following sequence $W^o_0, ... W^o_m$ and that this relationship, although unknown, is defined entirely within the data set. Various methods can then be used to correlate the two sets of values. In the case of neural networks, $W^i \rightarrow W^o$ can be used as a training vector. Both windows are shifted along the time series using a fixed step size s (Figure 39.5).

The choice of window and step sizes is critical to the ability of any prediction system to identify regularities and thus approximate the hidden relationship accurately. Quite often, some preprocessing of the data set is required to obtain a sensible starting point for n, m, and s.

Two types of forecasting are valuable in normal operating conditions in currency trading:

1. *Multistep prediction.* First, there is the requirement for long-term fore-casting that aims to identify *general* trends and *major* turning points in a currency exchange rate. In multistep prediction, the system uses a set of current values to predict the value of the exchange rate for a fixed period. The prediction is then fed back to the network to forecast the next period. We show that neural networks can use their smooth

interpolation properties to produce extremely good multistep predictions, even with difficult training datasets.

2. *Single-step prediction.* For the single-step prediction there is no feedback. The network predicts the exchange rate value one step ahead of time but uses the actual rather than the predicted value for the next prediction. Single-step prediction serves two purposes. First, it is a good mechanism for evaluating the adaptability and robustness of the prediction system by showing that even when its prediction is wrong, it is not dramatically wrong and that the system can use the actual value to correct itself. Second, it can act as an alarm generator and would allow traders to buy or sell in advance of a price increase or decrease. We show that neural networks are very robust and adaptive prediction systems, but careful network design and training are required to achieve reasonable turning point prediction in noisy data.

In the following section, we describe the use of the CLS+ procedure for identifying underlying regularities in time series. The system described here is designed and trained to predict the exchange rate between the U.S. dollar and the deutsche mark.

Training and Test Sets

The *training set* and *test set* consist of currency exchange data for the period 1988 through 1989, on hourly updates for the 260 trading days.

The first 200 items of the data set were used for training, while the second part was used for testing. The problem is particularly difficult to solve since the training set has a positive slope (i.e., general increase of the exchange rate), while the test set has a negative slope (i.e., a general decrease; see Figure 39.6).

The choice of window and step sizes is critical to the ability of any prediction system to identify high-order regularities in time series and thus approximate the hidden correlations accurately. Quite often, some preprocessing of the data set is required to obtain a sensible starting point for the sizes of W^i, W^o, and the step sizes. For our simulation, we use the following parameter values:

$$n = \text{size of } (W^i) = 12$$

$$m = \text{size of } (W^o) = 1$$

Figure 39.6

Training and Test Set

The data set consists of currency exchange data for the period 1988–1989 on hourly updates, that is, 260 trading days.

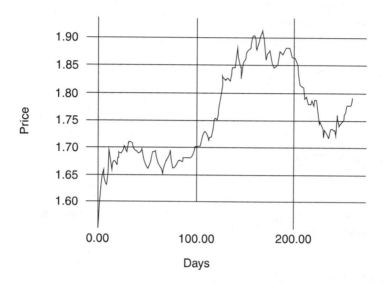

$$s = \text{size of (step)} = 4$$

The rationale behind this is that a day's trading ($n = 12$) would capture the underlying regularities quite accurately and would eliminate much of the noise. The rationale behind the small size of $m = 1$ is to avoid overloading the smooth interpolation properties of the learning procedure. Moreover, the overall effect of $s = 4$ is to take the moving average over a four-day period. This would dampen the effect of trading near the beginning and end of the week where the processing of backlogs might affect the markets and introduce further noise.

The resulting training set consists of overlapping snapshots of the time series, each of length 12 hours, moving along the curve at an interval of 4 hours. More formally:

$$t_0: \quad W^i_0 = \{V_0, ..., V_{11}\} \quad \rightarrow \quad W^o_0 = \{V_{12}\}$$
$$t_1: \quad W^i_1 = \{V_4, ..., V_{15}\} \quad \rightarrow \quad W^o_1 = \{V_{16}\}$$

$$t_j: \quad W^i_{\ j} = \{V_{j+s}, \ ...,V_{j+n}\} \quad \rightarrow \quad W^o_{\ j} = \{V_{j+n+1}\}$$

The overall size of the training set, therefore, is given by:

$$d \times y \times n \times s = \frac{2}{3} d \times n \times s = \frac{2}{3} 260 \times 12 \times 4 = 8{,}236$$

The intermediate size of the *training set* and *test set* makes the problem nontrivial and also allows for extensive tests of learning speed and generalization performance.

In our simulation experiments, we investigate the influence of varying learning time and varying the learning rate on the convergence and generalization performance. We start with the multistep prediction.

Multistep Prediction

For the multistep prediction, the network would use the inputs of the past 12 hours of trading to predict the value of the exchange rate for the $(12 + 1)^{th}$ hour. The prediction is then fed back to the network to forecast the next value. This process is repeated for all the values in the last 60 trading days of the year 1989.

The result of the multistep prediction is shown in Figure 39.7. The prediction for the general trend in the exchange rate is very accurate. The network predicted a sharp fall and then a rise in the exchange rate. For the first 30 days, the prediction is very accurate, both in terms of trend and in terms of absolute values. The network predicted a turning point at approximately the time that it took place and estimated correctly the pace of the recovery.

The problem as defined by the training data alone is particularly difficult to solve since the training set has a positive slope (i.e., a general increase of the exchange rate), while the test set has a negative slope (i.e., a general decrease).

Evaluation

Although the prediction performance of the network is intuitively quite accurate, a more rigorous evaluation would be required. It is generally difficult to quantify the prediction performance of such systems, and evalu-

Figure 39.7

Multiple-Step Prediction

The solid line shows the whole time series, while the dotted line shows the exchange rate predicted by the neural network for the days 200 to 260.

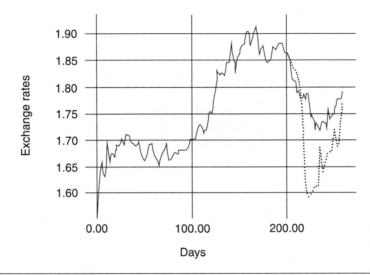

ations are often applicant dependent. The evaluation we use here is based on a simple trading strategy:

> We buy or sell in advance according to the prediction. We buy or sell when the system predicts a turning point. The volume of the transaction can be fixed or variable, that is, proportional to the predicted rate of change. Certain market imperfections such as transaction costs and the cost of borrowing are assumed away.

We define the following:

P_{t_0} = Actual price at time t_0 the decision time.

P_{t_k} = Actual price at the time t_k, which according to the predictionis a turning point.

$P^{*}_{t_k}$ = Predicted price at time t_k, which according to the predictionis a turning point.

λk = Amount of units bought or sold. For transactions with fixedamounts of money, we use $\lambda = 1$.

p_i = Profit that the system makes for transaction i. This can be negative as well as positive.

The profit is then related to the predictions as follows:

$$p_i = (P_{t_0} - P_{t_k})\lambda k \qquad (11)$$

The network has predicted one major turning point and four minor ones (Figure 39.7). The first was to occur approximately 30 days ahead of prediction, while the second would occur approximately 10 days later, and so on. According to the strategy outlined above, we would have made six transactions: at the 200th, 230th, 240th, 245th, 255th, and 257th. The corresponding profits are given by direct substitution in (11).

$$p_1 = (P_{t_0} - P_{t_k})\,\lambda k = (1.87 - 1.72)\,\lambda k = 0.15\lambda k \qquad (12)$$

$$p_2 = (P_{t_0} - P_{t_k})\,\lambda k = (1.72 - 1.72)\,\lambda k = 0\lambda k \qquad (13)$$

$$p_3 = (P_{t_0} - P_{t_k})\,\lambda k = (1.72 - 1.72)\,\lambda k = 0\lambda k \qquad (14)$$

$$p_4 = (P_{t_0} - P_{t_k})\,\lambda k = (1.78 - 1.72)\,\lambda k = 0.06\lambda k \qquad (15)$$

$$p_5 = (P_{t_0} - P_{t_k})\,\lambda k = (1.78 - 1.78)\,\lambda k = 0\lambda k \qquad (16)$$

$$p_6 = (P_{t_0} - P_{t_k})\,\lambda k = (1.79 - 1.78)\,\lambda k = 0.01\lambda k \qquad (17)$$

Thus, for fixed $\lambda = 1$, there is an overall positive profit p of 22 percent on the amount of monies invested in the transactions, that is:

$$p = p_1 + p_2 + p_3 = (0.15 + 0.05 + 0.02)\,k = 0.22k$$

A more sensible strategy is to make the number of units bought or sold proportional to the predicted changes in prices. In this case, profits on correct predictions are increased but so are losses on incorrect predictions. The choice of this strategy is directly related to the confidence in the robustness of the system. As we shall see later, there are good reasons to have a high level of confidence in the prediction accuracy of the network.

A sensible measure for λ is the ratio between the current price and the predicted one. This ratio is often suitably scaled by a factor c, dependent on the degree of confidence in the prediction system:

$$\lambda = \frac{P_{t_0}}{P^*_{t_k}} c \tag{18}$$

Using (18) and (12, 15, 17), we obtain a more realistic estimate of the profit. For $c = 1$, we have:

$$p = p_1 + p_2 + p_3 = (0.175 + 0.064 + 0.01) \, k$$

$$= 0.25k$$

For this type of prediction system, it is often sensible to scale λ by values of $c > 1$ near the beginning of the prediction and to use values of $c < 1$ as the prediction gets further away. In our case, such scaling would have increased the profit c-fold.

Single-Step Prediction

For the single-step prediction, there is no feedback. The network predicts the exchange rate value one hour ahead of time, but uses the actual rather than the predicted value for the current hour.

Figure 39.8 displays the results for the single-step prediction in which the input values are the values of the observed time series. The prediction is quite accurate in that it follows the actual prices closely. Even when it makes a mistake with respect to predicting a turning point, it is capable of adjusting itself as soon as the actual price is made available at the next cycle. This type of performance measure is often cited by researchers to indicate the robustness of the system. In practical terms, however, this is of little use, as the system has to predict ahead of time the exchange rate price.

To analyze the behavior of the system further, we compare the "gradients" of the two curves to identify turning points (strictly speaking, these are first differences, not true gradients, because the time series are not continuous).

Define t as the number of turning points in the curve, p as the number of perfect matches on turning points, within two time steps, and s as the

Figure 39.8

Single-Step Prediction

The solid line shows the whole time series, while the dotted line shows the actual exchange rate produced by the neural network for the days 200 to 260.

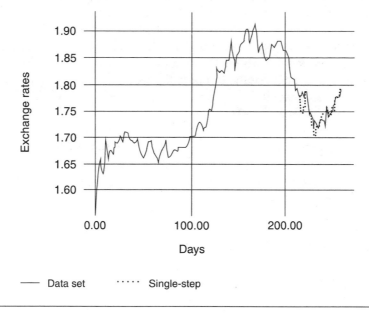

— Data set   ..... Single-step

number of slope corrections within two time steps. The following measures are of interest:

$a = \dfrac{p}{t}$ is the prediction accuracy of the system at the turning points.

$r = \dfrac{s}{t}$ denotes the robustness of the system and shows how well the system adapts its prediction in response to real events.

For the simulations in our single-step prediction, we obtain the following:

$$a = \frac{p}{t} = \frac{18}{26} = 0.69 (19)$$

$$r = \frac{s}{t} = \frac{23}{26} = 0.88 \tag{20}$$

The measures in (11) and (12) show that the system predicted correctly 69 percent of the turning points, and when it was wrong it corrected its prediction within two time steps 88 percent of the time. A closer analysis of those results showed that 90 percent of the correctly predicted turning points are in the positive direction. The main reason for the poor performance of the system lies in the training data itself, which generally follow a positive trend, but the test data follow a generally negative trend (Figure 39.6). In general, this problem need not arise. It is possible to select a more representative training set, one that contains both negative and positive trends, except for its availability.

The overall result is good. The network under evaluation here was designed to identify *major* rather than *minor* turning points and was carefully trained to avoid overfitting the noise. In practice, short-term prediction networks would be trained to overfit.

COMPARISON TO OTHER TECHNIQUES

Since 1973, with the implementation of the floating exchange rate system by the industrialized countries, a large amount of research work has been carried out in an attempt to explain the movements of exchange rates. In this section, we compare the performance of classical smoothing techniques and fixed geometry networks with that of the CLS+ procedure.

Statistical Forecasting

For these purposes, we use three smoothing techniques typical of those employed in everyday use by financial institutions: simple autoregression, and exponential smoothing methods.[10] In order to make these methods work at all, we found that this was necessary to reduce the noise in the data set and have compiled *daily* observations by taking the average of our *hourly* data set.

Exponential Smoothing. Exponential smoothing is a convenient way of expressing the forecast y_{t+T} in terms of exponentially smoothed statistics.

If the time series is not flat but has linear trends, *second order* exponential smoothing is used. This can model the trend and hence exponentially smooth the de-trended data set. The *second order* exponential smoothing model is given by:

$$y_{t+T} = \left(2 + \frac{\alpha T}{1-\alpha}\right)S_t - \left(1 + \frac{\alpha T}{1-\alpha}\right)S_t(2) \tag{21}$$

where $S_t(2) = \alpha S_t + (1-\alpha)S_{t-1}(2)$, T is the time trend, and:

$$S_t = \alpha y_t + (1-\alpha)S_{t-1} \tag{22}$$

where $0 < \alpha < 1$ and y_{t+T} denotes the exchange rate. The statistic $S_t(2)$ is called the double smoothed statistic and is a smoothing of the smoothed values. $S_t(2)$ gives an indication of the trend of the averages S_t over time. Hence, its inclusion in the model accounts for a linear trend of y_t with time. The estimated values for the parameters are $\alpha = 0.62$ and $T = -0.0015$.

The predicted values for y_1 are depicted in Figure 39.9a. They form a straight line *sf*1 of positive slope and fail to pick up the change of pattern in the actual data.

If the time series is neither constant nor linear with time, it is best to use a triple exponential smoothing model. Higher-order exponential smoothing models exist, but the difficulties in computing the forecasting equation for models of an order higher than the three are considerable. It is generally accepted that unless a time series is extremely volatile, third-order exponential smoothing would suffice. The *third-order* exponential smoothing model is given by:

$$y_{t+T} = \left[6(1-\alpha)^2 + (6-5\alpha)\alpha T + \alpha^2 T^2\right]\frac{S_t}{2(1-\alpha)^2}$$

$$-\left[6(1-\alpha)^2 + 2(5-4\alpha)\alpha T + 2\alpha^2 T^2\right]\frac{S_t(2)}{2(1-\alpha)^2}$$

$$+\left[2(1-\alpha)^2 + (4-3\alpha)\alpha T + \alpha^2 T^2\right]\frac{S_t(3)}{2(1-\alpha)^2}$$

Figure 39.9

Multiple-Step Prediction Using Statistical Methods

a. Second-order exponential smoothing
b. Third-order exponential smoothing
c. Autoregression

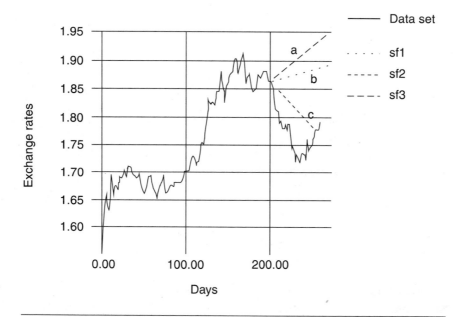

The *triple smooth statistic* $s_t(3)$ is, in a sense, describing the average rate of change *of the average rates of change*. It is computed as follows:

$$S_t(3) = \alpha S_t(2) + (1 - \alpha)S_{t-1}(3)$$

The predicted values for y_t using third-order exponential smoothing are depicted in Figure 39.9b. Again, they form a straight line *sf2* of positive slope and fail to pick up the change of pattern in the actual data.

The main problem with exponential smoothing is that essentially they perform piecewise linear approximation and find it quite difficult to model "volatile" time series. An additional obstacle is that an a priori estimate of the degree of nonlinearity of time series is required in order to select the order of smoothing. In practice, this is not always readily available.

Autoregression. The autoregression forecasting methodology consists of two main parts: a large class of time series models and a set of procedures for choosing one of these models to use for forecasting. The class of *autoregressive integrated moving average* models (ARIMA) contains all time series of the form:

$$y_t = \sum_{i=1}^{p} \varphi_i \, y_{t-i} + \varepsilon_t - \sum_{j=1}^{q} \theta_j \, \varepsilon_{t-j} \tag{23}$$

The first summation term in (23) is the autoregressive part of the model, with the second summation term being the moving average part of the model. The terms ε_t, ε_{t-1},...,ε_{t-q} are the current and past q error terms of the series. The constants φ_i are called the autoregressive parameters of the model, and the terms in θ_i are the moving average parameters.

We have used several autoregressive models, with the best being a purely autoregressive model with four lags. The estimated equation from the 200 observations is listed below:

$$y_t = 0.00972 y_{t-1} + 1.37448 y_{t-2} - 0.54810 y_{t-3} + 0.16870 y_{t-4}$$

with regression parameters $R^2 = 0.99$ and D. W. = 2.03.

Using the above estimated coefficients, we predicted the exchange rate for the remaining observations. The predicted values form a straight line of negative slope, as shown in Figure 39.9c. This model provides the most satisfactory forecasts among classical forecasting methods, and using (11) would give profit of 9 percent.

Fixed Geometry Networks

Fixed geometry networks are sensitive to network size, to training times, and to the choice of control parameters for the gradient descent. We have experimented with several configurations of standard back-propagation networks. The best result was obtained with a network of a single layer of 32 nodes, trained for 4,500 iterations, and $\lambda = 0.4$. The predicted result is shown in Figure 39.10.

For the first 20 days, the prediction is very accurate, both in terms of trends and in terms of absolute values. The network predicted a turning point slightly earlier than it actually took place and overestimated the

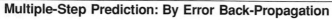

Figure 39.10

Multiple-Step Prediction: By Error Back-Propagation

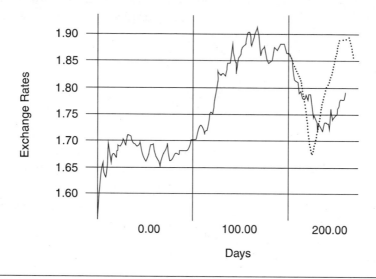

strength of the recovery. As expected, the smooth interpolation properties of back-propagation eliminated the short-term noise in the prediction.

Using the evaluation procedure in the previous section (11) and (18), the corresponding profit levels are 18 percent for fixed k and 20 percent for variable k and scaling factor $c = 1$. This is much better than the statistical techniques but not as accurate as with the CLS+ procedure.

The same type of prediction was possible with several network configurations of fixed geometry networks. However, as one varies network size, so one must vary training times appropriately; we were not able to establish a linear relationship between the two. In general, it is not possible to have an a priori estimate of these two parameters. Another interesting discovery was that almost all fixed geometry networks developed two attractor dynamics: If the network was overfitting, it would predict a curve with a shape similar to that in Figure 39.9 but with a smaller periodicity; if the network was underfitting, it would predict a curve that was in effect averaging the time series (i.e., with a larger periodicity but much smaller amplitude and a mean around 1.82). Interestingly, there was no smooth transition from one attractor dynamics to another; the change would happen within a single iteration (around the 4,000th pass through the data set).

CONCLUSIONS AND FURTHER WORK

One of the main problems with neural network design is that a priori no realistic estimate can be made of the number of hidden units that are required to solve a problem. We have presented a new strategy for dynamically configuring a feedforward multilayered network for any function. The CLS+ algorithm is designed for general purpose, supervised learning for neural networks. With respect to previous approaches to learning in a layered system, such as back-propagation, our approach presents a completely new way of addressing the problem. The geometry, including the number of hidden units and the connections, is not fixed in advance but generated by the growth process.

The CLS+ algorithm offers the following advantages over network learning algorithms currently in use:

- ❖ There is no need to guess the size and the connectivity pattern of the network in advance. A network (though not optimal) is built automatically.

- ❖ The CLS+ procedure convergence learns fast. In back-propagation, the hidden units engage in complex calculation before they settle into distinct useful roles; in CLS+, each unit sees a fixed problem and can move decisively to solve that problem.

- ❖ At any given time, we train just one unit in the network. The rest of the network is not changing, so the results can be cached.

The principal differences between the CLS+ algorithm and other learning architecture are the dynamic creation of hidden units, the way we add units to a single layer with a fixed input and output layer, and the freezing of units as we add them to the network. An interesting discovery is that by training one unit at a time, instead of training the whole network at once, we can speed up the learning process considerably.

We have explained the different parts of the application and the relationship between them. The result is good. For multistep prediction, the network learns the problem well and makes at least 20 percent profit.

This compares well with normal trading strategies, which normally achieve levels of profit between 2 percent and 5 percent.

The system described here is designed and trained to predict the exchange rate between the U.S. dollar and the deutsche mark, but it is easy to see how to apply the methodology to other time series problems. The next step will be to train the network for a realistic trading environment. For example, the current model assumes that there is a risk-free rate of interest at which borrowing (and lending) takes place.[11] In addition, taxes and other market imperfections (such as transaction costs) are assumed away.[12]

ENDNOTES

1. A. S. Weigend, B. A. Huberman, and D. E. Rumelhart, "Predicting the Future: A Connectionist Approach," Stanford University Technical Report, Stanford-PDP-90-01. Submitted to the *International Journal of Neural Systems*.

2. T. Komoto et al., "Stock Market Prediction with Modular Neural Networks," proceedings of the IJCNN-90, San Diego, 1990.

3. S. E. Fahlman and C. Lebiere, The Cascade-Correlation Learning Architecture. Carnegie Mellon University. *Technical Report CMU-CS-90-100*, 1990.

4. M. Mezard and J. Nadal, "Learning in Feedforward Layered Network: The Tiling Algorithm," *J. Physics A.* 22 (1989), pp. 2191–2203.

5. S. I. Gallant, "Three Consecutive Algorithms for Neural Learning," Proceedings of the 8th Annual Conference of Cognitive Science Society.

6. M. R. A. Frean, "The Upstart Algorithm: A Method for Constructing and Training Feed-Forward Neural Networks," Technical Report, Department of Computer Science, University of Edinburgh, 1989.

7. A. N. Refenes and S. Vithlani, "Constructive Learning by Specialization," *Proceedomgs ICANN-91*, Helsinki, June 1991.

8. Y. Le Cun, *Generalization and Network Design Strategies* (University of Toronto, 1985).

9. M. Minsky and S. Papert, *Perceptrons: An Introduction to Computational Geometry.* Cambridge, MA: MIT Press, 1969.

10. W. Mendenhall, et al. *Statistics for Management and Economics.* Boston, MA: PWS-KENT Publishing Company, 1989.

11. One possible candidate for this rate is short-term treasury bills because they are fixed in nominal terms and the probability of default is practically zero. However, in an inflationary environment, there is always uncertainty about the real rate of return.

12. We would like to thank S. Vithlani for implementing a simulator for the CLS+ procedure and Dr. G. Karoussos of Credit Swisse & First Boston for his advice on financial forecasting models.

NAME INDEX

SUBJECT INDEX

813